WATERLOO
NEW PERSPECTIVES

WATERLOO
NEW PERSPECTIVES
The Great Battle Reappraised

DAVID HAMILTON-WILLIAMS

John Wiley & Sons, Inc.
NEW YORK CHICHESTER BRISBANE
TORONTO SINGAPORE

First published in the United States by John Wiley & Sons, Inc., 1994

First published in the UK by Arms & Armour Press, an imprint of Cassell PLC, London.

Library of Congress Cataloging-in-Publication Data:

Hamilton-Williams, David.
    Waterloo : new perspectives / David Hamilton-Williams.
       p.   cm.
    Includes bibliographical references and index.
    ISBN 0-471-14571-8 (paper)
    1. Waterloo, Battle of, 1815. 2. Napoleon I, Emperor of the French, 1769-1821 – Military leadership. 3. France – History, Military – 1789-1815. I. Title.
DC244.H35 1994
364.1'32'0973-dc20

Cartography by Malcolm Barnes

Designed and edited by DAG Publications Ltd.
Designed by David Gibbon; edited by Michael Boxall.

Printed in the United States of America
10 9 8 7 6 5 4 3 2 1

Contents

List of Maps and Diagrams

*This book is dedicated
to my wife, Sally-Ann,
and my sons,
Oliver and Magnus*

Foreword

BY THE MARQUESS OF ANGLESEY
FSA, FRHist S, Hon DLitt
Author of *A History of the British Cavalry*

John Codman Ropes, an impartial American scholar, prefaced his magisterial account of the Waterloo campaign with these words: 'One would suppose that the theme had been exhausted.' Ropes was writing almost a century ago. Today, 178 years after 'the acknowledged master of modern warfare' was decisively overthrown and with thousands of further volumes in numerous languages having been added to the world's library shelves in the interim, the reader of yet another chronicle is entitled once again to question the need for it.

I will wager that no one who reads David Hamilton-Williams' 'new perspectives' approach will doubt that the reassessment he offers is an essential step towards the truth. Definitive, of course, it is not, for how can there ever be a complete picture of any human activity in which large numbers of participants are killed and of which the majority fails to give an account?

The military historian can only hope to add veracity, and to correct lies and inaccuracies. In this case, the author's chief tool has been the careful, exhaustive examination of a cache of letters, hitherto unconsulted, or at least not made use of, by generations of researchers and writers. It has taken him a good decade to perform this task, while at the same time looking with a critical eye at many hundreds of other sources.

The letters were all written to Captain William Siborne, who is here accused without much exaggeration of committing 'a crime against history'. Siborne's own history of the campaign, and his son's later publication of just 180 of the hundreds of letters his father received, have had an enormous influence on historians over the years.

The Introduction to this brilliant reappraisal describes in full the circumstances of Siborne's 'crime'. In short, the Captain depended all too often on pecuniary assistance from the officers whose accounts he solicited. That he was therefore prone to use the often self-justificatory stories of those who financially sponsored his work and tended to ignore others cannot be doubted. The proof is here. The purpose of the letters was to inform Siborne of the various units' dispositions during the battle for the two military models which he designed, constructed and displayed, and which rendered him impecunious. The selectivity of his son's *The Waterloo Letters* compounded the 'crime'.

The Sibornes' sins, grievous though they were, are acknowledged, nevertheless, as in no way diminishing the value of the narratives contained in the letters. Indeed, it is arguable that at least as deplorable a delinquency has been committed by those of us – for I, too, am guilty – who have repeatedly treated as gospel those parts of the letters which were published, without troubling to inspect the originals, as the author has done.

The chief object of this book is to present a coherent recital of the political and military course of events during those momentous weeks which ended in Bonaparte sailing for St. Helena, based on the fresh evidence so painstakingly accumulated. Purely as an account of the battles, it has few equals. Exciting and fast-moving, nowhere in the text does it trouble the reader with polemical outbursts or dry-as-dust quibbling. In the copious notes, however, there is a rich mine of supporting information. It is on this that he who wishes to observe the machinery which drives the reappraisal should concentrate. It is a most rewarding task; these notes make clear the vast extent of David Hamilton-Williams' studies. One of his laments is that nearly all histories of Waterloo are guided by too national an outlook and are therefore gravely unbalanced. He avoids this trap by paying great attention to sources from all the numerous combatant countries. Incidentally, in doing so, he has judiciously amended the libels perpetrated by many British writers on the behaviour of some of the non-British troops under Wellington's command. There were certainly instances of giving way, even of cowardice, but so there were among a few of the raw, unblooded British battalions.

Though for some tastes perhaps a little too spellbound by the Emperor, the author recognises his faults. Wellington does not escape unscathed, but the warts are exposed with great fairness. Not everyone will agree with the importance attached to these imperfections, but the deification often bestowed on him is given short shrift. The characters and actions of Blücher and Gneisenau are well described.

It pleases me that the part played in the great battle by the commander of the Allied cavalry turns out to be just as I described in my biography of him.

Anglesey

Plas Newydd, Anglesey,
July 1993

Preface

'After the publication of so many accounts of the battle of the 18th of June, it may fairly be asked, upon what grounds I expect to awaken fresh interest in a subject so long before the public. Can I reconcile the conflicting statements which have already appeared in print? Can I add to the information which most of my countrymen already possess concerning this memorable epoch? Or can I present that information in a compendious and lucid form, such as the general reader may still want? Something in all these ways, I hope I have accomplished.' So wrote Sergeant-Major Edward Cotton, late of the 7th Hussars and for many years official Waterloo battlefield tour guide, in the preface to his *A Voice from Waterloo*, published in 1849. Cotton felt that, during the nearly thirty-five years since the battle, so many accounts of the event had already been published it was incumbent upon him to justify his addition to the list.

The author feels similarly bound. This book is an attempt to tell the truth about what happened during the Hundred Days. Of the almost innumerable accounts and analyses on this subject over the past 178 years, a common thread seems to run throughout: that is, the partiality of their point of view. And partiality, like the blind men inspecting the elephant, even when possessed of good intent, cannot approximate the truth.

British accounts, for reasons which will be seen, have tended to magnify out of all proportion the accomplishments of the very modest numbers of British soldiers, even to the extent of ignoring completely the Hanoverians, Brunswickers, Nassauers and Netherlanders who made up the bulk of Wellington's army, and to play down shamelessly the role of the Prussians. There are also several prevalent French versions of the story which, in an attempt to preserve the myth of Napoleonic infallibility, have heaped blame upon various of his generals. Likewise, there are German accounts dwelling on the Prussians' experiences, and on the profound contempt with which the Prussian Chief of Staff viewed the English in general, and Wellington in particular. Even the name of the climactic battle cannot

11

be agreed upon: it is known to the British as Waterloo, for the place 2½ miles from the battlefield where Wellington had his headquarters; to the French, it is Mont St-Jean, after the ridge and hamlet upon which the enemy had disposed itself; and to the Germans, is is La Belle Alliance, for the inn at the centre of the French position at which, at the end of the day, Blücher proposed the name to Wellington as appropriately commemorative of their successful alliance.

The standard British version of Waterloo began to take its definitive form between 1839 and 1845, after Captain William Siborne had received permission from the then Commander-in-Chief to canvass the surviving officer veterans of the campaign as to their views of what occurred. For reasons of sycophancy, veniality, and national prejudice, Siborne, in the models and history resulting from his researches, wilfully suppressed and distorted facts. He omitted whatever was unflattering about any of the officers who financed him during his work, or which did not accord with a hagiographic portrayal of the Duke, or was less than Homeric in its account of the actions of the British army.

The Siborne version became the 'Bible' on Waterloo, not only for English-speaking writers, but others as well, although its authenticity was not universally upheld at the time. Lieutenant-Colonel Charles Chesney, Professor of Military Art and History at the Royal Imperial Staff College, who made a lifetime study of the Napoleonic campaigns and taught the subject to British staff officers, wrote in the introduction to his *Waterloo Lectures* (London, 1868), p. 3, that: 'The popular English version of the great battle which gives its name to the campaign of 1815 is hardly less a romance than the Famous Waterloo chapter in Victor Hugo's *Les Miserables*, over which our critics have (with good reasons) made merry.'

It was during two years of study of this primary source material that the author began to see glimpses of the true picture. Inevitably these led to the pursuit of many other lines of inquiry which involved the author in a further four years of research. This phase focused on the diplomatic policy of the British Government from 1789 to 1831. In searching through State papers, including those of the Foreign Office, Cabinet and Treasury, and mountains of correspondence of politicians of the period, the author discovered new ground to his knowledge hitherto neglected by military historians. The well-known maxim of Clausewitz came forcibly to mind that 'It is clear ... that war is not a mere act of policy but a true political instrument, a continuation of political activity by other means'. Much of what had seemed inexplicable in the events of the day was clarified when viewed with military-political stereoscopy.

These revelations led the author to devote another four years to examining material from the archives of the other nations that had participated in the great conflict. Some archives, particularly in The Netherlands and Germany, were destroyed between 1939 and 1945, but fortunately copies of certifiable authenticity had already been made of much lost material. Also, it became evident that Siborne had not been alone in his selective approach to history. The eminent French *fin de siècle* Napoleonic historian, M. Henri Houssaye, had chosen his sources carefully to shed only a warm light on his hero.

It became apparent to the author, and his publisher, that the body of material accumulated over this ten-year period, and covering political as well as military perspectives, would not admit to treatment in a single volume. It was therefore decided to produce three books, each a separate entity, which taken together would shed new light on the latter phase of the Napoleonic period, 1813 to 1821, from the events leading up to the Emperor's first abdication to his eventual murder through the connivance of the governments of several of the Allied powers.

The campaign of 1815 is treated first, in the present volume, largely as a military episode, because it was the critical point in this mature phase of Napoleon's career, determined as it was by what happened before, and determining in turn the protracted denouement to the life of the man who gave his name to his age. The second, *The Fall of Napoleon: The Final Betrayal*, currently in preparation, will cover the campaigns of 1813 and 1814 in arresting detail, but will also recount the remainder of Napoleon's life in the light of previously suppressed facts concerning terrorism, intrigue, and governmental duplicity which alone can make sense of the course of events. The third book, *Joachim Murat: The Last Campaign, 1815*, will treat in full of the Neapolitan campaign in its military and political aspects, leading to the judicial murder of Napoleon's brother-in-law.

The author has sought to let the story unfold from the amalgamation of facts gleaned by the method of judging historical evidence on the same grounds as juridical evidence: that is, whether it constitutes the testimony of a creditable witness. The author has tried to avoid chauvinism, not being distracted by the flapping of the Union Jack, the *Drapeau Tricolore*, or any other flag, and his investigation has held no brief for or against Napoleon, Wellington, Blücher, or any of the other principal characters.

The author must, however, in good conscience, declare a sentiment, born of his long researches. Although in the consideration of the deeds of the Napoleonic, or for that matter any other, era there is ample cause to apportion blame for acts of commission or omission, particular odium seems to attach to the House of Bourbon. The reign of this House was founded upon an act of betrayal by Henry of Navarre who, to secure the throne, renounced for a second time the Protestant faith he had intermittently championed during the French wars of religion. For two centuries, until the Revolution, he and his progeny had battened parasitically on the vigorous body of France. Of the two scions of the House during the Napoleonic period, Louis de Bourbon, Comte de Provence, and later Louis XVIII, lacked the intelligence or malevolence to be truly evil, while his brother Charles, Comte d'Artois, possessed in abundance those qualities of will and turpitude which made him a mortal danger to those whom he chose as enemies, and a blight on the people subjected to him. It is largely the pernicious effect of men like d'Artois, arising throughout history from the catacombs of humanity's more bestial nature, which prompted Voltaire to remark morosely that history is nothing but the *tableau* of crimes and misfortunes.

The author, therefore, unable to remain emotionally aloof from his subject, admits to a contempt for such men who were, in this twilight of the age of enlightenment, the principal and most repugnant examples of an atavistic tendency among those at the summit of the moribund feudal society of France to try to restrict the growth of individual liberty which their countrymen had enjoyed in greater measure under Napoleon than they had known since the time before Caesar set his defiling foot on their fertile soil.

In contrast, the author's sympathies lie with the men who formed the armies and the families who mourned their loss: they whose unheralded gallantry and sacrifice underlay and supported the more prominent achievements which are the stuff of most history, including this one.

David Hamilton-Williams, March 1993

Acknowledgements

It is always difficult for an author to express due gratitude to the many people who, during the research and writing of his book, have helped by giving so unstintingly of their time and patiently answering the multitude of questions put to them. This is especially so as answers inevitably open new lines of inquiry, leading to supplementary questions and further involvement.

No idea is genuinely new. It is rather a development or improvement on other people's formulations. Over ten years of researching this book, I have read many hundreds of works, many of some antiquity. My researches have been built on clues sometimes found by others long ago. I feel in duty bound therefore to acknowledge first my debt to the works of my historical antecedents.

Of those contemporary authorities whom I have consulted, I have the honour to thank: HIH the Prince Napoleon, whose recommendation to various French historians and institutes opened difficult doors for an Englishman wanting French information about the Campaign of 1815; the Most Hon. the Marquess of Anglesey, who kindly gave me his expert advice and answered a myriad of questions on theoretical situations, particularly involving cavalry; the Countess Elizabeth Longford, who was gracious enough to provide me with authoritative information regarding the first Duke of Wellington; His Excellency Archbishop Luigi Barbarito, Papal Nuncio, for arranging for me to have access to Vatican archive material; and Dr Otto von Habsburg, for information on his Austrian imperial forebears.

Dr David Chandler, of RMA Sandhurst, has for ten years been kind enough to correspond with me and has aided me greatly through his sponsorship, for which I acknowledge and thank him (again!) with all my heart. Without the help and encouragement of my dear friend, Philip J. Haythornthwaite, author, historian, Napoleonic authority, and good Samaritan, this book would not have seen the light of day. It is with sadness that I must extend my sincere acknowledgement to: the late Brigadier Peter Young, for the benefit of his knowledge; the late Major-General B.P. Hughes, for information on weaponry; and the late Michael Glover, for advice on some of Napoleon's marshals. Professor Tullard, M. Jean-Marcel Humbert, and M. Jacques Logie patiently took the time to answer many questions on Napoleon and his army's command structure. M. Logie generously supplied me with photocopies of rare extracts of French primary source material, some previously unknown in English-language histories. My old friend and mentor, Dr Nico Vels Heijn, of Zeist, Holland, has given me authoritative advice, material and guidance on the diplomacy and army of the United Netherlands of 1815. Colonel Cyril Desmet, friend and late Head of War Studies of the Ecole Royale Militaire in Brussels, guided me expertly over the field of Waterloo on several occasions, even taking me along the rough track (unimproved since 1815) used by the Prussians. Dr Natali Bogomoloboy, of the History Museum of Borodino and the Panorama, kindly researched and obtained for me previously inaccessible Russian state archive material dealing with the campaigns of 1813-15 and the Vienna Congress.

I should like to thank the following foreign institutions and staffs for their expert help and guidance: the Archives Nationales de France, for Napoleon's correspondence, prefectural reports, bulletins, and copies of *Le Moniteur* 1814-15; the Archives Militaires du Service Historique de l'Etat-Major de l'Armée de France; Colonel Paul Willing of the Hotel National des Invalides, for later printed works and information on Napoleon's final return to Paris; Lieutenant-Colonel Zwitzer of the Military History Section of the Koninklijke Landmacht (Royal Netherlands Army); Dr J.G. Kerkhoven, Director of the Koninklijke Nederlands Leger-en Wapenmuseum - 'Generaal Hoefer' (Royal Netherlands Military Museum - 'General Hoefer'); Dr Major Ostertag of the Militargeschichtlisches Porschungsamt (Military Historical Research Department) of the German Army; Dr Karl Holz of the Geheimes Staatsarchiv Preussicher Kulturbesitz (Prussian State Archives), Berlin; Dr Gudrun Fiedler of the Neidersachersisches Hauptstaatarchiv (State Archives), Hanover; Dr A. von Rohr of the Landeshauptstadt Hanover, for pre-1840 published material; Dr Christof Romer of the Braunschweigisches (Brunswick) Landsmuseum; Dr P. von Groeben of the Staatsarchiv Weisbaden (Nassau), for manuscript material and other documents; the Kriegsarchiv Wein (War Archives, Vienna), for material, advice, and direction; and the Landeshauptstadt Wien (Vienna Central Museum), for references to diplomatic sources.

I am indebted to all the following British regimental archivists for documents on Waterloo: Brigadier (retd.) R.J. Lewedon, The Royal Artillery Institution; Major (retd.) E.C. Weaver, MBE, The Grenadier Guards; Colour-Sergeant R. Rogers, The Coldstream Guards; Major (retd.) Jim Grant, The Scots Guards; Lieutenant-Colonel A.D. Meakin, The Household Cavalry; Lieutenant-Colonel S.W. McBain, The Royal Scots; A.J. White, Lancaster City Museum (custodian, 4th Foot); Brigadier J.M. Cubiss, CBE, MC, The Prince of Wales's Own; Norman Holmes, The Royal Welsh Fusiliers; Lieutenant-Colonel Jack Reilly, The Royal Irish Rangers; Lieutenant-Colonel H.L.T. Radice, MBE, The Gloucester Regiment; Major S. Tipping, The Queen's Lancashire Regiment (30th Foot); Major W.H. White, The Duke of Cornwall's Light Infantry; Lieutenant-Colonel W. Robins, OBE, The Duke of Wellington's Regiment; Lieutenant-Colonel E.G. Bostock, The Queen's Lancashire Regiment (40th Foot); Colonel the Honourable W.R. Arbuthnott, The Black Watch; D.L. Jones, Chelmsford

Borough Council (custodian, 44th Foot); Colonel J.S. Cowley, Yorkshire Light Infantry; John Willoughby, The Royal Green Jackets; Lieutenant B. Owen, The Welsh Regiment; Major D.I. Mack, The Royal Highland Fusiliers; Lieutenant-Colonel A.A. Pairrie, Queen's Own Highlanders; Captain C. Harrison, The Gordon Highlanders; Colonel J.R. Baker, The Royal Green Jackets (95th); Major J. Garbutt, 13th/18th Royal Hussars; Lieutenant-Colonel R. B. Merton, The Royal Hussars; Captain C. Boardman, 5th Royal Inniskilling Dragoon Guards; William Boag, United Service Museum (Scots Greys); Major J.T. Hancock, Royal Engineers (and sappers and staff corps); Roy Eyeions, Royal Army Medical Corps; C.W.P. Coan, Royal Corps of Transport (Wagon Train).

Also, I must express appreciation to: the staffs of the British (Museum) Library, the British Museum Manuscript Department, and the British Museum Map Library; Mrs Mavis Simpson of the Ministry of Defence Library, Whitehall; Richard Tubb, Librarian of the Royal United Services Library; Elizabeth Cuthbertson, Registrar of the Royal Archives - Windsor; The Public Record Office, Kew; Sue De Bie, Librarian of the Sandhurst Military Academy Library; Sally Magnusson of the Royal Engineers Museum Archives; Jenny Wraight of the National Maritime Museum, Greenwich.

For their expert help in translating old military texts, my thanks to: Brigadier Trofair of the Austrian Embassy; Colonel J. Smit of the Royal Netherlands Embassy; Captain H. Stradiot of the Royal Belgian Embassy; and Captains Reinhart, Ort and Mai of the Embassy of the Federal Republic of Germany. Major and Mrs Holt, of Holt's Battlefield Tours, Sandwich, Kent, have my gratitude for escorting me around the Waterloo battlefield (in absolute luxury), sometimes deviating from their planned route to an obscure part of the field for my sole benefit. For his photographic reproduction of rare map details and the use of photographs from his collection, my thanks to Richard Ellis, of Old Town Studios, Swindon. My sincere thanks to Stephen Dewey for making sense of my hieroglyphics; and my gratitude to Michael Boxall for editing the manuscript. Penultimately, I should like to express my deep gratitude to my publisher, Rod Dymott, for having faith in me throughout the long gestation of this book.

Because of space restrictions I have not included a bibliography in this book. However, as every work, manuscript, and source, without exception, is fully cited in chapter notes, the reader will be able to follow up any point of interest.

Finally, my appreciation to my wife, Sally-Ann, for her endless patience and understanding, and to my young sons, Oliver and Magnus, for their consideration of my need for quiet.

Inevitably, I must state that, while I have sought and received the expert advice of many, all conclusions, statements, errors and omissions fall to me alone.

David C. Hamilton-Williams, March 1993

The Siborne model – although the figures are wrongly placed, the ground is perfectly reproduced. The top illustration shows the view looking from behind the farmhouse of La Haye Sainte towards La Belle Alliance.

The lower view is from the same spot but towards Château Hougoumont. The viewer can appreciate the distance between it and La Haye Sainte and the extensive ground the château complex covered. (Photographs by courtesy of Richard Ellis)

Introduction:
Captain William Siborne

'Some errors obtain such firm possession of people's minds,
that it is extremely difficult to root them out, and, in consequence, they are sometimes
transmitted from age to age as acknowledged truths.' – A field officer
in *The United Service Journal*, June, 1839, p. 198.

N o one Englishman, not even the Duke of Wellington himself, has had so great an influence on the English-language historiography of the Battle of Waterloo as Captain William Siborne. So heavy has been Siborne's hand on the memory of the event that all histories of it to date, including those written by historians of the other nations involved, depend fundamentally on his interpretation.

To understand the way in which Siborne perverted his posterity's understanding of such an important event, and his reasons for doing so, it is appropriate and helpful to begin with a brief history of the evolution of the Captain Siborne who committed this crime against history. Siborne arrived in this world at Greenwich (fittingly, as both he and his meridian were to assume the role of prime demarcator in their respective fields) on 18 October 1797. He was educated as a gentleman-cadet at the Royal Military College, Great Marlow, and at Sandhurst (after its move). At the time of Waterloo, he was 18 and was serving as an ensign in 1st Battalion, 9th Foot. He did not fight in the battle because his unit did not arrive on the continent until afterward, but he served during the British army's subsequent occupation of Paris.

While on duty in Paris, Siborne saw the military models at Les Invalides and was greatly impressed with them. He began advocating the use of such models for the planning of operations; and in this he was far in advance of his time. Indeed, it is probable that his true talent lay in the field of topography. Already, by 1822, he had published two books on the subject of military topography, expounding '... The importance of Topographical Modelling in a military point of view...'

In 1830, Siborne was a lieutenant and an assistant military secretary to the British army Commander-in-Chief in Ireland. When he received news that the Belgian authorities intended extensive building on the battlefield site, Siborne conceived the idea of creating a topographical model of the field exactly as it was on 18 June 1815. To this end he petitioned the Commander-in-Chief of the Army, Lieutenant-General Lord Hill, who gave official sanction for the project and the promise of financial support.

Siborne spent eight months on the battlefield, staying at La Haye Sainte farmhouse, to carry out his topographical research. When he returned from the continent, he requested of Hill and received further permission to canvass all the surviving British officers who had fought in the battle. He conducted this canvass of necessity by correspondence, using an in-depth questionnaire designed to elicit details of the officers' roles in the battle, as well as information on the locations and dispositions of other units, and the type and condition of the ground and crops in the vicinity of their positions.

Great interest was generated throughout the British officer corps in the model and its development. Eight years after its inception it was completed, and was displayed in the Egyptian Hall, Piccadilly, from 4 October 1838. The model, to a scale of nine feet to a mile, was of considerable size: 27 feet 4 inches in length, and 19 feet 8 inches wide, with a surface area of 240 square feet. It was and remains to this day an impressive piece of craftsmanship. With some 70,000 figures, it is supposed to portray the situation right across the field at 7.15 p.m., when the Imperial Guard was about to assail the Allied line.

In 1844 Siborne decided to build another model, depicting another critical point in the battle, but on a larger scale than the first. The second model eventually measured 18 feet 7 inches, by 7 feet 9 inches, and was on a scale of 15 feet to a mile for terrain, and 1 inch to 6 feet for buildings and figures. It was to show the sublime (from the British perspective) moment when Uxbridge's cavalry charged d'Erlon's corps, utterly routing it. The second model required further technical investigation and appeared in the Egyptian Hall in 1845, alongside its predecessor. Also in 1844 Siborne wrote and published his two-volume *History of the War in France and Flanders in 1815*, containing minute details of the Battles of Quatre-Bras, Ligny, Wavre and Waterloo. This tome was supposed to be based on the enormous collection of letters and other primary source material which he had amassed during the preceding fourteen years. A large atlas covering the campaign and each engagement followed. In 1891, Major-General Herbert Siborne, son of William, published *The Waterloo Letters*, which contained 200 extracts of letters sent to his father. The published works of the Sibornes, *père et fils*, became, on their appearance, the definitive English language account of the battle.

Over the years, many writers and historians have attempted to present other interpretations of the great event, prompted by the anomalies which arose from treating the Siborne account as truly definitive. However, to make such an attempt in the latter part of the nineteenth century, and especially in Britain, was considered as the rankest heresy and, which was worse, ungentlemanly. An attack on Siborne was seen as an attack on the integrity of the British officers who had provided Siborne with their accounts. In 1899 Sir Herbert Maxwell wrote *A Life of Wellington*. In dealing with the Battle of Waterloo, Maxwell showed the forces of The United Netherlands as having played a more prominent part than had been credited to them by Siborne or Sibornic historians. In fact Maxwell had the effrontery to contradict Siborne's characterisation of The Netherlands troops. At once, no less a personage than Sir Charles Oman, Chichele Professor of Modern History at All Souls College, Oxford, rebutted Maxwell in the most vitriolic terms. Oman's article, 'The Dutch-Belgians at Waterloo', appearing in the prominent magazine *Nineteenth Century*, [1] accused the Dutch-Belgian forces not only of having been cowardly and of little use to Wellington, but of having been traitorously sympathetic to France and Napoleon. As an example of their alleged cowardice, Oman cited the actions of van Merlen's brigade at Quatre Bras. According to Oman, who rested of course on Siborne: 'There is no discredit to the brigade in having been repulsed, but it is an unfortunate fact that it could never be rallied sufficiently to make it possible to conduct it to a second charge. Out of the 1,080 sabres which it contained, only 22 had been killed and 146 wounded, but there was a dreadful deficit of 203 'missing' i.e., nearly a fifth of the men had absconded to the rear.' [2] Oman vouched for the authority of Siborne's interpretation on the basis that no one else had access to the amount of eye-witness information which had been made available to Siborne by the British officers who had been on the spot. Oman concluded on a note of challenge that anyone who disagreed with Siborne's 'irrefutable evidence should consult the wealth of data collected by Siborne'. Oman, by virtue of his stature as the pre-eminent Napoleonic historian of the day, and by his unanswerable challenge, deterred others from venturing into the realm of the apocryphal.

During Siborne's lifetime, and that of his son, no one in that more honour-conscious age would have presumed so far as to ask to inspect the letters in Siborne's collection. After all, Siborne had solicited the letters with the blessing of the army Commander-in-Chief, and, as a serving officer, Siborne was a gentleman, as were all the men with whom he had corresponded. One gentleman would not seek to read the correspondence of another; and if the enquirer were not a gentleman, he had no right to expect his request to receive any consideration. That is why Oman's challenge was unanswerable at the time, and Siborne's interpretation was deemed accurate on trust.

At the end of the last century the Siborne descendants donated the whole of William's voluminous correspondence to the Manuscript Department of the British Museum (now the British Library). There, for nearly a century the material has lain relatively undisturbed. The present author, however, decided to take up, albeit belatedly, Oman's challenge; not because he was feeling at all ungentlemanly (for such 'gentlemanliness' can be nothing more than the last refuge of a partisan), but from a desire to get closer to the truth. From 1985 to 1988, therefore, the present author spent nearly eight hours of every weekday in the British Library, laboriously transcribing the more than 700 manuscript letters that had been sent to Siborne. Further, in donating their forebear's archive material to the nation, the Siborne family included all the Captain's personal correspondence pertaining to his models. (It is fortunate indeed that Siborne was enough of an

21

historian to keep his own letters.) Thus, for the first time Siborne, as well as his work, came under scrutiny.[3]

A new picture began to emerge; one which had not been shown since 1830, a period of 160 years. The investigations carried out by the present author[4] were taken up by Dr David Chandler, Head of War Studies at Sandhurst Military Academy, resulting in a composite chapter on Siborne as an historian and model maker[5] for the National Army Museum's 1990 publication, *The Road to Waterloo*, marking the opening of a permanent gallery to exhibit the larger Siborne model.

Scrutiny of Siborne's own correspondence relating to the development of his models revealed a sad and sordid story of a man pursuing an obsession to the detriment of his health, wealth and, ultimately, his good name. In 1833, Captain Siborne, already heavily engaged in his project, was informed by the British government of the day that public funds would no longer be provided to finance what was a private endeavour being carried out in the hope of private gain (monies to be paid by the public to view the model).[6] The government agreed only to settle his account to date. Determined to continue, Siborne raised a private loan of £1,500, an enormous sum at the time. He was thus able to continue his work for a further period, although it represented a considerable burden in addition to his military duties, and there was also the worry of carrying such a large debt. By 1836 he was in an extremely embarrassed financial situation. In desperation he decided to try to raise loans from some of the veteran officers with whom he had been in correspondence, to be repaid from the proceeds of the eventual fee-charging exhibition. One such request, which may be seen in the manuscript collection,[7] asked the recipient for £5, but was amended to read £10. Sir Richard Hussey Vivian, who had commanded 6 Cavalry Brigade at Waterloo and was, when solicited, Siborne's own commanding officer, agreed to lend him £1,000.

From now on the objectivity which had marked Siborne's approach to his project became a luxury he could no longer afford. He felt constrained to enlarge the roles played by his benefactors, and correspondingly to suppress the evidence of other officers that tended to contradict those who had paid. He pressed on with the preparation of the model, haunted by the spectres of a bankrupt's disgrace and the debtors' prison. The completed model was placed on exhibition in 1838, but it never made enough money to pay half its cost. Nor did his 'investors' see their loans repaid, although Siborne tried to repay them with coin of a different stamp.

A plan of the model was shown to the Duke of Wellington, who wrote of it to a friend: 'No drawing or representation as a model can represent more than one moment of an Action, but this model tends to represent the whole action: and every Corps and Individual of all the nations is represented in the Position chosen by Himself. The Consequence is that the critical Viewer of the model must believe that the whole of each army, without any reserve of any kind, was engaged at the moment supposed to be represented. This is not true of any one moment or event or operation of this Battle; and I was unwilling to give any sanction to the truth of such a representation in this model, which must have resulted from my visiting it, without protesting against such erroneous representation. This I could not bring myself to do on [any] account; and I thought it best to avail myself of my absence from London, and of Indisposition, never to visit it at all.' [8] One cannot help speculating on how much Sibornic absurdity the world of Napoleonic history might have been spared had the Duke been ungentlemanly enough to have made his opinion public at the time.

With the financial failure of the first model, Siborne remained deeply in debt. To ameliorate his situation, he decided, with a perverse persistence, to make another model such as the one which had already nearly ruined him and had consumed years of his life. The second model, too, was a failure as a speculation, and served only to increase Siborne's heavy weight of debt. However, the campaign history which he produced in 1844 became at once a best-seller in military circles around the world. Naturally the book, which had been written to support the models, could not contradict what they showed.

The way in which Siborne selectively edited the manuscript material made available to him over the years of his correspondence, and the use he made of other sources, constitutes a catalogue of errors of historical sin and omission. In the first instance, he used only British sources, although even the most rabid 'patriot' would be prepared to admit that other nations were represented on the field. Siborne did not consult any Dutch, Belgian, Hanoverian, Prussian, Nassau or Brunswick sources. Apart from the letters of British officers, he was content to rely on *The Despatches of Field Marshal the Duke of Wellington*, edited by Lieutenant-Colonel Gurwood (1836), and Ludlow North Beamish's *History of the King's German Legion* (1832, 1837).

Siborne's only communication with a Frenchman was with the Prince of Essling, Duc de Rivoli, and son of the illustrious Marshal Massena. The Prince had served as aide to his father during his campaigns. Although he was certainly capable of answering Siborne's questions, he was taken aback by their basic nature. He expressed his surprise and gave some advice with a dry humour which may have been lost on his correspondent '... as you are a Lieutenant of the line, I cannot understand how you do not understand the elementary evolutions of infantry, that you are inquiring of me. It is my advice to you, to consult with the Duke of Wellington on these matters, for it is a subject that I know he understands, better than any other General'.[9] This was undoubtedly sufficient to discourage Siborne from pursuing his enquiries of the Prince. Siborne had never seen any active service, having spent the majority of his career in uniform as a military secretary or on secondment. He therefore had little understanding of strategy or tactics: that is, what a battle is intended to achieve, and how it is fought. He had asked the Prince to explain the difference between '*Colonne de Bataillon*

23

par Division' and *'Colonne de Division par Bataillon'*. The first was the order for a French division to go forward on a small two-company frontage by battalions, with proper intervals between them. This was the customary formation for a French infantry advance during the Napoleonic period. The second formation, which was used at Waterloo by Marcognet's and Donzelot's divisions, involved a division going forward on a broad battalion-wide frontage: that is, six companies across. Thus, a division so disposed would have its eight battalions lined up one behind another, with each battalion three-ranks deep, making a divisional depth of 24 ranks. Siborne, having been snubbed by the Prince of Essling, enquired no further, and in his history all the French divisions went forward 'in the same old way', that is, in *Colonne de Bataillon par Division*.

Upon its publication, Siborne's history created great controversy, especially among those who knew better. Major Macready of the 30th Foot, after several unanswered letters to Siborne, attempted to call upon him to discuss certain points in the narrative, but Siborne was never 'at home'. Macready was so upset by Siborne's account of the 30th at Waterloo, supposedly based on the testimony of an officer of the 30th, that he felt compelled to write several analytical articles, published in the (Royal) *United Service Journal* between March and June of 1845. [10] Macready challenged Siborne to produce a letter, 'any letter', from any officer of the 30th, that would corroborate Siborne's account of the actions of the 30th that day. Macready further said that he, Macready, had canvassed the recollections of all the five then surviving field officers of the 30th who had served at Waterloo. Curiously, none had chosen to take up Siborne's offer to purchase a subscription to the model venture, and none had subsequently received a questionnaire from Siborne. In his published reply to Macready, Siborne did not name the mysterious officer, but implied that he was of general's rank. Siborne put forward in support of his version of Waterloo the fact that General Halkett had viewed the model and had not criticised it, implying that Halkett had been the source for the contended account; although in fact he had not been. Macready argued that such an equivocal answer did not substantiate a statement of fact in a book purporting to be a history. Siborne sidetracked the issue with what would later be called stonewalling. Macready may perhaps have been mollified eventually, for when the next edition of the *History* came out it had been amended slightly to conform with Macready's version of the role of the 30th.

Relying heavily as he did on Wellington's published *Despatches*, Siborne also took on board the mistrustful attitude toward the Dutch and Belgians that was voiced often in the Duke's correspondence. The mistrust was completely without foundation, and was based on 'intelligence' provided to Wellington by General, later Marshal, Clarke, Duc de Feltre, who had been Napoleon's Minister of war from 1807 to 1814, when he conspired in the Emperor's betrayal. The most damning 'evidence', which caused the British Cabinet to warn Wellington to be wary of the Dutch and

Belgians, came from the man who had played Iago to Napoleon's Othello, Joseph Fouché, Minister of Police in Paris. Fouché sent Lord Castlereagh a copy of the 28 April 1815 issue of *Le Moniteur*, in which all Belgian and Dutch veterans and volunteers were invited to join Napoleon's army. In his accompanying note, Fouché added that Napoleon had supposedly said to Marshal Davout, then Minister of War: 'In this way I shall get eight or ten thousand soldiers.' [11] In fact, in 1815 Napoleon acquired only 378 assorted men from the Low Countries, who were considered fit only for garrison duty. Not a single Netherlands soldier deserted. After Waterloo, Wellington had the good grace to acknowledge the contribution of the Netherlanders. In 1831, however, the rebellion of the Belgians against Dutch rule, aided as it was by French troops, was inevitably cited by those inclined to see it so as further proof of at least Belgian perfidy.

A highly respected Dutch senior officer, General van Knoop, was disgusted by Siborne's treatment of his sovereign, King William II, who had been the Prince of Orange in 1815, and by Siborne's general portrayal of the actions of the Dutch and Belgian troops. By Royal authority, van Knoop published *Beschouwingen over Siborne's geschiedenis van den oolog in 1815* (Observations about Siborne's history of the war of 1815) (Breda, 1846). This scholarly work was immediately re-published by the French (Paris, 1846). In it, van Knoop examined every specific charge made against Dutch or Belgian troops, making judicious use of the actual divisional reports written immediately after the battle; reports which Siborne had not read. He was able to demolish Siborne's case against the United Netherlands forces. Van Knoop concluded that Siborne's defamatory remarks had been prompted by his desire to amplify the part of the British army at the expense of their allies. His book was never published or publicly discussed in Britain. To this day, the British Library does not possess a copy. Siborne even omitted a divisional account of the actions of Saxe-Weimar's brigade, not because of prejudice but because he did not bother or could not afford to obtain a translation of the German-language account sent to him. On the back of this account he simply pencilled fallaciously, 'from an unknown K.G.L. (King's German Legion) officer.' [12]

In writing his history, Siborne had sought to supplement his meagre knowledge of strategy and tactics with advice proffered by various of his paying correspondents. Sir James Shaw Kennedy, who had been on the British Quartermaster-General's staff at Waterloo, in discussing Siborne's views in the context of his own account, was generous enough to say that 'Siborne's account of the Campaign has very great merit ...', but he felt compelled to offer a detailed critique, velvet-gloved as it was: '... But Siborne fails in three respects: 1st, he was not well acquainted with the higher principles of the higher parts of war [command]; 2nd, he failed to separate the salient points of the battle of Waterloo... [and] 3rd, he was led into misapprehensions as to the effects of the cavalry attacks; and his views altogether respecting the cavalry attacks were erroneous and defective. I am aware that without it being in the slightest degree his fault, there were circumstances of importance on which he had not, and could not obtain, information.' [13]

Perhaps nearest the mark was the criticism of Siborne's book by Lieutenant-Colonel Charles Chesney, Professor of Military Art and History at the Royal Imperial Staff College in 1868: '... it has the essential faults of a national history written soon after a great war. Much that is in it would never have been inserted had the work not been largely dependent for support at its publication on the British Army.' [14]

With the possible exception of Professor Chesney, Siborne's critics, including the Duke of Wellington, Major Macready, General van Knoop and Sir James Shaw Kennedy, did not seem to fathom his chief motivation for distorting his history as he had – namely, the tyranny of financial necessity. In 1848 Siborne produced a campaign atlas which depicted on a series of beautifully executed maps the positions of the various forces throughout the 1815 campaign. Again, however, Siborne remained trapped in the web he had spun. After the expensive failure of the second model he faced mounting pressure and threats from his creditors, particularly a jeweller named Samuel Watts, who had made and assembled most of the larger model figures, and who was threatening Siborne with imprisonment for debt if he failed to settle his bill within a month. To raise money quickly, Siborne produced the atlas. He was able to do so in a short time because his principal map, of Waterloo, was based on another man's work, done years earlier. Immediately after the battle of Waterloo, a Belgian engineer, W.B. de Craan, by order of King William, made a map of the field. Working from 1815 to 1816, and with official information from all the divisional officers of all the Allied forces involved, provided through King William, de Craan produced a topographical map showing the positions of all the units of both sides where they stood at the start of the battle. Wellington inspected the map and approved it. The map was later presented to the British Royal Family, and some time afterwards Wellington wrote a memorandum on the map for King William IV, who had asked him for an explanation of the Prussian role. Wellington prefaced the memorandum by stating: 'I have looked over the plan of the ground of the battle of Waterloo, which appears to me to be accurately drawn.' [15] In 1831 the official copy of the de Craan map resided at Horse Guards. Siborne sought and received permission then to have a copy made of it for his use. [16] In producing his atlas, Siborne had simply to move the pieces around, so to speak, to conform with his models and history. And conform he was obliged to do; in order to protect his reputation and be able to pay his debts, he was obliged to persist in what he knew to be historical perjury.

A gross example of the errors contained in the Siborne model of the battle relates to his positioning of Bijlandt's brigade. Comparison with the brigade's position on the de Craan map, based on Netherlands' divisional accounts written two days after the event, shows the difference between the plausible and the ridiculous. For Siborne's position, based on the decades-old recollections of British officers, to be accepted, one would also have to accept that the Duke of Wellington and General Picton, not to mention General Perponcher, were capable of committing the most elementary error in disposing men on an open forward slope in the face of an enemy heavy in cavalry and artillery. Two days earlier, on 16 June, Wellington had been critical of the Prussians for putting men on an exposed forward slope. Such has been the pernicious effect of Siborne and his spurious authority that this false placement has been allowed to stand until this past decade.

Further, in being asked to accept Siborne's model, the viewer (or reader) would be expected to accept that Wellington fought the battle of Waterloo with only one line on his left, while on his right he had two lines and a reserve. One would also have to ignore Shaw Kennedy's expert testimony that Wellington always fought in two echelons, or lines, and a reserve, as he had done throughout the Peninsular Campaign. Shaw Kennedy's duty at Waterloo had been to ensure that the disposition of Wellington's army was carried out in accordance with the Duke's orders. The de Craan map accurately shows the Anglo-Allied army arranged as it actually was, with two lines and a reserve on both the right and left.

Even if Siborne had attempted fairly to portray the battle in accordance with the information supplied to him by the British officers who responded to his questionnaire, he would still have fallen victim to a fallacy based on a partial view. By taking the testimony of only British officers, Siborne restricted his primary source material to accounts of the action as seen almost entirely from one side of the field, and for only part of the time. Readers may demonstrate for themselves the truth of the first part of this fallacy in a simple and graphic way. Take any representation of the Anglo-Allied disposition at the outset of the battle.[17] Photocopy it, white-out the symbols representing all the Dutch, Belgian, Nassau, Brunswick, Hanover and KGL units, then photocopy the altered copy. The reader will thus have a map showing only the positions of the British units under Wellington's command. It will at once be apparent that, for the most part, British officers being asked to comment on the evolution of the battle could only have given an impression of what was occurring on Wellington's right. In the canonical material promulgated from the Sibornic 'church', there is normally nothing meaningful said about the fighting in the Smohain-Frischermont-Papelotte area because British officers for the most part did not see it and were not affected by it. With regard to the second part of the fallacy, during the latter part of the day, of the few British units remaining on the left, there were fewer still whose officers were unscathed. In some cases sergeants were in command of companies. Therefore the British accounts touching on the Allied left side of the battle tended to fall silent as the day wore on. There is little in Siborne's history regarding the left, and even less regarding the left after about 2 p.m. Consequently, in Sibornic treatments of

Waterloo, the narrative tends to pursue a major theme on the right through-out the day, while its minor theme on the left inexplicably subsides below the threshold of the reader's awareness.

Not surprisingly the sins of the father were taken up by the son. Major-General Herbert Siborne edited his then deceased father's papers in 1890–1. In 1891, the celebrated *Waterloo Letters* was published. With these, Herbert no doubt sought, out of a praiseworthy filial devotion, to embellish the memory of his father. In the preparation of the book, he employed a method which his father would have recognised. He prepared edited extracts of 200 of the 503 letters that were in William's collection. Anything which seemed to disagree with the content of the Siborne models and history or detract from their reputation as pillars of the temple of late-Victorian belief in British martial invincibility was omitted. One letter, appearing on pages 350–2, written by Captain Mountsteven of the 28th, had been lightened by a complete paragraph, which exists in the manu-script copy (B.L. Add. MS. 34703, 19 August 1839). In the excised para-graph Mountsteven related how he had stopped his men from firing on a body of Dutch-Belgians who had charged forward to attack d'Erlon's retreating Frenchmen. Siborne Junior could not allow this to stand as it contradicted Siborne Senior's contention that all the Netherlanders in that part of the line had already run away in the other direction. In some cases also, an earlier and more candid letter by a respondent would be left aside in favour of a later, substantially altered letter from the same officer, after the officer had agreed to be gilded in exchange for gold. Siborne *fils* also ignored accounts from journals written almost immediately after the event, using instead differing accounts written much later when memory was occluded by the haze of time.

With regard to the Kiplingesque jingoism rampant in Victorian Britain, it should be said in mitigation of condemnation of Siborne that at least he could plead financial necessity, but no such excuse could be made available to Professor Oman and his ilk. For them are reserved places on a lower level of purgatory than that upon which Siborne's shade may yet linger. If Siborne was an opportunist, Oman was an intellectual bigot whose academic training should have held him above the mire of the inter-pretation of history through base emotion. In the matter of his charge of cowardice laid on The Netherlands troops, Oman knew of but refused to consult any Netherlands reports, accounts, memoirs or diaries dealing with Quatre Bras. Pilate-like, Oman raised the question of Netherlands' cow-ardice, but did not seek the answer. If he had wished he could have found the honest answer to why there were 203 reported 'missing' among the Netherlands cavalry in a single charge of the battle on the 16th. The leading (Belgian) regiment of Netherlands light horse wore green uniforms and spoke French. Having charged the French, they were riding back to their lines to regroup and were closely pursued by French lancers, also wearing green uniforms. Both Belgian and French cavalry were shouting excitedly –

in French. British soldiers newly arrived at the Quatre Bras position, who had not previously been integrated with Netherlands forces, understandably mistook the whole crowd galloping toward them for French and fired several volleys in their direction. In keeping with the general maxim of the day, 'aim for the horses', most of the resulting casualties were among the Belgians' mounts. Because of the generally disorganised state that the Anglo-Allied army had been thrown into by Wellington's multiple movement orders issued on the night of 15th/16th, these dismounted Belgian troopers were unable to obtain remounts until after the 18th. Thus these men were therefore counted as missing, in the sense that they were not available for active duty. The bravery of The Household Brigade at Waterloo is undoubted, and is readily acknowledged by both the biased and the unbiased among English-language and other historians. How would it appear, though, if The Household's conduct had been scrutinised in the same way as Siborne, Oman and their fraternity had done with the Netherlanders? A total of 1,416 Household sabres were reported present at the start of the battle on the 18th; and at the end, 114 were reported as killed, 264 wounded and 245 missing. And this after eleven charges, while the Netherlands' casualties were suffered in only one charge. Using Oman's criterion of judgement, one would have to conclude that The Household cavalry, having suffered a far lower ratio of losses per charge than the Netherlanders, had been far less aggressive. The true solution to this riddle is of course that The Household cavalry were not fired upon by their own side as they were recalled to re-group, disordered and vulnerable.

Siborne did not even have the sense of purpose of an honest bigot in his calumniation of the Dutch and Belgians; instead, he backed into it circumstantially, just as he had with other wrong turnings which once taken had to be pursued. The choice of the Netherlanders as scapegoats for anything that seemed to have gone wrong in the campaign had already been made before Siborne entered the lists. From 1815 to 1816, in the first flush of victory, British panegyrists had tried to appoint the Prussians in the role, but Blücher's strong representations to Wellington frustrated them. By shortening their range somewhat they found in the Netherlanders a target which could not bring to bear as heavy a weight of counter-battery fire as could the Prussians. Siborne simply followed the path of least resistance.

To the catalogue of Siborne's more serious crimes may be added a petty misdemeanour: that of sycophancy. The only Netherlands army officer whom Siborne deigned to anoint with his blessing was the Prince of Saxe-Weimar, who 'behaved well'. Only the most jaundiced eye could see an attempt to curry favour in the coincidence of this favourable exception being made in a book dedicated to Queen Victoria, who was related by marriage to the House of Saxe-Weimar-Coburg-Saalfeld.

It is small wonder that Siborne's history was received with hyperbolic praise by like-minded men when it was published in 1844. The April edition of *The United Service Journal* of that year declared: 'Since the

6,000 years the world has existed never a more important work has been published than Siborne's.' The Lord may have created the world, but Siborne had re-created Waterloo. However, whereas the Lord looked on His creation and found it good, Siborne's was imbued to the core with the sin of deliberate flouting of the cardinal rule of historiography: the balanced search for truth. Siborne broke the rule, and in so doing wronged many good men and deceived many others. His book was more than a bad book; it was a bad deed.

CHAPTER 1

The End and the Beginning

'A man's worth is no greater than the worth of his ambitions.'
- The Emperor Marcus Aurelius Antoninus, *Meditations*, c.AD 170.

By 1814, the Emperor Napoleon had ruled France absolutely for fourteen years. His empire, the largest European political entity since the western Roman Empire, stretched from Brest to Poland and from Spain to Denmark. It encompassed parts of Illyrian Croatia and Serbia. Italy, Naples and the greater part of the German principalities were client provinces. Napoleon had created vassal kings of Saxony, Bavaria, Württemberg, Westphalia, Spain, Holland, and Naples. He had elevated, throughout his vast Empire, princes, dukes, counts and barons. Prussia, Russia, Denmark, and Norway had been his allies. The Emperor of Austria, Francis I, was his father-in-law and grandfather to his son, the King of Rome.

Now, on 1 April 1814, Napoleon was in his Imperial palace at Fontainebleau, while within the walls of Paris were the armies of Russia, Prussia, and Austria, awaiting his attack. Traitors had betrayed Paris to the enemy by deliberately making it indefensible.[1] In fact, Napoleon faced two opponents in 1814: the foreign and the domestic enemies of his dynasty. His chief foreign foe was Great Britain, which had fought him on land and sea and had continually bribed other continental states to fight him. Britain had been at war with France since 1 February 1793, with a brief hiatus during the period of the Peace of Amiens in 1802-3. King George III had called the Peace of Amiens 'an Experimental Peace'. It had been forced on him by his war-weary parliament. King George's Prime Minister, William Pitt, who had already resigned on an unrelated matter of political principle, wept when the conclusion of the Peace was announced by his successor. During the brief life of the treaty Pitt's party and the King had maintained an unrelenting policy of non-compliance with its terms. This soon produced the desired effect of provoking Napoleon into renewing the war, and Pitt was returned as Prime Minister in 1804. Pitt feared Napoleon more than Napoleon knew. Napoleon assumed that Britain simply resented French commercial competition on the seas. But it was the threat to Britain represented by Napoleon's military genius coupled with the expansionary impulse of post-revolutionary France which made Pitt and his government the Emperor's implacable foes. In this respect the Britain of Pitt mirrored the Rome of Cato. The great Censor would end every speech in the Senate by declaring that Carthage must be destroyed; in like wise did Pitt rail in Cabinet and Parliament against Napoleonic France.

Twice during its revolution France had tried to invade Britain, once in Ireland and once in Wales. These attempts were disturbing to Britain, especially when the Irish foray coincided with local rebellion, but they did not represent serious dangers. Napoleon, upon his assumption to power, had applied his enormous talent to the problem of mounting such an invasion. By his possession of Belgium, and the great inland port of Antwerp, Napoleon posed the greatest threat that Britain had faced since William the Conqueror. 'Antwerp is a pistol pointed at the heart of England', Pitt declared to Parliament, and he was right. In the time between the failure of the Peace of Amiens in 1803 and September 1805, Napoleon had massed his Grande Armée of 178,000 men along the French coast facing England. At Brest Marshal Augereau commanded 13,500 men. Napoleon's army of 135,000 men was disposed from the Pas de Calais to Belgium, with a concentration around Antwerp. Pitt, using the wealth of Britain, had bribed Austria and Russia to form a coalition to attack Napoleon in the rear, distracting him from the planned invasion.

In September 1805, Napoleon awaited on the Channel coast the arrival of the Franco-Spanish fleet under Villeneuve, who had slipped out of Toulon past Nelson's blockading ships. Napoleon did not intend to mount his real invasion of England on the south coast as was generally believed by the British public. He intended that Villeneuve's fleet, together with part of his army, would attempt a cross-Channel attack as a diversion that would preoccupy British land and naval forces. His main invasion force would embark in a flotilla of specially built boats from Antwerp and the Scheldt estuary. With a favouring wind, as was prevalent at that time of year, this flotilla would in twelve hours have reached the Thames estuary. They would land near Tilbury, take London, then if necessary take in the rear the British forces – mainly poorly trained militia – defending the south coast beaches. The task of Villeneuve's fleet was twofold: to assist the diversionary assault on the English south coast, and, more importantly, to screen the main invasion force from the British fleet based on Channel ports. Like Caesar, Napoleon was no sailor; he was applying to his seaborne invasion the same strategy he used on land.

Admiral Lord Nelson, in a secret memorandum to Pitt in 1801, had declared that if Napoleon attempted to invade by the Scheldt-Thames route during or some time after September in the year, he would in all probability effect a landing. Nelson explained that this would be so because the equinoctial gales which spring up in the North Sea during this period would make an uninterrupted blockade of the Scheldt estuary impossible. At the onset of a gale the British blockading ships would have to seek shelter in their Channel ports and roads. When the gale had abated the ships would require at least twelve hours to reassemble on station. During those vital twelve hours Napoleon would in Nelson's estimation have enough time to get his flotilla across the North Sea and make an unopposed landing.[2]

As it happened, of course, Villeneuve's fleet did not reach the Channel, but was defeated by Nelson at Trafalgar, and Britain's purchased allies were persuaded to march on France. Napoleon felt obliged to abandon the invasion attempt for the time being. Without Villeneuve's fleet he had no diversionary attack and no screen for his Antwerp flotilla. Also, he did not feel he could risk being engaged in England while a sizeable Austro-Russian force was marching on his capital. Napoleon therefore marched his Grande Armée away from the coast and led it to the great victories at Ulm and Austerlitz, which established at a stroke his dominance of the continent.

Pitt and his successors believed firmly that only Napoleon's removal from power would ensure Britain's security. Toward that end, and particularly to keep large French forces away from the Channel coast, Britain fomented coalition after coalition against Napoleon. In 1805, Pitt elaborated the theme of British anti-Napoleonic policy in a treaty with Russia.[3] The sections of the treaty touching upon Britain's security were embodied in several secret protocols, considered so sensitive that they were not even included in the draft put before Parliament for fear that Napoleon might learn of them. According to these protocols, Britain and Russia were committed to restoring the House of Bourbon to the French throne, creating a British-dependent client kingdom of Holland, and establishing in Belgium a military barrier consisting of fortified cities and towns, such as Antwerp, Mons and Ypres, which could hold an advancing French army long enough for a British expeditionary force to be assembled and landed behind the barrier.

The British governments of the period so feared the threat of invasion by Napoleon that they twice ordered the Royal Navy to attack the fleets of third countries against the possibility that Napoleon, with his well-known swiftness, might gain control of them before they could be put beyond his reach. The first such pre-emptive strike was against the Dutch fleet in the Texel in 1805. The second, against the Danish fleet in Copenhagen harbour in 1807, was more drastic. Neutral Denmark was under pressure to join Napoleon's Continental System. On the assumption that the Danes would not be able to resist Napoleon's invitation, Britain dispatched a fleet. When the Danes proved as reluctant to 'lend' their fleet to Britain as to France, the British fleet bombarded the trapped Danish fleet and the Danish capital, causing considerable loss of life and damage to property. A combined sea and land assault on the Danes resulted in the British fleet returning home with such Danish ships and naval stores that had survived the bombardment. A proper receipt was given for the 'loan' and the British Prime Minister professed surprise and dismay to Parliament when the King of Denmark and Norway allied his nation with France.

Thus Britain and France conducted a mutual siege. Britain pursued a blockade of France and her allies by sea. Under its terms foreign goods could only be landed in ports occupied by, or friendly to, France after a licence and British duty had been paid in a British port. Britain had more ships than all the other European navies combined and so was able to enforce the blockade by stopping and searching neutral vessels. This policy in itself caused a war with hitherto neutral America in 1812. Napoleon had responded to Britain's naval blockade with his Continental System, which attempted to embargo any British goods reaching the mainland of Europe. All British imports were to be seized, any British captured, civilian or otherwise, were to be considered as prisoners of war, and any European country that opened its ports to Britain was liable to invasion. In consequence of this policy, Napoleon invaded Naples and removed its pro-British Bourbon ruler. He also took from the Pope the temporal lands of the Romagna because the pontiff refused to close its ports. And in the Iberian peninsula, Napoleon sent armies into Bourbon Spain and Portugal to stop those countries allowing British goods to be landed. In 1812, Napoleon invaded Russia in part to stop her breaking the embargo by supplying vital naval stores to Britain – pine tar, spirits, and timber for masts and spars. Further, unlike the indecisive Danes, the Russians, perhaps recalling the fate of the Dutch fleet seized by Pichegru's cavalry in 1795, sent their entire Baltic fleet, which would have been icebound in winter, to England to keep it out of Napoleon's reach.

The chief domestic enemy of Napoleon's dynasty during this period was the Bourbon Comte d'Artois, brother of the executed King Louis XVI and second in the old line of succession to the throne. To keep the royalist cause alive d'Artois had established a terrorist organisation in Jersey in 1791,[4] run along Masonic lines and financed by the British Government. Pitt, in his ruthless determination to destroy Napoleon, disbursed money to d'Artois' group through the secret service fund without the knowledge of Parliament.[5] From 1800 to 1805, this royalist organization attempted no fewer than six times to assassinate Napoleon. The most famous occasion, or infamous from a Bonapartist point of view, was the 'infernal machine', a huge bomb which exploded in Paris, in the Rue Sainte-Nicaise, within moments of Napoleon's carriage passing it. This horse-drawn bomb killed more than 22 people, maimed another 56, and demolished half the buildings in the street.

In 1812, Napoleon marched a mixed army of 500,000 men into Russia to coerce the Tsar into complying with his embargo. As a consequence of internal politics Napoleon – against his own inclination – decided to retreat from Moscow at the onset of winter. He arrived back in Paris on 18 December 1812, but only 58,000 of the Grande Armée got back with him. In Paris he found that a *coup d'état* mounted by General Malet, and aided by d'Artois' organisation, had almost succeeded in taking control of the capital and forming a provisional government.[6]

As the new year 1813 began, all over Europe the crowned heads celebrated the demise of the feared warlord following his disastrous retreat from Moscow. Prussia had been browbeaten into joining Russia in liberating Europe from Napoleon's yoke. In fact the Tsar hoped to parade triumphally in Paris in revenge for Napoleon's capture of Moscow. He also planned that if instead he had to come to terms with Napoleon, he would keep all the Polish territory then occupied by Russian forces. This at least would give him a satellite buffer zone along the traditional invasion route into Russia from Europe. In 1805, King Frederick William III of Prussia had agreed not to join Russia and Austria in their attack on France in return for possession of King George's patrimony, Hanover. The next year, 1806, however, in response to a series of annexations and indignations which included Napoleon's offer to return Hanover to King George in exchange for peace, Prussia declared war on France. The Prussian army, developed by Frederick the Great, had been feared in Europe for its successes against the armies of France, Russia, Austria and the lesser German states. But in his war against Prussia and Russia in 1806-7, Napoleon shattered the Prussian army in a lightning campaign lasting less than a month. Prussia suffered the additional humiliations of the occupation of Berlin and the loss of almost all its territory. Napoleon, brooking no rival in Germany, had reduced the Prussian state and army to a level of impoverishment. Now, in 1813, the Prussian king was promised by Russia substantial restitution of what he had lost, plus the kingdom of Saxony whose stature had been elevated above that of Prussia by Napoleon, the further to humiliate the Prussian king.[7]

Austria had risen against Napoleon in 1809 and been badly beaten and bankrupted as a result. The Austrian Emperor, Francis, had then given his daughter, Marie-Louise, in marriage to Napoleon. Within a year the French Emperor had a male heir of Habsburg blood. In 1813 Austria sat on the fence to see how events would develop.[8] The general celebrations of Napoleon's demise were, of course, premature. Early in 1813 he raised another army of 400,000 men with which to regain his lost position. Suddenly, he erupted into the German plain and trounced the Russo-Prussian forces there, driving them out of Dresden and back across the Elbe,[9] but was obliged to grant a temporary armistice because he had outstripped his supply lines.[10] He was then presented by his father-in-law with a diplomatic blackmail. Austria would use its rapidly assembling army of 300,000 to support a peace plan if Napoleon would give up his domination of the Confederation of the Rhine and his claims on Poland and Austrian Italy. If Napoleon agreed Francis would force Russia and Prussia into negotiations; if not, Francis would join the other emperors against his son-in-law. Napoleon was disgusted by this 'family stab in the back'. He spurned Francis' threat and embarked on a brilliant campaign that was hampered by having to fight on three widely divergent fronts and by a lack of suitable army commanders. As Napoleon marched and countermarched on extended lines of communication, he found that for every gain he made his subordinates suffered three losses. At Dresden on 25 August 1813, when Napoleon returned to the city, he found it besieged by three monarchs,

Russian, Prussian and Austrian, and their armies totalling 251,000 men. As he appeared in the city through the pouring rain, a great cheer arose from the French lines which demoralized the enemy. The next morning Napoleon attacked the besieging armies with 98,000 men. The great allied force was seized by panic and was routed with the loss of 40,000 killed, wounded or captured. Napoleon was striken with fever and diarrhoea caused by exhaustion and exposure during his forced march to Dresden in torrential rain, and so could not supervise the pursuit. One of the French commanders, Vandamme, left to his own devices, led his men into a Prussian trap and effectively lost a corps, thus muting his chief's victory. Eventually Napoleon decided to fight on interior lines around Leipzig, Saxony's second city. There he concentrated his three armies and waited for the enemy to come to him.

Lord Castlereagh, Britain's Foreign Secretary, had envoys at the allied Headquarters, attached to each of the three sovereigns of Russia, Prussia, and Austria. Their reports showed that the alliance was one in name only. Each of Britain's allies had its own aims and aspirations, as indeed had Britain. Castlereagh was further taken aback to find that the allied European monarchs had little interest in Britain or her part in the conflict, save for her financial backing. After all, they saw not one British soldier in the main theatre facing Napoleon; Wellington's army in the Iberian peninsula was viewed as of little importance. Further, Britain's naval policy, termed its 'maritime rights',[11] was considered to be high-handed. Russia, the only ally with a seagoing navy, had great sympathy with the position of the United States which in 1813 was still at war with Britain over Britain's assertion of its maritime rights. None of the allies, it appeared, had a single war aim in common.[12]

Castlereagh was also offended that Metternich, Austria's Foreign Minister, had offered Napoleon a negotiated peace about which Britain had not been consulted[13] and by which Britain would have been left isolated. But Austria was motivated by two main concerns. First, it was thought essential that the Austrian army sustain no serious losses. The army was needed to police the empire, keeping its diversity of ethnic populations under control. Also, Austria would need a substantial army in being as a strong card at the post-war conference to rearrange the political boundaries of Europe. The second main concern was that Austria only wanted to weaken Napoleon sufficiently so that he would accede to their demands. They wanted a strong, if subdued, Napoleon in control of France after the war as a counterbalance to potential Russian or Prussian efforts at aggrandizement. Metternich respected Napoleon's achievement in unifying France after its revolution and especially his halting of the spread of dreaded revolution across Europe. To Metternich Napoleon represented order and stability. Furthermore, Napoleon's first-born son, heir to the French imperial throne, was grandson to Metternich's sovereign.[14] For all these reasons Metternich prevailed upon Francis, as the sovereign with the largest force in the field, to choose the rotund Prince Schwarzenberg, master of deliberation and consensus, rather than the warlike and capable general Archduke Charles, to be the supreme allied commander.

The great Battle of Leipzig was fought over the three days of 16-18 October 1813. During the battle Austria and Russia fell out because the Austrians were reluctant to fight in a decisive manner. As a result of the defection of some of his allies at a critical juncture, Napoleon was forced to retreat. The only avenue open was a single bridge over the River Elster, Metternich having arranged for this route to remain unblocked to ensure Napoleon's escape back to the French border.[15] After Leipzig, Metternich nearly tricked the impressionable young British envoy Lord Aberdeen into agreeing a peace treaty which would not only leave France in possession of Belgium, but would asserted that France had maritime rights equal to those of Britain.[16] The British Cabinet was sufficiently shocked by this development to send Lord Castlereagh, the Foreign Secretary, to the allied Headquarters to represent Britain. Castlereagh had been vested by his Cabinet colleagues with a wide authority amounting to *carte blanche*. He bribed his impoverished allies with five million pounds in gold, an incredible sum for the period, and blackmailed the Tsar over Russia's fleet which was being held in British custody for the duration.[17]

Using this combination of carrot and stick, Castlereagh engineered an Allied policy of attacking France until Napoleon would agree to accept the return of France to its 'ancient', or pre-revolutionary, borders, which excluded Belgium. Britain's allies favoured offering Napoleon a France confined within its 'natural' borders, the Pyrenees, the Alps and the Rhine. The continental allies did not regard Belgium as of any importance. The Emperor of Austria, who did not think in terms of sea power and who had owned Belgium before the French revolution, would have been content to have it remain in the family, first with his son-in-law and later with his grandson. But adherence to 'natural' borders in this case would have left Antwerp and the Scheldt within France. Such was the Machiavellian character of alliances in Europe of that period (and, indeed, in most places and periods throughout history), that Castlereagh could not be so candid as to reveal that the British Government viewed Belgium as Britian's strategic Achilles' heel and would feel obliged to fight on indefinitely as long as it remained in hands as unsafe to British interests as Napoleon's.

When the Allied armies invaded France in 1814, Napoleon was inspired to fight one of his most brilliant campaigns. The Duke of Wellington was of the opinion that if Napoleon had been allowed to continue he would undoubtedly have won. In one engagement Napoleon faced 100,000 Allied soldiers with only 30,000 men and the Allies remained most of the day in a defensive position fearing his attack. Napoleon then casually withdrew his small army from this dangerous position apparently without fear of interference from his enemy. At Montereau on 17 February, with fewer than 60,000 men, Napoleon threw an Allied army of 120,000 into headlong flight. In these victories he was aided by Austria's politically motivated preference for retreat rather than running the risk of losing its army. A crisis arose when Austria and Russia argued over their respective war aims. Austria threatened to withdraw from the coalition and make a separate peace with Napoleon,[18] but Castlereagh persuaded Metternich that, if Austria carried out its threat, it would have no voice in the settlement discussions following the likely Allied victory. To induce Francis to fight on toward the goal of replacing his son-in-law with the Bourbon claimant, thus disinheriting his daughter and grandson, Castlereagh assured Metternich that Britain would provide additional funds to bankroll Austria and would support her against the claims of Russia and Prussia. Such support, Castlereagh told Metternich, would also be forthcoming from a Bourbon France. After all, he reasoned, the Austrian Emperor could retain possession of the French Emperor's acknowledged heir, his own grandson, and hold him in pledge. Therefore any Bourbon monarch installed on the French throne would be obliged to comply with Austrian wishes or the Austrian Emperor could take up arms in the time-honoured cause of dynastic war: in this case to secure for his grandson his French imperial inheritance.[19]

Austria agreed secretly to this arrangement, which Castlereagh explained to his Prime Minister only in the vaguest language, to hide Britain's post-war political commitment to Austria. Russia, however, had no wish to see a Bourbon replace Napoleon. When the Tsar and his late father had given sanctuary to the Bourbons after the French Revolution, the Tsar had come to know them; and with familiarity came contempt. The homeless French Bourbons later took up residence in England, no doubt encouraged to do so by the chilly atmosphere in Russia. The Tsar, in 1814, wished to see Napoleon replaced by a regency for the young King of Rome or by the Crown Prince of Sweden, the ex-Marshal Bernadotte, installed as the Tsar's puppet.

Now events proceeded at a rapid pace and by devious turns. Baron Vitrolles, one of the Comte d'Artois' agents, arrived at the Allied Headquarters with a letter from Prince Talleyrand. Talleyrand, once Napoleon's Foreign Minister but now his nemesis, urged in his letter that the Allies advance to take Paris. The Tsar was happy to accept any assistance from within Napoleon's capital, but told Vitrolles that he would not support a Bourbon restoration. Vitrolles then departed, supposedly to see d'Artois in Nancy, where he was attempting through his agents to give the appearance to the Allied sovereigns that the French people were all royalists at heart. In fact Vitrolles accompanied Metternich and Francis to Dijon, where the Austrian Emperor and his Foreign Minister were going ostensibly to secure the safety of their persons during such a dangerously fluid situation. Once in Dijon Metternich and Vitrolles arranged through d'Artois that the numerous royalists in Paris would support Talleyrand in his efforts to subvert Napoleon's position. Talleyrand's price to the Allies for his treason covered both eventualities. If the Allies won, Talleyrand and his collaborators would retain their Napoleonic titles, receive a suitable cash payment and keep whatever offices they had held. In the event that Napoleon prevailed, or if the Allies came to some arrangement with him, Talleyrand and his collaborators would be guaranteed immunity and safe passage from France as part of any peace terms. The Allies agreed to Talleyrand's conditions, and Castlereagh said he was prepared to suppy the required payment, but was unable to pay the large sum directly from the secret service fund. Austria agreed to 'launder' the money, receiving the sum from Britain as though it were part of its subsidies and paying it on to Talleyrand. Thus Castlereagh was able to conceal these sordid arrangements from Parliament and the British public.[20]

Napoleon then sent a letter to the Empress that had fatal consequences. In it he revealed his intention to strike northward then east, cutting across the rear of the Allied armies nearest Paris and severing their communications. This, he felt, would cause them to halt their advance or even recoil into defensive positions. As he traversed the Allied rear, Napoleon intended to gather troops from the garrisons of border fortresses. With his augmented force he would attack the disconcerted Allied armies piecemeal and send them scuttling yet again back toward the Rhine. The messenger carrying this most indiscreet letter was captured by Prussians under the command of Field Marshal von Blücher and a copy was sent to Allied Headquarters. On the strength of its information, coupled with Talleyrand's advice, the Tsar decided to move the armies forward to capture Paris when Napoleon was several days' march into his intended sweep.

An Allied force of cavalry 10,000 strong manoeuvred to screen the march on Paris and to make Napoleon's men think it was acting as the advance guard of the Allied army. In the meantime Talleyrand had lost no time in suborning many prominent figures in Napoleon's government. That a man of Talleyrand's political stature and known astuteness was openly opposing Napoleon persuaded them that their master's cause must indeed be lost and that they too should follow the old French maxim of *sauve qui peut*. Among the more than 800,000 souls living in Paris in 1814 was the largest royalist community in France. These people were at once set to work pasting up anti-Napoleonic and anti-war posters, and generally spreading dissent. The wealthy royalists precipitated a run on the banks and refused credit in their establishments, thus creating a cash crisis in the capital. Napoleon's Minister of War, General Clarke, and the garrison commander, General Hulin, together with the Chief of Police, Baron Pasquier, turned their coats at Talleyrand's solicitation. Napoleon had left his inept brother, Joseph, in Paris as Lieutenant-General of the Kingdom. Joseph was prevented by the turncoat Ministers from carrying out measures to defend Paris. As the Allies approached Paris a paralysis seemed to overtake the civil services and departments controlled by the turncoats. Joseph was unable to raise more than 12,000 National Guardsmen, while unknown to him tens of thousands of volunteers were being sent out of Paris by General

Clarke to parts of France remote from the capital or the Emperor.[21] Joseph was obliged to arm half his men with pikes because he had been told that there were no serviceable muskets to be had. In fact 20,000 good muskets were stored in the Paris magazine, but these were said to be awaiting repair.

Joseph had been frightened by the conspirators into believing that Paris was indefensible. In a panic he repeatedly pressed the Empress to write to Napoleon asking him to make peace on any terms. Napoleon, infuriated with his brother's craven attitude, suspected him of treason and instructed the Empress to keep away from him. Believing that all was up with his illustrious brother, Joseph contacted his brother-in-law, Bernadotte, the Crown Prince of Sweden,[22] through his wife's sister, the Crown Princess, who was living unmolested in Paris. Bernadotte advised Joseph to make only a token defence. This advice accorded with the plans of the conspirators.

Napoleon, attacking the Allied cavalry screen, soon realized that there was nothing behind it. While awaiting some development, he received a warning from his Postmaster-General, Count Lavellette, to return immediately to Paris, as '... there are men in league with the foreigners encouraged by what has happened in Bordeaux, they are raising their heads, supported by secret intrigue. The Emperor's presence is vital if he wants to keep his capital from being handed over to the enemy. There is not a moment to lose.' Bordeaux, in the southwest of France, had been betrayed to Wellington's advancing Anglo-Portuguese force by its royalist mayor who was a leading member of d'Artois' organization. The mayor and his secret 'regiment' of fellow royalists had made a theatrical occasion of their treachery by their effusive greeting of the Duc d'Angoulême, d'Artois' son, and their giving of the city to him for King Louis XVIII.[23] The propaganda value of this act to Talleyrand in Paris and to Castlereagh was immense.

Alerted by Count Lavellette, Napoleon ordered his army to march on Paris and raced ahead himself, accompanied only by his personal guard. Paris is bisected by the River Seine, which is joined by a tributary at the south-east edge of the city. Thus, from Fontainebleau on the south-easterly approach to Paris around to the north-easterly approach there are forty miles and two rivers intervening. Napoleon hoped that if the northern defences of Paris were held for a day, he could, as he had done at Dresden, enter the besieged city from the south, followed at their best speed by his army. He could then rally the citizens, organize a combined force and sally forth to deliver the Allies a stunning blow.

As a result of Napoleon's foray to the north the Allies' communications had been cut. Not one cannon or musket-ball had reached them for eleven days. The Allies did not have enough ammunition for the 33-hour bombardment they calculated would be needed to force the surrender of the city. Further, as the Allied army had been reduced to 180,000 men, it was not numerous enough to hold the city's full perimeter.

On 28 March, Joseph acted out a charade before the Council of

Ministers, reading from an outdated letter from Napoleon to himself, purporting it to be a current order from the Emperor. By this means the Empress and many government officials were induced to flee Paris. Their decision was, of course, approved by General Clarke and the other conspirators. General Clarke also deliberately stationed a mobile artillery park of heavy field pieces in the south of the city, away from the scene of the impending battle. Marshals Marmont and Mortier alerted Paris that they were retreating on the city before the Allied advance. On their arrival Joseph placed the command of the city and its defence in Marmont's hands, wishing to distance himself from it.

The next day, the 29th, found a city demoralized by royalist posters announcing the departure that day of the Empress and the government. With the citizens having been prevented from arming or volunteering to fight, Marmont had next to nothing with which to confront the Allies and no time to take stock of the situation and prepare a defence. No earthworks had been dug and no wooden ramparts erected, although there was plenty of labour and wood available. Although Napoleon had ordered the strategic heights of Montmartre to be fortified with redoubts and 600 heavy calibre cannon, Generals Clarke and Hulin had neglected to do this and the cannon remained stored in the arsenals. Marmont himself placed 30 cannon on Montmartre, but Clarke removed the National Guardsmen who were assisting the few trained gunners manning the cannon, with the result that only six cannon could be employed.

Marmont's defence was superb, given the material, or rather the lack of it. The Allies, expecting no resistance, were blooded. But no sooner had Marmont decided to withdraw from the northern suburbs to man the walls of the city, than Joseph sent him an order either to hold his position in the suburbs until the Emperor should arrive, or to surrender.[24] Joseph thereupon rode out of Paris to join the Empress. Marmont arranged an honourable surrender which would allow his forces to withdraw southward from the city, with their equipment, to join their advancing Emperor. At dinner that night Talleyrand convinced Marmont that all was lost with Napoleon and the war. He suggested that Marmont follow his example and agree to accept high office under a restored Bourbon monarchy. Talleyrand produced documents signed by the Allies and d'Artois attesting to the Allies' approval of these terms. Marmont was seduced and agreed to betray his Emperor. A messenger then arrived from Napoleon with his order to Marmont to refuse to sign any surrender document. The message informed him that Napoleon was only four hours' away and would be in the city by midnight. Constant in his treachery, Marmont expedited the withdrawal of his troops and advanced the planned hand-over of the city to the Allies. This, of course, was not known to Napoleon.[25]

Napoleon heard the incredible news of Marmont's withdrawal at Juvisy. At Fontainebleau he awaited his army. From there he would attack the Allies in Paris and recapture the city. He knew that the Allies were in a difficult situation. They would have to defend a 14-mile front and the circumference of the city, with a largely hostile population of 800,000 at their backs. Indeed the Allies did fear that if Napoleon attacked there would be an insurrection such as had occurred at Reims[26] which could trap their army in Paris. Accordingly Schwarzenberg and the Tsar made plans to evacuate northward toward Belgium and the relative safety of juncture with another Allied army still in that vicinity.

Napoleon's plans for an attack were thwarted by Talleyrand. Talleyrand, however, having duped the Tsar into appointing him head of a provisional government,[27] had started printing masses of copies of a decree declaring Napoleon removed from office and warning soldiers to adhere to the new government or be treated as traitors. Coupled with an effective whispering campaign started by royalist agents, this did much to undermine the morale of many of the officers in Napoleon's army. His marshals, led by Ney, mutinied and refused to attack Paris. Napoleon tried to convince them that his fall would mean a return to pre-revolutionary standards and that their prominent positions would be much reduced. When they still refused to fight, Napoleon in desperation offered to abdicate in favour of his son. For a time it seemed as though this gesture might bring his marshals into line.

Talleyrand, hearing of Napoleon's efforts to retain the loyalty of his marshals, became concerned that he might lose his newly created position as head of the provisional government. He arranged for Marmont to betray his corps, which was acting as advance guard to Napoleon's army. As they advanced by night the men of Marmont's corps believed they were moving forward to attack positions. At first light they discovered that they were actually in a trap surrounded by Allied forces. The soldiers of Marmont's corps assaulted their officers, whom they blamed for their predicament. Marmont's corps was thus held in check, but was still under arms and could still pose a threat to the Allies if Napoleon should mount an attack.

Although shocked by the news of the fate of Marmont's corps, Napoleon remained at Fontainebleau while his army concentrated around him. He did not alter his plan of attack in light of Marmont's action, but still intended to attack on two fronts. A small force would cross the Marne and the Seine above Paris to launch an assault by way of Meaux. His main body would make a direct approach from Fontainebleau. Napoleon hoped that the Allied army, in trying to meet his multiple threat, would become dispersed in the great labyrinthine city. Also he trusted that, as had occurred at Reims, the civilian population would rally to him and aid in the discomfiture of the enemy.

In Paris, the Tsar was heartened by Napoleon's offer to abdicate, but was still fearful that, despite the defection of Napoleon's marshals, the soldiers of his army and the people of Paris might still fight. The Tsar felt it expedient to offer Napoleon a treaty. In return for an unconditional abdication and immediate ceasefire, Napoleon could become sovereign of Elba, retaining his current title. The Tsar was prepared to offer further minor concessions if the broad intent of the treaty were preserved. Napoleon's marshals accepted the Tsar's offer on Napoleon's behalf. Most of them then went to Napoleon at Fontainebleau to persuade him to agree. Ney, however, had already gone to offer his allegiance to Talleyrand's provisional government.

Napoleon felt unable to fight without the assistance of his senior commanders and he feared it was too late to reverse the effects of the civil treachery of Talleyrand and the royalists in Paris. Accordingly, he grudgingly agreed to abdicate on terms, 'I abdicate, but I yield nothing.'[28] His terms were that: the new French government would guarantee his personal and family property; he and his family would be paid annual pensions, with his amounting to two million francs, in return for which he would return the treasury and the crown diamonds; his wife and child be provided with passports to join him on Elba; he be given a bodyguard of 1,000 men of all arms; the cannon and stores of the fortress of Elba be under his control; and, finally, the frigate of his choice, HMS *Inconstant*, be given to him as his personal property. The Tsar agreed to Napoleon's terms on behalf of the Allies, and Napoleon, together with Prussia, Austria, Russia and the French Bourbons, signed a treaty embodying the terms. Castlereagh, who had remained at Dijon working with Metternich to arrange a Bourbon restoration, was furious with the treaty, and although he was obliged to accede to it, he did not sign.[29]

Earlier, Napoleon had sought asylum in Britain. No doubt the idea of life as an English country gentleman seemed congenial to him in his circumstances. Instead, upon his abdication, Castlereagh offered Napoleon a commissioner to escort him on his journey to Elba and to remain there as long as Napoleon required his services. The appointment went to a Colonel Campbell, who was given a broad authority.[30] The other Allies also appointed commissioners after their own fashions; the Russian commissioner had been charged on pain of losing his head to keep Napoleon safe during the journey to Elba. Nor were the fears leading to these precautions unfounded. When Napoleon left Fontainebleau for Elba on 20 April 1814 the Comte d'Artois, Lieutenant-General of his brother's Bourbon Kingdom of France, had ordered agents to arrange assassination attempts at Orange and at Avignon.[31] These were to be carried out under the cover of staged popular demonstrations. The attempts were unsuccessful thanks to the vigilance of the Allied commissioners and the effectiveness of the disguise Napoleon adopted.[32] After he arrived safely on Elba he dismissed all the commissioners except Campbell, upon whose services, and those of the Royal Navy, he continued to rely for protection.

With Napoleon off stage the Allies were eager to carve up his former Grande Empire. But before they could begin Castlereagh cleverly arranged for all of Britain's war aims to be met through separate private discussions with the foreign minsters of each ally. In return for his promise of support at the congress to be held in Vienna, Castlereagh extracted from each their agreement that Holland be made a kingdom, and that Belgium be fortified as a military barrier. Further, Castlereagh reasoned, as Britain had no territorial claims whatsoever to make at the congress and was prepared to restore all captured colonies of her former enemies, there would be no need to raise the issue of Britain's maritime rights.[33]

Louis XVIII presided over the Bourbon restoration. He was old, haughty in manner, obese and suffered so severely from gout that he could hardly walk. He was married, but had fathered no children, having instead a predilection for his male favourites. As a result of having spent many years living in exile in England he had formed an admiration for the system of government by ministers of the crown. He did not understand the nature of the sovereignty in England however. He had been brought up to believe in the divine right of kings, as had his brother and heir, d'Artois. A condition of Louis' investiture had been that he sign a charter providing for a constitutional government. He agreed, of course, but when Talleyrand presented him with it he refused to sign it on the grounds that it had been formulated by an unlawful assembly. He then appointed a commission of selected royalists to produce a different charter, one that provided for a legislature but without legislative power.[34] With the King returned, many hundreds of *émigré* nobles at once set about regaining the property that had been taken from them by the state nearly a quarter century earlier. By 1814 these lands had been sold and in many cases resold many times. The current owners of these lands would naturally resent seeing them confiscated. By such measures the inept Bourbons managed within six months to alienate almost the entire population of France, except the roughly nine per cent who directly benefited from their rule.[35] Royalists who had fought in the Allied armies or in the underground against Napoleon were elevated. D'Artois and his two sons, the Ducs de Berry and d'Angoulême were doing a brisk business in the selling of honours and titles.[36] The army, the Napoleonic nobility and the Imperial civil servants were treated by the Bourbons and their repatriated *émigré* supporters as enemies. The Imperial Guard, which had been the most renowned and feared fighting unit in Europe, was redesignated into line units. Antiquated laws were reintroduced, and educational opportunity was restricted, as before the revolution, to the sons of the privileged.

At the Congress of Vienna the Alliance disintegrated, largely because of the machinations of Castlereagh. As part of his private arrangement with Metternich he had agreed that Talleyrand, representing Bourbon France, be seated at the table as an equal. This violated the terms of the Treaty of Paris, which had laid down that the participants be limited to Britain, Austria, Russia and Prussia, and that France be specifically excluded. The Tsar learned of Talleyrand's duplicity before he left Paris for Vienna and was greatly offended by it. This, coupled with insults offered to the Tsar publicly by Louis in Paris, had decided the Russian autocrat in favour of supporting Napoleon's wife, Marie-Louise, as regent for her son, Napoleon's heir.[37]

In Vienna the Tsar set forth what he expected from the proceedings: primarily that Poland should become a constitutional monarchy under himself. This ostensibly independent entity would in fact be a buffer state firmly under Russian control, to guard the traditional invasion route to Russia from the west. Additionally he wanted his ally, the King of Prussia, to have all of Saxony as recompense for Prussia's sufferings and humiliations since 1806, but more importantly as recompense for Russia's gain of Prussian Poland. Finally the Tsar expected that Austria would regain all its territory lost since the French Revolution together with some further compensations. All this he assumed was a foregone conclusion, requiring merely an assent among the respective Foreign Ministers and some discussion as to the finer points.

But Austria had other interests which were largely opposed to those of Russia. Austria did not want Russia to take all of what was Poland, nor did she want Prussia to have all of Saxony, and for the same reason. Russia, Prussia and Austria were competitors for control of eastern Europe, and Austria did not want great lengths of common border with her dangerous adversaries. Metternich had no intention of allowing Prussia to absorb the buffer state of Saxony and thereby lengthen its border with Austria from 150 to 500 miles. Neither did he want Russia's 100-mile border with Austria to be approximately tripled in length, placing Russia within striking distance of Vienna. Additionally, autocratic Austria would feel distinctly uncomfortable with even a nominally constitutional political entity so close to its ethnically diverse subjects, possibly providing them with an inspiration to press for their own autonomy. Austria also wished to re-assert its pre-Napoleonic influence over the lesser German states. Napoleon had dissolved the welter of German principalities, dukedoms and archbishoprics, and recast them into a few much larger states such as Westphalia. These in turn, together with such older large German states as Bavaria and Hanover, were then amalgamated by Napoleon into a Confederation of the Rhine, largely to simplify control over this strategic area. However, Prussia also wanted to exercise influence over the German states. As early as 1813 the Prussian General von Gneisenau had written to Castlereagh soliciting his support for Prussia's ambition to extend its sway westward. At the time Castlereagh had seemed sympathetic in principle,[38] but in 1815 in Vienna the Prussians found him definitely opposed. Castlereagh's volte-face from Prussia to Austria in this matter was dictated by his indebtedness to Metternich for the Austrian Foreign Minister's help in arranging the Bourbon restoration in France. This meant that at the peace conference Metternich could also count on the support of the adaptable Talleyrand, attending as King Louis' Foreign Minister.

When the Tsar had placed his cards on the table at Vienna, Talleyrand opposed him in everything on the grounds of legitimacy. Talleyrand maintained that the legitimate King of Saxony should not be removed for having supported Napoleon. This, he remarked pointedly, was something which even the Tsar had done, '...it being a question of dates'. The Tsar lost his temper, stung no doubt by the truth of Talleyrand's words, redolent as they were of the humiliation of the raft on the Niemen. When Castlereagh attempted to side with Talleyrand and Metternich the Tsar spoke to him in a peremptory manner: 'I shall be King of Poland, and the King of Prussia shall be King of Saxony.' He reminded Castlereagh that there was a Russian army of about 480,000 men in and around Poland and Saxony, and he invited Britain to remove them if it could.[39] In Castlereagh's pre-conference planning, Talleyrand's role at the table was to be simply to aid Britain and Austria. But Talleyrand hoped, by his contentious attitude, to split the alliance, thereby increasing the prestige of Bourbon France and building credit for himself with his new master, Louis. Castlereagh wrote to Wellington, in Paris as British Ambassador, asking him to instruct Louis to require that his Foreign Minister take his direction from Castlereagh. In fact Louis had sent Talleyrand to Vienna with instructions that reflected Louis' own dynastic concerns, including pressing for the removal of Murat from the previously Bourbon throne of Naples. Murat, who had married Napoleon's sister and had been his outstanding cavalry commander, had deserted his brother-in-law after Leipzig in order to keep his throne, and had joined the Allies upon Austria's offer of an alliance. Castlereagh had acceded to this arrangement at the time, but worked discreetly with Talleyrand and Metternich to find a pretext for deposing Murat and restoring the Neapolitan Bourbon monarch.

At Vienna Castlereagh was carrying out his own policy, against the wishes of his Cabinet colleagues, Parliament and the British public. He put it to Metternich that Austria would have to yield on one of its main objections to ensure the other. Castlereagh proposed that Prussia be permitted to take all of Saxony provided that Prussia would join Austria, Britain and France in opposing the Tsar's ambitions in Poland.[40] Metternich agreed to Castlereagh's proposal, provided that Prussia sided actively with the others against Russia. The Prussian Foreign Minister, Karl von Hardenberg, agreed with Castlereagh, but when the Prussian King, Frederick William, was confronted by the Tsar on the matter, Frederick William denied that Prussia had any objection to the Tsar's plans. Metternich undiplomatically told the Tsar that Austria had as much right to create a dependent state in Poland as did Russia. The Tsar replied that Metternich was the only person rude enough to address him in such a manner. For a time war clouds seemed to be gathering over the conference. Prussia asked Britain and France to officiate the ceding of Saxony to Frederick William. Castlereagh said that he could not do so above board and in advance, but that if the Prussians moved into Saxony, Britain would acquiesce, being incapable of doing otherwise. Metternich, however, still opposed such a Prussian move, adding that Austria would resist it by force if necessary.

In Britain, the government and Parliament were becoming extremely concerned by the reports of the direction of Castlereagh's diplomacy. Britain had spent £700 million in defeating France and had gained all her war aims in the Treaty of Paris. No one could understand why the Foreign Minister appeared to be steering the country into a war with Russia over matters that affected none of Britain's interests.[41] Further, sentiment in Parliament and among the British public supported the view that the King of Saxony should not be dethroned for having supplied troops to Napoleon's armies, something which others including Prussia had also done under the same duress. Also, in Britain, the Tsar was seen as a champion of liberty for his role as principal sovereign in the coalition that had succeeded in bringing down Napoleon. Britain approved of the Tsar's avowed intention to unify Poland in the form of a British-style constitutional monarchy. Parliament had lost patience with Castlereagh's deferential attitude towards the wishes of the French Bourbons. To foster acceptance of the Bourbons by the French and to enlist Bourbon aid for the peace conference at Vienna, Castlereagh had ensured that the Treaty of Paris required of France the payment of no war indemnities. The Treaty did not even require the restitution of the art treasures looted by France's victorious armies from its European neighbours.

In Vienna the complexion of the Congress was anything but peaceful. The Tsar again lost his temper upon hearing of the British and Austrian attempt to bribe Prussia to join them in opposing his plans for Poland. The Prussian Foreign Minister told the Tsar that he had only consented to this because Metternich had stated that the Tsar had offered to abandon support for Prussian claims to Saxony in exchange for a free hand in Poland. The Tsar challenged Metternich to a duel over this bald lie, but the Austrian Emperor interceded to prevent bloodshed. In the meantime the British Cabinet specifically instructed Castlereagh to avoid taking any position that could provoke a war; and Castlereagh proceeded to ignore these instructions. Prussia stated that it would consider any further refusal to recognize its right to Saxony as tantamount to a declaration of war. Russia had already passed control of the part of Saxony it had occupied to a Prussian army of 80,000 men. In and around Poland were about 200,000 Russian soldiers, and a further 230,000 were marching towards its border. Austria, for its part, had raised an army of 300,000, of which 180,000 were regular soldiers and 120,000 were untrained and virtually unarmed conscripts. The main Austrian force of 100,000 men was disposed in Italy watching Murat's army; the conscripts were deployed near the Polish border; and the rest faced Saxony.

On 3 January 1815 Castlereagh, Talleyrand and Metternich signed a secret treaty obligating their respective countries to support one another in the event of a war with any other country. In so doing Castlereagh had flagrantly disobeyed his most recent instructions. In the event of war he had committed Britain to supply 150,000 soldiers or the equivalent in financial support. In the event of a continental war in 1815, however, Britain could field only 40,000 men. Many of the best British troops, such as Wellington's peninsula veterans, were still committed to the war in America. Additionally there was unrest in England and Ireland requiring the presence of troops, and half the government's annual revenue was needed to reduce the country's enormous war debt. Further, if Prussia declared war it would certainly overrun King George's new Kingdom of Hanover and possibly even Belgium; and the Tsar might be prompted to send the Russian Navy, recovered from Britain in 1814, to the aid of America. And all this for a nation, Poland, which had already been partitioned between Russia, Prussia and Austria before the French Revolution. A rump of Poland, Napoleon's Duchy of Warsaw, was wanted by the Tsar as a buffer on the invasion route which Napoleon had used only two years earlier. In this matter the Tsar was as resolved to fight, if necessary, as Britain had been over the neutrality of Belgium throughout the Napoleonic Wars. Parliament did not believe Castlereagh's assertion that the issue of Poland represented a threat to the peace of Europe. What he could not admit was that his opposition to Russia over Poland was a quid pro quo with Metternich for Metternich's support over the deposition of Napoleon, which Austria had not desired. Austria, remembering its past glory, sought to use British influence and wealth to regain its former dominance in central Europe. Castlereagh, not wishing Parliament or the British public to learn of the machinations he had indulged in under his broad commission of 1813-14, had no choice but to repay Metternich.

This tense situation, with large armies manoeuvring near borders, was defused when the British Cabinet made it known to the Tsar, through a deliberate and judicious leak to the Russian Ambassador in London, that Castlereagh's actions did not represent the policy of the British Government.[42] Disavowed in this way, Castlereagh was obliged to come to terms with the Tsar. Prussia, without Russian backing, had to be content with a fifth of Saxony which excluded both Saxon capitals. In compensation Britain ceded Prussia some territory from Hanover and Belgium. The Tsar also gave Prussia a small slice of Poland.

Frederick William and his generals naturally felt betrayed by Castlereagh. The Tsar was left feeling mistrustful of Britain because of Castlereagh's inexplicable animosity. Emperor Francis felt that he had been deceived by Castlereagh into relinquishing the Habsburg claim to the French throne, under a diminished Napoleon, for assurances which Britain had failed to honour.[43] Such was the political situation among the Allies at the beginning of March 1815. Not one trusted the others, and all the continental Allies particularly mistrusted Britain, due primarily to the mishandled Machiavellian intrigues of Britain's Foreign Secretary.

Napoleon, since his arrival on Elba, had busied himself with reorganizing and fortifying his island empire. He was well aware that agents of the Comte d'Artois were seeking to assassinate him. He was also aware that

King Louis was trying to have him removed to some more distant island than Elba, in contravention of the Treaty of Fontainebleau. Napoleon knew of the rising level of unrest in France in reaction to the corruption and reactionary tone of Bourbon rule, but he was more concerned that Louis was breaking the treaty and the Allies were doing nothing to enforce its terms. Louis was refusing to make the stipulated annual payment to Napoleon of two million francs. Also, in violation of the treaty, Louis had expropriated Napoleon's personal property. Further, passports had not been issued which would have allowed Napoleon's wife and child to join him. Although he still had enough hidden wealth to ensure his safety on Elba for another two years, he was more concerned that if the Allies did not require Louis to carry out his treaty obligations, Louis might soon feel secure in using the French Navy and royalist troops to capture or kill him. Indeed it was Louis' intention to see Napoleon dead by any means possible. Napoleon of course was not temperamentally inclined to await events. He sent emissaries to Vienna to ask for Louis' compliance. The Tsar, who felt that Louis' behaviour cast dishonour on the Tsar's own signature on the treaty, was the only sovereign to acknowledge the justice of Napoleon's complaint. Louis indicated vaguely that if Napoleon would agree to live at some other unspecified place he would pay the pension. Napoleon decided that if Louis would not honour the treaty, he himself was released from its obligations. According to the international conventions of the age, Napoleon had followed the recognized procedure for seeking a redress of a breach of treaty. As he had not received it, he was free to reassume, if he could, his position before the treaty had been signed. Napoleon decided to visit Louis outside Paris with his army.

Since Napoleon's departure from France, republican and imperial elements had been driven into a firm opposition to the Bourbons and their fanatical royalist supporters, soon to be known as 'Ultras'. D'Artois had transformed his underground terrorist society into a political police force, called the 'Verdets', after their green livery.[44] The harsh, repressive measures of d'Artois' Verdets had created a strong antipathy among many French. Also, the strenuous efforts of royalist *émigrés* seeking to regain possession of their former estates had instilled fear and resentment among the many who stood to lose all they had. After the restoration of the Stuart monarchy in England, Charles II prudently had not attempted such a reversal of the transfer of property that had occurred during the English Civil Wars. Louis had obviously not become acquainted with this aspect of English history during his long exile in England. To the many royalists who had lent sums of money to the Bourbons during their exile, Louis and d'Artois offered repayment in the form of lucrative appointments to government positions, fostering resentment among those thus displaced.

The France to which the *émigrés* had returned was much changed. Palaces had been turned into museums, great monuments such as the statue of Louis IV had been demolished, the city suburbs and bridges renamed. The populace had no inbred fear of the nobility, nor were they subservient. On assuming power Napoleon had healed the breach with the Catholic Church. Long used by the nobility as a tool to keep the people obedient, its ranks had been filled by subservient bishops and priests – like Talleyrand, lesser sons who would not inherit the land, but who had been raised to magnificence on the backs of the poor. The Revolution had swept these parasites away, but with them had gone the good priests in the provincial backwaters. This was one of the causes of Vendéen and Chouan risings, or more properly, religious wars.[45] In his famous *Concordat*, Napoleon had removed these abuses, restored the Church and, indeed, permitted religious freedom to all creeds. French Protestants were given freedom of worship, the Jewish people, long persecuted, were given established rights, and Napoleon had his troops demolish the old ghetto gates in Rome and in all other cities of his empire. The priests were now the servants of the people, not the masters. The old nobility were attempting to reverse everything that the Revolution and Napoleon had changed.

Common sense should have told them that by trying to turn the clock back, they were only setting the scene for a second revolution and for exactly the same reasons. The people of France were now more educated, articulate and politically informed than during the enforced feudalism of the past, and they had a better standard of living. The Bourbons, in their arrogance, were believing their own propaganda. They failed to realize that, having been brought back by Allied bayonets which had now departed, they had little or no power base from which to suppress any insurrection – except the army.

Since his return, however, Louis had treated the army harshly. The élite Imperial Guard had been broken up into line units. The Old Guard infantry, renamed Grenadiers of France, had been posted to provinces remote from the capital and treated with contempt. Tens of thousands of officers had been put on half pay, and had rarely been paid even that. Officers seen in cafes were often abused and set upon by gangs of royalist louts.[46] The Bourbons recreated the old royalist guard, the Maison du Roi. They also reconstituted the Swiss Guard, whom the people loathed; that the King should entrust the protection of his person to foreign mercenaries was deeply offensive to the army and the people. Experienced officers were removed to make room for young and old royalists who had never heard a shot fired in anger and were incapable of commanding a corporal's guard. Louis lavished half his military budget on his small, exclusive Household Guard of royalists; their uniforms and horses cost five times as much as those of the line, and each trooper of the Guard ranked as an officer in a line regiment.

Napoleon's Marshals fared variously under the restoration, but on the whole not well. Marmont was appointed captain of a troop of the Guard that was nicknamed the 'Judas Company' by Parisians. Soult, to the disgust of the other ex-Marshals, did his best to ingratiate himself with the

Bourbons, and for his pains had been appointed Minister of War. Davout, who had held Hamburg since 1813, only surrendering when he was satisfied that Napoleon had indeed abdicated, was internally exiled. Macdonald was content to receive the pay of a duke and marshal while carrying out the duties of a colonel. Ney, however, was not finding life under Louis to his liking. The son of a cooper from Saarlouis, he had joined the King's Hussars while still a youth and by the time of the Revolution had risen to sergeant-major. The Revolution opened the path of advancement to merit, rather than pedigree, and he rose to General of Brigade, then of Division. By the time he had forced his Emperor and benefactor to abdicate, he was styled 'Michel Ney ... Duke of Elchingen, Prince of the Moscowa and Marshal of France, a Chevalier of the Order of St. Louis ... Grand Cordon of the Legion of Honour ... The Iron Crown of Italy and the Order of Christ'.[47] Not surprisingly, the St. Louis distinction was bestowed on Ney after the restoration and it took precedence over the rest. Louis also made Ney a Peer of France which allowed him to retain all his titles as though bestowed by Louis, but because all these titles were less than 30 years old he was required to give precedence on all occasions to members of the old nobility, who would walk before him and his wife. Ney had been called '*le plus brave que les braves*' by Napoleon and had been the darling of the army rank and file. His reputation for bravery was legendary. During the retreat from Moscow Ney brilliantly commanded the rearguard of the stricken army. His personal courage and determination saved the lives of many French soldiers. The army looked to him as its symbol. Under Louis, Ney was reduced to shepherding the aged Duc d'Havre from the review of one military unit to another. D'Havre was one of the King's intimates who wanted to be a soldier. At nearly eighty he was given a general's commission, but liked to be addressed as 'Marshal'. Ney was required to parade troops back and forth while the senile d'Havre, who stood bent over like a hairpin, cackled with pleasure. D'Artois avoided Ney as though he were a leper, and his wife was ill received at court. Things had indeed turned sour for Ney, as Napoleon had predicted to him in 1814. Even his sons were discriminated against. The academies and polytechnics established by Napoleon for the bright children of France were reserved for the sons of the old nobility. Even the orphans of soldiers killed in Napoleon's campaigns felt the malice of the Bourbons. The children were put out to the parishes, and their establishments returned to the royalists who had once owned them. The veteran pensioners of The Invalides were likewise to be discharged, with a licence to beg, as was the practice in England.

D'Artois's two sons, the Ducs de Berry and d'Angoulême, had naturally received rapid promotion in the restoration army. They tried to ape Napoleon by chatting to the men and tweaking their ears as the Emperor had done, but to no avail; the men were not deceived by their condescension. The soldiers well knew that Napoleon and his marshals had gained advancement the hard way and had shared the privations of the common soldier. The Bourbon dukes, however, did not even know how to load a musket. The army, like the French people in general, felt betrayed. They knew they had not been beaten in battle and wondered why they should have to suffer the arrogance and ignorance of the Bourbon and other royalist officers who had been set over them. At one review, de Berry remarked to a distinguished officer, 'The French soldier must be happy these days. His long campaigns are over, and we have peace.' He was shocked by the officer's reply, 'Do you call peace a halt in the mire?'[48] The irate Duke tore off the officer's epaulettes and had him cashiered, but the sentiment behind the officer's reply remained widespread through the ranks. The soldiers hated their new Bourbon masters, just as they knew their new masters despised them. The troops were kept short of rations, uniforms and pay, and were housed in appallingly antiquated barracks. These were all things which 'He' would never have done. By comparison with the Emperor the Bourbons seemed all the worse. In the army, in the villages and in the towns, the songs of the Revolution were recalled and sung anew. The conditions for revolution in France in 1815 had developed rapidly; all that was needed was a precipitating event, as in 1789.

Louis' government did not function. He had given France an absolutist charter[49] by which all legislative power remained with the King. He had delegated this power to Ministers, on the English pattern, but Louis had no conception of how a government should be organized or function. He had no Cabinet, no Prime Minister, and, of course, there was no collective responsibility. At meetings of the Council of Ministers, d'Artois dictated policy without even the slightest regard for the legal niceties. Ministers had access to the King through Count Blacas, the King's favourite and Grandmaster of the Wardrobe. Blacas acted as would a modern personal secretary, determining who was permitted to see Louis. The Finance Minister, Baron Louis, said of his meetings with the King: 'What is the good of making reports to him? You might as well make them to a saint in a niche. I simply give him ordinances to sign, and he signs them.'[50] Before Wellington left his position at Paris as British Ambassador to replace the recalled Castlereagh in Vienna, he described the Court of Louis to Lord Liverpool as paternal anarchy: 'There was no ministry, only ministers.' The country continued to function, but only because the system of government evolved by Napoleon had not yet been completely destroyed.

Four events precipitated a second revolution. First, the King's Minister in the Chambers indicated the King's sympathy for the claims of the old *émigrés* to land restitution. Secondly he allowed his brother d'Artois to behave like a dictator. D'Artois, who liked his 'English' Sundays, ordered the cafes to be closed on Sundays without reference to the Chambers for legislation. He encouraged the Church to re-introduce many of its old customs, for example religious processions to the sites of martyred royalists, executed by the State. Not only was this illegal -the statutes having not been revoked – but the people had no feeling of collective guilt for, in their opinion, a bunch of traitors who, like Cadoual, had received their just deserts. Thirdly, the Duchesse d'Angoulême, d'Artois' daughter-in-law and niece, insulted Ney's wife. Passing her in a corridor of the palace with another marshal's wife, she addressed the princess thus: '... and you must be Madame Ney', implying that in her eyes the princess was but a commoner. When Ney heard of this he rode straight away to the palace. Booted and spurred and covered in mud, he strode into the King's apartments unannounced. He pushed the guards aside, saying 'Out of my way, lackeys!' Thrusting past the King, he entered d'Angoulême's rooms and in the language of the barrack room told her what he thought of her, her manners, her ridiculous pedigree and the fat king and all his relatives. With that he strode out again. When the news of this encounter hit the streets and the army, France went wild.[51] The bubble had burst. The King and his livid family could neither arrest nor punish him in any way. Had they attempted to do so the Parisian mob would have stormed the palace. In the cafes the soldiers joked and ridiculed the royal family, and their derision carried like a wave to the provinces. One colonel of hussars exclaimed at the price of his meal, with a wink to the room, 'In Paris for a napoleon you can get a whole fat pig' The final event that pulled down the Bourbon house of cards was an invasion. On 1 March 1815, the Lilliputian Elban army, commanded by its emperor, landed at Fréjus in the south of France.

CHAPTER 2

The Return of the Eagles, Which Fly from Steeple to Steeple

'These are the times that try men's souls. The summer soldier and the sunshine patriot
will, in this crisis, shrink from the service of their country; but he that stands it now,
deserves the love and thanks of men and women.' - Thomas Paine, 'The American Crisis.
No. 1.' in *Pennsylvania Journal*, 19 December 1776.

Napoleon left Elba on 26 February after having carefully made his plans for his return to France. His invasion armada consisted of his three Elban ships, *Inconstant*, *Saint-Esprit* and *Caroline*. To support him in his attempt to reconquer France, Napoleon had with him on board 1,100 soldiers, 40 horses, two cannon and his famous green coach; probably the smallest invasion force in history to endeavour to conquer a nation of 50 millions – but undoubtedly the most successful.

Before embarking Napoleon had, as was his custom, arranged a diversion to mask his true intentions. During the twenty years of his prominence, Italians had been united under French control of their peninsula and had begun to develop a sense of national identity. Following Napoleon's forced abdication, the Italians had found themselves again under Austrian domination and had lost the relatively greater freedom to which they had become accustomed under him. Italians of all classes, including the army and the professions, were anxious for Napoleon to land and lead them in a campaign that would repeat his earlier successes.

On the Italian mainland only a few miles from Elba was the independent Kingdom of Naples. This kingdom in the southern part of Italy had been known as the Kingdom of the Two Sicilies when Napoleon removed its Bourbon king, Ferdinand. On the throne of the newly established Kingdom of Naples Napoleon at first placed his brother Joseph, and then his brother-in-law Joachim Murat, his brilliant cavalry marshal. Murat had been with Napoleon from the days in Paris when, in 1795, he brought up the cannon with which Napoleon administered the 'whiff of grapeshot', and had received numerous rewards and titles for his services. Although loved by his subjects Murat was not tolerated gladly by the longer-established dynastic sovereigns of Europe, especially the Bourbons who had held the Neapolitan throne he now occupied. Murat was aware that, although the Allies had stopped fighting Napoleon, Bourbon France had not. He was aware too that Britain had not yet ratified his peace treaty even though he had fulfilled its terms. In fact Castlereagh, Metternich and Talleyrand had been plotting to organize an invasion of Naples to remove him in favour of the Bourbon claimant.[1]

Metternich had been persuaded by Castlereagh and Talleyrand that Napoleon could easily land in Murat's Naples, and at the head of its army move north, raising the discontented Italians to augment his force, then march on Vienna to recover his family. He might then turn west towards France. It was Louis who was the motivation behind this scheme against Murat. He was committed to trying to restore his Bourbon cousin to the Neapolitan throne, which he felt was his family's by right, by ousting a hated Napoleonic usurper.

If Louis' plot were to succeed, Napoleon knew it would leave him surrounded by hostile Bourbons in Naples, Sicily, Spain and France. Napoleon encouraged Murat's own fears in letters to him and to his wife, who was Napoleon's sister. Napoleon pointed out to them that their only hope lay in his restoration to power in France.[2] He urged his brother-in-law to advance as far as the Austro-Italian border as soon as he heard that Napoleon had returned to France. As an incentive he promised Murat most of northern Italy.[3] Napoleon then waited until the British Commissioner, Colonel Campbell, made one of his frequent trips to the Italian mainland for relaxation, and sailed for France.

On landing he moved with his customary speed, striking out at once for Grenoble. On 5 March Monsieur Chappe, brother of the inventor of telegraphy, delivered a sealed letter to Baron Vitrolles at the Tuileries Palace in Paris. Vitrolles immediately handed it to Louis. The King asked Vitrolles if he knew of its contents. When the perplexed baron replied in the negative, Louis said: 'Well I will tell you. It is a revolution once more! Bonaparte has landed on the coast of Provence. Have this letter taken to the Minister of War, so that he can come and speak to me at once and decide what steps are to be taken.'[4] When Marshal Soult, the King's Minister of War, and d'Artois and his sons had arrived before the King, Soult outlined the steps he thought should be taken. Already there were some 30,000 men in the South, ostensibly placed to take part in an invasion of Naples, but also occupying a strategic position as a result of the threat of war with Russia and Prussia in January. With the National Guard in the area, the King had 60,000 men with which to crush Napoleon and his thousand. Soult recommended that d'Artois take command of the 30,000-man army and that Marshal Ney, with the Duc de Berry, raise a second army from local troops and National Guard in the Franche-Comté area around Besançon. The Duc d'Angoulême, Soult suggested, should go to Nîmes to take command of regular troops and National Guard there. Thus, as Napoleon advanced, the three forces, totalling 60,000, would converge on Napoleon and destroy him.[5]

Soult's plan appealed to d'Artois, who was pleased to have the opportunity to be in at the kill of Napoleon, and at the odds of 60 to 1 it must have seemed something like a fox-hunt. Soult further advised the King to pass ordinances mobilizing the rest of the National Guard so that a reserve army of 120,000 could be assembled around Paris as a last-ditch defence. The royal family also published, through Soult, an ordinance which is known by its date, the royal ordinance of 6 March. It enjoined all Frenchmen to, '...fall upon Napoleon Bonaparte, declared a traitor and rebel for having introduced himself by force into the department of the Var, to apprehend and convey him forthwith before a military tribunal'. In other words, if caught, Napoleon would be taken before a drum-head court-martial, tried as a rebel, and shot.[6]

By 6 March, the date of the royal ordinance, Napoleon had reached Gap, a day's march from Grenoble, the headquarters of the local military district. Already peasants who had heard of his landing were joining him, making of his march a cavalcade resembling a royal, or rather imperial, procession. At Gap the people erected a liberty tree, something not seen since the Revolution. The people sang revolutionary songs and shouted, 'Down with priests! Down with the aristos!' in scenes strongly reminiscent of the early, popular days of the Revolution. Seigneurial pews in churches were ripped out and thrown on bonfires.

General Marchand, the district military commander at Grenoble, had at his disposal the 5th and 7th Regiments of the Line, each of three battalions, the 3rd Engineer Regiment and the 4th Hussars. Marchand dispatched one battalion of the 5th with a company of engineers, under Colonel Lessard, to blow up the bridge at Ponhaut with a view to halting Napoleon's progress and effectively trapping him. When Lessard's command came into contact with Napoleon's advance guard, Lessard hastily withdrew, taking up a blocking position across the defile at Laffrey. The next day the two forces, each numbering about one thousand, were drawn up within musket range of each other. But Napoleon had no intention of allowing Frenchmen to fire on fellow Frenchmen. The scene which followed was as crucial and dramatic as that of Ney's dressing down of the royal family. Napoleon walked forward alone from the ranks of his men of the Old Guard, approaching the levelled muskets of the 5th. He presented the figure so well known to the soldiers of the French Army: a small man carrying a riding-whip, wearing the green uniform of Colonel-in-Chief of the Chasseurs of the Guard, a tricorn hat and old grey riding-coat. He walked forward to well within the effective range of the smooth-bore muskets of the period. No soldier could have failed to hit him, but no soldier fired. Napoleon is said to have addressed them, saying, 'Soldiers of the 5th, will you fire on your Emperor?', but in fact he may not have had time to say anything, for the whole line before him erupted in a rapturous welcome. The soldiers wept, overcome with emotion, and shouted 'Vive l'Empereur!' and 'He has come back!'. Soon after this first bloodless victory, Napoleon, reinforced by the battalion of the 5th, was nearing Grenoble when the 7th Regiment of the Line was seen advancing toward him under the *tricolore* with an Imperial eagle surmounting it. The Colonel of the 7th, Charles de la Bedoyère, had kept these proscribed emblems hidden since the Bourbon restoration. Napoleon made Bedoyère a general, and his aide, General

Marchand, had the gates of Grenoble closed against Napoleon and his further augmented force, and ordered the garrison's cannon to prepare to fire. But Marchand's men balked. They were in fact trapped between Napoleon's advance guard outside the walls and the irate populace of Grenoble within. Marchand's royalist artillery officer told his commander that he feared that he and his men would be torn to pieces by the citizens if they fired. The officer shouted to Napoleon's men that he would surrender if they would guarantee his safety from the people.[7] The town gates were soon demolished by blacksmiths and wheelwrights of the town, and were laid at Napoleon's feet as he entered Grenoble.

The next day, 9 March, Napoleon issued a proclamation which within days had been posted in every city, town, village and hamlet in France:

'Soldiers!

We were NOT defeated: two men risen from our ranks betrayed our laurels, their country, their prince, their benefactor. Those whom we saw for twenty-five years, scouring all Europe to raise enemies against us, who spent their lives fighting against us in the ranks of foreign armies, execrating our fair France, would they lay claim to command and manacle our eagles, they who could never withstand their gaze? Must we endure that they should inherit the fruits of our glorious labour, that they should seize our honours, our goods, and that they should trample on our glory? ... Soldiers! In my exile I heard your voice! ... tear off those colours which the nation has proscribed, and which served for twenty-five years to rally all the enemies of France! Put up your tricolore cockade! you wore it in our greatest battles ... Do you think this handful of arrogant Frenchmen can stand the sight of them? They will go back to where they came from, and there, if they so wish, they can reign, as they claim to have reigned for nineteen years! Your goods, your ranks, your glory, the goods, the ranks, the glory of your children, have no greater enemies than these princes whom foreigners imposed upon us. They are the enemies ... Victory will advance at the charge; the eagle, with the national colours, will fly from steeple to steeple all the way to the towers of Notre Dame...'[8]

The power and truth of the content of this proclamation struck a chord of grievance and discontent which resonated throughout France.

Already, in the north, there had been an abortive attempt at a *coup d'état*, led by several of Napoleon's former generals, Lefebvre-Desnouëttes, d'Erlon, and the brothers François and Henri Lallemand. The coup was betrayed by one of the conspirators, the dangerous and highly duplicitous

Joseph Fouché, Duc d'Otranto. Fouché had once been Napoleon's Minister of Police and head of the secret police, but had been dismissed in 1809 for intriguing with foreign powers. Coming to a position of power during the Revolution, he had been one of the regicides who signed the death warrant of Louis XVI, and the instigator in the removal of Robespierre. During the nearly twenty years that he held the dual posts of chief of police and head of the secret police, Fouché had amassed a great deal of confidential information on the crimes or indiscretions of many people. These compromised people, in all levels of society, were blackmailed into acting as Fouché's agents. He was desperate to gain favour with the Bourbons and once more have a prominent position in government, something he knew he could not hope for under Napoleon. In 1814 Fouché helped the Bourbons to regain power, and so had kept his titles and indeed his life, but he remained personally unacceptable at court. To gain the necessary degree of acceptability, Fouché infiltrated the coup conspiracy, even helping to plan it, then, as a proof of loyalty, betrayed it to the King.[9]

Marshal Soult, in his zeal to show loyalty to his new master, had announced to the royal family and the army that the captured conspirators would quickly be tried and shot. Soult then proceeded, on his own initiative, to issue a proclamation against his former master:

> 'Soldiers, That man Buonaparte, who recently in the face of all Europe abdicated an usurped Power of which he made so fatal a use, has now landed once more on French soil, which he ought never to have seen again. What does he desire? Civil War. Whom does he seek? Traitors. Where will he find them? Will it be among those soldiers whom he has deceived and sacrificed so often, by misleading their valour? Will it be in the bosom of those families, in whom his very name is still sufficient to inspire terror? ...'[10]

On 6 March Napoleon was still deep in the South of France, two weeks' march from Paris. Soult expected, with the unfolding of his plan, a summary conclusion to the problem of Napoleon. This of course was devoutly wished for by Louis, and anticipated with varying degrees of enthusiasm by the sovereigns and Ministers. The diplomats in Vienna first learned of Napoleon's departure from Elba in a dispatch from the Austrian Consulate in Genoa, delivered to Metternich on 7 March, a week after the landing at Fréjus. Its information was succinct: 'The English Commissioner Campbell has just entered the harbour enquiring whether anyone has seen Napoleon at Genoa, in view of the fact that he had disappeared from the island of Elba. The answer being in the negative, the English frigate without further delay, put to sea.'[11] Metternich naturally informed his Emperor, Francis, and his fellow Ministers at the Congress. The Allies decided to use armed force if Napoleon attempted to upset the delicate equilibrium of

Europe. At this point no one in Vienna knew where Napoleon had gone. Talleyrand assumed that he would land somewhere on the Italian coast. Metternich, writing of the event many years later, claimed to have replied, 'No, he will make straight for Paris.' On 12 March Talleyrand received official confirmation that Napoleon had landed in France on the 1st. He also received a copy of the royal ordinance of 6 March. When the assemblage received this news from Talleyrand they felt as he did that Louis' forces would soon crush Napoleon's pathetic attempt, and that the 'rebel' would be tried and shot.

On the next day, 13 March, to sanction the expected summary execution of Napoleon, Talleyrand had drafted a document in which the powers assembled declared Napoleon outside the law, '... Buonaparte had destroyed the only legal title on which his existence depended: by appearing again in France, with projects of confusion and disorder, he has deprived himself of the protection of the Law'.[12] This instrument, issued with the signatures of the Ministers of the Allied powers, and in effect sanctioning the killing of Napoleon out of hand, would, Talleyrand hoped, make it easier for his Bourbon monarch to portray the eventual disposal of Napoleon to the French people as an act beyond reproach. But according to the standards of legality then obtaining, the case for declaring Napoleon *'hors de la loi'* is extremely weak. Napoleon had thus far used no force other than that of his charismatic personality. Also, as Napoleon was the sovereign of Elba, he could not be considered a subject of the French king, and therefore could not be in rebellion against him. The terms of the Treaty of Fontainebleau had first been broken by Louis, and redress was not forthcoming from the guarantors of the treaty; therefore Napoleon was no longer in honour, or international convention, bound by them. Thus, for Louis, in his ordinance, to refer to '... Napoleon Bonaparte, declared traitor and rebel ...' was an early nineteenth-century example of The Big Lie, a phenomenon that would often appear in the twentieth century. However, as we have also seen in our century, this technique can be most effective. The Bourbons put forth this view of Napoleon backed up by some rather tortured logic. Napoleon, they said, was simply a general of the Revolution, which, since the then monarch had not sanctioned it, had not occurred. Napoleon was therefore rightfully one of the King's officers, owing him allegiance; and he could be tried and executed for failing in this duty.

Castlereagh immediately took up the Bourbon view of Napoleon, and from 6 March it became the policy of the British Government to refer to Napoleon as General Bonaparte. Castlereagh and the Cabinet, at this point, had great hopes that Napoleon would simply be apprehended by the enormous preponderance of force seemingly available to the Bourbons, and judicially murdered.[13] The Duke of Wellington, to his later regret, was induced to sign the Bourbon declaration proscribing Napoleon. To its credit the British Parliament repudiated the base document.

Three days before the representatives of the Allied powers signed the proscription, Napoleon had reached Lyons with 4,000 infantry, a regiment of Hussars, several *ad hoc* battalions and twenty cannon. Within the walls of Lyons were Monsieur, the Comte d'Artois, and Marshal Macdonald, with fewer than 3,000 men. The Bourbons, frightened of intrigue, had so widely billeted the 30,000 men of the Army in the South that they could not be concentrated in time to bring overwhelming odds to bear against Napoleon. Yet again he had moved more quickly than his adversaries. In Lyons crowds were roaming the streets chanting the old slogans and singing the old songs of the Revolution. Unnerving cries of 'Death to Artois, death to priests!' and 'Vive l'Empereur!' went up as mobs attacked the homes of prominent royalists. The general scene may have been reminiscent of 1793, when the mob had marched through Lyons from Marseilles to Paris, bearing their ropes and knives and exuding revolutionary fervour. D'Artois, in a pathetically ill-directed act of desperation, was reduced to attempting to bully a lone dragoon on parade into shouting 'Vive le Roi', but the soldier refused. By the morning of 10 March the Lyons garrison had gone over to Napoleon and d'Artois was riding for his life to Paris. Marshal Macdonald, like Horatio, stood alone holding the city's bridge, but his altruistic though futile gesture soured into ignominy when the 4th Hussars charged the bridge. The Marshal dropped his unfired musket and vaulted into his saddle, escaping only just in time to avoid the slashing sabre cuts of Hussar Sergeant Lecourbe, who nevertheless returned from the engagement in possession of a French marshal's hat.

At nine o'clock in the evening of the 10th, Napoleon resumed the issuing of imperial decrees as sovereign Emperor of France for the first time since his abdication. He ordered all badges, insignia and emblems of the House of Bourbon to be removed immediately, as had been required under the revolutionary laws. The *tricolore* was reinstated as the national flag. The Bourbon laws restoring lands to royalist émigrés was annulled. Further, all émigrés on the proscribed list of the Revolution who had returned to France, including of course the Bourbons, were to leave the country at once or suffer the prescribed penalty. All military commissions, feudal titles and patents of nobility granted by Louis were nullified. The hated Swiss Guard was abolished. All Bourbon changes to the laws and the operation of the Courts of Justice were reversed.

Napoleon left Lyons on 13 March, the day of the Declaration of the Congress of Vienna. With him marched eleven regiments of infantry, two of cavalry, a regiment of engineers, several *ad hoc* volunteer battalions and fifty cannon: a total of nearly 18,000 men. At the same time in Paris, the Comte de Blacas was offering, on Louis' behalf, 20 million francs to Austria is she would invade Naples as France's ally; this was ten times the amount of the pension Louis had refused to pay Napoleon to keep him on Elba. It can only have been with foreboding that, later on the 13th at the Tuileries, Louis received his brother d'Artois, covered in horse sweat and mud, and bearing the disastrous news of the royalist débâcle at Lyons.

The news of 'His' return spread all over France, and the enthusiasm it aroused was irresistible. Spontaneous insurrections broke out against the Bourbon government. In the Isère four royalist châteaux were attacked by National Guard and peasants. At La Sône the royalist mayor attempted to prevent the raising of the *tricolore* and was shot dead by his own guard. In Brittany, Dauphiné, Languedoc and Lyonnais patriots formed federations of 'liberty and equality'; and students, 'children of the Empire', demonstrated and formed battalions of *fédérés*, reviving the old volunteer units of the Revolution. Even in the royalist strongholds of the Vendée and Chouan the people, who had been promised the removal of the offensive *octroi* and *droits réunis* taxes, erupted into violence against the government, pillaging the homes of tax officials, beating, and in one case murdering, the officials and burning their record books. Napoleon himself was surprised by the extent to which the spirit of the Revolution had entered into the minds of the French people. The Bourbons and their adherents could not undo history; the Revolution had been paid for in blood – but the price had been paid. The clock of progress would go forward – only damage could occur by trying to force it backward.

On 12 March a Parisian mob had hung a huge placard from the victory column in the Place Vendôme, which read, 'From Napoleon to Louis XVIII, My good brother, there is no need to send me any more soldiers. I have enough.' Later the same day, Louis' Minister of the Interior, M. l'Abbé Montesquiou-Fézensac, announced in the Chambers, 'Gentlemen, the most recent piece of news which we have to communicate to you is that Marshal Ney, who is very satisfied with the good spirit of the troops under his command, is advancing through Lons-le-Saunier.' Ney was now seen by the royalists as their salvation. There was no more talk of 'upstart', 'common scum' and 'Madame Ney'; it was rather of how the 'Hero of Krasnöe' was going to destroy the presumptuous Corsican. Since the incident with the Duchesse d'Angoulême, Ney and his wife had left Paris and were living on his country estate. Ney only learned of his command when a messenger reached him from Marshal Soult with instructions for him to report to the War Office. Ney and Soult shared a mutual antipathy which had arisen during their time in Spain, with the result that they barely spoke to each other. Upon his arrival at the War Office, Ney was told that Napoleon had returned to France with a small following and was threatening civil war. He was ordered to report to Besançon where he would receive further orders from General Bourmont. Ney thought that this was insulting because Bourmont was one of d'Artois' royalist myrmidons, and in rank was quite junior to a marshal.[14] Ney told Soult that he was going to see the King, to which Soult replied that the King was indisposed. Ney realized that Louis' 'indisposition' was a consequence of his earlier outburst, but he was not prepared to save Louis' throne without being asked to do so by the King in person. Ney was duly admitted to the King's presence, and Louis was all smiles and attention. He appealed to Ney to stop Napoleon's rash adventure and thereby save all the lives that would be lost in a civil war. Ney, although a principal of the Treaty of Fontainebleau, had not been told that the stipulated pension payment to Napoleon had not been made. Perhaps Ney did not realize the fact of human nature that a turncoat is not thereafter trusted by either side. Ney then made the promise which hindsight has shown to have been unlikely of fulfillment, 'You are right, Sire, France must not have a civil war. Bonaparte's enterprise is madness. I am leaving at once for Besançon, and if need be I will bring him back in an iron cage.' This light-hearted and, as events were to prove, lightly meant *bon mot* gained a wide circulation in Parisian royalist circles through the agency of the Comte de Blacas. The royalists could only hope that Ney would be the 'bravest of the brave' when confronting his former master.

Although Marshal Soult was a man of strong resolution and ability, Louis could hardly have given him this crucial command. Since Napoleon's abdication, Soult's earnest efforts to become a good royalist had thoroughly alienated him from almost the entire army. Earlier in the year Comte Exelmans, an officer in the French Army, disgusted with the intrigue to oust Murat from the throne of Naples, wrote to him offering his services. His letter, carried by Lord Oxford, was seized and read by d'Artois' secret police. Soult, as Minister of War, relieved Exelmans of his command and ordered him to retire to his country estate, but Exelmans refused; his wife was expecting a child, and he had no intention of leaving Paris at such a time. Soult ordered Exelmans' arrest on charges of disobedience, oath breaking and treason. Informed in time of the arrest order, Exelmans went into hiding, and through the press demanded a court-martial. He had not, he maintained, committed treason; France was not at war with Naples; he had not disobeyed a military order; the internal exile he had refused was manifestly illegal except as the result of a trial; and he had not broken any oath. A court-martial was convened. Exelmans appeared, accompanied by many fellow officers and a huge crowd. The general officers presiding acquitted Exelmans of all charges; Soult and his new royal masters were much chagrined; and the army saw in the once illustrious marshal of their beloved war leader a treacherous enemy.

In an additional act which caused widespread offence in the army, Soult had issued a ministerial order addressed to all junior officers who had applied for the Order of St. Louis, as holders of the Napoleonic Legion of Honour were entitled to do. The Order of St. Louis was being introduced to supersede the Legion of Honour; and the Legion award was to be degraded to a meaningless civilian decoration. Soult's communication to the junior officers pointed out that applications for the St. Louis were being submitted without an accompanying declaration of faith.[15] Such a declaration, of course, would serve to affirm the officer as a true adherent of the Catholic

Church, thus debarring the many Protestant and Jewish officers who had received the Napoleonic award. This requirement also served to taint the St. Louis with the odium of bigotry. Further, the whole business of superseding the Legion award implied a disrespect for the patriotic acts of the soldiers who had received it.

Nor were the Exelmans affair and the St. Louis test the only insults which Soult offered to his former comrades. He refused an appointment to General Travot on the grounds that he had not returned to its 'rightful' royalist owner his estate, which he had purchased for a quarter of a million francs. It was also known that he intended to execute the highly regarded generals who had attempted a coup in the north. In all, Soult, at the head of a French army in March 1815, would have been very lucky not to have been shot in the back.

For the defence of the capital from Napoleon and his ever-growing army, Marshal Oudinot was ordered to summon troops from the northern departments, including the Grenadiers of France, the renamed Old Guard. All the way to Paris the Marshal harangued the men to be loyal to Louis, but the nearer the column got to Paris the more the men made clear their lack of enthusiasm for the Bourbon fleur-de-lis and anyone who wore it. Indiscipline and insubordination became rife; and this from the Old Guard whose *grognards* (grumblers) had maintained perfect order throughout the appalling retreat from Moscow. At length, Oudinot pleaded with the men, asking whether they would follow him. Officers and men replied pointedly that they would, provided that he led them in the right direction. Not since the chaotic days of the Revolution had soldiers agreed to orders on terms. France in March 1815 was rapidly reverting to a revolutionary condition. In Paris the royalist gangs, which until very recently had been accustomed to preying upon ex-Imperial officers while the gendarmes looked the other way, now found themselves the target of attacks by bands of workers from the faubourgs. Many of these noble thugs were found hanging from lampposts, as in 1793.[16]

On 10 March Ney reached Besançon to find the situation quite different from the picture painted by Soult and the King. He discovered that more than half the garrison had already gone over to Napoleon, that Lyons had gone over without a shot fired, that d'Artois and Macdonald had fled to Paris, and that Bourmont's true function was to spy on him on behalf of d'Artois. That night two officers known to Ney arrived with two letters for him from Napoleon and Comte Bertrand. Ney was apprised of Napoleon's reasons for his return to France, especially the history of Louis' disregard for the letter and spirit of the Treaty of Fontainebleau. In his letter Napoleon asked Ney to rally to him at Chalons, 'I shall receive you as I did after the Battle of Moscow.' On that occasion Napoleon had bestowed on Ney the title of Prince de la Moskowa. Bertrand's letter asked Ney to avoid causing civil war as the nation was happy to receive back its rightful emperor. Ney's choice was not difficult. In the past Napoleon had had occasion to castigate him for bad judgement in the field, once saying, 'He had less sense than a drummer boy.' Ney could accept this from a man with whom he had risen through the ranks and whom he recognized as his superior in military ability. Also, Napoleon had raised Ney as high as it was possible for him to go and had always treated him and his family with respect. The Bourbons, however, had treated Ney with mistrust and condescending tolerance punctuated by instances of slight. Ney himself had been subjected to insult, as had his wife; and his sons had been deprived of the opportunity of an education. And now, with the revelations contained in Napoleon's letter, Ney was striken with remorse over his decisive role in forcing Napoleon's abdication and paving the way for the Bourbon restoration.

The next day Ney informed Bourmont that he was declaring for the Emperor, giving him explicit reasons.[17] In the Place des Armes at Lons, Ney addressed the soldiers and people who had gathered to hear him, 'The cause of the Bourbons is lost forever! The legitimate dynasty chosen by France is about to re-ascend the throne. It is to the Emperor Napoleon, our sovereign who has the RIGHT to rule over our beautiful country...'[18] Before Ney could finish his speech the crowd erupted with hysterical acclaim. And with his change of heart the last plausible hope the Bourbons might have had to retain power evaporated.

Soult determined that the place to concentrate forces for the last-ditch stand before Paris was in the area of Melun, south-east of the capital. There both roads from Lyons could be blocked. The composition of the force assembling around Melun was a shambles. In March 1815 the regular French Army consisted of 122,000 men – on paper. But some 30,000 in the south had already gone over to Napoleon's banner. From the rest of France a variety of regular units and National Guard were moving toward the rendezvous near the capital. In the meanwhile Marshal Soult was replaced by General Clarke, Duc de Feltre and betrayer of Paris in 1814, whom Louis considered more reliable. Clarke did not alter Soult's strategy, but the manner in which he deployed his forces probably guaranteed the failure of that strategy. He placed untrained but politically correct royalist regiments in the first line, while units of Napoleonic veterans were placed in the second. The Duc de Berry arrived to assume command. He saw himself in the mould of military greatness, but as he wandered about the camp, wearing a uniform and enlarged epaulettes of his own design, chatting to the men with a false *bonhomie*, he must have presented to the veterans a figure of pathetic diminution in comparison with the compelling presence of the emperor they had been proud to follow.

Among the royalist formations there was much dispute over the conflict between the military chain of command and the Courtly order of precedence. Ought, for example, Colonel, le Duc Fitzjames take orders from General, le Comte de Chabrillon? After all, the Duke was a first gentleman of the chamber, while the Count was merely a gentleman of honour. Would it not degrade the Court for the Duke to obey the Count? It is often

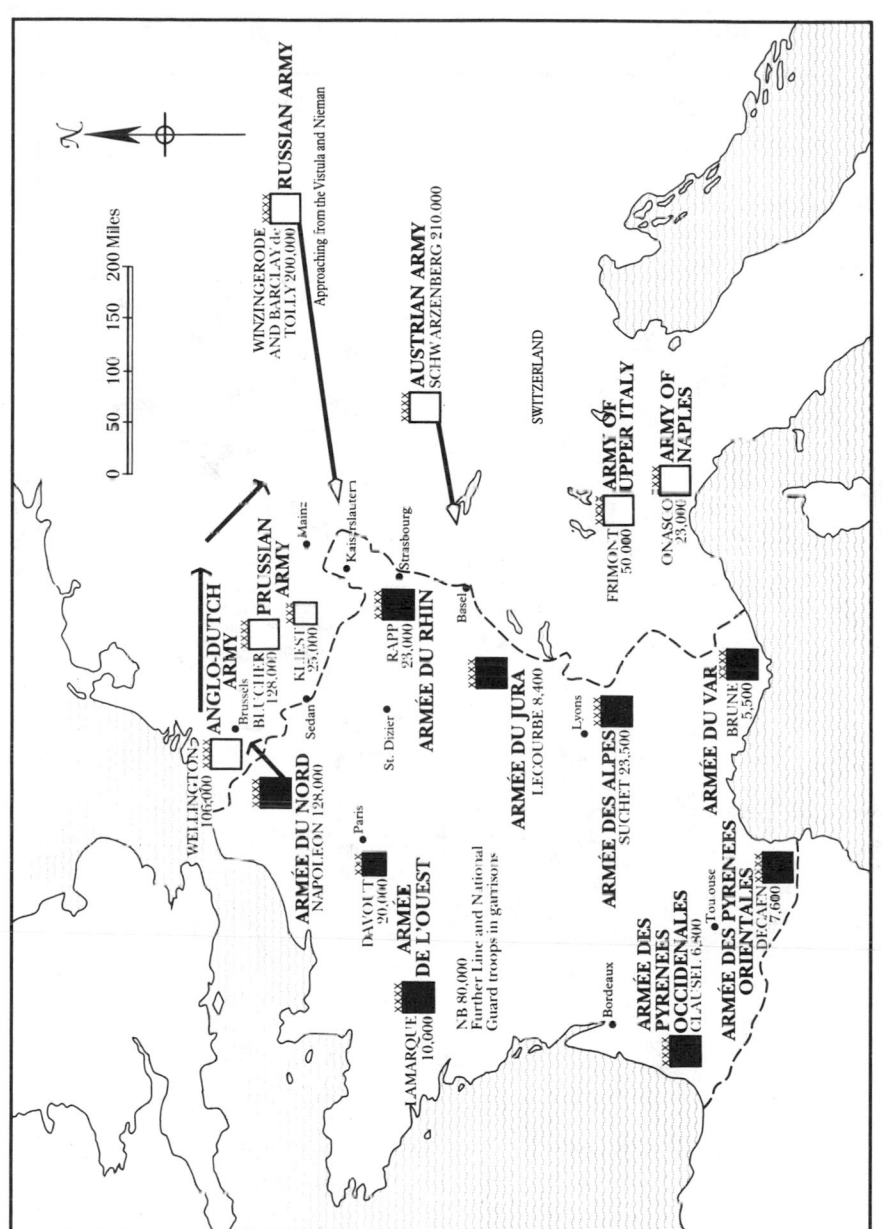

N

0 50 100 150 200 Miles

RUSSIAN ARMY

WINZINGERODE
AND BARCLAY de
TOLLY 200,000

Approaching from the Vistula and Nieman

AUSTRIAN ARMY
SCHWARZENBERG 210,000

SWITZERLAND

**ARMY OF
UPPER ITALY**
FRIMONT 50,000

**ARMY OF
NAPLES**
ONASCO 23,000

**ANGLO-DUTCH
ARMY**

**PRUSSIAN
ARMY**

BLÜCHER
128,000

KLEIST
25,000

• Mainz

• Kaiserslautern

• Strasbourg

RAPP
23,000

ARMÉE DU RHIN

• Basel

WELLINGTON
106,000

• Brussels

Sedan •

ARMÉE DU NORD
NAPOLEON 128,000

St. Dizier •

ARMÉE DU JURA
LECOURBE 8,400

• Lyons

ARMÉE DES ALPES
SUCHET 23,500

ARMÉE DU VAR
BRUNE 5,500

DAVOUT
20,000

• Paris

**ARMÉE
DE L'OUEST**

NB 80,000
Further Line and National
Guard troops in garrisons

LAMARQUE
10,000

• Bordeaux

**ARMÉE DES
PYRÉNÉES
OCCIDENALES**
CLAUSEL 6,800

Toulouse •

**ARMÉE DES PYRÉNÉES
ORIENTALES**
DECAEN 7,600

Napoleon's Plan of Campaign

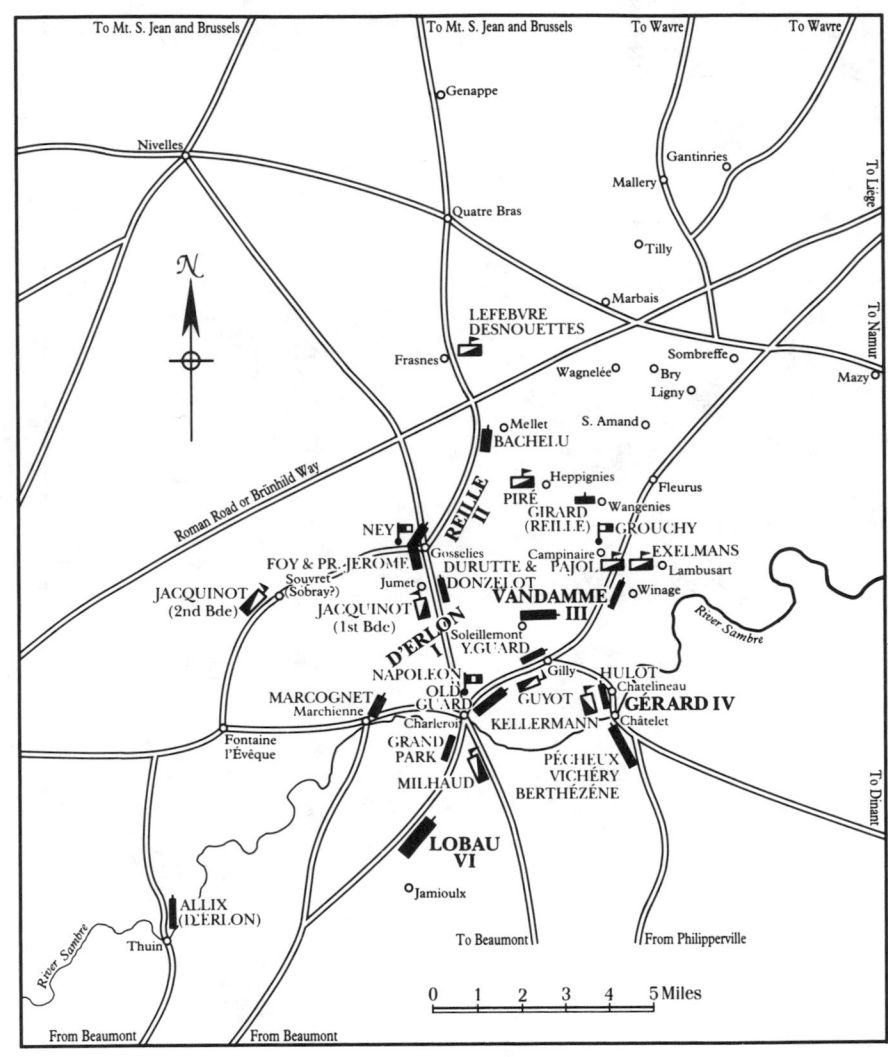

To Mt. S. Jean and Brussels To Mt. S. Jean and Brussels To Wavre To Wavre

Genappe

Nivelles

To Liège

Gantinries

Mallery

Quatre Bras

Tilly

To Namur

Marbais

N

LEFEBVRE
DESNOUETTES

Frasnes

Wagnelée   Sombreffe

Bry   Mazy

Ligny

Mellet   S. Amand

BACHELU

Roman Road or Brünhild Way

Heppignies   Fleurus

PIRÉ

GIRARD   Wangenies

NEY   (REILLE)   GROUCHY

REILLE   II

FOY & PR. JÉROME   EXELMANS

Gosselies   Campinaire   Lambusart

DURUTTE &   PAJOL

Souvret   DONZELOT

JACQUINOT   (Sobray?)

(2nd Bde)   Jumet   VANDAMME   Winage

JACQUINOT   III

(1st Bde)   River Sambre

D'ERLON   I

Soleillemont

Y. GUARD

NAPOLEON   Gilly   HULOT

MARCOGNET   OLD   Châtelineau

Marchienne   GUARD   GUYOT   GÉRARD IV

Charleroi   KELLERMANN   Châtelet

Fontaine
l'Évêque

GRAND
PARK

MILHAUD   PÉCHEUX
VICHÉRY
BERTHÉZÈNE

To Dinant

LOBAU
VI

Jamioulx

ALLIX
(D'ERLON)

Thuin   River Sambre

To Beaumont   From Philipperville

0   1   2   3   4   5 Miles

From Beaumont   From Beaumont

Dispositions of Napoleon's army on the night of 15 June

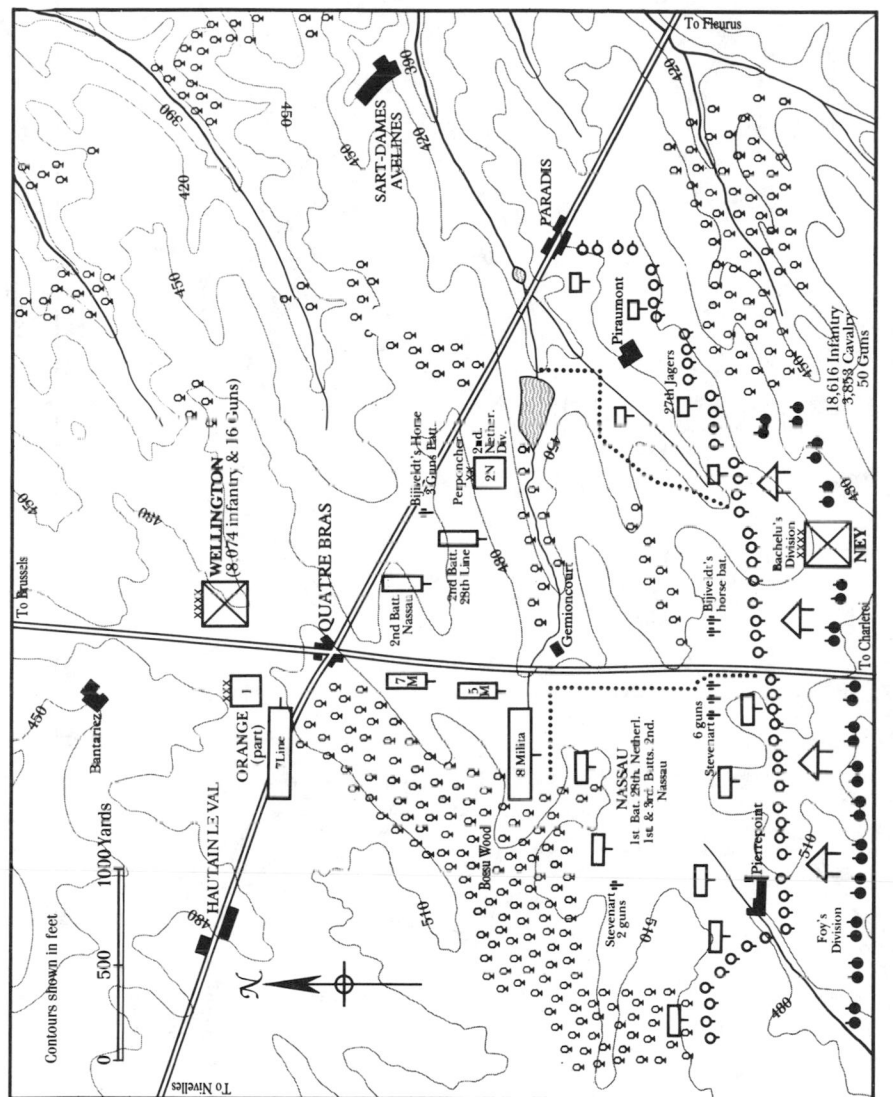

Quatre Bras: Situation between 10 a.m. and 3.30 p.m. 16 June

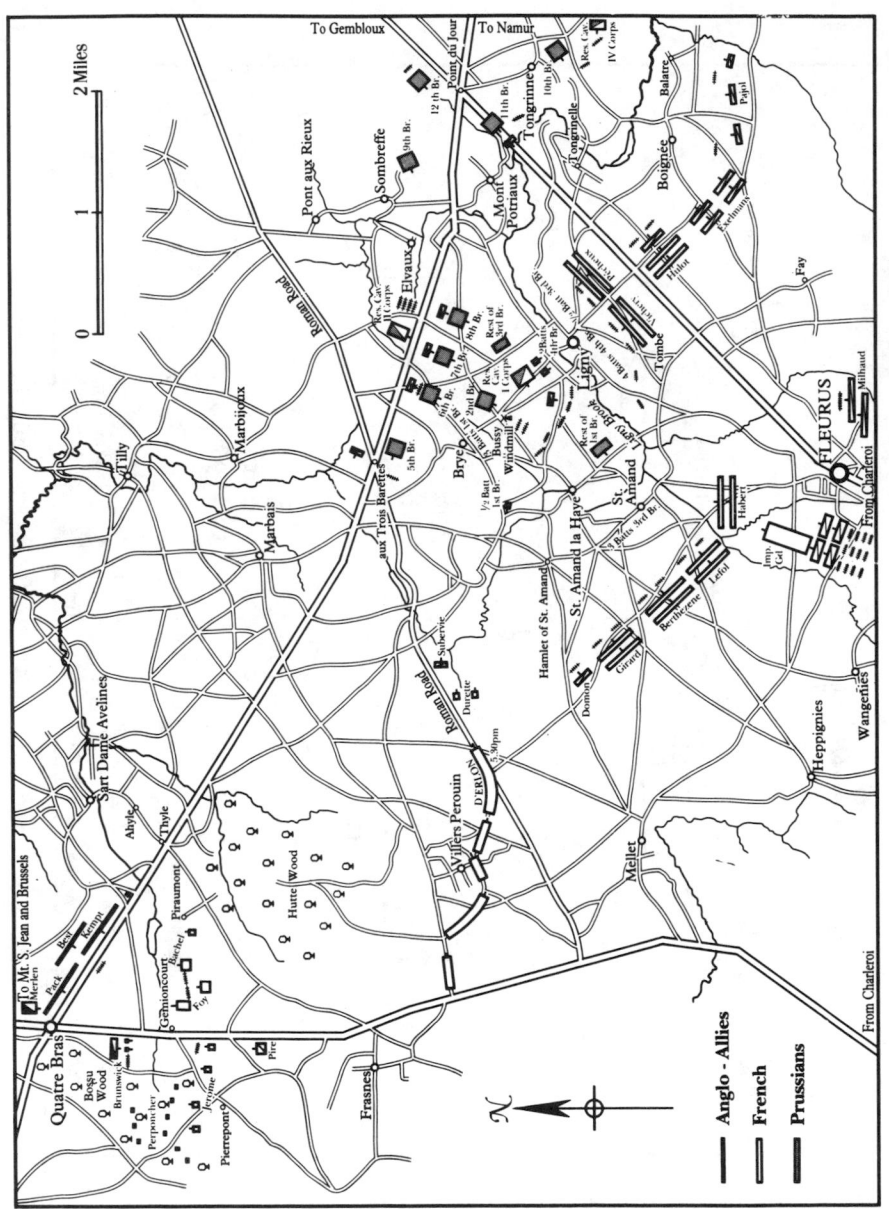

Battlefields of Ligny and Quatre Bras at 2 p.m. 16 June

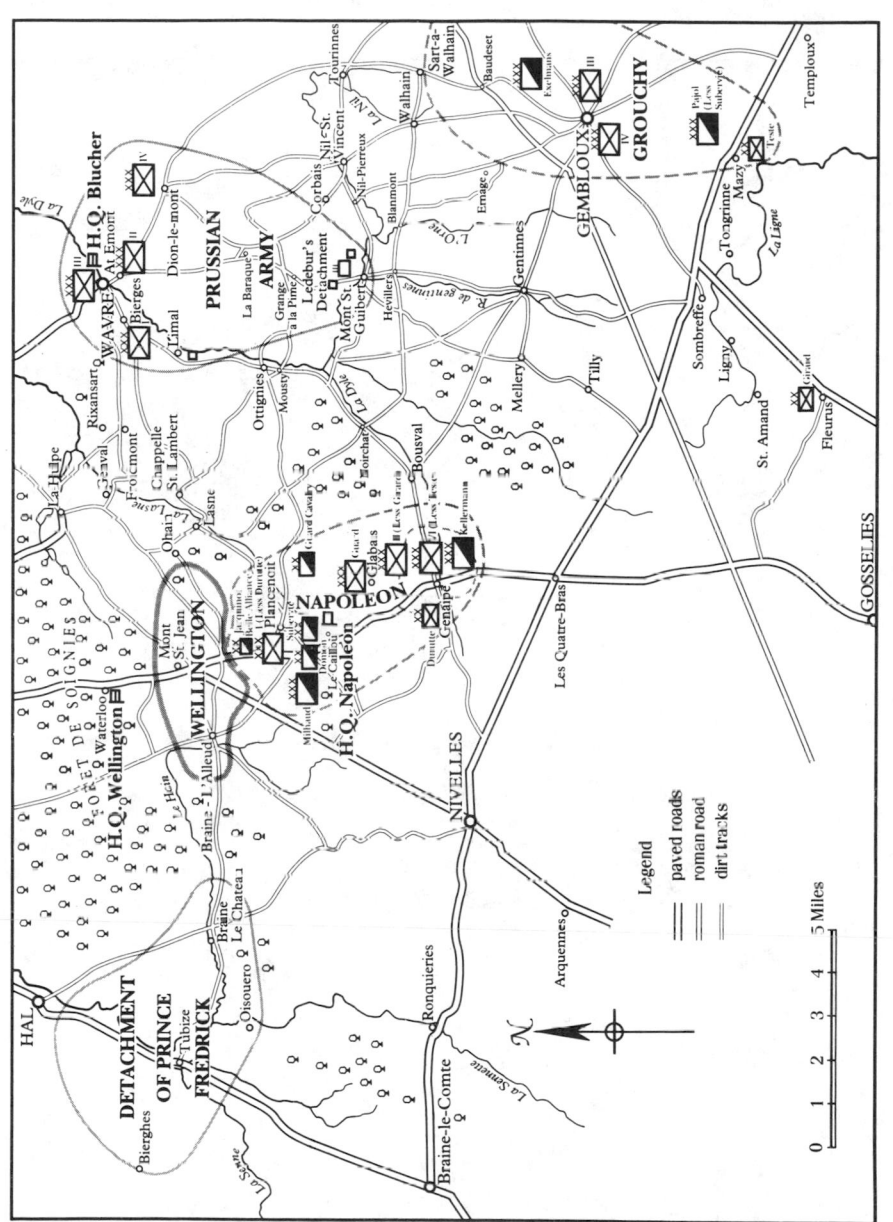

Positions of the Armies, 17 to 18 June

Legend

paved roads
roman road
dirt tracks

0 1 2 3 4 5 Miles

Detail from a Ferraris & Capitaine map of 1797 which shows the appalling country road and terrain over which the Anglo-Allied army had to move towards Quatre Bras. Owing to the final orders changing the destination, Braine-le-Comte became a congested bottleneck with hundreds of wagons, baggage mules and artillery intermingled with cavalry and infantry divisions, all straining to reach Quatre Bras.

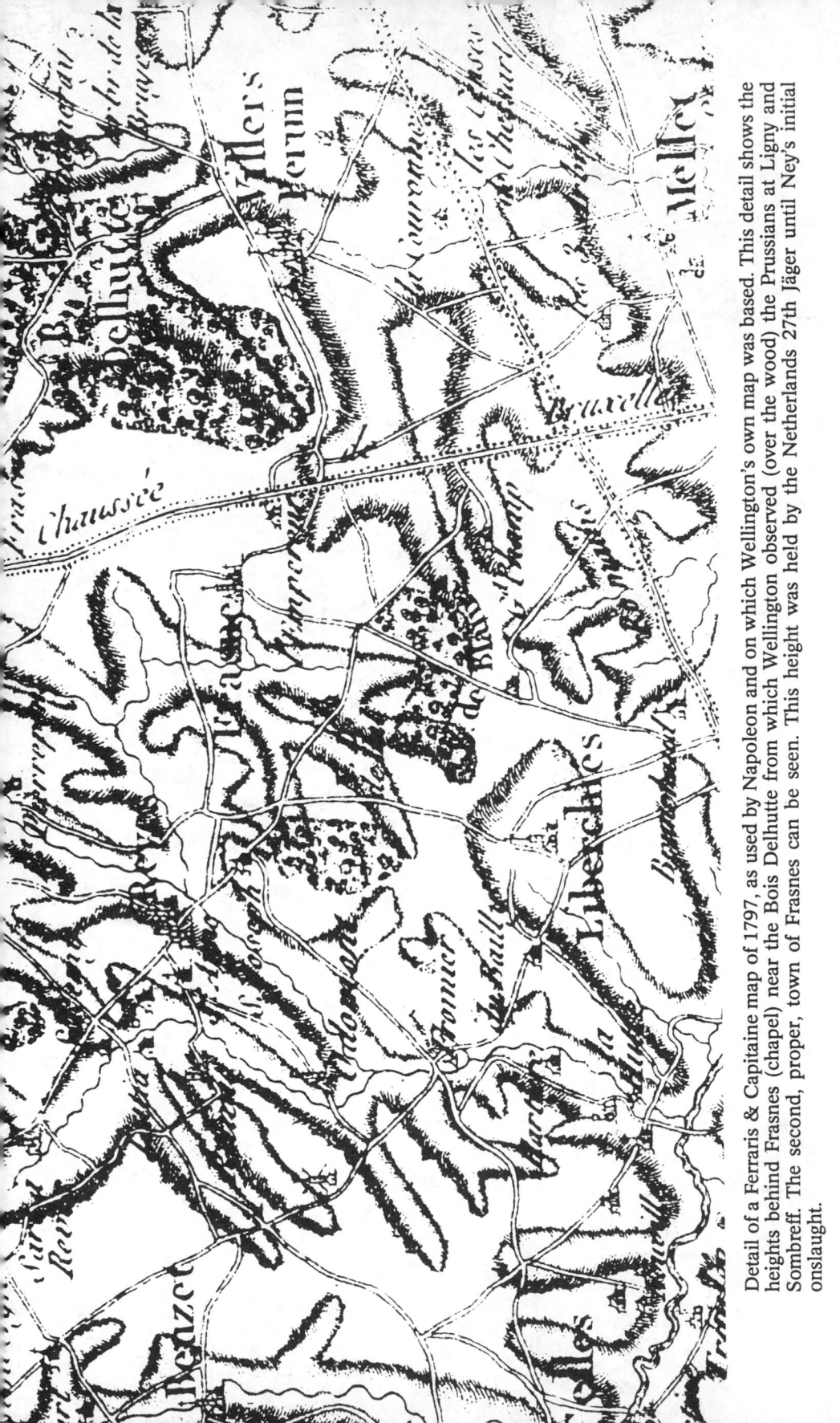

Detail of a Ferraris & Capitaine map of 1797, as used by Napoleon and on which Wellington's own map was based. This detail shows the heights behind Frasnes (chapel) near the Bois Delhutte from which Wellington observed (over the wood) the Prussians at Ligny and Sombreff. The second, proper, town of Frasnes can be seen. This height was held by the Netherlands 27th Jäger until Ney's initial onslaught.

Detail of a Ferraris & Capitaine map of 1797 showing Hal and the Waterloo position. In the event of defeat, Wellington intended to retreat via Hal. The wooded area around Waterloo can be seen below the hollow dip in the Smohain, Papelotte and Frischermont area.

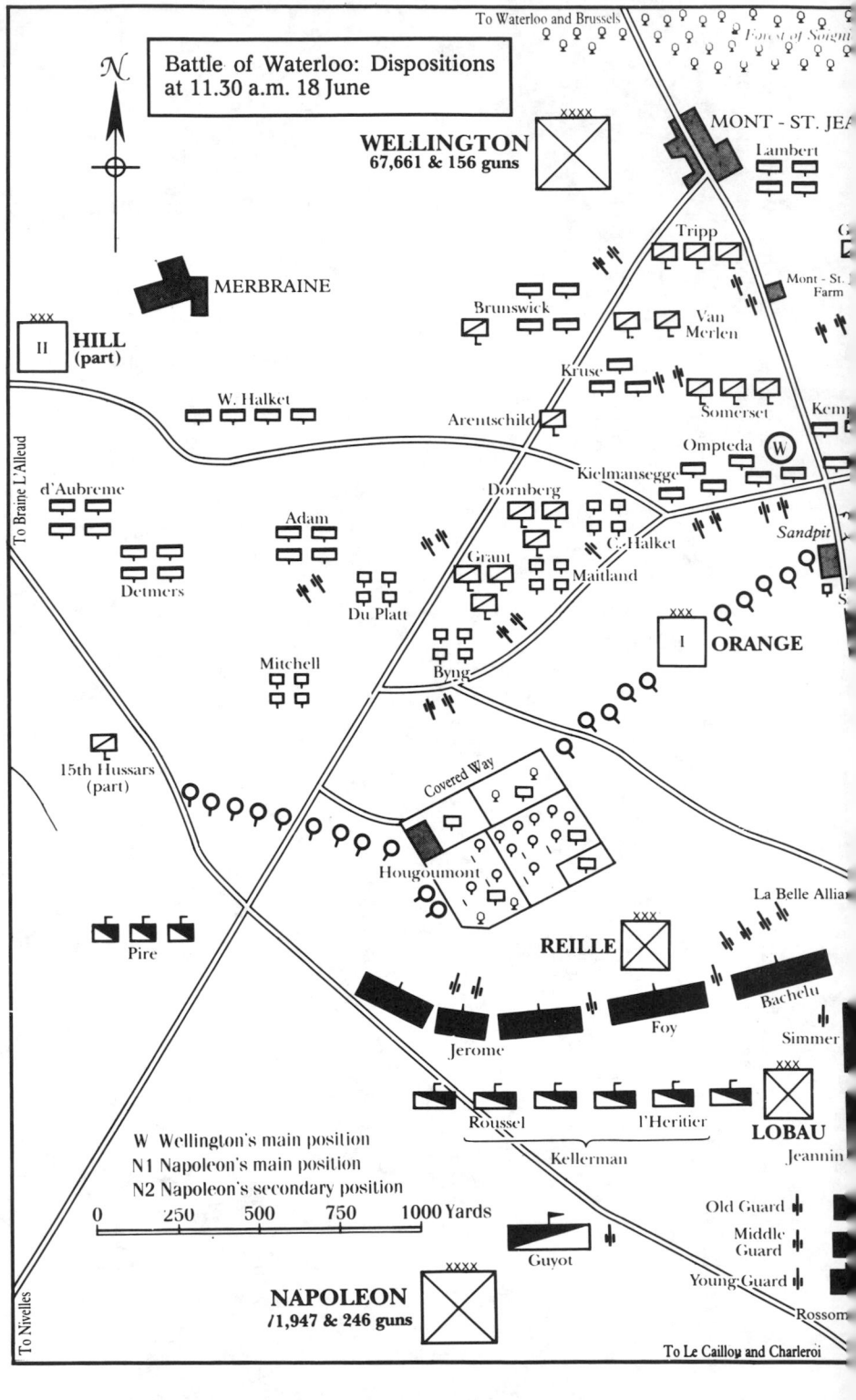

Battle of Waterloo: Dispositions at 11.30 a.m. 18 June

N

To Waterloo and Brussels

Forest of Soigne

MONT - ST. JEAN

WELLINGTON
67,661 & 156 guns

Lambert

Tripp

Mont - St. J Farm

MERBRAINE

Brunswick

Van Merlen

G

HILL
(part)

Kruse

Somerset

Kem

W. Halket

Arentschild

Ompteda

W

d'Aubreme

Dornberg

Kielmansegge

Sandpit

Adam

Grant

C. Halket

Maitland

Detmers

Du Platt

Byng

ORANGE

Mitchell

15th Hussars
(part)

Covered Way

Hougoumont

La Belle Allia

Pire

REILLE

Bachelu

Jerome

Foy

Simmer

LOBAU

Roussel

l'Heritier

Jeannin

Kellerman

W Wellington's main position
N1 Napoleon's main position
N2 Napoleon's secondary position

0   250   500   750   1000 Yards

Guyot

Old Guard

Middle Guard

NAPOLEON
/1,947 & 246 guns

Young Guard

Rossom

To Nivelles

To Le Caillou and Charleroi

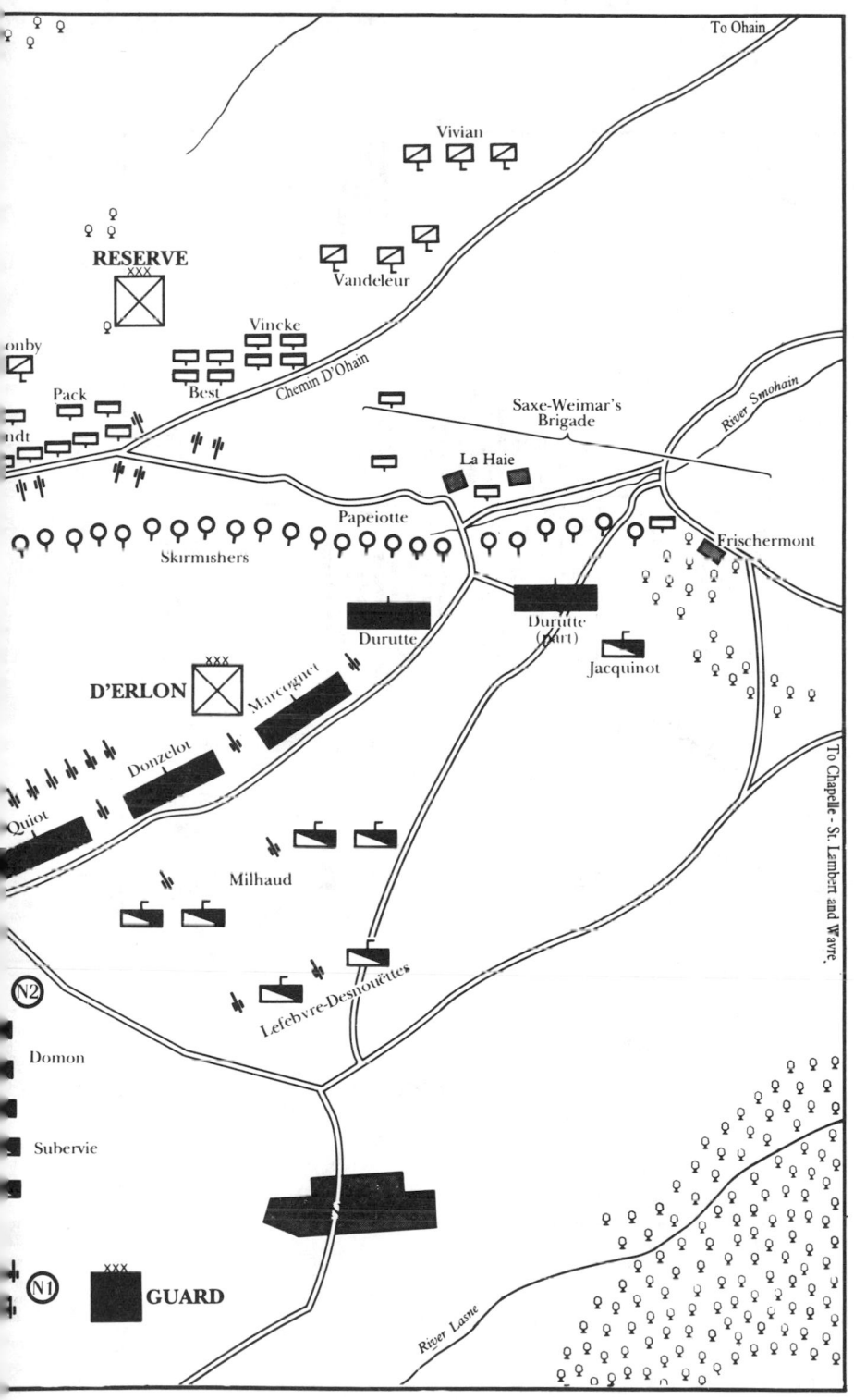

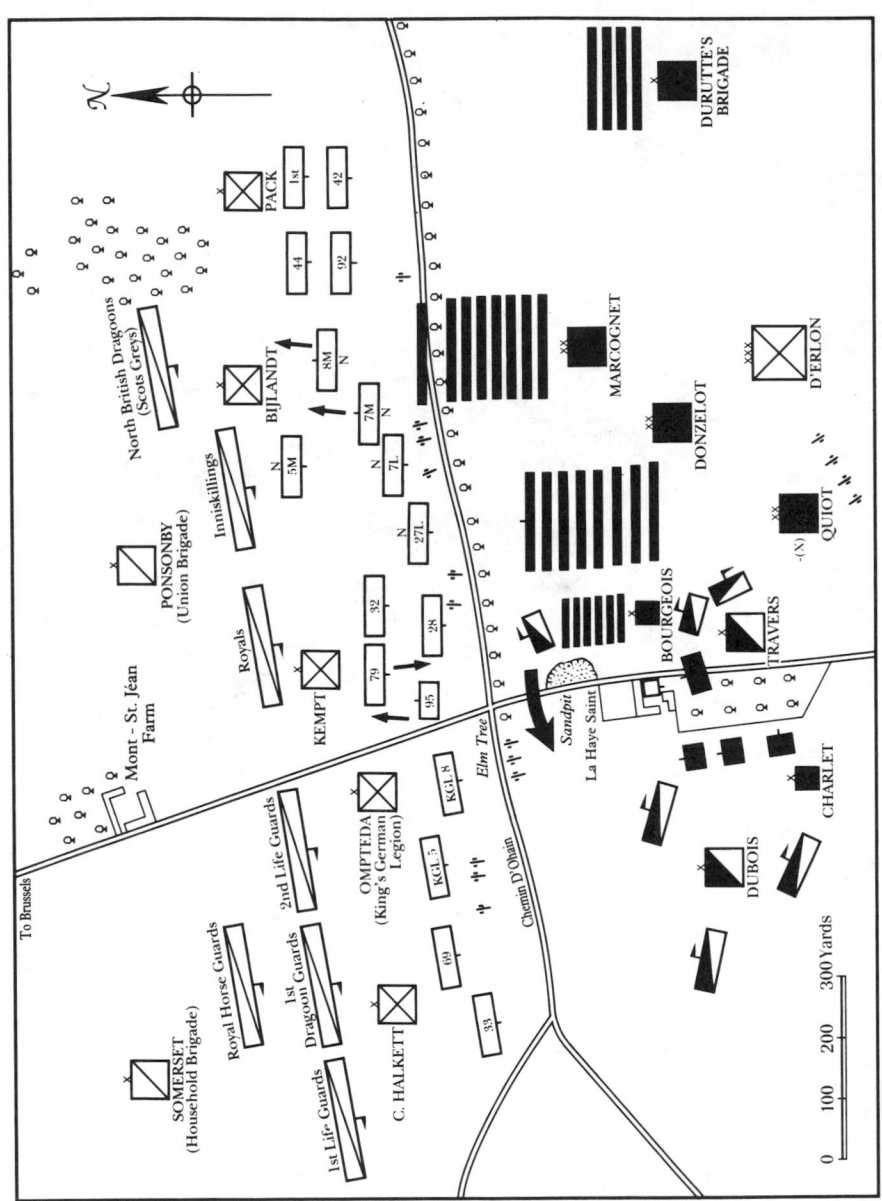

Battle of Waterloo, phase one: d'Erlon's attack, showing the irregular French column formations

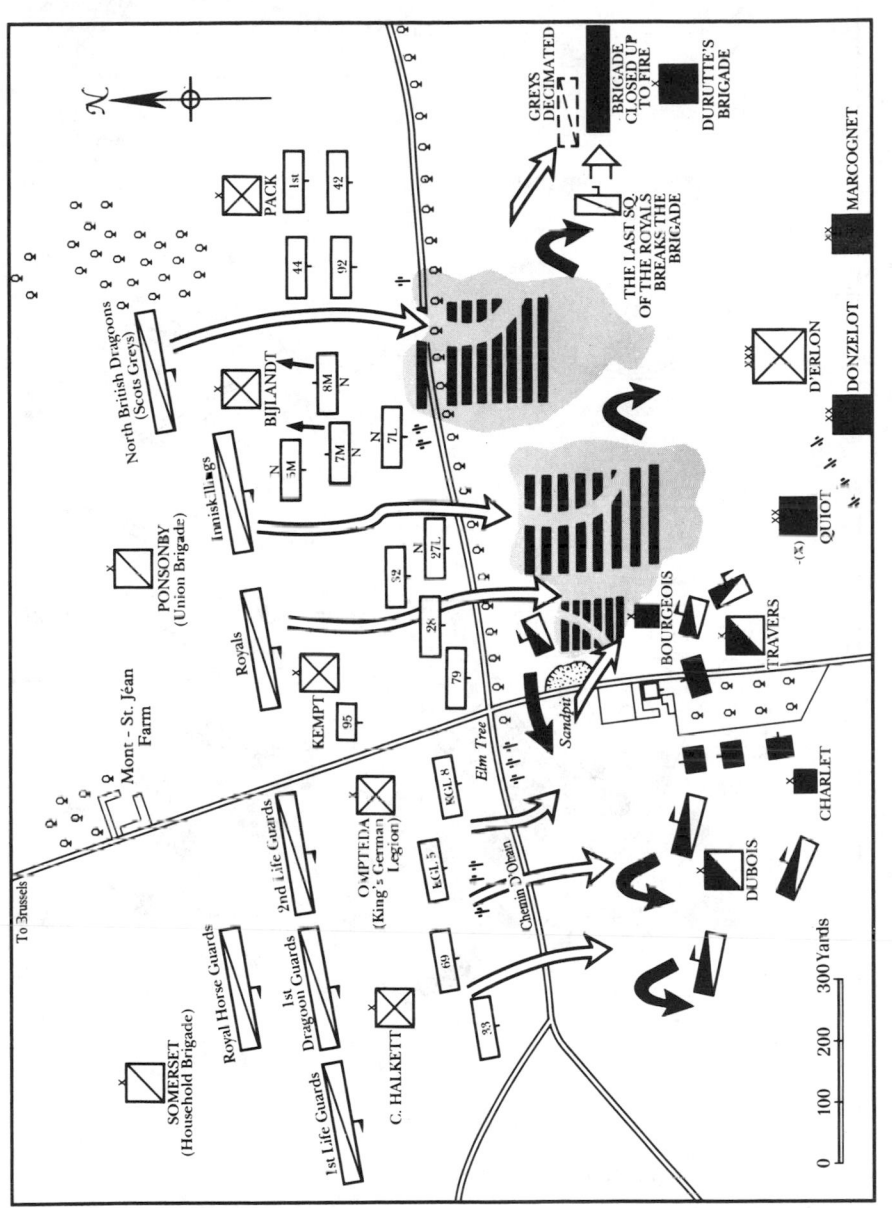

Battle of Waterloo, phase two: Uxbridge's cavalry charge, showing the destruction of the French columns and the 'breaking' of Durutte's Brigade by the last squadron of the Royals

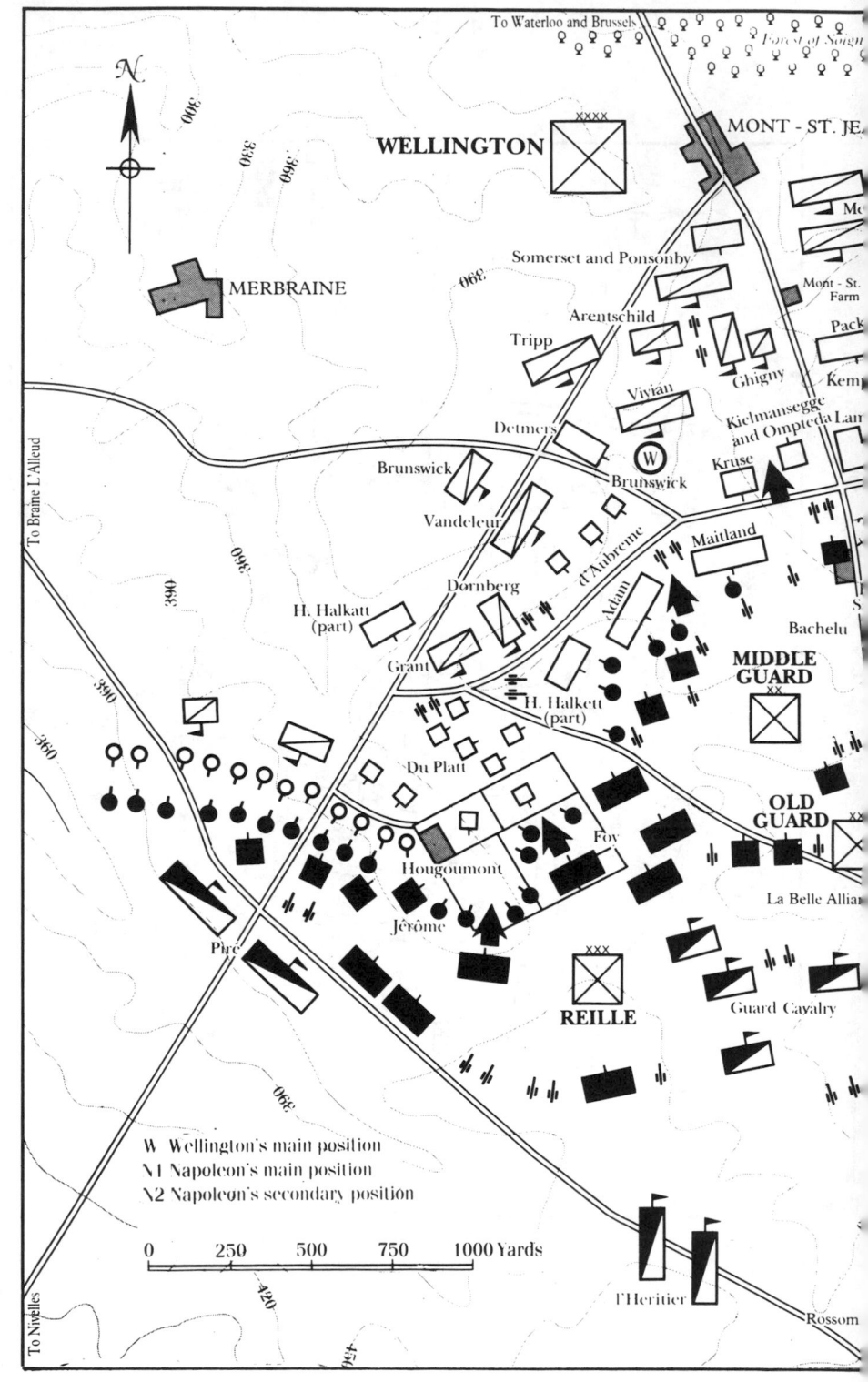

To Waterloo and Brussels
Forest of Soign

WELLINGTON

MONT - ST. JE.

Mo

Mont - St.
Farm

Somerset and Ponsonby

Pack

MERBRAINE

Arentschild

Tripp

Ghigny

Kem

Vivian

Kielmansegge
and Ompteda Lam

Detmers

Kruse

Brunswick

To Braine L'Alleud

Brunswick

W

Vandeleur

d'Aubreme

Maitland

Dornberg

H. Halkett
(part)

Adam

Bachelu

Grant

**MIDDLE
GUARD**
XX

H. Halkett
(part)

**OLD
GUARD**

Du Platt

Hougoumont

Foy

La Belle Allia

Jérôme

Piré

REILLE
XXX

Guard Cavalry

W Wellington's main position
N1 Napoleon's main position
N2 Napoleon's secondary position

0   250   500   750   1000 Yards

To Nivelles

l'Heritier

Rossom

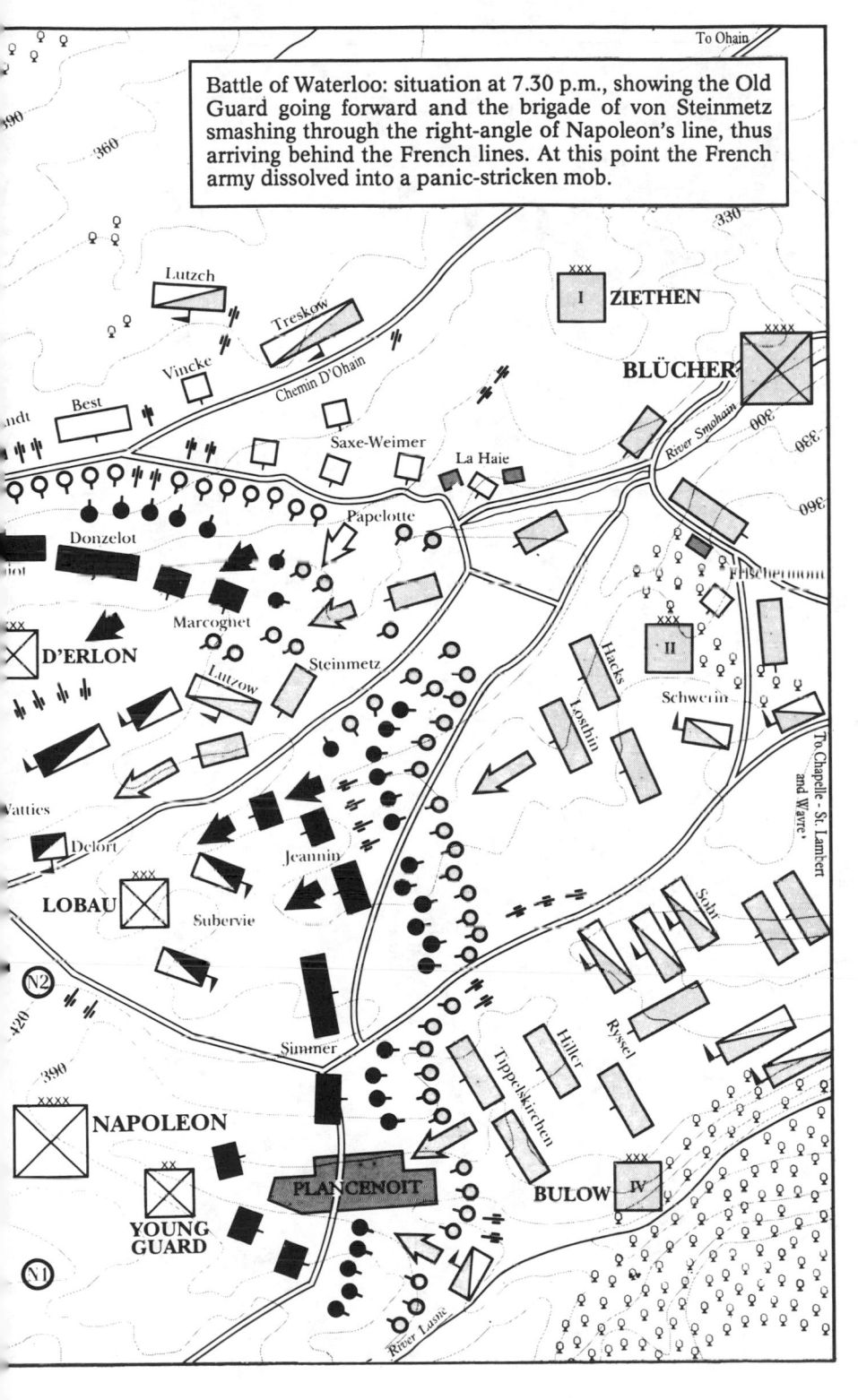

Battle of Waterloo: situation at 7.30 p.m., showing the Old Guard going forward and the brigade of von Steinmetz smashing through the right-angle of Napoleon's line, thus arriving behind the French lines. At this point the French army dissolved into a panic-stricken mob.

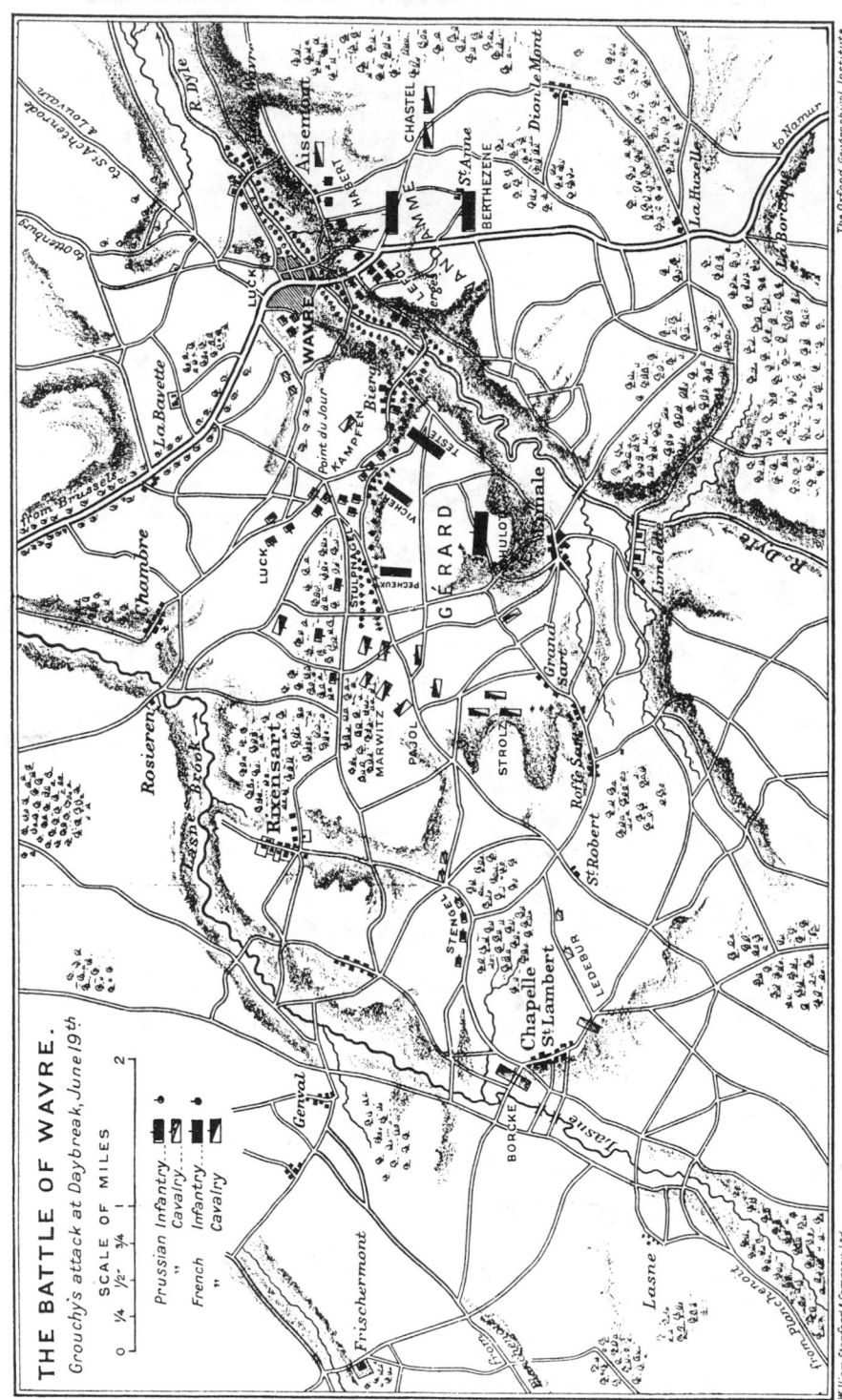

THE BATTLE OF WAVRE.
Grouchy's attack at Daybreak, June 19th.

SCALE OF MILES

Prussian Infantry......
"   Cavalry......
French Infantry......
"   Cavalry......

William Stanford & Company, Ltd.,

The Oxford Geographical Institute.

Battle of Wavre: Grouchy's attack at daybreak on 19 June

said that decision is the responsibility of command. It may well be that de Berry was happier to concern himself with making rulings in this ethereal realm, rather than face up to the awful problem of meeting the greatest general of the age on the field of battle, especially when that general's soldiers would be both facing him and behind him.

Reports reaching de Berry of the size of Napoleon's army indicated that it was growing almost hourly. Perhaps to try to reassure himself, de Berry decided to go among the veterans of the rear echelon. When he stopped at a campfire, as Napoleon had often done, and asked the men for some of their soup, a sergeant replied darkly, 'You have come too late, Sir. You will find it cold.'[19] At this point, de Berry, as his father had done before him, decided to exercise the better part of valour. He mounted his horse and rode straight to Paris. Following His Grace's lead, most of the royalist first line made off during the night.

By 16 March, fifteen days after Napoleon had landed, his proclamation at Lyons had reached most parts of France. The atmosphere almost everywhere was as though an election had been held and the results were being declared. In the large town of Clamecy a gentleman of military bearing, in riding-habit and top hat, rode up before the *hôtel de ville*, tied his horse, mounted the steps, put on his spectacles, and shouted to the people in the street for attention. A crowd soon gathered. The man identified himself as General Allix, who was on half pay. He then read out Napoleon's proclamation. The royalist mayor summoned the town guard; and shortly a lieutenant and a file of twelve men arrived with muskets at the ready to arrest the traitor. General Allix removed his spectacles and announced, 'In the name of the Emperor, I assume command of the town of Clamecy! All of you present here, I call upon to put up the national colours immediately, and to regard all as enemies who do not wear it.' As the crowd roared its approval, *tricolores* sprouted from the twin spires of the town church, and the squad of gendarmes saluted and promptly removed their Bourbon emblems. Thus was the town of Clamecy captured for Napoleon by one man.[20]

In Paris, Louis, in desperation and probably with unconscious irony, invoked the revolutionary law of 4th Nivôse, Year IV, which punished with death any one who recruited for an enemy or rebel.[21] This law had been promulgated to combat the efforts of Louis' own brother and uncle who were recruiting in Coblenz during the early days of the Terror. Louis, upon his return, had declared all such laws void, but that could be overlooked in the present emergency. On 16 March he went to the Chambers and declared that he could, at 60 years of age, do no better than to die in defence of France. As he spoke, his Finance Minister, Baron Louis, was arranging on his king's behalf for as much Treasury gold and Crown jewellery as possible to be packed into ammunition wagons. He also laboured to convert all available money and government stocks and bonds to foreign bills of exchange payable on London. If Louis could not continue to be a king in France, he certainly intended to continue living like one in England.

The next day Louis appeared in the Chambers wearing the insignia of the Legion of Honour and told those present, 'We might have to be supported by the bayonets of our allies.' This remark summed up Louis' only claim to the throne of post-revolutionary France: the armed force of like-minded reactionary monarchs. Louis' audience, the royalist Chambers, would certainly have favoured the use of any means to maintain their king and their own positions. Louis also enjoyed solid support in the Faubourg Saint Germain, the very name of which was synonymous with the aristocracy of the *ancien régime*. But it was felt necessary to quadruple the force of royalist National Guards patrolling Saint Germain, because virtually everywhere else there arose the spectre of a second revolution. The thrill of liberation coursed through the populace, while the shadow of the guillotine fell across the minds of the nobility.

The 10,000-man *Maison du Roi*, the King's Household Guard, composed of the flower of French chivalry, would in the time of Roland and Charlemagne have stood sword in hand around the person of their king and died where they stood. Of course, in those heroic days, the king would still have been there to defend. As it was, though, in the days of the eighteenth Louis, nobility embodied only the cold ashes of those radiant virtues of honour and sacrifice by which, at its best, it had illuminated the Dark Ages. Word soon circulated through the Paris aristocracy, including the personnel of the *Maison du Roi*, that the royal family was hurriedly liquidating its assets. There was a run on the Paris banks as the aristocracy too sought to obtain bills of exchange for their endangered wealth. The re-emigration of the *émigrés* began in earnest. By 19 March the *Maison du Roi* had been reduced to about 4,000. A true and justifiable panic had seized the minds of most royalists. In their imagination they could see again the tumbrils and '...a certain movable framework with a sack and a blade in it, terrible in history'.[22]

When Marshal Macdonald, summoned urgently, arrived at the Palace wearing civilian clothes, he found a number of coaches being held in readiness for instant flight. Louis was terrified that if he stayed any longer he might be apprehended by bloodthirsty republicans, as his late brother had been at Varennes in 1791, and suffer his brother's fate. Macdonald served him well by taking his departure arrangements into his own steadier hands. Macdonald ordered that the coaches be taken away and brought back after dark. He also arranged a military review for the next day and announced that the King would address the Chambers later that day. By now Napoleon was at Auxerre, one day's march from Fontainebleau where he had signed his conditional treaty of abdication less than a year before.

At midnight, Louis shuffled down the steps of the Tuileries and into his coach as quickly as his gouty legs would allow. In later years a famous painting would depict Louis' departure in a romanticized fashion, with his loyal family and followers imploring him to stay. In fact many royalists were already on the roads north-east of Paris, making for the Belgian border. Such was the haste of Louis' flight that a Count in the royal guard galloping behind his coach burst his money-belt with the result that its contents of diamonds worked down his trousers and into his boots where he allowed them to remain, lacerating his flesh, until the party had reached its destination.

Next morning the less astute royalists, such as Chateaubriand, who had delighted Paris at the Restoration with his vitriolic pamphlet against Napoleon, awoke to find the King gone, having left them all to their fate. The news in Paris was that Napoleon had reached Fontainebleau. In reporting these events, foreign newspapers did not touch upon the ignominious rout of the Bourbons or the popular acclaim with which Napoleon was received. Instead they reported the Bourbon line that it was the working of a conspiracy by Napoleon to subvert the army and use it to overawe the people into acquiesence to 'the Tyrant, the Usurper'.

Paris did not descend into anarchy with the collapse of the monarchy. Napoleon's civil service continued to function as it had over the past year. The Comte de Lavallette, on his own initiative, resumed his former position as Postmaster-General and wrote to Napoleon asking him to come at once to Paris. General Sebastiani, with a small cavalry force, rode to Melun to order the leaderless soldiers there to return to barracks. Only one recorded act of violence connected with this disbandment occurred, when an 18-year-old royalist, Lieutenant M. Negre de Massais, who had not been apprised of the true state of affairs, became enraged at the soldiers' acceptance of Sebastiani's order. Out of pique, he tore off his epaulettes, shouted at his men and threw his insignia at them. The insignia struck a veteran, who in turn boxed the boy's ears so hard he fell to the ground in tears. The men shouted 'Vive l'Empereur!' and marched off. On 20 March at nine in the evening, Napoleon arrived at the Tuileries, two weeks and five days after setting foot on the shores of France. During that time his men had not fired a single shot or sustained a single casualty.

Napoleon was under no illusions about the magnitude of the task ahead of him. Without entertaining any hopes he wrote to each of the Allied sovereigns, offering conciliatory terms as the basis for peace. He proposed to renounce his claims to Poland, Germany, Italy, Belgium and Holland. His letter to the Prince Regent of Britain, however, was returned unopened at Castlereagh's direction. Lord Liverpool, the Prime Minister, was not interested in seeking a *modus vivendi* with Napoleon. His foreign policy, inherited from William Pitt, was based on having a weak, pliable Bourbon monarch on the French throne, not a dynamic figure like Napoleon. The British establishment feared Napoleon, not only for his ability to threaten Britain militarily, but also for the republican political ideas which spread in the wake of his conquests. Britain had fought implacably and at great expense for twenty-five years to try to contain the ideological contagion of the 'Rights of Man', first clearly expressed in the American

Declaration of Independence in 1776. The colonies in America had been lost to this contagion, but it could not be allowed to flourish so close to home. During the early days of the French Revolution, republicanism had spread to Britain and had begun to take root in the form of Jacobin clubs and workers' societies. These domestic threats to privilege were dealt with by the expedient of transportation.[23] America, which had long been used for this purpose, was no longer available, so the poor wretches were now sent to Australia.[24] Equally, the external threat could not be tolerated. Britain – that is, the government and ruling class, the average person having no political voice as yet – was not prepared to co-exist with a Napoleonic France on any terms. The mere existence of a republican state across the Channel was too dangerous. This view was shared by the delegates to the Congress of Vienna who had expected at first that Louis, with command of the French Army, would easily deal with Napoleon and his battalion-size force. The delegates, representing as they did nations controlled by reactionary governments, did not contemplate that the French people and soldiers as individuals might so readily become actors in the drama. In the event of a civil war breaking out in France, the Allies intended to assemble some 200,000 men on the border to strengthen the royalist hand. They had not considered that the French nation as a whole might be prompted by Napoleon's mere presence to rise up and reject the Bourbons.

On 12 March the Duke of Wellington wrote home enclosing a copy of the declaration of outlawry against Napoleon and outlining the Allied military plan to bring to an end his re-animation. First the Austrians would assemble an army of 150,000 men in Italy to protect Vienna from any advance either by Murat from Naples or by Napoleon. On the upper Rhine a force eventually totalling 200,000 would be formed of Bavarians, Württembergers, Badeners and a few Austrians, under the command of Prince zu Schwarzenberg. Also on the upper Rhine, the Prussians would field a corps of 25,000 men under von Kleist. A Russian army of 200,000 led by the Tsar would begin marching towards the Rhine. On the lower Rhine a Prussian army of 120,000 would assemble. And finally, in The Netherlands a combined Anglo-Dutch force would be comprised of 25,000 British and German Legionaries and 25,000 Dutch. Wellington, not wishing to act as a supernumerary to either the Tsar or Prince Schwarzenberg, accepted command of the Anglo-Dutch army. The Allies informed Britain that their treasuries were so depleted that they would require subsidies in accordance with the Treaty of Châtillon. This treaty obliged each of the Allies to support the others for a period of twenty years after the Peace of Paris. Under its terms Britain agreed to supply each of her allies with a cash payment of £20-30 per man for each man fewer than the 150,000 that Britain would field in the event of war.[25] As Britain's army on the continent fell short by 125,000, this subsidy amounted to more than three million pounds. After so many years of war Britain's financial situation in 1815 was precarious. A third of the annual revenue was required to be set against the national debt and accrued interest. Britain was borrowing gold from foreign banking houses to finance the coming campaign of 1815. Castlereagh told Wellington in confidence that '...unless some system of this kind [levying half of the cost of the war from France in reparations] be agreed upon ... We shall be bankrupts, and driven from the field in three months.'[26]

An unforeseeable accident occurred in Paris which furthered distrust among the Allies. Talleyrand's deputy for foreign affairs, the Marquis de Jarcourt, in his haste to leave Paris, had left behind all his state papers. Among them was the secret treaty of January 1815 between France, Austria and Britain, against Russia and Prussia. Napoleon summoned the Russian Ambassador, who had not yet received his passport to leave France. He was permitted to make his own copy of the treaty to take to the Tsar in Vienna. Alexander, when he had seen the copy, called the Allied commissioners and confronted them with the document. King Frederick William of Prussia and his generals were as shocked as the Tsar had been. By this treaty Britain had not only reneged on its agreement with Prussia over Saxony, but had been ready to ally herself with the old enemy, France, and the vacillating Austrians in war against Prussia and Russia. The Tsar appeared to dismiss the matter and left for his forward headquarters in Germany. But he wrote to his brother Constantine[27] that he had no intention of throwing away any more Russian lives on behalf of foreign machinations. He would accept the British subsidy and make haste slowly towards France. Let Austria first show that she meant to fight and suffer losses. He would not make great efforts to reinstate the Bourbons who had insulted him and had tried to rob him of Poland. In any case, if Napoleon were to prevail, the Tsar had no doubt he would offer Russia the whole of Poland to secure a peace treaty.

Like Russia, its ally and enemy, Austria too had no intention of losing her army fighting Napoleon. The possible loss of Italy was her chief concern; and accordingly its greatest force was kept there. Because Austria had, within the previous three months, threatened both Russia and Prussia with war, she could not afford to lose an army defeating Napoleon and then be faced with a Hobson's choice of holding down Italy or opposing any aggression by Russia or Prussia. In any case, if Napoleon were victorious, Austria would return Napoleon's wife and son, retain part of Italy, and have a strong son-in-law in France to side with Austria against her rapacious neighbours to the north and east. For the moment the Austrian Emperor would concentrate on the immediate problem of Murat in Naples, and await developments.

Thus the burden of prosecuting a war against Napoleon in 1815 fell to Britain, The Netherlands and Prussia. The Prussians had no wish to see their country again reduced in size as a result of Napoleonic victory. The Prussian generals wanted to see Napoleon destroyed; they wanted to harry and waste France, recover their stolen art treasures, and blow up the Pont d'Iéna in Paris. The new king of The Netherlands had no wish to give up his crown to Napoleon, and his Dutch and Belgian subjects did not want to see their own country again become so many French departments. And the British Government, having incurred £1,000 million of debt in opposing him, would not be satisfied with any eventuality which left Napoleon in control of France.

Immediately upon his regaining control of the government, Napoleon embarked with his renowned energy on a dual programme of domestic reform and national defence. He drew up a charter, the *Acte Additionnel*, as an amendment to his Imperial Constitution. In it he gave France a two-tiered Chamber, with legislative power, to which Ministers were responsible. The Act also protected individual liberty, abolished slavery in all French colonies, and disallowed in perpetuity any claims on state lands by *émigrés*. In effect the Act provided for a constitutional monarchy, or rather, *imperium*. Napoleon also reorganized the finances of the state. He instructed banking houses to cancel all bills of exchange given to the Bourbons and to civil servants. He recovered some 50 million francs which Baron Louis, the Bourbon finance Minister, had expropriated to fund his own speculations on the Bourse but which he had neglected to take with him. Napoleon raised a loan on foreign banks of 150 million francs, using the state forests as security. The remainder of his personal fortune Napoleon applied to state finances and the equipment of a much expanded army fit to meet the gathering Allied forces.

The Army of France, as the Bourbons had left it, consisted of a complement of 200,000 – on paper. Of these, 32,800 were listed as on leave, to avoid having to pay them. Fully 82,000 were listed as deserters, the majority of whom simply did not want to serve under the Bourbons.[28] Napoleon issued a decree for all these missing men to rejoin the Colours. By June, 82,446 had returned to their units and a further 23,448 were at their depots awaiting equipment. Of 114,000 men missing, only 8,105 had not responded. Napoleon tapped additional military manpower by ordering the formation of forty battalions of sailors from the largely idle French naval forces. The mobile National Guard was mobilized in accordance with laws of 1791, 1792, 1805 and 1813 which entitled him to bring the Guard up to war strength for national defence. This measure produced another 200,000 men under arms. Lazare Carnot, whom Napoleon had wisely appointed Minister of the Interior, was the 'organizer of victory' whose organizational genius had been crucial to Republican France's unexpected victories against the First Coalition. Carnot told the Chambers that, given time and equipment, France could field an army of two and a half million men.

By 15 June, 234,720 National Guardsmen had been summoned, and 150,000 were already assembled. From his surplus of regular army officers on half pay, Napoleon assigned many to train the National Guard up to regular army standards. He well remembered how, at La Fère-Champenoise in 1814, a division of these untrained men had blundered into the entire Allied army. The division assumed a square formation and fought a stubborn retreat for sixteen miles, assailed by almost the whole of the Allied cavalry, 20,000 horsemen. The Guards were only compelled to surrender when the entire Russian and Prussian Guard infantry blocked them and reduced them by cannon fire.[29]

Napoleon also asked the Chambers to call out the conscripts for 1815, but they refused, thus exercising one of their new rights given to them by him. Marshal Davout, now Minister of War, pointed out that the conscripts had in fact been called out in 1814, but had not completed their assembly before Napoleon's abdication. When the Chambers were informed of this they decided that, as the call-out of 1814 had been lawfully balloted and as those called out had not been dismissed, it was proper now to recall them. By 11 June, one week later, 46,419 of these conscripts had assembled. The prefect of the Aisne reported, 'The conscripts of 1815 have joined in three days with amazing readiness, there have been an additional 18,200 volunteers.'[30] The call to arms in the Aisne may have been aided by memories of the advance the year before of the Allied armies of liberation which pillaged the land and filled the cemeteries.[31]

In fewer than eight weeks from his entry into Paris, Napoleon had raised a field army of 284,000 men. As an auxiliary force he had 220,000 mobile National Guardsmen. Thus by 10 June he had 504,000[32] men under arms. By the beginning of October this figure would have risen to 800,000 without a new conscription. But having the men was only part of the need; equipment was the other. 'The salvation of the nation depends on the number of muskets and bayonets we can shoulder,' Napoleon wrote to Davout.[33] The equipage of the army had suffered greatly under the destructive neglect of the Bourbons. The men were in need of everything: muskets, bayonets, greatcoats, uniforms, boots and leather equipment; the cavalry needed horses, saddles, harness, pistols and uniforms; and the artillery needed gun carriages and ammunition wagons.

With Napoleon's abdication and the demise of the Empire with its system of preferential tariffs, France had suffered mass unemployment and inflation. The Bourbons had aggravated this situation by shipping grain to England for hard currency. Napoleon was able virtually to eliminate unemployment, at least in the short term, and address the desperate need for military equipment by almost literally putting the nation to work fitting out its soldiers. The old cry of 'La patrie en danger!' went out across France; foreign armies were again massing to invade and attempt to thwart the will of the French people. In every city, town and village the people worked around the clock. Tailors, seamstresses and clothiers made uniforms – Paris alone producing 1,250 a day. Tanners, leatherworkers, cobblers and glovemakers produced 195,000 pairs of boots and other leather equipment. Thousands were occupied in producing munitions. All cartridges had to be made by hand, each requiring paper manufacture, gunpowder production and the moulding of lead balls. At the Vincennes arsenal alone, 12 million cartidges were made in eight weeks. Wheelwrights, coopers, carpenters and metalworkers produced hundreds of gun carriages, wagons, ambulances, mobile forges and bridging wagons. The prefects of the departments assembled armourers, watchmakers, gunsmiths, cabinetmakers, brassworkers and jewellers to manufacture and repair muskets. They produced 40,000 a month. The cutlery firms in Moulins and Langres supplied 110,000 bayonets, 17,000 sabres and 14,879 heavy cavalry swords. Napoleon ordered twelve francs to be paid for every musket turned in that had been found after the battles of 1814. A total of 11,035 muskets of various calibres were thus obtained, with gendarmerie muskets being given in exchange, to keep the army's ammunition uniform. Napoleon required each department to provide 8,000 suitable horses, to be paid for in cash on delivery. He requisitioned half the gendarmerie horses at 600 francs each, knowing that the local gendarmes could replace them with good horses for about 450 francs each. This scheme produced 4,250 trained heavy cavalry mounts with little delay, making a total of 55,500 horses requisitioned in eight weeks.

By 12 June Napoleon had raised 280,000 well-trained soldiers for his field army. Most had fought in at least one campaign. Many had been prisoners of war, released after Napoleon's abdication: veterans from Spain, men from prison camps in England, Prussia and Russia. Troops from the beleaguered French garrisons in Poland, Saxony and throughout the German states had also returned. Davout's garrison of Hamburg had come home in good order. The mobile National Guard was officered entirely by thousands of experienced regular officers, most of whom had themselves risen through the ranks. All men, regular and National Guard, 504,000 and growing daily, were fully equipped with muskets, bayonets, ammunition and cannon.

All this had been accomplished in only eight weeks. No better fact can be advanced to refute the Bourbon assertion that Napoleon's return to power had been a sort of army coup foisted on an unwilling people. The army with which Napoleon faced the approaching Allies was experienced, highly motivated to prove themselves and defend their country in battle, well equipped, large enough to accomplish their task, and was supported to the hilt by the vast majority of the French people.

CHAPTER 3

The United Netherlands:
The Allies Assemble

"'Do you not see your country is lost?" asked the Duke of Buckingham. "There is one way never to see it lost," replied William, "and that is to die in the last ditch."' - King William III of England and Prince of Orange, 1650-1702. Burnet, *History of his Own Times* (1715), i, p. 457.

The Duke of Wellington arrived in Brussels from Vienna in the early hours of 5 April 1815. The Royal Commission appointing him Commander-in-Chief of all British land forces, dated 28 March, had reached him en route at Coblenz. In the pompous and fussy language of Courtly pretension, it charged him '...to be Commander of our Forces serving on the Continent of Europe during our pleasure. You are therefore carefully and diligently to discharge the said trust of Commander of our Forces by doing and performing any and all manner of things thereunto belonging.'[1] However, Wellington was appalled by the weakness of 'our Forces' on the continent in 1815. The effective and, by British standards, sizeable army he had built so laboriously in the Peninsula from 1808 to 1814 had been broken up, many of the best troops being sent to America or discharged. The British troops immediately available upon Wellington's arrival in The Netherlands were fifteen battalions and a detachment of rifles; a mere 8,200 men. Within a fortnight every soldier who could be spared was sent from Britain; another 17,500.

Of other nationalities, there were a variety of units. The King's German Legion, formed when King George's Electorate of Hanover had fallen under French control, was at a nominal strength of 7,500 men, but was rife with desertion in expectation of disbandment.[2] Additionally, 15,000 Hanoverian militiamen had been raised from the regained electorate, now elevated to the dignity of a kingdom. The United Netherlands' new army of 29,500 men, under the titular command of the Prince of Orange, was more under Wellington's guidance than control. The King of The Netherlands had stipulated that his army remain a separate entity.[3] The Duke of Brunswick, brother-in-law of the Prince Regent of England, had offered his Black Corps of 6,700 men in return for a subsidy, which was paid. The twin duchies of Nassau also contributed 7,300 men. Most of Wellington's army therefore spoke either German or Dutch, which he did not. The units from Hanover, Brunswick, Nassau and The Netherlands, although under his orders, had their own chains of command. Each also had its own supply train and methods of training. Wellington could hardly credit the motley of forces with which he was expected to face Napoleon.

73

Since Wellington's departure from the army in 1814, the British Government had removed 47,000 well-trained men from its establishment. The Royal Ordnance, a body independent of the army, but controlling the army's artillery and supplying its small-arms ammunition, had discharged 7,000 irreplaceable artillerymen.[4] The line cavalry also had been drastically culled. With Napoleon's abdication, many of the army's best units and first battalions of infantry had been sent to America and Canada to fight the Americans. Now that news of the Peace of Ghent, ending the War of 1812, had reached the British forces there, they would be returning, but would they arrive in time? The Crown Prince of Württemberg wished to place his 25,000 men under Wellington's command.[5] These élite troops had fought for Napoleon from 1805 until 1813, and then had fought valiantly against him in the last two campaigns, as had the troops of Hesse-Darmstadt and Hesse-Cassel. The British Cabinet hoped also that General von Kleist's 25,000-strong Prussian corps might be placed under Wellington, but all such proposed subordinations involving German- or Prussian-controlled troops were vehemently opposed by the Prussian delegate on the combined Allied War Council, General von Knesebeck. He objected on the grounds that these were German Confederation troops which should be under either Prussian or Austrian command. After its recent experience at the Congress of Vienna, Prussia mistrusted British motives. Thus Field Marshal, the Duke of Wellington had assembling under his command in the new United Netherlands fewer than 25,000 British, 29,500 Netherlanders and some 36,500 Germans from four different states, with very few veterans among any of the units.

Wellington's problems were further complicated by administrative obstructiveness at home, by people of social rather than military prominence who resented the Duke's rapid rise through battlefield promotion and the extraordinary independence of action he had enjoyed through his success and remoteness. Chief among these was HRH Frederick Augustus, Duke of York and Albany, Commander-in-Chief of the British Army. Frederick Augustus, second son of George III, had been out of office during Wellington's ascendancy because of a scandal involving the sale of officers' commissions by his mistress, Mary Anne Clarke. Frederick Augustus was a poor field commander who inspired the famous nursery rhyme about the Duke of York and who had led the disastrous Flanders expedition of 1793-5 in which Wellington had served as a regimental colonel. Wellington would later tell his intimate friends that it was in this campaign that he 'learnt what not to do'. Now with Frederick Augustus again Commander-in-Chief and Wellington, although a Field Marshal and Duke, his subordinate, Frederick was determined that during this present campaign, at least, he would assert his authority. While assisting Wellington with his genuine administrative ability, the Duke of York intended from the outset not to allow Wellington any greater latitude than any other commander would be permitted. In a letter to Wellington which arrived with his commission, Frederick Augustus instructed his field commander:

> 'On all subjects relating to your Grace's command you will be pleased to correspond with me or with my Military Secretary for my information, and your Grace will regularly communicate to me all vacancies that may occur in the troops under your command; and as the power of appointing to commissions is not vested in you, you will be pleased to recommend to me such officers as may appear to you most deserving of promotion, stating the special reasons where such recommendations are not in the usual channel of seniority.'[6]

This officious letter continued with instructions on the proper procedure for courts-martial and sentencing, citing two incidents that had occurred in Wellington's command after he had returned to England in 1814. This was intended no doubt to be irritating because Wellington was well known to be a stickler in these matters. The letter concluded in the same petty tone by reminding Wellington to ensure that his headquarters staff keep accurate records.

Fortunately for Wellington, the Duke of York's Military Secretary, Major-General Sir Henry Torrens, was devoted to the Peninsula hero and assisted him to the limit of his authority. The news from home, however, was not promising. Because war had not been declared, the militia were not permitted to replace the regular troops in Britain and Ireland that were to be sent to The Netherlands. In several letters and a memorandum, Torrens informed Wellington of the parlous state of unpreparedness into which the British Army at home had been placed since the Duke's departure for Vienna:

> 'At the period of the definitive peace with France last year, all the Dragoon regiments in the service were reduced to the amount of 320 men and 400 horses each, and the Hussars to the amount of 480 men and 530 horses each. The reduced state of these corps has, therefore, rendered it totally impracticable to afford a field establishment beyond three squadrons of 120 men and horses and five dismounted men each, for every regiment of cavalry ordered on service ... [I]t now remains to be seen what force can be further collected before the arrival of the troops from America; and it is difficult to speak with any accuracy on this subject, unless it were ascertained in the first place whether the English and Irish Militia which still remain to be embodied in Ireland can be LEGALLY kept up without

a fresh ballot and secondly, whether the government decide upon the reassembly or ballot of all the militia that have already been disembodied.'[7]

Torrens attached a complete breakdown of all the troops that Wellington could count on receiving. On his arrival in The Netherlands Wellington had 18,536 soldiers of all arms, and 2,340 cavalry and 7,050 infantry had been ordered to join him from England. This would give him some 27,926 men, nearly 3,000 of whom were in Belgian hospitals. Torrens added that 1,250 cavalry would be sent as soon as the legal protocol involving the militia had been followed. Sometime in May 6,000 infantry should arrive in The Netherlands from America, with another 1,500 from Canada in June, and a further 10,000 from that province by September, making a total in that month of 47,735.[8] But until September Wellington could only hope to have about 30,000 of his countrymen under his command on the continent, provided that the militia would be called out in England and Ireland.

While the newly formed war council in Vienna formulated plans of attack, Wellington in Brussels, with his diminutive British Army and polyglot collection of Allied soldiers, was unable to halt the enforced discharge of veterans in England. This apparent absurdity occurred because in Parliament, the Opposition critic, Samuel Whitbread, put the question to Lord Castlereagh: 'Are we at peace or War?' Castlereagh, in his attempts to prop up the discredited Bourbon monarchy, tried to maintain the fiction, also put about by Louis, that Napoleon had ousted Louis by a military coup, and that therefore Wellington was required under the terms of treaties to support the Allies in restoring Louis to the French throne. As this meant attempting to reverse the manifest decision of the French nation by force of arms, Parliament balked. Sir Francis Burdett rose to say that it was impossible,

'...weighing the language of the noble lord, to catch his counsel, – whether he advocates peace or war? If I translate his words to signify the expediency of watch and ward, that we may not be taken unawares, I agree; but if he is proposing to plunge this country into a sea of blood to reinstate the Bourbon line in France, I should but poorly do my duty in this House, did I not lift my voice protesting against so ruinous an enterprise! Sir, I am old enough to call to mind the first frenzied speeches to the same ends. The outcome of which was to make this man [Napoleon] the object of your present apprehensions, with such power and might as could withstand all of Europe banded against him... Shall, then, another twenty years of sacrifice blight this land to make another Bourbon King? Wrongly has Bonaparte's excursion been called an adventure, a rude

excursion into France – Who ever knew one sole and singular man invade a nation of thirty million strong, and in a
few days gain its full sovereignty, against that nation's will!
– the truth is this: the nation longed for him, and has
obtained him ... No man can doubt that this Napoleon
stands as Emperor of France by the will of the French people. Let the French people settle their own affairs.'

Samuel Whitbread then rose again to attack Castlereagh and the Government over the so-called declaration of 13 March. Who had authorized
Wellington to sign it on Britain's behalf? By what law of Britain was it promulgated?

'The Declaration signed at Vienna against Napoleon, is in
my regard abhorrent, and our Country's character defaced
by subscribing to its terms! If words have any meaning at
all, it incites to assassination; it proclaims that any [one]
meeting Bonaparte may lawfully slay him; And whatever
language the Allies now decide, in that outburst, at least,
war was declared! The noble lord to-night would second it.
He urges that we arm, then wait for just as long as the
other powers are ready, and then – pounce down on
France!'

Such indeed was the Government's intention. Whitbread carried the House
in indignation:

'Good God! then, what are we to understand? ... what is
this new aggression urged on for now, if not to vamp
[patch] up and restore the Bourbon line? The wittiest man
who ever sat in this house [Richard Sheridan], said that
half our nation's debt had been incurred in efforts to suppress the Bourbon Power, the other half in efforts to
restore it, and I must deprecate a further plunge for ends so
futile! Why, since Ministers craved peace with Bonaparte
at Châtillon, should they refuse him peace now on the
same terms?'[9]

The Parliamentary debate ended without resolution. Parliament
would not degrade itself by declaring war on a single man. Until Liverpool
and Castlereagh accepted that Napoleon was again the head of state in
France and declared war on France as a nation, no funds could be voted for
the military and the militia could not be embodied. Thus, by offering the
suggestion that the Government's bellicosity be redirected against the
French nation from its champion, the Parliamentary Opposition suggested

that, for all its expressed antipathy to the substance of the Government's crusade against Napoleon, it would be mollified if the form were acceptable.

In the meantime Wellington through Torrens attempted to obtain his old commanders, in whom he had confidence. In this too he was thwarted. Many of his trusted field officers were in America or otherwise unavailable. To fill supernumerary staff appointments the Duke of York at the Horse Guards was sending out young men of influential families, who had little or no staff or even military experience, further exasperating Wellington. Lord Combermere, who had served as Wellington's cavalry commander in the Peninsula, was requested urgently by the Duke. Indeed, Combermere, expecting Wellington to want him and assuming that the Duke's preferences would be respected, had already written to Wellington in anticipation of his recall, '... I shall at all events make my arrangements for joining you in as short a time as possible after I am appointed to the command of the British Cavalry'. But this was not to be. The Duke of York and his brother, the Prince Regent, appointed instead William Paget, Earl of Uxbridge. Like Wellington, Uxbridge was a career soldier, and an experienced cavalry commander of the highest ability. He had earned fame for his superb rearguard cavalry actions in Spain during the lengthy retreat of Moore's army to Corunna in 1808-9. He had won two important engagements, slowing the French advance and enabling the British Army to escape at Sahagun and Benavente. There was, however, a compelling personal reason for Wellington not to want Uxbridge under his command.[10]

Writing home to General Lord Stewart, Wellington complained, 'I have got an infamous army, very weak and ill equipped, and a very inexperienced Staff.'[11] In April 1815 Wellington's entire British contingent of six regiments of cavalry and 25 battalions of infantry did not exceed the size of one French army corps. Fifteen of the infantry units were '...weak corps and inefficient battalions', at strengths of less than 500 men each on average[12] out of a full complement of 18,413. And all this time Wellington and the Government were powerless to prevent the continued discharge in England and the Low Countries of veterans of the previous campaign.

On 6 April Wellington wrote to Lord Bathurst, the Colonial Secretary, explaining his humiliating situation and the overly sanguine appraisal of his command that he had sent to Prince Schwarzenberg, the overall commander of the Allied armies. Wellington's anger is apparent:

> 'Your Lordship will see by my letter to Prince Schwarzenberg, in what state we stand as to numbers. I am sorry to say I have a very bad account of the Netherlands troops and the king appears unwilling to allow them to be mixed with ours ... Although I have given a favourable opinion of ours to General Schwarzenberg, I cannot help thinking, from all accounts, that they are not what they ought to be

to enable us to maintain our military character in Europe. It appears to me that you have not taken in England a clear view of your situation, that you do not think war certain ... You have not called out the militia, or announced such a measure in parliament, by which measures your troops of the line in Ireland or elsewhere might become disposable.'[13]

Of course, if the militia were called out they could replace many line units that were tied down to various domestic policing jobs, releasing the line units for Wellington. Further, if the militia were embodied, a part of the Mutiny Act appended to the Embodying Act could extend the period of service of the soldiers being discharged. Short of embodiment of the milita, Wellington was sent only a single brigade of heavy cavalry and four battalions of infantry from Ireland, and that against strenuous representations by the local Military Commander to Horse Guards. In Britain and Ireland in 1815, high inflation, the operation of the Corn Laws and unemployment had resulted in sporadic rioting. Unlike her continental neighbours, Britain had no police force at this time, and law enforcement was the responsibility of magistrates and private enterprise. In an emergency such as a riot, a magistrate had the power to summon the military. The Government was therefore reluctant, in troubled times, to send abroad any more troops than was absolutely necessary, especially cavalry, which were used for crowd control in the towns and for customs duties patrols along the coast.

To Wellington's urgent requests for the embodiment of the militia and the retention of veterans due for discharge, the Duke of York replied through his Adjutant-General:

'Having the honour to lay before the Commander-in-Chief your Grace's letter of the 28th ultimo, with its enclosure, I have received His Royal Highness's commands to signify that the men whose period of service had expired must necessarily be discharged, as their services can only continue under authority of a Royal Proclamation.'

As a further insensitive measure the Duke of York, in his capacity as Colonel-in-Chief of the Guards, changed the order dispatching the experienced 1st Battalion Grenadier Guards to Wellington, substituting in their stead the 3rd Battalion.[14]

Lord Liverpool, in an effort to find a means by which to overcome the objections of Parliament to mobilizing the British Army against an individual by broadening the issue to war with France, sent two Cabinet members, Lord Harrowby and Mr Pole, to seek the advice of Wellington and King Louis. In the Memorandum of Questions sent with these emissaries, Liverpool asked Wellington, 'Do the Allies consider themselves under their declaration as at war with France, or for what further deliberation does this decision wait; and when may it be expected? Where are the Sovereigns now expected to be, and what are their intended intentions [*sic*]?'[15] In the end, but too late to help Wellington, Castlereagh and the Cabinet acquiesced and on 9 May brought forward a weak bill permitting local militia to volunteer to release the old militia. A fortnight later a second bill embodying the old militia was hurried through. This bill's preamble stated, '...there is an immediate prospect of war with France'.[16]

In addition to frustrations generated by the political contention of Parliament and personal friction with his commander-in-chief, Wellington had also to contend with the diplomatic complexities of relations with the Dutch and Germans. By the Treaties of Utrecht in 1713 and Rastatt in 1714 which brought to an end the Wars of the Spanish Succession, the seven northern, Protestant Dutch provinces of the Spanish Netherlands were recognized as the Republic of the United Provinces, while the ten southern, Catholic Belgic provinces passed into the control of the Austrian Habsburgs. At that time a principal concern of the Dutch and British was for the creation of a military barrier of fortified towns in Belgium against the inroads of expansionist Bourbon France. A century later, a similar concern would underlie the peace aims of the Dutch and British with respect to expansionist Republican-Imperial France. The character of French ambition regarding neighbouring lands since the time of the Sun King could have been summed up in the French expression, '*La plus ça change, la plus c'est la même chose*'.

In 1795 the Austrian Netherlands and then Holland were overrun by a fervent French Republican army. Although at first happy to have been liberated from the dead hand of the past, the Dutch, who had been ruled quasi-monarchically by the Stadtholder, the Prince of Orange-Nassau, and the Belgians, soon felt the rapacious hand of the Gallic hegemony. In 1806 Napoleon created the Kingdom of Holland so that his younger brother Louis could occupy its throne. This apparent elevation in status, and its implication of independence, appealed to the proud Dutch, whose bitter struggle for independence from Spain had been epic and whose capable fleet had dominated the Thames estuary in 1666. Perhaps Napoleon had a certain admiration for the people who had achieved a naval feat against 'perfidious Albion' such as had eluded him in 1805. In 1810 Louis Bonaparte had abdicated when Napoleon gave him a touch of the hitherto loose rein regarding enforcement of the Continental System. Until then the Dutch had fought alongside French troops as willing allies. With Louis' departure the Kingdom of Holland was incorporated into Imperial France as a province under a Governor-General. The Dutch were appalled when 15,000 of their soldiers perished in Napoleon's disastrous Russian campaign. Resistance grew until in 1813, with the approach of the Allies, the Dutch rose under the cry of '*Orange Boven*'.

The Walloon Belgians too had chafed under twenty years of French rule. They felt oppressed by the weight of Imperial demands and, though co-religionists and French speakers, they resented Napoleon's impositions on their Church and his treatment of the Pope. When an Austrian Governor-General, De Vincent, was appointed to the province on 5 May 1814, the Belgians looked forward to re-incorporation within the Austrian fold, but by secret agreement with Castlereagh the Emperor Francis had renounced his claim. The province was ceded to Holland in the London Protocol of 21 June, and William of Orange received the government on 1 August 1814. The Vienna Congress ratified William's position as King of the United Netherlands and Archduke of Luxemburg on 9 June 1815. William promised the Belgians that Brussels would be his second capital, enjoying an equal amount of his time, and from August 1814 to June 1815 the Belgians were happy with the arrangement.[17]

At first the British Government had not been in favour of William of Orange being King of The Netherlands. They preferred his Oxford-educated son, also named William. 'Slender Billy', as the younger William was nicknamed, had been commissioned as a colonel in the British Army and had been an aide-de-camp to Wellington in the Peninsula; he had no intention of being a party to any effort to supplant his father. Britain's mistrust of the elder William stemmed from his appeal some years earlier to Napoleon to restore to him the Duchy of Orange-Nassau, but opposition abated with the proposed engagement of the younger William to Princess Charlotte, daughter of the Prince Regent.

With Napoleon's return from Elba in 1815, the new United Netherlands Army was mobilized on 17 March. King William placed his 29,566 men under the command of his son, William, the Crown Prince of Orange. Until Wellington's arrival in The Netherlands from Vienna the Crown Prince, as a commissioned British General, also commanded the few British troops already present there. From Cabinet correspondence Wellington expected that when he reached The Netherlands he would assume command of all Allied forces present. After all, as Field Marshal in Spain he had enjoyed just such a breadth of control. But King William was reacting to the treatment that had been accorded him and his country. Britain had initially opposed his selection as King and had only acquiesced because they expected to control him as a puppet. Further, Britain had not returned many of the Dutch colonies seized during the late war, and the compensatory payment carried the stipulation that it be used towards the fortification of Belgian towns and citadels of the proposed military barrier, the work to be carried out under British supervision. In 1814, when Wellington was on his way to Paris, Lord Bathurst requested him to 'inspect and report on their progress and their defensive capabilities'. As an additional insult to William, when Louis XVIII fled France as Napoleon neared Paris, the Dutch king was obliged by British Cabinet pressure to offer Louis refuge, against his own wishes and provoking Napoleon's wrathful attention. On top of all this, King William found himself being subjected by Wellington to a lecture on the Duke's view that the King's army was unreliable and that its officers had treacherous leanings.[18]

The collapse of the Bourbon monarchy in 1815 shocked and surprised Wellington. He feared that the Belgians and Dutch would defect to Napoleon if he advanced in their direction. His attitude was shaped by the society he kept as Ambassador in both Paris and Vienna, as well as by his own reactionary proclivities. Those with whom he associated had minimized the seriousness of Napoleon's landing in southern France and their reports were coloured by wishful thinking. Wellington was stunned by the magnitude of popular French resentment of the anglophile Bourbons. When General Clarke, who had been Louis XVIII's Minister of War, and Napoleon's before that from 1807 to 1814, arrived in Ghent with the fleeing French king, he had brought with him the complete order of battle of the French Army, together with equipment and armaments statistics, to establish his bona fides with the Allies. During his time in Napoleon's service Clarke had been responsible for both Holland and Belgium as imperial provinces; and he had come to know the prominent Dutch and Belgian officers then serving under the French flag. In a lengthy memorandum,[19] several letters and a newspaper report, Clarke warned Wellington against trusting these officers. He was certain that they would rally to Napoleon as events progressed. Wellington was disposed to believe him and tried to induce King William to replace most of his officers with 'reliable German ones'. Wellington further offended King William and his Dutch and Belgian subjects, both civilian and military, by proposing that the key ports be garrisoned by 'trusted British and Hanoverian troops', while The Netherlands forces occupied the first-line Belgian fortresses.[20] In making these suggestions Wellington was seeking ways to ensure the fulfillment of the British Cabinet's requirement that the North Sea ports, especially Antwerp, be denied to any enemy or potential enemy of Britain's. To the Netherlanders, however, it appeared that Wellington was primarily concerned to ensure his line of retreat and safe embarkation in the event of a serious reversal, just as in the Peninsula he had held the Lines of Torres Vedras to keep the port of Lisbon open behind him. In exasperation Wellington wrote to Lord Bathurst:

> 'They are completely officered by officers who have been in French service ... You will see in my despatch of this date the arrangement which I have made with the King for the defence of this country in case the armies should move forward. I have had the greatest difficulty in making this and indeed every other arrangement with him ... In consequence of the arrangement for the defence of his country he will take away from the operating army 7,000 or 8,000 men, which he proposes to place under the command of

Prince Frederick, a fine lad of eighteen years old. He then intends, as I understand, that all the remainder should be under the Prince of Orange, notwithstanding the remonstrances I before made with the Prince's consent against this arrangment, as placing in too great a mass *all the youth and treason of the army. He has given me no command over his army*, and everything is a matter of negotiation, first with his son and then with himself; and although he is I believe, a well-meaning man, he is surrounded by persons who have been in the French service. It is very well to employ them, but I would not trust one of them out of my sight, and so I have told him. They manifest the greatest desire to get us out of Antwerp and Ostend; but unless I am ordered to evacuate these places, I shall not quit them. You'll see what has passed between the King and me about having English governors in these places; I don't know anything of the persons he has named to those situations.'[21]

The Dutch and Belgians found Wellington's sceptical attitude all the more unfathomable because of its singularity. Although the Tsar had offered Wellington a post on the joint Allied command staff, none of the other Allies had offered him the field command of their armies. Additionally, they must have wondered how Wellington could seek to apply to them a standard of loyalty far more rigid than that then prevalent; more rigid in fact than Britain had applied to herself; for had not John Churchill – before becoming Duke of Marlborough – served in turn both the Stuart James II and his supplanter, William III of the same House as the present William, King of The Netherlands? Among Wellington's comtemporaries on the continent, von Gneisenau, von Scharnhorst, and other Prussian generals had been born in Hanover, the Electorate of the British king. General Pozzi di Borgo, the Tsar's adviser, was a Corsican, as was Napoleon Bonaparte, who had entered French service. General Wilhelm von Dornberg, commander of Wellington's 3 Cavalry Brigade, was a Hanoverian officer who had refused to join the King's German Legion in Britain when Hanover fell to France. Instead he served in Napoleon's forces, becoming commander of King Jérôme's Guard cavalry in the Napoleonic State of Westphalia. Von Dornberg had only returned to Hanoverian service after Leipzig, yet he was trusted. Why should not Dutch and Belgian officers, whose experience had been similar, also be trusted?

Certainly King William preferred to trust the defence of his kingdom to his own subjects rather than to foreigners. His Royal Council were also determined that The Netherlands' soldiers would be commanded by its own generals. In the minutes of its meeting on 30 April 1815 Councillors van Hogendorp and van Limburg Stirum summed up the national mood:

'It is inconceivable that if the situation was reversible, that
England would turn over her army to a Dutch commander.
Neither would she tolerate a Dutch garrison in Dover and
the Tower of London, on the grounds that the Dutch commander mistrusted the English generals to hold them on
grounds of suspected treason. Britain has an estimated
militia and regular force left in its islands of 80,000 men.
Why do they not then provide Lord Wellington with an
Army? surely if they cannot trust him to do so [command
troops], why must we risk our only army and our country?
We do not have a Channel and a navy to act as our
defence. If Britain wants Lord Wellington to have an army
– let her provide one.'[22]

Indeed, when the shoe had been on the other foot after 1688, the English of
all classes had been intensely resentful of William III's Dutch favourites and
Dutch guards.

As a consequence of its refusal to recognize and declare war on
Napoleon's new French state, the British Government was unable to send
Wellington more troops, so it resorted to the application of financial pressure on William to give command of his army to Wellington. Wellington too
exerted pressure amounting to blackmail; thorough in his methods, he also
tried to intimidate William. In a letter sent via the Prince of Orange, he
emphasized two points regarding his request that Netherlands troops be
detached from the field army and used to garrison the fortified military barrier and Ghent, which was doubly important to the British Government: as
a supply depot, having access to the sea by ship canal, and as the refuge of
Louis XVIII:

'His Majesty should in my opinion, consider that he has
but a small, and very young army to oppose a possibly
numerous and well disciplined one; that he has a large
extent of country to cover but lately brought under His
Majesty's government, whose inhabitants are supposed by
some not to be very well disposed towards it. I know of no
mode so well calculated for the defence of such a country
by such an army, as works well chosen.'

Wellington then speciously posed the question, if the French maintained
garrisons of some 15,000 in their own border fortresses and the Allies did
not in turn man their own border fortresses, and the Allies were to advance
into France past the French fortresses, what would stop the French garrisons from making a mass sortie to occupy Brussels? For Wellington even
to have voiced such a disingenuous supposition is indicative of his low
regard for his Netherlands allies. No commander worth his salt would leave

garrison forces in his rear without investing them. Adamant in his intention to prevail, Wellington pressed his point to King William with a thinly veiled threat:

> 'This is my decided opinion regarding these posts, and it rests with His Majesty to occupy them or not, as he may think proper. As far as the King's Allies will be concerned, *I shall take measures to render it a matter of total indifference to their particular interests, whether the enemy does or not occupy Bruxelles as soon as we shall have advanced.*'[23]

Wellington was implying that he would be prepared to influence the movements of the Allied armies in such a way that Brussels would deliberately be left vulnerable to Napoleon. Such a calamity would destroy the fragile integrity of William's new United Netherlands.

Reluctantly, William yielded to the extent of appointing Wellington Field Marshal of The Netherlands Army,[24] bringing all Netherlands forces under the Duke's direct command. But there were provisos attached to the King's acquiescence. Netherlands forces could not be mixed with other nationalities; they were to remain at all times under the operational control of Netherlands commanders. Wellington could not remove any Netherlands officer from his position without the King's consent, except for those military offences recognized by Netherlands law. Also, and perhaps the most irritating, Wellington was required to pass all his orders through the King, the Prince of Orange, or the Prince's Chief-of-Staff. Not surprisingly, Wellington, as a field commander accustomed to freedom of action, was particularly piqued by this, as is evident in a letter he wrote to the Prince of Orange on 8 May concerning a report he had received directly from The Netherlands commander General Behr at Mons:

> 'It appears to me that the general had misunderstood the King's order; at least, he has not understood it as I do. I understand that all reports are to reach me in the usual channel; that is to say, they ought to go first to your Royal Highness, and your Royal Highness would send such as you would deem it necessary I should have knowledge of. It would be quite impossible for me to attempt to conduct the details of the Dutch army [under the King's constraints]. That which I recommend therefore to your Royal Highness is, that you should give an order explaining that of the King, in which you should point out in what channel the reports are to be made. You should submit it to his Majesty first, and let me see it. Those reports then that I should beg your Highness to communicate with me are

those in which the British or Hanoverian troops may be concerned, or the permanent garrisons and ports of the country, or the enemy. The orders from the Government will remain as directed by the King. I will settle this day the distribution of the army in corps, and its cantonments ...'[25]

Nor were the stipulations of King William unique; the non-British majority of the Allied forces concentrating in The Netherlands and environs were only available to be placed under Wellington's command on the satisfaction of a welter of similar restrictive provisos which resulted in a dangerously complex chain of command. This situation arose largely because of the impetus given to the nationalistic aspirations of the German states when the French destroyed their hitherto feudal structure. The Duke of Brunswick's Black Corps, 6,700 men of all arms, would fight under Wellington's orders, but only on condition that they were not dispersed or commanded by other nationals. The German regiment, Orange-Nassau, recruited from King William's Nassau territories, and numbered 28th of The Netherlands Line, was in Netherlands service together with the 2nd Light Regiment and a company of volunteer rifle-armed Jägers. These Orange-Nassau units, numbering 4,481 men, constituted 2 Brigade of the 2nd Netherlands Division. Since the Peace of 1814 the Vienna Congress had redivided the Napoleonic Duchy of Nassau into its separate component states. The Duke of Nassau-Usingen and Nassau-Weilberg had sent Wellington the 1st Nassau Regiment under the command of Major-General von Kruse. Although classed as a regiment, this unit included three battalions and a staff, for a total of 2,900 men. It was thus larger than most British brigades. Wellington had hoped to amalgamate the 1st with William's two other Nassau regiments to form a division, but the King objected. He had not been consulted by the Duke of Nassau and in any case he felt that the removal of the two Nassau regiments from The Netherlands Army into a Nassau Division would weaken the coherence and *esprit de corps* of the fledgling Netherlands Army.[26] In the end Wellington resolved to constitute von Kruse's regiment as an independent contingent.

Nationalistic fervour was also evident in King George's new Kingdom of Hanover. The Hanoverians were waiting expectantly for the disbandment of the King's German Legion. This unit, comprising Hanoverian soldiers who had preferred to fight for their Elector, George III, rather than Napoleon, had since 1803 been virtually a part of the British Army and had received Wellington's high praise for their performance in the Peninsula. Indeed Wellington's own orderly sergeant had been seconded from the Legion. The new Kingdom of Hanover wanted these veteran soldiers to form the core of an army. With the reappearance of Napoleon, however, Hanover had agreed to leave with Wellington its King's German Legion troops and to send him the 15,000 men of its Landwehr, or militia. This entailed the payment to Hanover by Britain of a subsidy of £50,000 per month.[27] Wellington, anxious to raise the strength of the Legion's eight weak battalions, wanted to recruit for them from the Hanoverian militia. The Governor-General of Hanover, His Royal Highness Adolphus, Duke of Cambridge, brother of Wellington's Commander-in-Chief, offered Wellington 5,000 men from the militia, but on conditions unacceptable to the British Cabinet: that the Legion become at once a Hanoverian unit; that Britain continue to pay the current level of subsidy as well as the cost of equipping, uniforming, feeding and paying the 5,000 militia at Legion rates; and lastly, that six months after the end of hostilities the entire Legion, together with its guns, horses, and equipment, be handed over to Hanoverian control.[28]

In the circumstances Wellington had no choice but to reduce the eight battalions of the Legion from ten companies each to six. The supernumerary officers and non-commissioned officers were transferred to the Hanoverian militia. This arrangement was far from ideal; for as Wellington had rightly pointed out, it is easier and more effective to absorb green soldiers into well-trained veteran units than to put experienced officers and NCOs in charge of inexperienced units such as militia.[29]

In a letter dated 28 April to his younger brother Henry, Wellington made evident his misgivings about the lack of co-operation he was receiving from his governmental and royal superiors in Britain:

'We have here including the Dutch, about 60,000, and we are in close communication with the Prussians on our left. They promise us more men from England; but it appears to me as if they were afraid there to touch the question of war, and that they have most unaccountably delayed all their warlike preparations. The consequence is that the peace opinions are gaining ground fast; and I agree with you in thinking that if we leave Buonaparte alone, we shall have him more powerful than ever in a short time ...'[30]

Wellington had better luck in the appointments of his British divisional and brigade commanders, most of whom had served under him in the Peninsula. He was granted his request that his military secretary, Lieutenant-Colonel Lord Fitzroy Somerset, '...write to Lieutenant-Colonel Grant of the 11th Regiment, to beg him to come out with the intention of employing him at the head of the Intelligence department, which I hope will be approved of; and Lieutenant-Colonel Scovell at the head of Military communications.'[31] Grant, on arrival, was sent deep into French territory to liaise with French royalists, to observe covertly French troop movements and concentrations, to learn, in the event of large-scale movement towards the Belgian border, the avenue or avenues of approach, and to communicate his intelligence at once to Wellington. By this means Wellington hoped to be able to avoid being outflanked or outmanoeuvred by Napoleon, the master of military movement.

For the rest of his staff, Wellington had: Sir Edward Barnes as Adjutant-General, Colonel Sir George Wood as commander of artillery, Lieutenant-Colonel Sir James Carmichael Smyth in charge of Engineers, and Mr. Dunmore, of the Treasury Commissary Services, as Commissary-General. The final post, and one of great importance, was Quartermaster-General, effectively Chief of Staff. This post was currently filled by Sir Hudson Lowe who had already consigned himself to oblivion in his commander's estimation. One of the idiosyncrasies of Wellington's style of command was that he insisted upon an immediate answer from his officers in response to any question he might put to them, however particular. On arrival in The Netherlands, during a routine inspection of troop cantonments Wellington had asked Lowe 'Where does that road lead to?' Lowe, instead of replying at once, became flustered and fumbled with his maps. Wellington, in disgust, called Lowe a 'damned old fool' and rode on. The Duke's more astute generals never allowed ignorance of the facts to delay their response. On being asked by Wellington, 'How many rounds of ammunition have we?', one general promptly replied, 'four hundred and twenty', remarking to a fellow officer that the number could always be adjusted later.[32] This foible of Wellington's, and his officers' pandering to it, would later have embarrassing consequences. Wellington had Lowe replaced. He would have preferred to have Sir George Murray, his old 'right arm' in this capacity, but Murray had been sent to Canada. Torrens issued an urgent recall, but it would be some months before Murray would be available. In the meantime Wellington's old Deputy Quartermaster-General, Sir William Howe de Lancey, agreed to suffer the 'indignity'[33] of returning to his former post without having been offered the full command.

It could be said that, like Napoleon's, Wellington's greatest asset was his administrative ability. By strength of will, the judicious use of political pressure and an understanding of human nature, Wellington soon had complete command of all the troops at his disposal. As part of his arrangements to accommodate the letter of the limitations placed on him while frustrating their spirit, Wellington adopted the continental corps system. It was Wellington's custom to fight his army using the division as the largest tactical unit. In The Netherlands he organized his forces into three corps: I, under the Crown Prince of Orange, with General Constant de Rebecque as Chief of Staff; II, under Lieutenant-General Lord Hill;[34] III, the army reserve corps, under his own command. These corps, however, were to be administrative entities only. By this means Wellington was able to satisfy the respective force contributors that their own troops were under the command of their own officers, while at the same time giving himself the ability to intermingle units and himself exercise direct command over the whole. King William and his war council, headed by General Janssens, did not object to a British corps commander issuing orders to a Netherlands division within his corps because the Prince of Orange, as a corps commander, enjoyed the same authority over the British and Hanoverian units within his corps, such as the British Guards Division.[35] The Dukes of Brunswick and of Nassau were content for their troops to be in the reserve corps under Wellington's personal command. The cavalry and horse artillery were placed under the command of the Earl of Uxbridge, except for The Netherlands cavalry which, until the morning of 18 June, was under the orders of the Prince of Orange. Further, Wellington had managed to arrange that nominally British divisions be formed of intermingled brigades (see Appendix II), averaging one brigade each of British, King's German Legion, and Hanoverian Landwehr. Only the Guards Division was wholly British because its battalions were roughly twice the normal British line battalion strength.

By June Wellington's army numbered 107,000 men and 216 guns, including garrison troops. At last he had a force with which, in conjunction with a Prussian army, he could consider confronting Napoleon, even though his country had provided less than a quarter of the troops under his command. On 3 June Thomas Creevey, an Opposition Member of Parliament visiting Brussels with his family, met Wellington and Sir Charles Stewart, the British Ambassador, outside the official British residence. In the course of their conversation Creevey asked Wellington how he evaluated his situation. Wellington remarked, 'By God! I think Blücher and I can do the business.' Then, pointing to a passing British soldier, he added, with disgust at Parliament's delay in mobilizing the militia, 'There! – it all depends on that article whether we do the business or not. Give me enough of it, and I am sure!'[36]

Relations with the Prussians were to prove more difficult for Wellington than those with the Dutch. At first, however, the prospect for co-operation based on something like comradeship seemed good. Wellington, fearful of being attacked by Napoleon before having had time to consolidate his heterogeneous force, had written to von Gneisenau on 6 April requesting urgently that the Prussian Army of the Lower Rhine move into Belgium to help him guard the border and to be close enough so that the two armies could support each other. Von Gneisenau replied the next day unambiguously and positively, '...rather may you count, Your Grace, on the support of all our available forces in the event of your being attacked. We are firmly determined to share the lot of the army which is under Your Excellency's command.'[37] Wellington had already communicated with von Kleist, the commander of the Prussian army corps concentrating on the lower Rhine, on 9 May, to arrange communications between the two armies by way of the outposts of The Netherlands troops (most importantly on Wellington's left), and through the Prince of Orange. Also letter posts were established at certain places, notably Mons.[38]

Soon, however, mistrust clouded the scene. On 8 April Castlereagh had written to Wellington with news that Napoleon was planning to divide the Allies by revealing to Prussia the contents of the secret treaty of 3 January in which Britain had agreed to side with France and Austria against Prussia and Russia in the event of war over the issues of Saxony and Poland. Castlereagh advised Wellington that, if asked, 'My own notion is, that it is better to be silent, unless Russia or Prussia should enquire as to the facts.'[39] On the same date, von Gneisenau wrote to Wellington asking him for an explanation of the treaty, a copy of which had been discovered on the person of a French official. Wellington informed Lord Bathurst:

> 'I enclose copies of a further correspondence which I have had with General Gneisenau. Having learnt that General Gneisenau had found upon M. Reinhard, the Under Secretary in the foreign office at Paris, who had been arrested at Aix-la-Chappelle, a copy of the Treaty of Vienna of the 3rd January last, which has created a good deal of jealousy and ill-temper in the minds of Prussian officers, I thought it proper to send Colonel Hardinge, who is here, to remain at General Gneisenau's headquarters; and I have desired him to explain confidentially the circumstances under which the treaty had been concluded.'[40]

Considering his violent opinion of the Dutch and Belgians' supposed unreliability, it is interesting to speculate what might have been Wellington's reaction had it been he rather than von Gneisenau who learned apparently by accident of a secret agreement by an ally to collude with a conquered enemy against Britain's interests. Later in the century under Bismarck and his *realpolitik*, the Prussians would demonstrate how well they had learned from this incident that there was no room for concepts of honour in the Machiavellian world of European balance-of-power politics.

Since Napoleon's return to France, Prussia had been mobilizing its Army of the Lower Rhine. On 17 March Field Marshal Prince von Blücher von Wahlstatt received a reply from the Prussian King Frederick William to his request to resign. Blücher had made his request in protest at the treatment of Prussia by its so-called allies at the Vienna Congress; but before doing so, he had written to Gneisenau, the King's Chief of Staff, of his intention, remarking, 'It honours and rejoices me to have shared in the war that is ended, but my chief satisfaction is in not having shared in the peace that has been concluded. We drove in a fine bull and have got in return a dried-up old cow.'[41] King Frederick William replied simply, 'I have been unable to grant your request to be discharged.' Gneisenau had already pointed out to Blücher, 'Permit me to make the following observation, Field Marshals of the Prussian Army are not allowed to resign.'[42] For Blücher, the other shoe dropped on the 19th when another letter arrived from the King appointing him to replace Kleist in the command of the Prussian Army of the Lower Rhine. Blücher left Berlin at the beginning of April and reached

Koblenz on the 16th. En route he wrote to his wife, 'Tomorrow I go to Luttich, where I shall find my headquarters. Hostilities have not yet begun. They cannot long be delayed ...'[43]

Blucher arrived in the area of Liège on 21 April. There he found his army in the process of both mobilization and reform. Before the crisis of Napoleon's return, King Frederick William had given orders for military reforms, to include the incorporation into the Prussian Army of the forces of its newly gained provinces and the Landwehr, or militia. The King had also decreed that compulsory military service, introduced by General von Scharnhorst for the duration of the war of the Fourth Coalition against France,[44] be established by law as the basis for all military recruitment.

Blücher's experience on joining his command was markedly different from Wellington's. He found a field army of four corps, of four brigades each. The King's re-organization had resulted in a Prussian army of seven permanent corps, each having four brigades; and the brigades were numbered consequtively throughout the army; thus, I Corps had 1 to 4 Brigades, II Corps 5 to 8, and so on. V, VI and VII Corps were designated for home defence.

Lieutenant-General Count von Gneisenau, the Quartermaster-General and Chief of Staff of the Prussian Army, enjoyed a status unique among his peers in other European armies of the period. Unlike his French and British counterparts, for example, who merely transmitted the orders of the commander, Gneisenau actually held the command of the army jointly with the commanding general. This dual command structure existed also at corps level. In his capacity, Gneisenau would co-operate with the commander in developing a plan of campaign (strategy), including the movement of the army and decisions as to when and where to fight. During battle the commander would have tactical control, but the Chief of Staff could overrule the orders of the commander if he believed them to be contrary to standing orders of the King. The Chief of Staff had his staff attached as additional adjutants to the various levels of command down to brigade, to ensure smooth and correct compliance with his orders.

Gneisenau was bitterly disappointed not to have been given command of the army, but the King, although he thought very highly of him, believed, rightly, that Blücher's charisma with his troops and his dogged determination to beat Napoleon at any cost were overriding considerations in ensuring victory. Gneisenau could be content, though, to have been given a post in essence senior to Blücher's. On 29 March, writing to Gneisenau through his Cabinet, confirming his appointment, the King gave the following instructions: '...I cannot, in view of the distance from the area of operation, give you any definite orders as to how you should act in case of unforeseen events but I must leave it to you to make such arrangements with the Duke of Wellington as suit the circumstances and to act in agreement with him in all things.'[45]

The King knew that it would be necessary to make specific and obligatory the requirement for his army to co-operate with Wellington and his command. Even before the revelation of the secret treaty of 3 January Gneisenau and most of the Prussian officers were deeply mistrustful of the British, and of Wellington in particular. In 1813 Gneisenau had written to Castlereagh soliciting his and Britain's help in elevating Prussia to dominance in a new German federation to replace the Napoleonic Confederation of the Rhine. Castlereagh had sent him a diplomatically worded reply which was taken as a promise of support. Later Castlereagh had indicated that the Prussians were wrong to have assumed that his approval 'in principle' represented a committment of his government. Gneisenau and his fellow officers were further aggrieved by what they considered Britain's betrayal over the compromise settlement on Saxony worked out at the Congress of Vienna, by which Prussia received only a small part of the territory demanded,[46] and the news of the secret treaty against Prussia was the last straw. They wanted nothing more to do with the British, who seemed prepared to take the field alongside the enemy, France, to deny the Prussians what they considered rightfully theirs. And Wellington had been Ambassador to France, then Castlereagh's replacement in Vienna, during this time. It was obvious to them that he had been one of the principals in the creation of the treaty.[47]

Despite the insults which they felt had been offered to them, the Prussians were in dire need of British financial subsidies and Wellington held the British purse-strings. So King Frederick William ordered his officers to co-operate; and they, being good officers, would obey, within the considerable latitude he had allowed. His instructions to Gneisenau continued: 'While I empower you to do so [overrule Blücher, if deemed necessary] and assure you of my fullest confidence in you, I also make you responsible for acting with all prudence and the most careful consideration in every matter affecting the future of Europe.'[48] Such confidence from a sovereign is a two-edged sword which can cut one way in victory, but quite another in defeat. Nevertheless Gneisenau was effectively vested with the ultimate control of the Prussian Army that would take the field against Napoleon.

Blücher had met Wellington in London in 1814, and saw in him a fellow soldier. He cared little for the political niceties; so far as he was concerned Wellington, like himself, could fight and beat the French, as their records proved.

Towards the end of May 1815 Blücher and Gneisenau reported that their army was mobilized and, although not all units were in place and at full strength, for operational purposes they were ready. As ordered, Gneisenau had contacted Wellington after the Duke arrived in The Netherlands. Wellington requested that the Prussians move into the area Sambre – Maas. The Prussians did so, on the assumption that The Netherlands would assume responsibility for their supply. The supply problem for the Prussian

Army, severe at the best, became critical when the army left German soil. On enemy territory, it, like the French Army, was organized largely to live off the land, but when among friends it needed hard currency to pay for its requisitions. And Prussia, after the cruel deprivations suffered at the hands of the French in the campaigns of 1813-14, had none to spare. General von Grolman, Gneisenau's own chief of staff, wrote of this situation:

> 'The strenuous efforts of the campaigns of 1813-14 had so exhausted the strength of the state that, on the return of Napoleon, which called for even greater exertions, only materials actually needed for battle, such as men, horses, arms and ammunition, could be acquired, despite our every sacrifice. Ordnance and supply depots in the wider sense were out of the question. Pay had to be owed the troops ... It was under these circumstances that the Prussian army occupied widely scattered cantonments in Belgium ... which was dictated by necessity. In these cantonments it was only possible by dint of rigid organization and frugality to provide the soldiers with a three-day supply of bread and food and to make a similar provision for the supply columns.'[49]

Blücher was obliged to ask Wellington for a loan to cover the most urgent requirements, in return for moving his army on to Belgian territory.

Thus, by the end of April to the beginning of May 1815, the Prussian army was in cantonments alongside Wellington's Anglo-Allied army. Together these armies presented a front from Ostend to Namur and down to Dinant in the Ardennes, about one hundred miles in length and about forty miles in depth. Wellington's communications with England ran through Ghent, Bruges and Ostend, as well as Antwerp. Blücher's communications with Berlin ran through Namur and Liège to Maastricht and Cologne on the Rhine.

Both Wellington and Blücher feared only that Napoleon might strike them before they had completed the combination of their forces. Events were soon to prove them fully justified in this fear.

A Pleasant Disposition

'If I am able to determine the enemy's dispositions while at the same time I conceal my own then I can concentrate and he must divide. And if I concentrate while he divides, I can use my entire strength to attack a fraction of his. There, I will be numerically superior. Then, if I am able to use many to strike few at the selected point, those I deal with will be in dire straits.' - Sun Tzu, *The Art of War*, c.500 BC, tr. Griffith.

Since his return to France from Elba Napoleon had raised an army of half a million men. Virtually the whole of France had been mobilized to equip them. This had at least temporarily removed unemployment at a stroke. Napoleon had re-established the nation's finances after the state treasury had been plundered by the departing royals and royalists. He had established a new government and given the country a new constitution by the *Acte additionnel*. France was placed in a good immediate posture of defence, and the authorization had been given for the repair of fortifications and other defensive works throughout the country. It was time for Napoleon to organize his army, appoint commanders and prepare to take the war to the enemy before they could bring it to France.

Among senior commanders, there were few marshals available to call upon. Newly created Marshal Grouchy, who had helped Napoleon consolidate his position after his return, was given command of the cavalry of the main field army. Marshal Brune, who had immediately rallied to Napoleon in March, was assigned to command the Army of the Var, holding the important area based on that department, guarding the Mediterranean coastal invasion route into France. Marshal Suchet, who had also been prompt in deciding his loyalties in March, received command of the Army of the Jura, based on Lyons and covering the passes on the Swiss border which led on to the plain of Langres. It was by this route that the Austrians advanced around the natural river barriers of north-eastern France, and retreated when necessary, in 1814.

Marshal Mortier, Napoleon's old commander of the élite Young Guard, had been honoured by Louis and made commander of the 16th Military District, based on Lille. In early March of 1815 Mortier had frustrated Count d'Erlon's attempt to take the city's garrison over to Napoleon. He had also ignored Davout's repeated orders to arrest Louis, considering instead in his simple soldierly fashion that his duty lay in supporting the leader of the moment. Mortier had in fact escorted Louis safely into exile. When Mortier arrived at The Tuileries in answer to the summons of his new master, Napoleon greeted him with some humour as 'Monsieur le Blanc'[1] and appointed him first to command of the cavalry, then of the newly raised Young Guard for the forthcoming campaign.

Marshal Ney, having fully converted back to the imperial fold, was sent on a tour of inspection to keep him at some distance from Napoleon, who found it hard to forgive him for insisting on his abdication at Fontainebleau in 1814 instead of helping him to secure the decisive battle. Ney's emotional nature had further muddied the waters for him when he was prompted to make the gratuitous announcement to Louis about returning with Napoleon in an iron cage. In the early days of the Empire Napoleon had taken a genuine interest in Ney and his career and had real affection for him. He respected Ney's courage, bravery and, until 1814, his loyalty. It was the sense of personal betrayal that Napoleon felt with regard to him, and which would take time to heal, that Ney did not understand. He felt that because he had effusively declared his allegiance to his old chief, he ought to have a clean slate with which to make a new start.[2] This complex and mutually unsatisfactory emotional clash of expectations between Napoleon and Ney would cause grave problems in the coming campaign.

Marshal Berthier, Napoleon's long-serving chief of staff and right arm, had throughout Napoleon's military career, translated his chief's garbled, sometimes imprecise, requirements into clear orders. On learning of Napoleon's return Berthier had attempted to rejoin him. Travelling from his castle at Bamberg in Saxony, where he was living in exile, Berthier was prevented from crossing the French border by the Allied authorities. He returned to Bamberg where, on the orders of the Comte d'Artois, he was murdered by defenestration. Although d'Artois' agents reported Berthier's death as a suicide,[3] the Comte was well aware of Berthier's value to Napoleon and would certainly have made every effort to deny Napoleon the services of his brilliant chief of staff.

The death of Berthier was a heavy and irreparable blow to Napoleon's chances of success in the campaign of 1815. There was no one who could take the place of 'the Emperor's wife'. During his reign Napoleon had failed to decentralize his command structure or to develop a staff system, such as the Prussians had devised, that could offer clarification and guidance to field commanders and co-ordinate subordinate commands with Napoleon's headquarters. His generals for the 1815 campaign, unable to grasp his strategic intentions, would therefore be in the unenviable position of having to follow his orders blindly. They would fear to use initiative, in case of failure. Those few generals capable of independent command were either dead – like Lannes, killed in battle in 1809, or needed elsewhere – like Davout, whose commanding personality, absolute loyalty and iron resolve Napoleon felt were essential on the scene in Paris to hold the capital, the indispensable nerve-centre of the empire, against the likelihood of a repeat of the intrigue and betrayals of 1814. Davout would be sorely missed from the field army where those same qualities could often make all the difference to the outcome of a battle and a campaign. Suchet, too, would be missed, but his record in Spain and other theatres had proved him well suited to his role of defending France's only dangerous mountain frontier, supported by the reliable Brune.

Then there was Soult. Napoleon considered the propaganda value of having Louis' ex-Minister of War back within his ranks; he was another marshal who had not remained aloof from Napoleon upon his return. Also Soult was a good field commander. In his last campaign in Spain in 1814, Soult had disputed every foot of ground with Wellington. But Soult had more deeply offended Napoleon than Ney or any of the other marshals. Further, he was detested by the entire army, but especially his fellow generals who had not forgotten or forgiven his central role in *l'affaire Exelmans*, nor his efforts to have Generals d'Erlon, Vandamme, Reille, Dumas, Lefebvre-Desnouëttes and the brothers Lallemand shot for their part in an attempted coup in the North in support of Napoleon. Had Napoleon been defeated upon his return there is little doubt that these executions would have been carried out. The army also remembered Soult's ill-treatment of General Travot. Napoleon would also have found it difficult to overlook the enthusiasm with which Soult sought to assist the Bourbons in apprehending him after his landing in the South, or his proclamation of 8 March in which he referred to him as a madman, a usurper and a warmonger. Altogether there was a great deal in Soult's recent behaviour to warrant his imprisonment or exile by Napoleon, rather than his employment.

The only reason that Soult had sought such employment[4] was that he had been dismissed as Minister of War at the eleventh hour in favour of the even more compromised General Clarke. Soult, although a professed royalist, but embittered by Louis' dismissal, did not have the integrity of a Marshal Macdonald or a St-Cyr to retire from public life and remain faithful to his oath to 'the worthy heir of the great Henri's virtues'. Seeing the precipitate collapse of the Bourbon position in France as Napoleon advanced bloodlessly toward Paris, Soult had begun to fear that he had backed the wrong side. He approached Napoleon, not out of conviction, but from a desire to protect his titles, position and income. He gave the age-old excuse that, as a soldier, he was only following orders in what he had done under the Bourbons. Napoleon knew that in no circumstances could Soult be entrusted with an independent command. Having turned his coat twice already without difficulty, he could easily do so again, and perhaps at a critical moment as had Marmont. Nor, remembering the Malet plot, could he chance leaving Soult behind him in Paris. So having decided to make use of Soult, he could only take the man with him on campaign. He gave Soult Berthier's job, for which Soult had experience as an independent commander and as Minister of War. In that capacity Napoleon could keep an eye on him.[5]

Napoleon had no difficulty in finding good fighting generals for both divisional and corps commands. There was no need no confine his search to marshals; a marshal was after all only a general who had been given a dignity. In fact since 1813 Napoleon had noticed that his marshals, loaded with honours, wealth and position, no longer had the incentive to risk all they had acquired on the field of battle; there was no more they could hope to attain. It was with this in mind that Napoleon took the first opportunity to elevate a new man, Grouchy, to the marshalate, and to take away the baton from Marmont, Augereau and Victor, whom he felt had failed to live up to the honour. This was an object lesson for the new corps commanders, three of whom, Reille, Vandamme and d'Erlon, no doubt received their commands as a reward for the personal risks they had run for their emperor in the recent coup attempt. The lesson was that the Emperor alone could create a marshal and bestow all that went with the baton, and that he could also withdraw the honour. The new corps commanders would see that, like Grouchy, they too had the opportunity to reach that highest level. The criterion was a resounding triumph in battle. They would therefore be eager to fight and win. In Napoleon's army, unlike that of the Bourbons, the path of promotion was open to all. The Legion of Honour, degraded to a civilian award by Louis, was again the highest acknowledgement for acts of exceptional valour in war, and was open to all ranks.

The new army commanders were all experienced generals. It says something for their élan – their aggressive leadership in attack – that almost all the new divisional and corps commanders had reached the rank of general during the Revolution. In the early years of the Revolution a general had to be victorious or risk arrest and execution as an enemy of the people. During that period, in one year alone, 668 French officers of high rank were placed under arrest. Of these, 62 were guillotined for cowardice or simply for not winning a battle, 100 were imprisoned, 188 dismissed and 36 demoted to the ranks. Some 282 senior officers avoided such fates by being successful.[6] Most of those who commanded corps, divisions or brigades in 1815 had been among that surviving 282. In them the will to succeed was second nature.

For his Armée du Nord, the field army for the campaign, Napoleon appointed to corps command: General d'Erlon[7] I Corps, with 20,000 men at Valenciennes; Reille II Corps, with 25,000 at Avesnes; Vandamme III Corps, with 20,000 at Rocroi; Gérard IV Corps, with 15,000 at Metz; Lobau V Corps, with 10,000 at Laon. The Imperial Guard of 20,000 at Compiègne and Paris would be under Napoleon's personal command, and four reserve cavalry corps of about 3,500 each around Avesnes would initially be under the command of Marshal Grouchy. Together these corps numbered about 128,000 men.

Of the independent commands which would occupy positions for the aggressive defence of France during the coming campaign, while Napoleon manoeuvred the Armée du Nord: General Rapp, Napoleon's long-serving aide and one of the most frequently wounded of the fighting generals, was given an independent corps command, designated the Armée du Rhin, of 23,000 men; General Lecourbe, the Armée du Jura, with 8,400; Marshal Suchet, the Armée des Alpes, with 23,500; Marshal Brune, the

Armée du Var, with 5,500; General Decaen, the Armée des Pyrénées Orientales, with 7,500; General Clausel, the Armée des Pyrénées Occidentales, with 6,800; and General Lamarque, the Armée de l'Ouest, with 10,000. Also, Marshal Davout would hold Paris with its garrison of 20,000 and its National Guard. The departmental National Guards, totalling 81,000 men, would secure their areas of the interior. A further 133,200 men were either due to report, were receiving training or were awaiting equipment before being dispatched to line regiments, the Imperial Guard, or the mobile National Guard.[8] Altogether, at the begining of the campaign of 1815, France had produced 504,000 men under arms.

THE DÉPARTEMENTS OF FRANCE, 1791–1815

Opposing Napoleon and France were the Allied forces. In Belgium the Duke of Wellington commanded 107,000 men of the Anglo-Allied army, made up of British, Hanoverians, Dutch and Belgians, together with contingents from Brunswick and Nassau. On the Belgian border with the German States was the Prussian Army of the Lower Rhine, commanded (at least nominally) by Prince Blücher, with 128,000 Prussians and other Germans, including contingents from the states of the former Confederation of the Rhine and from Saxony, which had been unwillingly incorporated into the Prussian Army by the Vienna Congress. Close to Blücher was General von Kleist with a Prussian corps of 25,000, keeping watch on the French fortress of Sedan. The main Austro-Allied army, under Prince Schwarzenberg and composed largely of Bavarians, Württembergers and other former Confederation troops, and less than 50 per cent Austrians, totalled 210,000, but was a long way from striking distance of France. It was placed to be able to support the Austrian army of 75,000 under Frimont in Italy, guarding against an attack by Murat from Naples, possibly in conjunction with French forces from the South of France. In any event Schwarzenberg had been ordered to delay an advance towards France until the Russians came up.

The Russian armies of Witzingerode and Barclay de Tolly, numbering 200,000 men, had begun their westward march from the Rivers Vistula and Niemen on 5 April, and were still on Russian and Polish soil in late May. The Tsar was in no hurry to commit his troops before the Austrians had advanced. It was his intention to let others bear the casualties in 1815, as Russia had done from 1812 to 1814.

Spain and Portugal were supposed to supply 80,000 men to invade France across the Pyrenees, but Napoleon did not consider this likely. King Ferdinand of Spain already had enough trouble controlling his people without forming a sizeable army which might turn on him and the Spanish Bourbons as the French army had done with the French Bourbons.

Napoleon's plan for his campaign to defend France and his regained position against the gathering Allied forces was brilliantly conceived. He had said, '...The scheme of campaign often contains the plan of battle: none but superior minds can appreciate this ...' By this he meant that the strategy for his campaign would be based on the same plan he would use for the decisive battle. Essentially he would seek to pin down one element of the enemy forces with a smaller force, while using his larger force to engage and defeat another element. Then he would move swiftly to attack and destroy the pinned down enemy force.

In this Grand Strategy, Napoleon had arranged for the front armies which were guarding France's borders to be disposed in three lines of battle. In the first line were fortresses, fortified points and earthworks placed at important locations such as towns, cities, passes and river crossings. These static defences would have to be overcome, thus depleting and delaying an enemy advancing over the frontier. Behind these and supporting them would be a second line of mobile troops who would counter-attack when the direction of an enemy advance was known. The third line would be Napoleon's own field army, the mass of decision, which would break through the enemy's line and turn his flank.

The borders of France were closed by land and sea. The gendarmerie and border guards were tripled to prevent unauthorized persons from crossing or putting to sea. Behind this screen Napoleon assembled his field army and the other front armies took their assigned positions. Clausel and Decaen guarded the coastal avenues from Spain. Brune's small force was sufficient to hold the narrow coastal strip from Italy, backed by the fortified towns of the region. Lecourbe watched the vital invasion route from the Basle valley to the Langres plateau.[9] Centrally placed behind Brune and Lecourbe, and able to support either of them, was Suchet, who could also destroy piecemeal any forces attempting to defile through the Alpine passes. In the event of the main Allied thrust being aimed at the Langres plateau, as in 1814, both Suchet and Rapp could combine with Lecourbe to defend the Langres with 54,000 men. Even with four times that number, the Austrians would not be able to deploy a fighting front against them of more than 40,000.[10] On Rapp's left, he was in contact with the main fortresses from Strasburg to Lille. Davout's force in Paris could serve as a reserve if needed. Lamarque occupied a position from which he could suppress any royalist uprisings in the Vendée or Chouan regions, oppose any British landings in support of risings or as diversions to aid Wellington, or support Clausel and Decaen. And behind the north-eastern fortresses Napoleon assembled an experienced and well-equipped field army.

North-eastern France is flat and therefore difficult to defend. It was there during May and June of 1815 that Napoleon began concentrating his army. By the 14th he had discreetly positioned I and II Corps around Maubeuge and Beaumont on the Belgian border opposite Thuin. In front of Beaumont, opposite Charleroi, were III and VI Corps, with the Imperial Guard infantry corps, the Guard cavalry corps and the reserve artillery. Next to Philippeville was IV Corps.

A disaster of the first magnitude now occurred. King Joachim Murat of Naples, Napoleon's brother-in-law, had advanced the Neapolitan Army northward up the shank of the Italian peninsula towards Milan in support of Napoleon's strategic plan. For this march Murat had been obliged to divide his army into two parts, advancing on both sides of the central spine of the Appenines, to forestall any Austrian attempt to outflank him and threaten Naples and his army's line of communication. Finally, faced by the Austrians with overwhelming odds, Murat was unable to concentrate his divided force. His two Neapolitan forces retreated separately; Murat, with the Adriatic part of his army, fell back to Macerate. The Austrians closely pursued both Neapolitan forces. At Tolentino during 2 and 3 May Murat fought and defeated his pursuers, but was prevented from exploiting his victory when a third Austrian force, of which he had no knowledge, threatened to cut his line of communication. Murat was obliged to conduct a prolonged retreat, pressed closely by the Austrians. His efforts to disengage from the three Austrian forces which continually outflanked his demoralized Neapolitans were unsuccessful; he eventually arranged a surrender and fled to Marseilles.[11]

Napoleon was furious that Murat had been decisively beaten. The Austrians were now much freer to move forces against France. He refused to see his brother-in-law and rejected his offer to command Napoleon's cavalry. Thus, Murat, probably the finest cavalry commander in history, was left idle in the South of France when he would be desperately needed in the North.

Napoleon decided to attack Wellington and Blücher while they were waiting for the Austrian and Russian armies to reach the French border. He hoped to defeat each of them in detail, but was prepared as always to adjust his plan to circumstances as they unfolded. His primary aim was to push Wellington into the sea, knocking Britain out of the war on land. If Blücher were defeated the Prussians would fall back on their communications to the east. Wellington, in this event, would fall back on his communications westward towards the North Sea coast. Then, after dealing with Wellington and driving Louis out of Ghent and William out of Brussels – thus gaining an immense political advantage – he would turn and pursue Blücher. In so doing he would turn the right flank of the Allied armies. The remainder of the Allies, held on the border by the French front armies, would find Napoleon advancing on them indirectly, threatening to roll them up. They would have to fall back or risk having their communications cut. Napoleon hoped that with luck he might catch the Allied armies between himself and the 54,000 men Suchet would be bringing up behind them (see chart of this strategy). Otherwise, Suchet's men, together with those still mobilizing, could augment the field army to double its size. Napoleon hoped that Lord Liverpool's government, faced with yet another protracted, financially crippling war with Britain acting as the Allied pay master, would fall. Without British money the Allies could not pursue a war. At this point, Napoleon was certain, the Allies would come to terms. Such, in essence, was Napoleon's strategy for the campaign of 1815: a plan which differed little from his plans of campaign in 1813 and 1814.[12]

Although Napoleon displayed his customary military genius in the planning and preparations for his attack on the Allies in Belgium, he also allowed one of his most dangerous enemies to occupy an important post in Paris. On his return Napoleon had been struck by the depth of republican sentiment evident among the French people. Even if he had not returned it is probable that a second revolution would have occurred. In the light of this great strength of republicanism, Napoleon appointed as Minister of Police a man who was highly regarded by the republican element in the Chambers for the fact that he had voted for the death of Louis XVI. Napoleon knew that Fouché had corresponded with the Allies, but he did not know that he was a royalist agent who worked closely with the Comte d'Artois. It was Fouché who had infiltrated the group, which included d'Erlon and Vandamme, that had planned the abortive army coup in March. Although Napoleon mistrusted Fouché, he had no legal power under the new constitutional monarchy to have him arrested[13] nor, having just appointed him, did he wish to alienate the Chambers by removing him. Strangely, Napoleon evidently thought that this man, whom he mistrusted, would be a good choice to put down the uprising being fomented in the Vendée by royalist agents[14] and to uncover royalist plots in Paris. Thus, out of apparent expedience, Napoleon left in a key position in Paris a man whom he suspected of being a royalist and a traitor.[15]

Napoleon decided that he must open his campaign in Belgium by 14 June, his spies[16] having informed him that Wellington's and Blücher's forces were not concentrated, but widely dispersed. These Allied armies were not expecting to be attacked without warning and so were disposed in cantonments to cover a front between Tournai and Liège about ninety miles long and with a depth from the border to Brussels of almost forty miles. Napoleon calculated on his maps that it would take the Allies in Belgium six days to concentrate on either flank or two to three days to draw together on a central line covering Brussels.[17] He decided that his attack should fall on the junction of the two armies.

If the Allied armies in Belgium had already been concentrated or were under a single overall commander, attacking their junction would have been folly. But Napoleon's intelligence agents had told him that neither army commander was in overall control. At the point of contact there was no great concentration of forces to delay an advance. The bridges over the Sambre were intact and had not been mined. Charleroi, the main town where the Sambre would be crossed, was the only one on the entire border lightly garrisoned and without any proper fortifications. Each army commander had made adequate provision for an attack on his own immediate front, but neither had provided for an attack on the outlying flank adjoining his ally, each having assumed that the other would cover this unlikely possibility.

From the beginning of June until the 14th, Napoleon drew a heavier curtain over the north-eastern border area. Patrols were increased, strangers arrested and any unauthorized persons were turned back. Also numerous false deserters were sent across the border to feed misinformation to the enemy.[18] Their reports, when collated with the reports of any genuine deserters, Allied or royalist agents, or peasants who used little-known crossings, would serve to confuse the Allies and, because so much of the information they were receiving would be contradictory, cause them to discount anything they might learn of genuine French movements in the border area. Further, because Napoleon knew that royalist agents would keep the Allies constantly apprised of his whereabouts, he delayed leaving Paris until the latest possible date.

Concentrating on a 16-mile front was Napoleon's army, totalling 128,000 men, with 366 cannon. Across the frontier, Wellington had forces of 107,000 including garrison troops, with 216 cannon, and Blücher had 128,000, not including von Kleist's corps, with 312 cannon. The Allies outnumbered the French by nearly two to one, but Napoleon hoped to strike at the point between the Allied armies before they could concentrate and combine, thus seizing a central position from which he could fight each Allied army separately.

He had planned as far as he could; the rest would depend on circumstance. If, when his forces struck the Prussian outposts around Charleroi, Blücher again adopted his tactics of 1814 and retreated,[19] Napoleon would attack Wellington, who appeared more vulnerable because of his wider dispersal. If Blücher stood, he would defeat the Prussians first, then turn on Wellington. The moment was near when the campaign would have to start. To wait too long was to risk the Allies realizing or guessing his intentions and thwarting them by moving to combine forces. Accordingly, at 2 a.m. on 11 June, hoping to escape the notice of royalist agents, Napoleon left Paris in his coach with his staff and escort, heading north to the army he had assembled in the border area around Philippeville and Maubeuge.

Wellington, between his arrival in Belgium and June, had cantoned his army to cover the area from Ostend on the coast to Binche adjoining 1 Brigade of the Prussian I Corps. His wide disposition was of course dictated by the necessity to safeguard the ports of Antwerp and Ostend, in accordance with his secret instructions, and to protect Louis in Ghent and William in Brussels.[20] Wellington had never faced Napoleon before, but had studied his campaigns and battles well enough to know that complex and unexpected manoeuvres were not out of the question. Napoleon might try to hold him at the border with a small force, while outflanking him along the coast with his main force, seizing the ports and cutting his communications. If that happened Wellington could not rule out the possibility that Napoleon might seek to encircle his army as he had encircled Mack's at Ulm in 1805. On the other hand Napoleon could try to punch straight through to Brussels by way of Maubeuge and Mons. Added to these strategic considerations was the necessity, when disposing forces to remain in place for a period of time, to canton them as widely as was prudent to ease logistical problems and spread the burden of their presence on the civilian population more broadly.

Wellington had therefore made the following dispositions. He maintained his headquarters at Brussels, cantoning his reserve in the vicinity. This comprised the British 5th and 6th Divisions, the Nassauers under von Kruse, and the Duke of Brunswick's Corps. The Prince of Orange commanded I Corps, with his headquarters at Braine-le-Comte, Cooke's 1st Guards Division at Enghien, Alten's 3rd Division at Soignes, Perponcher's 2nd Netherlands Division between Nivelles and Quatre Bras, and Chasse's

3rd Netherlands Division at Roeulx. II Corps, under Lord Hill, had its headquarters at Ath with Clinton's 2nd Division, and Colville's 4th Division at Oudenarde. Stedman's 1st Netherlands Division at Sotteghem and Anthing's Indonesian Brigade at Alost were under the nominal command of Prince Frederick of Orange. Between Ninove and Grammont, along the River Dendre, were most of the British and King's German Legion cavalry and horse artillery under the Earl of Uxbridge. Collaert's Netherlands Cavalry Division was headquartered at Roeulx, with Trip's 1 Brigade and Ghigny's 2 Light Brigade at Havre, and van Merlen's 3 Brigade at St-Symphorien. Patrolling the border between Tournai and Mons were von Dornberg's 3 Hanoverian Light Cavalry Brigade, and from Mons to the Prussian outposts between Binche and Fontaine-l'Evêque were van Merlen's 3 Netherlands Light Cavalry Brigade. Patrolling the border near the coast, around Ostend, Nieuport, Ypres, Menin to Mons, were the garrisons of the towns in the vicinity, such as General Behr's force at Mons.

On Wellington's left, between April and May, the Prussian Army of the Lower Rhine settled into cantonments.[21] Von Ziethen's I Corps had its headquarters at Charleroi, with von Steinmetz's 1 Brigade at Fontaine-l'Evêque watching the border and river crossings from the last Netherlands outpost to Marchiennes, Pirch II's 2 Brigade covering the crossings between Marchiennes and Campinaire, Donnermarck's 4 Brigade downriver between Campinaire and Namur, Jagow's 3 Brigade some seven miles back at Fleurus in reserve, Roder's corps cavalry reserve farther back at Sombreffe, and Lehmann's corps artillery reserve behind Roder at Gembloux.

II Prussian Corps, under Pirch I was headquartered at Namur, where Blücher's Army Headquarters was also located, and which was defended by Tippelskirch's 5 Brigade, with Langen's 8 Brigade at Huy, Krafft's 6 Brigade back at Thorembey-les-Béguines, Brause's 7 Brigade at Heron, Jurgass's reserve cavalry brigade at Hannut, and Rohl's corps artillery reserve around the hamlets of Eghezee and Barriere behind Namur.

Thielemann's III Corps had headquarters at Ciney in the Ardennes forest, with Kamphen's 10 Brigade there as well, and Borch's 9 Brigade at Asserre, Luck's 11 Brigade at Dinant, Stulpnägel's 12 Brigade in reserve at Huy, Hobe's corps reserve cavalry between Ciney and Dinant, and Mohnhaupt's corps artillery reserve in the forest between Ciney and Asserre. Hobe's cavalry covered 11 Brigade at Dinant and watched the front of the forest, with sections posted as far as Namur.

Finally, back at Liège were von Bülow's IV Corps headquarters and Hacke's 13 Brigade, with Ryssel's 14 Brigade at Waremme, Losthin's 15 Brigade at Hologne, Hiller's 16 Brigade at Liers, Prince William of Prussia's corps cavalry reserve in front of Tongres, and Bardeleben's corps artillery reserve at Gloms.

The Prussian troops had to be quartered in this fashion in order to be able to keep watch on three sectors of the front: Binche to Namur, Namur to Marche, and Marche to Liège. Although the first of these sectors was considered the most likely to be attacked, the others had also to be watched in case the French should advance through the Ardennes, threatening the army's communications with the German States. Also, although widely dispersed, as were the Anglo-Allied troops, the Prussians found supplies of food and forage in short supply, for which they blamed the Dutch authorities. Gneisenau wrote urgently to von Boyen, the Prussian Minister of War, 'The problem of food supplies in this devastated [from the previous year] country between the Maas, Moselle and the Rhine is daily causing me greater anxiety. I consider we have reached the point at which we should quit this area and look for somewhere else where we may find the wherewithal to sustain ourselves.'[22]

Wellington managed to obtain a credit arrangement which alleviated the Prussians' hardships. But Blücher was impatient to advance. It would considerably ease his logistical problems if his army could live off the land in France rather than having to become further indebted to the British to pay the Dutch for their maintenance on friendly soil. Even more, though, Blücher's experience of Napoleon over the past two years had taught him that it was folly to leave the initiative with the French emperor, especially if one's army was so widely dispersed. Blücher therefore arranged to see Wellington at Tirlemont on 3 May.

In the meantime Blücher had had a mutiny with which to contend. In 1813, after the Battle of Leipzig, the Saxon king, Frederick Augustus, who had been Napoleon's staunchest ally and had fought with France at Leipzig, was imprisoned in Berlin. In a fruitless attempt to allay the wrath of his Prussian gaolers, Frederick Augustus called upon those Saxon troops who had deserted the French eagles or had been captured to serve in the Prussian army. At the end of the war in 1814, these troops attached to the Prussian army had been left in the new Rhine provinces. News reached them of the insulting treatment of their captive king and the partition of the homeland. Now it had been announced that those regiments that had been raised in the parts of Saxony which the Vienna Congress had given to Prussia against their king's will would become Prussian regiments and their soldiers Prussian subjects. The Saxon division was to be divided: part becoming Prussian, and part remaining Saxon. Naturally those units designated to become Prussian objected; they were not cattle to be bought and sold. A further provocation was offered in the form of an unwelcome change of commander. General von Lecoq was replaced by General von Thielemann. He was a Saxon who had been a divisional commander in the Saxon army when Saxony was allied to France. In 1813 he had been in command of the garrison of the key fortress of Torgau when, contrary to the instructions of Frederick Augustus and in disobedience of Napoleon's order to join him, he betrayed his men and his position to the Allies. Initially he had been taken into Russian service, but then had again transferred his loyalties to Prussia for service as a general. Not surprisingly he was heartily despised by most of the Saxon troops.

Many of the Saxon regiments given to Prussia, including the provisional Garde Regiment, were composed of units of ancient lineage, such as the Lieb-Grenadier-Garde battalion, the König's battalion, and all the grenadier companies of the remaining regiments. In general the Saxons had no love for Prussians; so to be told that their proud units were simply to be subsumed into the Prussian army was deeply offensive to them. A number of officers and men of the Saxon regiments went to Blücher's headquarters on 2 May to protest the decision. With mutual animosity between Prussian and Saxon smouldering, the situation was ominous. Blücher refused to see the Saxon deputation, ordering them to disperse. A stone was thrown through a window of Blücher's headquarters, and the old field marshal was bundled out the back door by his staff. Gneisenau soon ordered a Prussian regiment to surround and disarm the protesters.

At first Blücher was sympathetic to the Saxons. To his wife that evening, he wrote, 'The mistake was that these people have not been treated with kindness.'[23] Gneisenau took another view of the rebellious Saxons, feeling that on the eve of a campaign leniency was ill advised. The army contained several non-Prussian contingents from the newly acquired provinces, Rhinelanders, Westphalians, and regiments from Berg and other Saxon territories, which might be encouraged to make their own demands upon their new masters. Additionally the Saxon officers and men in question had refused to obey Gneisenau's and Blücher's orders. Prussian military regulations demanded the severest punishment.

When Blücher convened a court-martial, Prussian hatred for the Saxons had been whipped up by the Prussian general officers. The court ordered seven Saxons to be shot at once in front of their regiments and the flag of the élite Leib-Grenadier-Garde to be publicly burned. Wellington's liaison officer with the Prussians, Lieutent-Colonel Sir Henry Hardinge, reported to his chief the cruel treatment the Saxons received:

> '...it was explained [to the Saxons] that if each battalion gave up four leaders of the mutiny, it would be the means of preventing the shooting of one man of each company. Four were therefore produced of one battalion, and three of the other. The seven men were shot; and the eighth, who was taken by lot from a most culpable company, being a very young man, was pardoned by Prince Blücher. At Namur orders have been given for the disarming of the battalion of Saxon Guards and burning the colours ...'[24]

To make matters worse the flag to be burned had been embroidered personally by the Saxon Queen.

To burn a regimental flag which had not been taken in battle as punishment for the actions of a minority was a dishonourable contravention of the accepted standards of military behaviour of the day. General von Borstell, commander of the Prussian III Corps, was perhaps the highest-ranking officer in the Prussian army to voice his objection to this sordid act. Blücher immediately relieved him of his command, placed him under arrest and sent him back to Berlin, for conduct prejudicial to the army and disputing an order from a superior officer. Command of III Corps was given to General Pirch I. Borstell, although a favourite of the king's, was tried by a court-martial in Berlin and imprisoned.[25] In terms of discipline at least, the Prussian army was once again the army of Frederick the Great.

Blücher wrote personally to Frederick Augustus of Saxony, requiring him to inform the Saxon soldiers in question, Frederick Augustus's former subjects, to obey Prussian orders, or else: 'I shall restore order by force even if I be compelled to shoot down the entire Saxon army.'[26] The King's reply was a proclamation to the soldiers that the separation was not in accordance with his wishes and advising them to accept their fate and make the name Saxon something to be proud of. His other response to Blücher's arrogant letter was to inform the British consul that either his troops be removed from Prussian control or he himself would withdraw them.

Given the circumstances of this sad episode and the general resentment felt by the Saxons, the Allies had little doubt as to which side in the coming campaign the Saxons would like to see victorious. Gneisenau, mindful of how the defection of the Saxons from Napoleon at a crucial point in the Battle of Leipzig contributed greatly to the Allied victory, decided to send all 14,000 Saxons in the Prussian army back to Germany. He was not prepared to take the chance of the Saxons taking revenge on Prussia by performing a similar defection in the other direction. It will be appreciated that this act did little to instil *esprit de corps* in the troops of the other former Confederation states forcibly incorporated into the Prussian army.

The day after the mutiny Blücher and Gneisenau met Wellington at Tirlemont, about equidistant from Brussels and Namur. Blücher spoke to Wellington about the necessity of advancing into France as soon as possible. Wellington agreed, but both commanders were bound by their respective governments to conform to the decision of the war council sitting at Vienna, and by whose agreement Field Marshal Prince Schwarzenberg was supreme commander, as in 1813 and 1814.[27] Schwarzenberg had informed Wellington that the Allied armies would begin a concerted movement towards Paris on about 20 June.[28]

At Tirlemont Wellington and Blücher agreed that in the unlikely event of their each being attacked by Napoleon they would concentrate and combine. Wellington's army would mass on its own left, around Gosselies, leaving it as before to the Prussian right. Blücher's army would concentrate on its right around Fleurus. General von Müffling was present and recorded it agreed that after Wellington had bivouacked within the triangle Frasnes-Quatre Bras-Nivelles – in other words, assembled on his own left – then Gosselies for Wellington and Ligny for Blücher would be the ideal points from which both armies, in battle order, could best act in concert.[29] It is apparent from these decisions that Wellington and Blücher expected, in the event of an advance by Napoleon, to attack him as he crossed the Sambre, when his army would necessarily be vulnerable.

To ensure co-ordination and co-operation each commander appointed a liaison officer to be attached to the other's headquarters. General Müffling, an experienced staff officer with sound battle experience, was to be sent to Brussels and Lieutenant-Colonel Sir Henry Hardinge, of the 1st Foot Guards, to Namur. Wellington and Blücher realized that they would need two to three days to accomplish their concentration towards a position between their fronts, but both believed that either Napoleon would fight a defensive campaign as in 1814 or their own intelligence would give them timely warning of an agressive enemy build-up.

Although Wellington and Blücher had met and agreed a contingency plan in the event of Napoleon's attacking them, they were constrained in several ways from taking the initiative and advancing or even concentrating and combining. Formally, they were both under the direction of Schwarzenberg, who in turn was chosen by Prince Metternich and the Austrian Emperor to carry out Austria's ambivalent and dilatory policy concerning Napoleon. Additionally, and confidentially, Wellington had his instructions from London regarding Antwerp, and Gneisenau had his from Frederick William making him '...responsible for acting with all prudence and the most careful consideration in every matter affecting the future of Europe,' in other words, to safeguard the integrity of his army: virtually the same brief given to Schwarzenberg, and the same policy of preservation being followed by the Tsar.

Gneisenau warned Müffling to be careful of Wellington and to be sceptical of his motivations, '...for from his relations with India, and transactions with the deceitful Nabobs, this distinguished general had so accustomed himself to duplicity, that he had at last become such a master of the art, as even to outwit the Nabobs themselves'.[30]

In trying to determine Napoleon's intentions the Allies had a great advantage in the person of Joseph Fouché, Napoleon's Minister of Police and the Comte d'Artois' agent. He had managed, through one of his own agents, to send to Wellington by way of Castlereagh in London the entire order of battle of Napoleon's army, down to the last horse.[31]. Furthermore General Clarke, who had been instrumental in the betrayal of Paris to the Allies in 1814, had managed when leaving Paris in 1815 to take with him status reports on the French army. With these two documents Wellington and the other Allied leaders had a complete picture of the forces at Napoleon's disposal, their equipment and their positions on 2 May.

Wellington's confidence was enhanced by the knowledge that his reliable head of intelligence, Colonel Grant, was across the border in France, in contact with d'Artois' agents and with orders not to risk capture by sending any information other than whether Napoleon should concentrate his army in the north and if so, where and by what route it was moving.

After their conference at Tirlemont Wellington and Blücher felt they were prepared. As May turned to June and no apparent French concentration had occurred in the north, the commanders began to feel that perhaps, as in 1814, Napoleon had left them to deplete their strength investing the 42 strong points en route to Paris, and that when he had dealt with the Austrians, sending them home, he would perhaps turn back to face them.

Napoleon's efforts to mislead the Allies and mask his true plans were succeeding. On his orders French garrisons around Lille manoeuvred to create the impression that forces were concentrating there. Napoleon was clearly able to fathom and exploit Wellington's strategic concern about a French seaward sweep around his right flank. In contrast, along the border in the vicinity of Charleroi, the French had broken up the roads and taken other measures of a defensive nature.

Because the Cabinet had refused to declare war against France as opposed to war against Napoleon, Wellington was constrained from sending patrols across the frontier, and thus was denied his most immediate source of intelligence on the situation to his front. The vigilant Netherlands cavalry under van Merlen had captured several French reconnaissance patrols, but were obliged by Wellington's order to escort them back across the border. This exasperating charade continued until as late as 13 June, when the Prince of Orange wrote in frustration to Wellington, 'I am going to send back the prisoners this morning with a letter to Count d'Erlon, according to your wishes.'[32]

However, despite not being able to patrol into France and despite the flood of fake information from bogus deserters, the reliable evidence the Allies were able to gain showed a concentration of French troops between Maubeuge and Philippeville. One of the more cryptic items of earlier information was passed by Wellington through Hardinge to the Prussians: 'May 7th, 1815, Wellington to Sir H. Hardinge: Communications with foreign countries [by Frenchmen] is forbidden on pain of death, which looks as if an attack was intended.' By 16 May Wellington was able to disclose in his memorandum to Allied leaders, based on Fouché's information, that the French field army contained '...not less than 110,000 men', adding that 'There are a great number of troops about Maubeuge, Avesnes, etc.'. And on the 19th Wellington was able to inform his cavalry commander, Lord Uxbridge: 'I have a most formidable account of the French cavalry. They have now 16,000 *Grosse Cavalerie*, of which 6,000 are Cuirassiers. They are getting horses to mount 42,000, heavy and light.' On 7 June the Allies were sufficiently alarmed to issue instructions to the governors of all the

Belgian fortresses to proclaim a state of siege as soon as the enemy should enter the Low Countries. On the 12th General Dornberg, Wellington's officer responsible for collating intelligence from the border, wrote from Mons to Lord Fitzroy Somerset for Wellington's information that Bonaparte was expected at any minute at Avesnes, that Soult had passed through Maubeuge, that the forces between Philippeville, Givet, Mezières, Giuse, and Maubeuge amounted to more than 100,000 troops of the line, and that the general opinion in the French army was that the arrival of Napoleon at Avesnes would be the signal for the beginning of hostilities.[33]

Notwithstanding this full and highly accurate information, the Allied leaders in the north began to think that theirs was going to be but a secondary theatre in the war. By 14 June both commanders had booked full diaries of social activities. Wellington was planning to attend several cricket matches and gala balls, particularly the Duchess of Richmond's on the evening of the 16th. Blücher had likewise made several social engagements for the same period. On the 13th Wellington wrote to General Lord Lynedoch:

> 'There is nothing new here. We have reports of Bonaparte's joining the army and attacking us; but I have accounts from Paris of the 10th, on which day he was still there; and I judge from his speech to the Legislature that his departure was not likely to be immediate. I think we are too strong for him here.'[34]

Gneisenau, too, had come to this conclusion, believing that Napoleon's thunderbolt would fall first on Schwarzenberg, to knock the Austrians out of the war, as he had attempted in 1814, while the Allies in the north waded through the fortress belt. Gneisenau wrote to Berlin on 9 June: 'The enemy will not attack us but will retire [south] as far as the Aisne, Somme and Marne in order to concentrate his forces,'[35] adding on the 12th, 'The danger of an attack has almost vanished.'

That morning, however, at 2 a.m., Napoleon's green coach, followed by its escort, clattered out of Paris, heading north to Avesnes.

CHAPTER 5

'A Dependable Article': The Rival Commanders and their Tactics

'Infantry, cavalry, and artillery are nothing without each other. They should always
be so disposed in cantonments as to assist each other in case of surprise.' – Napoleon,
The Military Memoirs of Napoleon, 1831, tr. d'Aguilar.

To understand better the campaign of 1815, it will be helpful to pause to assess the contending generals and their methods of warfare. Napoleon, of course, was the pre-eminent military genius of his day; the conqueror who had schooled a generation of generals in the art of war. His rise had been swift and irrefutable: if not Alexandrian, possibly Caesarian in its boldness and self-justifying authority. From an obscure captain of artillery at 23, he rose to be general of brigade at 24, major-general and army commander at 26, leader of a successful coup d'état at 31, and emperor at 35. The scope of his genius was far ranging, taking in civil matters such as political administration, education, law and science. Many of his reforms in these areas, such as the Code Napoleon, have survived to the present day. He sought to emulate Charlemagne and the Roman emperors, and notwithstanding Talleyrand's spiteful remark to the contrary, he gave his name to his era.

Napoleon governed his empire and army personally from wherever he happened to be, whether in a magnificent palace or a tent on the field of battle. With the aid of a portable filing system he always had access to a wide range of information, from the general to the very detailed, collected from many sources and kept up to date by his staff. With this at his fingertips he was able to decide with confidence matters both civil and military as they came to his attention.

In June 1815, aged 46, Napoleon had already ruled France as a republic and an empire for fourteen years until his forced abdication in March 1814. Now, having been refused a peaceful coexistence on any terms by his implacable enemy, the British Government, and its subsidised allies, he had little choice but to fight a swift campaign which would bring the Allies to terms before they could combine massively against him as in 1814. He realized that the greatest threat would come from a combined Anglo-Allied and Prussian army advancing on Paris from the Low Countries over terrain which had already seen the passage of many armies, and would see many more in years to come.

In planning the campaign he relied on the basic strategic conception which had served him well many times before when faced with numerically superior forces, the manoeuvre of the central position. This was essentially Napoleon's application of the Roman maxim of divide and conquer. The danger inherent in this strategy was that if the enemy did not divide, one could be trapped.

The French army, which was the instrument of Napoleon's will, had changed radically over the years since the Revolution. In the infancy of the new era, the army was still the small, well-drilled professional force that was adequate for the French monarch to use in the prosecution of the small-scale, dynastic campaigns of the 18th century. This well-disciplined army, called '*Les Blancs*' for their Bourbon white uniforms, could maintain tight linear formations to deliver a volley, and perform the evolutions required to form a square or a marching column of route. To meet the urgent offensive and defensive requirements of Republican France, however, a much larger army was required. Largely through the organizational efficiency of Lazare Carnot, hundreds of thousands of men were recruited, but there was neither time nor sufficient NCOs to train such a multitude. These citizens in uniform were simply armed and ordered to attack the enemy in massive assault columns. After several reversals in which untrained masses were rebuffed despite their numbers, Carnot instituted the demi-brigade which combined two battalions of recruits with one of regulars.

On the attack, the demi-brigade advanced in a new formation consisting of a line of regulars to provide firepower and discipline and a column of conscripts on each side to give weight to the attack. The three columns were preceded by experienced soldiers, called variously *voltigeurs* (vaulters), *chasseurs* (hunters) and *tirailleurs* (sharpshooters), in skirmishing order, who would harass the enemy ranks with sniping fire. This mixed order of attack proved highly successful against the traditional armies of Europe and was much favoured by Napoleon. In this, as in other areas such as artillery, experimentation and reform had begun well before the Revolution. Also born of necessity was the policy of having Republican armies live off the land when on foreign soil. The Republic could not afford to provision its large armies, so they foraged and requisitioned locally for many of their needs, both for food and fuel and for guns and other military equipment.

Among the monarchical armies it was the custom of the period to draw up for battle in two lines, each consisting of regiments or battalions deployed two or three men deep. The soldiers' muskets were smooth-bore weapons that fired a round ball. They could not be aimed in any meaningful sense at any target beyond 25 yards' distance. This of course was the reason for the tactic of massed fire. Commanders would wait until their troops had closed to about 100 yards of the enemy or less before giving the order to open fire. The volley delivered by 400–600 muskets had the effect of a great shotgun, cutting down many individual soldiers within the large target presented by the enemy formation.

One of the reasons for the considerable early success of the French mixed-order form of attack was that the skirmishers were able to approach often to within 20 yards of the enemy lines. At that range they were certain to hit someone with almost every shot. Apart from thinning the enemy ranks, this point-blank sniping had a demoralizing effect on the enemy, who had to stand shoulder to shoulder and take it, without being able to return fire. In the early campaigns the armies of France's enemies did not themselves deploy skirmishers and their commanders refused to allow individual fire in return or to waste a volley on such a widely dispersed target as skirmishers.

From 1800 to 1805 Napoleon consolidated the old armies of the Republic into a unified force, the *Grande Armée*. The soldiers of this supreme instrument of Napoleon's ambition were trained to perform all the drills and evolutions practised by traditional armies, but to these Napoleon added his own refinements, gained through reflection on his experiences of the Revolutionary wars. In his infantry, each regiment was composed of from two to five battalions, each of which was made up of six companies, four of the line, one of *voltigeurs*, and one of grenadiers (élite infantry, originally armed with grenades). During the early period the strength of a company was 140 men, although in the 1815 campaign 100 was normal. The grenadier units were formed of the biggest and most experienced men of the battalion and they provided the impetus in assault. The light troops tended to be small and agile, but after 1807 they lacked long-range sniping capability because Napoleon withdrew their rifles, considering their rate of fire too slow. Both the grenadiers and the *voltigeurs* were considered to be élite, and men of the line companies aspired to join them.

French cavalry was divided into three classes: light, line, and heavy. Each regiment of the army had a nominal allocation of four squadrons of cavalry, each comprising two troops of 60-65 men. The light were employed primarily in scouting, screening and harrying routed enemy forces; they were differentiated by their weapons into lancers and others. Napoleon had introduced the lance into his army in 1809 and promoted its training and use. Two of his élite Guard regiments were Lancers. A lancer had advantages in attack. Able to impale a standing or mounted enemy by the force of his forward impetus, he could also make stabbing thrusts at men crouching or lying flat on the ground, something virtually impossible for sword- or sabre-armed cavalry. Against an infantry square the long reach of the lancers made them uniquely able among cavalry to inflict casualties on the enemy within the bristle of bayonets. The French lancer was also taught, when outnumbered in a mêlée, how to keep the enemy at bay by sweeping the lance, and to use the iron-shod base to strike at the face of an enemy. Light cavalry divisions were attached to each of Napoleon's corps.

The second class, the line, consisted of dragoons. Originally intended to fight as either a cavalryman or a mounted foot soldier, the dragoon was armed with a heavy cavalry sword, pistols, and musket and bayonet rather than a cavalry carbine. Napoleon had used the dragoons as both light and heavy cavalry, but in 1815 they served as heavy.

The third class, the heavy, were the *cuirassiers*, who were heavy in the literal sense. Mounted on powerful horses, they were large men who wore steel back- and breastplates (*cuirasse*) and a helmet, and were armed with a heavy straight sword, pistol, and later a carbine. Their armour gave them a great deal of protection against sword and sabre.

Napoleon usually kept the heavy cavalry corps, of *cuirassiers* and dragoons with their attendant horse artillery and staff, under his direct command. These big men, mounted on the heaviest horses, riding boot to boot in a thundering mass, would gallop in on their emperor's order to counter-attack enemy cavalry, punch a hole in the enemy line, or burst wide a breach made by infantry columns.

The artillery arm was divided into foot and horse. In the French Army each division of foot had at least one battery of eight guns, usually six 8pdrs and two howitzers. Corps commanders usually had several additional batteries in reserve, and there was usually an Army artillery reserve. Horse artillery batteries normally consisted of six light guns. These batteries could move into position quickly, unlimber, fire and move away before the enemy had time to deliver counter-battery fire on to their position. When attached to a cavalry unit engaging infantry squares, horse artillery could be decisive, unlimbering at point-blank range and devastating the dense infantry formations with canister, or grapeshot as it was sometimes termed.

In his generalship Napoleon was a firm believer in the superiority of aggression over passivity and attack over defence. In the form of attack that he would usually mount against an enemy line of battle, a basic pattern may be discerned. A preliminary bombardment by artillery would thin the enemy ranks and cause confusion as they prepared to meet his approaching columns. The columns, preceded by clouds of skirmishers, would attempt to pierce the enemy line, which would already have been significantly thinned by the bombardment and the sniping of the skirmishers. Often the enemy line would break and rout at the point of attack before the columns had come to close quarters. In any case, if the enemy line were broken, the foot would hold the shoulders of the gap while heavy cavalry rode in, turning to right and left to roll up the enemy line. Following the heavy, the light horse would swarm through to sabre and harry the disorganized enemy, giving them no chance to rally or withdraw in a coherent body. Such an attack could be either a diversion, to induce the enemy to commit his reserves, or the main thrust, and ideally the enemy would be suffering the further anxiety of not knowing which it was. If it were the main effort, the breakthrough, once achieved, would be exploited by additional troops following the attack columns. By 1815, most of France's enemies had learned by bitter experience the efficacy of Napoleon's battle tactics and had made efforts to adopt them. The sole exception was the British Army, which fought differently and had never been beaten by Napoleon's standard method of attack. [1]

Among the reforms of the army begun before the Revolution was the development of the *corps d'armée*. Napoleon saw the value of this reform, adopting and developing it into what has been called his secret weapon.[2] The Napoleonic army corps was a well-balanced unit comprising all arms: infantry, cavalry and artillery, with attached engineers, auxiliary trains and a headquarters staff. The corps was in effect an army in miniature, although its size, anywhere from 5,000 to 40,000 men, could rival that of many 18th-century armies. The corps would be made up of a number of infantry and cavalry divisions, each of two or more brigades with attached artillery. As Napoleon's corps structured army went into battle against a traditionally organized enemy force, each of his corps, being a complete fighting force, could go into action without delay as soon as it arrived on the field. When Davout, one of the pre-eminent corps commander of the period, brought his men by an epic forced march directly into the fray at Austerlitz, he undoubtedly stopped the great Russian envelopment of the French right which would have threatened to cut across Napoleon's line of communication and make his position untenable. The size of a corps could vary and would depend on several factors, such as its particular task and the ability of its commanding general. To his step-son, Eugène de Beauharnais, Napoleon in 1809 commented, '...a corps of 25,000–30,000 men can be left on its own. Well handled it can fight or alternatively avoid action... an opponent cannot force it to accept an engagement, but if it chooses to do so it can fight alone for a long time.'[3]

The corps, with their ability to engage much larger enemy forces, were essential to the working of Napoleon's two favoured types of campaign strategy: the manoeuvre of the central position and the envelopment. The manoeuvre of the central position was favoured by Napoleon when confronting two separate enemy armies of a significantly greater combined size than his. Perhaps the classic examples of this type of campaign occurred at the beginning and the end of Napoleon's military career: in the opening phase of the Italian campaign of 1796 and in the opening (and, for Napoleon, unexpectedly decisive) phase of the campaign of 1815. In the 1796 campaign he manoeuvred his forces between those of Beaulieu and Argenteau and by a combination of boldness and the use of interior lines defeated each in turn. The fighting power of the Napoleonic corps was most dramatically illustrated during the lightning campaign against Prussia in 1806, when Marshal Davout alone with his three-division corps routed the main part of the Prussian army. By the campaign of 1815, however, Napoleon's attempt to execute another textbook manoeuvre of the central position miscarried, for a variety of reasons which will be discussed at length in succeeding chapters. One reason may be noted as pertinent here, though; it is that, since 1806, the Prussians had learned the value of corps organization and had wholeheartedly adopted and improved upon it.

The Imperial Guard Corps were Napoleon's praetorians, the *corps d'élite* of his army, and his ultimate reserve. Like the others it comprised all arms, but the infantry of the Grenadiers and *Chasseurs* of the Old Guard were perhaps the most famous. These were the *grognards* (grumblers) who were selected for the Guard individually by the Emperor himself on their records, character and long service throughout many campaigns and battles. The tradition of the Old Guard had grown since 1800; the men enjoyed a reputation for fearlessness and invincibility; and they inspired terror in the hearts of the enemy merely by the sight of the serried ranks of their great bearskin shakos as they stood waiting ominously behind the field of battle. Before 1812 Napoleon seldom committed the Old Guard infantry unless it were vital, as in 1814. When committed they would usually spearhead the final attack, which would restore the spirits of the French line and encourage them to redouble their efforts, for they had the reputation of never having retreated. Often, seeing the Old Guard in reserve, the enemy would hold larger numbers of his own men in reserve, even if these were sorely needed elsewhere.

The Guard Cavalry, divided into a light and a heavy division, was also an élite unit, but was used more frequently. The main fighting element of the Guard was the Young Guard, which was considered more expendable and whose ranks as they thinned were filled by worthy veterans from the line. The Old Guard recruited mainly from the Young. The men of the Old Guard had to be warriors indeed to have been chosen to enter its ranks; and all were fanatically loyal to their emperor, and enjoyed better rates of pay and special privileges. The rank and file of the line did not resent the Guard, for most hoped one day to join it; they merely joked good naturedly that the Guards donkeys ranked as mules.

The artillery of the Guard was likewise composed of the élite gunners of the army. Its horse artillery could move, unlimber, fire, limber and move again in half the time of most other horse artillery. The foot artillery of the Guard were equipped mainly with 12pdr cannon, the 'Emperor's beautiful daughters' as they were affectionately known. These usually formed the army's artillery reserve and Napoleon often used them as a core around which he would build his 'grand batteries', sometimes totalling almost 100 guns. This massed artillery was used in battle to batter a hole in the enemy line.[4] Napoleon, having begun his military career as an artillery officer, had an understandable interest in artillery and had encouraged in his generals the aggressive use of this arm.

In 1807 at the Battle of Friedland, General Senarmont had initiated the 'case-shot attack'. This artillery general took 30 guns from his battery of 36, split them into two wings and advanced them alternately toward the Russian enemy. As each wing fired, the other advanced to a new, more forward position. After six volleys his artillery had advanced to within 250 yards of the Russian line. They then fired case-shot, the anti-personnel weapon of the period, consisting of tin canisters filled with some 85 lead

116

balls larger than musket-balls. On leaving the muzzle these spread into a wide shotgun pattern. Often a single ball would kill more than one man or horse. At 150 yards, Senarmont's gunners double-shotted their cannon, firing two canisters at a time. The effect of 30 guns firing in this way at point-blank range was terrible. Rank upon rank of Russians were cut down, leaving great bloody swaths in their line. This daring and imaginative, if awful, use of a modest number of cannon gained Napoleon the victory that an entire army corps had failed to achieve.

In his campaigns Napoleon made brilliant use of his corps system to try to ensure that when manoeuvring against the enemy, when disposing for battle and while fighting a battle, his army remained balanced, so that all arms could act in support of one another whenever required. The corps system was also integral to the execution of the strategy upon which Napoleon would base a campaign. Broadly his campaign strategies were of two types: the manoeuvre of the central position, his 'inferiority' strategy, used when he faced an enemy or enemies whose numbers were significantly greater than his; and the manoeuvre on the rear, his 'superiority' strategy, when the tables were turned.[5]

For the campaign of 1815 Napoleon, heavily outnumbered, chose to use his inferiority strategy. By it he hoped to overcome the advantage enjoyed by the Allies according to their application of the 'law of numbers': basically that a much larger force, acting cautiously and in concert, will eventually defeat a much smaller force by the effect of attrition over a series of engagements, even if the smaller force should 'win' each engagement.

Napoleon planned to move against the two Allied armies in Belgium in such a way as to drive a wedge between them, taking for himself the central position, before they were able to concentrate or combine. He would use two corps to hold one enemy in play, while attacking the other with his advance guard aggressively enough to prevent it from disengaging. He would then develop his attack against the second enemy by using his reserves to extend his line, causing the enemy to do the same to avoid being outflanked. Then he would draw one corps from the force holding the first enemy and force-march it across interior lines to the inside flank of the second enemy. Either he would turn the second enemy's flank, or by maintaining severe pressure exhaust the enemy's reserves. At this point, using his own uncommitted reserves, his mass of decision, including possibly the Guard and heavy cavalry, he would breach the second enemy's line and rout them, using light cavalry to harass their retreat. With the second enemy broken, he would leave a corps to follow up and prevent them from rallying, and turn the rest of his forces upon the first enemy, repeating the process that had broken the second. In this fashion, Napoleon, with a single army, could defeat two armies, each as numerous as his, that were intent on converging on him.

Napoleon's personal high command structure, when he developed it, was more advanced than that of his opponents. When he arrived at a place, his command centre would be established. This included a travelling library in partitioned boxes which would be stacked in a makeshift study. The army muster rolls, amounting to twenty volumes, would be easily accessible. On these rolls were details of every unit in the army: strength, location, ammunition and food supplies on hand.[6] In the Emperor's makeshift study notebooks were kept and updated daily, giving the location of each unit, its level of training and its battle record. Also included were detailed records on each officer and NCO. These personal records were no doubt an aid to Napoleon's famous ability when with his troops on parade or on the march to tweak the ear of a veteran and say, 'Sergeant [so-and-so], do you remember how hard we fought at Arcola?' This personal touch helps to explain the strength of the bond between him and his army. He was able to strike an emotional chord in his men by the resonance of which they would be inspired to die for their beloved Emperor, even when in the later years they had lost their blind faith in him. Wellington said of Napoleon, 'His hat on the field of battle was worth 40,000 men.' Napoleon himself rated the value of his presence much more highly, as when he wrote to St-Cyr: '...I alone am worth another 100,000 men.'[7]

In his study, in addition to his library, Napoleon would have two tables. On one would be placed a huge, detailed map, lit at night by twenty candles. His cartographer would have outlined clearly the important topographical features such as rivers and mountains. Coloured pins were placed and replaced in the map to record the latest known positions of his and the enemy's formations. A compass, set to measure a day's march, and a scaled ruler lay by the map ready for Napoleon's use. Many recorded accounts relate that Napoleon and his chief of topography would hit their heads together while crawling across the map on their hands and knees, intent on its features.[8] On the other table were stacked reports by Napoleon's Chief of Staff containing summaries of the latest positions of all his army units, daily status reports from each of his corps, a daily report on enemy positions, and intelligence reports culled from the interrogation of local inhabitants and captured enemy soldiers and couriers and from the analysis of captured enemy mail. All this information was examined by Napoleon personally. With this two-table system he was able to calculate to within a few hours the time by which any given unit, or his entire concentrated army, could arrive at a given place. This was crucial to the brilliant timing which so often gave him victory.

Napoleon's Chief of Staff, his invaluable right hand for more than twenty years, had been Louis-Alexandre Berthier, whom Napoleon had elevated to Marshal of France, Prince of Wagram, and sovereign Prince of Neuchâtel. During all Napoleon's campaigns, including Egypt, Berthier had been at his side directing the movements of the army. He was an administrative genius, probably the greatest chief of staff in a century, whose solid attention to detail was a perfect foil to Napoleon's mercurial and impulsive character. He could listen to the avalanche of words poured out by

Napoleon in his staccato fashion and, without needing to commit the unthinkable sin of interrupting the Emperor's flow, could follow its direction. He could then write down the orders, stating clearly the essence of Napoleon's stream of consciousness dictation, supplying ringing Napoleonic phrases at the appropriate points, and correcting the place names Napoleon usually mispronounced. The clear copy of his orders which Berthier would then present to Napoleon would instantly be recognized by the Emperor as the expression of his mind.

Berthier also had developed his own system for the handling of orders and returns. For example, any order sent would be numbered and dispatched in triplicate using three messengers travelling by different routes. The three copies of the order were signed out in a book recording time of departure, name of the intended recipient and name of carrier. Each messenger was charged, upon delivery of the order, to obtain a receipt bearing the signature of the recipient and the time of receipt. When the messenger returned to headquarters, this information was recorded in the order book. Naturally if one or two messengers returned to headquarters with receipts and one or two did not, Berthier would know that the order had been received, but that the other messenger(s) would have to be found to determine whether the order had fallen into enemy hands and thus been compromised.

Napoleon's advanced command system functioned well even on the move. In his last campaigns of 1813 and 1814 his coach had become something of a legend in France and Germany. Napoleon, never the best of horsemen, travelled by coach over distance. This, apart from being more comfortable, allowed him to make full use of the thing he knew was most precious – time. In his coach, accompanied normally by Berthier, he could dictate orders and messages, discuss his plans with his chief of staff, or sleep. Many historians have remarked on how the Emperor would go without sleep, sometimes for as many as 36 hours at a time, basing their assertion on the positions of his nightly headquarters. But his coach, specially sprung and drawn by six large grey limousine horses, contained a pull-out bed on which Napoleon could and did sleep. The coach was also specially fitted with a folding writing top, numerous partitioned and locked boxes, a hand-operated printing press, his mobile treasury, a small armoury of weapons and his travelling library. The coach could only seat two, and the other occupant was invariably Berthier.

On the move it was an impressive sight. Painted Imperial green, it had two coachmen on top and Napoleon's personal servant on the box. Outriding the team of horses were three ex-drivers of the Imperial Guard horse artillery in Imperial livery. Four *chasseurs* of the Imperial Guard rode in pairs before the coach, while behind it rode the Imperial train: a troop commander at the head of twelve pairs of *chasseurs* and behind them a varying number of general officer orderlies, liaison and orderly officers, equerries and other attendant personnel. The cavalcade that accompanied the coach could number from 50 to 250 men.

At night the coach was illuminated by five lamps which gave it a demonic appearance as it raced through sleepy hamlets. The drumming of so many hooves would generally alert the population to its approach some ten to fifteen minutes before it burst upon them. While it was moving, if Berthier wanted to make a communication he would put his arm out of the window and beckon the troop commander, who would send up a rider to the window. Cantering abreast he would receive the written or verbal message.

If Napoleon ordered the coach to halt so that he could relieve himself or examine a map or the country at first hand, an established ritual was enacted by his guard. First, the four *chasseurs* ahead of the coach dismounted, fixed bayonets to their carbines, and formed a square around their Emperor as he stepped down to carry out his purpose. Within moments, the other twenty-four troopers would have joined their comrades, enlarging the square. If required, a folding chair and a table would be placed within the Emperor's field sanctum, and perhaps a fire lit. Only Berthier was permitted access to Napoleon at these times. Napoleon's horse would be brought up and held at the ready by a page. The interlude would end when Napoleon ordered 'To horse!' and either mounted his horse to make a reconnaissance or re-entered the coach, and the entourage would proceed.[9]

Among Napoleon's travelling train of attendants there were two kinds of aide-de-camp: those attached to him directly, and those attached to the staff of his Chief of Staff. Napoleon's own aides were ADCs first-class, men of the rank of general or colonel who themselves would each have several aides. These first-class ADCs would relieve or replace commanders in emergencies, mount special operations with *ad hoc* units, form the artillery into grand batteries and generally act as the Emperor's voice. In this last capacity the General ADC would carry Napoleon's verbal messages or orders to avoid the possibility of written orders falling into the hands of the enemy or being misconstrued. By a special decree of 1 June 1815 French army commanders were to obey such verbal orders 'as if from the Emperor himself'.[10] The Chief of Staff's aides were ADCs second-class, twelve orderly officers of the rank of major, captain or lieutenant who performed missions as required or carried messages and orders.

In 1815, Napoleon fielded the best army – in terms of the quality of its rank-and-file – that he had commanded since 1807. The soldiers were all French and the vast proportion were veterans, many of whom had been repatriated from prisoner-of-war captivity or isolated garrisons after the 1814 Peace. Even many of the recruits of 1814 had had a baptism of fire in the campaign of that year. Those who had remained under arms during the Bourbon restoration had been drilled and put through much practice of manoeuvres during the past year. Morale, or *élan*, was high as the 1815 campaign drew near. The troops were pleased to have their Emperor back. They felt that they had regained their honour and their pride. They knew what they would be fighting for and the outcome of the campaign mattered to them personally.

The Prussian commander, Field Marshal Gebhard Leberecht von Blücher, Prince of Wahlstadt, was seventy-two years old in 1815, extreme old age for the period. He was born near Rostock in Mecklenberg in 1742 and joined the Swedish army when he was fourteen. He had fought against Prussia[11] until he was captured. Colonel Belling, the commanding officer of the 8th (later 9th) Hussar Regiment which had captured him, decided that young Blücher had the makings of a good hussar and used his patronage to get him a commission in the regiment. Hussar Blücher was the very model of his type, both in and out of the saddle: he displayed a fiery temper, was loud-mouthed and profane, gambled, drank heavily and chased women. Unfortunately for his immediate career prospects, his reputation had preceded him when he rashly wrote to his adopted monarch, Frederick the Great, requesting promotion and threatening to resign if refused. The great Frederick wrote on Blücher's intemperate letter, 'This officer can go to the devil!'

After Blücher had spent fifteen years as a farmer, Frederick William II acceded to the Prussian throne and Blücher returned to his regiment as a major of hussars. By 1794 he had become Chef de Regiment, with the rank of major-general. During the Revolutionary Wars he and his hussars were often in the van of the army; and Blücher became an expert in the role of the advance guard, even taking time to write a textbook on this difficult branch of field operations.[12] Attacking had become his forte and, as was customary for the commander of the advance guard when moving off, he would point his sword and give the order '*Vorwärts!*'(Forward!). By 1813, within the Prussian army he had gained the nickname '*Alte Vorwärts*'(Old Forward).

Earlier, in the débâcle of 1806, after Prussia had declared war on France, Napoleon had required only six weeks to destroy the fighting ability of Frederick the Great's much vaunted Prussian army, which was hampered by reliance on obsolete 18th-century linear formations and an antiquated command structure. Unable to withstand the onslaught of Napoleon's innovative corps-structured army, the Prussians were destroyed piecemeal by French tactics.

Blücher was one of the few generals in the defeated Prussian army to survive the catastrophe with his reputation not only intact but enhanced. As the role of light cavalry such as hussars was to act as advance guard in an advance, so it was to cover the rear of the army in retreat. Blücher commanded the rearguard in 1806, fighting a series of ferocious actions to avoid envelopment by pursuing French forces. Eventually, at Lübeck, with his back to the Baltic and having fought on for several hours after his ammunition had run out, he was compelled to surrender.

Napoleon, wishing to meet such an exceptional commander, took an immediate dislike to Blücher, reacting naturally to the evident hatred he felt directed towards himself from the defiant Prussian general. Then, for the second time, Blücher was retired from the military for having incurred the displeasure of a sovereign; during the years of French dominance over Prussia, Napoleon ensured that he remain out of uniform. But in 1813, with the loosening of the French grip on Prussia, he returned to the Colours. His intense hatred of the French, and of Napoleon personally, for the humiliation suffered by his army, his country and his monarch, augmented his innate aggressiveness, making him ruthless and indefatigable in battle. Even in defeat, Blücher was formidable, regrouping quickly and returning to the attack as soon as possible.[13] On the strength of his successes in the campaigns of 1813 and 1814, Blücher became the foremost Prussian general. He was second only to Wellington among Allied commanders in the victories he had gained from the French, but unlike Wellington he had faced Napoleon in battle many times, on one occasion even beating him.

The Prussian army of 1815 was the product of years of fundamental reform initiated as a result of the humiliation of 1806. In this reform the Prussian General Staff had been inspired by, but had improved upon, Napoleon's organization of the French army. During the five years following 1806 in which Prussia was noncombatant, the General Staff had had time to analyse Prussia's mistakes and Napoleon's successes. The outcome of the review was a remodelled army structure, taking the all-arms corps system of the French one step farther, and a doctrine of aggressive attack. The basic combined-arms tactical fighting unit of the new Prussian army was the brigade (in 1815 roughly equivalent in size to a division in other European armies).[14] The Prussian army was organized into corps, each comprising nominally three or four brigades. The brigades, consecutively numbered throughout all the corps, had three regiments: one line, one *Landwehr* and one from the new provinces. The highly trained line regiments were intended to form the solid core of each brigade, serving as an example to the other regiments. The regiments had three battalions each: usually two musketeer and one fusilier. All Prussian soldiers were taught to aim before firing, but the best marksmen were placed in the fusilier battalions. Fusiliers were trained to operate both in skirmish order as light infantrymen and in line formation. Attached to a fusilier battalion would normally be several companies of *Jäger* (hunters), rifle-armed volunteers who provided their own uniforms of distinctive green and black, an early attempt at camouflage. Their rifled weapons gave them an advantage in range and accuracy over their French counterparts, who were not rifle-armed. For the most part foresters and hunters, or the sons of good families, the *Jäger* equipped themselves and served at their own expense, receiving in return a commission either at the end of the campaign or when merited. These volunteer *Jäger* companies supplemented the existing *Jäger* or rifle battalions of the army, which were distributed to the corps for use by the brigades.

Cavalry for a Prussian corps consisted nominally of two brigades of three to five regiments each. Cavalry brigades were either light or heavy, and like the French the Prussian cavalry had regiments of lancers, called *Uhlans*. Most of the militia cavalry were also armed with lances, making the Prussian cavalry proportionately heavier in lancer units than the French. Two light regiments in a corps would be available for reconnaissance and other varied duties, including escort and liaison. In battle the corps' heavy regiments would normally be massed to form a cavalry reserve.

Of artillery, a Prussian corps usually had twelve batteries of 6pdr and 12pdr cannon, each battery made up of eight pieces as in the French artillery. Corps artillery was a mix of horse and foot; and the corps commander would allocate the batteries of each type to his brigades according to the tactical role he had assigned to the brigade.

In addition to taking the army tactical fighting unit down a level from corps to brigade/division, the Prussian General Staff had also refined the battle tactics to be used by the brigade. They abandoned linear formations in favour of assault columns which attacked closed up and could in a minute form into square without the tedious necessity of forming it from a battalion in line or a spaced column of companies. Then, after the threat had been repelled, their squares could open again concertina fashion and resume their advance.

According to the new Prussian tactics, a brigade advance would be led by a first line of *Jäger* and fusiliers in skirmish order. These marksmen would snipe at officers in the enemy line and drive in the enemy pickets. The skirmishers would be followed closely by several of their own companies in line. This line would support the skirmishers against opposition or form the base for the skirmishers to fall back and form squares if counterattacked. In the next line would be fusilier battalions to provide further firepower, lengthening or reinforcing the skirmish line. Behind the second line would be its supporting companies. In the third line would be tight assault columns composed of three musketeer battalions, supported on each flank by a half-battery of foot artillery. The fourth and final line would be a reserve of two battalion assault columns deployed to cover the gaps between the three columns of the third line so that they could pass through and attack or outflank any enemy positions that might have stopped the third line. On the flanks or at the rear of the brigade formation would be a cavalry regiment (if attached), supported by a battery of horse artillery, to exploit any rupture of the enemy line. Also on each flank of the brigade would be at least a half-battery of foot artillery. In addition, a brigade could normally call on the support of its corps' heavy cavalry division, usually held in reserve, with its horse artillery. The corps heavy cavalry could exploit the attack, defend brigade artillery, counter-attack enemy cavalry, and act as a rearguard with the fusiliers in the event of a withdrawal.[15] Thus the advantage of the Prussian army's reforms in structure and fighting doctrine derived from all-arms flexibility at one full organizational level lower than that of the French corps, and tighter formations capable of more rapid manoeuvre. A new model Prussian brigade applying the new tactics could therefore cause as much trouble for a French corps as the French corps had done for traditional armies a generation earlier.[16] Although these changes had borne fruit in the campaigns of 1813 and 1814, the ability of the Prussian army to fight in this fashion at the outset of the 1815 campaign was limited because units assigned to its corps, together with replacements and reserves, were still arriving at the front during, and even after, the decisive battles of June.

The architect of these effective reforms, and of the reform of the Prussian General Staff itself, had been Major-General Gerhard von Scharnhorst, who was mortally wounded at Lützen in 1813. Scharnhorst began his military career as one of King George's Hanoverians, but as a captain of artillery he left Hanoverian service after the disastrous campaign of Flanders in 1794. During the following years he became a respected military theorist, writing several books and essays on the theory and art of war. In 1801 he entered Prussian service as a lieutenant-colonel, with a patent of nobility and twice his Hanoverian salary. He taught at the War Academy in Berlin where a young officer, Karl Maria von Clausewitz, was his protégé. Senior British army officers had wanted Scharnhorst to head Britain's new military academy,[17] but the invitation was not extended because of growing friction between Britain and Prussia in 1805, when Napoleon had offered Hanover to Prussia to purchase its neutrality. Scharnhorst rose rapidly to the rank of major-general. In 1806, when Chief of Staff to the Prussian army commander, the Duke of Brunswick, he suffered the frustration of having his advice ignored, and endured the anguish of witnessing the débâcle which followed. At the beginning of that fateful campaign Scharnhorst had written prophetically: 'What ought to be done, I know only too well; what is going to be done, only the gods know!'[18]

The Prussian army of 1806, which Napoleon had been able to defeat so swiftly and utterly, was still the army of Frederick the Great, looking backward to the glories of those days. The military hierarchy and staff structure, too, were relics of the Seven Years War, having various councils and civilian departments, each with an independent voice in its sphere of army activity and each outside the control of the army commander or his chief of staff (who had only an administrative or advisory role). In fact the anatomy of the Prussian army command structure in 1806 was identical with that of the British army throughout the Napoleonic period.

With the help of Gneisenau, Scharnhorst convinced King Frederick William that the old system had to be reformed drastically. The King established the post of Minister of War and a General Staff office for the army. Essentially all officers of the General Staff were obliged to undergo a uniform course of staff training so that they would all be able to understand the new requirements for the method of operation of the chief of staff function within the army. They were taught logistics, movement, supply, all the modern theories of tactics, strategy, and planning, and to use maps in the way Napoleon did. This training was eventually extended down to regimental staff level, producing in the army a large body of staff officers skilled in the application of Scharnhorst's innovations. Every staff officer in the Prussian army was assigned specific duties, but also understood his function in relation to the army as a whole. In contrast to the practice of other armies of the period, the Prussian staff officer's duties were not shared by different departments and civilians, all of whom would in turn have had assistants and aides. The arrangements in other armies were cumbersome, inefficient and prone to break down under stress. The staff of the Army of the Lower Rhine was lean and correspondingly efficient. There were only fifty-eight staff officers in Blücher's army, serving under the orders of the commander's Chief of Staff, Gneisenau (whose title translated as Quartermaster-General and Chief of Staff of the Army, but was usually referred to as the Chief of the Staff).

As Chief of Staff Gneisenau had a unique status. Unlike his French or British counterparts, Berthier (or Soult) and De Lancy, who simply transmitted the commander's orders, Gneisenau and his corps chiefs of staff held dual authority with the commander. It was the chief of staff's job to plan and advise on strategy, move the army or corps, and plan an attack. Gneisenau had staff attached as additional adjutants to the corps and brigade headquarters within his army to ensure that commanders fully understood and complied with their orders.

The Prussian army of 1815 facing Napoleon was vastly different from the antiquated force he had so easily overawed at Jena in 1806. It was an army which could look back to a victory over Napoleon at Laon in March 1814, less than a year earlier. No more would Prussian troops present themselves in static lines as targets for French corps-level tactics. As a consequence of the reforms of Scharnhorst, Gneisenau and Yorck the Prussians now had more sophisticated methods and a superior organization. In the tactical sense, they could do everything the French could do, but more efficiently: their skirmishers were rifle-armed and more numerous, and were closely supported by assault columns, cannon and cavalry; and all at brigade level. Further, the Prussian army was inspired, not by a mental construct such as *élan*, but by one of the most potent spurs to sustained violence – revenge. The honour of Prussian arms, lost at Jena, would be restored in Belgium.

The commander of the Anglo-Allied forces in Belgium was Field Marshal Sir Arthur Wellesley, Duke of Wellington, and second son of the Earl of Mornington, an Anglo-Irish peer. Wellington was 46 years old in 1815, the same age as Napoleon. His rapid rise in rank in the earlier part of his military career was facilitated by his ability to take advantage of the purchase system for obtaining commission and advancement which operated throughout the period in the British army. By this system an interested gentleman could buy a commission and after serving the minimum stipulated period at that grade could buy the next higher grade, and so on up to general officer, which was gained by appointment on the basis of seniority. The idea behind the system was that an officer who had invested capital in his career would take an interest in it and make it his profession. Occasionally an ageing officer, to fund his retirement, would sell his commission at an inflated price to a rich young officer who wished to accelerate his advancement.

Obviously such a system was unlikely to produce a competent body of officers. It attracted for the most part rich dandies who wanted a smart uniform to be seen in, but did not want to be involved in the sordid business of fighting or learn the mechanics of their profession. Many officers had to pay their senior NCOs to teach them drill, the use of weapons and how to give orders. Inept second, third or subsequent sons, disinherited from their family estates by primogeniture, would thus come into command of regiments, while experienced officers of merit who lacked the funds would be denied promotion.

Arthur Wellesley was a rare exception who, although he took advantage of the purchase system to rise from ensign to lieutenant-colonel in seven years, was nevertheless a true professional. His first active command was in the ill-fated expedition to Flanders in 1794-5 under the Duke of York. Wellesley concluded this campaign commanding a brigade and recorded experiences almost identical with those of the then Captain Scharnhorst. Wellesley's often-quoted remark was that he had learned nothing '...except what one ought not to do, and that is always something'. In 1798 he accepted a post in India where his elder brother was Governor-General, and rose to major-general. His experience of campaigning in India with its difficult terrain of deserts, jungles, mountains and rivers (given to rapid flooding in the monsoon season) taught him important lessons in logistics and the husbanding of his forces. In India reinforcements were hard to come by in the field, and so too was battle experience, for heavy losses meant a long, laborious retirement and a lengthy period of obtaining and training recruits. Wellesley learned to be solicitous of the welfare of his valuable men. He made certain that they were well supplied with all the 'necessaries'. He made it his business to know all he could of his craft: the weight a man could comfortably carry on his back, the number of wagons needed for a given task, the amount of fodder required to sustain a given number of horses for a given time. Wellesley came to understand the logistics of moving an army through hostile terrain better than any of his British contemporaries. Certainly he made errors; but, as he said, the important thing was to learn from them. He gained his military reputation in India at the Battles of Seringapatam in 1799, and Assaye and Argaum in 1803, in which his awareness of ground aided his victories. Wellington explained the diligent, ground up method by which he gained his ability to command men in the field:

'One must understand the mechanism and the power of the individual soldier, then that of a company, a battalion, a brigade and so on, before one can venture to group divisions and move an army. I believe I owe most of my success to the attention I always paid to the inferior part of tactics as a regimental officer. There are few men in the Army who knew these details better than I did; it is the foundation of all military knowledge.'[19]

From 1805 to 1807 Wellesley was back in England, where he was given command of a battalion in the south-east during the invasion scare. In 1807, in command of a division, he took part in the expedition to neutralize the Danish fleet and was appointed Chief Secretary for Ireland. In 1808 he was promoted to lieutenant-general and sent out with an expeditionary force to Portugal. There he inflicted a defeat on the French at Rolica, but was unable to follow it up because he was superseded in command by two lacklustre generals. Three days later, however, Wellesley again commanded a force at Vimeiro because his superiors had elected to spend the night aboard ship. Again, he inflicted a resounding defeat on the French, but could not follow it up because his two superior officers arrived on the scene. In this instance the senior British general, instead of exploiting the victory and seeking the capture or destruction of the French, agreed – against Wellington's advice – to negotiate the infamous Convention of Cintra by which the beaten French were actually transported back to France under arms aboard British ships. When outrage at home resulted in both his seniors being called back to face a commission of inquiry, Wellesley was caught in the same net. He was later exonerated, though, and returned to the Peninsula in overall command of the Anglo-Portuguese forces in place of General Moore, who had died during his retreat to Corunna.

Wellesley's great administrative abilities now came to the fore. Taking the creaking, Frederickian, traditional British army under firm control, he turned it into an efficient, responsive fighting force which defeated one French force after another, damaging in the process the reputations of many of Napoleon's best marshals. Wellesley was wise in using terrain to advantage, and that of the Peninsula, although rugged and sparse, was more congenial than that of India, where the 'Sepoy General' had become adept at moving through inhospitable territory inhabited by a hostile population. In the Peninsula, Wellington, as we will now call him, had the advantage of a population that was not only friendly to him but was in arms against the French. He appreciated the value of these allies and advocated the secondment of British officers to instruct Spanish and Portuguese soldiers in his tactics.

Before Wellington could defeat the French in Iberia, though, he had to do battle with the British War Office. The British army of the period was run by a daunting tangle of military, civilian and political departments. The army was one entity, but its ordnance another. Ordnance comprised artillery (manufacture, transport and manning), small-arms ammunition production and the Royal Engineers and Corp of Sappers and Miners. Ordnance was as distinct from and independent of the army as was the Royal Navy. It had its own commander, a political appointee, who assigned guns, gunners, ammunition and engineers for the assistance of army commanders (see chart). An ordnance officer was appointed to army headquarters and, should a matter arise which conflicted with the officer's standing orders from the Ordnance Board, he would be required to write to the Board for clarification before complying. The degree of local initiative taken on these matters would depend on the character of the officer and his relationship with the commander.

The Commander-in-Chief of all British land forces, appointed by King George, was Frederick Augustus, Duke of York, the King's second son. He was assisted by a military secretary, the Quartermaster-General, and the Adjutant-General, whose roles were to provide him with a staff, and arrange for troop movements, supply and routes.[20] As an example, the Adjutant-General would designate a regiment to go abroad, the Quartermaster-General would designate the route of march and port of embarkation, the military secretary would apply to the Navy for transport over the sea, and the civil department would approve the arrangements. The authority for political direction in military affairs and the appointment of field commanders fell to either the Secretary of State for War or the Secretary of State at War, depending on whether the country were actually at war at the time.

The complications of the administration of the British army must have seemed infuriatingly Gordian to the straightforward military minds of field commanders such as Wellington. The funding of his army was supervised by the Treasury Department through the Paymaster-General. The Treasury Department also appointed an Auditor-General to supervise the Commissary in Chief who in turn appointed his own men to the headquarters and divisional staffs to arrange contracts of supply. These men issued and paid for all manner of supplies, wagons, food and so forth, but were not directly responsible to the field commander. Medical services were under a Medical Board which was divided into three parts. The first was the Apothecary-General whose post was hereditary, a Royal Warrant having been granted to an ancestor of his by George II to be '...the perpetual furnisher, with remainder to his heirs, of all medicines necessary for the general land forces of Great Britain'.[21] If this cosy monopolistic arrangement seems a virtual guarantee of inefficiency, in another way the rest of the Medical Board, the Physician-General and the Surgeon-General, presented a worse picture. These two departments fought an internecine bureaucratic war over the proper demarcation of their roles and duties. The whole system was a clerical nightmare and Wellington must have been

Right: Napoleon; print after Meissonier showing the Emperor's escort and Imperial aide-de-camp (Philip J. Haythornthwaite collection).

Below: Napoleon; print after Meissonier showing Napoleon with his entourage moving along with a column of infantry. (Author's collection)

Right: A rare eye-witness sketch of the Battle of Ligny. St. Amand is in flames; the hamlet of Petite St. Amand can be glimpsed through the smoke, with the conflagration of Ligny at the top right. In the foreground the Young Guard is marching to the attack. Napoleon can be seen in silhouette on the height above Ligny, with the Old Guard about to assault that town. (Author's collection).

Below: A view by the same artist of the Battle of Ligny; the Prussians can be seen falling back to Brye, while in the distance the spire of Sombreffe can be seen. Girard's troops are attacking from Wagnelée, and the Prussians are falling back to escape encirclement, the French having just broken through their centre (Author's collection).

Opposite page, bottom: Brunswick troops in action at Quatre Bras; they are fighting in line with their right on the Bossu wood, which loops around behind them. In the background the Duke of Brunswick falls from his horse mortally wounded (after Richard Knötel).

Left: Louis XVIII; engraving after Isabey. Louis, trying to mimic Napoleon, took to wearing epaulettes on his coats and adopted a military bearing (Philip J. Haythornthwaite collection).

Left: Tsar Alexander; engraving by H. Meyer from a drawing taken during his trip to Britain in 1814 (Philip J. Haythornthwaite collection.

Right: Emperor Francis II
(Francis I of Austria);
engraving by Meyer after A.
Dumont (Philip J.
Haythornthwaite collection).

Right: King Frederick
William III of Prussia;
engraved in 1814 by Blood
after I. Bolt (Philip J.
Haythornthwaite collection).

Left: King William I of the United Netherlands; unsigned engraving published in 1815 (Philip J. Haythornthwaite collection).

Left: The Crown Prince of Orange; engraving after Joseph Oderaere (Philip J. Haythornthwaite collection) Right: Lord Castlereagh; engraving by T. W. Harland after Lawrence (Philip J. Haythornthwaite collection)

Left: Prince Metternich; engraving by T. W. Harland after Lawrence (Philip J. Haythornthwaite collection)

Left: The arch-traitor Talleyrand; engraving by Engleton after Gérard (Philip J. Haythornthwaite collection)
Right: The Duke of Wellington; engraving by W. Say after Thomas Phillips (Philip J. Haythornthwaite collection)

Left: The Comte d'Artois. Print after John Kay, made during Artois' residence in Edinburgh. Artois (right) is wearing the French royalist uniform with the cross of St. Esprit; the figure on the left wearing a British general officer's uniform is Lord Adam Gordon, commander-in-chief of forces in Scotland (Philip J. Haythornthwaite collection).

Right: Fouché the betrayer (Philip J. Haythornthwaite collection).

Right: Marshal Ney; by Gérard (Author's collection).

Left: Field Marshal Prince
Blücher von Wahlstadt;
engraving by T. W. Harland
after F. C. Gröger.
Above: Napoleon at Juvisy,
30 March 1814, ten miles
from Paris, is told by General
Belliard of the impending
surrender of the capital.
(Author's collection).
Right: The 'turncoat'
Marshal Soult; print after
Rouillard.

Left: Major-General Baron Constant Rebecque; Chief-of-Staff of Allied I Corps; engraving after Hofmeister (Philip J. Haythornthwaite collection).

Left: Lieutenant-General Baron de Perponcher-Sedlnitzky, the commander of the 2nd Division, who with General Constant de Rebecque disregarded Wellington's order to abandon Quatre Bras (Author's collection).

Right: The Prince of Saxe-Weimar, commander of 1 Brigade of Perponcher's division (Author's collection).

Right: Lieutenant General Baron de Chassé, commander of the Netherlands 3rd Division. His masterly use of Krahmer's horse battery and Detmer's brigade in repulsing part of the Imperial Guard's attack in the last stages of Waterloo was acknowledged in writing by Lord Rowland Hill on 20 June 1815 (Author's collection).

Left: The Duke of Brunswick; after Ackermann, 1819 (Philip J. Haythorn-thwaite collection)

tempted at times to take a sharp Alexandrian sword to it; but in fact he found himself answerable to a score of civil servants and others, and was sometimes unable to function because of the unwillingness of a departmental officer to interpret his standing orders without specific approval from Britain.

Such was the parlous state of the British military establishment of the period that, without Wellington's rise to the position of foremost British land commander, it is most doubtful whether Britain would have attained the military pre-eminence she was to enjoy for nearly a century. In the Peninsula Wellington was able to wrestle with military administration until he had managed to make it reasonably compliant to his will. Distance from Britain and the delays and difficulties of travel were exploited by him. He arranged, for example, to have obstructive departmental representatives left at cities many miles from his headquarters so that an 'acting representative' more amenable to his wishes would have to be found.

Staff duties at Wellington's Peninsula headquarters were divided between the departments of the Adjutant-General and the Quartermaster-General, and the functions of each were supposed to be clearly defined. The Quartermaster-General's department allocated quarters, routes of march, and conveyance, while the Adjutant-General's handled equipment, discipline, intelligence gathering, and prisoners of war. Wellington kept both departments under firm control, but thanks to the ability of his QMG, Sir George Murray, that department absorbed much of the AG's duties. Attached to Murray and his counterpart were the inevitable and numerous aides: Assistant-Quartermasters and Adjutants-General (AQMGs and AAGs in military jargon), who in turn were assisted by deputy assistants, or DAQMGs and DAAGs. These aides were generally drawn from the regiments on the recommendation of the officer requiring them, normally with little or no pertinent training or preparation for their new duties. The QMG and AG assigned deputies and assistant deputies to the divisions and brigades to facilitate the transmission of their orders, but the effectiveness of the aides was hampered by their lack of staff training. General Le Marchant had helped set up the first royal military college in 1802, but by 1815 only 4 per cent of army officers had passed through it.

Wellington caustically summed up the administrative situation in a classic letter to the War Office (with copies to a host of other departments):

'Gentlemen: Whilst marching to Portugal to a position which commands the approach to Madrid and the French forces, my officers have been diligently complying with your request which has been sent by H.M. ship from London to Lisbon and then by despatch rider to our headquarters. We have enumerated our saddles, bridles, tents, and tent poles, and all manner of sundry items for which His Majesty's Government holds me accountable. I have despatched reports on the character, wit, spleen of every officer. Each Item and every farthing has been accounted for, with two regrettable exceptions for which I beg you your indulgence. Unfortunately, the sum of one shilling and ninepence remains unaccounted for in one infantry battalion's petty cash and there has been a hideous confusion as to the number of jars of raspberry jam issued to one cavalry regiment during a sandstorm in western Spain. This reprehensible carelessness may be related to the pressure of circumstances since we are at war with France, a fact which may come as a bit of a surprise to you gentlemen in Whitehall. This brings me to my present purpose, which is to request elucidation of my instructions from His Majesty's Government, so that I may better understand why I am dragging an army over these barren plains. I construe that perforce it must be one of the alternative duties, as given below. I shall pursue one with the best of my ability but I cannot do both. 1. To train an army of uniformed British clerks in Spain for the benefit of the accountants and copy-boys in London, or perchance, 2. To see to it that the forces of Napoleon are driven out of Spain.'[22]

Through the force of his personality, reinforced by the political and popular support his victories attracted, Wellington won his battle with Whitehall; his approach to combat in the military sphere was no less deliberate or self-assured. Noting the way in which Napoleon had inflicted devastating defeats on the continental nations with his strategy of outmanoeuvring them, Wellington had stated at the outset of the Peninsula struggle:

'...they [the French] may overwhelm me, but I don't think they will out-manoeuvre me. First, because I am not afraid of them, as everybody else seems to be; and secondly, because if what I hear of their system of manoeuvre, is true, I think it is a false one as against steady troops. I suspect all the continental armies were more than half-beaten before the battle was begun – I at least, will not be frightened beforehand.'[23]

Wellington's weapon, the British army of the period, was composed of regiments of from one to three battalions (although two was normal). The terms regiment and battalion were loosely interchangeable in the British army. Usually only one battalion of a regiment went to war, while the second served as a reservoir of replacements for the first and was consequently weak in strength and lacking in experienced men. Ten companies comprised a British battalion, eight of the line and two flank – one grenadier and one light. Companies had a nominal strength of 100, but most seldom mustered more than 40 to 50 in Wellington's time, with the exception of those of the Guards, light infantry, and Highland regiments, which often approached full strength.

British infantry fought in a two-deep line as opposed to the customary three-deep line of the continental armies. This was due more to lack of numbers than tactical intention. A third rank was normally only possible to form at the expense of the length of a unit's frontage.

The soldiers of the British line were armed with a smooth-bore musket commonly known as the 'Brown Bess'. Because of the lack of spin on the projectile, the path of any given ball was unpredictable; their effectiveness lay in their use in mass. About 100 yards was a good range, although the balls would still cause casualties at 200, and the odd spent ball might kill at 300. A test was carried out at the Tower armouries on a target six feet high and 50 yards long, representing a battalion of foot, and one the same length but eight feet six inches high for cavalry. At 100 yards, 75 per cent of a volley registered as hits on the infantry target and 82 per cent on the cavalry. At 200 yards the figures were 37 and 50 per cent respectively; and at 300 yards only 18 and 29 per cent. Of course these test volleys were fired under ideal conditions, in perfect weather and without the stress of battle.

The round lead ball fired by these muskets was not a 'humane' projectile like the modern pointed bullet, nor did it lack penetrating power. Tests carried out with the ¾-ounce ball showed that at 25–100 yards it required five inches of solid oak to stop it, and at 300 yards 3 inches of oak or 18 inches of packed earth. Wounds inflicted by a musket-ball in the trunk or head were almost always fatal (except from a spent ball), while a wound to an arm or leg bone usually resulted in amputation. Canister, larger than musket-balls, caused horrific damage, smashing off arms and legs of men and horses, literally cutting them to pieces.

The rifle used by the British troops and their Hanoverian allies was the Baker. Its spirally grooved barrel imparted spin to the bullet, giving it a deadly accuracy. It had a shorter barrel, and sights and could be set to kill at 300 yards. Also it allowed its user the great advantage of cover in that it could be loaded and fired from a prone position.

Light infantry tactics had been pioneered by Lieutenant-General Sir John Moore, who was killed at Corunna in 1809. In 1815 many regiments were designated light infantry and as such they moved more quickly than a regular line regiment, fought in skirmish order when required, were more selective in their recruiting, and were deemed élite units. These formations were supplemented by companies of the 95th Rifle Regiment. The 95th comprised three battalions, but was generally parcelled out among the brigades. Like the German *Jäger*, the 95th wore a dark-green uniform and their equipment was black; they were armed with the Baker rifle. These units were not copied from the Prussians, but were the result of indirect

German influence. During the War of American Independence King George hired many mercenaries from the German States. The rifle-armed *Jäger* units among these mercenaries inspired the British army to adopt camouflage clothing, black equipment, and the use of rifle-armed flank companies to counter American sharpshooters. In turn the success of these British light troops in America influenced the development of similar units in Prussia. General Scharnhorst, architect of Prussian military reform and the man Britain had wanted to run its military academy, wrote in a paper that: 'The English recognized that they lacked the skill for dispersed fighting, particularly in broken terrain. Each battalion was, therefore, given a light (flank) company.'[24] In introducing rifle-armed light troops, General Moore may have been influenced by what he saw during his service in America, and in so doing he rendered a great service to his army and to his successor as Britain's premier fighting general, Wellington.[25]

Wellington's artillery was of the same type as the French, but of a smaller calibre, and his batteries were smaller than either the French or Prussian, having six pieces to their eight. Guns and gunners were under the control of the Master General of the Ordnance. The munitions ranged from ordinary shot to secret weapons. The various weights of roundshot could achieve different velocities and varying ranges, depending on the number of bounces a shot might take. It was possible for a shot to pass through several files of men, reducing many to pulp, then bounce and repeat the carnage in another file until spent. Common shell consisted of shot that had been hollowed out, filled with gunpowder and fuzed. The gun would be aimed by a sighter and its firing would (ideally) ignite the fuze which was timed to explode the shell at its desired point of impact, showering deadly metal fragments over the enemy. Canister was fired at close range and caused tremendous damage. Carcase was an incendiary shell filled with a solidified mixture of pitch, tar, sulphur and other volatile substances, usually fired from a howitzer, a short-barrelled gun with a high trajectory. The howitzer fired carcase and spherical case into troop formations, woods, over walls and into buildings.

Spherical case was one of the secret weapons available to Wellington in 1815. Invented by Lieutenant Henry Shrapnel, RA, and first used in 1803, this half-hollow shell packed with musket-balls and powder would be fuzed to explode above enemy troop formations, with the intended devastating effect. Wellington had come to appreciate the value of this new munition in the Peninsula.

The other secret weapon was the rocket, which had been used to great effect in 1807 during the siege of Copenhagen and at Leipzig in 1813. A rocket troop was mobile, like the horse artillery, firing their rockets from a variety of tripods and launchers. Rocket warheads ranged in size from small to a massive 32-pound charge, and included explosive, shrapnel and incendiary variants. At Leipzig the rocket battery commanded by Captain Bogue opened fire on an advancing French division. The French had no inkling of what to expect from the unconventional battery when suddenly out of the blue a flame appeared travelling towards them at an incredible speed, followed by others, all within seconds. A volley of six 32pdr rockets exploded over the division, showering the dense formations of men with canister balls. Lieutenant Strangeways recorded that '... the column was blown asunder like an ant-heap'. The Russian General Wittgenstein, aghast at the sinister flight of the rockets and the carnage of the massacre of the French division, wrote of the rockets: 'They look as if they were made in Hell, and surely are the devil's own artillery. It was beyond any hope to expect these Frenchmen to advance into this unholy barrage'. Rockets remained an unstable and marginal form of artillery during the Napoleonic Wars, but when they worked, as at Leipzig, their effect was out of all proportion to their size.

Wellington's third arm was his cavalry, comprising light and heavy dragoons. The British cavalry of 1815 was well drilled, but had little experience of battle. The majority of veteran troopers had been discharged in 1814, and there had been much movement of officers between regiments through commission purchases and an influx of new officers. The British Government was reluctant to let cavalry go abroad, preferring to have them available at home for policing and customs duties. With the exception of the Household units, British cavalry was hobbled by this dual role which inhibited their training and, together with other factors, made them most unreliable in battle.[26] Wellington mistrusted his cavalry which, once launched, tended to career across the battlefield out of control, its ill-trained officers leading their men as though at a fox-hunt, disregarding order, discipline and objectives. Wellington once wrote to Lord Hill of the cavalry's poor performance in battle: 'It is occasioned by a trick our officers have acquired of galloping at everything, and then galloping back as fast as they gallop at the enemy.'[27]

Further, there was no clear division of roles recognized by the British cavalry as there was in the cavalry of the continental armies. Officers of both light and heavy cavalry tended to see themselves solely in the undeniably glorious role of leader of the charge of the heavies, with horses belly to the earth and sabres outstretched. More mundane but no less important activities such as scouting, reconnaissance and screening were neglected in favour of making contact and conducting all-out charges. Fortunately, within the Anglo-Allied army in Belgium, Wellington had many experienced King's German Legion and Netherlands cavalry officers who carried out these other aspects of horse soldiering for him with considerable skill.

There were, of course, British cavalry commanders of great merit, true professionals like Wellington himself: the Earl of Uxbridge, Lord Combermere and the late General Le Marchant. But these officers could only do so much with a generally neglected cavalry arm which was kept weak by government policy, the purchase system and the absence of a proper training school. In this period, only the Household cavalry had a riding school; and it was this, together with its status, better grade of recruits and constant training, which gave it an edge on other mounted regiments.

The tactics employed by Wellington in the campaign of 1815 had their origins, not unnaturally, in the Peninsula, where he had learned what to do in fighting the French. In Iberia, faced with greatly superior French forces, he had been obliged to develop defensive strategies and tactics while he patiently built up an Anglo-Portuguese army capable of offensive operations. He evolved his classic defensive battle, in which he obliged the French to attack him in a position of his choosing. Ideally, he would have his infantry drawn up behind a low ridge, or even a slight fold in the ground, lying out of sight. In this way they were well protected from the French preparatory artillery barrage. Gunners of the day had to aim by sight, so not having a visible target meant firing blind or not at all. Therefore most of the French solid shot would pass overhead or hit the forward slope and bounce over, while their shells would largely burst on the forward slope. This trick often spared Wellington's men the heavy losses and demoralization of standing in the open being shot at by artillery.

After the preliminary barrage the French would advance and Wellington would deploy his light infantry well in front of his lines, usually fronted by several companies of riflemen in skirmishing order. His better armed skirmishers would generally outshoot the French skirmishers, making the no man's land between the armies untenable for French light forces or horse artillery. Wellington's light screen would give ground slowly in the face of the advance of the French heavy assault columns, inflicting sniping casualties on them all the while. Then the light troops would disappear over the crest of the ridge. At the last moment before the French gained the crest, Wellington's line of infantry, at full strength and unshaken, would come into sight before them, advancing in complete silence. At a range of between 25 and 100 yards they would level their muskets and deliver a devastating volley into the double company fronted French columns, then with a terrible shout charge the shattered French formations with the bayonet.[28] Generally the French assault troops would rout before contact. Wellington's infantry officers would then quickly call back and re-form their men in case another volley were required. Routed French troops would be followed and subjected to harassing fire by Wellington's light troops as they recrossed no man's land.

At the first warning of an enemy cavalry attack Wellington's infantry would form squares in a chequered pattern so that the squares could support one another. Unless horse artillery were brought up, squares formed of unshaken troops were almost invulnerable to cavalry, largely because horses could not be induced to impale themselves on bayonets.[29] Wellington used his cavalry to counter-attack and maintain pressure on routed French troops. This would be followed by a general advance against the broken French force to dislodge it from its position. This technique of defensive warfare, designed to conserve his own troops and avoid battles of attrition, rewarded Wellington with almost unbroken success in the Peninsula from 1808 to 1814.

When he arrived in Portugal the British army there had operated with a brigade of two or more regiments as its largest formation. Wellington later organized divisions of several brigades, with attached artillery. He also created an élite division of light troops to act as the advance or rearguard of his army. He did not use the corps as a tactical unit, as did the French and Prussians. His creation of corps for the Anglo-Allied army in Belgium in 1815 was simply an administrative device to integrate his heterogeneous forces.

The Anglo-Portuguese army which Wellington had forged into a highly effective force was, of course, disbanded after the Peace of 1814. And since then many of his veterans had been sent to America or been disbanded, and the Duke of York's return to command of the British army had reduced Wellington's influence at Whitehall. The Anglo-Allied army of 1815 bore no resemblance to Wellington's Peninsula army,[30] and the circumscription of his authority closer to home in Belgium was a far cry from the freedom of action he had enjoyed in far-away Iberia.

Of the Anglo-Allied force, the Brunswick contingent, under its own duke, had some veterans, but were for the most part raw recruits. The tactics of the Brunswickers were the same as those of the British alongside whom they had been fighting since 1809. Brunswick light formations consisted of battalions trained along British lines and an élite *Jäger* unit armed with both rifle and musket (one for sniping and the other for more rapid fire). Brunswick cavalry were hussars with an attached squadron of lancers, and were well trained. The Nassauers under von Kruse fought in the French fashion, with a three-deep line, and using assault columns behind a skirmish screen.

The Netherlands army had adopted the British two-deep line, largely as a consequence of the influence of the Prince of Orange's experiences in British service. The majority of Netherlands officers had learned their trade all over Europe and in Spain and Russia under Napoleon and were highly experienced. Their army was very young and consisted mostly of recruits. It was made up of 38 battalions and 23 cavalry squadrons. The infantry included battalions of regular line troops, light infantry (*Jäger*), and militia. The militia was formed partly of volunteers and partly of conscripts. The Belgian components of the army, whose reliability was expected by many to be as doubtful as their loyalty to their new Dutch masters, made up only three cavalry regiments and six of the 38 infantry battalions of the Netherlands army; and in the event not one Belgian soldier deserted to the enemy.

The Anglo-Allied army numbered fewer than 30,000 British officers and men, drawn mostly from the untrained second battalions of regiments whose first battalions had gone to America. With them were 77,000 Allied soldiers: untrained Brunswick and Nassau levies, and the whole of the new United Netherlands army, whose own administration and commanders resented Wellington's overall command. From his arrival in Belgium Wellington had less than two months to form these various and contending elements into an army. It was, he said, 'An Infamous Army', of which fewer than one-third were the red-coated 'Articles' on whom he had told Mr. Creevey the outcome of the campaign would depend.

CHAPTER 6

12–14 June

'All warfare is based on deception. Therefore, when capable, feign incapacity; when active, inactivity. When near, make it appear that you are far away; when far away, that you are near. Offer the enemy a bait to lure him; feign disorder and strike him.' - Sun Tzu, *The Art of War*, c.500 BC, tr. Griffith.

Wellington and Blücher now seemed convinced that Napoleon intended to open his campaign in the south, as in 1814. The fear that he might first attack in the north, expressed by the two leaders in April and May, seemed to have receded. As their armies grew in size, and with the expectation that Austrian and Russian armies would soon close up to the French border, they looked forward to advancing into France as part of a concerted movement of about half a million Allied troops.

For this reason both the British and Prussian commanders forbade the destruction of the main and subsidiary bridges across the Sambre on their front, even in the event of an attack, for they were confident that any such attack would only be diversionary and they knew that they would need every bridge for their eventual advance into France. General Baron Behr, of The Netherlands army, commanding the Allied garrison at Mons, had requested of Wellington that he be allowed to pull down a building and a tree which were obstructing the field of fire near part of the city walls and destroy a bridge. On 11 June Wellington wrote to the Prince of Orange on this matter, 'I do not think I can authorize the destruction of the house without referring to the King... regarding the use of the bridge on the canal of Condé... Foreign officers are too apt to order measures of the kind complained of without necessity; and I shall be very obliged to your Royal Highness if you will order General Behr to allow of the use of the bridge in question by the inhabitants of the country.'[1]

Prussian senior commanders were similarly forbidding on the subject of defensive measures. Their forces were to hold the bridges on their front, but their engineers were not to destroy or even mine them. General Pirch II, commanding 2 Brigade, requested authority to destroy all secondary bridges within his sector and to mine the main Charleroi bridge. His corps commander, von Zeithen, refused permission, issuing specific orders for the bridges to be occupied only. In his General Order of 2 May Zeithen elaborated on his prohibition, 'The passages over the Sambre, within the sphere of each respective brigade, will continue to be occupied until the brigades receive orders to retire from their points of assembly.'[2]

The Anglo-Allied troops were also losing their edge. By 12 June they had spent weeks standing-to in response to false alarms, rounding up

French patrols only to return them to French territory, and carrying out the tedious daily routine of arranging their equipment ready for attack or movement. Their edge of readiness was being blunted by a growing complacency that no action was imminent. Farther back from the border area British officers cantoned comfortably in and around Brussels had more or less taken root. Captain Mercer of the Royal Horse Artillery noted in his journal that, 'Everyone breakfasted in his own apartment. At 10 a.m. watering order parade and inspection of horses, etc. Then, after visiting the billets and getting through any casual business I was at liberty, and, mounting my horse, employed the morning exploring the country. In the evening we all assembled to our social meal. Those who had been up to Brussels (or, as we used to say, 'Up to town') usually brought some news, or at least gossip.'[3]

During this period drill and training continued. The Brunswick Corps practised field manoeuvres, its élite rifle-armed *Jäger* detachment putting the recruits of the light battalions through their paces in skirmishing and marksmanship.[4] The British Guards Division at Enghien, although not on orders to move at a moment's notice, had nevertheless made provision for rapid assembly and had increased musketry practice for the recruits who made up the bulk of its light companies. Lieutenant-Colonel Macdonell of the Coldstream Guards offered his men the encouragement of an increased ration of 'liqueur' for good results. This brought down on Macdonell a mild reprimand from Wellington's Adjutant-General for expending company ammunition instead of applying by the submission of the correct signed form to Army headquarters for practice ammunition to be allotted from a separate park.[5]

Senior Allied complacency regarding the possibility of a French offensive in the north continued into June. No Allied patrols were sent into French territory despite a constant flow of intelligence indicating French troop movements near the border. With the combined Allied strength in Belgium now more than double that of the French field army, it was felt that Napoleon would not attack the Allied dispositions there. The view among the senior Allied commanders was that Napoleon would almost certainly open his campaign to the south, against Schwarzenberg. On the Franco-Belgian border the more junior Allied commanders, who would have to take the initial shock of a French attack, were understandably less sanguine.

From the pens of senior British officers on the eve of battle, there is every indication that, at least on their own front, they were confident that the initiative rested with the Allies. As late as 13 June Colonel Sir William Gomm, a staff officer with Picton's 5th Division, wrote, 'I shall be well contented to remain in Brussels till the campaign opens, but I fear we shall be pushed forward in a few days by troops arriving from England.'[6] Even on 15 June, the very day that Napoleon attacked the Prussian army, Wellington wrote to the Tsar stating that he intended to take the offensive at the end of June or the beginning of July in accordance with the agreed overall Allied plan.[7] On the same day Wellington also wrote to Metternich, discussing the proposal that, during the forthcoming invasion of France, occupied areas should be handed over to French royalist officers who would then be responsible for requisitioning supplies for the Allied armies on the authority of the King of France.[8] On the 13th Wellington wrote to General Sir Henry Clinton, commanding the British 2nd Division, to say that at the request of the divisional commanders who had served under Wellington in the Peninsula, he intended to renumber the British divisions, restoring to them their old Peninsula numbers.[9] Such a change would inevitably cause significant confusion for a period of time, and if carried out when an enemy attack was known to be imminent could well be expected to result in fatal delays in the transmission of orders and messages in the ensuing battle. That a commander of Wellington's experience should have contemplated such a major administrative reshuffle at that time is probably the strongest evidence available that the senior Allied commanders were unaware of Napoleon's true intentions for his campaign of 1815 on the eve of the opening of the campaign.

The British Prime Minister, Lord Liverpool, writing to George Canning on 13 June, expressed an appreciation of the situation formed from Wellington's reports to the Government: 'We may now be in daily expectation of hearing that the Allied armies have entered France. The operations will probably begin on the upper Rhine, as the most distant point from Paris; but we know that the Duke of Wellington and Blücher are both ready to move; and fortunately there subsists between them the most perfect union and cordiality.'[10] While there is little reason to credit a 'perfect union and cordiality' between Wellington and the Prussian commanders, it does seem that they were of one mind in their belief that Napoleon was bound to protect Paris by disposing his mobile forces south of the capital, roughly as he had done in the campaign of 1814. This crucial misapprehension was apparently fuelled by a lengthy dispatch Wellington and Blücher had received from Prince Schwarzenberg, the supreme Allied commander.

In his dispatch, Schwarzenberg mainly sought to co-ordinate the projected offensive operations of each of the Allied armies as they moved into France from the border. He favoured a concerted advance on the broadest possible front to bring the full weight of the much larger Allied forces to bear simultaneously on Napoleon's army. This strategic view, shared by the other Allied commanders, derived from several concerns: a healthy respect for the almost superhuman generalship of their adversary, a firm intention to avoid heavy casualties and a general awareness of the dangers of dependence on lines of communication which were too few or too long, such as those that had failed to sustain Napoleon's *Grande Armée* during its disastrous 'Moscow Campaign'.[11]

Although the intent of Schwarzenberg's dispatch was unarguable, it included several enclosures detailing the strengths of the Allied armies and their approximate positions. At his headquarters in Heidelberg he had developed his estimates of the positions of the massive Austrian and Russian armies, based on his optimistic interpretation of position reports, into locations on a map. Unfortunately his estimates were highly misleading. The enclosures gave Wellington and Blücher the impression that the Austrian and Russian armies would be ready to cross the French border by the end of June, a month earlier than they actually did.

Among the junior Allied officers there was concern that, the alarms of April and May having passed without incident, their superiors had allowed a prudent caution to give way to an unjustified euphoria. Even the intelligence that a French corps had been brought up from Lille and Valenciennes into the area of Maubeuge and that the French IV Corps had moved up from Metz had not had any sobering effect on the euphoria of the senior commanders. One Prussian officer who had already served in three campaigns against Napoleon and one under him felt that, so far from the initiative resting with the Allies, an attack by the French must be considered as imminent. It was not until some years later that the officer, Colonel von Clausewitz, Chief of Staff of von Thielemann's III Corps, recorded his concern that, 'From this moment onwards one could no longer count with any certainty on receiving a second warning before the outbreak of hostilities and it was therefore high time to gather forces in greater strength and to dispose them in such a manner that every corps could reach the field of battle in twenty-four hours at the outside.'[12]

Junior commanders in the Anglo-Allied forces shared Clausewitz's sense of urgency. On 9 June General Constant Rebecque, Chief of Staff of I Corps, issued orders to the Netherlands divisions to improve their preparedness. Such an order was not needed, though, at least by Lieutenant-General Baron de Perponcher-Sedlnitzky, commanding the 2nd Netherlands Division. He was disturbed by reports he had received from patrols and on 9 June issued an order of his own:

'In accordance with instructions from HRH the General-in-Chief the division must be ready to march at any moment. For this purpose His Excellency the General of Division orders every battalion, until further orders, to assemble in the cantonment of its headquarters every morning at exactly 5 o'clock and to remain there under arms till seven o'clock in the evening.

'When the commanding officer of the battalion at seven o'clock in the evening has not received further instructions, he will dismiss all to their respective cantonments until the next day. Nothing shall be left in the cantonments, all the vehicles will be packed, because at the first drumbeat all will have to march leaving nothing behind. The troops will bring their food with them and the commander of the battalion will make an equal partition of the houses nearest to the assembling point, where the cooks will prepare the meal by groups. Then the troops one fifth at a time, will be allowed to withdraw for a quarter of a hour to eat their meal.

'When the commanders of the battalions by first roll-call at 5 o'clock in the morning have ascertained that their whole battalion is present, they will have the arms piled and will instruct the men not to go far and will make sure of this by repeated roll-calls. His Excellency the General of Division orders the cantonment of the 60 horses of the Train at Reves to be evacuated and the whole company of horse artillery to be concentrated at Frasnes. The whole artillery will every morning at five o'clock get under arms and remain so until seven o'clock in the evening. One half of the horses will at five o'clock come to the [artillery] park and be put to the limbers, the guns being limbered up. Meanwhile the other half will remain in the stable harnessed to relieve the horse-teams at noon and to remain there till seven o'clock in the evening.'[13]

Perponcher's prudent soldierly reaction to the reports of his patrols would have an incalculable impact on the course of events in the days to come.

Napoleon, in his famous carriage and accompanied by his entourage, left Paris in the early hours of 12 June to join his army near the Belgian border. Arriving at Laon at midday, he was dismayed to find Marshal Grouchy there with the Reserve Cavalry Corps. Marshal Soult, apparently by a gross oversight, had neglected to issue orders for this corps to concentrate at the front. Napoleon already had reason to lament the loss of Berthier. However, upon receipt of Napoleon's peremptory order to move up, Grouchy gave his emperor no reason to regret having given him the baton, force-marching his entire corps sixty miles in 36 hours. By the night of the 14th the Reserve Cavalry was in position.

Alighting unannounced at Avesnes on the 13th, Napoleon expected to receive news that the rest of his field army had reached their allotted concentration points around Beaumont near the border, but found that this had not yet been fully accomplished. To meet the paramount need for secrecy in the build-up of his field army on the Belgian border, he had issued complex marching orders to some of his corps. While it was comparatively simple to move the three central corps in secrecy, the same could not be assumed for the convergence of units on the right and left flanks obliquely across Allied fronts toward the same place. Napoleon knew that d'Erlon's I Corps, marching eastward from the Lille-Valenciennes area, and Gérard's IV Corps, marching north-westward from Metz, would be observed. He therefore had devised elaborate plans designed to deceive the Allies into misinterpreting what they would see. Demonstrations between

Lille and the coast had given Wellington concern that the French might try to cut across his lines of communication with Ostend and Antwerp or even seize those ports which, by his secret instructions, Wellington was to hold. The movement of d'Erlon's corps was noted by the Allies, as evidenced by a letter from the Prince of Orange to d'Erlon. However, perhaps because senior Allied commanders were thinking too exclusively of their own offensive plans, d'Erlon's movement was viewed as a defensive redisposition. Gérard managed to move his corps in near secrecy by a skilful use of the difficult terrain in the vicinity of the Ardennes forest to mask his right flank.

Napoleon's orders for 14 June concerned the final groupings of the corps for the coming campaign. Reille's II Corps, the lead corps of the left wing, was to bivouack around Leer, as close to the border as possible. His corps cavalry were to watch all the border crossing points while remaining as unobtrusive as possible. The bivouacs of Reille's troops were sited so that the light of their fires would be screened by hills, ridges or woods. D'Erlon's I Corps, completing the left wing, were bivouacked at Solre and maintained the same precautions against detection. Both corps of the left were under orders to be ready to move at dawn (about 3 a.m.) on the 15th.

The centre of the army was to bivouack around Beaumont. Vandamme's III Corps would be several miles to the north, with orders to keep watch on the border. Lobau's VI Corps was positioned behind Vandamme, and the Imperial Guard Corps behind Lobau, with the Guard Cavalry south of Beaumont. The town of Beaumont itself was free of troops, except for the 1st Grenadiers of the Guard, who were to act as the Emperor's bodyguard. Beaumont had therefore become Napoleon's headquarters for the start of the campaign. Well behind Beaumont Grouchy's four reserve cavalry corps were so placed as to be able to support either of the two forward wings. Like the left, the centre was under orders to be ready to move at 3 a.m. on the 15th.

Gérard was ordered to have his corps at Philippeville by the 14th and be ready to move up with the rest of the army at dawn on the 15th. Napoleon also issued precise orders as to the supplies of ammunition and the amount of supplies of all types that were to be carried. The Engineers and bridging train were to be at the front of the army in case the bridges over the Sambre were found to have been destroyed by the Allies, as the rapid forcing of the Sambre was vital to the success of the campaign. Finally Napoleon gave instructions that all his operational orders be treated as secret, as the entire campaign would obviously be jeopardized if the Allies were to learn of his intentions.[14]

Before Napoleon left Paris he had been informed that Marshal Mortier, whom he had intended to command the Young Guard, had asked to be excused from service with the army in the campaign as he had developed a severe attack of sciatica. Whether the Marshal's infirmity was physiological or political, Napoleon would have to go into battle without his 'big mortar'.

Also before leaving Paris, Napoleon had instructed Marshal Davout to send a message to Marshal Ney, who was living at his home in the country. Napoleon's note read, 'Send for Marshal Ney and tell him that if he wishes to be present for the first battles, he ought to be at Avesnes on the fourteenth.' Ney was surprised at this offhand summons, for he had been kept away from Court since Napoleon's reinstatement as Emperor, kept away from Court and from any military involvement. However, the reaffirmation of trust implicit in the note was enough to convince Ney that Napoleon had forgiven him his gratuitous 'iron cage' remark. Without waiting for his horses or equipment to be made ready, Ney set off in his fast carriage to join the army at Avesnes, pausing only to collect his close friend and chief of staff, Colonel Heymes.

On their arrival at Avesnes Ney and Heymes found Napoleon in a garden, 'walking up and down, deep in meditation and oblivious to the fine view over the valley'. When Napoleon caught sight of the two men he was the soul of cordiality, embracing Ney and slapping Heymes on the back. He invited Ney to dinner, during which he discussed the victories he expected to win over the Allies and his optimism that the campaign would be a resounding success. What Napoleon did not discuss with Ney, however, was anything of his plans or immediate intentions; which is not surprising given that Ney had twice turned his coat. Trust betrayed is not rapidly regained; and Ney's earnestness could not force the pace. Too little time had passed since Ney had been the King's man to mollify Napoleon's prickly temperament. Ney, for his part, did not wish to risk chilling Napoleon's unexpected but welcome warmth by pressing him about the impending campaign.

It could be argued that Napoleon had decided to wait until the campaign had begun before telling Ney his plans, in case Ney should be tempted to desert with them to the enemy. It is inconceivable that Napoleon would have overlooked the matter. Perhaps he sought to humble Ney further, before bringing him dramatically into play in the opening moves of the campaign. Napoleon would certainly have wanted to make use of Ney's aggressive spirit and his power to motivate the rank and file to whom Ney had become a hero after the epic part he had played during the retreat from Moscow. Whatever the reasons, by not taking Ney into his confidence at Avesnes, Napoleon made a mistake which was to give rise to serious consequences on the road to Brussels.

The next morning, 14 June, an element of farce was added to the sad story of the Emperor and the Marshal. As part of his plan to deceive the Allies, Napoleon delayed as long as possible his departure for Beaumont. When he and his entourage abruptly left Avesnes Ney was taken by surprise. The previous evening, as he had not had the opportunity to speak privately with Napoleon, Ney had not told him that he had travelled from home without horses. Ney had assumed that he would be able to borrow or purchase mounts from the army at Avesnes. He had therefore already sent his travelling coach back home. He now found that the country around Avesnes had been heavily requisitioned of horses by the army units that had already passed through. With great difficulty he managed to find a peasant's cart and nag to transport him and Heymes to Beaumont. The delay in reaching the front in this humiliating fashion became a handicap to Napoleon's chances of success in executing his manoeuvres to gain the central position between Wellington and Blücher.

During the evening of the 14th Napoleon drew up detailed orders of march for the next day, including the objectives to be attained during the day. The Army of the North would advance in three columns, the cavalry divisions of Domon and Pajol providing a tactical screen. Domon, for example, was to '...advance along the Charleroi road'. His orders further stated that 'Patrols will be sent out in every direction to reconnoitre the country, and to capture the enemy's advance posts; each patrol will consist of not less than fifty men. Before marching off General Vandamme will make sure that the cavalry are provided with small-arms ammunition.'[15]

Reille's II Corps would lead the left wing, moving off at 3 a.m. from Solre-sur-Sambre to its first-day objective of Marchiennes by way of the bridge at Thuin. Reille's orders stated:

'He will march to the bridge at Marchiennes, and will arrange to reach that place before 9 a.m. He will cause all the bridges over the Sambre to be guarded, and will allow no-one to cross them, the piquets which he leaves will be relieved in due course by I Corps; but Count Reille will do his utmost to forestall the enemy at the bridges, in order to prevent their demolition, and especially to seize that of Marchiennes, which will enable him to cross to the other bank, and which he will arrange to have repaired if it has been damaged. At Thuin, and at Marchiennes, as well as at the villages en route, Count Reille will interrogate the inhabitants, so as to get the latest news of the enemy's situation. He will cause letters in the post-offices to be seized, and will open them, forwarding any information thus gained to the Emperor.'[16]

D'Erlon was to march his I Corps in support of Reille's II Corps and be prepared to assist them if necessary. His orders also stated:

'He will keep one cavalry brigade in [his] rear to screen himself and to keep up connection, by small posts, with Maubeuge. He will also push patrols beyond this town in the direction of Mons and Binche; they are to advance right up to the frontier so as to get news of the enemy, and are to report immediately anything [that] is ascertained ...

Count d'Erlon will occupy Thuin with a division, and if the enemy had destroyed the bridge there, it is to be repaired at once, and a bridge-head will be traced and constructed on the left bank ... The division at Thuin will be responsible also for the bridge at the Abbey at Aulne.'[17]

III Corps, under Vandamme, bivouacked on the frontier north of Beaumont, would lead the right wing and consequently had to move off first. Vandamme would advance directly on Charleroi, supported by Gérard's IV Corps marching up from Philippeville. Gérard's initial orders were later changed so that he would advance on Châtelet, some four miles downstream of Charleroi, and secure the bridge there. This would put him in a position to outflank any Prussians retiring from Charleroi. Napoleon's orders further stated:

'Lieut.-Generals Reille, Vandamme, Gérard and Pajol, will connect with one another frequently by patrols and will time their advance so as to arrive at Charleroi together, and concentrated. As far as possible, they will attach to their respective Advance Guards those officers who speak Flemish, so that they may interrogate the inhabitants and thus gain information, but these officers will give out that they merely command patrols, without alluding to the Grand Army in the rear. Lieut.-Generals Reille, Vandamme and Gérard will arrange that all the Engineers belonging to their corps march in rear of the leading Light Infantry regiment, and the Engineers will be accompanied by all necessary material for the repair of Bridges; the Lieut.-Generals will order their Engineer officers to repair all bad places [in roads and tracks], to open up all lateral communications, and to bridge those streams that would wet the infantry when fording them.'[18]

Lobau's VI Corps was to follow up and support Vandamme's III Corps: 'His orders of march will be identical with that laid down for III Corps, and the same orders will hold good for his troops.' Marshal Grouchy's Heavy Cavalry Corps would advance in support alongside the infantry columns of III and VI Corps, ready to use its weight where needed. 'Marshal Grouchy will be careful to use lateral roads for their advance, marching on each side of the main road used by the infantry, in order to avoid crowding; and also that his cavalry may preserve a better formation.'[19] The third part of the army, the reserve, consisted of the Imperial Guard Corps, led by the Young Guard Division, followed by the Middle and Old Guard, and finally the Guard Cavalry. To help ensure a swift seizure of the north bank of the Sambre, Napoleon adjusted his orders so that, 'The Marines, the Sappers of the Guard, and the Sappers of the reserve, will follow the leading regiment of III Corps (d'Erlon). Lieut.-Generals Rogniant and Haxo will march at their head .... If the enemy is encountered they will not be engaged, but Generals Rogniant and Haxo will use them for bridging rivers, constructing bridge-heads, opening up communications, etc.'[20]

Concerning himself, Napoleon stipulated that 'The Emperor will accompany the Advanced Guard on the Charleroi road. The Lieut.-Generals will take care to keep his Majesty informed of their various movements, and to transmit all information which they happen to collect.'[21] Napoleon also set down extensive orders as to the composition of the bridging trains with their pontoon boats, dividing them into three groups following the columns and capable of being called up quickly if needed by the engineers.

In his efforts to forestall any hindrance to the smooth unfolding of his plan, Napoleon gave orders concerning the impedimenta of his army. No vehicle of any type – baggage cart, ambulance, wagon or officer's carriage – beyond those allowed for – would be permitted to accompany the columns. The Army of the North's objective for 15 June was to concentrate around Charleroi, cross the Sambre unhindered, and advance beyond it sufficiently to put both Allied armies off balance before they could manoeuvre to support each other. Napoleon knew that time would be precious. All baggage without exception was placed under the Director-General of Transport, and no wagon could leave its assigned position without a signed chit. The orders read: 'The Emperor commands that all transport vehicles found in Infantry, Cavalry, or Artillery columns are to be burned, as well as the vehicles in the baggage column which leave their allotted place and thus change the order of march, unless they have previously obtained special permission to do so from the Director-General of Transport. For this purpose a detachment of 50 Military Police will be placed under the orders of the Director-General of Transport; and the latter officer is personally responsible, as well as the officers of the Military Police and also the Military Police themselves, for the due execution of these arrangements on which the success of the Campaign may depend.'[22]

With his copious and explicit orders drafted, copied and dispatched from headquarters by 2 a.m. on the 15th, Napoleon was content with his arrangements. Starting at 3 a.m., at half-hourly intervals, the corps of his army would converge from their points of departure, spread over a 20-mile arc, on the vicinity of Charleroi, ready for battle. Tactical surprise was essential to catch the enemy unaware and effect the crossing of the Sambre with little resistance, and most importantly little loss of time. By the end of the 15th, Napoleon hoped to be in a position to decide his next move. If Blücher should make a stand behind the Sambre he would fight him. If he fell back before the French advance, Napoleon might decide to bring Wellington's Anglo-Allied army to battle and capture Brussels, which Napoleon viewed as a strategic prize of great political value.

In all these detailed and comprehensive orders, however, there was not one word concerning Marshal Ney. Napoleon obviously intended to open the campaign without Ney's involvement, even though he would have been perfectly suited to a task such as the seizure of enemy-held bridges, especially if Charleroi were held in force by the enemy. Ney had in fact received his title, Duc d'Elchingen, in 1805 for his key role in the dramatic capture of the vital bridge and town of that name held by a heavy force of Austrians. It is ironic, perhaps even tragic – at least from his own perspective – that a man like Napoleon, whose genius in military matters was unparalleled in his time, should have been so prone to disastrous errors of judgement in his decisions as to whom to trust and whom to distrust. Here was Napoleon on the eve of launching the most crucial campaign of his career. With him, incompetently or traitorously filling the key post of chief of staff, was Soult, who would have had Napoleon shot upon his return from Elba, and whom the rank and file in their good common sense loathed. Left marooned at Avesnes was Ney, next to Napoleon himself the most important man in the French Army, who was truly his emperor's man, and whom the army loved. Like a hero of classical Greek tragedy, Napoleon allowed his pride to overwhelm his judgement, out of pique he left the indispensable Ney to find his way forward in a farm cart, just as he had left the incomparable Murat idle in Marseilles.

Throughout 14 June, as 120,000 French soldiers assembled with their attendant horses, wagons and *matériel*, not even Napoleon's vigilance could prevent some intelligence of their presence from reaching the enemy. Indeed, the forward elements of the Prussian army were within gunshot of the border in front of the French forces. Across this narrow middle ground on the night of 12th/13th, a French soldier – not Marshal Ney, as Napoleon might have feared, but a drum-major – deserted, being taken at an outpost of the Prussian 1 Brigade, I Corps. This man was interrogated by the commander of the brigade, General von Steinmetz, at his headquarters at Fontaine-l'Evêque. The deserter revealed that Napoleon had been at Maubeuge with his Guard and Reille's II Corps and that he intended to attack the Prussians on either the 13th or the 14th. Steinmetz immediately passed this information to his superior, General von Ziethen, at I Corps headquarters in Charleroi. During the 12th Ziethen had been receiving much information concerning the French forces across the border, most of it false information generated by the French themselves, such as 'King Murat' being at Avesnes and 38,000 National Guardsmen without artillery sighted between Givet and Maubeuge.[23] Evidently Ziethen was able to discern the wheat of truth among the chaff of spurious reports, for he ordered his brigade commanders to draw in their troops, leaving only sufficient exposed forward to hold the vital Sambre bridges. He intended to be able to assemble his corps in battle order at the shortest possible notice, which is all he would receive if Napoleon were indeed across the river preparing to attack.

The system of communication between the Anglo-Allied and Prussian armies was still operating well. Zeithen received an accurate report from van Merlen's cavalry posted in the vicinity of Mons that there were now only weak French outposts in front of The Netherlands positions and that the cloudy sky was underlit by the glow of hundreds of watch-fires in the area of Beaumont, Marpent and Solre-sur-Sambre.[24]

Taking these reports, together with one from Colonel von Clausewitz that two divisions of Gérard's IV Corps had definitely been sighted moving from Sedan and Mezières towards Philippeville, General Gneisenau grew alarmed. He now had evidence of at least three different French corps, I, II and IV, converging on an area in front of thinly deployed Prussian forces which were more or less papering over the gap between the Prussian and Anglo-Allied armies.

At Mons Major-General von Dornberg was in command of the Hanoverian cavalry, with responsibility for outpost duties and the collation of intelligence on the border. Dornberg had been a colonel in Jérôme Bonaparte's Westphalian army until he switched allegiance to the Allies in 1813, when he was appointed to his Hanoverian command. It was Dornberg who had relayed Merlen's information to Ziethen and to Wellington at Brussels. At about this time Dornberg received vital information from a French royalist agent and sent a précis of what he felt were the pertinent facts in a letter to Wellington which he dispatched at 3 p.m: 'My Lord, I have just now got the following intelligence, which I copy literally [that is, in the original French]: "The headquarters-staff of the 1st Corps d'observation is en route to the Sambre... General d'Erlon is in attendance. Bonaparte's military kitchen was yesterday at Avesnes; he had not arrived himself. The troops are concentrating near Maubeuge and Beaumont. I estimate the army to be about 80,000 men around Beaumont and 100,000 men between there and Philippeville. Every division has six or eight [artillery] pieces. The three cavalry divisions attached to the I Corps d'observation from Cambrai and Valenciennes have passed behind Avesnes and through the town making for Maubeuge ... There are less than 100 men at Bavay."' [25]

Throughout history, when, at the crux of great events, the weight of decision has fallen on an individual, some have borne it well and have been accorded the laurels of heroism; others have failed and been branded traitors or made scapegoats. Had Dornberg simply passed on verbatim everything the agent had told him, perhaps with a covering note, he might not have become a hero, but he would certainly have avoided the ignominious obscurity into which he was cast after the event. What he had not seen fit to include from the original was the conclusion that from the dispositions of Napoleon's troops it was certain that they were heading for the Charleroi bridges and the broad paved highway, the *Chaussée*, which ran between the Allied armies straight to Brussels. More importantly he failed to advise Wellington that the French agent had been sent by Wellington's man behind the lines, his Chief of Intelligence, Colonel Grant.

Grant enjoyed Wellington's complete trust; like his chief, he was a veteran of the Peninsula, where he had acted in a similar role. Wellington had expressly asked the Duke of York's permission to appoint Grant as his chief intelligence officer, and had sent him, as a spy in uniform, into France where he had been able to make effective use of French royalist agents provided by the Comte d'Artois. Grant's orders were to inform Wellington if Napoleon approached the border, the strength of troops Napoleon had with him, and the route by which he intended to cross the border.

Unfortunately, Dornberg, although an important intelligence officer under Wellington's command, had no knowledge of Colonel Grant's mission or of the importance Wellington placed on information from Grant. For some time Dornberg had been receiving a mass of information from Frenchmen calling themselves agents, some of which was accurate; but much of it was false information from bogus agents or fiction provided by enterprising men who saw an opportunity to make money. It is evident that Dornberg did not view Grant's message as distinct from the run of doubtful material he had been seeing. Accordingly, he had sent Grant's agent back to him to convey Dornberg's apparently arbitrary opinion that the Charleroi route was highly unlikely. In his letter to Wellington, in place of the vital part of Grant's information, Dornberg included a paragraph to the effect that the French cavalry pickets in front of Valenciennes had been withdrawn and that the garrisons of Lille and Dunkirk had marched out and in passing Valenciennes had cried out 'Vive l'Empereur!'. Dornberg added as a postscript, '*Le Moniteur* has not arrived, but your Lordship will have seen in the *Journal de Paris* that Bonaparte left it in the night from the 11th to the 12th instant.'[26] Dornberg may have misapprehended a crucial report from his commander's agent in the field, but at least he had read the enemy's newspapers.

Dornberg's letter reached Wellington at about 9 p.m. on the 14th. Anglo-Allied Headquarters had been bombarded with much conflicting and implausible information as to the strength and movements of various French units and the whereabouts of Napoleon and the Imperial Guard from many self-styled 'agents'. Less than three weeks earlier, Wellington had written to Lord Bathurst, the Secretary for War, expressing his general view of such agents in the course of discussing a candidate recommended to him by Bathurst:

'There is a good deal of charlatanism in what is called procuring intelligence, as in everything else. I do not know how Mr. _____ has discovered that my channels of intelligence are of doubtful fidelity. I should find it very difficult to point out what channels of intelligence I have; but probably Mr. _____ knows. You may send him to me and I will try him; but I suspect he will not be worth the half-pay you will have to give him for the loss of his valuable time. You have two good correspondents, one from whom Lord Castlereagh sent me the other day two original letters, and the other respecting whom I have a letter from you of the 18th. Nothing else that I have seen from those employed by me, or others is worth having.'[27]

This latest report from Dornberg, attributed to yet another French agent, was unlikely to be given much credence. It is not surprising that no action was taken, or indeed even contemplated, in response to its receipt. Had Dornberg mentioned that the information came from Grant, Wellington would undoubtedly have sent several aides galloping to Mons on fast horses to extract the full text of Grant's message from Dornberg, and upon being apprised of Grant's conclusion Wellington would certainly have ordered his army to move at once to its agreed position in support of Blücher. As it was, however, Wellington issued no orders, as he had in his opinion no reliable intelligence which would cause him to alter his conviction that Napoleon was no longer preparing to attack his army but would instead open his campaign to the south.

At the headquarters of the Prussian Army of the Lower Rhine at Namur on the evening of the 14th, Gneisenau and Blücher were uneasy with the sighting reports from Ziethen and Clausewitz indicating that at least three French corps were concentrating before the thin dispositions of I Corps. Judging correctly that this signalled a large-scale French attack, the two commanders decided to concentrate their army in the Sombreffe-Fleurus area. Accordingly, they agreed that Pirch's II Corps would be ordered to march from the vicinity of Namur, Thielemann's III Corps from Ciney by way of Namur, and Bülow's IV Corps from Liège. Ziethen would be ordered to hold the Sambre bridges as long as possible and conduct a fighting withdrawal to Fleurus, disputing every foot of ground. If he could delay the French long enough, the rest of the Prussian army, and especially IV Corps, which had the farthest to march, could assemble in its agreed position and combine with Wellington's Anglo-Allied army to destroy Napoleon. Ziethen would also be ordered when first attacked to inform Wellington by a message to be sent to the *letter post at Mons*.[28] Having concluded his conference with Gneisenau, Blücher retired to bed, leaving his Chief of Staff to draw up and send the necessary movement orders to the corps commanders. Gneisenau found himself in a dilemma which had its roots in Prussian military tradition and recent history. Since the time of Frederick the Great, the Prussian army's chain of command was rigidly structured according to seniority of rank, like the British Army. For this reason King Frederick William, wishing to arrange matters so that Gneisenau could exercise effective control of the Army of the Lower Rhine, had appointed corps commanders of inferior rank to Gneisenau, with the exception of Bülow. In Berlin it had been assumed that Napoleon would repeat the previous year's strategy of defending France in the south and that, therefore, the Prussian forces would advance on a broad front into France with Bülow operating independently as a link between Blücher's army and Kleist's corps. In addition to Bülow there were other generals in the field near the main army senior in rank to Gneisenau and holding independent corps commands: von Tauenzien, hero of Wittenberg, commanding VI Corps and Kleist, hero of Laon, where he had been instrumental in Blücher's repulse of Napoleon (admittedly aided by favourable odds) in 1814.

It was Laon, or rather its aftermath, that must have been foremost in Gneisenau's mind as he considered how to phrase orders to Bülow, his senior, which he rather than Blücher would have to sign. Following the Battle of Laon on 9-10 March 1814, the Prussians had had an opportunity to pursue and perhaps destroy Napoleon's defeated and much smaller army. The opportunity was squandered, however, because Blücher, in overall command, fell ill and Yorck, commanding a corps, refusing to take orders from Gneisenau, his junior, set off for Berlin on 'sick leave'.[29] Only an urgent plea, written by Blücher with Gneisenau holding the pen in his hand, induced Yorck to return to the field.

To avoid a repetition of the embarrassment of the Laon episode, at which Bülow was also present as a corps commander, Gneisenau, unwilling to awaken Blücher for his signature, wrote the movement order to IV Corps couched in the most subservient phrasing: 'I have the honour humbly to request Your Excellency to be kind enough to concentrate the IV Army Corps under your command tomorrow, the 15th ... Your Excellency had doubtless better make Hannut your headquarters.' Upon reflection, Gneisenau, having dispatched the orders, still felt sufficiently anxious at the possibility of another Laon to follow up the order with a further letter amplifying the first: 'I have the honour respectfully to request your Excellency to concentrate the IV Corps to-morrow, the 15th inst., on a small space of ground near Hannut. Reports to hand strengthen the previous tidings that the French continue to concentrate larger forces in front of us, and that we ought therefore to expect that they will take the offensive immediately... The headquarters of the Prussian Army still remains temporarily at Namur, but your Excellency should move your headquarters to Hannut.'[30]

With Gneisenau's order expressed as a request, Bülow was bound to comply, but with a measure of delay which could be explained partly by Gneisenau's understatement of the urgency of the situation (in case the present alarm proved to be yet another false one) and partly by the probability that he, Bülow, while appreciating the military wisdom of the move, needed to indulge in a slighting gesture to salve his pride. In any case neither general wanted IV Corps to force-march through the night of 14/15 June; Bülow, because he had been marching his men all day and felt that as the order did not emphasize time as being of the essence they could wait until morning to concentrate; and Gneisenau, because he was greatly concerned to avoid the possibility of finding himself in the position of having induced a superior general to force-march his men all night for nothing.

Gneisenau then summoned Colonel Hardinge, the British liaison officer to Prussian headquarters. Gneisenau instructed Hardinge to inform Wellington that the Prussian army was starting to concentrate in anticipation of an attack by Napoleon. In a note sent from Namur at about 10 p.m. Hardinge wrote: 'A report from General Ziethen of this day's date, just received, encloses a letter from General Merlen of the Belgian Army this morning, in which he states that the troops collected at Maubeuge are in movement from thence on the road to Beaumont, being provided with eight days' provisions and forage. At the time General Ziethen wrote (presumed to be at twelve or one to-day) he had received no information of any movement of the enemy by their right ... General Gneisenau credits the intelligence he had received from different quarters of the arrival of the two divisions of the 4th Corps from the neighbourhood of Thionville at Sedan and Mezières on the 12th. The corps of General Kleist has been directed upon Arlon. In case of necessity the 3rd Corps from the environs of Ciney can be assembled at this point in fourteen hours; and the 4th Corps from Liège is prepared to move on Hannut. The prevalent opinion here seems to be that Buonaparte intends to commence offensive operations.'[31]

Hardinge's letter would probably have reached Brussels after 3 a.m. and Wellington would probably not have been awakened to read it. Hardinge had not mentioned that the Prussian army was concentrating in the Sombreffe-Fleurus area, the position agreed upon with Wellington in the event of a French attack. By the same courier Gneisenau had sent a letter to General von Müffling, the Prussian liaison officer at Anglo-Allied Headquarters. But Wellington was not prepared to take any action to concentrate to his left without corroborating information from Colonel Grant. With his secret orders from the British Government to hold Antwerp at all costs, he would not be lured away from the coast by rumours of enemy movements, especially when, as he believed, Napoleon was not present. Wellington therefore issued no orders for concentration. Indeed, feeling confident that Napoleon must now be in the south, he had not even ordered increased reconnaissance patrolling along the border.

Blücher and Gneisenau at Namur were much nearer to the front than was Wellington at Brussels, and were able to gain a more immediate and realistic picture of the threat developing across the border. Gneisenau, writing late in the night of the 14th to his friend Justus Gruner in Berlin, expressed the frustration which the Prussian army had felt since late May in not at once advancing into France: 'We are still standing idle here while the enemy is increasing his strength. The blame for this lies in our suspicious policy. General Ziethen, who commands our corps closest to the enemy, has today reported that (1) Bonaparte reached Maubeuge last night, (2) the 2nd French Corps under Reille has already arrived in Maubeuge, (3) the Guards coming from Avesnes have joined Bonaparte, (4) troops have already crossed the Sambre and the frontier villages are full of them. Orders have already been issued for our corps to concentrate and prepare for any eventuality.'[32]

So by midnight on 14 June Gneisenau had succeeded in preparing the Prussian army for an immediate attack the next day. Ziethen's corps, which was in the direct path of Napoleon's expected advance, had not only been alerted, but had been given precise orders. Napoleon, who would get up at 2 a.m. and begin his march to the Sambre crossings an hour later, was not to enjoy the important element of tactical surprise which he had done so much to achieve.

At about the same time, not far away in France, Colonel Grant's courier had finally reached him by a circuitous route, having had to hide frequently from French patrols. Grant learned that Dornberg had dismissed his information that Napoleon would imminently attack at Charleroi as 'highly unlikely' and had refused to send it on to Brussels. Grant had no choice but to try to take the intelligence through to Wellington himself. The difficulty in achieving this was apparent: to avoid being shot as a spy if taken, Grant was wearing his uniform of a Colonel of the British 11th Foot,[33] but between him and Mons was an alert French army of more than 120,000 men.

CHAPTER 7

15 June

'Everything which the enemy least expects will succeed the best ... In the same way, if he places himself behind a river to defend the crossing and you find some ford above or below by which to cross, this surprise will derange and confuse him.' -Frederick the Great. Instructions to his Generals, 1747.

'You will not be in a Worse Situation, nor your arms in less Credit if you should meet Misfortune than if you were to Remain Inactive.' - Major General 'Mad' Anthony Wayne. Letter to George Washington, November 1777.

At 3.30 a.m. on 15 June 1815, advance elements of Napoleon's army crossed the French frontier at Thy, Leers and Cour-sur-Heure. The army was disposed in three principal columns: on the left, the corps of Reille and d'Erlon marching via Thuin and Marchiennes; in the centre, Vandamme, Lobau, the Imperial Guard and Grouchy's cavalry reserve marching by way of Ham-sur-Heure, Jamioulex and Marcinelles; and on the right, Gérard's corps marching by way of Florennes and Gerpinnes. The Emperor had arranged everything in his orders, which are justly considered as model (see Appendix I), but they did not take into consideration human error and failings. Soult, unlike the late Berthier, did not dispatch more than one messenger to carry each order from headquarters. Neither did his staff record accurately whether orders had been received. These procedural omissions allowed the situation to occur in which the messenger sent from headquarters at night with the definitive orders of march for Vandamme lay unnoticed in a ditch with a broken leg, sustained when his horse tripped in a hole and rolled on him. As a result the order was not delivered; Vandamme did not know that orders had been issued to him; headquarters did not know the orders had not been received; and Vandamme's III Corps, the lead corps of the central column, remained in bivouac.

Napoleon learned of this mishap when a messenger from Lobau's VI Corps informed him that VI Corps had begun its march as ordered, only to come soon to a halt behind the stationary III Corps. He quickly issued duplicate movement orders to III Corps, then directed the Marines and Sappers of the Imperial Guard to side-step the two lead corps and proceed to lead the advance of the centre column. Napoleon did not place too much importance on this incident, shrugging it off as 'un funeste contretemps'(an unfortunate mishap).

More serious, and of greater consequence, was the fact that Gérard's IV Corps on the right was also stationary. The lead division of the corps, the 14th Infantry Division, was commanded by General Louis Comte de Bourmont who, it may be remembered, during Napoleon's advance from

Grenoble had been appointed by the Comte d'Artois to supervise Ney's operations in attempting to stop his former master. De Bourmont was a dyed-in-the-wool royalist who had fought for the Bourbon cause in the Vendée in 1794 and had assisted in the bombing attempt on Napoleon in 1800. In 1807 he had taken advantage of an amnesty for royalists under which he was able to join the imperial army. He served in several campaigns, during which he passed military information to the Allies. Upon Louis's restoration in 1814, de Bourmont had stood high in royalist circles and had only volunteered to rejoin Napoleon's cause in 1815 because d'Artois again wished him to act as a royalist agent within Napoleon's camp. When de Bourmont volunteered, Marshal Davout refused to accept him, writing to Napoleon via Count Bertrand: 'I cannot sit idly and watch this officer wear the uniform of this country; his treasonous statements concerning the Emperor are well known to all; the brigade and regimental commanders of the 14th Infantry Division despise him. Who would trust such a man?'[1] General Gérard had interceded on de Bourmont's behalf and Napoleon had permitted the appointment.

In his orders Napoleon had appreciated that the right column would be slower than the others, because of the distance it had had to travel to reach the Belgian frontier and its need to close up after such a long march at a fast pace. But the delay on the right in the early hours of the 15th was due to treason rather than exhaustion. De Bourmont had led his division over the border as far as Florennes, where he had halted. Then, on the pretext of wanting to reconnoitre ahead, he had ridden forward with his complete staff and an accompanying squadron of lancers. When this cavalcade had passed the advanced French cavalry outposts, de Bourmont sent the lancers back with a letter for General Gérard: 'I would have resigned and returned home had I thought I should be left free to do so. This seemed so unlikely, that I am obliged to ensure my liberty by other means ... I shall never be seen fighting in the ranks of the foreigner ... They will not get any information from me which could injure the French army, composed of men whom I love ...'[2]

De Bourmont and his staff, who shared his sympathies, then donned the proscribed Bourbon white cockade, which they already had in their possession, and rode as fast as they could to the nearest Prussian outpost, requesting to see Prince Blücher. Giving the lie to the assurances he had made in his letter to Gérard, de Bourmont offered Blücher the operational orders of the French army. Blücher was contemptuous of de Bourmont as a traitor and said so. When Gneisenau, who was grateful for such a godsend regardless of its background, pointed out diplomatically to the old warrior that de Bourmont was wearing the white cockade, Blücher erupted in fury, shouting in de Bourmont's face, 'Cockade be damned! A dirty dog is always a dirty dog!'[3]

Von Gneisenau now knew the exact orders for the French IV Corps and the general orders for the rest of Napoleon's army. There was no longer any doubt in his mind as to Napoleon's intentions. All haste was made in assembling the Prussian army at Sombreffe, ready to join the Anglo-Allied army which the Prussians assumed would assemble on their right in the area of Nivelles-Frasnes-Quatre Bras as arranged at the Tirlemont conference.[4] It was now vital that Ziethen delay the French as long as possible to give the Prussian army time to assemble.

The vacancy in the command of the French 14th Division was filled by General Hulot. De Bourmont's treachery became known and provoked furious anger throughout the ranks of IV Corps. The men remembered Marmont's betrayal of his command in 1814 and revived the deep mistrust of senior officers which that earlier episode had fanned. Hulot harangued his division with promises of loyalty and even Gérard felt it advisable to spend nearly an hour riding up and down giving assurances. By nightfall word of the defection had spread throughout the army, with a similar disquieting effect on the men, who for the most part felt an uncomplicated loyalty to their country and their emperor.

The advance of the French left and centre columns was proceeding about one hour behind schedule. The first Prussian outposts south of the Sambre to come under attack, at about 5 a.m., were elements of Pirch II's 2 Brigade, when General Domon's light cavalry, leading the centre column, engaged an outpost company at Ham-sur-Heere. While part of the French cavalry held the Prussian outpost in place with skirmishing fire from their carbines, two squadrons circled right and left around the outpost to cut it off. The Prussian company commander attempted a staged withdrawal by sections, but found his way blocked and was obliged to surrender.

At the same time, the advance guard of Reille's II Corps, comprising five cavalry squadrons, two light infantry regiments and three guns, leading the left column, attacked a Prussian battalion holding Thuin village and environs. The Prussian commander skilfully kept the superior French force at bay for nearly an hour, then attempted to withdraw by companies. Informed that the battalion was encircled, he launched a desperate bayonet charge to his rear in an effort to break out, and in this his brigade was supported by two Prussian hussar squadrons. But the hussars were driven back with great loss by the French cavalry, who also cut the encircled battalion to pieces, forcing the remnant to surrender.

General Ziethen, commander of the Prussian I Corps, covering the Sambre crossings centred on Charleroi, had decided to sacrifice his outposts south of the river to buy time. The outposts, including those at Ham and Thuin, were to delay the French advance as long as possible and were not to be supported in any significant way by detachments from his brigades. He could not afford to compromise the fighting integrity of his corps. His dilemma was that to fall back before the French army too slowly was to risk piecemeal envelopment of his corps as greatly superior French forces swirled around his positions; while to fall back too quickly was to risk allowing the French army, already concentrated and advancing, to come upon the Prussian army as it concentrated only a short distance behind I Corps and the river.

Ziethen knew from the French army orders delivered to Blücher by de Bourmont that 2 Brigade was defending the main bridges Napoleon intended to use in putting his army across the Sambre. Accordingly he ordered Pirch II to decline any serious engagement; to fall back behind the Sambre and hold the river line as long as possible; then, when his river positions had become untenable, he was to fall back behind Charleroi and take up a position at Gilly blocking the road to Fleurus. In 1815 the terrain around Gilly and the road leading from Gilly to Fleurus favoured defence. On each side of the Fleurus road was a deep gully, making it almost impossible for troops to advance along the road in any sort of order. In the rear of the position, toward Fleurus, were several woods, Bois de Gilly, Bois de Lobbes and Bois de Soleilmont, which ran together to form a sizeable area.[5] Before Gilly ran a swampy brook which spread into the adjacent fields. The Gilly position was the last at which 2 Brigade would stand and hold before falling back to Fleurus to join the rest of I Corps.

Because of the direction of the French advance, the Prussian 1 Brigade, commanded by General Steinmetz, was only vulnerable at Thuin. Ziethen ordered Steinmetz to fall back toward Gosselies, keeping in contact with Pirch II's brigade, to protect each other's inner flanks. Ziethen then ordered Donnersmarck's 4 Brigade, Roder's Corps Cavalry Reserve, and Lehmann's Corps Artillery Reserve to join Jagow's 3 Brigade at Fleurus to form a large corps reserve which could assist 1 and 2 Brigades in delaying the French or move to extricate either if it became imperilled.[6]

The new Prussian light infantry tactics (see diagram overleaf), together with the brigade structure, honed to a fine edge in the campaigns of 1813 and 1814, now began to prove themselves in the campaign of 1815. The troops of 1 and 2 Brigades used every cover provided by nature or the hand of man, thickets, hedges, fences, walls and outbuildings, from which to snipe at the French advance guard. The French, of necessity, had to winkle out each sniper or wait until their supports came up. In either case the Prussians gave ground, supported by their reserve companies. These tactics slowed the pace of the French advance to just one mile an hour.

It was therefore not until about 8 a.m. that Pajol's cavalry arrived at the bridge in the town of Charleroi. They found that the Prussians had barricaded it with every piece of furniture and bric-à-brac imaginable. From the north bank the Prussians maintained a galling fire on the French, shooting from behind the barricade and from cover nearby, including loopholes cut in the roofs and walls of the houses facing the bridge. As a result of Vandamme's late start (because his orders had failed to reach him on time), there was no infantry on hand in Charleroi to assist Pajol in forcing the bridge. Pajol tried a direct assault on the barricade with both mounted and dismounted hussars using carbines, but they were no match for the Prussian light infantry and rifle-armed *Jäger*. Pajol had no option but to keep up a demonstration without suffering too many losses. Upriver at Marchiennes, where the French left wing column was to cross, the bridge there also was barricaded and tenaciously held by elements of 1 Brigade.

At 11 a.m. Napoleon arrived in Charleroi at the head of the Imperial Guard Marines and Sappers, with the Young Guard Division, to find the Prussians still denying the crossing to his army. He at once ordered the Guard Marines and Sappers to clear the bridge, which they did, bayonetting the Prussians off the barricade and dumping the impediments into the river. Pajol's horsemen, with the pent-up anger of three hours' impotence

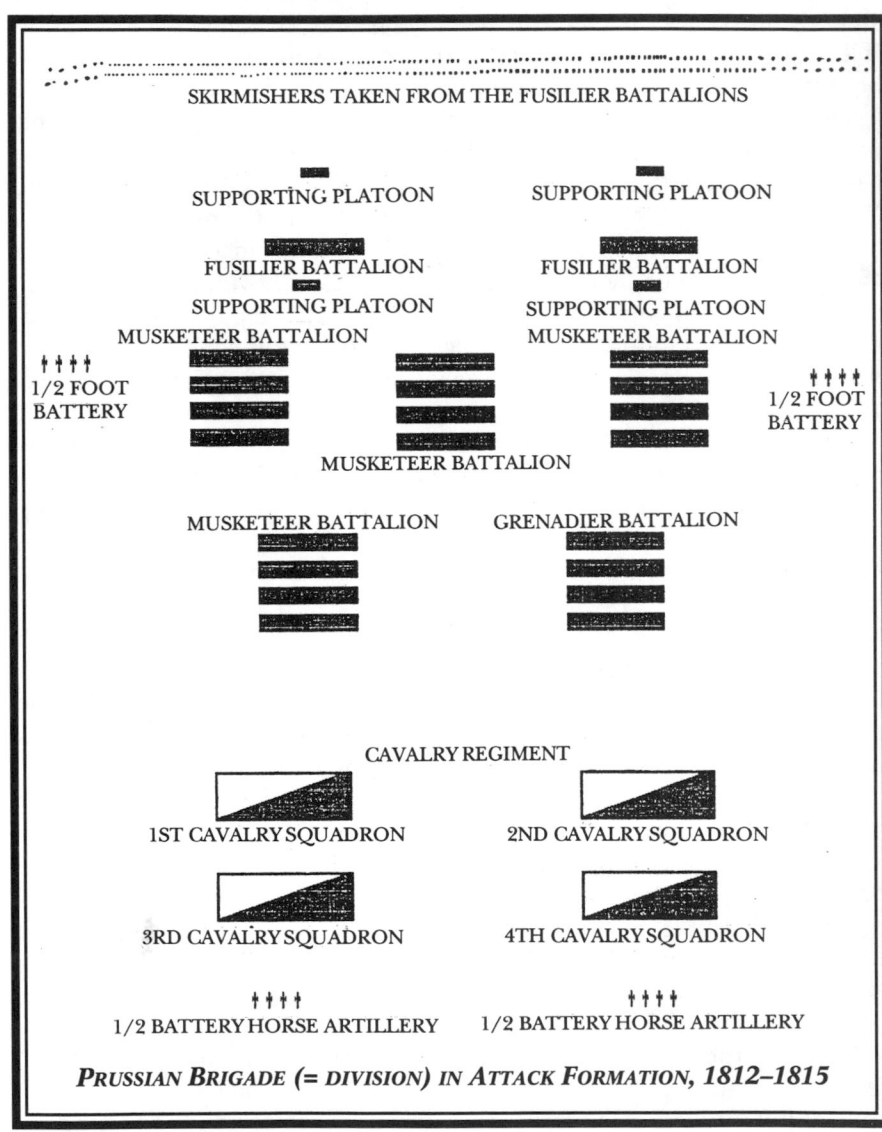

PRUSSIAN BRIGADE (= DIVISION) IN ATTACK FORMATION, 1812–1815

and no doubt some embarrassment before their Emperor, charged across and straight up the winding street which runs on to Brussels. Yet despite the eventual forcing of the bridge, the single battalion of the Prussian 2 Brigade which had held Charleroi, halting for three hours the centre column of Napoleon's army, retired in good order to the Gilly position.

Steinmetz, as instructed, now abandoned Marchiennes, leaving one battalion to hold it long enough for the rest of 1 Brigade to withdraw toward Gosselies and make contact with 2 Brigade's flank. The battalion left holding the bridge at Marchiennes finally fell back when the French 2nd Light Infantry Regiment made an all-out attack on the elaborate defences.[7] They, too, retired in good order.

To ensure that his brigade and its battalion rearguard were neither enveloped nor routed in withdrawing, Steinmetz dispatched a fresh infantry and cavalry regiment ahead to Gosselies, thereby observing the sound principle that in rearguard actions the withdrawal of engaged units should be covered by troops already in position.

At this juncture Pajol's cavalry erupted from Charleroi, blazing up the Brussels road and threatening to come between the two retiring Prussian brigades. Ziethen, aware of the danger, sent forward an infantry regiment and two cavalry regiments, supported by horse artillery, to prevent Steinmetz from being cut off. The appearance of this new Prussian force caused the French to pause to evaluate the situation and gave Steinmetz the time he needed. He should have closed in more to the east to find Pirch II's right flank, but he decided wisely, in light of circumstances, to disregard his orders and retreat instead by the Brussels road to Gosselies, to reach Fleurus by a more circuitous route.[8] He realized that Ziethen had miscalculated 1 Brigade's line of withdrawal. If Steinmetz had obeyed his orders and moved by way of the Bois de Jumet, the French cavalry would have been free to continue up the Brussels road. They could then have turned east above Gosselies and either participated in an attack on I Corps from three sides or possibly even turned I Corps' right flank, to envelop it. With I Corps out of the way, Napoleon could then have attacked the Prussian army as it concentrated around Sombreffe.[9] Steinmetz's sound judgement under pressure denied Napoleon this great opportunity and gained precious time for Blücher and, indirectly, for Wellington.

With the bridges at Charleroi and Marchiennes, and the several crossings above Marchiennes cleared, French troops were pushing across the Sambre as quickly as they could funnel through the crossing choke points. Vandamme's corps was defiling through Charleroi. The leading divisions of Reille's corps were crossing at Marchiennes and keeping close on the heels of Steinmetz's rearguard. The flow of French troops over the Sambre was slowed by the few narrow bridges in the area. The bridge at Marchiennes was especially narrow, and it was not until well into the afternoon that the rear of Reille's corps had crossed, and it was about 4.30 p.m. before d'Erlon's corps began crossing behind Reille.[10] In his orders (see

Appendix I) Napoleon had made pontoon bridges available to the leading corps commanders, but they had been forgotten.

Blücher, secure in the knowledge that Napoleon's entire army (whose order of battle he had received from Wellington) was crossing the Sambre on his front and concentrating above and around Charleroi, signed precise and imperative orders to his corps commanders. At noon on the 15th he sent instructions to Bülow which stated:

> 'The enemy opened the campaign this morning, and he is driving our outposts from Charleroi. Buonaparte is present with his Guard, and that is the reason why I desire your Excellency to push on at all speed with your corps, as soon as it has rested at Hannut, but at the latest to march forward at an early hour tomorrow morning, and to move to Gembloux. Your Excellency should inform me exactly of the time you attain that place. I am moving my headquarters to Sombreffe today, and there I await further information.'[11]

Over Blücher's signature, Gneisenau had ordered Bülow to Gembloux, rather than Sombreffe, in accordance with the plan arrived at during the Tirlemont conference: that, in the event of Napoleon's advancing to come between them and reach Brussels, the Anglo-Allied and Prussian armies would co-operate by drawing up in an extended line of battle which would have them in contact on their inner flanks, with Wellington's right covering Nivelles and Blücher's left on Gembloux. Bülow's corps was to form the Prussian left. By this deployment the Allies would be able to cover all the roads leading to Brussels from the district around Charleroi, and whichever part of their line Napoleon attacked, other Allied units could move to attack the French flank or rear. Gneisenau did not know, however, that in reply to his previous and more courteous order, bearing the Chief of Staff's signature, Bülow had written explaining that as there appeared to be no urgency he would move off on the morning of the 16th. This alarming message was delayed in reaching Gneisenau because the Army Headquarters was in transit from Namur to Sombreffe. Thus 24 hours were lost in rectifying Bülow's unwarrantably sanguine appreciation of the situation. Meanwhile, Pirch II's II Corps and Thielemann's III Corps actually reached their designated areas around Sombreffe within 24 hours of receiving their movement orders: a very creditable feat.[12]

With the French across the Sambre in strength, Pirch II had to retire his brigade generally from the river line. Accordingly he withdrew his infantry from Châtelet, several miles downstream of Charleroi, replacing them with cavalry which could obviously retire at the gallop if necessary. Pirch II concentrated his brigade at Gilly and deployed them for battle. He blocked the Fleurus road and placed *Jäger* to cover the barricade. On the wooded heights by the Abbey de Soleilmont, overlooking the valley through which the Fleurus road ran, Pirch II had arranged four battalions of infantry and one battery of artillery. The artillery was parcelled out along the line in four sections of two guns each, one of the sections sited to rake the right-hand roadside gully with canister.[13] Near Lambusart he placed another three battalions of infantry in reserve, supported by a regiment of dragoons. This reserve would support the line if necessary, but also disrupt any French attempt to outflank the Gilly position by putting a force across the Sambre downstream of Châtelet. Pirch II's extended dispositions were intended to give the impression that the position was manned by a corps rather than a brigade. The enemy was meant to believe that they were seeing only part of the force; the rest being hidden in the woods.

Part of Pajol's I Reserve Cavalry Corps had followed in the wake of Pirch II's rearguard battalion and was joined by Count Exelmans' cavalry division. The French cavalry halted before Gilly, having driven the Prussian rearguard into the line arrayed against them. Marshal Grouchy, in command of the reserve cavalry and present before Gilly, considered that cavalry alone could not assault the Prussian position. He returned to Charleroi to request infantry support from Napoleon.

Napoleon had situated his headquarters temporarily at a small château near the Charleroi bridge and was to be found sitting outside an inn, la Belle Vue, giving orders and receiving progress reports from his corps commanders. As Grouchy approached, Marshal Ney rode up accompanied by his aide, Colonel Heymes. Among the soldiers filing through the town came the cry '*le Rougeaud!*' (for his red hair and ruddy complexion) and speculation that things should now pick up. Since the 13th Ney and Heymes had been making their way very slowly from Avesnes to Beaumont, where they had purchased two chargers belonging to the invalided Marshal Mortier. Ney was not unaware of the fact that Napoleon had not bothered to send a patrol to find him or make horses available for him. His mood on coming face to face with his Emperor again can only be speculated upon. Napoleon, for his part, greeted Ney in an *ave atque vale* manner which made it clear he would not grant forgiveness short of Ney's self-redemption on the field of battle: 'Bonjour Ney, I want you to take command of I and II Corps. I will give you besides, the light cavalry of my Guard, but do not make use of it. Tomorrow you will be joined by Kellermann's cuirassiers. Now go and drive away all the enemy along the Brussels road and take up a position at Quatre Bras and await further orders.'[14]

Doubtless Napoleon also explained his overall dispositions to Ney, now that he had given him command of a third of his army. Additionally, because Ney had not been mentioned thus far in any of the army's orders, neither d'Erlon nor Reille, the commanders of I and II Corps, would have had any knowledge of Ney's presence or his new authority over them. It was for this reason that Napoleon gave Ney his Imperial Guard Light Cavalry Division, under Lefebvre-Desnouëttes. Its presence in Ney's train would be absolute proof to d'Erlon and Reille that Ney did indeed have his authority from the Emperor. Of course a complete division of élite cavalry as escort would also provide Ney with personal protection in hostile country until he could form a headquarters staff and delegate cavalry from his own force for this duty. It must have struck him as quite a contrast from making his way unaided by farm cart!

Ney took command at a serious disadvantage. He had not been involved in the planning of operations for the campaign, and he had little or no idea where his two corps might be. In fact they were strung out along seventeen miles of rutted roads between the other side of Thuin (the tail of d'Erlon's corps) and Gosselies (the head of Reille's). Gosselies was being held by a reargaurd of Steinmetz's brigade. Units of Pajol's cavalry were confronting the Prussian force at Gosselies, but could not dislodge them. The cavalry commander had sent back to army headquarters in Charleroi for infantry support, and Napoleon had pushed Reille's corps up the main Brussels road towards Gosselies in response. Ney, meanwhile, was forced to formulate a command structure on the hoof. Using some of the Imperial Guard cavalry on loan to him as orderly dispatch-riders, Ney sent word to both d'Erlon and Reille of his appointment to command of the left and requesting current information on the positions and strengths of their divisions, their artillery and their trains.

At Charleroi, Grouchy told Napoleon that the Prussians were holding Gilly in strength; he estimated about 20,000 men in a strong position. Napoleon, not certain of what Blücher intended to do, rode to Gilly with Grouchy at about 3.45 p.m. to see for himself whether Grouchy faced a Prussian corps. About half an hour earlier, the Young Guard, under General Duhesme, had arrived in front of Gilly, having leapfrogged Vandamme's delayed III Corps along the route of march from the frontier. III Corps was now moving up through Charleroi and into attack formation ahead of the Young Guard, which was of course part of Napoleon's army reserve and not to be blunted against enemy rearguards. Napoleon reckoned that there were not more than 10,000 Prussians in the positions behind Gilly: a fair estimate, as Pirch II's brigade had numbered approximately 7,700 before the fighting began, had lost about 700 so far in retreat, and had been reinforced by 550 cavalry, the 6th *Uhlans*, sent by Ziethen.

In the same peremptory fashion as he had given Ney the left wing, Napoleon now gave Grouchy command of the right. Grouchy must have displayed signs of the hesitancy exhibited by a man entrusted with responsibility beyond the scope of his confidence, because whereas Napoleon had simply given Ney his objective and the means to attain it, he told Grouchy how to achieve his. He advised him to fix the Prussians with a frontal assault by one of Vandamme's infantry divisions and one of Pajol's cavalry regiments, then to send Count Exelmans' dragoons to ford the stream near the mill of Delhatte and take the enemy in flank. The retreating Prussians might then be followed up as far as Sombreffe, where Grouchy should take up position and await further orders.[15] With the benefit of hindsight, Napoleon might have done better to have given the right to either of Grouchy's corps commanders: Vandamme, who had had the nerve to insult Tsar Alexander while his prisoner, or Gérard, who would soon prove the soundness of his battle instincts.

Having assessed the problem at Gilly and provided for its solution, Napoleon returned to his headquarters at Charleroi to receive reports and intelligence from patrols. From here he was to co-ordinate the movements of the columns as they crossed the Sambre and formed into the right and left wings and central reserve. Two hours passed before Napoleon, having heard no sound of battle from the direction of Gilly, called for his horse and rode there again, accompanied by his personal cavalry escort, the *Escadrons de Service*, which was composed of one squadron of Imperial Guard Dragoons, one of the mounted Grenadiers of the Guard, one of the Chasseurs of the Guard (whose uniform he wore as Colonel), and one of the Red Lancers of the Guard.[16] He soon discovered that as a result of a disagreement between Grouchy and Vandamme as to how the operation should be executed, two hours had been spent in positioning troops and waiting for Exelmans' messenger to confirm that his horse had effected a crossing upstream.

Napoleon was exasperated that Grouchy's excessive caution had wasted two precious hours, when it was clear that the Prussian force was only a rearguard. Grouchy had six times the Prussian numbers, but still hesitated. Having realized that telling Grouchy what to do was not enough, Napoleon proceeded to do it for him. At once, he ordered the battery which Grouchy had already sited at the front of his line to open fire on the Prussian guns. Vandamme, free of Grouchy's cramping restraint, obeyed with relish Napoleon's order to attack, sending forward three columns of infantry to push the Prussians aside with the bayonet. The cannonade and assault had the effect that Napoleon had predicted and the Prussians abandoned their positions. As a rearguard it was not their duty to be trapped or annihilated, but to give ground as slowly as possible. They had stopped the French right wing for nearly three hours, until the Emperor himself had had to deal with them; it was time to fall back on the I Corps position at Fleurus.

The Prussian 2 Brigade was now in a precarious situation. They had to try to withdraw in the face of a greatly superior French force, heavy in cavalry, and directed by Napoleon in person. As if that were not enough, they were exhausted, having been in action since 3 a.m. (it now being just after 6 p.m.), and had more that five miles to cover before reaching the I Corps position at Fleurus. Napoleon observed that the Prussians were attempting to escape into the woods behind them while their cavalry screened them from Exelmans' dragoons. He ordered his aide, General Letort, leading the Dragoons of the Guard, to take the entire *Escadrons de Service* and '...to charge and crush the Prussian infantry'. These élite cavalry, with Letort at their head, dashed across the stream and up the gully, close to the Fleurus road where the incline was slightest, and crossed in front of Vandamme's columns.

The four Prussian battalions withdrawing from the Gilly positions were trying to reach the edge of the woods, where three battalions of 2 Brigade were in position to cover them. The appearance of the Guard cavalry took the retreating Prussians by surprise. They attempted to form battalion masses (a type of square) and continue moving in those formations. Two masses gained the woods, but the other two were cut to pieces by the Guard cavalry. In this mêlée General Letort was killed by a bullet probably fired by a *Jäger*. The Guard cavalry then renewed their attack, eager for revenge, and Exelmans' dragoons, who had succeeded in repulsing the *Uhlans*, drove one of the Prussian battalions from the woods, having taken it in flank. In desperation, Pirch II pulled the remnant of his battalions back toward Lambusart to rally there, but the French gave him no respite. Exelmans' cavalry, supported by a brigade of Pajol's, followed up the Prussians with part of Vandamme's corps close behind. Ziethen used all his remaining cavalry to stem the French pursuit long enough for Pirch II's infantry to withdraw with their guns to Fleurus.

When Marshal Grouchy came up to Vandamme on the Fleurus road, he was fired with the enthusiasm he should have had earlier. He ordered Vandamme to mount an immediate attack on the Prussians at Fleurus. Vandamme, already exasperated with Grouchy for wasting so much time before Gilly, said that his troops were exhausted from marching and fighting since 4 a.m. and that, in any case, 'He would not take orders from the commander of the cavalry.'[17] Vandamme had not yet been notified of Grouchy's appointment to command over him.

Thus, the French right wing, then comprising III Corps and the Young Guard, came to a halt for the night of the 15th around Lambusart, with Grouchy's headquarters at Campinaire and the cavalry of Pajol and Exelmans covering the front. Grouchy had failed to achieve his objective for the 15th – Sombreffe.

Although it was not clear at the time, General Bourmont's defection earlier in the day had played a large part in the failure to reach Sombreffe. With the time lost in realizing what had happened to Bourmont, finding a replacement for him, and reassuring the troops, IV Corps did not approach the bridge at Châtelet until 3.15 p.m. The bridge was deserted, Pirch II having already withdrawn his men to Gilly. Had Gérard arrived there two hours earlier, he might have been in a position to threaten the flank and rear of the Gilly position. In that event, Pirch II would have had to abandon Gilly much earlier than he did, and the French right wing would undoubtedly have reached Sombreffe as ordered. This would have disrupted Blücher's concentration, necessitating a general Prussian withdrawal. As events unfolded, though, Gérard had managed to pass only

Hulot's 14th Division over the narrow bridge, and his other divisions were already bivouacking on the southern bank of the Sambre.

When Napoleon had seen the Prussians giving up their position at Gilly he returned to Charleroi. He conferred with Soult and consulted his maps to determine the current positions of the rest of his army and the known placements of the Allies, based on reports from patrols.

On the French left wing, Ney, on leaving Charleroi with Napoleon's appointment and orders to reach Quatre Bras, had hurried to the head of Reille's corps advancing on Gosselies, leaving Colonel Heymes to form a headquarters staff and catch up with him. Steinmetz's 1 Brigade was taking up positions at Gosselies to block the Brussels road. At Jumet, about a mile in front of Gosselies, the 1st Hussar Regiment of Pajol's cavalry met the Prussian 6th *Uhlan* Regiment and 24th Infantry Regiment sent there by Ziethen to cover Steinmetz's movement. The *Uhlans* attacked the French hussars and drove them back in disorder, only to be attacked in turn by the advance guard of Reille's corps, including Piré's Lancers and elements of Girard's infantry division, with accompanying horse artillery. Jäger Henri Niemann, a mounted skirmisher of the 6th *Uhlans*, related his account of the action: '... we passed through Galy [Gilly] and took position on the other side of it. Napoleon came nearer with his army; firing began. My heart began to beat, but I soon forgot I might be shot. By Command of General Ziethen we engaged the French; but it was nothing more than a feint; they retreated before us. Not yet having removed our wounded from the field, they renewed the fight with a stronger force. We were obliged to cover our retreat, and a hail of balls in screening our artillery from the enemy's attack was not very pleasant.'[18]

Reille, on being informed by his hussars of the presence of Prussians in Gosselies, urged his corps forward. Aware that large French forces were approaching, Steinmetz had been withdrawing his brigade north-westward from Gosselies toward Heppignies to make a wide movement to the I Corps concentration at Fleurus. He had left an infantry regiment and the *Uhlans* in Gosselies to cover the withdrawal, but when he saw French troops issuing from Gosselies in a direction which would threaten to cut his brigade's escape route, he sent several battalions and his *Jäger* to drive the French back into the town. Detaching a strong force of light troops to provide cover from houses and outbuildings north of the town, he succeeded in withdrawing his troops in stages, the *Uhlans* screening each stage.

The Prussian rearguard actions before both developing wings of the French army were brilliantly conducted and successful, but at a cost. According to Trooper Niemann: '... it was of no use to make a long face; we lost in all about three thousand men. Towards evening of that day our brigade, four regiments of cavalry reached Fleurus; we bivouacked before the town, but a further order came to break up. We marched through Fleurus and bivouacked on the other side that night. I would have paid five francs for a glass of water.'[19]

Before the French left wing the Brussels road appeared open. When Marshal Ney arrived at Gosselies about four hours of daylight remained. Ney, who had by then been under orders for only two hours, had a command spread out over twelve miles of road, with Marcognet's division still crossing the Sambre at Marchiennes and Allix's not yet across at Thuin. Although his corps had written orders and he verbal ones from Napoleon to keep in contact with the right, Ney did not know where Grouchy was. In the circumstances he decided to halt the advance of Reille's corps and ordered all but one squadron of Lefebvre-Desnouëtte's Imperial Guard light cavalry division to reconnoitre ahead to Quatre Bras as a means of fulfilling his objective for the 15th. Bachelu's division and some of Piré's cavalry were to follow and take an advance guard position at Mellet. Girard's division and the rest of Piré's cavalry were assigned to pursue Steinmetz's brigade west as far as Wangenies because Ney could hear gunfire from that direction. General Foy and Prince Jérôme, on arrival at Gosselies, were to halt and close up around the town to form a reserve to support either of Ney's flanks until I Corps came up and Ney was able to assess whether the enemy was near in any strength. After giving these first orders to his new command, Ney spent time in discussion with Reille, reading his orders, consulting the available maps and generally orienting himself.

Towards 5.45 p.m the Lancers of the Imperial Guard approached Frasnes, two miles south of Quatre Bras, and were met with cannon fire from a battery of horse artillery. The village was occupied by advance guard outposts of the 2nd Netherlands Division, Major Normann's 2nd Battalion, 2nd Nassau Regiment and Captain Bijleveld's Dutch horse artillery battery. Normann had heard the sound of battle from Gosselies and had ordered his men to stand on the alert. The ensuing action was recorded by Captain Bijleveld in his diary:

'Towards the end of the afternoon we were attacked by French Lancers, but the precautions I had made with Major Normann, commanding the 2nd battalion of Nassau infantry, ... frustrated the intentions of the French. I marched my battery of eight pieces out of the park and through a part of the village on the high road which passes through the midst of Frasnes. Major Normann with his battalion followed my movements and sent one company ... to stop if possible the Lancers in the village. As soon as I had arrived with my battery on the high road outside of Frasnes, I placed my battery in position viz. the two howitzers on the road and three guns on either side in the fields, ordering them to load canister. The infantry drew up in line to the left and right. In this position Major Normann recalled his light company by bugle-call, which company was followed by the French.

'The French cavalry debouching from Frasnes was fired upon by canister by the whole battery which killed and wounded several men and horses. They retired to the village and sent out reconnoitring patrols. Our position might be turned and the French seeing this sent a column to the right [the French left] wing to cut off our communications with Quatre-Bras, being at a distance of a quarter of an hour from both of them. The infantry then leaned with their right wing upon the wood [Bois de Bossu] which extends from Quatre-Bras to Hautain-le-Val, the left wing of the battery covering Quatre-Bras. In this position the cavalry did not risk to attack us any more. They posted sentries; we did also, maintaining our position till the next morning.'[20]

Lefebvre-Desnouëttes promptly sent to the rear for infantry support, and Bachelu's advance division sent forward a battalion, but the light was fading. Lefebvre-Desnouëttes was obliged to bivouac at Frasnes, from where at 9 p.m. he dispatched a report to Marshal Ney: 'When we reached Frasnes, in accordance with your orders, we found it occupied by a regiment of Nassau Infantry (some 1500 men), and 8 guns, as they observed that we were manoeuvring to them, they retired from the village where we had practically enveloped them with our squadrons, General Colbert (commanding the Lancers) even reached within musket shot of Quatre-Bras on the high road, but as the ground was difficult, and the enemy fell back for support to Bossu wood and kept up a vigorous fire from their eight guns it was impossible for us to carry it ...' He added information that he had obtained from prisoners and the villagers: '... the troops which we found at Frasnes had not advanced this morning and were not engaged at Gosselies. They are under orders from Lord Wellington, and appear to be retiring towards Nivelles. They set alight to a beacon at Quatre-Bras, and fired their guns a great deal. None of the troops who fought at Gosselies this morning have passed this way, they marched to Fleurus. The peasants can give no information about a large assembly of troops in this neighbourhood, only that [there was] a park of artillery at Turbize, composed of 100 ammunition wagons and 12 guns; they say that the Belgian Army is in the neighbourhood of Mons, and that the headquarters of the Prince of Orange are at Braine-le-Comte. We took about 15 prisoners, and have 10 men killed and wounded. Tomorrow if it is possible, I shall send a reconnoitring party to Quatre-Bras so as to occupy that place, for I think the Nassau troops have left it. A battalion of infantry has just arrived, and I have sent orders for it to bivouac with Bachelu's division, it will rejoin me tomorrow morning.' He evidently expected Ney to be riding back to Charleroi to confer with Napoleon, because he added: '... I have not written to the Emperor [to whom, as a Guard commander, he was directly responsible], as I have nothing more Important to report to him than what I am telling your Excellency.' And a footnote stated: 'I am sending you a Non-Commissioned officer [with the report] to receive the orders of your Excellency, I have the honour to observe to your Excellency that the enemy has shown no cavalry in front of us; but the artillery is light artillery [that is, horse artillery, normally attached to cavalry].'[21]

On receipt of this report at about 9.45 p.m.,[22] Ney rode to Quatre Bras. He arrived there as darkness was falling, but he could see Netherlands pickets out in strength. He returned to his headquarters at Gosselies to form a strategy, close up his dispersed corps, and try to elicit some guidance from Napoleon. The Emperor had indicated that he should have reached Quatre Bras, but that would not now be possible until the next morning. Lefebvre-Desnouëttes had reported the crossroads lightly held and his opinion that the enemy would abandon their positions there before morning. If so, *tant mieux*; if not, on the morning of the 16th Ney would have overwhelming force to bring to bear in occupying the position, if that was what the Emperor still required.

In setting the first-day objectives for the right and left wings, Napoleon had hoped to rupture the weak join between the two Allied armies which, according to his latest intelligence, had not even begun to concentrate. If Napoleon could push in quickly and anchor his left on Quatre Bras and his right on Sombreffe, he could sever the communications between the Allies. Then, because of the proximity of his battle-ready army, the separated Allies would have to draw back away from Napoleon – and each other – to concentrate, leaving the road open to Brussels, the primary strategic objective of his campaign. Now, by the night of the 15th, Napoleon's troops had carried the first tactical objective of crossing the Sambre, although against stiffer opposition than he had expected, and had achieved forward positions far enough ahead to ensure that the Allied armies could not unite in front of him. His greatest concern in this situation would be to have his army straddling a river, then to be obliged to fight a superior Allied force without his full force and with the river at his back. He could not have been content that a sizeable part of his army – part of I Corps, the whole of VI Corps, the Grand Artillery Park and most of IV Corps – were bivouacked south of the Sambre that night.

However, in much he was content. Marshal Grouchy's reports from the right indicated that large bodies of troops were massing between Ligny and Sombreffe. If this were Blücher concentrating his army, alone and so near, Napoleon would engage him next day. On the left, all the reports coming in from patrols regarding Wellington's army indicated that the forward divisions, Chasse's 3rd and Perponcher-Slednitsky's 2nd Netherlands Divisions, had not concentrated. Only one brigade of Perponcher's division held Quatre Bras. Napoleon's spies[23] kept him fully informed of the Anglo-Allied dispositions, so he knew that Wellington had yet to concentrate and therefore could not attack him except from Quatre

Bras or above. To confirm the reports of his spies, Napoleon had ordered d'Erlon to send cavalry patrols towards Binche and Mons, for if Wellington were concentrating in front of him or in conjunction with Blücher, Allied patrols in this area would have been withdrawn and Mons put in a state of siege – but they had not been.

From his headquarters at 11 p.m. on the 15th Marshal Ney wrote to Marshal Soult, Chief of Staff, at Napoleon's:

> 'I have the honour to report to Your Excellency that, in accordance with the Orders of the Emperor, I have advanced with the Cavalry of General Piré and the infantry of General Bachelu to Gosselies this afternoon, to dislodge the enemy from this point. The enemy made only a slight resistance. After an exchange of 25 to 30 cannon-shots he fell back through Heppignies to Fleurus. We have made 500 to 600 Prussians prisoner from the corps of General Ziethen.
>
> 'This is the situation of the troops: General Lefebvre-Desnouëttes, with the lancers and Chasseurs of the Guard, at Frasnes. General Bachelu with the 5th division at Mellet. General Foy with the 9th Division at Gosselies. The Light Cavalry of General Piré at Heppignies. I do not know where General Reille is. General d'Erlon has sent to inform me that he is at Jumet with the greater portion of his Army Corps. I have just sent him instructions prescribed in Your Excellency's letter of today's date. I annex to my letter a report received from General Lefebvre-Desnouëttes.'[24]

Ney's report illustrates the persistence of the predicament Napoleon had placed him in at the outset of the campaign. At 11 p.m. he did not know the whereabout of Reille, his II Corps commander. Nor did he know that it was Girard's 7th Division he had sent to Wangenies to link the inner flanks of the right and left wings, or that he had passed on Napoleon's order of 4 p.m. that d'Erlon was to close up with Reille at Gosselies.[25] D'Erlon's corps, following Reille's, had not seen any action during the long day, nor had they been able to keep up with II Corps. Although d'Erlon had written to Ney that he was at Jumet with the greater part of his corps, this was an exaggeration. D'Erlon actually had with him there Durutte's and Donzelot's divisions, and one of Jacquinot's cavalry brigades. The other brigade of cavalry, having sent out the patrols toward Binche and Mons, was bivouacked three miles west at Souvret, while Marcognet's division was still back at Marchiennes and Allix's was at Thuin, twelve miles away by road.[26]

At close on midnight Ney arrived at Charleroi, where he had a supper with Napoleon and a few others. Napoleon could only give him a broad outline of his plans as he would not be able to see clearly what was happening until daylight revealed the Prussian intentions.[27] During this meeting Napoleon criticized Ney for having deviated from his orders, which had been to drive the enemy in front of him along the Brussels road, instead of weakening his column by detaching Girard and part of Foy's cavalry to chase Steinmetz toward the sound of gunfire. This criticism seems capricious, for he could equally have censured Ney for allowing a retreating enemy to break contact. Perhaps it was simply spleen: the iron cage coming to the surface again. While this indulgence by Napoleon of his disappointment in Ney's past actions cannot have done much to help Ney to look to the morrow with a clear mind, its effect on another marshal present was profound. Grouchy later recorded his deep impressions of Napoleon's insistence on his generals following his orders to the letter. The seed planted in Grouchy's mind would soon bear terrible fruit for Napoleon.[28] Ney returned to Gosselies, spent some time reviewing reports of troop positions, and then snatched a little sleep.

In the early hours of 16 June Napoleon considered which course of action he would pursue that day, depending on what sunrise revealed. If Blücher were concentrating, and all evidence seemed to show this, he would seek to bring the Prussians to battle with his right wing, drawing aid from the left, which would be placed to block any intervention in the battle by Wellington as well as to enter the right wing battle on the enemy's inner flank. Then, having beaten Blücher, Napoleon could shift his weight to the left to deal with Wellington. Circumstances would dictate. It might be that the Allies had again adopted the policy they had employed during the 1813-14 campaigns: Schwarzenberg, the supreme Allied commander, could have directed that any Allied army finding itself alone and facing Napoleon would refuse battle, withdrawing in front of him to wear down his army in fruitless marches and countermarches. If Blücher employed this tactic on the 16th, Napoleon would leave Grouchy to maintain contact with the Prussians, while turning on Wellington with the left wing and reserves and seeking to drive him into the sea. If Wellington and Blücher should both fall back to join forces behind Brussels, Napoleon could advance directly to Brussels along the high roads from Quatre Bras and Gembloux simultaneously.

The coup of capturing Brussels in the face of two Allied armies could change the political atmosphere throughout the Allied coalition. The *émigré* King Louis would flee from Ghent to Britain, and the newly installed King William of the newly created United Netherlands would have to give up Belgium and hope to hold on to the Dutch throne. If he had not already fought Blücher and Wellington before Brussels, Napoleon would fight them after securing the Belgian capital, unless they had not already gone home. Then, if necessary, he would march across the Rhine and start moving south to threaten the rear and communications of Kleist's Prussian corps and Schwarzenberg's Austro-German army. It would be likely at this point that the coalition would dissolve, with each member reassessing its interests: in Britain, those in favour of accommodation with Napoleon would seek to bring in a government sympathetic to this idea, and with it the termination of Britain's financing of its continental coalition partners; in Prussia, ardent young nationalism would have to suppress a natural desire for revenge on France; in Russia, the Tsar would be prepared to recognize Napoleon in return for Napoleon's acquiescence in Russia's keeping Poland and her efforts to reach the warm waters of the Mediterranean through the Bosporus; in Austria, the Emperor would welcome his son-in-law in control of a strong but neighbourly France in return for Napoleon's guarantee of the integrity of Austria's borders against Prussian or Russian encroachment; and in Spain and Portugal, the sovereigns would simply be hoping to experience Napoleon's benign neglect. And from all the Allies Napoleon would expect to receive acknowledgement of the legitimacy of his claim to the French throne – be it imperial or constitutionally circumscribed – as the expression of the will of the French people; or, for the more traditionally minded, by the irrefutable right of conquest.

In Brussels the morning of the 15th dawned fair, and the Duke of Wellington awoke unencumbered by any awareness that Napoleon, a few hours earlier, had set his army in motion across the frontier with the intention of marching it the short distance to the congenial city where the Duke lay. Wellington had not been troubled by the eviscerated message he had received the day before from General Dornberg; after all, it was only from some unreliable French agent, and not (he believed) from his own man, Colonel Grant. And he had dismissed the report from Colonel Hardinge that the Prussians were massing in expectation of an imminent French attack as their overreaction to dubious intelligence of the situation across the border.

The Duke spent the morning attending to some correspondence which makes clear his equanimity. He wrote to Sir Henry Clinton with a view to renumbering the British divisions in Belgium as they had been in the Peninsula: the 2nd to become the 6th; the 3rd, the 5th; the 6th, the 4th, and so on. Then Wellington wrote to the Tsar[29] on the subject of the forthcoming concerted advance of the Allied armies into France due to begin at the end of the month.

Captain William Verner, a well-connected officer of the 7th Hussars, was looking forward to the Duchess of Richmond's ball that evening, having acted as postman to deliver the invitations. The Duchess had confided in Captain Verner that Wellington had assured her: 'Duchess, you may give your ball with the greatest of safety.'[30] Captain Mercer of the Royal Horse Artillery shared his brother-officer's appreciation of life cantoned around Brussels and his commander's assumption that the campaign would commence with an Allied advance: 'In spite of my eagerness for more active service, it was not without regret that I saw the time approach when I expected to leave the tranquil abode of Strytem.'[31] The 2nd Foot Guards at Enghien were ordered to furnish a corporal's guard, equipped with two days' rations, for the Duchess's ball, while their light company assembled with two hundred rounds of ammunition for target practice.[32] In all, life behind the front for the Anglo-Allied army on the morning of the 15th was still governed by social activity for the grand and camp routine for the common.

On the frontier, however, as the morning wore on, events took a disquieting turn. Ziethen, in accordance with Blücher's orders, had instructed his brigade commanders, if attacked, to send word both to himself and to the inter-army communication post at Mons. Acting on this order, at 8 a.m. Steinmetz had sent a messenger to General Behr at Mons.[33] The messenger was able to avoid the French lancers sent by d'Erlon to patrol around Binche and Mons. A picket of these lancers near Autreffe was reported to Dornberg by van Merlen. Another lancer patrol approached close enough to Mons to be engaged in a skirmish by the two companies of 2nd Battalion, 95th Rifles. Lieutenant Eyre, with the rifle companies, related: '... on the fifteenth our regiment were on outpost duty on the French frontier near Mons and were getting into play with some French lancers when we were ordered to retire ...'[34]

In accordance with Wellington's directions to General Behr,[35] Steinmetz's reports were to be forwarded from Mons to the Prince of Orange at Braine-le-Comte; he, if he saw fit, would send them on to Wellington at Brussels. Thus, Steinmetz's report of being under attack by overwhelming French forces, sent at 8 a.m., was relayed by Behr from Mons to the Prince's headquarters at Braine-le-Comte at 10 a.m. The Prince was not at his headquarters and would not be back all day, having left early on rounds, and would then go to Brussels to army headquarters, staying on to attend the ball in the evening. However, General de Constant Rebecque immediately relayed the message to Wellington's Adjutant-General, Lieutenant-Colonel Sir George Berkeley, attached as liaison officer to the Prince's headquarters. At 2 p.m. Berkeley sent a letter to Wellington's Military Secretary, Lord Fitzroy Somerset, advising him that 'HRH the Prince of Orange having set out at 5 o'clock this morning for the advance posts and not yet being returned, I forward the enclosed letter from General Dornberg. General Constant desires I would inform you that reports just arrived from different quarters state that the Prussians have been attacked upon their line in front of Charleroi; that they have evacuated Binche, and mean to collect first at Gosselies. Everything is quiet upon our front; and... [Chasse's] 3rd division of the Netherlands is collected at Fay. He sends you also the copy of a letter from the Commandant at Mons [Behr].'[36]

Behr's letter stated that Major-General Merlen had received a report from General Steinmetz at Fontaine-l'Evêque indicating that Steinmetz had had confirmation of a French attack that morning on Pirch II's 2

Brigade centred on Charleroi, and that cannon along the entire Prussian line had fired the pre-arranged warning signal. Steinmetz had carried out his orders to alert Wellington's army,[37] but the warning had to travel a long way to reach Wellington: seven miles from Charleroi to Fontaine-l'Evêque, another seventeen to Mons, fourteen more to Braine-le-Comte, and a further twenty to Brussels. Berkeley had sent on the message to Wellington post-haste, together with a similar dispatch from Constant Rebecque to the Prince of Orange.

At three in the afternoon of the 15th, a messenger from General Ziethen rode into General von Müffling's courtyard in Brussels and hurried inside to deliver his dispatch concerning the French attack. Müffling at once went to see Wellington and, as he relates:

> 'The Duke of Wellington, to whom I immediately communicated the news, had received no intelligence from the advance post at Mons. I put the question to him Whether and where he would concentrate his army, as in consequence of this news, Field Marshal Blücher would concentrate his forces at Ligny, if he had not already taken up this position. The Duke replied: "If all is as General Ziethen supposes, I will concentrate on my left wing, i.e., the corps of the Prince of Orange; I shall then be à la portée [within range] to fight in conjunction with the Prussian army. Should, however, a portion of the enemy's forces come by Mons, I must concentrate more towards my centre. For this reason I must positively wait for news from Mons before I fix the rendezvous. Since, however, the departure of the troops is certain, and only the place of rendezvous remains uncertain, I will order all to be in readiness, including the Brunswick corps in reserve, and will direct a brigade of light cavalry to Quatre-Bras." Orders were dispatched accordingly about six or seven o'clock.'[38]

Despite this accumulation of evidence for concluding that Napoleon was indeed advancing into Belgium (which Wellington now accepted), the Duke was not yet willing to act on the assumption that his forces were devoted entirely to the advance through Charleroi. Was the Charleroi attack the main French thrust, or was it only one or two corps fixing Blücher in position while the main weight fell elsewhere? If Charleroi were a feint, Blücher would have the measure of the French without Wellington's help. Until he had heard from Colonel Grant, Wellington did not dare concentrate his army too far to his left, in the Nivelles -Quatre Bras area agreed at Tirlemont, until he was assured that the main French advance would not materialize around Mons, heading for Brussels and Antwerp; and he would only be assured by his trusty Grant.

At 5 p.m. Dornberg's report and Baron Behr's communication from Steinmetz arrived at Wellington's headquarters in the train of the Prince of Orange. The Prince was able to add that he himself had heard the sound of gunfire earlier that morning while touring the forward Netherlands positions. On the strength of this reinforcement of the earlier warnings, Wellington was prompted to issue his first set of movement orders. As a precaution he would now concentrate his forces on Nivelles where they would be in a position to move quickly to block a French advance on Brussels by the high roads from either Charleroi or Mons, and also be within range to support Blücher. De Lancey was instructed to issue the following orders, timed for 5 p.m.:

'1. General Dornberg's Brigade and the Cumberland Hussars to march this night upon Vilvorde and bivouack on the High road near that town.
2. The Earl of Uxbridge will be pleased to collect the cavalry this night at Ninhove, leaving the 2nd Hussars looking out between the Scheldt and the Lys.
3. The 1st Division to collect this night at Ath and adjacent, and to be in readiness to move at a moment's notice.*
[see endnote]
4. The 2nd Division to collect this Night at Ath and adjacent, and be ready to move off at a moment's notice.*
5. The 3rd Division to collect this night at Braine-le-Comte, and to be in readiness to move at the shortest notice.*
6. The 4th Division to be collected this night at Grammont with the exception of the troops beyond the Scheldt, which are to be moved to Audernarde [Oudenarde].*
7. The 5th Division, 81st Regiment, and the Hanoverian Brigade of the 6th Division to be in readiness to March from Bruxelles at a moment's notice.*
8. The Brigade at Ghent [Lambert's] to March to Brussels this evening.
9. The Duke of Brunswick's Corps to collect this night on the high road between Bruxelles and Vilvorde. The Nassau troops to collect at daylight to-morrow morning on the Louvain road, and be ready to move at a moment's notice. The Hanoverian Brigade of the 5th Division to collect this night at Hal, and to be in readiness at daylight to-morrow morning to move towards Bruxelles, and to halt on the high road between Alost and Assche for further orders.
10. The Prince of Orange is requested to collect at Nivelles the 2nd and 3rd Divisions of the Army of the Low Countries; and should that point be attacked this day to move

the 3rd Division of British Infantry upon Nivelles as soon as collected. This movement is not to take place until it is quite certain that the enemy's attack is upon the Prussian Army, and the left of the British Army.*

11. Lord Hill will be so good as to order Prince Frederick of Orange to occupy Audernarde with 500 men, and to collect the 1st Division of the Low Countries, and march to Sotteghem, so as to be ready to march in the morning daylight.*

12. The Reserve Artillery to be in readiness to move at daylight.'[39]

These orders were issued without urgency and do not reflect an expectation of imminent action. Only the Prince of Orange was given any instructions as to what to do in the event of being attacked .When the Prince, arriving early in Brussels for the ball, received these orders, he immediately dispatched them back to Braine-le-Comte. The Netherlands forces at Frasnes did not come under attack by Ney's advance guard until after Wellington's movement orders had been drafted, but in any case news of the fight at Frasnes had not reached Brussels when the orders were sent out.

Lieutenant Basil Jackson, a Deputy-Assistant Quartermaster-General of Wellington's Staff Corps, was walking casually in the park in the centre of Brussels at 7 p.m. when, as he relates:

'... a soldier of the Guards, attached to the QuarterMaster-General's office, summoned me to attend Sir William De Lancey. He had received orders to concentrate the Army towards the frontier, which until then had remained quiet in cantonments. I was employed, along with several others for two hours in writing out 'routes' for the several divisions, foreign as well as British, which were despatched by orderly Hussars of the King's German Legion, steady fellows who could be depended on for so important a service... This business over, which occupied us till after nine, De Lancey put a packet in my hand directed to Colonel Cathcart ... "I believe you can find your way in the dark by the cross roads to Ninove," said Sir William. "Let this be delivered as soon as possible." ... Here let me stop for a moment to commend the practice in our service of having plenty of well mounted Staff Officers ready to convey orders at the utmost speed. On that portentous night in question several chiefly belonging to the Royal Staff-Corps ... were employed in conveying duplicates of the instructions previously forwarded by the Hussars, in order to guard against the possibility of mistake.'[40]

No sooner had these orders been dispatched than further information from Gneisenau reached Müffling, as he recounts: 'The Field Marshal
[Blücher] informed me of his concentrating at Sombref [sic], and charged
me to give him a speedy intelligence of the concentration of Wellington's
army. I immediately communicated this to the Duke, who acquiesced in
Blücher's dispositions. However, he could not resolve on fixing his point of
concentration before receiving the expected news from Mons, but he
promised to give me immediate notice when this arrived.'[41] As Müffling
knew nothing of Wellington's secret instructions to cover Brussels, and
more importantly Antwerp, he could not have understood his apparent reti-
cence in the face of such clear evidence. Certainly Müffling was not
impressed with Wellington's equivocal reply, and knew that his commanders would view it with similar dismay, especially in light of the strained
relations between Prussia and Britain. Müffling, concerned for the safety of
his army, may have reminded Wellington of the Tirlemont agreement of 5
May. He had already said to the Duke: 'You may depend upon this: when
the Prince [Blücher] has agreed to any operation in common, he will keep
his word, should even the whole Prussian army be annihilated in the act;
but do not expect more than we are able to perform; we will always assist
you as far as we can; the Prince will be perfectly satisfied if you do the
same.'[42] At about 10 p.m., after his worrying conversation with Wellington,
Müffling made out his report to Gneisenau, leaving part blank '... to add in
conclusion the places of rendezvous ...' and then, hoping soon to receive
from Wellington the all-important information, he '...kept a courier in
readiness at my door'.[43]

At the same time Wellington received news from both Dornberg
and Constant Rebecque of the attack on the Prussians at Charleroi. In
response the Duke issued a set of after orders, timed at 10 p.m., containing
the following directives: 'The third division of infantry to continue its movement from Braine le Comte upon Nivelles. The 1st division to move from
Enghien upon Braine le Comte. The 2nd and 4th divisions of infantry to
move from Ath and Grammont, also from Audernarde, and to continue
their movements upon Enghien. The above movements to take place with
as little delay as possible.'[44]

As this indicates, Wellington's intent in his after orders was to con-
centrate his army around Nivelles, rather than the agreed Nivelles–Quatre
Bras, because of his doubt as to the meaning of the French attack at
Charleroi in the absence, as he still believed, of word from Colonel Grant.
After writing the after orders and reflecting on the seriousness of the situa-
tion as he now saw it, Wellington wrote two letters, to the duc de Berry and
General Clarke, duc de Feltre, to inform Louis that Charleroi was
menaced.[45]

At Braine-le-Comte General Constant Rebecque had received
Wellington's initial order to assemble the 2nd Netherlands Division at Nivelles. To obey this order would have been to leave Quatre Bras undefended

and the high road to Brussels open to the French. Further, he had received a report from 2nd Division commander General Perponcher which made compliance with Wellington's order seem most ill-advised.

As a consequence of an injury sustained by his superior, Prince Bernhard of Saxe-Weimar, Colonel of the 28th (Orange-Nassau) Netherlands Regiment, was in command of 2 Brigade, Netherlands 2nd Division. Prince Bernhard, stationed at Genappe, had disposed the three battalions of 2nd Nassau Regiment around Quatre Bras, with Major Normann's battalion of that regiment and Captain Bijleveld's horse battery at Frasnes. As soon as the Prince heard firing from Frasnes and saw the alarm beacon alight, he moved with his remaining four battalions and *Jäger* company towards Quatre Bras. There he deployed his men and had them commence a rapid fire to create the impression that they were a larger body of troops. At 9 p.m. the Prince sent an account of the day's action to General Perponcher at Nivelles which concluded: 'I must confess to your Excellency that I am too weak to hold out here long. The two Orange-Nassau battalions have French muskets, and each man has only ten cartridges. The volunteer *Jäger* have carbines of four different calibres and only ten cartridges per carbine. I will defend as well and as long as possible the posts entrusted to me. I expect an attack by the enemy at daybreak. The troops are animated by the best spirit. The Battery has no infantry cartridges.'[46] Perponcher was appalled to learn of Bernhard's situation and immediately placed his 1 Brigade around Nivelles in a posture of defence and immediately sent Captain Baron de Gargen to report to General Constant Rebecque at Braine-le-Comte.

On the strength of de Gargen's report, Constant Rebecque took it upon himself to disregard Wellington's order, sent through the Prince of Orange.[47] He discussed the situation fully with Perponcher, who agreed with his decision and ordered his entire 2nd Division to concentrate at Quatre Bras by morning. Constant Rebecque then wrote, at 10.30 p.m., to inform the Prince of Orange of this decision: 'At this moment Captain Baron de Gargen has arrived from Nivelles, reporting that the enemy has shown himself at Quatre-Bras. I have thought it my duty to take it on myself to instruct General de Perponcher to support his second brigade with the first, and to warn the third division and the cavalry in order to support them if necessary.'[48] He sent this message post-haste to Brussels with instructions that it be put into the hands of the Prince of Orange. As he indicated in his letter, he had had the foresight to alert the other Netherlands forces in the area of impending attack.

Wellington, before going in to the Duchess of Richmond's ball, saw Baron Müffling and said to him: 'I have got news from Mons, from General Dornberg, who reports that Napoleon has turned toward Charleroi with all his forces, and that there is no longer any enemy in front of him; therefore orders for the concentration of my army at Nivelles and Quatre Bras are already dispatched.'[49] Constant Rebecque's report reached the Prince of

Orange at the ball, and of course the Prince at once apprised Wellington of its contents. The ball, which had been proceeding in a muted atmosphere,[50] broke up after supper. Wellington called for his map of the area, but was told that it was at Braine-le-Comte,[51] so he borrowed the Duke of Richmond's set of maps. As he studied the terrain he began to realize that Napoleon's tactics of disinformation and posturing on the coastal flank might have been a blind. His chagrin must have been considerable, and of course his recorded expression of it is famous: 'Humbugged, by God!'.

Wellington sent immediate orders to move his army reserve forward. The 5th and 6th British Divisions, the Nassau contingent and the Duke of Brunswick's corps, all of which had been ordered to be ready to march at a moment's notice, were to go to the crossroads at Mont St-Jean and await further orders. Wellington still believed that he was not in possession of Grant's intelligence, and even at the eleventh hour was reluctant to commit the army to full concentration. From Mont St-Jean the army reserve could march towards Quatre Bras or Nivelles, depending on developments. The Earl of Uxbridge ordered all officers at the ball to return to their regiments as soon as possible, although those committed to the next dance were permitted to complete it rather than allow the event to conclude with an unseemly general exit.

Müffling, after receiving from Wellington the information on concentration that he had been awaiting, had returned to his house to complete his letter to Gneisenau, which he sent off after midnight. At about the same time Gneisenau was receiving Müffling's 7 p.m. dispatch, from which he learned that: 'As soon as the moon rises the reserves will march; and, in case the enemy should not attack Nivelles, the Duke will be in the region of Nivelles with his whole force in the morning to support your Higness.'[52] This report seemed to indicate that Wellington planned to support Blücher from a distance of seventeen miles. When Gneisenau received Müffling's second dispatch, however, he noted that: 'Müffling also reported about midnight to the Prussian Commander-in-Chief that the allied army would be concentrated in twelve hours, and that at ten o'clock on the following morning 20,000 men would be at Quatre Bras, and the cavalry corps will be at Nivelles.'[53]

Having made his further dispositions Wellington retired at 2 a.m., intending to rise early to ride to the front. He had hardly got to sleep before he was roused by Lord Fitzroy Somerset, who admitted Dornberg and De Lancey. During the day Dornberg had received several urgent reminders from Wellington that Dornberg should inform him at once on receipt of any news from Colonel Grant or his agents. The terrible truth finally dawned on Dornberg that he had already received Grant's intelligence at about midday on the 14th and, in relaying it to Wellington, had failed to give the full message or to say it was from Grant. Not surprisingly Dornberg rode at once from Mons to tell Wellington of the error. Wellington 'shot up' in bed[54] and sent De Lancey to order the whole army to move with all haste on Quatre Bras.[55]

Lieutenant Basil Jackson returned to Brussels from his dispatch ride to Ninove at about 4 a.m. and by the early light of dawn saw the army reserve marching through the city and being joined by the Brussels garrison which had stood to in the park an hour earlier, and recognized General Picton riding down the line of his men. Jackson remarked of the passing parade: 'In a few minutes the troops broke into sub-divisions, and I waited, near the Hotel Bellevue, to see them pass. First came a battalion of the 95th rifles ... in their sombre green dress and black accoutrements. The old 28th followed ... The Royal Highlanders, the brave 42nd ... The 79th and the 92nd, also in full Highland costume, were there ... I lingered to see the whole of that noble division of veterans pass.'[56] So, as the day of the 16th dawned on Lieutenant Jackson as he watched Wellington's reserve marching south past the Hôtel Belle Vue in Brussels, it dawned also on the Emperor Napoleon as he strode past the Belle Vue Inn at Charleroi and called for his horse and escort to ride north.

CHAPTER 8

16 June: 2 a.m. to 2 p.m.

'There is an ancient rule of war that cannot be repeated often enough: hold your forces together, make no detachments, and, when you are ready to fight the enemy, assemble all your forces and seize every advantage to make sure of success. This rule is so certain that most generals who have neglected it have been punished promptly.' - Frederick the Great, Instructions to His Generals, 1747.

Marshal Ney left Napoleon's headquarters at Charleroi at about 2 a.m. on 16 June without having received any direct orders concerning his role in this campaign to defeat the seventh coalition raised against France. Napoleon had said that he would send Ney his orders later that morning after collating all the reports he had received and deciding his plan of operations. After Ney left, Napoleon slept for two hours and arose at 4 a.m. to check the French and enemy troop positions shown on his map table (updated continually by his staff). As nothing had changed during the night he began drafting the operational orders for the 16th: orders which would reflect the plan he was developing for the conduct of the campaign.

In the light of intelligence that had come in during the night, Napoleon decided that he would make a rapid advance on Brussels as the first phase of the campaign. To ensure that this manoeuvre should not be interfered with, however, it would first be necessary to push the Prussians back on their communications east of Gembloux to deny them the use of the Namur–Wavre-Brussels high road. For although denied the Namur–Sombreffe–Quatre Bras–Nivelles road, the Allies could otherwise use the road through Wavre to concert their operations in front of or behind Brussels. Napoleon had learned nothing of the troop movements under way throughout the Anglo-Allied army. The only troops of Wellington's that the French had observed were The Netherlands units at Quatre Bras, which were not present in strength when night had fallen, and those at Mons, which had not moved.

Napoleon concluded that Wellington was acting with circumspection and had fallen back on Brussels to be better able to cover Antwerp and Ostend and secure his lines of communication with the ports. Consequently he decided that a rapid advance on Brussels would give him a triple advantage. First it would hasten Wellington's apparent strategic concentration to the rear, and in so doing increase the distance between him and Blücher, making it more difficult for the Allies to act in concert and easier for Napoleon to deal with them one at a time. Secondly he could obtain the great political prize of entry into The Netherlands' only recently acquired

ausing both 'King' Louis and King William to flee Belgium. happen in the face of superior Allied forces could be a tremendous effect at home among the Coalition members, hose who were unenthusiastic in their purpose. And, ssels Napoleon could move against Wellington, forcing d be destroyed or hurriedly embark his British troops erlands and German allies to their fate. In either case en offer King William the same choice he had given the en Elector oi Saxony in 1806: join me as an ally and keep your throne or lose it when I annex your country. Napoleon would then have eliminated an enemy and increased his force by 30,000 Netherlands troops. With this army he could turn on Blücher and ensure his destruction. He could then cross the lower Rhine and be well placed to advance into Hanover, threaten Berlin and turn right to put himself in the rear of the Allied armies still massed on the French borders. At this point, he was certain, the Allies would come to terms.

At 8 a.m. on the 16th, Napoleon sent a personal letter to Marshal Grouchy,[1] confirming his verbal appointment to command of the right wing of nearly 45,000 men. The units placed under Grouchy were : Vandamme's III Corps. Gérard's IV Corps and the cavalry corps of Pajol, Exelmans and Milhaud. The letter informed Grouchy that each of these commanders had been notified that they were now under Grouchy's direct command.[2] Napoleon went on to give Grouchy guidance and an insight into his plans:

> 'If the enemy are at Sombreffe I desire to attack them; I
> wish to attack them even if they are at Gembloux, and also
> to occupy this position; my intention being, after gaining
> possession of these two positions, to set out by night and
> to co-operate with Marshal Ney and my left wing in a
> stroke against the English. Thus do not waste a moment,
> because the more rapidly I Manoeuvre the more favourable
> it will be for the rest of my operations. I presume that you
> are at Fleurus. Keep in constant communication with Gen-
> eral Gérard so that he can support you in an attack on
> Sombreffe, if that is necessary. Girard's Division [the 7th of
> II Corps] has moved to Fleurus; do not use them at all
> unless it is absolutely necessary, because it will have to
> march all night. Also leave my Young Guard and all its
> artillery at Fleurus.'[3]

It is evident that, at this stage, Napoleon was not expecting his right to find more than a rearguard in the area of Sombreffe. He intended that they would drive off the Prussian rearguard, seize the Namur-Brussels road and advance that night on Brussels. He personally would probably join Ney and the left. If Wellington took up a position between Quatre Bras and Brussels, the French right wing could still seize the capital and then attack Wellington from the rear.

Napoleon also explained his objectives in greater depth in a letter to Marshal Ney:

'... I am sending Marshal Grouchy with the 3rd and 4th Infantry Corps to Sombreffe. I am taking my Guard to Fleurus, and I shall be there myself before midday. I shall attack the enemy if I find him there, and *I shall clear the roads as far as Gembloux. At that place, according to circumstances, I shall come to a decision* – perhaps at 3 p.m., and perhaps this evening. My intention is that, immediately after I have made up my mind, you will be ready to march on Brussels. I shall support you with my Guard, who will be at Fleurus, or Sombreffe, and I shall wish you to reach Brussels tomorrow morning. You will set off with your troops this evening, if I make up my mind early enough for you to be informed of my intention by day, and then this evening you will cover three or four leagues [eight to ten miles] and reach Brussels by 7 a.m. tomorrow morning ... I should desire to have with me the Division of Guard [Cavalry] commanded by General Lefebvre-Desnouëttes .... I do not wish to cause General Lefebvre-Desnouëttes to make unnecessary marches, since it is probable that I shall decide to march on Brussels this evening with the Guard ... You understand how much importance is attached to the taking of Brussels. From its capture certain things would happen, because such a quick and sudden movement would cut the English Army from Mons, Ostende, etc. I desire that your dispositions may be well conceived, so that at the first order your eight divisions will take the road to Brussels.'[4]

It is clear from these letters to his wing commanders that, at 8 in the morning of the 16th, Napoleon did not expect either Wellington or Blücher to make a stand against him. Perhaps he thought the Allies would still govern their actions by the tactic of withdrawing before a French army led by him in person.

Napoleon's orders to Ney noted that the Emperor had sent his set of orders on to Ney before the Chief of Staff sent his detailed instructions because Napoleon's own messengers were better mounted. He therefore included some detail on the dispositions he wanted Ney to make until ordered to begin his advance on Brussels: '... 1st Division 2 leagues [5 miles] in front of Quatre Bras [or at about Maison du Roi], if it is not inconvenient; 6 infantry divisions around Quatre Bras, and a division [Girard's] at Marbais, in order that I can move it myself to Sombreffe, should I need its assistance, besides it will not delay your march.'[5]

By instructing Ney to assume the defensive posture outlined in these orders Napoleon meant to ensure that his left wing was placed to accomplish several tactical requirements. The division thrown forward as far as the vicinity of Maison du Roi would hold open the Brussels road and deny Wellington the use of the old east-west road running from near Nivelles to the Brussels road at Genappe. The concentration of six of Ney's infantry divisions at Quatre Bras would assemble the bulk of his fighting strength in a compact mass, within a day's march of Brussels. Also, if Wellington should move to support Blücher, Ney would be astride the routes Wellington would have to take, and in sufficient strength to chew up the Anglo-Allied units as they came along from Nivelles or Brussels. Finally, Ney would be able, if called upon, to march down the Quatre Bras-Sombreffe road to support Napoleon against the Prussians.

Napoleon went on to explain to Ney more of his grand tactical scheme for the campaign:

'I have adopted for this campaign the following general principle, to divide my army into two wings and a reserve. Your wing will be composed of four divisions of the I Corps, four divisions of the II Corps, two divisions of Light Cavalry, and two divisions of the Corps of the Count of Valmy [Kellermann]. This ought not to fall short of 45,000 to 50,000 men. Marshal Grouchy will have almost the same force, and will command the right wing. The Guard will form the Reserve, and I shall bring it into action on either wing just as the actual circumstances may dictate. The Major-General [Chief of Staff] issues the most precise orders, so that when you are detached you should not find any difficulty in obeying such orders as you receive; *general officers commanding corps will take orders directly from me when I am present in person*. Also, according to circumstances I shall draw troops from one wing to strengthen my Reserve ...'[6]

Napoleon had no intention of seeking a decision on both wings at the same time. His forces were far too weak to sustain such an effort. He aimed to seize Brussels first, then deal a decisive blow at each opponent one at a time, by using one wing to block and the other to hold until he could use his reserve, and borrow from the holding wing sufficient forces to destroy his opponent. Then he would reverse the equation by leaving enough men to follow up the defeated force while shifting the bulk against the other.

In any case he believed that serious fighting would not occur at this stage. He felt certain that his careful plans and elaborate deceptions had misled his enemies. Indeed, he had taken Wellington by surprise[7] and might have surprised Blücher too, had it not been for the alertness of Ziethen's outposts and the confirmation of de Bourmont's treachery. As it was, Blücher was at that moment (early morning of the 16th) anxiously awaiting the troops of II, III and IV Corps. Napoleon, confident that Grouchy would have no more than one Prussian corps to deal with at Sombreffe, ordered Lobau's VI Corps to halt at Charleroi so that it could more easily move to whichever wing with which Napoleon decided to advance. His decision would be determined by which wing he felt had the better opportunity to make the dash to Brussels; the taking of the capital was more important to Napoleon at this stage than seeking a decisive battle. That was the reason for his emphasis in his letter to Ney: '... You understand how much importance is attached to the taking of Brussels. From its capture certain things would happen, because such a quick and sudden movement would cut the English Army from Mons, Ostende, etc.' Thus Napoleon's Belgian campaign of 1815 was to open with a manoeuvre of the central position, but with the difference that the objective was not initially to achieve a decisive victory in battle against superior forces, but to outmanoeuvre them to achieve a political victory.

For the French, the first work on the morning of the 16th was largely organizational, although from 5 a.m. at Quatre Bras a brisk exchange of fire had developed between pickets of Saxe-Weimar's and Bachelu's forces. Marshals Ney and Grouchy spent the early hours trying to concentrate their wings. In the absence of orders to the contrary from Napoleon, Ney instructed d'Erlon to concentrate his badly straggling corps around Gosselies, while Reille was to group his around Frasnes. Napoleon had ordered Vandamme and Gérard to close up on Fleurus and place themselves under Grouchy's orders. Kellermann, with his cavalry corps, was to go to the left wing and place himself under Ney's orders. And Napoleon, with his headquarters and the Imperial Guard, was on his way to Fleurus.

At Sombreffe, Blücher's plan was simple: to give battle, aided by a significant force to be sent by Wellington. Müffling's last letter had reassured him on this crucial point. Accordingly he ordered the two nearest corps, Pirch I's at Le Manzy and Thielemann's at Namur, to close up on Sombreffe from their bivouacs. Blücher and Gneisenau were also confident that Bülow's corps was by now close enough to reach Sombreffe that day. They had not received Bülow's message stating that as there was no urgency he would not make a start until the morning of the 16th. It was not until then, however, that Bülow received Blücher's imperative order to march at once and realized the danger facing the Prussian army. Although Bülow would move heaven and earth all day to force-march to Gembloux as ordered, by nightfall his advance guard would only have reached Baudeset.

The morning of the 16th found most of the units of the Anglo-Allied army starting to receive Wellington's 10 o'clock (p.m. of the 15th) after orders and his subsequent orders to concentrate on Quatre Bras. That they should just be getting these orders was not surprising. As Genral Müffling, with his experience as an army Quartermaster-General, pointed out:

> '... the movements of the combined Anglo-Dutch-Hanoverian army were arranged, and the hours calculated, from the moment the cavalry orderlies were despatched from Brussels, to the time which the army would take to assemble at one or other of three places of rendezvous. The calculations themselves were not known to me; but, as was ultimately seen, they were made on the assumption that the orders could be transmitted at the rate at which they could be delivered by day, but not by night. This mistake occurs too often in calculations. In dark nights orderlies cannot ride fast on cross roads; in various cantonments they find every one sunk in deep slumber; and delay in arriving at the rendezvous is the inevitable consequence of a calculation grounded on the time it will take to execute an order by day, and not by night.'[8]

The 'inevitable consequence' was manifest throughout the vast area of the Anglo-Allied cantonments. Captain Mercer of the Royal Horse Artillery, attached to the British cavalry contingent at Strytem, had not received the first orders issued between 5 and 7 p.m. on the 15th, which told him '... to collect at Ninove this night, ready to move at a moment's notice'. It was in the early hours of the 16th that he received the more urgent 'After-Order of 10 o'clock'. As Mercer related in his Journal: '... I was sound asleep when my servant ... awoke me *en sursaut* [with a start]. He had brought a note which an orderly hussar had left, and ridden off immediately. The note had nothing official in its appearance, and might have been an invitation to dinner, but the unceremonious manner in which the hussar had gone off without his receipt looked curious. My despatch was totally deficient in date, so that time and place were left to conjecture; its contents pithy – they were as follows viz.: "Captain Mercer's troop will proceed with the utmost diligence to Enghien where he will meet Major McDonald who will point out the ground on which it is to bivouack tonight." '[9]

Wellington's three sets of orders, issued over the evening and night of 15/16 June, had overwhelmed his staff; in their panic to issue and deliver them they failed to write clear, dated dispatches, and the dispatch-riders often failed to wait for receipts, with repercussions which would be felt later. To pursue the example of Captain Mercer's experience, he was caught unprepared by the after order, not having received the first order, and its sketchiness left ample room for erroneous interpretation: '... That we were to move forward, then, was certain. It was rather sudden, to be sure ... but the suddenness of it, and the importance of arriving quickly at the appointed place, rather alarmed me, for upon reflection I remembered that I had been guilty of two or three imprudences. First all my officers were absent; secondly, all my country waggons were absent; thirdly, a whole division (one-third of my troop) were absent at Yseringen.'[10]

Mercer admitted in his Journal that valuable time was consumed in assembling his troop, and in having breakfast before setting off. He had not gone far, moreover, before reaching the limits of the topography with which he was familiar:

> 'We cleared the village and marched some miles well enough, being within the range of my daily rides; but, this limit passed, I was immediately sensible of another error – that of having started without a guide, for the roads became so numerous, intricate, and bad, often resembling only woodman's tracks, that I was sorely puzzled, spite of the map I carried in my sabretache, to pick out my way. But a grave error still had I to reproach myself with, and one that might have been attended with fatal consequences. Eager to get on, and delayed by the badness of the roads, I left my ammunition waggons behind, under charge of old Hall, my quartermaster-sergeant, to follow us, and then pushed on with the guns alone, thus foolishly dividing my troops into three columns – viz. the guns, ammunition waggons, and the column of provision waggons under the commissary.'[11]

Although Mercer may have been more candid than most in confessing his faults, his experience was typical.[12] At Soignies, when on the 15th the first rumours of enemy movement had come up from the border area, Ensign Nevill Macready of the Light Company of the 30th Foot had been ordered with his company to form a picket around the village of Naast, two and a half miles in front of Soignies. On returning to Soignies the next morning for the company rations, Macready found his regiment had gone in the night. He did not know that the regimental commander had received his after order and in his haste to comply with it had forgotten his light company. Macready wrote: 'I ran into a house and asked, "Where are the troops?" "They marched at two this morning," was the chilling reply. "By what road?" "Towards Braine le Compte"... We were most unpleasantly situated; ignorant whether we were left by mistake or design, and dreading equally the consequences of quitting our post without orders, or the division being engaged during our absence. Our commissions were safe by remaining where we were; but we were determined to risk them, and all the hopes of young ambition, rather than be absent from the field of glory.'[13]

Sir John Colborne (later Field Marshal Lord Seaton), commanding the 52nd Light Infantry, attached to Adams' brigade in Sir Henry Clinton's 2nd Division, received orders in the evening of the 15th to quit Quevres-au-Camp and move that night on Enghien. Colborne, who had had much experience of outpost duty, convinced Clinton not to activate his orders until first light at 4 a.m. on the 16th: '... Night was coming on, and I observed, "I'll undertake to say, from my experience, that if you march to-night, considering the circumstances – a strange road, darkness, the expectation of coming into contact with the enemy – you won't go two miles." And so it turned out. Our Division did not march till morning, and before we had gone three miles we came up with stragglers and regiments halted, and passed several divisions in great confusion.'[14]

Sir William Howe De Lancey simply did not have enough riders[15] to transmit in the proper fashion the great mass of orders, after orders, and supplementary orders Wellington had generated because of his initial uncertainty and belated awakening to the true situation. It was impossible for most of the riders delivering the 5 to 7 p.m. orders to have returned to headquarters in time to go out again with the after orders of 10 o'clock, which meant a delay in dispatch or the use of other riders who would not know the terrain so well. Further, the orders had to be sent on from the various corps, divisional and brigade headquarters, until they finally reached small units like Mercer's, cantoned in obscure hamlets dotted across the dark Belgian lowlands. Orders were received out of order, and some were not received at all. Many sets of later orders did not catch up with the correct units until those units had been some time on the march and had got closer to Braine-le-Comte and Nivelles. The mounting congestion on the narrow country roads gradually engulfed and jumbled a great part of Wellington's formations.

Nor were General Officers of the Staff often any the wiser than their counterparts in the field. General Sir Augustus Frazer, commanding the Horse Artillery and billeted near army headquarters, wrote a letter to his wife at 6 o'clock on the morning of the 16th: 'I have been sleeping sound. We have a beautiful morning. I have sent to Sir George Wood's [commander of the Royal Artillery] to hear if we are to move, which I conclude we are of course to do. I sent Major Bean orders yesterday by express to march to Vilvorde [5 to 7 p.m. orders], or any village in its neighbourhood in which he could establish his troop ... I have just heard that the Duke moves in half an hour. Wood thinks to Waterloo, which we cannot find on the map: this is the old story over again. I have sent Bell [Lieutenant William Bell, Staff Adjutant] to De Lancey's office, where we shall learn the real name, &c. The whole place is a bustle. Such jostling of baggage, of guns and of waggons. It is very useful to acquire a quietness and composure about all these matters; one does not mend things by being in a hurry.'[16] With sympathy for General Frazer's predicament, it is easy to imagine the difficulties likely to have been encountered by an orderly rider attempting to deliver subsequent orders to a unit with the address of 'some village in the neighbourhood of Vilvorde'.

Before Wellington left Brussels with a small party for Quatre Bras, he instructed De Lancey to prepare a current estimate of the locations of all the army units, which De Lancey was to bring with him when he followed. De Lancey produced a memorandum (see Appendix III) giving the 'dispositions' of the units as of 7 a.m. on the 16th. Not having obtained receipts for many of the orders, De Lancey was obliged to make educated guesses at the whereabouts of most formations, based on assumptions as to time of receipt of orders, speed of assembly, and rate of movement. Altogether, the De Lancey Memorandum was a specious document to which Wellington was to give unwarranted credence.[17]

On his way to Quatre Bras Wellington stopped at the edge of the Bois de Soignes near the farmhouse of Mont St-Jean to talk to General Picton, whose 5th Division remained halted in the woods as instructed in the after orders of 10 o'clock. Wellington ordered Picton to march on to Genappe and halt there. In Wellington's mind there still remained some doubt as to whether Napoleon might after all be feinting to the Allied left to force them to uncover their right and the Mons-Brussels high road. From Genappe Picton could march west along the Vieux Genappe road (the road Napoleon had ordered Ney to block) if it were necessary to counter a French column coming up from Mons.

During the early hours of the morning of the 16th, on the advice of General Constant Rebecque, the Prince of Orange had taken steps to strengthen the Netherlands' position at Quatre Bras; as he reported to King William: 'I ordered the third division, as well as the cavalry and the English divisions, to advance to Nivelles, and the second [Netherlands] division to support the position at Quatre Bras. Only a part of the second division could move at once, seeing that the brigade of Major-General de Bijlandt could not leave Nivelles before the arrival of the other divisions there.'[18] Bijlandt's 7th Line Battalion, about 700 men, was assigned to cover Nivelles until relieved, but did arrive at Quatre Bras before the serious fighting began.

When Wellington arrived at Quatre Bras he found it defended by 7,373 men and sixteen guns. Apprised of the situation and the measures taken, the Duke complemented General Perponcher on his dispositions. Perponcher had left Nivelles for Quatre Bras at two that morning, with the 27th Jäger and the 8th Militia Battalions. On the way they met a patrol of 50 Silesian hussars under the command of First Lieutenant Zehelin. These Prussian soldiers had been cut off during their retreat the day before, and agreed to accompany Perponcher and assist him. On arriving at Quatre Bras Perponcher had approved Saxe-Weimar's dispositions, but had extended them to give the impression of greater strength.

In truth, though, the position was still only lightly held when Wellington arrived. Since first light at about 4 a.m., it had been under pressure from the French. Ney had sent out probing patrols, some in considerable strength. These were to keep The Netherlands troops fully occupied all morning, until Ney eventually launched his attack. Perponcher's Chief of Staff, Colonel van Zuylen van Nyevelt, related the action of the morning and early afternoon:

'At five o'clock the 27th Battalion of Jägers was placed in the first line to [the] left of the Charleroi road, and both the flank companies of this battalion, relieving the 3rd Battalion Nassau, were distributed over its left wing, where they were able to watch the movements of the enemy. The 8th Battalion National Militia remained in reserve in the centre of the Second Brigade behind the houses of Quatre Bras.

'The 2nd Nassau having sent out picquets, soon followed by all the men of the battalion, fell in with a few cavalry patrols of the enemy and some picquets, who retired after a few shots had been exchanged. This battalion took up its stand on the high ground in the rear of Frasnes [chapel, not village], one company guarding the village, two others holding the edge of the wood. By this movement the battalion commanded nearly the whole of the wood of Bossu ... In the course of reconnoitring, the detachment of Prussian Hussars made a few splendid charges on the cavalry of the enemy, whom they forced to retreat, themselves losing four men and thirteen horses. This detachment having soon after heard of the whereabouts of its own army corps, left the Division and went to Sombref [sic] ... At 6 o'clock two companies of the left wing, which was occupied by the 27th Jägers, were told to seize a height [the height of Frasnes chapel itself], from which the enemy could watch our movements. They succeeded ... at several points little skirmishes took place, the artillery sending from time to time a volley to keep off the enemy ... At seven o'clock the enemy began to reconnoitre our position by making a few cavalry charges, which were however, repulsed with loss on his side ... Up to now the enemy had not appeared in great strength; the troops against whom we had to fight consisted, besides part of the infantry of the line, of Chasseurs of the Guard, Lancers and mounted artillery of the Guard ... The 2nd Battalion Nassau having been exposed to fire since the previous day, was at 12 o'clock relieved by the 3rd Battalion and sent to

Quatre Bras to rest and have its meal. Whilst these incidents were taking place, the Third division had reached Nivelles and there relieved the [7th Line] battalion of our division which had been left for the protection of the town.

'The Artillery was [initially] placed as follows: Two 6-pounders and a howitzer of the mounted artillery [Bijveldt's] on the road to Frasnes; one 6-pounder and one howitzer on the right side of that road; and the other 3 6-pounders of that battery on the road to Namur. The two howitzers and four of the 6-pounders of the foot battery [Stevenart's] were placed in front of Quatre Bras close to the troops of the second line; Lieutenant Winsinger, with two 6-pounders, supported the right wing of the First Line ... Two companies of the 27th battalion *jägers* were placed farther to the left, and a number of Tirailleurs [sharpshooters] along the wood of Villers-Perwin in order to watch the movements of the enemy ... In the meantime large bodies of the enemy had come into sight, the Tirailleurs keeping up a well sustained fire along the line ... About 2 o'clock the 7th Battalion of the line was also placed in a compact column on the plain, but soon afterwards it received orders to take up a position first behind the wood, afterwards on the right of it. The 7th Battalion of Militia followed in their traces and crossed the wood ... At the same time the 5th National Militia was ordered to take a stand somewhat more to the left on the Chaussée [high road] of Charleroi, and guard a farm situated alongside that road.'[19]

When the Duke of Wellington arrived at Quatre Bras a little before 10 a.m., he witnessed the repulse of the last French patrol. He later recorded his observations of the situation before Quatre Bras:

'I found there the Prince of Orange with a small body of Belgian troops, and two or three battalions of infantry, a squadron of Belgian dragoons [actually Zehelin's Prussian Hussars], and two or three pieces of cannon, which had been at Quatre-Bras since the preceding evening. It appeared that the picket of this detachment had been touched by a French patrol, and there was some firing, but very little; and of so little importance that, after seeing what was doing, I went on to the Prussian army, which I saw from the ground [that is, the height behind Frasnes chapel] was assembling upon the field of Saint Amand and Ligny, about eight miles distant.'[20]

Before riding over to see Blücher, Wellington sent ahead a letter to him:

> 'Upon the heights behind Frasnes
> June 16th, 1815, at half past ten.
>
> My Dear Prince,
> My Army is situated as follows. Of the corps of the Prince of Orange, one division is here [around Frasnes chapel] and at Quatre Bras, the remainder at Nivelles. The reserve is on the march from Waterloo to Genappe, where it will arrive at noon. The English cavalry will be at the same hour at Nivelles. Lord Hill's Corp is at Braine-le-Comte. I do not see any great force of the enemy in front of us, and I await news from Your Highness, and the arrival of troops to decide upon my operations for the day. Nothing has appeared in the direction of Binche, nor on our right.
>
> Your very obedient servant
> WELLINGTON'[21]

The estimates in Wellington's letter were of course derived from the De Lancey Memorandum, and if the units given in it were not where it put them, based on immediate compliance and daylight speed and precision of movement, the fault (as De Lancey might have seen it) lay with Wellington for the eleventh-hour nature of their issue and for not having moved his headquarters nearer the frontier on the 14th at the first definite signs of trouble.

In the meantime General Müffling, who was in Wellington's entourage, spoke to Lieutenant Zehelin, informing him of the whereabouts of the Prussian army. Then, just after 1 p.m., Wellington and his party, accompanied by Zehelin and his hussars, rode over to find Blücher and Gneisenau. At Brye, near a windmill, Wellington found the two Prussian commanders observing the French army massing to the front of their position. There could be no further doubt in the Duke's mind as to the whereabouts of Napoleon and his main force.

The Prussian position was well chosen. Viewed from Fleurus, the terrain seemed to allow the French an easy approach over an undulating plain and a series of low ridges to the villages of Brye, Mont Potriaux and Tongrinne, and behind them, the important Quatre Bras-Namur lateral road. Having dislodged the weaker Prussian force, the French could push them back beyond the Brussels-Namur high road – their immediate objective. In front of the villages, however, hidden from view in a hollow, was the meandering Ligny stream, about fifteen feet wide and four feet deep, with steep banks lined with thick undergrowth. Also along this natural trench was a series of habitations: Wagnelee, the hamlet of St-Amand, St-Amand la Haye, Ligny, Tongrinelle, Boignée and Balatre. Ligny itself contained a number of significant obstacles: two large farms, a ruined château and a church surrounded by a cemetery with high walls. The Prussians had prepared defences along the the Ligny, barricading and loopholing the buildings and walls of the habitations to transform them into ten bastions along the line of the stream. The bulk of the Prussian force was deployed on the ridges behind, ready to engage the French wherever they attempted to cross the water obstacle. The Prussian position was formidable.

Napoleon had arrived at Fleurus at 11 a.m. His engineers had built a platform around the mill from which he could survey the ground before him. The Prussian position appeared quite weak. The Ligny and all that lay along it were hidden from view. All he could see between Fleurus and the Prussians was a vast plain rippling with corn.[22] As far as he could tell the only Prussian troops deployed in line of battle were Ziethen's four depleted brigades and Roder's cavalry. Pirch II's and Theilemann's corps were just beginning to assemble on the heights behind Sombreffe and Tongrinne. Napoleon realized then that he was facing more than just one Prussian corps. He assumed from the disposition of the visible troops that Blücher had chosen to make a stand here while the remainder of his army assembled behind it. Closer examination revealed that his right flank was open, having no natural protection, and could be vulnerable to a decisive strike. It seemed obvious to Napoleon that, in attempting such a forward concentration and deployed as he was, Blücher was expecting assistance from Wellington. If Blücher, Napoleon reasoned, had intended simply to fall back on his communications, he would have deployed his troops perpendicularly across the Fleurus road in readiness to give ground. Napoleon was now clear as to his plan for the battle: if he struck hard at Blücher's right and destroyed it before Wellington could arrive to support it, he might drive the Prussians in disorder back to the Meuse and be free to drive on Brussels and destroy Wellington if he stood anywhere short of Dover.

Having decided what he intended to do, Napoleon set about the task of organizing his forces. On arrival he had found only Vandamme's corps, with Pajol's and Exelmans' cavalry corps, and Milhaud's division, now attached to the right. He sent orders for Gérard's corps to come up at once. In his haste Gérard and his staff rode ahead of the column and veered towards Prussian outposts, where he was nearly captured. Napoleon also ordered up the Imperial Guard, with both its cavalry divisions, Lefebvre-Desnouëttes' light division having been recalled from Ney in exchange for Kellermann's *cuirassiers*. Napoleon also hoped that Lobau's corps might have crossed the Sambre and be able to arrive in time to join the battle. In addition he intended that Ney should deploy one of his corps around Quatre Bras to prevent Wellington from aiding Blücher, and send the other corps down the Namur road to roll up Blücher's exposed flank.

When Wellington found Blücher and Gneisenau at Brye, the three Allied commanders discussed how to concert their efforts to meet what was undeniably an imminent attack by Napoleon's main force against the Prussian army. At this point Wellington knew that only a small part of his army was near enough to support the Prussians in time: the 2nd Netherlands Division of 8,000 men were at Quatre Bras, but were engaged by French forces; and reserve elements – Picton's division and the Brunswick and Nassau contingents – totalling another 17,500. From Quatre Bras Wellington had sent a galloper back to urge these units on to support the Prince of Orange at Quatre Bras.[23]

Relying on the value of Wellington's letter, Blücher and Gneisenau naturally assumed that by 4 p.m. they would be joined by several Anglo-Allied infantry divisions and cavalry, and possibly by Wellington's entire army.[24] General Müffling's letters to them of the night before had not mentioned Wellington's delay, but rather gave reason for undue optimism by reporting that he was concentrating nearer to Nivelles. Neither had Müffling told his superiors that Wellington had not ordered any real concentration until his After Orders of 10 o'clock.

Wellington, speaking French – in which he was fluent, having been at school in Belgium and France – asked his Prussian counterparts: '*Que voulez-vous que je fasse?* [What do you want me to do?].'[25] Müffling, who acted as translator for the discussion, later recounted the exchange of views between Wellington and Gneisenau (principally), including Müffling's own contribution to Allied Grand Tactics. Müffling wrote:

'... that the Duke had the best intentions to support the Field Marshal, and that he would do all they wished, provided they did not expect him to divide his army, which was contrary to his principles. As few troops had yet arrived at Quatre Bras, and the English reserve [which was directed thither] could not reach it before four in the afternoon, *it seemed to me important that Wellington's troops should concentrate in front, somewhere beyond Frasnes, from thence advance in a straight line towards the Prussian right (Wagnelee) and there forming a right angle with the Prussian position, immediately encircle Napoleon's left wing.* General Gneisenau shook his head at this proposition but I do not know what objections he had to make to it. Now, to the Duke's question, he replied, that the most desirable plan for the Prussian army would be, for the Duke, as soon as his army assembled at Quatre Bras, to march off to the left of the Chaussée to Namur, and place himself at Brye in rear of the Prussian Army as a reserve.'[26]

Gneisenau, sensing that Ligny was a strong natural position, would be satisfied, if he had enough reserves, to let Napoleon blunt his army assaulting it, expending French reserves at a higher rate than the Allies would have to expend theirs. Wellington's army would be used as the mass of decision to exploit any weakness appearing on either of Napoleon's flanks or any exposed part of his line.[27] Müffling recorded that neither ally was happy with the other's proposal:

'... nor could it be accepted by the English leader, who had Dutch troops under his orders; because in taking a flank march to the left of Quatre Bras, he must give up the two roads leading from the enemy to Brussels, and expose the capital of Belgium, which was contrary to his instructions [Müffling did not know of Wellington's underlying instructions regarding the ports]. The Duke looked at his map, and did not answer one word. I saw how much he disliked the proposition, and therefore made the following observations: "According to this proposition the English army must wait till the whole is assembled, in complete inactivity, at Quatre Bras, at a distance of 12,000 paces from the Prussians, without being able to render them the least assistance. *If, however, the English army advances to the point where the Roman road intersects the Chaussée from Quatre Bras to Charleroi [one German mile and a half; six English miles], they would not then be more than 6,000 paces from the Prussian right wing, and by deploying to the left, they would touch upon Field Marshal Blücher, and have favourable ground for fighting and manoeuvring.* The Corps of the Prince of Orange will have a little farther to march to the point of intersection specified, from Nivelles than from Quatre Bras; and the right wing from Ath is even nearer the former." In this manner I avoided publicly mentioning the Duke's erroneous calculations as to the time in which his army would be assembled, as well as Gneisenau's incorrect calculation as to the arrival of the English army at Bry [sic]; and the Duke eagerly caught my proposal saying, "Je culbuterai ce qu'il y a devant moi à Frasnes, me dirigant sur Gosselies [I shall overthrow what there is before me at Frasnes, in going on to Gosselies]." General Gneisenau refuted all that was said in favour of this movement by these few words: "It is too long and insecure; the march from Quatre Bras to Bry is, on the contrary, safe and decisive." The Duke replied: "Well I will come, provided I am not attacked myself."'[28]

It is apparent from this badly served conversation that Wellington expected that his entire army would have arrived at Quatre Bras by 4 p.m., for he would hardly have thought to advance through Frasnes toward Gosselies with the few divisions he knew were then at or near Quatre Bras. It is equally apparent that Gneisenau expected Wellington with substantial forces to come to the aid of the Prussians, and that he would think Wellington had agreed to use the Quatre Bras-Namur road. Müffling had failed in his duty as translator and intermediary because, while aware that each ally misunderstood the other and that both were relying upon De Lancey's erroneous estimates of the location of Wellington's army, he did not disabuse them of their misconceptions. With his experience and from his knowledge of Anglo-Allied dispositions, Müffling knew that it would be well into the evening before Wellington had something like an army assembled at Quatre Bras. And yet Müffling allowed Gneisenau to assume that Wellington had ordered his concentration upon first being notified of a French attack by Gneisenau through Müffling, and that Wellington's army should therefore be largely assembled at Quatre Bras within a few hours. With less justification than Gneisenau, Wellington, too, believed he would soon have very substantial forces at Quatre Bras, with which he could advance on Wagnelee to attack Napoleon's left flank and rear. After making his final remark, Wellington and his party, including Müffling, set out back to Quatre Bras, and Gneisenau and Blücher were left with impressions that would later precipitate them into near disaster.

Since 4 a.m. on the 16th Marshal Ney had been trying to close up his forces. D'Erlon, below Jumet, had two divisions with him and two still struggling to come up to him, with Allix only having crossed the Sambre by 5 a.m. Reille, on Ney's orders, had sent Bachelu's division up to Frasnes to support Lefebvre-Desnouëttes' cavalry, provide a skirmish line and assist in a reconnaissance to determine whether the enemy were still at the crossroads.

Napoleon had written his orders to his two wing marshals between 8 and 9 a.m. Because Ney was to be in command of the detached wing that day and not under his Emperor's eye, Napoleon sent Ney's orders to be reinforced verbally by his Imperial ADC, General Count Flahaut. Flahaut explained to Ney that Napoleon had decided to fight the Prussians on the right. As to Ney's immediate movement orders, Flahaut wrote:

> '... I was directed to give them to Marshal Ney by word of mouth.[29] I therefore gave him as from the Emperor the order to move to Quatre Bras, to hold this important point in strength, and [should the enemy allow him to do so] to support with every man at his disposal the Emperor's offensive against the Prussian army. After giving him ... this order at about eleven o'clock, I went forward, and not far from Quatre Bras I met General Lefebvre-Desnouëttes with his cavalry. I stayed with him pending the arrival of Marshal Ney's forces, and we saw opposite us, some way off, some of the English staff [Wellington and party], who

195

seemed to be taking stock of the position. General Lefeb-vre-Desnouëttes ordered a few rounds of artillery to be fired on them, although they were out of range ... As regards Marshal Ney, he knew at 11 o'clock in the morning of the 16th, how much importance the Emperor attached to his being in possession of the position of Quatre Bras.[30]

The reports reaching Ney from Frasnes were, as is often the case with the view from the ground, partial and misleading. They told of Prussian cavalry assisting Nassau and Netherlands troops, apparently in no great strength. There was nothing about the presence of Wellington or British troops. Ney was faced with a dilemma. Napoleon had ordered him to take and hold Quatre Bras using six divisions, with one more thrown forward to Genappe. However, as it would take another two or three hours for d'Erlon to close up, Ney could only advance at present with three of Reille's divisions. To place just two divisions at Quatre Bras and one at Genappe would be to court disaster. Wellington could attack in strength from Nivelles or above Genappe, or from both directions, and Blücher might send a corps up the road toward Ney's right flank and rear. Ney, in going out on a limb to Quatre Bras with inadequate force, could easily be ground up between superior Allied forces coming from any or all of three directions. Napoleon, in drawing up his orders, had not expected the Prussians to offer immediate resistance, nor had he known that his left wing was so dispersed. Cracks were already beginning to appear in his plans. Had Ney been brought into Napoleon's confidence earlier, it is likely that he would have been able to ensure that his wing stayed in much closer order on the march. Ney certainly would have used all the available pontoon bridges to cross the Sambre.[31]

Ney decided to ride to Frasnes to reconnoitre the ground and to instruct Lefebvre-Desnouëttes to return to Napoleon at Fleurus when Kellermann relieved him. Before going he issued instructions to his corps commanders. Reille was to take Quatre Bras and hold it with two divisions while pushing another one as far as Genappe (his fourth division, Girard's, had already been detached to the right). D'Erlon was ordered to concentrate three divisions at Frasnes to constitute the left wing reserve, to observe the Prussians on the right, and to send to assist the Emperor if required. Also, as a precaution, and to maintain contact between wings, d'Erlon was to send a division and his corps cavalry to Marbais, equidistant from Quatre Bras and Gembloux.[32] A copy of Ney's orders was sent as a matter of routine to Marshal Soult.

It was noon before Reille's corps was closed up and ready to move forward. Lefebvre-Desnouëttes' cavalry reports led Ney to expect little or no resistance. Bachelu's infantry and Piré's cavalry would act as the advance guard, followed by Foy, and Prince Jérôme's infantry divisions. By

1.30 p.m. the van had moved beyond Frasnes, Foy passing there at about 2 p.m. and Jérôme at 2.30. The advance guard sighted The Netherlands' first-line positions at about 2 p.m. To the French left, in the Bois de Bossu, were two battalions of 3rd Nassau Regiment and the 1st Battalion of 28th Netherlands (Nassau). The two farms of Pierrepont were held by detachments of the 28th, and Stevenart's six guns were also visible in the area. To the French right The Netherlands 27th Jäger Battalion was positioned around Gemioncourt and Piraumont and back to Paradis on the Nivelles-Namur road. The 27th, with only two companies in reserve, was strung out thinly along an extended line of 1,000 yards. Ney, a master of the rearguard action, commented to Reille that the disposition of the enemy's left was rash, and that the attack would therefore begin on the French right, with Gemioncourt as the first objective. At 2 p.m. a French cannonade opened the French attack to take the Quatre Bras crossroads.

CHAPTER 9
16 June: Quatre Bras and Ligny

'What is the object of defence? Preservation. It is easier to hold ground than to take it. It follows that defence is easier than attack, assuming both sides are equal. Just what is it that makes preservation and protection so much easier? It is the fact that the time which is allowed to pass unused accumulates to the credit of the defender. He reaps where he did not sow. Any omissions of attack - whether from bad judgement, fear, or indolence - accrue to the defender's benefit.' - Major-General Karl von Clausewitz, *On War*, vi, 1832.

At 2 p.m. Ney began his attack to capture Quatre Bras. He and Reille had arrived in front of The Netherlanders' positions with the advance guard of II Corps a quarter of an hour earlier. Ney immediately recognized the importance of the Bois de Bossu on his left. The Emperor's orders were to hold the crossroads and prevent Wellington from joining the Prussians. Unless Ney held the wood as well, he would not be able to stop Wellington bypassing his position by way of the track from Hautain-le-Val to the Charleroi road above Frasnes. More immediately, it would be impossible to advance to the crossroads while the enemy occupied the wood along his left flank. Ney remarked to Reille: 'There is hardly anyone in the Bois de Bossu; we must take it at once.'[1] Reille, who had fought in more Peninsula battles against Wellington than had Ney, replied cautiously: 'It may turn out to be one of these Spanish battles, in which the English never appear till their own time is come. It would be prudent to defer our attack until all our troops have mustered here.'[2] Although Ney replied: 'Nonsense! The companies of voltigeurs can manage it alone!',[3] he nevertheless waited until 2 p.m. when Bachelu's other brigade had arrived and drawn up in columns to the right of the road. General Foy's division, following Bachelu's, was directed to the left of the road. Jérôme's division was still on the march between Gosselies and Frasnes; while General Piré's cavalry was split, with his regiments of *chasseurs à cheval* flanking the right of Bachelu's infantry, and his regiments of lancers placed in the rear of the gap between Bachelu's and Foy's divisions. In Ney's second line was Lefebvre-Desnouëttes' Guard Light Cavalry waiting for Kellermann to come up. And indeed Kellermann was already deploying his 1st Cuirassier Brigade to the left behind Foy, although his other brigade had been left farther back at Liberchies, off the Brussels-Charleroi Chaussée, and just above the Roman road leading to Wagnelee, whence it could move with d'Erlon's corps to support the Emperor if needed.

Ney, seeing merit in Reille's comment about the wood, decided to start the attack on the left of the Netherlanders' line around Piraumont, with the objective of reaching the Nivelles-Namur high road at Thyle, clearing the wood indirectly. He reasoned that, with his right on the road, the Netherlanders would be obliged to pull back their entire line and abandon the Bois de Bossu to avoid being outflanked. Perponcher had already provided for this eventuality, having ordered the Prince of Saxe-Weimar, commanding the right and the positions in the woods, to fall back if necessary on Hautain-le-Val, where his ammunition park was located and where he could regroup and be reinforced from Nivelles.[4]

Reille's corps artillery began a cannonade on the Netherlanders' left flank at just after two. This was followed by an assault with Bachelu's entire infantry division, supported by a brigade of Piré's cavalry and Jamin's 2nd Brigade of Foy's division; in all, 5,000 infantry, 1,000 cavalry and 42 guns. Foy's 1st Brigade was to act as a temporary reserve. The attack swept along on a front between the Charleroi road and the farm of Piraumont. Then Foy's 1st Brigade followed in echelon to Bachelu's left, and 900 lancers of Piré's other brigade moved up to sweep the Bois de Bossu.

The Prince of Orange with his 8,000 men and sixteen guns occupied a front of a mile and a half. The Prince's force was spread thinly so as to give an impression of strength and to cover the two strategic points at Quatre Bras: the primary one, the Nivelles-Namur road, which communicated between the two Allied armies; and the secondary, the Bois de Bossu, without which the road could not be held. As the defender, the Prince had to bear the defender's disadvantages of having to cover an entire front and of having to leave the initiative to the enemy. The 27th *Jägers* received the heavy French attack on the Prince's left, and gave ground grudgingly, disputing every foot with the French skirmishers. Bijeveldt's horse battery delivered one devastating volley of canister, slowing the French advance, only to receive an overwhelming and terribly accurate barrage of counter-battery fire from the French corps artillery. An ammunition limber was blown up and a howitzer disabled. Bijeveldt withdrew the remainder of his battery out of range rather than risk losing it all.[5]

On the east side of the road, roughly parallel to Bijeveldt, were the six guns of Stevenart's foot battery, which was to keep up a flanking fire against the French left as Bijeveldt was to do against the enemy's right. For several rounds, Stevenart's pieces inflicted severe casualties on Foy's supporting brigade and the other one advancing directly on the Pierrepont farms in front of the Bois de Bossu. Seeing the effect of Stevenart's guns on his troops, Ney ordered an immediate barrage on his position. Within minutes, as Colonel van Zuylen van Nyevelt observed: '... The Captain of the foot battery was killed, several officers killed or wounded, and the horses so rapidly shot down that it was scarcely possible to keep the guns moving.'[6]

In the meantime Lieutenant-Colonel Westenberg had advanced the 5th Netherlands Militia Battalion down the Charleroi road. Westenberg was a first-class officer who, before Napoleon's abdication, had commanded a battalion of the French Imperial Guard, formed of the former *'pupilles et vélites'* of the Guard of King Louis Napoleon of Holland. Westenberg had his men occupy the central building of the fortified farmhouse of Gemioncourt, the surrounding area and the open ground from the farmhouse to the edge of the Bois de Bossu. To his left the 27th *Jägers*, having pulled back, now held a strong position along the line of the Gemioncourt brook, which ran past the farmhouse, through a broken ground of shrubs and rocks and into the Materne pond near the Namur road. To Westenberg's right and rear he was supported by the 7th Line Battalion, with some of the remaining effective guns of the two batteries falling back behind this new line to regroup and then provide fire support. Visibility was limited for both sides because most of the fields between Frasnes and Quatre Bras had standing crops of tall wheat, rye and corn.

In front of the Bois de Bossu Foy's 1st Brigade was pushing Saxe-Weimar's skirmishers out of the Pierrepont farms and back into the wood. Two guns from Stevenart's battery, commanded by Captain Winzeringer, sheltered in the lee of the wood and poured canister into the approaching French. Foy sent a battalion around the southern tip of the wood to launch an attack on the Netherlanders in the wood, co-ordinated with the attack by the remainder of the brigade from the west side. Saxe-Weimar, with his two Nassau battalions and one battalion of the 28th Line, was soon forced to pull back to avoid being encircled. General Perponcher sent the 7th Netherlands Line and the 7th Militia to help Saxe-Weimar hold the vital wood, and sent the 8th Militia to support the 5th Militia at Gemioncourt.

Thus, at 2.45 p.m., with the battle 45 minutes old, Ney had advanced about 1,000 yards, or half-way, toward the crossroads, along the whole of the front between the Bois de Bossu and the Bois Delhutte. To maintain the integrity of his new line, running through the Bois de Bossu and Gemioncourt to Materne pond and the Namur road, the Prince of Orange had committed all his slender reserves save only two battalions and three guns.

At about this time Prince Jérôme's division of 7,800 men and eight guns arrived on the field. This addition increased Ney's force to 22,500 men and 50 guns. Of the inauspicious outlook from the Netherlanders' viewpoint at this stage, Colonel van Zuylen van Nyevelt wrote:

> 'In this position the Division had been entirely by itself and without cavalry all the time exposed to a heavy artillery and musket-fire, with alternate cavalry charges. We were losing already a great many men, when towards half-past two, more of the enemy [Jérôme], with a shout of 'Vive l'Empereur!', simultaneously charged our line on several points at once. We were expecting at every moment our cavalry, which did arrive soon after, but reinforcements of the English, Scotch and Brunswick troops, who had only been moved up from Brussels during the night of the 15th to the 16th, could not be expected for some time.'[7]

At 3 p.m. the Duke of Wellington and his staff arrived back at Quatre Bras from Brye. But where, Wellington enquired of his aides, was his army? The cavalry that the Duke had confidently predicted to Blücher and Gneisenau would be at 'Nivelles at noon' were, unknown to anyone at Quatre Bras, somewhere between Enghien and Braine-le-Comte, caught in the infernal confusion that had engulfed much of the Anglo-Allied army. Wellington's three sets of movement orders had brought the cavalry and horse artillery down from Ninove to Enghien, where they began to lose themselves in the morass that was the intermingled units of brigades and divisions of Clinton, Colville, Grant, Vivian and Arentschildt. The worst bottleneck was the stretch of 'road' between Braine-le-Comte and Nivelles, which was appalling, even by the undemanding standards of the day.

From Enghien to Braine-le-Comte and beyond, Wellington's lost legions played follow-my-leader, with very few commanders really knowing where they were going. Mercer, with his horse artillery, following the 23rd Dragoons, related:

'The 23rd floundered through ... with difficulty, and left us behind. How we got through with our 9-pounders, the horses slipping up to the shoulders between logs every minute, I know not ... About noon after threading through more mud and many watery lanes, doubtful if we were in the right direction, we came out upon a more open and dry country close to a park, which, upon enquiry, proved to be Enghien. To the same point various columns of cavalry were converging, and under a park wall we found Sir Ormsby Vandeleur's brigade of light dragoons, dismounted and feeding their horses. Here we also dismounted to await the arrival of Major McDonald; and as I looked upon my day's march as finished, deferred feeding until our bivouac should be established - another folly ... and at the point where the road to Braine-le-Comte by Steenkerke branched off from the one we were on. All the corps as they arrived, I observed took this road, and continued onwards ... having waited a good half-hour, and no Major McDonald appearing, I began to look around for some one to give me information, but no staff-officer was to be seen, and no one else knew anything about the matter. Corps after corps arrived and passed on, generally without halting, yet all professing ignorance of their destination. Pleasant situation this! ... I sought out the General [Vandeleur], whom I found seated against the bank ... Sir Ormsby cut my queries short with an asperity totally uncalled for, "I know nothing about you sir! I know nothing about you!" "But will you have the goodness to tell me where you are going yourself?" "I know nothing about it, sir! I told you already I know nothing at all about you!'"[8]

Mercer then decided to follow Sir Hussey Vivian's cavalry brigade which was already being followed by Major Bull's Royal Horse Artillery troop: '... Bull I found was, like myself without orders, but he thought it best to stick close to the cavalry, and advised me to do the same ... and about four in the afternoon [we] arrived at Braine-le-Comte, almost ravenous with hunger, and roasted alive by the burning sun.'[9] At Braine-le-Comte Mercer found several regiments drawn up in close column, cavalry dismounted, and all feeding:[10] 'Here as before I could obtain no intelligence respecting our march, the direction and meaning of which all I spoke to professed ignorance ... The country around Braine-le-Comte was pretty, the usual rich and wooded champaign extending to the foot of an abrupt ridge of hills ... at the foot of the hills, the straggling street of which we found so crowded with Baggage wagons of some Hanoverian or other foreign corps, that for a long while we were unable to pass.'[11] This was Estorff's Hanoverian cavalry brigade coming up from Mons with its attendant baggage train. Here Mercer's battery became entangled with: '... Groups of Dragoons and Hussars, mingling with our guns, etc., all scrambling up the steep ascent.[12] Mercer's account of his trek to the scene of action concludes when he was nearing Hautain-le-Val and the rumble of cannonade filled the air: '... It was here that Major McDonald overtook us, and without adverting to the bivouac at Enghien, of which probably he had never heard, gave me orders to attach myself to the Household brigade, under Lord Edward Somerset, but no instructions of where or when ... Just at this moment a cabriolet, driven at a smart pace, passed us. In it was seated an officer of the guards, coat open and snuff-box in hand.'[13]

Mercer's experience was typical of most travelling along that route.[14] Largely British units from Ninove, Grammont and Ath converged on Enghien, then their twisting column went on to converge with Hanoverian and Netherlands troops from Mons and the border areas at Braine-le-Comte. Many had halted at one place or another, in adherence to orders, only to move on at their own initiative when it became evident that they would receive no further orders where they were. The lengthening column of men, horses and equipment was joined at Nivelles by yet more Netherlands troops coming up from Binche and by the Nivelles garrison which had been ordered on when their replacements arrived. From Nivelles, all formed one great column of some 60,000 travelling on the single road to Quatre Bras.

At Quatre Bras The Netherlands Light Cavalry Brigade, under General Merlen, had arrived at 3 p.m., having covered nearly 25 miles from the border region around Binche, travelling at times in parallel with the French left wing. Captain van Bronkhurst, of the 7th Battalion, National

Militia, noted the Light Brigade's arrival because his brother Jan was in the 6th Dutch Hussars, commanded by Lieutenant-Colonel van Boreel.[15]

At virtually the same time as Merlen's brigade began to arrive by the Nivelles road, the vanguard of Picton's division came into view from the north along the Brussels road. Because Picton's column stretched back 4¼ miles, his men would be arriving piecemeal and would take several hours to deploy on the field ready to fight as a division. The 1st Battalion, 95th Rifles was naturally the leading regiment. Next to their commander, Colonel Sir Andrew Barnard, rode the Adjutant, Lieutenant Kincaid. The 1st/95th had been advancing at a quick pace since Genappe where they had begun to hear cannon. During this last leg of their march Kincaid recounted: '... we presently met a cart-load of Belgian wounded,' and upon arrival, he noted that:

> 'Quatre Bras at that time consisted of only three or four houses... The village was occupied by some Belgians, under the Prince of Orange, who had an advance post in a large farm-house [Gemioncourt], at the foot of the road, which inclined to the right; and a part of his division, also occupied the wood on the same side. Lord Wellington, I believe, after leaving us at Waterloo, galloped on to the Prussian position at Ligny, where he had an interview with Blücher ... When we arrived at Quatre Bras, however, we found him near the Belgian out-post; and the enemy's guns were beginning upon the spot where he stood, surrounded by numerous staff ... The moment we approached, Lord Fitzroy Somerset, separating himself from the Duke, said, "Barnard you are wanted instantly; take your battalion and endeavour to get possession of that village [Piraumont] ... but if you cannot do that, secure that wood on the left [Bois de Cherris], and keep the [Namur] road open for communication with the Prussians."'[16]

Kincaid's single battalion was unable to retake the village, which was fronted by almost two brigades of Bachelu's division. The Prince of Orange sent several companies of the 27th *Jäger* to assist the British battalion, but language proved a barrier to useful co-operation, as the officers of neither nationality could speak the other's tongue, and neither had enough French for a lingua franca. Sir Andrew tried to encourage the *Jägers* to march forward in line with his men, holding fire until within range of Bachelu's infantry, who were flanked by mounted French *chasseurs*. The commander of the *Jäger* detachment, Colonel Grunebosch, having spent an hour giving ground before the weight of the French advance, tried to indicate to Sir Andrew that the French strength at Piraumont was too great to assault frontally with a battalion plus a few *Jäger* companies, but could not make himself understood; then by gesture Sir Andrew indicated that the Dutch should march forward with his British troops; while Grunebosch and his officers tried to relate by gestures and by firing towards the enemy who stood unseen through the six-foot stand of rye, the French were within musket range and in greatly superior numbers. Sir Andrew insisted, but Grunebosch baulked, and the rifle battalion went forward unaccompanied, only to be repulsed at once by a massive volley. The battalion fell back to the Bois de Cherris, harassed by sniping fire from eight companies of French skirmishers. The 95th cleared the French pickets from the wood, and held it and the village of Thyle, with its supports on the Namur road.[17]

On Wellington's orders, Lord Fitzroy Somerset had meanwhile taken post by the Quatre Bras crossroads. From there he was giving orders to the arriving units of Picton's 5th Division to array themselves from the crossroads along the Namur road to join up with the 95th at the Bois de Cherris and Thyle. This would help prevent Ney from severing the road link with the Prussians and would reinforce the weaker flank of the Quatre Bras position. Picton's men deployed quickly, as they had only to march down the road, halt and turn right to be in line four-deep.

While Picton's men were lining the Namur road, Ney was applying the weight of his three divisions in an attempt to seize the Gemioncourt farm and the rest of the Bois de Bossu. Wellington, realizing the importance of the farm to the integrity of his centre, ordered the Prince of Orange to hold it at all costs. He also sent up the British 28th Regiment to support and garrison the farm complex. Gemioncourt was typical of Belgian farms of the period: it was built strongly of stone, with the main house and subsidiary buildings grouped around a central courtyard entered by a single wooden gate, so that from without the farm presented the thick, windowless outer walls of its buildings and high connecting walls. With the simple addition of loopholes, such a farm became a formidable bastion. General van Bijlandt, with the able assistance of Colonel Westenberg, had been trying to hold the farm and the 600 yards of open ground from there to the edge of the Bois de Bossu with 461 men of his battalion on a two-deep front. To clear these men from their position, Marshal Ney ordered Foy, one of the Emperor's most capable divisional commanders, to attack this overstretched Netherlands battalion with four battalions and a battery of artillery, with support from Piré's cavalry division. Colonel van Nyevelt recorded the ensuing attacks from the receiving end:

> '... As soon as the enemy became aware that we had received reinforcements, he redoubled his attacks on the farmhouse, which was defended by the 5th Battalion National Militia. His Royal Highness [the Prince of Orange] personally held command here, and waving his hat, he rode in advance of the troops, and directed several charges on the enemy, repulsing them with heavy losses...

The example of His Royal Highness, was followed by the staff of the Division, so inspired the 5th Battalion National Militia, which was under the command of Lieutenant-Colonel Westenberg, that they did miracles of Bravery; but one attack had scarcely been repulsed ere the enemy made another with fresh men and in larger numbers.'[18]

While Foy was delivering his ferocious assault on Wellington's almost transparent centre, on Wellington's right in the Bois de Bossu seven Netherlands battalions were as yet frustrating Ney's attempts to move up under cover of its trees to the crossroads. On the Duke's left, Kempt and Pack's brigades of Picton's 5th Division now lined the hedged and banked Namur road facing south towards fields of corn and the French. These brigades were supported at each end by divisional batteries and by a second line formed of Best's Hanoverian Brigade 100 yards to their rear.

The 5th Militia were unable to hold Gemioncourt farm and the intervening ground across to the Bois de Bossu. With the 5th Militia dislodged, the 28th also had to fall back, and the Anglo-Allied centre was in immediate danger of collapse. The Prince of Orange then led a counter attack on Foy's infantry with Merlen's brigade of cavalry, the Dutch 6th Hussars riding with their Prince, and the 6th Belgian Light Dragoons in support. This bold foray drove in Foy's *voltigeurs* and caused his regiments to form squares and rallying groups. But Merlen's brigade was then hit by the two full brigades of Piré's cavalry, which had been preparing to exploit Foy's incipient breakthrough. The Netherlanders were severely handled by the French lancers, the Prince's aide, Major van Limburgh Stirum, being badly wounded. Merlen's force retreated back towards the crossroads, closely pursued by Piré's force.

There then occurred one of those tragic incidents of war in which men die in error at the hands of friends. Seeing the Netherlanders in blue (hussars) and green (light dragoons) galloping wildly toward the crossroads and hearing them shouting in French (a warning that the French were behind them), the Scots of the 92nd and 42nd Highland Regiments along the Namur road mistook them for French and were ordered to open fire on them. Many horses in particular were brought down, as they presented the larger targets and cavalry dismounted is effectively *hors de combat*. Piré's troopers, picking their way around Merlen's stricken horse, came under fire on the left of the crossroads from Rogers' battery firing canister, and withdrew, being unsupported by infantry or horse artillery. Merlen posted the remains of his brigade behind the British left wing until remounts could be called up from Nivelles. Merlen was left to reflect with sadness on the losses his unit had suffered and with bitterness that more had been caused by their 'Scotch' allies than by the French.[19]

With the repulse of Piré, the Duke of Brunswick's corps began to arrive at Quatre Bras. It was now about 4 p.m. Wellington ordered

Brunswick to form up his leading squadrons of lancer and hussar regiments abutting the Bois de Bossu on high ground, about 800 yards in front of the crossroads overlooking the boggy lowland where the Gemioncourt stream issued from the wood. Behind this cavalry Brunswick was to concentrate his infantry, now appearing in strength down the Brussels road. With this disposition reinforcing the centre right, and with Picton's brigades covering the centre left, Wellington had temporarily relieved the threat to his centre, and protected the inner flank of the Bois de Bossu, although for the past two hours fighting had raged within the wood itself, during which time Saxe-Weimar's brigade had been augmented by almost all the remaining Netherlands reserves, seven battalions in all.

Nor was Wellington's respite to be more than temporary. Ney's forces now held a firm line along the course of the stream through Gemioncourt, and were within range for attempting to carry the crossroads in a general assault. In the wood, Saxe-Weimar was opposed by thirteen battalions, nearly 8,000 men, under Prince Jérôme, who had worked up through the woods and along its flanks to a line roughly level with Gemioncourt farm. Between the wood and the farm were eleven battalions of Foy's division, another 5,200 men. And from the farm to the Materne pond Bachelu had arrayed nine battalions, 4,000 men, into three columns. Behind these infantry formations, Piré had regrouped his fifteen squadrons, numbering 1,800. Ney had also deployed along his front six 8-gun batteries. In close reserve, Ney had placed Kellermann's brigade of 1,026 *cuirassiers*. As a general reserve, Ney also had d'Erlon's corps, two miles back at Frasnes: 18,782 infantry, 1,500 light cavalry, 46 guns, and Kellermann's other heavy brigade of 900 *cuirassiers*.

The pressure in the Bois de Bossu, together with Ney's general aggressive stance, induced Wellington to advance his left and centre to put Ney off balance. To this end he asked the Duke of Brunswick to move forward toward Gemioncourt and to link his right with the Netherlanders in the wood. Brunswick accordingly disposed his troops, with his two élite *Gelernte Jäger* companies reinforcing Saxe-Weimar's left flank. On their arrival the Brunswicker 2nd Light Battalion would support the British 95th Rifles along the Materne-Thyle line. The Duke of Brunswick himself would lead the advance on Gemioncourt, with two companies of skirmishers, followed by his *Leib* Battalion and 1st Line Battalion supported by his cavalry and horse artillery battery. Brunswick would leave his 2nd and 3rd Line Battalions as a second line in reserve.[20] At the same time, Wellington ordered Picton to advance his brigades in line abreast, in support of Brunswick's movement, with the intention of breaking up Bachelu's assault columns. It was Wellington's intention, if possible, to regain some of the ground the Netherlanders had had to yield earlier in the day, thus deepening his position in front of the strategic crossroads and also relieving pressure on the Netherlanders in the Bois de Bossu. Then, when the rest of his army had concentrated on Quatre Bras, he planned to move forward in support of the Prussian army.

Advancing through rye more than six feet high, Picton's brigades met Bachelu's columns at close range and quickly overpowered them with controlled volleys and a bayonet charge. Bachelu's men pulled back, and Picton's were left in possession of the exposed broken ground. Soon, however, the British infantry found their position becoming untenable as Ney had ordered his preponderant artillery to fire on them. Of more immediate menace, French lancers rode down on them supported by a horse battery which began to unlimber within 200 yards of their line. The action was recorded by Sergeant James Anton of the 42nd Highlanders:

'We were ready and in Line ... and forward we hastened, though we saw no enemy in front. The stalks of Rye, like the reeds that grow on the margins of some swamp, opposed our advance; the tops were up to our bonnets, and we strode and groped our way through as fast as we could. By the time we reached a field of clover on the other side we were very much straggled, however, we united in line as fast as time and our speedy advance would permit. The Belgic skirmishers [27th Jägers]retired through our ranks, and in an instant we were on their victorious pursuers.

'Our sudden appearance seemed to paralyse their advance. The singular appearance of our dress, combined, no doubt with our sudden Debut, tended to stagger their resolution: we were on them, our pieces loaded, and our bayonets glittered ... We drove on so fast that we almost appeared like a mob following the rout of some defeated faction. Marshal Ney, who commanded the enemy, observed our wild unguarded zeal, and ordered a regiment of lancers to bear down upon us. We saw their approach at a distance, as they issued from a wood, and took them for Brunswickers coming to cut up the flying [French] infantry; and as cavalry on all occasions have the advantage of retreating foot, on a fair field, we halted in order to let them take their way; they were approaching our right flank, from which our skirmishers were extended, and we were far from being in a formation fit to repel an attack, if intended, or to afford regular support to our friends if requiring our aid. I think we stood with too much confidence, gazing towards them as if they were our friends, anticipating the gallant charge they would make on the flying foe, and we made no preparative movement to receive them as enemies; further than the reloading of our muskets.'

At this point Wellington sent a dispatch-rider to warn the unsuspecting 42nd. As Anton recounts:

> '... a German [KGL] orderly dragoon galloped up, exclaiming, "Franchee! Franchee!" and, wheeling about, galloped off. We instantly formed a rallying square; no time for particularity: every man's piece was loaded, and our enemies approached at full charge; the feet of their horses seemed to tear up the ground. Our skirmishers having been impressed with the same opinion that these were Brunswick cavalry, fell beneath their lances, and few escaped death or wounds; our brave Colonel [Sir Robert Macara] fell at this time, pierced through the chin until the point reached his brain. Captain [Archibald] Menzies fell covered in wounds ... The grenadiers, whom he commanded, pressed round to save or avenge him, but fell beneath the enemies lances. Of all descriptions of cavalry, certainly the lancers seem the most formidable to infantry, as the lance can be projected with considerable precision, and with deadly effect, without bringing the horse to the point of a bayonet; and it was only by the rapid and well-directed fire of musketry that these formidable assailants were repulsed.'[21]

The 44th Regiment, which had been advancing in line with the 42nd, was saved from destruction when its commander ordered the rear rank to face about so that the regiment presented in effect a flat square to the lancers, firing to the front and back.

Wellington was obliged to order Picton's brigades to retire from their present positions, exposed as they were to cavalry and artillery, to the shelter of their original positions along the Namur road.[22] Wellington's forward movement had succeeded, only to fail for lack of adequate cavalry and artillery to defend and consolidate the new positions. At Gemioncourt and on the eastern side of the Charleroi road, the Duke of Brunswick had been doing well. His advance, too, had benefited from the cover of the tall crops. During this stealthy movement the Duke had walked his horse up and down while he puffed on his pipe and encouraged his men. However, this advance was also to be short-lived.

In the Bois de Bossu, French numbers and drive created a brief opportunity which the French were quick to exploit. Saxe-Weimar's men had been engaged continuously for many hours, including their skirmishing duties before the general attack. And fighting in a dense wood required a good deal more musketry and they were running out of ammunition. Saxe-Weimar arranged for his men to be relieved so that they could fall back on Hautain-le-Val to regroup and replenish.[23] As his men gave ground slowly under the unrelenting French pressure, his relief came up: the 7th of The Netherlands Line, the 7th and 8th Netherlands Militia, and the 1st Battalion, 28th Netherlands Line together with the Brunswick *Jägers*. At this critical moment of changeover, the French were able to dash forward 50 yards in a rush. This put the Duke of Brunswick's troops advancing in the open under the fire of Jérôme's men from the edge of the wood. Also the artillery which had been trained on Picton's troops was swung over to the Brunswickers. The Duke was killed in an attempt to lead his cavalry in pushing back the horde of French skirmishers crowding his men. Foy then launched an attack with his entire division. Major Prostler of the *Leib* Battalion tried to rally his men, but a French artillery section (probably horse) swept them with canister and they broke, reeling back toward the crossroads. The Duke of Saxe-Weimar observed this repulse from the wood and the next day wrote: '... whilst I was defending the wood, the enemy drove our left wing [Picton] as far as Quatre Bras, at this moment the brave Duke of Brunswick was killed by a ball which entered his breast. Several strong columns turned my right flank; I applied for orders to direct me how to proceed; but I received none, finding that I was surrounded on all sides, and that my ammunition of all my troops was exhausted, I retired in good order through the wood to the vicinity of Hautain-le-Val.'[24]

Ney now believed that he had broken Wellington's centre. He ordered Piré to follow up the withdrawal of Picton's brigades and the Brunswick corps with two brigades dashing up to the crossroads, one on each side of the Charleroi road. Wellington personally rallied the Brunswick hussars and, bringing up the mounted remnant of Merlen's cavalry, prepared to go forward to plug the gap. But before his cavalry was positioned to advance, Piré's superior forces struck, driving them and Wellington himself back beyond the crossroads. Wellington, to avoid death or ignominious capture, rode toward the 92nd Highlanders, whose L-shaped line had its long leg on the Namur road and its short one on the Brussels road. Calling out to the men to crouch low, he jumped his horse over their heads and found refuge behind them. Picton's division, back in position between Quatre Bras and Thyle, formed squares, and the 4,000 Brunswick infantry under Colonel Olfermann on the Allied right of the crossroads did the same. The sudden eruption of the French cavalry from the corn caught several regiments in open order. General Best's Hanoverian battalion in the second line was badly cut up, and the Brunswick 3rd Line Battalion was only saved by Brunswick lancers interposing themselves until the battalion could form a rallying square. Piré's troopers swirled around the squares, but received such a galling fire that they soon withdrew behind the Gemioncourt line.

Wellington's situation at Quatre Bras was now stabilizing. His infantry strength, some 20,000 men, was now about equal to that of Ney's attacking corps; but he was still inferior in cavalry and artillery, with one effective mounted brigade and 22 guns. But he hoped soon to redress that imbalance. He had observed that he faced only a corps, and a weak one at that. With his continual reinforcement, Wellington was confident that he would soon be able to mount a sustained offensive to regain all his lost ground. In the meantime he had sent gallopers back along the Nivelles road to urge on the mass of men struggling to reach him. Two brigades of General von Alten's division had reached Hautain-le-Val, and Cooke's Guards Division was about an hour behind them, while Kruse's Nassau contingent was fast approaching Quatre Bras along the Brussels road.

Alten's leading brigades were Count von Kielmansegges's Hanoverian and General Sir Colin Halkett's British (comprising the 30th, 33rd, 69th and 73rd Regiments). Ensign Macready, with the light company abandoned earlier in the rush to concentrate, was force-marching through the fields bordering the Nivelles road to get past Cooke's Guards. Macready's company came across Saxe-Weimar's 2nd Netherlands Brigade in fields near Hautain-le-Val, not far from the Bois de Bossu, reorganizing and replenishing.[25] Macready wrote of the encounter:

> '... A wood stretched in front of us and a half mile beyond them [Saxe-Weimar's men], and over it was a heavy cloud of smoke ... We loosened our ammunition, loaded, and went up to these men. They belonged to the Nassau Contingent, and had been driven from the wood [Bois de Bossu]. We made for it, and came up with a staff officer with long light hair, who had just escaped from the lancers. He told us our regiment had entered the field a quarter of an hour before, and they were on the other side of the wood which we must pass on its right a mile further yet, as the enemy occupied nearly the whole of it. This we were soon convinced of by several round shots coming from it, one which splashed mud and dirt over the whole company.'[26]

As the first of Alten's brigades arrived at Quatre Bras, so did a messenger from Gneisenau. The courier, Captain von Wussow, was carrying a duplicate message, and it was as well he had been sent, as the first runner, Major von Winterfeldt, had been shot by Bachelu's men, who were trying to force the 1/95th and Brunswickers out of Thyle on the Namur road. The canny Captain Wussow recounted his experience:

> 'I did not waste a moment in setting my horse to the gallop towards Thyle and Quatre Bras by way of Brye and Marbais. I changed horses belonging to a cavalry detachment which kept open the line of communication with the Duke between Wagnelee and Quatre Bras. By the village of Thyle ... the commander of the cavalry post here informed me

that the road on the far side of the wood [Bois Delhutte] had already been occupied by the French ... and that Major von Winterfeldt had been severely wounded there by enemy sharpshooters ... I turned right and left the main road ... I had to ride through enemy musketry, but managed to reach the English troops at Quatre Bras unscathed. Here I found the Duke of Wellington on foot, holding his telescope and watching the attack and movements of the enemy. General von Müffling stood beside him. I reported to him [Müffling] first the nature of my mission I had been entrusted with. The Duke turned to me and I said to him: "At the time I left the battlefield we were still holding all the villages we occupied behind the Ligny stream, from Sombreffe through Ligny, St. Amand la Haye and Wagnelee, in spite of constant French attacks and of alternatively losing ground and then regaining it. However, it appears that our losses have mounted heavily, and as the prospect of Bülow's corps coming to our support have entirely vanished, the most we can do is to hold the battlefield until nightfall. Any greater success is not looked for. Perhaps, a strong offensive by the English troops could prevent Napoleon from turning his full force against the Prussian army."... The Duke instructed me to tell Marshal Blücher that so far it had been extremely difficult for him to resist the heavy attacks made by superior French forces, but that with the reinforcements that had just arrived - he believed he now had about 20,000 men on the ground - he would try and launch a powerful attack which would benefit the Prussian army. I followed the success of the English army until Piraumont had been captured, then I rode back as fast as I had come. At the windmill of Bussy I reported to General von Gneisenau and gave him the Duke's reply.'[27]

While the Prince of Orange and the Duke of Wellington were fighting their desperate holding action against Ney and Reille's reduced corps, Napoleon had completed his preparations and at 3 p.m. launched his attack on the Prussian positions at Ligny. Having carefully surveyed the Prussian dispositions, Napoleon concluded that they stood awaiting Wellington to come down the road from Quatre Bras and form up on their right. In consequence, Napoleon realized, the Prussians had based their dipositions on an assumption: that Wellington would come in time and in enough strength to make a difference. At present, however, the Prussian right was unsecured and vulnerable. Napoleon had planned accordingly.

Gneisenau had ordered the disposition of the available Prussian forces on Blücher's authority. Ziethen's I Corps was again to absorb the shock of the French attack: four battalions of Steinmetz's 1 Brigade were placed at St-Amand la Haye and the Hamlet of St-Amand, with his other six in reserve behind the Ligny; three battalions of Jagow's 3 Brigade in St-Amand, with the remaining seven in reserve at the mill of Bussy; four and a half battalions of Donnersmarck von Henckels' 4 Brigade in Ligny, with two in reserve just behind the village; Pirch II's 2 Brigade, which had suffered the most in the retreat from the Sambre, in central reserve between the mill at Bussy and Brye; and Roder's I Corps cavalry reserve massed in a hollow behind Ligny village, except for the 1st Silesian Hussars, detached far to the right with a horse battery to co-operate with Wellington at Thyle in holding open communications between the Allied armies. I Corps artillery was sited on the slopes between the villages of Ligny and St-Amand la Haye, facing Fleurus and covering the lightly defended stretch of the brook between Ligny and St-Amand. Behind Ziethen, II Corps of Pirch I was arrayed along the Namur road. Tippelskirch's 5 Brigade was facing outward on the open right flank, covering the crossroads of Trois Barettes and the approach to it along the old Roman road which could well serve as a route for a French envelopment. Krafft's 6, Brause's 7, and Bose's 8 Brigades were next in line, placed just south of the road facing the ground between Brye and Ligny, with each brigade's attached cavalry behind it. The II corps cavalry and artillery reserves were just north of the Namur road, behind 7 and 8 Brigades. Thielemann's III Corps formed the Prussian left, with Kamphen's 10 and Luck's 11 Brigades holding the ground in and between the villages of Mont Potriaux, Tongrinne, Tongrinelle and Balatre. Borcke's 9 Brigade and Hobe's III Corps cavalry reserve were at Sombreffe, while Stulpnagel's 12 Brigade sat astride the main Gembloux road behind the Point du Jour crossroads.

Napoleon had decided to contain and hold the Prussian left with Pajol's I and Exelmans' II Reserve Cavalry Corps, adding to this screen some batteries of artillery and a few regiments of infantry. The bulk of his force was directed against the Prussian right and centre, on a front from the St-Amands to Ligny. As usual, he would engage the enemy all along the crucial front, probing and pushing to discover the weakest point; then when the battle had progressed, he would launch his reserves at the weak point, breaking the Prussian line there. Coincidentally, he would call for one of Ney's corps, roughly 20,000 men, to come in on the open Prussian right flank, forming the anvil upon which the sledgehammer blows of his attacking columns would smash Blücher's right and centre, leaving the Prussian left to recoil. This would leave the Allied armies completely sundered and with little recourse but to retire generally along their communications.

At 2.20 p.m. Grouchy's cavalry began to manoeuvre towards the Prussian left flank as a feint, while the four divisions of Vandamme's left (including Girard, detached from Reille) prepared to advance on a front opposite St-Amand la Haye and St-Amand. Gérard also launched two divisions against Ligny, to pin the forces there and attract some of the reserves drawn up on the hillsides behind the village. At Fleurus Napoleon watched these attacks develop, waiting for the opportunity to employ his Guard, arrayed next to him.

On Vandamme's front Lefol's division closed on St-Amand in three columns preceded by a swarm of skirmishers. Their passage through the fields of rippling corn did not attract the enemy's attention; that was reserved for the columns. Prussian cannon fired on them with deadly effect, the first shot alone killing eight men of one company. Nevertheless, to the drumbeat of the *Pas de Charge*, the French columns rushed forward, losing sorely to point-blank canister and musketry. St-Amand was held by the entire 29th Regiment, but all their efforts could not stop Lefol's men from coming to grips with them. After twenty minutes of furious 'no quarter' fighting among houses and gardens, the French had almost cleared their hated enemy from the village.

From his adjoining position General Steinmetz could see the peril threatening Jagow's front. Jagow's reserve battalions at the Bussy mill were too far back to support the 29th Regiment in St-Amand. Steinmetz quickly hurried forward four battalions from his 1 Brigade reserve behind St-Amand. With a ruthlessness which would in later years become his hallmark, Steinmetz turned his howitzers on the village before the last of the 29th had been able to disengage, turning it into a fiery shambles. Then, pushing forward all his guns firing canister, he advanced the four battalions in a vicious bayonet charge, retaking the blazing ruins of St-Amand.

Vandamme at once escalated the action by sending forward Berthezene's division to assault St-Amand, and Girard's against neighbouring St-Amand la Haye and the hamlet of St-Amand. Berthezene's attack, pressed in the teeth of stubborn resistance, succeeded in retaking St-Amand, while Girard's was intended to isolate St-Amand from local support by tying down Steinmetz's 1 Brigade. But, despite having lost 2,500 men, Steinmetz managed to regroup his remnant. Then, summoning his last reserve, his grenadier battalion, he again retook the whole of St-Amand except, ironically, the cemetery, from which the French could not be dislodged. With Steinmetz occupied with St-Amand, Girard quickly took St-Amand la Haye and the hamlet of St-Amand. This development threatened the already tenuous link with Wellington and Quatre Bras. Gneisenau at once sent word to Zeithen to retake these flank villages whatever the cost. He gave orders to Pirch II's reserve brigade to recapture St-Amand la Haye and the hamlet of St-Amand, and to support Steinmetz in St-Amand. The bitter fight for these confusingly named habitations see-sawed for some time, until in a supreme effort Girard succeeded in evicting the Prussians from the key hamlet of St-Amand, although in so doing he sustained a mortal wound.[28] In all, 39½ battalions were engaged in the struggle for the three St-Amands.

At Ligny, Gérard ordered Vichery's and Pecheux's divisions forward against the village, which had been barricaded and fortified by Donnersmarck's brigade as Charleroi had been by Pirch II only a long day earlier. Captain Charles François, of the 96th Regiment of the Line, 1 Brigade, 12th Division (Pecheux's), recounted the assault:

'When within two hundred yards of the hedges which concealed thousands of Prussian sharpshooters, the regiment took up battle order while still on the march. The charge was sounded and the soldiers went through the hedges. The 1st Brigade's left half-battalion, to which I belonged, went down to a hollow track blocked by felled trees, vehicles, harrows and ploughs, and we got past these only after considerable difficulty and under fire from the Prussians hidden behind the hedges, which were extremely thick. Eventually we overcame these obstacles and, firing as we went, entered the village. When we reached the church our advance was halted by a stream, and the enemy, in houses, behind walls and on rooftops, inflicted considerable casualties, as much by musketry as by canister and cannonballs, which took us from front and flank. In a moment Major Hervieux, commanding the regiment, and two battalion commanders, Richard and Lafolie, had been killed; another battalion commander, Blain by name, was slightly wounded and had his horse killed under him; five captains were killed and three wounded, two adjutants and nine lieutenants and sub-lieutenants were killed, seven wounded, and close on seven hundred rank and file killed or wounded ... The regiment [three battalions] lost two-thirds of its strength without receiving either reinforcements or orders, and we were obliged to retreat in disorder, leaving our wounded on the ground. We rallied near our batteries which were firing like hell at the enemy's guns ... Just as we were busy collecting the regiment, General Rome arrived and ordered us back into Ligny Village. The men, not at all disheartened by their failure, nor disturbed by the loss of nearly two-thirds of their comrades, shouted 'Vive l'Empereur!' and advanced. Captain Christophe had the charge sounded, our battalion re-entered the village, but was repulsed. It rallied and forced its way in three times more, only to suffer the same reverse each time.'[29]

The losses, however, were not all one-sided; more and more Prussian reserves had to be committed to the battle to hold the line of the Ligny brook.

With the battle well developed in the centre, and the thin Prussian right badly dented with the taking of the hamlet of St-Amand, the time was approaching when Napoleon would want to deliver the decisive blow which would shatter the enemy's right. To this end he was expecting the arrival of d'Erlon's corps, which would guarantee that the defeat of the enemy, of which the Emperor was confident, would be another Austerlitz. At 2 p.m. Soult had sent a message to Ney informing him of the then imminent battle at Ligny and giving Ney general orders:

> 'The Emperor desires me to inform you that the enemy has collected a Corps of troops between Sombreffe and Brye [This indicates Napoleon's continued ignorance of the Prussian obstacles along the line of Ligny brook], and at 2.30 p.m., Marshal Grouchy with the III and IV Corps will atack the enemy's positions. His Majesty's desire is that you will attack whatever force of the enemy is directly opposed to you, and after having driven it aside you will turn in our direction, so as to bring about the envelopment of that body of the enemy's troops whom I have just mentioned to you [the Prussian 'Corps of troops']. If the latter is overthrown first, then his Majesty will manoeuvre in your direction, so as to assist your operations in a similar way. Inform the Emperor forthwith of your dispositions, and all that goes to your front.'[30]

Having received Soult's communication before Picton's division entered the fight, Ney would have replied that all was going to plan and would have informed Napoleon that d'Erlon's corps was forming at Frasnes, presumably intending thereby to indicate that d'Erlon was available to Napoleon. Certainly, the letter would not have excited a sense of urgency or danger in Ney's mind. There had been nothing in Soult's wording to intimate that Napoleon expected to have to fight a full-scale battle. Soult had written that only a single Prussian corps opposed the Emperor, who had at his command two full corps (including a division of Ney's), three corps of reserve cavalry, and the entire Imperial Guard. It would have seemed to Ney that Napoleon had only to brush aside another Prussian rearguard before moving on to Gembloux and the Brussels-Namur road. Indeed, the Emperor had even offered to give Ney help if he finished the Prussians before Ney disposed of the motley of troops opposing him.

It must have come as a shock to Ney, therefore, to receive another letter from Soult, sent at 3.15 p.m. by two messengers, Colonel Forbin-Jason (who was first to reach Ney) and Colonel Laurent, who took a more circuitous route, in which the Chief of Staff explains that the Prussian corps is really most of the Prussian army, and announces disturbingly that Ney himself holds the key to victory:

'I wrote to you an hour ago to inform you that at 2.30 p.m., the Emperor would attack the position taken up by the enemy between the villages of S. Amand and Brye. At this moment the action is in full swing. His Majesty desires me to tell you that you are to manoeuvre immediately in such a manner as to envelop the enemy's right and fall upon his rear; the army in our front is lost if you act with energy. THE FATE OF FRANCE IS IN YOUR HANDS. Thus do not hesitate even for a moment to carry out the manoeuvre ordered by the Emperor, and direct your advance on the heights of Brye and S. Amand so as to co-operate in a victory that may be decisive. The enemy has been caught in the very act of carrying out his concentration with the English.'[31]

Ney was now in a quandary. Because he had not been given command of the left wing before the start of the campaign, he had been unable to ensure that Reille and d'Erlon kept their corps closed up. Therefore, on the morning of the 16th, Ney had been unable to advance on Quatre Bras with more than two divisions. Further, all indications from patrol intelligence and from the Emperor's morning orders were that Wellington would not be able to concentrate on the crossroads in time to deny it to him, and that in any case the French left wing was to play only an auxiliary role, remaining at Quatre Bras in readiness to advance on Brussels and arrive there 'no later than 7 a.m. on the 17th'. However, because of the initiative shown by The Netherlands army commanders, Constant Rebecque, Perponcher and Saxe-Weimar, Ney could not achieve his objective with a *coup de main.* Jérôme's division had not been available to press the attack on the Bois de Bossu until 3 p.m., and the advance through it was time consuming. Then a series of 'in the nick of time' arrivals served to prolong the Allies' defence of the crossroads: Merlen's cavalry brigade checked Ney long enough for Picton's division to deploy, and in turn be supported providentially by the Brunswick corps. Now Wellington was receiving divisional reinforcement by the hour. What was Ney to do? Soult had painted a vivid picture, but if Ney sent d'Erlon to assist the Emperor, it was inevitable that Reille's three exhausted divisions would be pushed back by Wellington's mounting superiority. This would allow Wellington to send a strong force down the Namur road to take the Emperor's position by surprise in flank and rear.

The only course of action Ney could see open to him was to send at once for d'Erlon's fresh 20,000 men and use them to smash the Allied formations at Quatre Bras, forcing Wellington's troops to withdraw towards Nivelles and Genappe. Ney could then deploy three divisions to hold the crossroads while sending light cavalry to harass the retreating Allies, and then send d'Erlon down the Namur road to fulfil the Emperor's plan.

Having come to this logical conclusion, Ney sent urgently to Frasnes for d'Erlon to bring up his corps to the French line at Gemion-court. D'Erlon had spent the previous night at Jumet. On the morning of the 16th he concentrated his corps and marched north along the Brussels road. At 2 p.m. he had only reached Gosselies, where he was held up because of reports from his cavalry patrols that an Allied force had been seen on his left flank. It took some time to establish that this sighting did not represent a developing attack from the direction of Mons. In fact the force had been Merlen's, heading for Quatre Bras. When the head of d'Erlon's corps reached the intersection of the Brussels road with the old Roman road, d'Erlon instructed his divisional commanders to march on to Frasnes while he rode ahead to find Marshal Ney and receive any further orders.

In the meantime Napoleon had been reflecting that Ney might not succeed in carrying out the movement of turning the corner at Quatre Bras but instead become enmeshed in an inconclusive fight with Wellington, with the result that d'Erlon's corps would not get over to support him in time. But Napoleon considered that Ney should be able to carry out his primary mission of keeping Wellington from joining Blücher even without d'Erlon's troops. He decided therefore that, as time was of the essence, he would send the necessary orders directly to d'Erlon by means of his own Imperial Aide de Camp, General le Comte de la Bedoyère.

On reaching Frasnes, Bedoyère found that d'Erlon was not present, so he gave the order to d'Erlon's Chief of Staff, General Delcambre, 'as from the Emperor', to turn right at once, advance along the Roman road, and attack the Prussian right. The order read: 'Monsieur le Comte d'Erlon, The enemy is falling headlong into the trap I have laid for him. Proceed immediately with all your forces to the heights of Ligny and fall on Saint Amand. Monsieur le Comte d'Erlon, you are about to save France and cover yourself with glory. - Napoleon.'[32] Delcambre immediately rode forward with an escort to return d'Erlon to his command, but before he went, he showed the Emperor's letter to General de Salle, commander of the Corps Artillery, and charged him to direct the other divisional commanders to get their men on the march in obedience to the Emperor's urgent order. De Salle later recalled his confusion over the content of the order: 'Having no map of Belgium before me, it is possible that I am transposing the names of the two villages. I rather think that it was 'at St. Amand', and 'fall on Ligny', otherwise I made no mistake.'[33]

This confusion over names, however, was to have incalculable consequences, as it would result in d'Erlon's corps appearing on the battlefield, not behind the Prussian right flank, but behind the French left. General Durutte, commander of the 4th Division, leading the I Corps column, realized afterwards that they had taken the wrong turning: 'The Emperor sent Count d'Erlon the order to attack the left (the right) of the Prussians, and to try and take possession of Brye. The 1st Corps passed near Villers-Perouin to execute this order.'[34] Just before Villers-Perouin, I Corps, directed by de Salle's interpretation of Napoleon's wording, turned right so as to pass to the south of Villers-Perouin in the direction of Ligny, rather than marching along the road passing the village to the north, which would have brought the corps on to the Roman road at a point just behind the Prussian right and in line to attack toward Brye. This decision was one of those which determined the course of the campaign.

When d'Erlon had been informed by Delcambre of Napoleon's order, he instructed his Chief of Staff to find and inform Ney while he rode back to join his corps. Ney had been anxiously awaiting the appearance behind him of d'Erlon's corps, when he was informed of the arrival before him of yet another fresh division of Allied troops (von Alten's 3rd).

On the other side of the Quatre Bras battlefield Wellington personally directed General Count von Kielmansegge's Hanoverian brigade of five battalions and a *Jäger* company to relieve the 1/95th Rifles, defending Thyle, and with them advance to retake the Piraumont farm buildings. Wellington also instructed Picton to advance General Sir Colin Halkett's brigade between the Charleroi road and the Bois de Bossu to a position, roughly where the Brunswickers had stood, from which they could support Picton's men and also link up with the Allied troops in the wood. Halkett's brigade took position in battalion squares in echelon from the 69th astride the Charleroi road, through the 33rd, the 73rd and, nearest the wood, the 30th. Wellington now had 29,000 men and, with the addition of Lloyd and Cleeve's field batteries, 42 guns. Thus he had achieved superiority of numbers, and knew that Cooke's division and the Nassau contingent would soon reach the field, followed in turn by still more units.

Ney was speechless with surprise and alarm when Delcambre informed him that in obedience to an order from the Emperor, d'Erlon's corps was marching off toward St-Amand to attack the Prussians. It was at about this anxious moment when Colonel Laurent delivered to Ney the repetition of Napoleon's exhortation of 3.15 p.m., reminding him that he still held the fate of France in his hands. How could the Emperor expect him to hold up an army with three battle-weary divisions? The Emperor could have no idea of the true situation he faced at Quatre Bras. Ney decided to countermand Napoleon's order to d'Erlon. He impressed on Delcambre that, pieces of paper notwithstanding, d'Erlon was under Ney's command unless the Emperor were present in person, and not by proxy. He warned Delcambre that if d'Erlon did not bring his corps back at once to support him, Wellington would overrun Ney's position and fall on Napoleon's flank. In fairness Ney could have added that the fate of France now lay in d'Erlon's hands. Delcambre set spurs to his horse and was away like a shot. To ensure that his recall order reached d'Erlon, Ney sent several of his aides by different routes[35] with instructions to bring d'Erlon and his men back with all haste, as though the fate of France lay in their hands.

During the lull at Quatre Bras, while Ney awaited d'Erlon, Wellington had been using the time to regain ground. Kielmansegge's Hanoverians had joined the 95th Rifles at Thyle, relieving the heavy pressure on them from Bachelu's troops and replenishing their Baker rifle ammunition. (The Hanoverian *Jägers* and light battalions were equipped with the Baker.) Going forward from Thyle, the Hanoverian 1 Brigade was subjected to a brief bombardment by 20 to 30 guns which were supporting Bachelu's positions. Kielmansegge threw out the Luneberg Battalion in skirmish order, followed by the Grubenhagen Field Battalion. In short order, these troops had stormed Piraumont and prepared to defend the farm and outlying buildings against a counter-attack. Kielmansegge also detailed the field battalions Bremen and Verden, preceded by his two rifle-armed field *Jäger* companies, to advance in columns of four into Thyle to take up defensive positions, with the Duke of York Field Battalion in reserve on the Namur road.[36]

On the right and centre of Wellington's line the Prince of Orange ordered Halkett's battalions into line; he reasoned logically that, if Halkett's men were to keep abreast of Picton's and support them in a general advance on Gemioncourt, they could bring more firepower to bear in line than in column or squares.[37]

Ney, learning of Wellington's activity at Thyle and Piraumont, decided to make another effort to reach the crossroads, which, even if it did not succeed, would serve to relieve the pressure Wellington was beginning to apply to Ney's position until d'Erlon could be retrieved. He ordered Kellermann to charge his *cuirassier* brigade at the crossroads. When Kellermann pointed out that he had, at the Marshal's order, only one brigade, Ney replied: 'My dear General, a supreme effort is now necessary; that mass of hostile infantry must be overthrown. *The fate of France* is in your hands. Take your cavalry and ride them down. Go! I will support you with all Piré's cavalry.'[38] Once again the fate of France had changed hands. Kellermann returned to his *cuirassiers* and, leading them off, ordered the Gallop, then the Charge, as 1,000 steel-clad heavy horsemen gained speed. Kellermann's onrush was to be followed closely by all Piré's remaining 800 cavalry, and the rest of the three infantry divisions, in an all-out effort to shatter Wellington's hold on Quatre Bras.

The men of Halkett's brigade were in the path of Kellermann's charge. The tall rye hid the onrushing *cuirassiers* from the view of the British infantry in line between the Charleroi road and the wood, but the drumming of 4,000 hooves could be heard plainly enough, and even felt in the soles of their feet. The 30th and 33rd Battalions formed square first. The 69th was about to follow suit when two companies were given a wrong order by Major Lindsay. He called for the 1st and 2nd Companies to 'Face to right about, in open column, and commence firing upon the cuirassiers.'[39] This blunder left one side of the 69th's square open. When the *cuirassiers* burst upon the malformed square, they were able to charge in and cut it up badly. The 69th's King's Colour was taken and its men broke for the woods. The 73rd were panicked by the fate of the 69th, and they too broke and ran for the woods. The 33rd, formed on a knoll, became the target of Kellermann's horse battery, which cut them up with canister, causing them to follow the others who had broken.

Wellington returned to the crossroads from his left to see Kellermann's horde approaching. Picton's men in line in front of the Namur road had formed square and were secure. At the crossroads Wellington formed two recently arrived Brunswick battalions in square across the high road. Major Kuhlmann's horse artillery battery, attached to Cooke's Guards division, had come on ahead. They unlimbered instantly and were protected by the Luneberg *Landwehr* battalion which was in front of them lining the storm ditches before the crossroads. Wellington, again seeking shelter within the square of the 92nd, directed their fire. Kellermann and his fine cavalry, having cleared away all opposition, reached Quatre Bras only to be met by a murderous fire of point-blank canister and musketry from all sides. Horses and men fell and died. Kellermann had his horse shot from under him and only escaped death or capture by grasping the stirrup leathers of the horses of two troopers who carried him to safety.[40]

Piré's cavalry attacked Picton's squares among the corn and rye. Although the lancers caused many casualties, the squares remained intact. At best this second charge bought some time for Kellermann's *cuirassiers* to retire. It was now about 6.30 p.m. Cooke's Guards division began to arrive, followed by the Brunswick foot battery. Wellington's force had swollen to 36,000 men and 50 guns. With a two-to-one advantage in men and rough parity in guns, Wellington decided to go over to the offensive. He intended to retake the positions his troops had held at the beginning of the day. Then, the next day, with his entire army concentrated on Quatre Bras, he would feel confident that he was in a position to support Blücher. Cooke's two brigades (Maitland's and Byng's) were sent into the Bois de Bossu, because by then Prince Jérôme's troops had moved up the wood far enough to begin shelling the Nivelles road.

Wellington's line moved forward. On his left was Kielmansegge's brigade at Piraumont, then Picton's division, with Best's Hanoverian brigade to its left. Between Picton and the Bois de Bossu was Halkett's regrouped brigade, the Brunswick corps, and The Netherlands' 7th Line and 7th Militia Battalions. The Guards were sweeping the wood, and beyond it Saxe-Weimar's brigade and The Netherlands 5th and 8th Militia Battalions advanced from Hautain-le-Val, pushing back the French who had been trying to cut the Nivelles road between the wood and Hautain-le-Val. It took the Guards two hours to reach the southern end of the wood, for the French had disputed every building, tree and shrub of it. When the Guards emerged from the edge of the wood in a broken line heading for the Pierrepont farms, they and the adjoining Brunswickers were pounded by artillery, then attacked by Piré's lancers and driven back into the wood.

One of Saxe-Weimar's battalions, similarly attacked by the French 7th *Cuirassiers*, sought refuge in the wood.

By 9 p.m, with the light waning, the struggle for Quatre Bras was ended for the day. Ney withdrew slowly and in good order toward Frasnes. Wellington's cavalry had begun to arrive in penny packets, but there was little light left, and being fatigued by their long march they were in no condition to dispute with Kellermann and Piré.

Ney had nothing to reproach himself for in the day's proceedings. Thrown into his command at the eleventh hour, with only three infantry divisions and three cavalry brigades, Ney had by skill and stubborn courage succeeded in fulfilling the intent of his original orders: he had prevented Wellington from aiding Blücher for the whole of the 16th. And of his decision to recall d'Erlon; although with hindsight it was evident that Ney did not need d'Erlon on the 16th, with the information available at the time Ney cannot be faulted for acting as he did. He could not have known that the enemy obviously concentrating right in front of him would take so long to achieve superiority and would not succeed in defeating his force. When Ney sent the recall order to d'Erlon in late afternoon, there were still enough hours of light left for an aggressive and preponderant Wellington to have pushed past him and reached Wagnelee or St-Amand.

Wellington had less with which to be content. He had fought the most confused battle of his career, more or less by accident. His staff had let him down badly over the concentration of his army. Fortunately, though, his Netherland, Brunswick, Nassau, Hanoverian, and British troops had all worked well together, managing to hold the crossroads and finish the day with an advance. But it was the nearest Wellington had come to suffering a major defeat, and he had still to face a better general than Ney commanding a much larger force.

Lieutenant Basil Jackson of the Staff Corps left Brussels for the battle area at 2 p.m. on the 16th. Near Mont St-Jean he fell in with a senior staff officer who was not to be hurried, even though the rumble of gunfire over the horizon was distinct. Jackson and his dilatory companion encountered Lieutenant-Colonel Sir George Scovell, Wellington's Deputy Adjutant-General, riding a lathered horse (he was probably urging on the marching units), but they could learn nothing from him of the situation ahead. When Jackson eventually passed through Genappe he began to see the human evidence of nearby battle moving north along the road towards Mont St-Jean:

> 'At length we cleared the long village of Genappe, and
> began to meet wounded men and stragglers, from some of
> whom we gathered whereabouts the troops were engaged,
> - our own I mean; for as to the Prussians, then fighting at
> Ligny, the cannonade of which battle resounded to Brus-
> sels, drowning the secondary action of Quatre Bras, we

remained in perfect ignorance respecting them. There was now quite a stream of disabled soldiers on the road, habited in red, blue or black; the latter being the uniform of the Brunswick troops ... Presently we fell in with a huge lumbering mass, which puzzled us not a little to make out what it was. This turned out to be a Dutch 12 pounder gun, upon which, and its carriage, were clustered a dozen or more of wounded men, with torn uniforms, bloody and dirty, many having head or limb bound up, and among them were two or three females ... a voice in the midst of this Dutch mass ... I discovered [was that of] ... Brough of the 44th, who told me his division (Picton's) had been severely handled, but had held its ground; that he himself had got hit, and was besides being knocked up by their forced march of twenty miles before getting into action, and was therefore but too happy to profit by the good nature of the Dutch drivers.'[41]

On arriving at Quatre Bras, Jackson made an appreciation of the situation:

'The shades of evening were creeping over the ground by the time we arrived at the scene of the action, we were too late to see Ney's last attack; bodies of the enemy seemed still to threaten our position, but, except by the artillery and skirmishers, there was no more firing. The Duke remained for some time near the [tip of] the Bois de Bossu, intently watching the dark masses in our front, which were then scarcely beyond the range of our most advanced field-pieces; but it was soon evident from their motions that the business of the day was over ... some of our friends, belonging on the Staff, gave us in the meantime, an account of the battle; all agreeing that the Duke had never before been so severely pressed, or had so much difficulty to maintain his position.'[42]

While Wellington had finally forced Ney back from Quatre Bras, winning the day tactically but losing it strategically, more dramatic events were being enacted five miles down the Namur road at Ligny. During the afternoon Vandamme had attacked and counter-attacked several times on his front between Wagnelee and St-Amand, and Gérard had been no less active against Ligny. At about 4 p.m. Napoleon massed the 12-pounders of the Imperial Guard artillery with the artillery of IV Corps before Ligny. The cannonade had soon reduced the village to a shattered inferno. Gérard sent his infantry in again, having transferred a brigade from Vichery's division on the left of the front to Pecheux's on the right. The village was contested fiercely house by ruined house, with high casualties for every yard gained or lost. At last the Prussians retired over the bridges spanning the brook which flowed through the village. There, among the rubble on the north bank, the Prussian defenders stood, reinforced by two reserve battalions posted on rising ground behind the houses. The Prussians were therefore able to bring two tiers of fire to bear on the bridge crossings. Two regiments of French stormed the bridges under murderous fire, driving in the Prussian sharpshooters lining the brook. Jagow sent a further four battalions into the north side of Ligny and they pushed the French back across the bridges. It was all Gérard could do to prevent the Prussians recapturing the south side of the village. A tremendous musketry duel then ensued at ranges under 50 yards, and in some cases virtually muzzle to muzzle, resulting in very high casualties but no ground gained by either side.

On the French right Grouchy had skilfully kept Thielemann's III Corps busy locally. By 4 p.m. he had driven the Prussians out of Boignee, and Hulot's (formerly Bourmont's) division had attacked Tongrinelle, causing Thielemann to retain his corps reserves to provide support, if necessary, for his engaged line.

By 5 p.m. among the villages and hamlets through which the Ligny brook ran in its first half-dozen miles, the sounds of battle were augmented by the heart-rending cries of the wounded, including the terrified screams of those being burned alive in the flaming wreckage of the houses.

Additional batteries were brought to bear on Ligny and the cannonade increased, but the Prussian line there held firm. Gneisenau had chosen his position well: a killing ground fronted by one and a half corps, with an equal number of reserves to feed slowly into the battle or to form a strong rearguard in the event of a reversal. Also, Gneisenau expected to be significantly reinforced. Bülow was due to reach the battlefield with 32,000 men that night or at first light on the 17th. But more immediately, and therefore more importantly, Wellington, he thought, had promised to deploy at least 20,000 men to aid them that afternoon. The arrival of either of these forces on either of Napoleon's flanks would give the Allies a decisive victory. To defeat Napoleon all the Prussians had to do was to hold him until Wellington arrived, or morning brought Bülow. Napoleon, too, in the late afternoon of the 16th, was eagerly awaiting reinforcement to tip the balance and give him the ability to gain a decisive victory.

But Napoleon and Blücher were in very different positions with respect to time: it was Napoleon's enemy and Blücher's friend. Napoleon was attempting to conquer superior forces 'caught in the very act of concentrating' by a *coup de main* employing the extremely risky manoeuvre of the central position. He had desperate need of d'Erlon's 21,000 men and 46 guns, which were positioned so ideally to march a few miles and deliver a crushing blow to the Prussians. Lobau's neglected 10,300 men and 32 guns would of course be valuable, but could not enter the field from as advantageous an angle. Blücher, unlike Napoleon, had only to hold his position until either Wellington or Bülow arrived. And of this he could be confident with 84,000 men and 224 guns to Napoleon's 58,000 and 210 guns. The Prussian commander's confidence must have been further bolstered by the information in his possession: Napoleon's order of battle, courtesy of Wellington, and his movement orders, courtesy of the contemptible de Bourmont. Blücher felt that he could afford to leave his right flank open because Napoleon was too weak to exploit it and, of course, Wussow had indicated that Wellington would come.

Napoleon was now only waiting for d'Erlon to fall upon the Prussian right rear in the neighbourhood of Trois Barettes before beginning his final attack. French troops all along the line from Wagnelee to Ligny would attack their fronts, and the Imperial Guard would rupture the angle in the Prussian line between Ligny and Mont Potriaux, driving in to isolate Thielemann and complete the double envelopment and capture of the other two corps. Grouchy would press his attack on Thielemann. The cavalry corps of Pajol, Exelmans and Milhaud would swirl through and around the field, decimating the routed remnant of the Prussian army fleeing towards Gembloux or Namur, and in the process capturing the Prussian commander and his staff.

Napoleon's hopes were not to be realized, however. At about 5.30 p.m. an orderly officer arrived from Vandamme with grave news. A large corps of enemy troops had been observed about three miles distant, threatening the French left. Vandamme's sorely tried men were falling into disorder as panic took hold of many. Vandamme had already brought Girard's division and artillery about face to confront this new adversary.[43] Vandamme added that unless Napoleon sent him some reserves he would be forced to retreat from St-Amand. Napoleon was perplexed. Had Vandamme taken d'Erlon's corps for the enemy? But d'Erlon should not have been there. Napoleon had not reckoned on d'Erlon's arrival on the field before 6 p.m. He immediately sent an aide to approach the mysterious column and establish its identity.

Pending this confirmation, Napoleon was obliged not only to postpone the final attack but to derange his reserves. He sent General Duhesme's Young Guard Division and the 2nd, 3rd and 4th *Chasseurs* of the Old Guard to support Vandamme. He also sent an aide galloping to Lobau to apprise him of the danger and urge him to bring on his corps as quickly as possible. Could a corps of Wellington's army have marched from Mons along the Roman road, cutting across the Brussels road below Ney, to attack Napoleon's force from the rear? Or had Wellington concentrated a great force at Quatre Bras to push through Ney and come down past Frasnes?

Gneisenau and Blücher at Bussy also received a sighting report from the Silesian hussars patrolling between Wagnelee and Thyle of a column estimated at 20,000 on the Roman road; d'Erlon's corps extended over a distance of five miles, and from its direction it appeared to both Napoleon

Right: Colonel Sir William Howe de Lancey; Wellington's deputy Quartermaster-General (Philip J. Haythornthwaite collection).

Right: The Earl of Uxbridge, Wellington's cavalry commander whose brilliantly timed cavalry charge destroyed Napoleon's plan of attack (Philip J. Haythornthwaite collection).

Left: General Sir Thomas Picton, commander of the most experienced portion of the British contingent. Picton was badly wounded at Quatre Bras, but kept the fact to himself, being killed leading the counter-attack on d'Erlon's ill-fated attack (Philip J. Haythornthwaite collection).

Right: Lieutenant-General Lord Hill, commander of II Corps of the Anglo-Allied army (author's collection).

Right: Lieutenant-General Count von Gneisenau, Chief of Staff of the Prussian Army (Philip J. Haythornthwaite collection).

Left: Lieutenant-General Count von Bülow von Dennewitz, Commander of IV Corps (Philip J. Haythornthwaite collection).

Left: Lieutenant-General von Ziethen; Commander of I Corps, whose fighting retreat on 15 June denied Napoleon both strategic positions – Quatre Bras and Sombreffe – and whose final intervention at Waterloo broke the cohesion of Napoleon's line (Author's collection).
Right: Marshal Grouchy; engraving by Wolf after Rouillard (Philip J. Haythornthwaite collection).

Above: Lieutenant-General Count Reille, the energetic commander of Napoleon's II Corps (Philip J. Haythornthwaite collection).

Above: General Gneisenau directs the Prussians to fall back on Wavre after being defeated at Ligny, thus enabling them to aid Wellington at Waterloo (Author's collection).
Below: Nassau troops and British Guardsmen hold the woods of Hougoumont as long as possible (Author's collection).

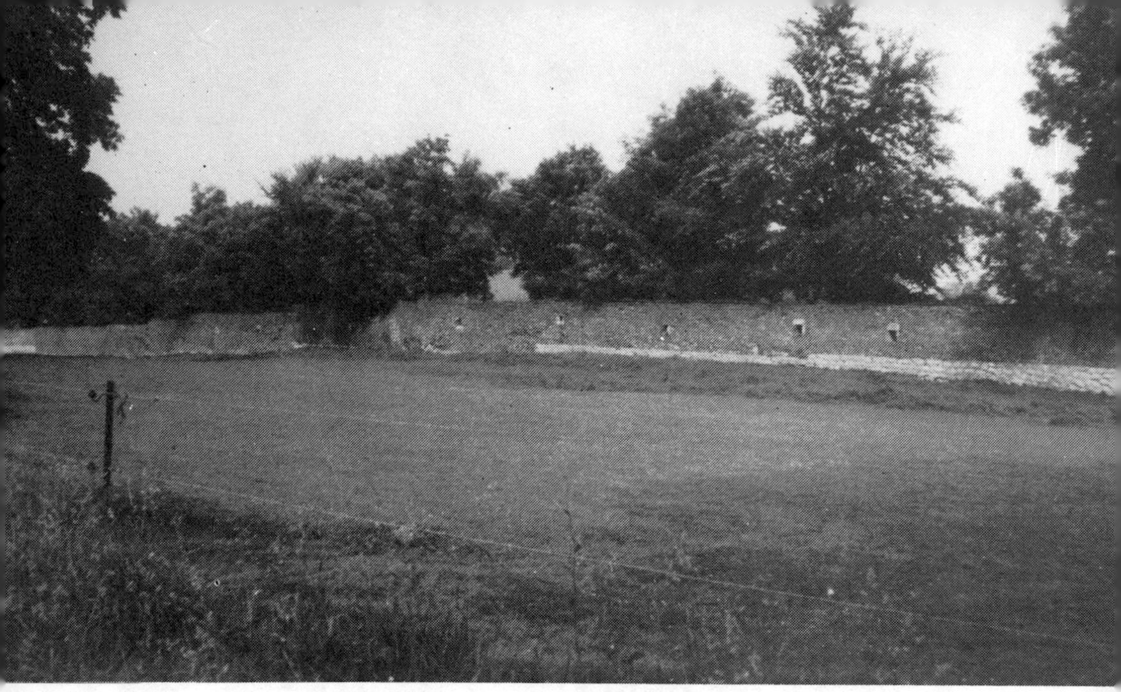

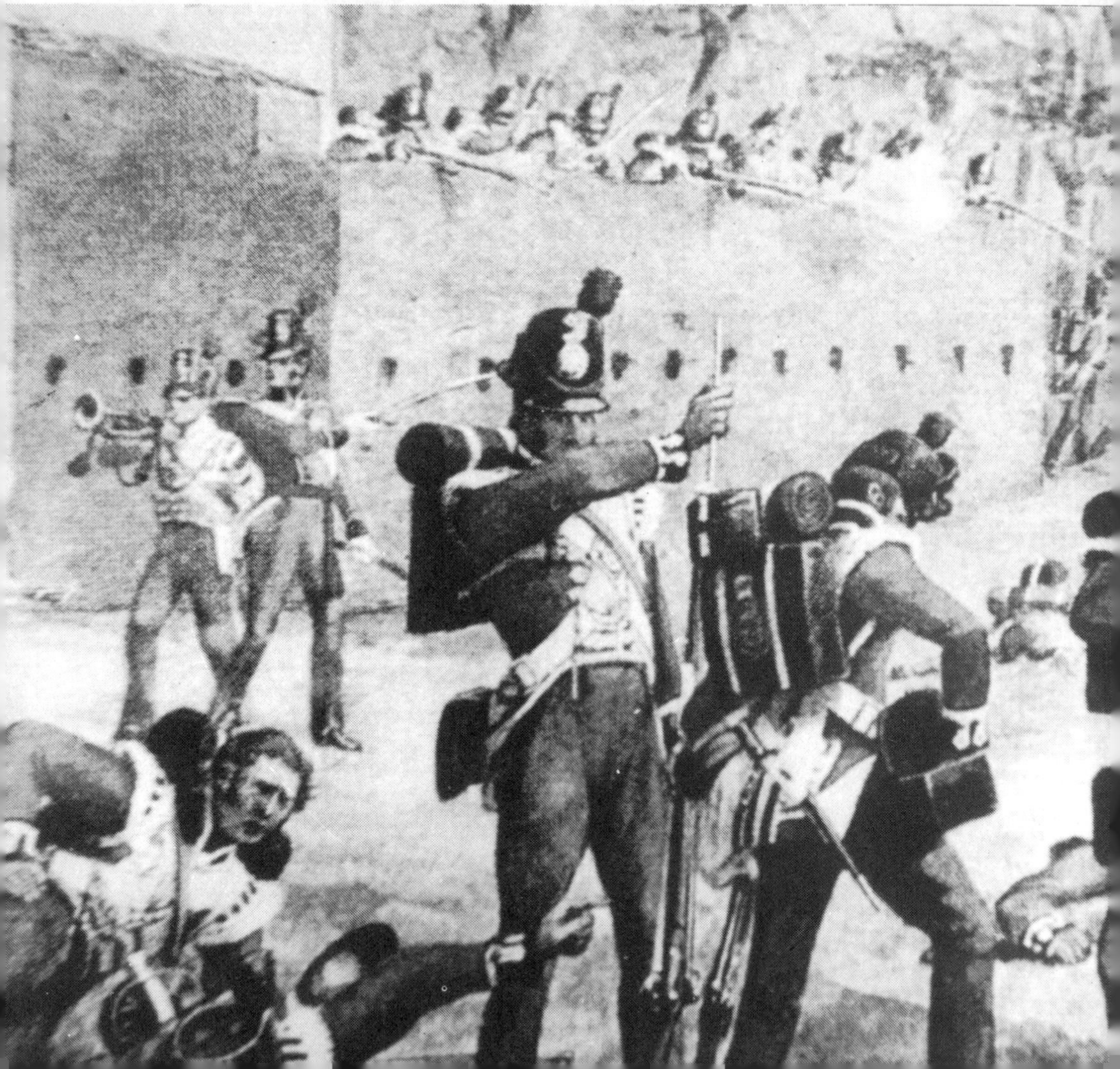

Top left: The loop-holed garden wall at Château Hougoumont; in 1815 trees grew where the wire fence now runs (Author's collection).
Left: British Guardsmen are pressed back from the Château woods to the main building. In their rear can be seen part of the loop-holed garden wall. Print after Simkin (Author's collection).
Above: The approach from the lane (still a dirt track) to the Farm of Papelotte. Around these hedgerows and walled buildings the Netherland and Nassau troops of Perponcher's 2 Brigade fought all day (Author's collection).

Above: Looking across the fields north-east from Papelotte to the buildings around ruined Frischermont. Note how the ground ascends slightly to the right; the whole area – Papelotte, Smohain and Frischermont – lie some 35 feet in a dip below the Waterloo skyline (Author's collection).

Below: The innocent landscape. Looking from the rear of Plancenoit (through the bushes behind the Prussian monument), you can see one dip to the right; out of vision in this photograph is the Papelotte, Smohain and Frischermont area beneath the dip behind the trees on the extreme right (Author's collection).

Above: The road leading from Plancenoit to Frischermont on which Pirch I's Corps advanced (Author's collection).
Below: Le Caillou, Napoleon's headquarters on 17 June (Author's collection).

Left: The defence of La Haye Sainte farm-house by Major Baring's Germans and Nassau troops (painting by Adolph North courtesy of the Niedersächersisches Landesmuseum, Hannover).

Bottom left: The Prince of Saxe-Weimar consults with his brigade staff at Smohain on 18 June. Note that the Nassau officers on the right wear Netherland uniforms. Although referred to incorrectly by British sources as the 'Orange-Nassau regiment', the regiment was in fact the 28th of the Netherlands Line and contained many Dutch soldiers as well as German. (Siborne referred to them as 'Orange-Nassaus' so as to further discredit the Netherlands forces.) The uniform, French in colouring and design, was mistaken by the Prussians at the end of the day, causing needless loss to the regiment by 'friendly fire'. (painting by J. Hoynck van Papendrecht, courtesy of the Koninklijke Nederlands Leger en Wapen Museum, Delft).

Below: The Prince of Orange at Quatre Bras, leading the 5th Netherlands Militia in a desperate counter-attack in an attempt to purchase time until Wellington's reserves could arrive (painting by J. Hoynck van Papendrecht, courtesy of the Koninklijke Nederlands Leger en Wapen Museum, Delft).

Above: 1.30 p.m. Dubois' Cuirassiers advance to cross the sunken road. Behind, in the middle of the picture, can be seen the sandpit and the knoll defended by the British 95th Rifles; behind it can be seen the all-out attack on the Allied left by d'Erlon's Corps (detail from the Belgian panorama by Louis Moulin, Author's collection).

Below: Marshal Ney leads forward d'Erlon's Corps to attack the Allied left; the Grand Battery is firing on the ridge behind (drawn by Jean Augé, Author's collection).

Above: After the failure of d'Erlon's attack, Ney is ordered to attack with the massed cavalry to break Wellington's centre (detail from the panorama by Louis Moulin, Author's collection).

Below: As the cavalry gallop towards the Allied centre, we can see the area encompassed by Château Hougoumont; smoke is rising from the burning buildings, and to the right the 'hollow way' is clearly seen (detail from the panorama by Louis Moulin, Author's collection).

Above: As the French cavalry press home their attack, the artillery of Captain Sandham see their limbers and caissons being driven away by inexperienced drivers hired from postillions, pot-boys, etc. (detail from the panorama by Louis Moulin, Author's collection).
Below: Wellington and some of his staff are seen here in the centre of a square (detail from the panorama, by Louis Moulin, Author's collection).

and Gneisenau to be ideally placed to fall at right-angles on the left flank and rear of the French army. And, looking in that direction Gneisenau could see that the enemy indeed was manoeuvring as though to receive an attack in rear of their left flank. He assumed that the French had identified the newcomers as Allied. At the same time Gneisenau received a request from Jagow for reinforcements for Ligny and replied confidently: 'Hold on for one half-hour longer, the English army is drawing near.'[44] Gneisenau believed that the British Field Marshal, who had won so many victories against the French, was doing what Müffling had suggested and Wellington had endorsed at 1 p.m. that afternoon, a few very long hours earlier.

Eager to take full advantage of the assistance being rendered by his ally, Gneisenau decided to do to the French army what Napoleon had planned for the Prussians. He would gather all his reserves from the centre, including Marwitz's brigade of Hobe's III Corps cavalry, and, with what he thought was all of Napoleon's reserves committed to supporting the French left, use his reserves to launch an attack in force on the French line between Wagnelee and St-Amand. Then, having broken through the French line there, the Prussian reserves would turn both left and right, enveloping separately the French right and centre which were contending with Zeithen and Thielemann, and the French left which was turned to face the arriving Allies.

While the Prussians prepared to leave their defensive positions and carry out this decisive attack, Napoleon's aide had recognized d'Erlon's corps as French and had so informed his Emperor. Napoleon guessed at what must have happened: when de la Bedoyère had reached him d'Erlon must have been farther south than anticipated and had therefore marched straight along the Roman road from the Brussels road, rather than joining it farther towards the Prussian positions as Napoleon would have expected him to do had d'Erlon already been around Frasnes. Napoleon assumed that d'Erlon would continue along the Roman road to Trois Barettes. The Prussians would not be surprised by d'Erlon, but would still have to deal with him, and that would serve Napoleon's purpose well enough. He accordingly ordered the rest of the Old Guard and the Guard cavalry to the height overlooking Ligny.

Suddenly, at 6 p.m., the Prussians began their offensive on the French left. Jurgass's cavalry squadrons surged forward against the hamlet of St-Amand, followed by Tippelskirch's 5 Brigade (which had been guarding Trois Barettes). Brause's 7 and Krafft's 6 Brigades closed in on St-Amand from three sides. Furious fighting erupted anew along this front, and only the reinforcements from the Imperial Guard saved Vandamme from being totally routed. As it was, the French left was everywhere pushed back. Then Domon's cavalry division and Colbert's lancers of the Imperial Guard charged and drove back Jurgass's squadrons. Girard's division had meanwhile turned around again towards the Prussians and entered the fray. By 7 p.m., thanks to the 8,000 fresh troops of the élite Guard which the

Emperor had sent him to fight the English, Vandamme had managed to hold the Prussians' advance.

At the same time, from his position with his Guard before Ligny, Napoleon could see that the Prussians had committed their reserves against his left in what seemed to him to be a futile gesture to keep open their communications with Wellington. He adjudged that the time had come to spring his own trap. Sixty cannon of Gérard's corps and the Old Guard bombarded the stricken village, smashing its rubble into smaller fragments and relieving many wounded of their pain for ever. The cannonade was followed immediately by an assault in two columns, each led by elements of the Old Guard. The left column was led by the 2nd, 3rd, and 4th Grenadiers, and the right by the 1st Grenadiers, 1st *Chasseurs* and the Sappers and Marines. The left column was supported by Napoleon himself with the Guard cavalry headquarters squadron (of regimental strength), and the right by Milhaud's *cuirassiers*. Finally Vichery's division followed the left, and Pecheux's the right.

Both columns, spearheaded by the Old Guard, the most feared and formidable soldiers of the day, soon penetrated the weakened Prussian defences. The Guard units of both columns then drove towards Sombreffe to isolate Thielemann, and Gérard's divisions attacked toward the rear of the Prussian line holding the St-Amands. In the Prussian army the shock of this breakthrough was profound. Gneisenau and Blücher had thought that Napoleon had sent his entire Guard to support his left against Wellington and preserve his line of retreat.

An account of the effect of the French incursion was given by Lieutenant Reuter, commanding the Prussian 12pdr battery No 6, assigned to I Corps but attached to II Corps, positioned between Ligny and St-Amand so as to be able to shell either place. Reuter recounts how French from one direction got within musket range of his battery by a ruse, then others took him by surprise:

> '... the battery had ... been engaged for some hours in its combat with the hostile guns, and were awaiting the order to follow up the movement of the 14th regiment, when suddenly I became aware of two strong lines of skirmishers, which were falling back on us from the village of St. Amand. Imagining that the skirmishers in front of us were our own countrymen, I hastened up the battery and warned my layers not to direct their aim upon them, but to continue to engage the guns opposite. In the meanwhile the skirmishers in question had got within three hundred paces of the battery. I had just returned to the right flank of my command, when our surgeon Zinkernagel called my attention to the red tufts on the shakos of the Sharpshooters. I at once bellowed out the order "With canister on the

skirmishers!" At the same moment both lines turned upon us, gave us a volley, and then flung themselves on the ground. By this volley, and the bursting of a shell or two, every horse, except one wheeler, belonging to the gun on my left flank, was either killed or wounded ... I meanwhile kept up a slow fire of canister, that had the effect of keeping the marksmen glued to the ground. But in another moment, all of a sudden, I saw my left flank taken in the rear, from the direction of Ligny brook, by a French staff officer and about fifty horsemen ... As they rushed on us the staff officer shouted to me in German, "Surrender, gunners, for you are all my prisoners!"'[45]

Gneisenau and Blücher were doubly staggered, by Napoleon's sudden appearance in their midst and by Wellington's more gradual disappearance from their view. The column which had been welcomed with jubilation when it had come along behind the French left had suddenly disappeared. It was now about 8 p.m. While the situation in the Prussian centre was critical, Gneisenau, having committed his reserves as the mass to encircle the French left, had denuded his centre. And although both its wings were holding firm, with a local superiority of numbers, not everything had been thrown into the battle; Kamphen's 10 and Stulpnägel's 12 Brigades were intact on the Prussian left, but were not available to form a rearguard as Napoleon's Old Guard now stood between them and the broken Prussian centre. The danger to the Prussians was that the developing rout of their centre would spread to units of the two flanks which were still standing firm.

It was then that Blücher saved his centre. The Hussar General, 72 years old, with a long span of years spent in the saddle, leading advance guards and bringing up rearguards, responded instinctively to the need of the moment. He collected all the available cavalry, 32 squadrons, and led them in repeated charges against the irrupting enemy forces. The French facing these charges held their fire until the horsemen were within point-blank range, and did terrible execution on them. The Imperial Guard continued to move forward slowly in square, firing on the Prussian cavalry whenever they drew too near. With Blücher, a Field Marshal and commander of the army, in the thick of the fighting, the Prussian soldiers were encouraged; their spirit and discipline flourished; they fought hard; and they were not routed. Napoleon might have won the day in that he was left in possession of the field; but he was denied a victory, in that the Prussian army was not broken. Both armies had committed themselves to an encircling attack, using the mass of 20,000 men that both thought were their own allies. Gneisenau and Blücher had ripped into Napoleon's left with fresh troops, intending to trap them against a wall of Allied troops. Napoleon had likewise hammered through the weakened Prussian centre only to find that the Prussians to his left were not held or encircled by d'Erlon's 20,000 men. Neither Blücher nor Gneisenau, nor a large percentage of the troops had been captured. Ligny had not been an Austerlitz or a Jena; but it could have been.

Like Gneisenau and Blücher, Napoleon was dumbfounded by the disappearance of the force which, in its walk-on part at the edge of the Ligny field, had been all things to all men. Why was not this force, which Napoleon knew to be French and therefore undoubtedly d'Erlon's, driving in the Prussian left? Why were not his cannon sweeping the Namur road, cutting down the dislocated Prussians? Compounding the mystery of d'Erlon's volte-face was the fact that he had left two full divisions, one infantry and one cavalry, at the high-water mark of his advance near Wagnelee, and that this still significant force, poised at the jugular of the Prussian army, was largely inactive. All that these two divisions would have had to do would have been to advance together along the Roman road towards Trois Barettes and they could still have accomplished much of what Napoleon had hoped for from d'Erlon's full corps.

It transpired that Delcambre, bearing Ney's recall order, had found d'Erlon at about 6 p.m. This of course placed d'Erlon in an unenviable position: to obey Ney, his direct superior, would be to disobey the Emperor, his commander-in-chief and sovereign, and vice versa. D'Erlon tried to obey both. He would substantially obey Ney, because, de la Bedoyère and his 'as from the Emperor' notwithstanding, Napoleon's orders of the 16th to his corps commanders had clearly stated that when the Emperor was with a wing of the army he commanded, otherwise the corps commanders were to obey the wing commander. Also, as d'Erlon later wrote of his quandary: 'I decided that as he [Ney] summoned me back, in direct opposition to Napoleon's will, the Marshal must be in extreme peril.'[47] But d'Erlon also wanted to do as much as he felt he could to obey the Emperor. The lead divisions of the column, Durutte's 4th Division and Jacquinot's cavalry division, which were then only half-a-mile from the Prussian left flank,[48] were therefore ordered to support the French flank which, in effect, they were extending; while d'Erlon had the rest of the column, whose rearguard was less than a mile from Marshal Ney, about face and march in response to Ney's summons.

The only instruction d'Erlon had left with Durutte was '... be Prudent'.[49] Jacquinot's cavalry had gone ahead to skirmish with Marwitz's troopers and the Silesian hussars, clearing the way for Durutte to advance his infantry rapidly along the Roman road (that is, in column, rather than having to scuttle forward in squares), only to discover that Durutte, having taken Wagnelee from a small Prussian rearguard, thus turning the Prussian right flank, had remained there. One of Durutte's brigade commanders, General Brue, was so exasperated that he shouted at his superior: 'It is unheard of, that we should stand here with folded arms, and witness the retreat of a beaten army, when everything shows we have but to attack to destroy it!' Durutte, feeling the weight of d'Erlon's admonition to be prudent, replied: 'It is lucky for you that you are not responsible.' And although Brue's riposte, 'Would to God I were! For we should be fighting at this moment!'[50] should have picqued Durutte's proven fighting spirit, caution prevailed and the 4th did not advance further. (Durutte and Jacquinot disposed of 5,400 men, who could have been more effective.)

D'Erlon rode swiftly back to his rearguard, Marcognet's 3rd Division, leaving Delcambre to see to the return of Allix's 1st, Donzelot's 2nd, and de Sale's corps artillery. D'Erlon had arrived at Frasnes by 8 p.m. and, as he recounted: 'On my return with [part of] my army corps to Frasnes, I took over the outposts to relieve the II Corps which had suffered heavy losses.'[51] It is probable that only the firm resistance of d'Erlon's fresher troops, who replaced Reille's exhausted men in the outposts and kept up a brisk skirmishing fire, deterred Wellington from pressing Ney further that night.

At Ligny Blücher's heroic action had allowed the two Prussian wings to withdraw in good order. An anecdote illustrative of how the Prussian centre was stabilized is told by Lieutenant Reuter, whose battery proved to be situated at the focus of the French attack and had been captured by French cavalry, only to be rescued by one of Blücher's charges. After that, Reuter recalled a conversation with his brigade commander, General Pirch II, and what then occurred:

> '"Truly sir," said I, "matters are not looking very rosy, but 12-pounder battery No 6 has simply come here to get into a position to check the enemy's advance." "That, then, is very brave conduct on your part," answered the general, "... cling to the position at all hazards, it is of the greatest importance. I will collect a few troops to form an escort to your guns." Whilst this short, but animated, discussion had been going on his brigade had come up close to where we were. He collected it up to cover us, and sent every one who was mounted to collect all retreating troops in the neighbourhood for the same purpose, while, as they came up, he called out to them, "Soldiers, there stand your guns, are you not Prussians!" During the time that a sort of rear-guard was thus formed, the battery had opened fire on the enemy's cavalry, which was coming up rather cautiously, and had forced them to fall back again. Later on a 6-pounder field battery and a half horse battery came up and joined us. The fight then became stationary, and as the darkness came on, fighting gradually ceased on both sides. During the course of the night this rearguard ... had come under the command of General von Roeder.'[52]

In one of the last actions of the day, as Gneisenau later reported to his king:

> 'A charge of cavalry led on by himself [Blücher], had failed. Whilst that of the enemy was vigorously pursuing, a musket-shot struck the field marshal's horse: the animal, far from being stopped in his career by this wound, began to gallop more furiously till it dropped down dead. The field marshal, stunned by the violent fall, lay entangled under the horse. The enemy's cuirassiers, following up their advantage advanced: our last horseman had already passed by the field marshal, an adjutant alone remained with him, and just alighted, resolved to share his fate ... The enemy, pursuing their charge, passed rapidly by the field marshal without seeing him: the next moment a second charge of our cavalry having repulsed them, they again passed him with the same precipitation, not perceiving him, any more than they had done the first time. Then, but not without difficulty, the field marshal was disengaged from under the dead horse, and immediately mounted a dragoon horse.'[53]

Nor was the fate of his field marshal Gneisenau's only problem as the day of the 16th began to fade. The army was effectively split into two sections. Most of I and II Corps had withdrawn north of the Roman road from between Wagnelee and Brye. Part of II and all of III Corps were at Sombreffe. Gneisenau had at first resolved that the former section pull back to Tilly, which was on a parallel with Quatre Bras, and the latter section retreat to join IV Corps at Gembloux and with them move on to Tilly to join the remainder of the army. On reflection, however, Gneisenau, feeling betrayed by Wellington and resentful of his unidirectional interpretation of Allied co-operation, and no doubt recalling in this context the treaty of 3 January, came to the view that it would be better for the Prussian army, after having regrouped at Tilly, to abandon any further thoughts of trying to act in concert with Wellington and fall back on new lines of communication towards the Rhine. One of Gneisenau's General Staff officers, Colonel von Reiche, later described the discussion regarding Tilly he had with Gneisenau on the Roman road, and the consequent decision, which would prove to be another of the turning-points of the campaign:

> 'Although it was almost dark I could still see my map clearly enough to realize that Tilly was not marked on it. Thinking it likely that a number of other officers would have the same map [Nouvelle carte Pays-bas, etc., réduite d'après celle de Ferraris], and that uncertainty and confu-

sion could easily result, I proposed that instead of Tilly another town lying further back but on the same line of march should be named as the assembly point - somewhere which we could assume would be shown on every other map. I remarked that even if two withdrawal points were detailed, they were in the same direction, so there would be no fear of confusion. Gneisenau agreed. On his map I found that Wavre was just such a place ... Next I stationed the staff officer I had with me, Lieutenant von Reisewitz, at the point [Trois Barettes] on the Roman road where the track now to be taken branched off, and instructed him to direct any troops who arrived to follow it. The detachments which had already taken the Roman road or the Namur road could not, of course, be recalled. In itself this was a bad thing, yet it had the advantage that the enemy would be deceived as to the line of retreat.'[54]

Allied fortunes, so endangered on the evening of the 16th, were to be redeemed by Reiche's perception and Gneisenau's endorsement of it. For in deciding not to retreat along the existing Prussian line of communication through Namur and Liège and instead go north, Gneisenau hoped to elude immediate pursuit, and thus gain the 36 to 48 hours he felt would be needed to re-assemble the army into an effective fighting force. The French, he hoped, would not be expecting the Prussians to retreat along the axis of the Brussels-Namur road, although ironically this was one of the two routes by which Napoleon intended advancing his army on Brussels. From Gneisenau's new temporary headquarters at Mellery, the highly efficient General Staff was active almost immediately upon arriving there from the battlefield. Never again would it take five days, as it had after Blücher's heavy defeat at Etoges in 1814, for the Prussian army to be able to fight again. As a priority, orders were issued to open a new line of communication through Tirlemont and Louvain, on Maastricht, Aachen, Cologne, Wesel and Münster to Berlin. From the early hours of the 17th, Prussian official couriers were dispatched to points along the new line, carrying orders to set up magazines of military stores, and to move the siege train up to Maastricht.[55] Had Blücher been fit and in command at this stage, he would probably have considered the decisive reason for withdrawing to Wavre was that it kept the Prussian and Anglo-Allied armies within a distance of each other so that they might still be able to combine against Napoleon. While he remained incapacitated from his ordeal on the field, Gneisenau, in keeping with his king's instruction, had assumed the authority of army commander in name as well as in substance. Where Blücher would have kept his mind on the problem of how to defeat Napoleon, Gneisenau was preoccupied with the episode of d'Erlon's corps, which he saw as Wellington's willingness literally to stand by and watch the Prussian army suffer a defeat. Gneisenau's attitude toward his 'ally' was evidenced by his failure until the 17th to inform Müffling of his decision to withdraw and of his selection of Wavre as his assembly point.[56]

On the Ligny battlefield during the night of 16/17 June General Zeithen was again given the duty of conducting a rearguard action. The last elements of the western section of the army and part of Thielemann's corps maintained posts between Brye and Sombreffe and along the Namur road. A very short distance through the darkness beyond these Prussian outposts were the French troops of Lobau's corps who had finally caught up with their army. Vigilance was keen on both sides of the no man's land. Even the battalions of the Imperial Guard in the French second line bivouacked in squares on damp ground without fires, ready for any eventuality. Napoleon was wary that, as at Laon on 9 March 1814, Blücher might launch a night counter-attack and turn his reversal into a victory.

Encircling the dark French bivouacs on the battlefield were the nearer and farther glows of the fires smouldering in the nine villages and hamlets that, for a day, had played unconsulted hosts to the contending armies. Dead men were everywhere, and the haunting cries of the wounded could be heard all around. Captain de Maduit, of the Grenadiers of the Old Guard, recalled the close and unrelenting nature of the battle:

'Ligny ... consisted of hand-to-hand fighting that lasted for hours together; and with this was combined, not a fusillade and cannonade carried out at ranges of some four or six hundred yards as occurred in most other battles, but these were replaced by point-blank discharges of musketry, and canister volleys fired at fifty yards' range. At Ligny, more than 4,000 dead soldiers were piled on an area less in measurement than the Tuileries garden, some 300 or 400 yards square ... The aspect of the cemetery at S. Amand was not a whit less terrible ... The gallant 82nd of the Line (Girard's division), almost to a man lay here ... One can picture the rage with which each side dashed against its foes.'[57]

Napoleon had returned to Fleurus by 11 p.m. In assessing his victory *manqué*, Napoleon adjudged that the Prussians had lost 16,000 men and 21 guns, with another 8,000 men of the centre fled in rout. Many of these were from the provinces newly acquired by Prussia. French losses at Ligny had been 11,000 men, and when Napoleon received Ney's reports on the results of the day he would learn of another 4,000 lost at Quatre Bras. He would not be able to decide his next move until the 17th, when he had learned whether Blücher intended to continue the fight in the morning. Wellington was within a distance to support him, and together the Allies could still field double his forces. If, on the other hand, Blücher had decided to retreat to the Meuse, Napoleon would try to bring Wellington to battle and take Brussels. All depended for the moment on the Prussians.

At Mellery, late in the night, a bruised and battered Blücher sat with Gneisenau and other senior Prussian officers. One of these officers recorded the scene in his diary:

> 'I found him [Blücher] in a farmhouse ... On the floor wounded men lay groaning. The General [Gneisenau] himself was seated on a barrel of pickled cabbage, with only four or five people around him. Scattered troops passed through the village all night long ... The dispersion was as great as after the battle of Jena, and the night just as dark – but morale had not sunk. Each man was looking for his comrades so as to restore order.'[58]

Blücher, as might have been expected, had his mind on the military situation and did not want to give up the fight: 'We've had a blow and must now straighten out the dent.' Gneisenau, writing that night to his king, expressed a bitter recrimination: 'On the 16th of June in the morning the Duke of Wellington promised to be at Quatre Bras at 10 o'clock with 20,000 men ... on the strength of these promises and arrangements we decided to fight the battle [at Ligny].'[59] The difference of opinion between the Prussian commanders was talked through at some length, as related by Wellington's liaison officer, Hardinge (who had lost a hand at Ligny that day): 'I was told that there had been a great discussion that night in his [Gneisenau's] rooms, and that Blücher and Grolmann [Chief of the Prussian General Staff] carried the day for remaining in communication with the English army, but that Gneisenau had great doubts as to whether they ought not fall back on Liège and secure their own communications with [Kleist in] Luxemburg. They thought if the English should be defeated, they themselves would be utterly destroyed.'[60]

Blücher had been adamant in his resolve to see the thing through. His hatred for Napoleon and the French outweighed any other factor. Also, he had given his word (to Wellington at Tirlemont), '... which was his sword and he was too old to break it!' In the end, however, Gneisenau was swayed by his own Quartermaster-General, Karl von Grolmann, who was persuasive on the advantages of concentrating on Wavre. He reasoned that from Wavre the Prussian army could consolidate safely and maintain a line of communication with Prussia, while still preserving the option to co-operate with Wellington if they so chose, and while covering one of the two main roads Napoleon might use to march on Brussels. If Wellington declined to cover the other Brussels road and instead headed for the coast, the Prussian army could, Grolmann concluded, fall back at once on Prussia, or conduct an offensive against Napoleon in conjunction with Kleist's corps of 25,000 men.[61] Grolmann's sound counsel prevailed and all the gloom of defeat evaporated as Gneisenau's headquarters were reanimated. Planning was set in motion and couriers sent to Bülow, Thielemann and Pirch I. Gneisenau did not hurry to inform Wellington and Müffling of the decision reached; after all, they had hardly given priority to keeping him up to date during the 16th.[62] First light on the 17th found the Prussian army on the road to Wavre, disorganized, but the only one of the three contending armies with a clear purpose.

CHAPTER 10

17 June: Strategic Withdrawal

'There are few Generals that have run oftener, or more lustily than I have done. But I have taken care not to run too far, and commonly have run as fast forward as backward, to convince the Enemy that we were like a Crab, that would run either way.'
– Major General Nathanael Greene to Henry Knox, 18 July 1781.

At 11 p.m. on 16 June Napoleon returned to his headquarters at Fleurus, realizing that yet again he had been robbed of his decisive victory. If only d'Erlon had come up on Blücher's flank and rear at the same time as the Guard had cleared Ligny – as he had expected – the Prussians would have been utterly crushed, not one man or gun of his right wing could have escaped the trap, the Prussian staff would have been captured, their army ruined as completely as at Jena, and probably beyond recovery. Such a victory would have shaken all Europe, ranking second only to Austerlitz in its political potential. In France it would have stirred the people to a fever pitch of enthusiasm and eliminated any opposition or waverers to the Emperor's cause.

Napoleon would now have to wait for morning and the reports of his corps commanders before he could properly assess the new military situation. One set of possibilities concerned the Prussians. How far and in which direction was Blücher retreating to regroup; and when he had done so, would he seek still to act in concert with Wellington or attack independently; would he retire to Prussia or head south to join forces with Kleist and perhaps Schwarzenberg? Other possibilities centred on the Anglo-Allied army. If Wellington were strong enough at Quatre Bras (as was indicated by Ney's having countermanded d'Erlon's detachment), would he remain within striking distance long enough after the Prussian withdrawal to be brought to battle separately; would he fall back to cover Brussels, with or without Blücher; or would he head for the embarkation ports on the coast? Before midnight, in an endeavour to learn as much as possible of the status of his enemies as early as possible, Napoleon instructed Grouchy to send out a cavalry reconnaissance in force eastwards before first light. He ordered Soult to send a similar force northward at the same time.

At Quatre Bras between 10 and 11 p.m., Wellington ordered the Prince of Orange to return to Nivelles, make an appreciation of the situation there, then go on to Braine-le-Comte to fetch his campaign map. The Prince, escorted by the battered 27th *Jägers*, arrived in Nivelles just before 2 a.m. There he wrote a hurried report to King William, which reflects some of the legitimate pride with which a son might tell his father of his praiseworthy actions that day:

'... As I managed successfully [to hold the crossroads] the Duke of Wellington had time enough to assemble a force to frustrate the enemy's intentions. The result of this attack was that after heavy fighting, which lasted to 9 p.m., we not only brought the enemy to a standstill, but also repulsed him slightly... Our troops remained bivouacking on the battlefield, where I intend to proceed soon, it being probable that Napoleon will again try to accomplish his plans of yesterday. The Duke of Wellington has assembled all possible troops at this point.'[1]

Wellington's force, increased by about midnight to 46,000, was bivouacked all around the Quatre Bras crossroads, with outposts at Frasnes chapel and the farms of Piraumont, Gemioncourt and Pierrepont. Content that Ney would remain quiescent for the night and convinced that French vigilance before Frasnes afforded no real opportunities for night action, Wellington and his staff rode back to Genappe for the night, confident that on the morrow he and Blücher would crush Napoleon between them.. Lieutenant Basil Jackson left an account of how he passed the night at Genappe at the inn where Wellington stayed:

'The next question was, quarters for the night – not for the troops who had so hardly fought, they had the cold ground for their bed with the canopy of heaven for a coverlet, and short commons for supper; but for the staff, who could go where they pleased, and get housed. Genappe, which was only about a couple of miles in the rear, would, we knew, be head-quarters, and thither I accompanied my fellow traveller and others. On entering the principal auberge, we found a long table, with covers laid for at least twenty persons, the arrangement of which an officer of the Duke's personal staff was superintending, as a sort of major domo; there were hampers of wine in a corner of the room, from which the officer in question was selecting bottles for the table. On observing my companion, whose rank entitled him to some consideration, he proposed that he should remain and sup with His Grace; the invitation however was declined, and we left the house ... It was about eleven, and I had just fallen asleep, when a tremendous clatter of horses in the street awoke and caused me to fly to the window in some alarm; which ceased when I found that the horsemen were moving in the direction of the enemy. I tried to recompose myself to sleep, but the incessant clatter of hoofs, jingle of steel scabbards, and rattle of artillery kept me awake for hours, as I thought. This was the whole, or nearly so, of the British and German Legion Cavalry, with some troops of horse artillery, which had moved from Ninove, by Nivelles, and were proceeding onward to Quatre Bras.'[2]

Wellington arose before first light on the morning of the 17th and attired himself in his usual field costume of a short blue frock-coat, short cloak of the same colour, light buff pantaloons, and Hessian boots, with his plain low cocked hat bearing the British black cockade surmounted by three miniature cockades representing Spain, Portugal and The United Netherlands.

Arriving at Quatre Bras before sunrise, Wellington checked and adjusted his dispositions, expecting at any moment to receive word from Blücher and Gneisenau as to what action they intended to carry out that day. The Quatre Bras position was precarious; there were still less than half the Anglo-Allied army present, the remainder temporarily halted between Nivelles and Braine-le-Comte; so Wellington was most anxious to apprise himself of the position and plans of the Prussians.

During the night, General Müffling had expected but not received any communication from Gneisenau. He did not count the message retrieved when Nassau soldiers had found the wounded Prussian Major von Winterfeldt, who had been hit during the afternoon while delivering a copy of Gneisenau's now moot request to Wellington for aid. At first light on the 17th Müffling sent several aides by different routes to find Gneisenau and obtain news and instructions. Wellington, too, had decided to send an aide to Prussian army headquarters. Between 6 and 7 a.m., Colonel Sir Alexander Gordon went down the Namur road escorted by a troop of the 10th Hussars, with orders to make contact with Blücher or Hardinge.

Situated as he was, Wellington would need to conform quickly to whatever movement the Prussians might make, or fall back before Brussels and there complete the concentration of his army. At the moment, with most of his army still strung out along the roads to the east, he was in no condition to accept battle. To his front was Marshal Ney with almost equal numbers of men, and on his open left flank was Napoleon with numerical superiority. Further, Wellington still feared that another French corps or larger force might be advancing up the Mons-Hal-Brussels road. If this nightmare came true, Wellington knew that his army would be destroyed piecemeal and the Low Countries lost. Prompted by this dark prospect, at about 9 a.m. Wellington sat on the ground and personally drafted contingency movement orders for a withdrawal, then gave it to one of his aides, De Lacy Evans, to copy out.

Colonel Gordon had been fortunate to avoid capture by French patrols. Eventually he found General Zeithen at Tilly organizing rearguard pickets. Zeithen told Gordon that the Prussian army was falling back on

Wavre to regroup and that it could do nothing for Wellington. Galvanized by this crucial news, Gordon immediately set off back to Quatre Bras.

While awaiting either a Prussian messenger or the return of his own, Wellington had allowed his men to cook breakfast. He was deep in thought when the Prince of Orange returned with his map and joined him. At about 10 a.m. Gordon arrived and dismounted from his lathered horse. When Wellington received this news he was dumbfounded. Müffling, who was present, was exquisitely conscious of the embarrassing position in which this development placed him:

'The Duke and I were both greatly surprised by this news. The Duke looked at me, as if he wished to ask whether I had known the thing and concealed it from him on good grounds. But on my saying quite naturally [and cleverly], "This is probably the account which the officer, who was shot down, was bringing me," and adding, "but now you cannot remain here, my Lord," he immediately entered with me as usual on the measures to be taken.'[3]

Wellington had already decided that if he were forced to withdraw, it would be to Mont St-Jean, where Picton had halted the previous morning. In 1814, on his way to Paris, Wellington had been charged with carrying out an inspection of the fortifications being constructed in the area as a military barrier against the French. He had at that time stated that if he were called upon to defend Brussels, Mont St-Jean would be the ideal position to take.[4] Now, in 1815, Wellington had been so called upon. Before he put into effect the draft movement orders he had written earlier, a Prussian staff officer arrived with a very welcome message to Müffling from Gneisenau.

Müffling's aides had reached Gneisenau above Mellery on the road to Wavre. In questioning them about the events of the 16th, Gneisenau and Blücher discovered that Wellington had been heavily engaged all day at Quatre Bras, having only just maintained his hold on the crossroads, and had had no opportunity or ability to aid his allies at Ligny by any route. It then became apparent to the Prussian leaders that the attack they had so unfortunately launched on the French left had been prompted by the appearance of a body of Napoleon's troops, not Wellington's. Gneisenau, while still unenthusiastic about the Duke, was magnanimous enough to admit to himself that he had misjudged him on this important matter. Accordingly he instructed a staff officer, Lieutenant von Massow, to tell Müffling that the Prussian army was still prepared to co-operate with Wellington, but from Wavre. Later Gneisenau wrote to his wife: '... Since the promised reinforcements did not arrive and some misunderstanding took place, we were forced to withdraw in order to combine our forces with the Duke of Wellington's army at some closer point. We retreated for one and a half hours. After today's march we closed in to the British Army and we will seek for another battle.'[5]

Calling for the campaign map which the Prince of Orange had retrieved from I Corps Headquarters at Braine-le-Comte, Wellington reviewed the withdrawal movement orders he had earlier given De Lacy Evans to prepare. Lord Hill was instructed to go to Nivelles, order the brigades of Colville's 4th British Division between there and Braine-le-Comte to remain at Braine, arrange for the baggage wagons clogging the road between those two towns to move back by way of Braine-le-Comte and Hal to Brussels, and finally to march with Clinton's 2nd British Division from Nivelles to Waterloo. Prince Frederick of Orange (younger brother of William, Prince of Orange, who had fought at Quatre Bras) was to march his command of Stedman's 1st Netherlands Division and Anthing's Indonesian Brigade from Enghien that evening to take up a position in front of Hal, supported by Colonel Estorff's cavalry brigade. To Major-General Colville he had written instructions to fall back with his division on the morning of the 18th from Braine-le-Comte to Hal. Colville was to be guided by the direction of the enemy advance, if any, whether he went directly to Hal or by way of Enghien, but Prince Frederick '... [was] to occupy with his [nominal] corps the position between Hal and Enghien, and ... defend it as long as possible.'[6] The Prince of Orange, acting on separate orders for The Netherlands forces, would send Constant Rebecque back to Nivelles to order Chassé's 3rd Netherlands Division and two Netherlander cavalry brigades to the Waterloo position by way of Nivelles. The Prince, on formal receipt of these orders, rode off at once to put them into effect.[7]

Wellington, humbugged by Napoleon as to the invasion, now showed his strategic brilliance. Having a clearer picture now of his troops' dispositions, he had personally ordered the vulnerable, strung-out section of his army to fall back and concentrate. Thus he safeguarded Brussels from attack by the Mons–Hal–Brussels road, and the Mons–Braine-le-Comte–Nivelles–Brussels road. The section of the army assembled at Quatre Bras would fall back holding the Charleroi—Brussels road, and the Prussians likewise, having denied Napoleon in the process the Gembloux–Wavre–Brussels road. This strategy frustrated Napoleon's use of the four principal routes to Brussels. At Mont St-Jean in front of Waterloo village and the forest of Soignies, Wellington's main force would hold the two roads to the capital that converged there; to his right Prince Frederick and Colville's secondary force the third road, and finally, to his left at Wavre, Blücher the fourth route. If Napoleon wished to take Brussels and its political advantage, Wellington knew that he would have no choice but to fight him there at Mont St-Jean – a position of his own choosing and with Prussian assistance giving him numerical advantage. In that case all that Napoleon had gained in his initial advance would be negated. Wellington also knew that, in the unlikely event of the Prussians failing him and his losing the battle, Hal would be the direction in which he would withdraw to the Scheldt and Antwerp. Prince Frederick's force would become the rearguard behind which he would rally his army before withdrawing.

Müffling instructed the courier, Massow, to inform Wellington in French of the message he had received from Gneisenau. The Duke put some questions to Massow and, on receiving satisfactory replies, declared: 'I am going to take up my position at Mont St-Jean. There I will wait for Napoleon and give him battle, if I may hope to be supported by a single Prussian corps. But if this support is denied me, I shall be compelled to sacrifice Brussels and take up *my position behind the Scheldt*.'[8] Wellington then wrote dispatches to this effect addressed to Blücher and Hardinge (of whose injury Massow had informed him) to be taken back by Massow. He then charged Uxbridge with command of the rearguard which would hold Quatre Bras while he turned his attention to organizing the withdrawal.

Several miles to the south of Quatre Bras, at Frasnes, in the middle of the preceding night, another staff officer had decided to return to his commander. General le Comte de Flahault, the Emperor's aide, had remained with Ney during the 16th and had supped with him late that night. Flahault wrote: 'I departed about one o'clock in the morning, not as the bearer of a message from him [Ney], but for the purpose of rejoining the Emperor at Fleurus. I arrived there before breakfast and gave him an account of what had happened on the previous day.'[9] Flahault was able to flesh out for the Emperor the brief dispatch Nay had sent to Soult at 10 p.m. on the 16th. Ney had written:

> 'I have attacked the English position at Quatre Bras with the greatest vigour; but an error of Count d'Erlon's deprived me of a fine victory, for at the very moment when the 5th and 9th divisions of General Reille's corps had overthrown everything in front of them [on the Allied left], the I corps marched off to S. Amand to support his Majesty's left ... Actually there have been engaged here [of French forces] only 3 divisions of infantry, a brigade of Cuirassiers, and General Piré's cavalry. The Count of Valmy [Kellermannn] delivered a fine charge, all have done their duty, except I Corps. The enemy has lost heavily; we captured some guns and a flag. We have lost about 2000 killed and 4000 wounded.'[10]

With the benefit of Flahault's elaboration, Napoleon understood the way events had unfolded at Quatre Bras, and why d'Erlon had turned back to return to Ney. Flahault would also have informed his Emperor of Wellington's weakness in cavalry and artillery on the 16th. In mitigation of Ney's repulse at the end of the day, Flahault wrote: 'I was close to Ney throughout the Quatre Bras engagement. Nobody could have shown greater courage, I might even say greater contempt for death, than he did.'[11] Thus, knowing Ney, and now knowing what he had had to contend with at Quatre Bras, Napoleon could be assured that he had done the best he could with the few troops from the two corps that were closed up and available.

Napoleon dictated to Soult new orders for Ney, timed between 7 and 8 a.m. Soult wrote to Ney:

> 'Marshal, General Flahault, who has just reached here [from Frasnes], reports that you are in doubt about the precise result of yesterday's operations on this wing. I [Soult] thought that I had already acquainted you of the victory which the Emperor gained. The Prussian Army has been routed, and General Pajol is now pursuing it along the roads leading to Namur and Liège. We have captured some thousands of prisoners and 30 guns ... The Emperor is proceeding to the windmill at Bry, past which runs the Namur and Quatre Bras high road; and, as it is possible that the English Army will engage your command, then, in such circumstances, the Emperor would march by the Quatre Bras road against the enemy in front of you, whilst you attack them in front with your divisions, which ought now to be concentrated; and in such an eventuality the hostile army would be annihilated immediately. Yesterday the Emperor remarked with regret that you had not massed your divisions; they acted spasmodically, and consequently you suffered disproportionate loss. Not one Englishman would have escaped if the corps of Counts Reille and d'Erlon had been kept together. *If Count d'Erlon had carried out the movement on S. Amand, prescribed by the Emperor, then the Prussian Army would have been totally destroyed*, and we might have captured 30,000 prisoners ... The Emperor hopes and desires that your seven infantry divisions and the Cavalry are concentrated, and that they occupy no more than a league [2½-3 miles] of ground, so as to have the whole force in hand, and ready for immediate action in case of need. His Majesty's intention is that you will take up a position at Quatre Bras, as you were ordered to do; *but if it is impossible to act in this manner send a detailed report immediately and the Emperor will move thither along the road already mentioned*; if, on the other hand, you are only confronted with a rear-guard, drive it off, and occupy the position. To-day is required for completing this operation, replenishing

ammunition, gathering stragglers and detachments ... The well-known [Prussian] partisan leader, Lützow, who has been taken prisoner, stated that the Prussian Army was lost, and that for the second time Blücher had jeopardized the Prussian Monarchy. – Soult.'[12]

Having dictated the substance of this letter for Soult to write, Napoleon rode to Ligny accompanied by Flahault. On and around the battlefield between Ligny and Sombreffe were Gérard and Lobau's corps, Vandamme, and the Guard, with the cavalry of Exelmans and Milhaud: some 70,000 men. Somewhere to the front of the French army was the Prussian army; but Napoleon did not know where. Behind Zeithen's rearguard screen, and aided by the dark night, the mass of disorganized Prussian units had broken contact with the French troops, and most had moved north. They had rested for a time during the night between Tilly, Gentinnes and Mellery, lighting no fires and moving on towards Wavre before first light. As they marched along several roads the wings of the Prussian army, which had been separated by the French attack at Ligny, came together around Mont St-Guibert. It was at this time also that Bülow's corps finally joined their comrades, swelling the size of Blücher's force to 300 guns and 90,000 men of whom about a third had not been put through the mangle of battle. And those who had fought at Ligny had been discomfited rather than defeated, and certainly had not been routed as Soult had blithely asserted in his interpretation of Napoleon's censure of Ney.

Napoleon now appeared to waste the morning promenading around the battlefield, but in fact he was waiting for the vital report – in which direction were the Prussians retreating? On this hung his next move. If Wellington were retreating and leaving only a rearguard, Ney should attain the crossroads by mid-morning; if not, the blow would fall on Wellington, not that he expected the Duke to be foolish enough to remain there. Napoleon would then have access to the two roads leading to Brussels that had been his objective on the 16th. He knew that Blücher still had a considerable force under his command, no doubt augmented by Bülow's corps. Under the circumstances any precipitous move against Wellington could – if Blücher emulated his actions of 1813-14 – find Napoleon caught in a vice. This was the reason for his delay.

At 2.30 a.m. on the 17th Grouchy, having been informed by his staff that advance cavalry pickets had reported the noise of wagons ahead of them on the high road to Namur, dispatched Pajol's light cavalry, supported by a brigade of Exelman's dragoons, to investigate. The Prussian force which had been heard was a mass of from three to eight thousand men of the Prussian centre who had been routed by the French attack. They had scattered before the General Staff could organize officers to direct them on to Tilly and Wavre. In the dark and without orders, the officers of these broken units had decided to withdraw their men along the army's line of communication. This large body inadvertently helped to confirm in the minds of the French that the Prussians were heading back towards Prussia. So these routed troops were able to perform an inestimable service to their army.

In searching for this unidentified Prussian force, Pajol missed his way in the dark, struck a different road and soon came up with a Prussian baggage train, an artillery battery and a squadron of the 7th *Uhlans*. Pajol's superior force quickly cut up this mixed group of the enemy and secured their guns and wagons, but continued along the Namur road no farther than Les Isnes, short of Temploux, as Pajol was unsure how far to press the search in this direction without specific orders. He then dispatched patrols along several roads to gather intelligence from their own observations and from questioning the inhabitants (this was the French-speaking part of Belgium).

By mid-morning of the 17th Pajol had received more sighting reports of bodies of stragglers, but this time heading northwards. He therefore set out in the direction of Louvain, reinforced by the 1st Hussars and Teste's infantry division of Lobau's corps, with two batteries of horse artillery sent by Napoleon. The Emperor had also ordered a general reconnaissance of all roads leading north and east. At the point where the Namur road crossed the Orneau brook Bereton's dragoons learned from peasants (subsequently proved to be correct) that the Prussian army was retreating by way of Gembloux. Bereton went there to investigate and found a strong Prussian rearguard. He sent a messenger at the gallop to Count Exelmans, who came up with three brigades of cavalry and two horse batteries. Exelmans rode forward and in the distance beyond Gembloux to the north he could see masses of troops, obviously Prussian, which he estimated (quite closely) to be 20,000 men of all arms. This distant body was Thielemann's corps marching along the Brussels-Namur road toward Wavre. Exelmans, with 3,000 troopers and no infantry, could not interfere with the withdrawing Prussians, even if he knew where to send for Pajol and his 1,400 cavalry. He had to content himself with keeping the Prussian force under observation, while reporting back to Grouchy.[13]

Grouchy was with Napoleon and his suite on the Ligny battlefield. Before they had set out from the Emperor's headquarters he had asked Napoleon for orders for the day, and Napoleon had answered tersely: 'I will give them to you when I see fit.'[14] As yet Napoleon had no positive news as to the exact whereabouts of the Prussians; they might be regrouping a mile or two back in order to attack with Wellington, or they might have retreated eastwards. Napoleon had divided his army into two wings and a central reserve and had attempted to hold up Wellington while destroying Blücher; Ney's mission had not failed in this respect. But d'Erlon's march and counter-march had not only deprived both wings of the 20,000 men [mass of decision] needed to defeat either Allied commander decisively, but worse, by his presence at Ligny, where Napoleon had ordered him to be, he had caused Napoleon to launch his attack too soon and unaided; further-more, by his appearance he had denied Napoleon the opportunity to delay until he could deploy a different force on the open Prussian flank.

D'Erlon's presence and counter-march had ensured that Napoleon attacked there without support, and this enabled the main Prussians to withdraw without having been damaged to any degree. So on 17 June Napoleon could not afford to make a hasty decision; this was the one draw-back of using the 'central reserve position' strategy; if it failed – as it had – Napoleon had to decide on which wing to throw his central weight. The wrong decision in the face of two enemies could be fatal: if Blücher were not withdrawing and Napoleon threw his weight prematurely on Welling-ton, Blücher might attack again on his other wing with three times his num-bers, crushing it and then aiding Wellington by falling on Napoleon's rear and communications, to encircle and entrap him. Napoleon had fought Blücher too many times in 1813 and 1814 to underestimate the new Pruss-ian army's resilience. Indeed, he had said of Blücher to Campbell, the British Commissioner on Elba: 'That old devil always attacked me with the same vigour. If he were beaten, he would, a moment later, show himself ready to fight again.'

Checking against his maps the intelligence reports he had received before and since the start of the campaign, Napoleon felt certain that Wellington had not yet completed his concentration, and was therefore still vulnerable. By the time he heard definitely of the current location of the Prussian army, he hoped also to learn that Ney had begun his attack on Quatre Bras, either confirming Wellington's withdrawal or pinning him in place. Depending on Blücher, Napoleon could then march his reserve from Marbais and the Ligny field to strike Wellington's open left flank – then on to Brussels.

While awaiting his cavalry reports Napoleon used this period of apparent inactivity to examine the ground and boost the morale of Van-damme and Girard's corps who had borne the brunt of one of the worst battles he had ever fought, involving bloody house-to-house fighting. Indeed, as he rode through St-Amand he was delayed for fifteen minutes while the heaps of mangled bodies were cleared to make a path for him and his entourage. But when he reached the bivouacs of the exhausted troops he was greeted with volleys and enthusiastic cheers on a par with their ferocity of the previous day.

By 11 a.m. Napoleon had come to a rapid conclusion from the reports he had thus far received. Pajol and Exelmans' initial reports indi-cated a Prussian withdrawal east of Gembloux and Namur towards their supply magazines on the Meuse. A patrol sent out by Napoleon towards Quatre Bras at 8 a.m. had returned with the intelligence that the 'English' were still there and that there had been a skirmish. (The British cavalry had disputed the ground with a French probing attack, rather than gradually yielding it as a rearguard would have done.) Napoleon concluded from these pieces of the puzzle that Blücher had in fact fallen back on his communications, but that against military logic Wellington was standing at Quatre Bras. Here was the opportunity he had hardly dared hope for: a gross error committed by an experienced general. The decisive battle of the campaign, missed on the 16th, could be gained on the 17th.

Accordingly Napoleon ordered Lobau to move his VI Corps (less Teste's division) to Marbais with Subervie's light cavalry for support. Also the Imperial Guard was to concentrate at Marbais. He left Vandamme and Gérard's men, and Girard's decimated division, at Sombreffe to recuperate, but he added Domon's cavalry division and Milhaud's *cuirassiers* to the force with which he would advance from Marbais when he knew that Ney had fixed Wellington by frontal attack. Including Ney's troops, Napoleon would have 72,000 men and 246 guns with which to destroy Wellington's much smaller force, weak in cavalry and artillery.

Further dispatches reached Napoleon from Pajol and Exelmans just after 11.30 a.m. Pajol reported that he was in front of Le Manzy on the Namur road, east of Sombreffe, where he had captured eight cannon and numerous wagons. This was welcome news. Exelmans' report, however, was disturbing. He informed his Emperor that he was riding with his two dragoon divisions and attached horse batteries to a position just above Gembloux: 'Where the enemy has massed itself.'[15] If the Prussians were massing above Gembloux they might be falling back on Wavre and then Brussels. On this Gembloux road, which ran almost parallel with the Charleroi—Brussels road, there were at least three routes by which Blücher could join Wellington (indeed, Napoleon had intended to use them himself). The worst possible scenario would be for Wellington and Blücher to fall back unhindered on both roads and concentrate together in front of Brussels. Not only would this deny him a chance of Victory and Brussels, but he would not be able to debouch his army from the forest of Soignies in the face of the combined armies that would destroy him piecemeal.[16] He would probably have to abandon his campaign in the north and march south back into France with the enemy at his heels.

This new factor in the equation had to be provided against. Now, having to assume that the Prussian army had retired northwards, and still being committed to his tactic of two wings and a reserve, Napoleon was obliged to detach from his army a force strong enough to harry the Prussians sufficiently to prevent them from assisting Wellington until Napoleon, with Ney, could find, fix and destroy him. The roles of Napoleon's wings had now reversed. Grouchy was summoned to perform this task, with 33,000 men, including 5,000 cavalry, and 96 guns. Napoleon's verbal orders to Grouchy were substantially: 'While I am engaged with the English, you must devote your energies to the pursuit of the Prussians. You will have under your orders the corps of Vandamme, Gérard, the division of Teste, the cavalry corps of Pajol, and of Exelmans.'[17] Grouchy was to 'keep a sword in the backs' of the Prussians while maintaining close contact with Napoleon's right.[18]

Grouchy had not long departed to organize his new command when Napoleon had misgivings as to the instructions he had given him. His task was vital, but Napoleon reflected that his verbal orders did not emphasize the need for extreme caution. The experiences of 1813 and 1814 had taught him that the Prussians in retreat would be quite capable of turning suddenly on Grouchy, especially at night, and annihilating him. Grouchy's role was to hold the attention of the Prussians, but he must ensure at all times that he could extricate himself. He was only to hazard his command in the event of Blücher's attempting to join Wellington. Feeling it essential to clarify this without delay, Napoleon did not wait until his Chief of Staff, Soult, could join him from Fleurus to dictate superseding written orders for Grouchy, but instead employed Soult's ever-present and reliable substitute, the Grand Marshal Count Bertrand. The order read:

> 'Marshal, proceed to Gembloux with the cavalry corps of Generals Pajol and Exelmans, the Light cavalry of IV corps, General Teste's infantry division (and of this latter you will be especially careful, for it is detached from its own corps) and the III and IV infantry Corps. You will reconnoitre towards Namur and Maastricht, and you will pursue the enemy. Observe his march and inform me of his movements, that I may penetrate his intentions. I shall move my headquarters to Quatre Bras, where the English still were this morning; our communications will then be direct by the Namur highroad. Should the enemy have evacuated Namur write to the General in command of the 2nd Military division, at Charlemont, to occupy the former place with some battalions of the National Guard and some guns, at present at Charlemont. The command at Namur will be given to a Major-General. It is important to discover what the enemy intend doing, whether Blücher is separating himself from Wellington, *or whether they meditate uniting to cover Brussels and Liège by risking another battle.* At all events keep your two infantry corps continually together within the limits of a league of good ground; and occupy each evening a good military position, which has several avenues of retreat. Place cavalry detachments between us so as to keep up communications with Headquarters. Dictated by the Emperor in the absence of the Major-general [Soult] – Grand Marshal Bertrand.'[19]

Napoleon would have been happier if he had been more certain of Blücher's location before taking action against Quatre Bras, where he supposed Wellington still to be, but he could not afford to let any more time pass. Time was on the Allies' side, not his. He had done his best to provide for contingencies. If the Prussian army had retired on Namur or along the Roman road towards Tongres, or both, and should subsequently move to support Wellington at Quatre Bras, Grouchy, by covering the Sombreffe –Gembloux area, would be well placed to delay them. Also, from there Napoleon felt that Grouchy would be able to detect a Prussian movement northward to make contact with a withdrawing Wellington. Napoleon's emphasis on maintaining cavalry communication reflected his concern that he be kept up to date with Grouchy's situation, as he had not been with Ney on the 16th. The contingency that Grouchy could not cover from his assigned position, of course, was that the Prussian army might already have gone north in parallel with Wellington.

Midday came and still Napoleon could hear no sounds of battle from Quatre Bras. Soult had ridden up from Fleurus, but with no fresh information from Ney, so an irritated Napoleon ordered Soult to send Ney another imperative message: 'The Emperor has just placed in position before Marbais a corps of Infantry and the Imperial Guard. His Majesty desires me to tell you that his intention is that you shall attack the enemy at Quatre Bras, and drive them from their position; the corps at Marbais will support your operations. His Majesty is going to Marbais, and awaits impatiently your report.'[20]

It would be appropriate here to point out that Marshal Soult had been of very little assistance in the campaign so far. No greater blow had been dealt to Napoleon in 1815 than the murder of Marshal Berthier. For eighteen years Berthier had been Napoleon's right arm. He had transcribed the Emperor's rapidly spoken thoughts so well that Napoleon could not distinguish the polished results from his own erratic dictation. He had managed the smooth movement and compliance by corps commanders swiftly and accurately, and ensured that Napoleon was kept up to date on all fronts. In an era when dispatch-riders rode horses, all orders were subject to inevitable delay and it was important not only to ensure their arrival but to know at what time they were received. Berthier used to send the same message by three riders taking different routes, and would not accept that an order had been received until he received a signed receipt. Soult was well acquainted with Berthier's methods, having had to comply with them for some fourteen years; he had had a large, vice-regal style of command in the Peninsula, and as the Bourbons' ex-Minister of War he had had vast experience in issuing movement orders to large bodies of troops equal in numbers to the present field-army of the North. Yet not only did he not keep an up-dated register as had the late Berthier, but he used fewer messengers than Berthier would have approved of – as witness the single messenger to Vandamme with his vital movement orders on the first day of the invasion. Further, he had not informed Ney on the night of the 16th as to the result of the battle with the Prussians. In his dispatch in the morning he stated: 'I thought I had already acquainted you of the victorry,' which patently he had not, as Count Flahault had informed the Emperor. These orders to Ney carried no sense of urgency; Ney was merely told to carry out his orders of the previous day, i.e., to capture and hold Quatre Bras, but with the rider that if it were: '... *impossible to act in this manner, send a detailed report immediately and the Emperor will move thither along the road already mentioned'*. The order ended by informing Ney that 'Today is required for completing this operation, replenishing ammunition, gathering stragglers and detachments'. Hardly an urgent summons to fix Wellington in position so that Napoleon could take him in flank with force and destroy him. Neither had he remembered to send out his own Chief of Staff, General Monthion, or any other officer to reconnoitre north in the direction of Tilly and Mont St-Guibert, as Napoleon had ordered. Had he done so Napoleon would have been apprised before 9 a.m. on 17 June of the true direction of the Prussian line of retreat. Much blame that would be unfairly heaped on the heads of Ney and Grouchy must be laid at the door of Soult, whose actions during the campaign cannot be excused by the bland statement that the position was not one to which he was used.[21]

At first light Marshal Ney had already reconnoitred the field of Quatre Bras, tested it with a skirmish in force and observed Wellington's 46,000-odd men well positioned. On 16 June Ney had already lost 6,000 men, 30 per cent of those actually engaged, in trying to take this nightmare of a position, flanked as it was along its entire length by a dense wood that could only enfilade his advancing flank if not taken by force. Under these circumstances Ney thought it would be better if Napoleon attacked from the left, which would cause Wellington to shift his weight and would make him fight on this open flank and at right angles before Ney attacked. Under these conditions Ney expected that Wellington would retreat and be cut up in the process. He had already sent Soult a detailed report to this effect, written at 6.30 a.m. from Frasnes, which he assumed must have crossed with his orders from Soult, and had covered the requested reply. In it Ney stated that Wellington was positioned well in front of Quatre Bras and was holding Bossu wood, Gemioncourt and Piraumont in strength. He, Ney, estimated the visible force in Wellington's first line as eight regiments (French regiments all had two to four battalions as opposed to the British average of one, thus Ney meant some 16 – 24 battalions) and 2,000 horse – in all, about 21,000 men.[22]

This report must have reached Imperial Headquarters no later than 8.30 a.m., given the distance from Frasnes to Fleurus. But because of bad staff work or worse, this letter, according to Soult, arrived at Fleurus after Soult had left, and was sent on after him first to Ligny, then to Marbais, reaching him only when he had got to Quatre Bras, six hours later. During all this time Ney had closed up his two corps on a small front as ordered, and had been waiting for the sound of Napoleon's guns before launching his own attack in support of the Emperor's, rather than deploy his troops in a costly frontal assault on Wellington's prepared positions which would automatically become untenable to the enemy (as Wellington had known) when attacked on their open left flank by Napoleon. Ney felt that the losses he would incur by a unilateral attack were unjustified in the circumstances, and because Soult had informed him that Napoleon had gained a victory over the Prussians and had ordered that this '... day was required for completing this operation' at Quatre Bras, and that 'the Emperor will move thither along the road already mentioned', Ney sat and awaited Napoleon's assistance.

So, as a consequence of Soult's poor system of communications, Ney and Napoleon were sitting waiting for the sound of each others' guns to fix Wellington in position,[23] while Wellington's army was withdrawing rapidly along three roads, away from the French and nearer to the Prussians.

Lord Uxbridge's rearguard at Quatre Bras had been in position, ready to repel the French attack they thought must come at any moment, since the withdrawal of Wellington's infantry and artillery had begun at about 10 a.m. By 1 p.m Uxbridge's troopers were still unemployed, and Wellington had had three invaluable hours to get men, horses and equipment about eight miles up one of the best roads in the country, a paved *chaussée* to Mont St-Jean and their pre-arranged positions. Wellington had detailed De Lancey and his staff to supervise the arrival of units, especially those coming up the Nivelles road, on the field at Mont St-Jean, ensuring that they reached their assigned positions. In this task De Lancey and his staff found invaluable the map of the area drawn in part by Major Oldfield of the Royal Engineers, based on the Ferraris and Capitaine sheets.

Units travelling up the *Chaussée* soon became congested at the small bridge which takes the highroad over the River Thy just before the town, and the problem was exacerbated by the narrow streets of the town itself. This bottleneck could have caused a disaster for any units still below it if the rearguard had come pounding up from Quatre Bras closely pursued by the French. Staff Corps officers such as Lieutenant Basil Jackson, acting as military police, directed the wheeled transport and their escorts through the town and sent half the infantry downstream less than a mile to cross at Ways la Hutte and half upstream to cross the Rivers Pontney and Dyle at Barrière. Certainly this vital information was sent back to Lord Uxbridge.[24]

At Quatre Bras action so long delayed began soon after 1 p.m., and at an accelerating pace. Napoleon had started his force forward with skirmishers of the 7th Hussars in the van. These were driven back as soon as they made contact with Uxbridge's cavalry. At once Napoleon drew up his force in line of battle with his artillery front and centre, infantry in the second line, and cavalry on both wings. At the same time, he sent an aide, escorted by a detachment of hussars, to Ney with an imperative verbal order to start his attack immediately. En route this detachment encountered Ney's cavalry because Ney had just received Soult's noon order and had already begun an advance in strength on the crossroads. The cavalry encounter was ill fated, for when the 7th Hussars escorting the Emperor's aide saw some Red Lancers of the Imperial Guard (whom Ney had retained) around Frasnes chapel, they mistook them for English and a skirmish ensued.

It was about then that the awful truth was laid before Napoleon. It came from the lips of a *vivandière* (camp-follower), formerly with the Anglo-Allied army, who was brought before the Emperor. She told him that Wellington's army had been retreating all morning, and that only a strong rearguard now remained at Quatre Bras.[25] Napoleon's anguish can only be imagined. If Wellington were not stopped in his retreat and pulled back before his army crossed the forest of Soignies and awaited Blücher, his campaign in the North would be paralysed, there would be no political prize of Brussels to overawe his enemies, no march on the Rhine to threaten the Allied right flank, no decisive victory. All could only be saved by pinning Wellington before he could reach the other side of Soignies, making him give battle and destroying him, and then on to Brussels.

With everything now at stake, Napoleon became the very embodiment of action. He mounted his horse and, with his escort squadrons of the Guard, Milhaud's *cuirassiers* and the rest of the light cavalry, accompanied by the Guard horse artillery batteries, galloped straight for the crossroads, leaving Soult to bring on the remainder.

At Quatre Bras Wellington's rearguard were still mystified. Captain Mercer, commanding one of the three horse batteries in the rearguard, wrote in his journal:

> 'It was now about one o'clock. My battery stood in position on the brow of the declivity, with its right near the wall of the farm, all alone, the only troops in sight being ... the picket and a few scattered hussars in the direction of Frasnes, Sir O. Vandeleur's light dragoons two or three hundred yards in our rear, and Sir H. Vivian's hussars away to the left. Still the French army made no demonstration of an advance. This inactivity was un-accountable.'[26]

At nearly 2 p.m. Wellington and Uxbridge observed Napoleon's escort of lancers and *cuirassiers* coming up the Namur road. Wellington handed over command at Quatre Bras to Uxbridge, saying: 'Well, there is the last of the infantry gone, and I don't care now.' Then, before putting spur to his horse, he enjoined Uxbridge not to engage seriously, but only to hold the position as long as he conveniently could.[27]

The Earl of Uxbridge had already instructed his cavalry commanders how they were to conduct the inevitable withdrawal. On the Nivelles side of the crossroads he had positioned General Dornberg's brigade, and had told Dornberg that when ordered to withdraw he was to cross the Thy just upstream of Genappe at Barrière. On the Namur side were Vivian's brigade, fronted by Vandeleur. These were instructed to cross the Thy east of Genappe at Ways la Hutte. In the centre Uxbridge had placed the heavy brigades of Somerset's Household Cavalry and Ponsonby's Union Brigade. These were to retire across the Thy by the highroad through Genappe, diverting the attention of their pursuers from the other two crossings. Finally, the 23rd Light Dragoons and the 7th Hussars would follow, screening the heavies.[28]

The morning of the 17th had begun with a refreshing light rain shower. Throughout the morning and early afternoon, however, the atmosphere had grown increasingly sultry and the sky had become obscured by laden thunderclouds. At about the time Wellington left the field Captain Mercer, standing by his battery, was treated to a dramatic spectacle, accentuated by the frisson of danger:

'I saw their whole army descending ... [the slope] in three or four dark masses, whilst their advanced cavalry picket was already driving back our hussars ... My situation now appeared somewhat awkward: left without orders and entirely alone on the brow of our position – the Hussar pickets galloping in and hurrying past as fast as they could – the whole French army advancing, and already at no great distance. In this dilemma, I determined to retire across the little dip that separated me from Sir O. Vandeleur, and take up position in front of his squadrons, whence after giving a round or two to the French advance I could retire in sufficient time through his intervals to leave the ground for him to charge. This movement was immediately executed; but the guns scarcely in position ere Sir Ormsby came furiously up, exclaiming, "What are you doing here, sir? You encumber my front, and we shall not be able to charge. Take the guns away, sir; instantly, I say – take them away!" ... when up came Lord Uxbridge, and the scene changed in a twinkling. "Captain Mercer, are you loaded?" "Yes, my lord." "Then give them a round as they rise the hill, and retire as quickly as possible. Light Dragoons, three's right; at the trot, march!" and then some orders to Sir Ormsby, of whom I saw no more that day ... I had longed to see Napoleon, that mighty man of war – that astonishing genius who filled the world with his renown. Now I saw him, and there was a degree of sublimity in the interview rarely equalled. The sky had become overcast since the morning, and at this present moment presented a most extraordinary appearance. Large isolated masses of thundercloud, of the deepest, almost inky black, their lower edges hard and strongly defined, lagged down, as if momentarily about to burst, hung suspended over us, involving our position and everything on it [in] deep and gloomy obscurity; whilst the distant hill lately occupied by the French army lay bathed in brilliant sunshine. Lord Uxbridge was yet speaking when a single horseman [Napoleon], followed immediately by several others, mounted the plateau I had left at the gallop ... their dark figures thrown forward in strong relief from the illuminated distance ... Lord Uxbridge cried out, ''Fire!-fire!' and giving them a general discharge we quickly limbered up to retire ...'[29]

Uxbridge's rearguard gave ground before the overwhelming French advance, literally being led by the Emperor in person, and the French had soon gained the crossroads.

Of Ney's force, d'Erlon was first to join Napoleon at Quatre Bras: 'The Emperor found me in front of this position, and in the gravest tone, said to me the following words which have ever remained engraved on my memory: "France has been ruined! Go, my dear general and place yourself at the head of this cavalry, and press the English rearguard vigorously!"'[30] One of his aides, General Gourgaud, says that Napoleon waited long enough to see Ney and tell him how surprised he was at Ney's delay in obeying his early morning orders.[31] Ney no doubt referred to his own letter of early morning and maintained that he had complied with his orders, and that he had only been awaiting the Emperor's attack. The conversation was probably not protracted.

Just as Napoleon prepared to set off up the Brussels road after Wellington, the heavy clouds massed overhead broke forth with a violent thunderstorm which brought sheets of rain on to the stage of human events. The game was escape and pursuit; the quarry had a long lead; but the hunter was driven; and the rain assigned a handicap to both parties. The chase was again led by Napoleon with his escort squadrons and the Imperial Guard cavalry and artillery. An officer of the Guard artillery left a vivid impression of the urgency with which Napoleon pressed on:

'One must have been a witness of the rapid march of this army on the day of the 17th ... a march that resembled a steeple-chase rather than a pursuit of an enemy in retreat ... to get an idea of the activity which Napoleon knew how to impress upon the troops when placed under his immediate command. Six pieces of the horse-artillery of the Guard, supported by the headquarters squadrons, marched in the first line, and vomited forth canister upon the masses of the enemy's cavalry, as often as, profiting by some accident of ground, they endeavoured to halt, to take position, and retard our pursuit. The Emperor, mounted on a small and very active Arab horse, galloped at the head of the column; he was constantly near the pieces, exciting the gunners by his presence and by his words, and more than once in the midst of the shells and bullets which the enemy's artillery showered upon us.'[32]

At Genappe, Uxbridge turned to blood the pursuers; the 7th Hussars charged the French lancers as they clattered through the cobbled streets, but as the lancers had a secure flank against the buildings and greater reach with their lances, they presented an invulnerable wall and, supported by more cavalry pushing them forward, forcibly ejected the 7th from Genappe. Lord Uxbridge, however, had determined the order of retreat precisely for such a contingency, and smashed into the disorganized lancers with the heavy 1st Life Guards who regained the *status quo*. But an Imperial Guard artillery piece was brought round to a side garden that enfiladed the position, and Uxbridge ordered a withdrawal before it could disable these cavalry. Throughout this dogged retreat rain fell in torrents with thunder and lightning, and men and horses were reduced to a walking pace because of the mud.

A premature dusk, brought forward by the weather, was descending when Napoleon arrived on the ridge where the inn La Belle Alliance was situated. Before him he could see a shallow valley and beyond it another ridge, lower and running north-east–south-west in parallel with the one on which he stood. Back from the brow of the lower ridge was the hamlet of Mont St-Jean where the Nivelles-Louvain road intersected the Charleroi–Brussels road. In the valley Brunswick infantry were making their best pace across the open ground, goaded by the sight of French cavalry massing on the ridge behind them. Along the base of the Mont St-Jean ridge Wellington's cavalry had formed a screen in strength. Was what Napoleon could see a rearguard stand to cover Wellington's army defiling through the Forêt de Soignies? Or had Wellington employed one of his favourite Peninsula tactics and arrayed his army behind the Mont St-Jean ridge? Napoleon had to determine the true situation without delay. Nightfall would favour the hunted, not the hunter. He ordered four horse batteries to be brought up and to open fire on the enemy. Twenty-four French guns were shortly in action, while Milhaud's *cuirassiers* formed up along the base of the Belle Alliance ridge, ready to charge across the valley at the enemy cavalry. Almost at once more than 60 guns sited along the length of the Mont St-Jean ridge opened fire in response to Napoleon's challenge. He had his answer, although he could scarcely believe it: Wellington had chosen to stand in front of the forest rather than behind it. He ordered Milhaud to pull back and his artillery to cease firing. They would need their ammunition the next day.[33]

Napoleon remained concerned that Wellington's deployment across the valley might be a ruse; that the wily Englishman might still retreat behind the forest as night approached. The Emperor remained on the ridge with his telescope observing the enemy until 8.30. As his corps commanders came up on his position and reported to him, Napoleon personally allocated them positions on the assumption that there would be a battle here next day. In the first line, he placed d'Erlon's I and Lobau's VI Corps. They occupied the area between the village of Plancenoit on the left flank and the large farm of Mon Plaisir on the Nivelles road on the right. Behind these corps, and covering them, were bivouacked Milhaud and Kellermann's *cuirassiers*. It was now dark, so Reille's II Corps halted at Genappe, and the Imperial Guard around Glabais, with the 1st *Chasseurs* of the Old Guard posted at the farm of Le Caillou, a mile and a half from the Belle Alliance inn. Between the front line and Reille's rearguard Napoleon had 72,000 men, including more than 15,000 cavalry, and 246 guns. But in his haste to fix Wellington in a position to fight, Napoleon's own army, forced-marching from Ligny and Frasnes, had become extended. Now that all Wellington's men had closed up on Mont St-Jean it was only the French who were impeded by the foul weather. It was with an impotent bitterness that Napoleon remarked: 'Would to God I had Joshua's power to stop the sun for two hours.' When he was satisfied that Wellington meant to pass the night in the neighbourhood and that his own dispositions were in order, he rode back to Le Caillou to read reports and consult his maps.

Also arrived at Le Caillou was a Sergeant de Mauduit, of the Imperial Guard Infantry, one of the Emperor's beloved *grognards*. He later recorded his grumbles about the steeplechase pursuit through the thunderstorm: 'The tracks were so deep in mud after the rain that we found it impossible to maintain any order in our columns ... The Emperor had selected the farm of Le Caillou, right on the main road itself, as Headquarters. One by one the regiments of his Guard came up, but each arrived there in a state of exhaustion. During all the marches and countermarches of that frightful night there was a real helter-skelter. Regiments, battalions, even companies became muddled ... we had constantly to push our way through quick hedges or deep ravines ... At about midnight the bulk of our regiment arrived ... our greatcoats and our trousers were caked with several pounds of mud. A great many of the soldiers had lost their shoes and reached the bivouac barefoot.'[34]

At Le Caillou Napoleon received disturbing news from General Milhaud. During the pursuit from Quatre Bras one of his cavalry patrols had sighted a Prussian column marching from Gery, near Gentinnes, toward Wavre. Napoleon was not unduly alarmed at this development because he had not yet received a report from Marshal Grouchy, who by now might well have caught up with Blücher.[35] Napoleon's overriding concern on the night of 17/18th remained that Wellington might attempt to slip back through the forest under the cover of darkness. But he reasoned that such an attempt could be forestalled if his own troops demonstrated a vigilant attention to their enemy through the night.

The Prussian army, of which Milhaud's men had caught a glimpse, pressed on to Wavre with stolidity and purpose. Captain Fritz of the Westphalian *Landwehr* wrote that night in his journal:

> 'In very bad weather we set off again in the morning to cross the Dyle. The mood of the troops was certainly grave, but not in the least disheartened, and even if one could have detected that we were on a retreat rather than a victory march, the bearing of all but a few isolated units was still very good. "We have lost once, but the game is not yet up, and tomorrow is another day," remarked a Pomeranian soldier to his neighbour who was grumbling, and he was quite right. The firm bearing of the army owed not a little to the cheerful spirit and freshness of our 74-year-old Field Marshal. He had had his bruised limbs bathed in brandy, and had helped himself to a large schnapps; and now, although riding must have been very painful, he rode alongside the troops, exchanging jokes and banter with them, and his humour spread like wildfire down the columns. I only glimpsed the old hero riding quickly past, although I should have dearly have liked to have expressed to him my pleasure at his fortunate escape.'[36]

Grouchy, the 'sword in the back' of the Prussians, had remained sheathed at Gembloux and bivouacked there for the night. Thielemann's III Corps, which Exelmans had observed earlier and whose back Grouchy should have been prodding, drew their own conclusions about the caution with which they were being followed rather than pursued. Thielemann's Chief of Staff, Clausewitz, later wrote:

> 'If we seem here to find so great a difference from the earlier methods of procedure adopted by the French, we must get a true picture of the changed conditions. The extraordinary energy in pursuit to which the brilliant results of Bonaparte's former campaigns were due, was simply pushing very superior forces after an enemy who had been completely vanquished. Now, however, Napoleon had to turn with his main force, and above all with his freshest troops, against a new enemy, over whom victory had yet to be gained. The pursuit [of the Prussians] had to be carried out by the IIIrd and IVth Corps, the very two who had been engaged in the bloodiest fight till ten in the evening, and now necessarily needed time to get into order again, to

recover themselves, and provide themselves with ammunition.'[37]

Clausewitz should also have mentioned the principal changed condition in this campaign – the absence of Berthier.

Wellington had made his headquarters in the inn at the hamlet of Waterloo on the edge of the forest, about as far behind his front line as Napoleon's was behind his. The army Wellington had managed to concentrate on Mont St-Jean was considerable – 68,000 men and 156 guns – but it was a polyglot amalgamation which was now confronted by Napoleon commanding superior numbers of veteran troops, including the Imperial Guard, many more guns, and a very heavy cavalry arm. Prince Frederick stood half-a-day's march to Wellington's right with 17,000 men and 30 guns, bivouacked for the night on the area Hal-Tubize-Braine-le-Comte. But Wellington could not call upon these men to reinforce him at Mont St-Jean; they were needed where they were to hold his line of retreat. Then, on his left, there were the Prussians. Blücher and Gneisenau had promised to support him from Wavre, but would their promise prove as impossible to honour as his own had been? By 10 p.m., however, a Prussian messenger had reached Müffling with a brief note for Wellington. Blücher and Gneisenau had delayed sending it sooner as they had feared for a time that their ammunition train might have been captured. Its arrival at 6 p.m., after having lost its way, ensured the ability of the Prussian army to aid Wellington. His earlier communiqué to them had frankly threatened to leave them to face Napoleon alone if they did not substantially support his stand at Mont St-Jean: '... *I hope to be supported by a single Prussian corps. But if this support is denied me, I shall be compelled to sacrifice Brussels and take up my position behind the Scheldt.*' Blücher replied: 'I shall not come with one corps only, but with my whole army; upon this understanding, however, that, should the French not attack us on the 18th, we shall attack them on the 19th.'[38]

Another Prussian dispatch arrived for Wellington at 2 a.m. on the 18th. Composed by Gneisenau and signed by Blücher, it gave details of how Prussian support would reach Wellington's position: 'Bülow's [IV] Corps will set off marching at daybreak tomorrow in your direction. It will be followed immediately by the [II] corps of Pirch I. The I and III Corps will also hold themselves in readiness to proceed in your direction. The exhaustion of the troops, part of which have not yet arrived does not allow of my commencing my movement any earlier.'[39]

Wellington realized that he would have to hold Napoleon until Bülow arrived, whenever that might be. If Bülow were unduly delayed, however, and Wellington's force were broken before help could arrive, he would retreat by way of Hal behind the Scheldt just as he had said he would. It was clear from Wellington's statements and actions that night that he did not expect to be able to repulse Napoleon unaided. In the early hours of the 18th, Wellington wrote some letters indicative of his concern. To Sir Charles Stuart, the British Ambassador in Brussels, he wrote: 'You will see in the [enclosed] letter to the Duc de Berry the real state of our case and the only risk we run. The Prussians will be ready again in the morning for anything. Pray keep the English [in Brussels] quiet if you can. Let them all prepare to move, but neither be in a hurry or a fright, as all will yet turn out well.'[40] The letter to the Duc de Berry advised him to move Louis and his court to the safety of the Citadel of Antwerp, from which he could easily embark on one of the British vessels stationed there, in the event of Wellington's having to retreat.[41] Another letter was sent to General Clarke, duc de Feltre, who as Napoleon's Minister of War had betrayed Paris in 1814.[42] Still another was written to the British Governor of Antwerp, ordering him to place the town and citadel in a state of seige, but to allow entry to Louis Bourbon and his party and to the prominent Britons who had accompanied the British army to Brussels.[43] Wellington's final letter, written at 3 a.m., was to a young woman of his acquaintance, Lady Frances Webster, in which he managed to be disingenuous: 'As I am sending a messenger to Bruxelles, I write to you one line to tell you that I think you ought to make preparations, as should Lord Mountnorris, to remove from Bruxelles. We fought a desperate battle on Friday [the 16th], in which I was successful, though I had but few troops. The Prussians were very roughly handled, and retired in the night, which obliged me to do the same to this place yesterday. The course of the operations may oblige me to uncover Bruxelles for a moment, and may expose that town to the enemy; for which reason I recommend that you and your family should be prepared to move to Antwerp at a moment's notice. I will give you the earliest intimation of the danger that may come to my knowledge; at present I know of none.'[44] It should be noted, however, that Wellington did not write a word of warning to King William, whose field marshal he was, and whose country he was supposed to be defending.

It was a very long night for Napoleon also. Fearing that his quarry might escape him, he rode out at 1 a.m., accompanied by Count Bertrand and his escort, to make the entire round of his front and examine Wellington's positions. He later wrote of this:

'It was my intention to follow the English army in its retreat and endeavour to engage it, despite the darkness, as soon as it was on the march. I walked along the line of main defences. The forest of Soignies looked as if it was on fire; the horizon between this forest, Braine-la-Leud and the farms of La Belle Alliance and La Haye was aglow with bivouac fires; complete silence prevailed ... On arriving near the wood of the Château de Hougoumont I heard the sound of a column on the march. It was half-past two. Now, at this hour, the rearguard would be leaving its position if the enemy were in fact retreating; but this illusion was short lived. The noises stopped. The rain fell in torrents. Several officers who had been sent out on reconnaissance, and some secret agents returning at half-past three, confirmed that the Anglo-Netherland troops were not making a move ... The day began to dawn. I returned to my headquarters well satisfied with the great error which the enemy commander was making and very anxious lest the bad weather should prevent my taking advantage of it. But already the sky was clearing. At five o'clock I noticed a few faint rays of that sun which, before setting should light up the defeat of the English army. The British oligarchy [Liverpool's government specifically] would be overthrown by it! France, that day, was going to rise more glorious, more powerful and greater than ever!'[45]

CHAPTER 11

18 June: Morning

'Four things come back not: The spoken word; the sped arrow; Time past; and opportunity.' – The Caliph Omar I, AD 582-644.

After inspecting his outposts Napoleon returned to Le Caillou at about 3.30 a.m. on the 18th and was handed the first dispatch sent by Marshal Grouchy since he had been detached. Dated Gembloux, 17 June, 10 p.m., it read:

'I have the honour to report that I have occupied Gembloux, with my cavalry at Sauvenière. The enemy, to the number of '35,000 men, continue to retreat ... From all reports to hand, the enemy appear to have divided at Sauvenière into two columns, one marching on Wavre via Sart-à-Walhain, whilst the other is heading for Perwez [in the direction of Hannut]. Perhaps it may be inferred that one portion is going to join Wellington, whilst the centre, under Blücher, retires on Liège; another column, accompanied by guns, has already retreated to Namur. This evening General Exelmans is pushing 6 squadrons of cavalry towards Sart-à-Walhain, and three to Perwez. When their reports are to hand, then if I find that the mass of the Prussians is retiring on Wavre I shall follow them, so as to prevent them gaining Brussels and to separate them from Wellington. If on the other hand all my information proves the principal Prussian force has marched on Perwez, then I shall follow them in that direction.

'Generals Thielemann and Borstell belonged to the Prussian Army that Your Majesty defeated yesterday; they were still here at 10 this morning ... On leaving this place they enquired how far it was to Wavre, to Perwez and to Hannut respectively.'[1]

Obviously Grouchy had misunderstood the role that Napoleon intended him to play. If he so much as suspected that the mass – or even a single corps – of Blücher's army were moving towards Wavre his job was to follow and stop them joining Wellington, either behind or in front of the Forêt de Soignies. In effect Napoleon expected Grouchy to play a role similar to Ney's when he was detached to take Quatre Bras: first, to pursue and harry the enemy; secondly, to prevent him intervening in Napoleon's main battle; and finally to provide a reserve if required. This was why Napoleon had explained to both Marshals in detail that '... for this campaign I intend to divide my army into two wings and a reserve' with the caveat that he would draw reserves from either if needed. To this end Napoleon had entrusted the Marshal with one-third of his army.

But Napoleon's system was no longer the precise military machine it once had been, and it was now breaking down. He had masterminded a strategy using a pivotal central position to attack two enemies. The plan was good in theory but the execution was flawed. Napoleon had failed to bring Ney into his confidence until hostilities had already begun, and even then he had failed to explain in detail what he required of Ney and what his exact role was to be. Thus his part in Napoleon's plan failed on 15/16 June through no fault of that Marshal. Likewise with Grouchy. Napoleon had not explained on the 17th the importance of the Wavre–Brussels road or what he expected of him save 'to keep a sword in Blücher's back' – which entailed harrying the Prussians to prevent their diverse units from rejoining – this Grouchy was trying to carry out as his letter confirmed. If Napoleon had confided his fears about Blücher's falling back via Wavre to join Wellington undoubtedly Grouchy would have moved swiftly in that direction. Napoleon was the master of the use of maps in his campaigns and he knew that Blücher would either retreat east or fall back towards Wellington and Brussels.

Napoleon had also failed since 1805 to innovate any changes in the Imperial army whose command structure and tactical ability had been allowed to stagnate. Where even the antiquated Austrian army had revised its ideas in the face of Napoleon's army and since 1805 had emulated it; and Prussia had gone farther with its general staff system and light infantry tactics; Napoleon still clung to the old system he had evolved at his ascension to power. He had not created a general staff structure that would ensure a smooth compliance with his orders at corps and divisional level, and a uniform staff able to grasp his strategy. Thus Grouchy and Ney were kept in the dark as to their respective roles. All movements emanated from the Master who reaped the prestige when they succeeded and allocated the blame to his commanders when they failed, thus preserving intact his personal aura of invincibility. He also kept his own counsel as to his personal fears lest they demoralize his subordinates. This system had worked well when administered by Berthier, who had had years to perfect it and who passed precise instructions to commanders in lieu of knowledge. But with his loss it just failed to function. In truth, Berthier had so understood Napoleon's thoughts and methods and had given such precise orders that a general staff had not been necessary. This campaign was the first in eighteen years in which Napoleon did not have his old chief of staff with him, and it is probable that he himself could not understand why his brilliant plans were not being brought to fruition.

Having read Grouchy's report, Napoleon did not send him any further orders. Instead he dictated several letters responding to mail he had received from Paris. Davout had written, warning of 'intrigues and obstruction' on the part of the republican elements in the Chamber, fomented in the Emperor's absence by Fouché.[2] Davout described a stormy sitting on the 16th when criticism of the conduct of the war had been voiced. Davout believed that 'the successes of the Army will be useful in raising the courage of the weak, and overawing the discontented'.[3] Napoleon would have seen in this information a reinforcement of his conviction that the swift accomplishment of the politically significant seizure of Brussels was of paramount importance.[4]

Between 7 and 8 a.m. an officer sent by Napoleon to keep Wellington's force under observation arrived from the advanced posts with word that the enemy was retiring. Napoleon sent an aide at once to d'Erlon, whose corps was alone in the first line (Reille's having not yet fully closed up on the field), instructing him to pursue. D'Erlon saw the situation differently: he perceived that Wellington was only repositioning his troops. Napoleon joined d'Erlon and, as d'Erlon related:

> 'The Emperor came immediately to the advanced posts. I accompanied him; we dismounted in order to get near the enemy's vedettes [pickets], and to examine more closely the movements of the English army. He perceived that I was right, and being convinced that the English army was taking position, he said to me: "Order the men to make their soup, to get their pieces in order, and we will determine what is to be done towards noon."'[5]

When Napoleon had dictated general movement orders for his attack formations, he had timed them for 6 a.m. But several officers had complained that the deep mud and general softness of the ground from the recent downpour would make very difficult the movement of men, horses and especially artillery pieces, each weighing several thousand pounds. They also pointed out that some of their men still had some distance to march before they could come into line, as they had bivouacked in and around farms in the area of Genappe and Glabais. Napoleon's own reconnaissance of the terrain confirmed this. At this moment the main road was the only passable route forward. Reille's corps had only begun to pass Le Caillou at 9 a.m., and the Guard, Kellermann's *cuirassiers*, and Lobau's corps were ranged behind them.[6] When he returned to Le Caillou Napoleon changed his general orders for 9 a.m. The revised orders were issued to Ney via Soult:

> 'The Emperor commands that the army will be formed up ready to attack the enemy at 9 am. General Officers com-

manding Army Corps will concentrate their troops, they will arrange that the arms are put into serviceable condition, they will permit the soldiers to prepare their soup, also they will cause the men to complete their meal by 9 a.m. to the minute, so that the whole force will be ready and formed up in battle array, and in the positions indicated in the Emperor's overnight order. The Lieutenant-Generals commanding both Infantry and Cavalry Corps will despatch officers at once to report to the Chief-of-Staff the positions now occupied by their corps, and these officers will also act as bearers of further orders.'[7]

At 8 a.m. Napoleon had breakfasted with several of his generals, including Count Drouot, commander of the Imperial Guard, Marshal Soult and the Duc de Bassano. After the meal he studied his Ferraris and Capitaine maps, spread out on the adjacent table[8] and announced to the generals: 'The army of the enemy is superior to ours by more than one-fourth. We have nevertheless ninety chances in our favour, and not ten against us.' Ney entered the room at that moment and exclaimed: 'Without doubt Sire, provided Wellington be simple enough to wait for you. But I must inform you that his retreat is decided, and that if you do not hasten to attack, the enemy is about to escape you.' Napoleon, having already satisfied himself that Wellington was only redeploying, replied: 'You are wrong, and it is too late now. Wellington would expose himself to certain loss. He has thrown the dice and they are in our favour.'[9] Soult urged him to send for part of Grouchy's force, but Napoleon, annoyed at such public faint-heartedness, retorted sharply: 'Because you have been beaten by Wellington, you consider him a great general. And now I will tell you that he is a bad general, that the English are bad troops, and that this affair is nothing more serious than eating one's breakfast.' To this Soult replied: 'I earnestly hope so Sire.'[10] It is doubtful whether Napoleon believed all he had just said, but he had long held it politic before his officers to speak disparagingly of the enemy. In 1809 he had written to this effect to his elder brother Joseph, whom he had installed on the thankless throne of Spain. He had counselled Joseph that it was foolish and contrary to the sound conduct of war to make remarks which give weight to the enemy, '... for to do so is to take it from oneself; in war morale is everything'.[11] Not long after this exchange Prince Jérôme, Napoleon's youngest brother, and Generals Reille and Foy arrived. Napoleon asked Reille's opinion of the English army. Reille, who had fought the English in the Peninsula longer than most French generals, replied:

'Well posted, as Wellington knows how to post it, and attacked from the front, I consider the English infantry to be impregnable, owing to its calm tenacity, and superior aim in firing [a reference to Wellington's use of rifle-armed light troops and large numbers of skirmishers]. Before attacking it with the bayonet, one may expect half the assailants to be brought to the ground. But the English army is less agile, less supple, less expert in manoeuvring than ours. If we cannot beat it by direct attack, we may do so by manoeuvring.'[12]

This honest piece of good advice was not at all what Napoleon had wanted from Reille. Prince Jérôme then contributed a highly pertinent item of gossip. The waiter at the inn in Genappe where he had stayed for the night had told him that when Wellington had stayed there he had overheard one of the Duke's aides speaking about the English army and the Prussian army linking up in front of the forest of Soignies. Napoleon dismissed this as impossible, according to his somewhat outdated understanding of his enemys' potential and his very imperfect knowledge of Grouchy's at-a-distance fighting stance, and then delivered to his no doubt startled audience, in the form of a pep-talk, an unprecedented insight into his plan for the coming battle:

> 'After such a battle as Fleurus [Ligny], the junction between the allies is impossible for at least two days; besides the Prussians are pressed by Grouchy's detachment, who are at his heels ... we are only too pleased that the English wish to accept battle. The battle which we are about to deliver will save France, and will be celebrated in the annals of the world. I shall make use of my numerous artillery, I shall launch my horsemen to compel the enemy to unmask; and, as soon as I am certain of the position held by the English, I shall advance straight against them with my Old Guard.'[13]

Napoleon began to realize why Wellington had not retreated behind the forest: he had chosen this position as suited to his tactics and because he expected Blücher to come across to his aid. This interpretation made sense of Grouchy's report and that of Milhaud concerning Prussian movements. However, Napoleon was not discomfited; he still expected Grouchy to prevent Blücher from interfering until he had destroyed Wellington. Then he could turn on Blücher and destroy him piecemeal.

Without delay he dictated to Soult a message for Grouchy, timed at 10 a.m.:

> 'Marshal – The Emperor has received your last report dated from Gembloux. You mentioned to His Majesty only two columns which have passed Sauvenières and Sart-à-

Walhain, nevertheless our reports state that a third column, a fairly strong one, has passed Gery and Gentinnes and that it was heading for Wavre.

'The Emperor instructs me to tell you that at this moment His Majesty is going to attack the English Army, which has taken up a position at Mont St. Jean, near the forest of Soignies; consequently his Majesty desires that you head for Wavre in order to draw near to us, and place yourself in touch with our operations and to keep up your communications with us, pushing before you those portions of the Prussian Army which have taken this direction, and which have halted at Wavre; this place you ought to reach as soon as possible.'[14]

Grouchy's dilemma of where to look for the Prussian army was resolved for him by this order. He was to march his force towards Wavre, detaching only some light troops to follow the Prussians to his right with orders to pick up stragglers and try to gain information. It is obvious from this order that Napoleon had taken seriously the news related by Prince Jérôme. It helped to explain why Wellington was sitting in front of Soignies: he expected significant support from Blücher. Napoleon would not otherwise have used the wording '... those portions of the Prussian Army which have taken this direction, and which have halted at Wavre'. There was as yet no definite proof that Blücher was at Wavre with the main part of his force, but Napoleon had worked out with his compasses and maps that, given the approximate time of departure of Blücher from Ligny, a large part of his army could have reached Wavre.

After dictating Grouchy's order Napoleon sent an order to Colonel Marbot[15] of the 7th Hussars to take up a position behind Frischermont and from there send out patrols to Lasne, Coutre and the bridges of Moustier and Ottignies. It is apparent from the strength of his detachment and its prescribed dispositions that Marbot was posted not to look for Grouchy but to give early warning of the approach of the Prussians. Marbot described receiving his orders:

'At the commencement of the action [the Battle of Waterloo], towards 11 a.m., I was detached from the division with my own regiment and a battalion of infantry, which had been placed under my command. These troops were posted on our extreme right, behind Frischermont, facing the Dyle. Particular instructions were given to me on the part of the Emperor by his aide-de-camp, la Bédoyère, and by a staff officer whose name I do not recall. They prescribed me to leave the bulk of my command always in view of the field of battle, to post 200 infantry in the Wood of Frischermont [Bois de Paris], one squadron at Lasne, having outposts as far as St. Lambert; another squadron, half at Coutre, half at Beaumont, sending reconnaissances as far as the Dyle, to the bridges of Moustier and Ottignies.'[16]

Napoleon would have been more concerned than he was at this moment had he known that Grouchy had not left Gembloux until 6 o'clock that morning, and that by 11 o'clock he had only reached Sart-à-Walhain where he had halted his force for breakfast. Grouchy of course was following Napoleon's orders of the 17th, and would not receive his new, more urgent orders until 4 p.m.

Napoleon's army began forming for battle as they arrived along the highroad. By all accounts this marshalling was spectacular: with the bands playing, the men shouting *'Vive l'Empereur!'*, the skilful evolutions of large bodies of colourfully uniformed men. It was not until 10.30 that the formations had been completed; the battle would be starting rather late in the day because of the mud and the distance many units had had to march from their bivouacs. Napoleon rode out into the assembled host and received a frenzied chorus of cheers which echoed across the valley to the waiting enemy.

With his telescope Napoleon again scanned the enemy's positions and the terrain over which he would fight the battle. Nature had provided the combatants with an arena bounded by the two opposing ridges, one surmounted by the inn of La Belle Alliance and the other by the Ohain–Braine-l'Alleud road which ran in parallel from north-east to south-west. From the centre of the French first line at La Belle Alliance on the southern ridge to the centre of the Anglo-Allied first line at the crossroads of the *Chaussée* and the Ohain-Braine-l'Alleud road on the northern ridge was a distance of about 1,300 yards. The ridges were separated by a shallow valley, with the Charleroi – Brussels *Chaussée* cutting through the middle of the battlefield at right angles to the ridges. The *Chaussée* follows the line of the watershed between the Dyle and Senne river systems. Running north-east from La Belle Alliance was an overgrown valley of broken ground which narrowed until dropping suddenly above the Papelotte farm, and continued towards Ohain as the valley of Smohain brook (which rose in a pond between the hamlet of Smohain and La Haye farm), part of the Dyle river system.[17] On the western side of the *Chaussée* numerous undulations of the ground running toward Braine-l'Alleud became the valley of Hain brook, also part of the Senne river system.

Seen from La Belle Alliance, the Brussels road dips into the valley between the ridges, then appears to rise steeply to the brow of the Ohain road ridge. But the apparent steepness is only an illusion of perspective. The incline ascending the Ohain road ridge from the valley is actually very slight; a horseman travelling north on the Chaussée could take it at the gallop without straining his horse. In the valley, on each side of the *Chaussée*, however, a horseman, or even a man on foot, would have encountered greater difficulties. Although when observed from a distance the ground seems to be uniform, when the observer is upon it, he finds that it has resolved into a mass of hillocks, hollows, depressions and banks.[18] This of course was why the *Chaussée* had been built along the watershed line. From La Belle Alliance the ground immediately behind the Ohain road ridge is not visible.

Features provided by the hand of man that are important to an understanding of the forthcoming battle were principally roads, buildings and ancillary plantings such as hedges and orchards. Of the roads, apart from the Brussels – Charleroi *Chaussée*, the other highroad was the one which ran from Mont St-Jean to Nivelles, diverging arrow-straight south-westward from the course of the Charleroi road. Several lesser roads running more or less at right angles to the Brussels – Charleroi road were also important. The Ohain road enters the battlefield paralleling the Smohain brook, then runs along the ridge to the north of the contested valley, before descending to Braine-l'Alleud. This road, and the Lasne road, which parallels the Smohain brook to the south and goes to Plancenoit, would later in the day provide the Prussians with routes of access to the battlefield.

The Ohain road, where it ran along the ridge, formed the feature upon which Wellington established his first line. The crossroads where it intersected the *Chaussée* naturally became the centre and focal point of his defensive dispositions, which enjoyed the advantage of some natural fortification. To Wellington's left of the crossroads for about a half to two-thirds of a mile, the Ohain road lay level with the ground, but was bracketed by high, thick hedges which formed an obstacle to cavalry. To the Duke's right of the crossroads, where the ground rises sharply, for about 400 yards the road passed between embankments five to seven feet high, forming a trench-like obstacle, before emerging level with the ground and descending gradually to Braine-l'Alleud.

A number of farmhouses, several hamlets, a gravel pit and two châteaux were situated in the area which was to become the no man's land. To the east, around the head of Smohain brook, was the hamlet of Smohain, the farmhouse of Papelotte, the larger farmhouse of La Haye and the stone Château de Frischermont with its park, situated about 600 yards from the Belle Alliance ridge. To the east of these buildings, and forming the eastern edge of the battlefield, was the large Bois de Paris. To the centre of the field, about 400 yards in front of the Ohain–Brussels crossroads and directly on the western side of the Brussels road, was the enclosed farmhouse of La Haye Sainte, a formidable stone structure similar to that of Gemioncourt, and flanked by a hedged garden on the southern side and a terraced kitchen garden on the northern. On the eastern side of the main road, some 200 yards nearer the Ohain crossroads, was a large sand and gravel pit which had partially excavated a hedged knoll which rose about nine feet above the level of the road. To the west of the battlefield, about 400 yards south of the intersection of the Ohain and Nivelles roads, was the complex of the Château Hougoumont, comprising a château, chapel and other buildings around a courtyard, formal gardens adjacent to the château, a hedged orchard in the north-east corner of the estate faced by hedges and a banked ditch, and a large wood to the south. The southernmost boundary of the Hougoumont estate was only 300 yards from the ridge of La Belle Alliance.

Upon this ground on the morning of Sunday, 18 June the armies of Wellington and Napoleon were arrayed. Napoleon's was drawn up in three lines, or echelons. The first line, formed along the Belle Alliance ridge, consisted of two corps. On Napoleon's right, from the Brussels road east toward Château Frischermont, was d'Erlon's I Corps. His four infantry divisions, Quiot's 1st, Donzelot's 2nd, Marcognet's 3rd, and Durutte's 4th, were side by side, each with one brigade behind the other in two lines. Between divisions, d'Erlon had placed artillery batteries. Jacquinot's light cavalry division, covering the flank of the right wing, observed the Frischermont to Papelotte area. On the left of the road Reille's II Corps was positioned in a like manner to d'Erlon's, with Bachelu's 5th, Foy's 9th and Prince Jérôme's 4th infantry divisions. (Girard's 7th had been so savaged at Ligny on the 16th that it had been left there.) The left wing was covered by Piré's light cavalry division, posted beyond the Nivelles road.

In Napoleon's second line, to the east of the Brussels road, behind d'Erlon, was Milhaud's IV Heavy Cavalry Corps, while to the west, behind Reille, was Kellermann's III Corps. Between Milhaud and Kellermann, Lobau was placed with Simmer and Jeannin's infantry divisions one behind the other just to the west of the road, and two cavalry divisions to the east, also in echelon. The third echelon consisted of the Imperial Guard Corps, commanded by Drouot. The Guard infantry, 24 battalions in columns, was placed astride the Brussels road near the farm of Rossomme, several hundred yards in front of the Emperor's headquarters at Le Caillou. To the east of the road, Lefebvre-Desnouëtte's Guard Light Cavalry Division was behind Milhaud's corps, and to the west, Guyot's Guard Heavy Cavalry Division was behind Kellermann.

In all, Napoleon was commanding some 71,947 men and 246 guns along a front of about 2½ miles. He had sent his engineer general, Haxo, forward to scout the terrain and the enemy's preparations. Haxo reported that Wellington had not constructed obstacles to his front, apart from an abatis on the Brussels road near La Haye Sainte and another one on the Nivelles road above Hougoumont. Napoleon made his final plan of attack.

Earlier, at 6 a.m., Wellington had left his headquarters at Waterloo and ridden up to join his army, in realization that the French attack could begin at any time that morning. The previous evening an awkward scene had unfolded. Lord Uxbridge, Wellington's second in command, had been concerned that, in the event of Wellington's being killed or incapacitated in the battle and Uxbridge having to take command, he did not know the Duke's intentions. Such was the barrier between the two men that Uxbridge felt it necessary to use an intermediary, General Count Don Alva, the Spanish representative, to broach the subject. The Duke then approached Uxbridge and said: 'Who will attack first tomorrow, I or Bonaparte?' Uxbridge replied: 'Bonaparte.' 'Well', replied the Duke, 'Bonaparte has not given me any idea of his projects; and as my plans will depend on his, how can you expect me to tell you what mine are?'[19] With which reply the hapless second in command had to be content. Wellington had, however, formed his plans. He intended to hold his present defensive position until Blücher arrived to take Napoleon in flank or rear. Failing this – if Napoleon broke him before Blücher appeared, or if Blücher did not appear at all – Wellington would fall back through Prince Frederick's force to the Scheldt. The Duke had made plain his plan to Blücher and Gneisenau in his threat to them of the 16th, and had intimated it in his warning to Lady Webster written only three hours before he rode to the front.

The force under Prince Frederick, 17,000 men and 30 guns, around Hal, covered the Mons-Brussels road against a French move to envelop Wellington's right or seize Brussels.[20] It was also ideally placed to cover a retreat on the Scheldt, forming the rearguard behind which he could withdraw and regroup.[21]

At Mont St-Jean Wellington and his long tail, including his staff, representatives of other Allied powers (such as Don Alva) and certain camp-followers such as the Duke of Richmond and his son, rode across the field to inspect the Anglo-Allied dispositions. On the previous evening Wellington had determined the position of each division and, in some cases, individual brigades. At daybreak there had been a flurry of activity as units used the growing light to find their assigned places. It was this reshuffling which had been misconstrued by Ney and others on the French side as a withdrawal. In disposing his force, Wellington had deliberately intermixed his nationalities to foster a greater cohesion and camaraderie among the disparate units.

The Anglo-Allied force arrayed on the northern side of the battlefield amounted to 67,661 men and 156 guns. Only 15,000 of the infantry were British, and of these only about 7,000 had ever heard a shot fired in anger; the remainder were inexperienced second battalions normally kept in Britain for domestic duties. (The 3rd Battalion of the 14th Regiment, for example, had almost no one in the ranks above the age of 22.) There were also 5,840 British cavalry and 2,967 Royal Ordnance personnel. Allied troops in Wellington's army included: 3,300 King's German Legion Infantry (perhaps best classed as auxiliaries to the British army); 2,000 cavalry and 12,464 infantry of Hanover, independent of their KGL compatriots; nearly 6,000 Brunswickers of all arms; 2,880 independent Nassauers; and 13,500 infantry, 3,200 cavalry and 510 artillerymen of The United Netherlands.

From the east of the Ohain road crossroads Wellington had placed his first and second lines. Saxe-Weimar's 2 Brigade of Perponcher's 2nd Netherlands Division was disposed with half its strength forward occupying Frischermont, Smohain, La Haye and Papelotte, and the remainder back along the Ohain road in reserve with a section of two guns (one each from Bijveldt and Stevenart's batteries). On the plateau behind the Smohain brook valley, covering the left flank, were the light cavalry brigades of Vivian and Vandeleur. Next in from the left flank on the line were the Hanoverian brigades of Vincke and Best. To their right, under Picton, was Pack's 5 Brigade in two lines (the British 42nd and 92nd Regiments formed in columns four deep in the first line, and 30 yards back the 1st and 44th in like formation). To Pack's right, also in the same formation but only two deep, was Bijlandt's 1 Netherlands Brigade under the direct command of General Perponcher.[22] This brigade was also formed behind the hedges bordering the Ohain road, with the 8th Militia, 7th Militia, 7th of the Line and 27th *Jägers* in the first line, and the 5th Militia in the second.[23] Right again from Perponcher, and shouldering the crossroads, was Kempt's brigade, with the 28th and part of the 95th in the first line and the 32nd and 79th in the second. A skirmish line was established on the left wing from the light companies of the first line, augmented towards the centre by three companies of the 1/95th Rifles, one on the knoll behind the hedge and two in and around the gravel pit. All along the front of the left the divisional artillery were sited behind the hedges: with Rettenburg's 6-gun Hanoverian battery to the right of Best; Bijveldt's 7-gun Netherlands battery to the right of Rettenburg; and Rogers' foot battery in front of Kempt. Behind Picton in the third line of the left was Ponsonby's 2 Heavy Cavalry Brigade of three regiments, and behind Ponsonby in the 4th line was Ghiny's 1 Netherlands Light Cavalry Brigade. Farther back, at Mont St-Jean, Lambert's 6 Infantry Brigade was due to arrive at 11 a.m. to provide a further reserve on the left.

To the west of the *Chaussée*, nearest the centre, was Alten's British 3rd Division in two lines of columns four deep. Next to the right was Opteda's 2 KGL Brigade, with the 1st Light Battalion and the 5th Line Battalion in the first line, and the 8th in the second. To Opteda's right was Kielmansegge's 1 Hanoverian Brigade, with the Lüneburg, Verden and Bremen Battalions in the first line, and York and Grubenhagen's in the second. Then were placed Halkett's British 5 Brigade, with the 2/73rd and the 2/30th Regiments to the front, and the 33rd and 2/69th behind. Right of Halkett was Cooke's 1st Guards Division, with Maitland's 1 Brigade, the 2/1st Foot Guards in front, and the 3/1st behind, then Byng's British 2 Brigade, the 2nd Coldstream Guards, and the 2/3rd Foot Guards, acting as reserve for Hougoumont, which was garrisoned by the four light companies of the Guards Division. To Byng's right, just past Hougoumont, was Mitchells' British 4 Brigade, with the 1/51st in front and the 3/14th and 1/23rd behind. On Mitchell's flank, a detachment of the 15th Hussars kept watch on Piré's horsemen. Farther still, in the area of Braine-l'Alleud was

Chassé's 3rd Netherlands Division. Around the village itself was Detmer's 2 Netherlands Brigade, with the 35th *Jägers*, 2nd Line Battalion, and the 4th, 6th, 17th and 19th Militia Battalions, and Krahmer's horse battery. To Detmer's right and in line with him was d'Aubreme's 2 Netherlands Brigade, with the 36th *Jägers*, 3rd, 12th and 13th of the Line, and the 3rd and 10th Militia Battalions.

In the third line of Wellington's right, nearest the Brussels road, was Somerset's heavy cavalry brigade. To Somerset's right was Kruse's Independent Nassauers in two lines of columns, with the 1/1st Nassau in front and the 1st and 2nd Nassau *Landwehr* Battalions behind. To their right was Arentschildt's light cavalry brigade, with Dornberg's to their right front. Following on to the right of Dornberg was Grant's light cavalry brigade. To Arentschildt's right rear was Du Plat's 1 KGL Brigade, with the 1st, 2nd, 3rd and 4th Line Battalions in line of columns. Behind Du Plat was Adam's British 3 Brigade, with the 1/71st, 1/52nd, 2/95th and 3/95th, also in line of columns.

Wellington's fourth line, farther to the right and roughly in line with Ghiny's brigade on the left, was van Tripp's Netherlands heavy brigade, with van Merlen's 2 Light Cavalry Brigade to van Tripp's right. To the right forward of Merlen was the Brunswick corps, in reserve, in two lines of columns four deep, with four battaliions in front and three in the rear; the Brunswick cavalry forward to the right of its infantry. The Brunswickers were almost in front of the hamlet of Merbraine. To the Brunswick right was Halkett's 3 Hanoverian Brigade, with battalions Bremervorde, Osnabruck, Quackenbruck, and Salgiter, in line of columns linking with Chassé at Braine-l'Alleud.

Batteries were arranged before the first line on the right: nearest the centre, Ross's battery on the high ground behind La Haye Sainte, with two guns facing down the *Chaussée*; Cleeve's battery in front of Alten's division; and Kuhlmann's and Sandham's placed in front of the Guards. Sympher's and Bolton's batteries were held in reserve, with Bean's, Sinclair's and Braun's, and five horse batteries (Bull's, Webber-Smith's, Whinyates', Mercer's, and Ramsay's) nominally attached to the cavalry but used when available as mobile field pieces.

Initially, Wellington deployed Major Baring and the six companies of the 2nd KGL Light Battalion (rifle-armed) to hold La Haye Sainte. To Hougoumont, besides the four light companies at first commanded by Lord Saltoun, he sent the 1/2nd Nassau Light Infantry Regiment of the 2nd Netherlands Division, some 700 men under Captain Buschen, and one light company (331 men) of the élite rifle-trained Hanoverian *Jägers* of Kielmansegge's corps. These additions placed about 1,500 men in defence of Hougoumont before the battle commenced.[24]

Captain (later General Sir) James Shaw Kennedy, acting on Wellington's Quartermaster-General's staff, explained why for this battle Wellington had the majority of the Anglo-Allied army adopt four-deep columns as opposed to the linear two-deep formation he had normally employed:

'The French cavalry had, on the 16th, proved itself very formidable at Quatre Bras in its attack ... That cavalry, in immensely augmented numbers, was now forming opposite ... and the ground between them and us presented no obstacle whatever. It was at the same time evident, from the way in which the French guns were taking up their ground, that the [army] would be exposed to a severe artillery fire. It was therefore, of the highest importance that the formation[s] ... should be such that ... [their] passing from line into a formation for resisting cavalry should be as rapid as possible ... To carry these views into effect the strong battalions formed each an oblong on the two centre companies, and when the battalions were weak, two were joined, the right-hand battalion of the two forming left in front, and the left-hand battalion right in front, each in columns of companies. The fronts of the oblongs were formed by four companies; the rear face of the oblongs by the same strength; and the sides of one company each, which were formed by the outward wheel of the subdivisions. It will be observed that, when a battalion forms oblong in this manner upon two centre companies, the formation is made in less than half the time in which it would form a square on a flank company [grenadier or light]; and the same applies to deployment.'[25]

Obviously the Allied army, well back, hidden behind the ridge of Mont St-Jean out of sight of the French gunners who needed a visual target to aim at, would not see the cavalry coming on immediately. And with the massed bombardment of some 400 cannon in total, and the heavy smoke from these, they might not be seen or heard as soon as would be required. So as a practical expedient the Allies adopted a four-deep formation that contracted the line but allowed fewer muskets to fire.

In the Peninsula, the French had used fewer cavalry, especially after 1812 when Napoleon repeatedly called on mounted units there for service on the eastern front. Additionally the use of massed cavalry in Iberia was largely prohibited by the terrain. But the impending battle would not be of the same character: the troops, the terrain and the tactics were all different.

Wellington had ordered Lieutenant-Colonel Carmichael Smyth of the Royal Engineers to strengthen the right wing in front of Braine-l'Alleud with an entrenched earthwork. Wellington may also have intended the crossroads at Mont St-Jean to be similarly protected and the road there to be broken up. (The farm of Mont St-Jean, however, was to be *hors de combat* because Wellington had designated it his main field hospital.) On the morning of the 17th Lieutenant Sperling of Smyth's command had ridden from Quatre Bras to Hal, where a company of Sappers and Miners was stationed. At 5 p.m. Sperling gave the captain in charge Wellington's order, by way of Colonel Smyth, to march at 6 p.m. to Braine-l'Alleud and construct the required field works. The captain and his company did not arrive there until well into the next morning because he claimed to have 'lost my way in the forest of Soignies' and retired for the night to Waterloo village to shelter from the rain. On arrival next morning, too late to perform his task, he was immediately placed under arrest.[26].

Wellington's army was now as ready as it could be and were only waiting for Napoleon to 'open the Ball'. Back in Brussels and Ghent there was little sign of the 'stiff upper lip' among the English expatriates and Bourbon exiles. One panic-stricken lady, Fanny d'Arblay, had rushed out at first light when the news had leaked from Wellington's letters and dispatches to Lady Webster and Sir Charles Stuart. She failed to obtain a passport from the military governor and returned home at 6 a.m., to be greeted by a hysterical friend shouting: 'Open your door! There is not a moment to lose!' They went to the wharf to try to purchase a passage on a barge to Antwerp, only to find that the barges had been commandeered to take the thousands of Allied wounded to Antwerp. Another lady, Caroline Capel, who had cheered on Picton's division as it had marched out on the night of the 15th, wrote: 'This has indeed come upon us like a Thief in the night – I am afraid our Great Hero must have been deceived for he certainly has been taken by surprise.'[27] Much panic was exhibited by these society Britons in their anxiety to get away, for they remembered Napoleon's Berlin Decree of 1806 which declared all British subjects, civilians or military, irrespective of age or sex, to be prisoners of war if taken on Imperial territory. But the good people of Belgium did not rise and beg to belong to France as Wellington and his officers had feared. Instead they ignored the embarrassing antics of the British and helped nurse their own and the British wounded, some 2,380 men who had arrived in torrential rain from Quatre Bras. At Ghent Louis XVIII declared: 'Let those who are afraid depart. For myself, I shall not leave here unless forced to do so by the march of events!' This sounded good to the foreigners and to himself, but Louis suddenly found that his gouty legs did not prevent him from constantly getting up to look out of the window, and, as in Paris, he took care that his valuables were packed up ready to go.

At Wavre, in the first hour of 18 June, Müffling's dispatch arrived, informing Gneisenau that: 'The Anglo-Allied army is posted with its right on Braine-l'Alleud, its centre upon Mont St. Jean, and its left on La Haye; with the enemy in front. The Duke awaits the attack, but counts on Prussian support.'[28] In answer to this, Gneisenau had sent the detailed reply signed by Blücher, which Wellington received at 2 a.m. The route by which

Prussian help would have to reach Wellington was a difficult one. Wavre was ten miles from Mont St-Jean. The roads between were narrow, rutted, dirt tracks across an area of broken ground, with many steep rises and falls, brooks to ford and woods to negotiate. A number of villages and hamlets dotted the forlorn landscape, representing a further hindrance as bottle-necks on the already slow roads. Wavre itself stood on the northern bank of the Dyle, and was linked to its southern suburb by two stone bridges. The Brussels–Namur highroad ran roughly north-south through the town, bisecting it. The Dyle, not normally deep, had been swollen by the recent heavy rain and was flowing full between its banks lined with hedges, trees and thickets. The northern bank of the Dyle at Wavre was slightly higher than the southern, making the river line well suited to defence from an attack from the south. Here at Wavre on the 17th, the Prussian army, or most of it, had concentrated. A force from Bülow's corps had been left at Mont St-Guibert to observe Grouchy. This force of 1,500 men, under Colonel von Ledebur, commanding the 10th Hussars, comprised his unit and the two fusilier battalions of light infantry from the 11th Fusilier and 1st Pomeranian *Landwehr* with a 2-gun section of No 12 Horse Artillery Battery.

During the Prussian withdrawal to Wavre I and II Corps, which had borne the brunt of the fighting at Ligny and before, with the loss of about 10,500 men, arrived with so little ammunition as to be considered non-combatant. It was not until, through the efforts of Lieutenant-Colonel von Sohr, the army ammunition train reached Wavre at 5 p.m. that these corps regained their ability to fight. Towards evening III and IV Corps also gained the Wavre area, with Bülow last and bivouacking his troops at Dion-le-Mont, south-east of the town.

During the evening of the 17th Blücher had sent Müffling his I'll-go-you-one-better reply to Wellington's plea for at least one Prussian corps, promising to assist with his entire army. Never one to do things by halves, was 'Old Forward'. Müffling not only received Blücher's letter but one also from Blücher's aide, Count Nostitz, which stated:

> 'General Gneisenau is aware and approves of the contents of this [Blücher's] letter. He requests you ascertain beyond doubt whether the Duke is firmly resolved to do battle in his present positions or whether he is merely engaging in a show which can only be of the gravest disadvantage to our army. Would you please let me have your views on the matter, as it is of the greatest importance that we should be accurately informed of the Duke's intentions, so that our own movements may be directed accordingly.'[29]

The reader will by now be aware that General Gneisenau did not trust the Duke of Wellington. His part at the Vienna Congress, in dealing with Metternich and Talleyrand to the detriment of Prussia's claim on Saxony, was only about five months old,[30] and his apparent failure to support the Prussians at Ligny only hours earlier was still vivid in Gneisenau's mind. It is hardly surprising, in light of these fresh incidents, that Gneisenau wanted assurances other than Wellington's own that the Duke would stand at Mont St-Jean. During the night of the 17th Gneisenau wrote a report to General Knesebeck, King Frederick William's principal military adviser:

> '... It is rumoured that the Duke of Wellington's left wing was attacked this morning [at Quatre Bras] but this has not been confirmed; he wants to accept battle at Mont St. Jean, near the entrance to the wood of Soignies; if we can give him two corps ... If information [Müffling's assurance] comes we will accept the Duke's request, let Bülow's corps join him together with the still complete battalions of the other army corps, and we will consider what to do with the rest.'[31]

Like Napoleon, Gneisenau was adept at reading maps. He could see very well the type of terrain which his army would have to cross to get to Mont St-Jean. He had no intention of allowing the army, which his king expected back in recognizable form, to become strung out over ten miles of difficult ground with Napoleon in front and Grouchy coming up behind, only to find that Wellington's force had not stood against Napoleon's veterans and had already fallen back westward. Gneisenau therefore arranged that Prussian troops would not be committed to battle against Napoleon unless Wellington were already firmly fixed to the ground and not easily able to withdraw.

So Gneisenau decided that Bülow and his IV Corps would lead the advance to Mont St-Jean. That Bülow, at Dion-le-Mont, was some ten miles from Chapelle St-Lambert while the war-weary Zeithen was only four, would serve Gneisenau's plan to delay the arrival of Prussian forces close to Napoleon until it could be ascertained whether Wellington had drawn his sword or drawn back. Bülow would have to march five miles to Wavre, then defile his entire corps over the two bridges, squeeze through the town and pass I Corps, before marching on to Chapelle St-Lambert.

Determined not to allow things to go wrong through misunderstanding, Gneisenau gave Bülow, over Blücher's reluctant signature, explicit orders:

> 'You will, therefore, at daybreak, march with the Fourth corps from Dion-le-Mont, through Wavre, in the direction of Chapelle St. Lambert, on nearing which you will conceal your force as much as possible [behind and in the

Bois de Paris], in case the enemy should not, by that time, be seriously engaged with the Duke of Wellington; but should it be otherwise, you will make a most vigorous attack on the enemy's right flank. The Second Corps will follow you as a direct support; the First and Third will also be held in readiness to move in the same direction if necessary. You will leave a detachment in observation at Mont St. Guibert; which if pressed, will gradually fall back on Wavre. All the baggage train, and everything not actually required in the field, will be sent to Louvain.'[32]

Bülow set out at daybreak on the 18th. Prussian cavalry patrols had already been sent ahead to scout St-Lambert and, at 10 a.m., had made contact with Captain Taylor of the British 10th Hussars. Bülow's lead infantry brigade reached Wavre at 7 a.m. and started filing across the Dyle and through the town. A fire broke out in the main street at about 8 a.m., causing great confusion, as it was feared that the ammunition train might catch fire and explode. It took three full battalions of the 14th Regiment to put out the fire, by which time IV Corps had been delayed for two hours, and did not clear Wavre until 10 o'clock. During the fire Gneisenau had refused to allow I Corps to advance ahead of Bülow. All had to wait until IV and then II Corps passed them. Bülow's advance guard reached St-Lambert at 10.30 a.m., and the main body at 12.30 p.m., but the rearguard (Rysscl's brigade) did not arrive until 3 o'clock.

At 11 a.m. Napoleon had completed his plans for the battle. It was to be literally a straightforward operation: no manoeuvring, but a brutal frontal assault. The Emperor's initial order read:

'To each Corps commander: directly the army has formed up, and soon after 1 p.m., the Emperor will give the order to Marshal Ney and the attack will be delivered on Mont St Jean village in order to seize the crossroads at that place. To this end the 12pdr batteries of the II and VI corps will mass with that of the I corps. These 24 guns will bombard the troops holding Mont St Jean, and Count d'Erlon will commence the attack by first launching the left division, and, when necessary, supporting it by other divisions of the I corps.

'The II Corps also will advance keeping abreast of the I Corps. The company of engineers belonging to I Corps will hold themselves in readiness to barricade and fortify Mt. S. Jean directly it is taken.'[33]

Napoleon intended that d'Erlon would sweep away Wellington's left flank then, turning his corps at right angles (*en potence*) to Wellington's line, and in conjunction with Reille's frontal attack on Wellington's right, roll up the enemy's left and centre sufficiently to permit seizure of the objectives – Mont St-Jean farmhouse and the crossroads hamlet of the same name. These seizures would have been virtually unopposed; as a field hospital the farmhouse had not been garrisoned or prepared for defence, and the hamlet had not been barricaded or garrisoned because as it was, with 17,000 men detached to hold Hal, Wellington's full force was barely adequate to defend the line Frischermont–Braine-l'Alleud. Further detachments to the rear of the line could not be spared.

With the Mont St-Jeans taken and the initial campaign objective of the highroad to Brussels at last secured, Napoleon expected that Wellington's heterogeneous army would begin to disintegrate and oblige him to retreat on his right flank towards Hal. This of course would drive a widening gap between Wellington and Blücher. Ney, as commander of the left wing, would harry Wellington's retreat with a single corps and some cavalry, while Napoleon would march straight up the *Chaussée* to Brussels with his Imperial Guard and two infantry corps. After his triumphal entry into the city, he would concentrate his central reserve in front of Brussels, in an ideal position to support either Ney or Grouchy. At this point, if not before, Napoleon felt confident that Wellington would embark for England and that Blücher would be forced to retreat back into Prussia. The military campaign would then in all probability be complete, and the fruit of it could be expected to fall freely. In Paris and around Europe Napoleon would be seen to have beaten the two most famous Allied commanders, who had enjoyed superior numbers. He would have retaken the long-contested, strategic area known as Belgium, causing the new King William to yield what the Vienna Congress had given him, and causing the old King Louis to take a short voyage across the Narrow Sea. Napoleon would be well placed to threaten the right flank of the other Allied armies approaching France, and there could be little doubt that they would retire without obliging him to march south on them. The Tsar and the Austrian Emperor Francis, his father-in-law, would, if allowed, put a noble face on it and agree to peace on terms advantageous to Napoleon; certainly he would regain custody of his son and heir. Most importantly for the prospects of a long-term peace, and probably most satisfying in a vindictive sense, Napoleon would expect the no-accommodation-with-Bonaparte party of Lord Liverpool – the party that had sustained seven coalitions against him over two decades and which had connived at the attempted murder of him and his family – to be sufficiently embarrassed by the failure and wasted expense of yet another coalition war effort and by the ignominious collapse of the reign of their Bourbon simulacrum of a king, that the British peace party would gain the ascendant and form a government.

Upon reflection Napoleon modified his inital orders. The Château Hougoumont would become a diversionary target. Its seizure would threaten Wellington's right and his line of retreat, perhaps causing him to commit reserves to bolster his right. Also the Grand Battery forming in the centre would be increased from 24 to 84 guns. Its sustained fire would reduce Wellington's centre to a shambles, easing d'Erlon's job of rolling up the enemy left. Consequently Ney pencilled on the orders: 'Count d'Erlon will note that the attack will be delivered first by the left instead of commencing from the right. Inform General Reille of this change.'[34]

At almost 11.30 a.m., just after Napoleon had taken up position near Rossomme, one of Reille's batteries opened fire on Wellington's positions above Hougoumont. (Wellington, it may be recalled, had ordered his batteries not to engage in counter-battery fire.) Prince Jérôme's 6th Division had been ordered to mount the diversionary attack on Hougoumont. His Chief of Staff, General Count Guilleminot, sent forward the division's 1 Brigade under General Baron Bauduin to carry out a frontal assault on the wood at the southern end of the Hougoumont estate. Seven battalions advanced in battalion columns in echelon, preceded by their light companies in extended skirmish order. At the same time Piré's lancers went forward along the axis of the Maison du Roi-Braine-l'Alleud road to a position across the Nivelles road, extending the French left flank partially to envelop the Hougoumont position. British officers with Peninsula experience were surprised to observe the French use of massed troops and the precision of their movements. In the Peninsula, with its rugged terrain, the French had rarely formed up in uniform order of battle as normally occurred on other European fields.[35]

During the short-lived French preliminary bombardment of the Hougoumont wood, Napoleon personally ordered Kellermann's two horse artillery batteries to go forward to give Bauduin's attack covering fire.[36] The French light infantry skirmishers charged into the wood with bayonets fixed, only to be decimated and driven back by the intense fire of three companies of the Nassau light battalion and the Hanoverian *Jägers* who, from the cover of the trees, suffered little in return for the casualties they inflicted. But the French massed formations came on in overwhelming strength, driving back the enemy skirmishers. By weight of numbers and constant outflanking from wherever the defenders' thin line was pierced, the French maintained a slow advance up through the wood toward the château, but at a high price. The Nassau and Hanoverian light troops fell back skilfully from tree to tree, as Saxe-Weimar had done in the Bois de Bossu two days earlier, taking a heavy toll of the packed French formations. Soon the French had also taken up open-order positions, and a point-blank musketry duel ensued, with the French gaining ground due to constant reinforcement from behind.

General Bauduin, conspicuous on horseback, was one of the early casualties, falling shot through. As in the Bois de Bossu, every tree and clump of bushes was contended. The dense foliage and growing pall of gunsmoke from the thousands of rounds fired made visibility in the wood extremely limited. The fire fight inevitably took its toll on an innocent third party, the wood itself. As one British officer watching the fight remarked: '... the trees in advance of the Château were cut to pieces by musketry'.

It took nearly an hour for Jérôme's 1 Brigade to clear the wood of its 600 German defenders, who on reaching the château fell back behind it into an area called 'the hollow way', which was hidden from the view of the French. The château and adjoining buildings were therefore uncovered and their defence rested on the efforts of the troops within – the light companies of the British Guards and three companies of the 1/2nd Nassauers.[37]
On clearing the wood, the disordered French troops found themselves only some 30 yards from the château complex and its adjoining garden wall. Possessed of the adrenalin of battle and out of control of the senior officers, the French troops at once charged the small British force standing between them and the buildings. The British disputed the open ground as best they could, but steadily drew back.

Soon hundreds of French threw themselves at the south gate of the complex and the 6-foot-high garden wall, only to be met by intense musketry from the Guardsmen and Nassauers firing point-blank. The defenders had loopholed the south-facing walls of the buildings and garden to such an extent as to make of the open space a killing ground. Even roof tiles had been removed to provide for sniping. The French pounded in vain on the huge wooden doors of the gate, and tried to boost comrades over the garden wall. Those who managed to get to the top were shot or bayoneted immediately. In desperation those French who had gained the walls tried to grab the barrels of the muskets poking through the loopholes, but most only received the ball. French dead lay in heaps before the walls and gate. Eventually those who could fell back to the comparative safety of the wood. It did not occur to the attackers, when frustrated on the south side of Hougoumont, to try another side. Had they circled around the left side to the north-facing main gate they would have found it open and relatively undefended.

Reille had not intended to assault the château but only to gain control of the wood. This would provide cover behind which a large force could be built up to assault the right of Wellington's line. That was the intention of the diversionary plan. The British Guards in the château buildings and the Nassauers in the garden, together numbering less than a battalion, were a severe nuisance, but if kept bottled up inside, beyond 150 yards' effective musket range, they would not be able to interfere with the development of the diversion.[38]

However, as has been demonstrated time and again in history, plans are often thwarted by the unpredictable action of human irrationality. Prince Jérôme now considered it a point of honour to capture the château. After all, he had lost some 1,500 men in the wood and before the south wall, including one of his generals of brigade. Accordingly Jérôme ordered General Baron Soye to advance his 2 Brigade into the wood to replace 1 Brigade, which would then move to turn Hougoumont's left side and attack the north gate. General Guilleminot remonstrated with the Prince about the folly of committing another 8,000 troops to the taking of the château which itself was militarily insignificant. Hougoumont, along its entire western side (left as the French saw it), was formed of the huge buttressed wall of a barn and outbuildings, without loopholes and virtually blind to the defenders. A division could have formed there to threaten Wellington's right flank in comparative safety. But Jérôme would not be deterred and 2 Brigade went forward into the wood. No one had thought of bringing up one of Kellermann's horse artillery sections to demolish the south gate and blow holes in the walls.

Soye's descent of the slope of the Belle Alliance ridge into the Hougoumont wood was observed by Wellington and Sir Augustus Frazer, who wrote of Wellington's reaction to this movement:

'I... was rejoiced to hear that his Grace had determined not to lose a wood, 300 yards in front of the part of the line, which was in reality our weakest point... Whilst looking about, remarking again that the weak point of our line was our right, and imagining that the enemy, making a demonstration on our centre and left, would forcibly seize the wood, and interpose between us and Braine le Leud [sic], would endeavour to turn the right flank of our second line [which was exactly what Napoleon wanted his enemy to believe] ... I met Lord Uxbridge, who very handsomely asked me what I thought of the position, and offered me the free use of the Horse artillery. In a moment Bell [Adjutant of the Horse Artillery] was sent for the Howitzer troop [Bull's], and I rode up and told the Duke I had done so. By this time the enemy had forced a Belgian battalion [actually the Nassauers] out of the orchard to the left of the wood, and there was a hot fire on a battalion (or four companies, I forget which) of the Guards, stationed in the buildings and behind the walled garden. The Howitzer troop came up, handsomely; their very appearance encouraged the remainder of the division of the Guards, then lying down to be sheltered from the fire. The Duke said, "Colonel Frazer, you are going to do a delicate thing; can you depend upon the force of your howitzers? Part of the wood is held by our troops, part by the enemy," and his Grace calmly explained what I already knew. I answered that I could perfectly depend upon the troop; and after speaking to Major Bull and to all his officers, and seeing that they, too, perfectly understood their orders, the troop commenced its fire, and in ten minutes the enemy was driven from the wood.'[39]

Under the bombardment of explosive howitzer shells Soye withdrew his brigade from the wood, and after regrouping proceeded by the left flank of the wood forward to the shelter of the blind left side of the complex. The howitzers continued to wreak havoc on Jérôme's 1 Brigade, still in the wood.

Above the château and facing towards Nivelles, Captain Mercer's horse battery had taken position after having been called up by Bell from its reserve location near the farmhouse of Mont St-Jean. He had been ordered to observe Piré's cavalry and to fire upon them if they advanced or otherwise menaced Mercer's position. But Mercer saw fit to disobey orders. He started a slow fire on Piré's light artillery batteries, inevitably drawing counter-battery fire from two of Reille's divisional batteries. When Mercer ceased firing, Reille's batteries no longer had his smoke to sight upon and they too ceased fire. This flagrant breach of his orders came to the Duke's attention when he noticed a projectile strike a French cannon. Wellington mistakenly assumed that the fire had come from Sandham's battery, and ordered the officer presumed responsible placed under arrest. The arrest was withdrawn when the officer in question and a fellow officer declared upon their honour that the fire had not been theirs. British officers had pledged their personal honour; the Duke was therefore persuaded of their innocence.

When Jérôme had led Soye's brigade around the left of Hougoumont, an attempt was made to carry the north gate by storm. The soldiers on duty there, suddenly alerted, opened fire on the attack column, but they were too few to repulse it. In the charge on the gate Colonel de Cubières, commander of the brigade's 1st Regiment and acting in command in place of Bauduin, was himself shot off his horse, severely wounded. Wellington, alerted to this attack, directed Byng to assault the column with his reserve, which sent them reeling back into the woods. The defenders managed to close the gates, but a giant of a Frenchman, Lieutenant Legros, smashed a door panel with an axe and reached through to unlatch the doors. Two dozen French soldiers got in before troops rallied by Lieutenant-Colonel Macdonell, commanding the château garrison, managed, after a titanic struggle, to wedge the gate shut. The French who had got in pursued the troops who had shut the gate as they retreated to the main building. Lieutenant Wilder of the 2nd Nassaus, attempting to escape the onslaught, entered the farmhouse and shut the door. As he did so, a Sapper of the 1st Regiment swung his axe, severing Wilder's left hand. The Hougoumont garrison had to kill the fanatical intruders to a man; only their drummer-boy survived.[40]

While the diversion around Hougoumont was producing the desired effect on Wellington, the massive Grand Battery of 84 guns which Napoleon had ordered was assembled on a spur some 250 yards south of La Haye Sainte on d'Erlon's front. The battery consisted of twenty 12pdrs of II and VI Corps, forty 8pdrs of I Corps, and twenty 12pdrs of the Imperial Guard foot artillery. At midday the Grand Battery opened fire with all guns simultaneously and the awesome roar overwhelmed the battlefield. About a dozen miles away at Walhain, Grouchy and his detachment heard the salvo. The Prussians, too, must have heard it although they could only surmise what it might portend.

At about the same time a messenger arrived at Rossomme with a letter from Grouchy to the Emperor, dated from Gembloux at 6 a.m. The time of the letter alone was terrible news. Grouchy had still been at Gembloux at 6 o'clock that morning! Napoleon's drawn sword had already wasted at least three hours of light. (First light in Belgium in June comes usually at about half-past three.) Grouchy, having become the personification of caution, had waited there until he heard from Pajol as to the outcome of Pajol's reconnaissance eastward before setting out northward in 'pursuit' of Blücher. Grouchy's dispatch informed Napoleon that:

> 'All my reports, and also the intelligence to hand, confirm me in the opinion that the enemy is falling back on Brussels in order to concentrate there, and to deliver battle after having effected his junction with Wellington. Namur has been vacated by the enemy, General Pajol has written to me to this effect. The I and II corps of Blücher's army would appear to be heading towards Chaumont. They left Tourinnes yesterday evening at 8.30 p.m., and executed a night march; luckily the weather has been so bad that they would not have been able to make good progress on the road. I start this very instant for Sart-à-Wahlain; whence I shall advance on Corbais and Wavre. I shall have the honour to write to you further from one of these villages.'[41]

Napoleon would have been even more alarmed if, when reading this letter, he had known that the old cavalry general had only reached Walhain at 11 o'clock – five hours to march five miles. Napoleon rode to a position just behind La Belle Alliance and consulted Soult. All was ready for the major offensive against the enemy left, but Napoleon felt it necessary first to dictate a hasty follow-up to Grouchy in an effort to motivate him. Soult drafted Napoleon's thoughts as:

> 'You wrote to the Emperor at 6 this morning that you would march on Sart-à-Walhain; your further plan was to proceed to Corbais, or Wavre. This movement is conformable to His Majesty's arrangements, which have been communicated to you. Nevertheless His Majesty directs me to tell you that you ought always to manoeuvre in our direction. It is for you to ascertain our exact whereabouts, to regulate your movements accordingly, and to keep up

your communication with us, so as to be prepared at any
moment to fall upon and crush the enemy's troops which
may endeavour to annoy our right flank. At this moment
the battle is raging in front of Mont St Jean, manoeuvre
therefore to join our right.'[42]

Before this letter was sent to Grouchy Napoleon received more startling
news, this time concerning the scope of Blücher's intentions. Colonel Marbot had captured a Prussian messenger delivering a letter from Gneisenau
to Müffling. The letter announced the imminent arrival at Chapelle St-Lambert of the bulk of IV Corps. Napoleon and his entourage scanned the
heights to the east with their telescopes, focusing on the area where the
faint dark shapes of columns of men could be seen. The captive Prussian
courier, who spoke French, enlightened Napoleon further: 'The troops you
see are the advance guard of General von Bülow. Our whole army passed
the night at Wavre. We have seen no French, and we supposed they
marched on Plancenoit.'[43]

    With his worst fears of the morning confirmed, Napoleon ordered
Soult to add a postscript to the message to Grouchy: 'A letter which has
just been intercepted states that General von Bülow is about to attack our
right flank. We believe that we notice this corps now on the heights of St.
Lambert. So do not lose a moment in drawing near to us, and effecting a
junction with us, in order to crush Bülow whom you will catch in the very
act of concentrating [with Wellington].'[44]

    Ever the gambler, Napoleon could see that the odds were lengthen-
ing against him, but he felt that the game was by no means lost. He still saw
it as 'seventy chances in his favour'. Jérôme's and Milhaud's intelligence
had been correct: Blücher did intend to join Wellington. Napoleon knew
that his hold on power in France would be seriously eroded if he were
forced to retreat and fight on French soil as in 1814; and that the outcome
could be the same as in 1814. The republican and royalist elements in the
Chambers would seek to engineer a repetition of the conditions that had
brought about his abdication. But there was still time to make all well. If
Wellington could be broken before the Prussian army had drawn up on the
field, Blücher would fall back (as indeed Gneisenau had instructed Bülow
to do if Wellington wavered). The road to Brussels might yet be opened.
The time was 1.30 p.m. Napoleon ordered Marshal Ney to lead the main
attack against the enemy left.

CHAPTER 12

18 June: 1.30 to 3.30 p.m.

'Those who face the dizzying heights and cross the dangerous defiles,
who can shoot at a gallop as if in flight, who are in the vanguard when advancing
and in the rearguard when withdrawing are called Cavalry Generals.'
– Zhuge Liang, *The Way of the General*, c. AD 210.

N apoleon, having returned to his position at Rossomme, awaited
the start of the decisive assault which Ney would lead. Turning
to Soult, the Emperor expressed his latest estimation of his
prospects:

'This morning we had ninety odds in our favour. We still
have sixty against forty, and if Grouchy repairs the terrible
fault he has made in amusing himself at Gembloux, and
marches rapidly, our victory will be all the more decisive,
for Bülow's corps will be completely destroyed.'[1]

To meet the developing Prussian threat on his right flank,
Napoleon ordered Lobau to take his VI Corps (lacking Teste, detached to
Grouchy) to take up a position from Durutte, on the right flank of the first
line to Plancenoit, facing east at right angles to the main line of battle.
Lobau's deployment would hold Bülow in check until Wellington had been
dealt with.[2]

To increase the pressure on Wellington's right, assisting d'Erlon
when he was ready to roll up the enemy left, Reille was ordered to commit
Foy's division to the fray around Hougoumont. Foy sent his first brigade
forward, under Colonel Tissot, to attack the right (as Foy saw it) of
Hougoumont in the area of the formal gardens. Foy's 2 Brigade was to wait
behind the wood, ready to support 1 Brigade. Tissot's attack was countered
by General Byng and 2 Brigade of Guards. Wellington also moved the Bre-
menvorde Battalion of Hanoverians from Du Plat's brigade, the Brunswick
Leib-Battalion, 1st Battalion, and their élite *avant-garde* light infantry (part
rifle-armed), to the north-west corner of the château to support the garrison
and help repel flanking attacks.[3] Eight companies of Guards, three companies of Nassauers, a battalion of Hanoverians and three battalions of
Brunswickers, some 4,277 men, were now arrayed against the 6,024 men of
Reille's 1½ divisions in the fight for Hougoumont. The Allies still held the
château and buildings, but the French had the wood and now the orchard,
presenting an implied threat to Wellington's line of retreat. Both sides per-
sisted in their mistaken belief that possession of the château and buildings

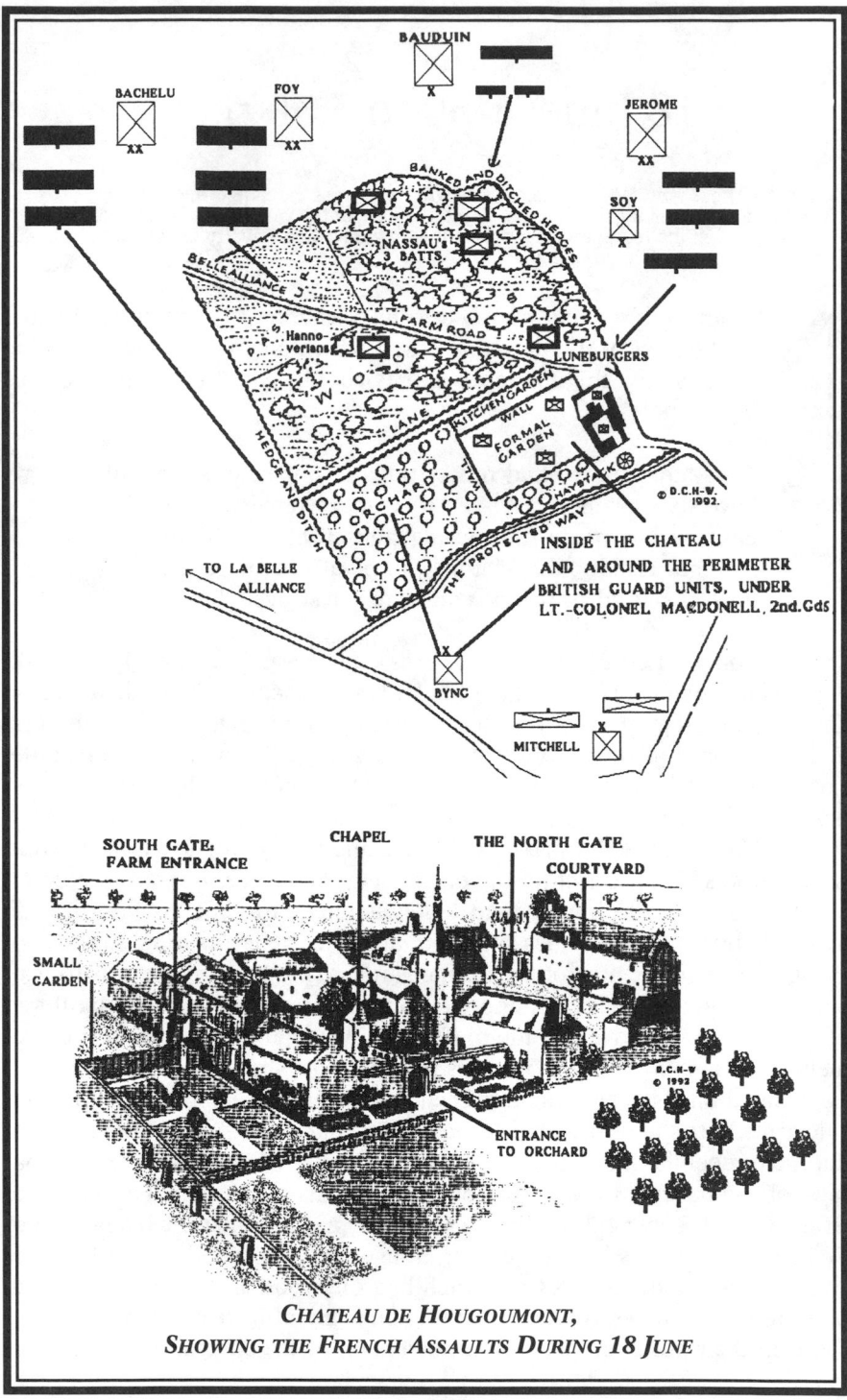

CHATEAU DE HOUGOUMONT,
SHOWING THE FRENCH ASSAULTS DURING 18 JUNE

was a requisite for control of the adjoining ground which either guarded or threatened the Allied right flank.

Earlier in the morning on Wellington's left, where d'Erlon would direct his attack, Bijlandt's brigade of the 2nd Netherlands Division had stood highly exposed, 150 to 200 yards in advance of Picton's division on a forward slope, in full view of the enemy. It had been put there as an outpost guard to the left flank of the army on its arrival on the field the previous evening. In war, as in other human endeavour, it is often true that complexity fosters error. The elaborate Anglo-Allied command structure required that De Lancey, Wellington's Chief of Staff, would have to consult his opposite numbers on the staffs of the other nationalities as to the movement of any of their respective troops. With the great press of business in arranging such a complicated army, Bijlandt's brigade had received no further orders, and therefore remained exposed as the new day wore on and the enemy prepared to attack. General Kempt described the brigade's deployment: 'The first line was composed of Dutch and Belgian troops, with the 1st Battalion of the 95th Regiment under Sir Andrew Barnard posted on a knoll on the right. The second line was composed of the 8th and 9th Brigades under Major-General Pack and myself.'4

Saxe-Weimar's 2 Brigade of the 2nd Netherlands, however, had received its instructions. Saxe-Weimar, who on the 16th had held Quatre Bras on his own initiative until reinforced, thus snatching the Allied cause from the jaws of potential disaster, was on the 18th entrusted with another important task. He and his men had been posted to hold the strategic buildings in the upper Smohain valley: Frischermont, Smohain, La Haye, and Papelotte. This position was very close to the French line, but because of its situation was not subjected to cannonade. According to Colonel van Zuylen van Nyevelt: 'The position of the second brigade was as follows: The 2nd and 3rd battalions under the direct command of the Brigadier – the Prince of Saxe-Weimar – occupied, together with the 28th of The Netherlands line [the Orange-Nassau Regiment], the extreme left of the Duke of Wellington's position; five companies held la Haye, Frischermont was held by the 28th [Orange-Nassauers], and the remainder of the 2nd Nassau Infantry formed up in column behind La Haye, acting as a support to the front line...'5 The Netherlands 2 Brigade also covered the Ohain road which was Wellington's vital link with the Prussian advance elements. Allied guns protecting the left flank were positioned on the higher ground behind the Smohain valley. Vedettes and patrols of Vivian's and Vandeleur's light cavalry brigades maintained constant communication with Saxe-Weimar's detached position which, like Hougoumont on the right, safeguarded one of Wellington's flanks.

When General Perponcher, commander of the 2nd Netherlands Division, arrived on the battlefield from the Prince of Orange's headquarters at about 11 a.m., he was alarmed to find Bijlandt's brigade, 2,500 strong, arrayed on the forward slope in a two-deep line extending 1,200

285

yards, almost the full extent of Wellington's visible left. Perponcher realized at once that Bijlandt's position was untenable. Although he might have wished to place these men behind Saxe-Weimar, as a second line in support, that ground had already been occupied on Wellington's direct order by the Hanoverian brigades of Vincke and Best. The dilemma was resolved when Wellington arrived just after 11 o'clock and was apprised of the problem by Perponcher.

It was Wellington's policy in defence not to reveal his positions to the enemy. Indeed, before leaving Brye on the 16th he had criticized the Prussians for exposing their men on forward slopes. Naturally he readily agreed that Bijlandt's brigade should fall back, and he ordered its deployment behind the Ohain road hedges in line between Pack and Kempt's brigades, which were drawn up in four-deep columns.[6] Of this movement Perponcher's Chief of Staff, Colonel van Zuylen van Nyevelt, later reported to King William:

> 'At twelve o'clock the whole of the first brigade (Bijlandt) and the artillery of the right wing moved farther back, in order not to hinder the evolutions of the English guns placed in their rear, and also to be less exposed to the fire of the enemy. Crossing the sunken road, the corps [body] formed itself on the northern side of the road in the battle array as before, supported on its right and left by the English and Scottish troops, the guns in line with those of the English.'[7]

Thus, by about midday, the forward slope between Saxe-Weimar and the gravel pit was covered only by skirmishers of the light companies of Kempt, Perponcher and Pack's divisions. The gravel pit and its knoll were occupied by three companies of the élite 1/95th Rifles. The adjutant of the 1/95th, Lieutenant Kincaid, described the situation of the riflemen:

> 'Immediately in our front, and divided from La Haye Sainte only by the great road, stood a small knoll, with a sand-hole in its farthest side, which we occupied, as an advanced post, with three companies. The remainder of the division was formed in two lines; the first, consisting chiefly of light troops, behind the hedge, in continuation from the left of our battalion reserve; and the second, about a hundred yards in its rear.'[8]

To Kincaid's right front, across the *Chaussée*, was the farmhouse of La Haye Sainte. This important strongpoint was occupied by the rifle-armed battalion of the King's German Legion under Major Baring. Behind the 1/95th, General Sir James Kempt's 8 Brigade began, ranged in two lines of battalion columns formed four deep. The need to be able to re-form against the masses of French cavalry had been made obvious at Quatre Bras. Left of Kempt, Bijlandt's brigade was deployed, but only two deep as a result of its losses. The 5th Netherlands Militia, severely depleted after its brave performance on the 16th, served as the second line reserve for Bijlandt's brigade and was situated centrally behind it. To Bijlandt's left was General Sir Denis Pack's 9 Brigade, deployed in two lines of battalion columns. Pack's men linked on their left with Vincke's 5 and Best's 4 Hanoverian Brigades. The third line of Wellington's left was composed of cavalry: the Union, or 2 Heavy Cavalry Brigade, commanded by Sir William Ponsonby, and including 1st Royal Dragoons, 2nd Royal North British Dragoons (known as the Scots Greys for their origin and the colour of their mounts) and the 6th (Inniskilling) Dragoons.

On the left since mid-morning the Allied troops and their officers had been watching with some apprehension as on the opposite slope of the valley, only about 750 yards away, teams of horses pulled gun after gun into position. The steadily growing battery seemed finally to stretch the length of the Allied left. The cannonade began at noon and continued for ninety minutes, raining shot and shell on the immobile Allies from Papelotte to slightly west of La Haye Sainte. The bombardment caused a large number of casualties. While some of the projectiles hit the forward slope and buried themselves in the soft soil or exploded harmlessly, most found their marks on the reverse slope of the ridge. Sergeant Robinson of the 92nd of Picton's division was well back from the front line and witnessed the carnage: '...At this time, our men were falling fast from the grape shot [canister] and shells that the French were pouring in amongst us, while as yet we had not discharged a musket.'[9]

The bombardment was felt keenly by the cavalry of the Union Brigade in the third line, who appeared to be receiving much of what was coming over the ridge. The whole brigade moved to its left in an effort to reduce the rate at which they were taking casualties. The Scots Greys in particular suffered. They had been placed in the second line of cavalry to support the Royals and the Inniskillings. Their leftward movement took them more out of harm's way, but in line with the other two cavalry regiments they had been positioned to support. One Greys officer's anecdote well illustrated the scene: 'We came out from the hollow ... the fire from the enemy's guns becoming too warm ... an unfortunate officer, I think of the Highlanders, who was brought down to this very ground, and was being carried in a blanket by five or six of his regiment, when a shell came and fell near them and destroyed the whole.'[10]

Even Kincaid, with his company of riflemen hidden in skirmish order behind the gravel pit, the knoll, hedges and trees, well before the target area, suffered losses: 'A cannon-ball ... came from Lord knows where, for it was not fired at us, and took off the head of our right-hand man.[11]

At about 1.30 p.m. Napoleon was satisfied that the cannonade had sufficiently disrupted Wellington's dispositions, especially where d'Erlon was to strike. He ordered Ney to commence the attack. The Marshal and his staff took post in front of I Corps, and Ney signalled d'Erlon to begin. With an intimidating tumult, the drums of the entire corps beat the *pas de charge* and the shout '*Vive l'Empereur!*' rose from thousands of French throats. D'Erlon's columns strode forward in echelon from their left, headed by General Baron Quiot de Passage's 1st Division, Colonel Charlet leading 1 Brigade, the 54th and 55th Regiments of the Line in the van. They crossed to the west of the *Chaussée* to assault La Haye Sainte, supported on their left by Dubois' *cuirassiers*. Quiot's 2 Brigade, 1st Division, under General Baron Bourgeois, comprising the 28th and 105th of the Line, advanced on the extreme left, next to the *Chaussée* and facing the gravel pit and knoll occupied by three companies of the 1/95th, on a two-company front (*colonne de bataillons par division*) of about 100 yards, the 28th leading, followed by the 105th.[12]

Two of d'Erlon's divisions, Donzelot's and Marcognet's, and one of Durutte's brigades, were deployed in a most unusual formation, not seen since the early days of the Republican armies. In the early morning a group of French generals had breakfasted with their Emperor at Le Caillou. Afterwards, and particularly bearing in mind Reille's disturbing remarks about the English army, some of the generals, principally d'Erlon, Reille, Lobau and Drouet, had convened to discuss the matter in some depth. They called upon their collective experience in facing the British in a set position. They were agreed that it would be of the utmost advantage to present their battalions in line prior to engaging them. They reasoned, correctly, that to try to deploy within musket range would be to court defeat.[13] In the light of this discussion, d'Erlon decided to deploy his 2nd, 3rd and 4th Divisions in '*Colonne de divisions par bataillon*':[14] that is, a complete division column presenting a battalion frontage, with one battalion behind another, at three-pace intervals. This would give each attacking division a five-company frontage (excluding the skirmishing company) in three ranks approximately 200 yards in length, allowing between 250 and 350 muskets to bear on the enemy instead of 50 to 60 in the case of battalion columns.

Thus, Bourgeois' 2 Brigade of 2,100 men advanced in two regimental columns. Next came Donzelot's division in the resurrected Revolutionary formation, some 5,000 strong. Margognet's 3,900 men followed, deployed as Donzelot's. Durutte's two brigades were split: 1 Brigade of 2,100 men, arrayed as Donzelot and Margognet's, but with a battalion frontage 12 files deep instead of 24. Durutte's 2 Brigade was deployed on a normal double company frontage, the 1st to support Marcognet, and the 2nd to assault the positions held by Saxe-Weimar's brigade. The 2nd's attack was supported by two batteries of horse artillery from Milhaud's corps and light cavalry from Jacquinot's division on their right flank.

As Bourgeois' regimental column of the 28th led the staggered line of d'Erlon's entire corps in the attack, the whole mass was preceded by a swarm of skirmishers, of brigade strength, made up of all the light companies of the advancing divisions. They were so numerous that the Allied soldiers mistook them for the 'First' attack.[15] Here then was a complete reversal of the familiar 'Peninsula battle', with the French advancing in line, about to be received by the British (and others) in column formation, and with the French skirmish line outgunning the Allies'.

As the corps moved forward at a brisk pace, the Grand Battery reopened a rapid fire, to inflict as much damage on the enemy as possible but also to heighten the psychological effect of this approaching mass. This was a classic Napoleonic technique, involving the expenditure of thousands of rounds, to damage and disrupt the enemy formations.

Charlet's 1 Brigade of Quiot's division, having crossed the *Chaussée*, engaged Major Baring's troops in and around La Haye Sainte. At the same time Bourgeois' 2 Brigade, 1st Division closed with the knoll and gravel pit. His men received a galling fire from the lethally accurate Baker rifles of the three companies atop the knoll and from the rifles of Major Baring's men in the La Haye Sainte farmhouse across the road. This pinpoint rifle fire immediately disabled the senior mounted officers of the leading regiment and inflicted very heavy casualties on the skirmishers, who had been allowed to advance to within 100 yards before the riflemen opened up on them. The skirmishers fell back on to their columns for support, thus further exposing the columns.

In the meantime the Allied gunners were also firing rapidly at the advancing enemy, who appeared to them as a single continuous ribbon of men, nearest on the Allied right, and rippling across the valley. If a roundshot ploughed into the thick mass, several files of men would fall back 'as if pulled by a rope'. And, each time, the men unscathed would step over the mangled remains of their comrades and close up. At 300 yards the Allied gunners double loaded with shot and canister which, like a giant scythe, cut swathes through the files of men, reducing entire ranks to a bloody rubble. Still the mass of French marched forward, quickening their pace through the muddy fields so as to be exposed to the cannon fire as briefly as possible. Despite Wellington's strict injunction, some Allied gunners yielded to the temptation to fire at the Grand Battery, thus wasting rounds which should have been directed at reducing the approaching columns. These errant gunners were quickly reprimanded by General Picton himself in language they could well understand.[16]

When Bourgeois' men came under unexpected heavy rifle fire from the hidden gravel pit, the knoll and La Haye Sainte, the leading column halted. Still under constant rifle fire from three sides, they redeployed to their right to avoid the unseen obstacle. This sudden halt and sideways movement temporarily checked Donzelot's division, who waited to see what was happening. Marcognet's troops, however, were not obstructed and did not stop. They soon overtook Donzelot's troops and outflanked the Allied riflemen, firing on them from the rear of the knoll position. When their senior officers had become casualties, the riflemen behind the knoll quickly withdrew to form up on their reserve.

Across the *Chaussée*, Charlet's 1 Brigade had started its assault on La Haye Sainte. The farm was close to the west side of the *Chaussée*, and included the house, barn, stable, kitchen garden and, to the south facing the approaching French, an orchard bounded by a thick hedge interspersed with trees. One side of the farmhouse abutted the road, and the garden to the north side was fenced on the road side and hedged on the other three.

Major Baring and his detached 2nd KGL Light Battalion had been assigned to hold La Haye Sainte. When he first saw the position upon his arrival there with his men after daylight, he was appalled:

> 'Important as the possession of the farm apparently was, the means of defending it were very insufficient, and besides, I was ordered, immediately on arriving there, to send off the pioneers of the battalion to Hougoumont, so that I did not have even an axe; for the unfortunate mule that carried our entrenching tools was lost the day before. As day broke on the 18th June, we tried by all possible means to put the place in a state of defence, but the Barn gate having been burnt [as firewood by Allied soldiers the night before] presented the greatest difficulty.'[17]

Lacking any tools, Baring's men did what they could. They tried to barricade the barn door, which faced toward Hougoumont to the west, with farm implements and anything to hand, but almost everything combustible had been burned during the wet night by other soldiers trying to dry their clothes. Baring's Germans could not build any firing platforms around the courtyard, nor could they loophole the thick walls of the buildings, their bayonets proving inadequate to the task. Yet at Waterloo, a large and fully equipped company of Sappers and Miners sat idle with their officer under arrest.

Baring had disposed his 376-man battalion with three companies in the orchard with him, two in the buildings and one along the garden hedges behind the buildings. Although the buildings of the farm sat upon higher ground, the orchard lay in a hollow. To the south of the hollow a slight elevation of the land concealed the approach of the French from Baring's view. It was over this elevation that Charlet launched his 2,000 men. Baring recalled the unequal contest at the outset:

> 'Some skirmishers commenced the attack. I made the men lie down, and forebade all firing until the enemy were quite

near. The first shot broke the bridle of my horse close to my hand, and the second killed Major Bosewiel, who was standing near me. The enemy did not skirmish for very long, but immediately advanced over the height, with two close columns, one of which attacked the buildings, and the other threw itself en masse into the orchard, showing

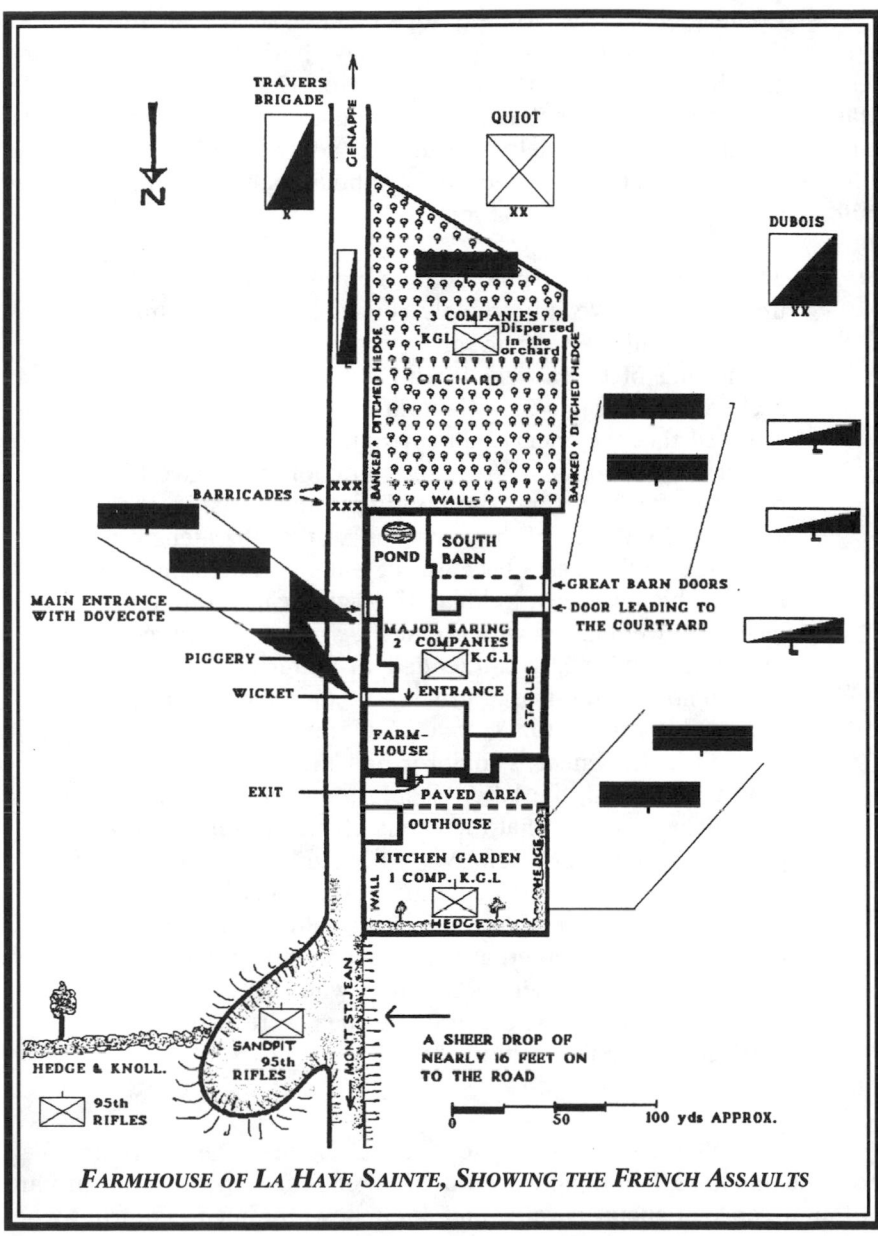

FARMHOUSE OF LA HAYE SAINTE, SHOWING THE FRENCH ASSAULTS

the greatest contempt for our fire. It was not possible for our small disjointed numbers fully to withstand this furious attack of such a superior force, and we retired upon the barn, in a more united position, in order to continue the defence. My horse's leg was broken from a musket-ball, and I was obliged to take that of the adjutant.'[18]

Count Kielmansegge, on the ridge behind La Haye Sainte with the Prince of Orange, the corps commander, saw Baring's predicament and realized that he was in danger of being overrun. He therefore ordered the Hanoverian light infantry battalion Lüneburg to come to Baring's assistance. Its commander, Colonel von Klencke, advanced his men in line to allow Baring's troops to fall back to the farmhouse behind their screen. The outcome was vividly related by Baring:

'Colonel von Klencke now came to my aid with the Lüneburg battalion. We immediately recommenced the attack, and had made the enemy give way, when I perceived a strong line of Cuirassiers [Dubois] form in front of the orchard; at the same time Captain Meyer came to me and reported that the enemy had surrounded the rear garden, and it was not possible to hold it any longer. I gave him orders to fall back into the buildings, and assist in their defence. Convinced of the great danger that threatened us from the Cuirassiers, because of the weakness of the hedge, which was easy to break through, I called out to my men, who were mixed with the newly arrived Lüneburgers, to rally around me, as I intended to retire into the barn. The number of the battalion which had come to our aid, exceeded, by many times, that of my men, and as, at the same time, the enemy's infantry had driven out my men from the orchard, the latter, seeing the Cuirassiers in the open field, imagined that their only chance of safety lay in gaining the main position. My voice, unknown to them, and also not sufficiently penetrating, was, notwithstanding all my exertions, equal to the task of halting my men and collecting them together; already overtaken by the cavalry, we fell in with the enemy's infantry, who had surrounded the garden, and to whose fire the men were exposed in retiring to the main position.'[19]

Baring's men, attempting to skirmish in the orchard, rather than hold the buildings, had rapidly been outflanked. The Lüneburgers, ignorant of the presence of enemy cavalry, had come down in line to confront what at first appeared to be a strong skirmish line. In a matter of minutes some of the French assault columns had bypassed these men and attacked the garden to their rear. As soon as Dubois' *cuirassiers* advanced, the Lüneburgers, instead of forming a square or retiring into the barn, ran back toward the ridge whence they had come. Dubois' men rode down the Lüneburgers, hacking and impaling many of Baring's intermingled Hanoverians as well. Baring, on horseback and with some of his men, was against his will swept along in the human tide that was the rout of the Lüneburgers and carried all the way back to the Allied first line on the ridge. Lieutenant Kincaid, observing this from the safety of the other side of the double hedge to Baring's rear, wrote that Baring had gone back to the safety of the Allied line 'like a shot out of a shovel'. The French *cuirassiers*, elated at their success in destroying the Hanoverian battalion, pursued the rout on to the ridge, but had to check as the sunken Ohain road loomed to their front.

On the eastern side of the *Chaussée* the outflanked companies of the 1/95th, closely followed by jubilant French skirmishers, withdrew at the run toward their reserve stationed in Picton's first line. The air of panic in their pell-mell retreat spread to the 1/95th's reserve. Without much ado they broke and ran back toward the comparative safety of the second line. Lieutenant Kincaid explained how the 1/95th reserve, much to his embarrassment, chose the better part of valour and how he came to face the French army alone:

> '... we had held the knoll longer than prudence warranted with the enemy already round both flanks, and we were consequently obliged to make the best use of our heels to get into position. I had just dashed my horse [forward] through a gap in the hedge (I was Adjutant) when I observed our reserve beginning to retire. Our 2 Field officers had been wounded the instant before, and the next in command at the moment, believing it to be intended that he should give his place to the [Allied] skirmishers and join the line [second], he put them in motion for that purpose ...'[20]

So the reserve of the 1/95th fell back before the retreating three skirmishing companies of the 1/95th which had intended to form up on their left, and all continued to retire towards Kempt's second line, except Kincaid, who sat his horse in isolation on the other side of the hedge.

Reaching the first line of the Allied position on Bijlandt's front, French skirmishers started a fire fight. Masses more skirmishers poured over the Ohain road in front of The Netherlands 27th and 7th Line Battalions and 7th and 8th Militias. Because Bourgeois's brigade had deployed to its right to avoid the gravel pit, and Donzelot's column had halted to avoid a collision with Bourgeois' men, Marcognet's division had taken the lead.

Several hundred yards behind Marcognet were Donzelot and Quiot almost in parallel, and Durutte's 1 Brigade not far behind. The Netherlanders fired at the multitude of enemy skirmishers at point-blank range and, although they had sustained heavy casualties in the fire fight, felt they were doing well when suddenly the French skirmishers in front of the 7th and 8th Militias fell back to reveal a French column which was just the other side of the Ohain road and was levelling almost 400 muskets at them. The volley at such close range destroyed the two militia battalions as coherent fighting units, causing massive casualties in dead and wounded. The French column with fixed bayonets then pushed on over the road and up the ridge. At this point in the road the cutting had given out and the small hedgerow presented no obstacle to their advance. The remnants of these two militia battalions, like the 1/95th, fell back on the second line.

Colonel van Zuylen van Nyevelt reported of the reversal:

'... In the meantime three columns advanced to attack our position under the command of Count d'Erlon, with the 105th regiment at their head. The enemy crossed the ravine, where he was outside the range of our fire, and drove back our skirmishers. Having approached us to within fifty paces, not a shot had been fired, but now the impatience of the soldiers could no longer be restrained, and they greeted the enemy with a double row, which caused the firing to be meagre and badly kept up whilst the downfall of some files made an opening to the enemy, through which he forced his way with his columns. Everything which was immediately in front of him was forced to give way but the pelotons [half-companies] on the wings with much cold bloodedness linked up with the adjoining troops. The enemy had now succeeded in passing our first line [Bijlandt's brigade and the 1/95th], and had arrived on the plain. The second line [Kempt and Pack] made ready to advance against him...'[21]

The controlled firepower of the French companies at the hedge had decimated Bijlandt's line and had caused some panic in Major Rogers' battery near them. One of Rogers' NCOs spiked a gun and the crew ran off,[22] following the others to the second line. At this point Donzelot's column arrived in front of The Netherlands 27th *Jägers* and 7th (Belgian) Line. Lieutenant Scheltens, an ex-Imperial Guardsman who was Adjutant of the 7th, recalled: '... The battalion remained lying down behind the road until the head of the French column was at a distance of a pistol-shot. The line then received the order to rise and commence firing. The French column, which was crossing the hollow road, committed the fault of halting in order to reply to our fire ... We were at such close quarters that Captain l'Olivier received the [paper] wad with the ball of the musket in his wound...'[23] The 7th Line did not retreat, but held its ground.

While the 7th Line stood, the 7th and 8th Militias had fallen back next to them, leaving a gap through which the French marched up toward the crest of the ridge. Picton and Kempt, some hundreds of yards behind the first line, were in a position to see what had occurred, as was Kincaid: 'Our first line, in the meantime, was getting so thinned, that Picton found it necessary to bring up his second, but fell in the act of doing it.'[24]

Kempt's and Pack's regiments were lying down to avoid presenting a target to French gunners. They were formed in columns of fours for easy movement and to allow the formation of a square in less than a minute in case of cavalry attack.[25] There was about 400 to 500 yards between Pack's and Kempt's brigades, with the 5th Netherlands Militia in the middle.

Picton had hurriedly ordered Kempt forward. Kempt enjoyed two advantages: the terrain, which allowed him to anchor his right flank on the *Chaussée* where it went through a steep cutting; and to shelter his right front behind the Ohain road cutting. His elevation also gave him an unhindered view of the battlefield. Seeing how close the enemy had come he at once sent his brigade forward, changing from column to line formation. He now had to his front only the French brigade advancing deployed 'in the same old way'. In the meantime Picton started to lead an advance on the left of Kempt's brigade, in front of the 28th Regiment.

General Pack, on the left, had also received Picton's urgent directive, and ordered his leading right-hand battalion, the 92nd, to advance in columns of fours. The urgency of the situation was reinforced within seconds by the sight of the retreating Netherlanders from the broken militia battalions running past, in some cases straight over the still prone British soldiers who had not yet been ordered to rise. The Scots and Inniskilling regiments, believing, as did their officers, that all people who had once been subjects of Napoleon would rather rejoin him than fight, were hostile and abusive. They had not yet seen what had driven The Netherlanders, Rogers' gunners, and the 1/95th back on the second line.

However, those Netherlanders who were not fronted by the massive French divisional column were wheeled back to protect their exposed flank by General Perponcher, and joined the left of Kempt's advancing brigade. The remnant of the broken Netherlands militias were rallied behind the 5th Militia by Perponcher's staff officers. As Colonel van Zuylen explained: '... Whilst the enemy was rallying his forces in great haste the nearest troops [Kempt's] of the second line attacked his flanks, supported in the movement by the Head of Staff, who had been able to rally about 400 men of the troops which had been forced to retire. They succeeded in driving the enemy back over the sunken road, pursuing him with the bayonet ...'[26]

From his relatively low position General Pack may not have been able to see what had happened at the hedge. He sent forward his four battalions in columns four deep, led by the 92nd, with the 44th in column behind, the 42nd to the left with the hedge enclosure to its front and Durutte's column 450 yards away, and the 1st Royal Scots to the rear of the 42nd. This formation allowed only the 92nd to engage the enemy during the brigade's advance, the 44th being in column behind it, the 42nd to its left with the hedge enclosure to its front, and the 1st Royal Scots in rear of the 42nd.[27]

As Kempt moved forward, the 28th, 79th and 32nd Regiments, together with the 7th, Netherlands Line, poured a volley into the two columns of Bourgeois' 2 Brigade which had just started to ascend the rise, having crossed through the barrier of the Ohain road and its pair of hedges. Major Calvert of the 32nd related: '... When the attacking force had crossed both hedges lining the meadow in the bottom, and had commenced ascending our position, the 32nd regiment poured in upon it a heavy fire succeeded by a charge. This the enemy did not wait to receive, but retired with precipitation, and getting entangled in the hedges on returning to their position must have suffered considerable loss. We halted and reformed at the first hedge ...'[28] This hedge was a most formidable obstacle and was as disruptive to the Allies as the French. Lieutenant Belcher of the 32nd recounted the next phase of the action: '... Immediately on passing the narrow road which ran along our front, the Ensign carrying the Colour was severely wounded. I took the Colour from him until another Ensign could be called. Almost instantly after, the Brigade still advancing, and the French Infantry getting into disorder and beginning to retreat, a mounted [French] Officer had his horse shot under him. When he extricated himself we were close on him. I had the Colour on my left arm and was slightly in advance of the division [a section or 'division', of his battalion]. He suddenly confronted me and seized the staff, I still retaining a grasp of the silk (the colours were nearly new). At the moment he attempted to draw his sabre, but had not accomplished it when the covering Colour-Sergeant named Switzer, thrust his pike into his breast and the right rank and file named Lacy, fired into him. He fell dead at my feet.'[29]

The fighting at the hedges bordering the road and fronting the French assault reached a critical stage. The arc of Kempt's brigade was wheeling into line, and the 79th added their fire to that of the 28th, then they crossed the hedges to charge home with the bayonet. The advance of the French regimental columns caused the 28th to divide into two wings.[30] The right wing fired into the column nearest them which was attempting to deploy in front of the 79th, and the left-hand wing delivered a deadly flanking fire into the other column. The left wing of the 28th was supported by the 7th Netherlands Line which had fallen back on the left of the 28th then advanced with it. This action was observed by Captain Scheltens of the 7th: '... The fire of the English very soon enveloped the column, which endeavoured to deploy instead of pushing on ... The battalion which had to cease firing ... immediately crossed the road and advanced. The enemy was taken in the Flank by Picton's [28th] regiment.'[31]

As this was happening, Pack's division, going forward in columns of four[32] with the intention of deploying behind the hedge, was met head on by Marcognet's division. Lieutenant Winchester of the 92nd related the action: '... Sir Denis Pack calling out at the same time, "92nd, everything has given way on your right and left and you must charge this column," upon which he ordered this regiment [four deep] to be formed and closed in to the centre. The regiment, which was then within about 20 yards of the column, fired a volley into them. The enemy on reaching the hedge at the side of the road had ordered arms and were in the act of shouldering them when they received the volley from the 92nd.'[33] The 92nd, however, still advancing with a reduced frontage (in fours in two companies), received a severe shock when they suddenly saw what was to their front. It was a French division (Marcognet's) in line on a battalion frontage. Now, unlike the situation in the Peninsula, the French line overlapped and outgunned the British. There was no time to deploy. The 92nd hurriedly closed up on their centre and fired a volley, but only about half their muskets – the first two ranks – could bear. The soldiers of the 45th Line of Marcognet's division took the British volley from fewer than 150 muskets, then halted, and after the command *'Appuyez à droite, serrez les rangs!'* (Bear to the right, close up!), delivered a volley from more than 400 muskets at less than twenty yards. Captain Duthilt, of the 45th, gave a rather condensed account of this successful French drive: '... Suddenly our path was blocked; English battalions concealed in a hollow road, stood up and fired at us at close range, we drove them back at the point of the bayonet and climbed higher up the slope and over the stretches of quick hedge which protected their guns. Then we reached the plateau and gave a shout of "Victory"...'[34]

The 92nd, reeling from the musketry of the French 45th, could not stand against a bayonet charge by a column of 4,000 men. This French breakthrough was detected by Uxbridge's ADC, Captain Horace Seymour: '... At the moment Sir Thomas Picton received the shot in his forehead which killed him, he was calling me to rally the Highlanders, who were moving up to their right of the high road.'[35] Meanwhile the 1st, 44th and 42nd were attempting to deploy behind the 92nd in restricted space and could not see the conflict.[36] It seemed as though Marcognet's division would establish itself on the plateau atop the ridge, wheel left, open out into a linear formation of eight battalions, and roll up Wellington's left.

This was the high tide of Napoleon's expectations. It appeared to him and his staff that his troops were about to overwhelm Wellington's left centre, and that everything was giving way on the Allied side. To the French left of the *Chaussée*, Dubois' *cuirassiers* had reached the Allied line above La Haye Sainte farmhouse. Quiot's 1 Brigade was attacking the farm buildings from three sides, while the defenders, numbering fewer than four companies, were trying to hold the barn without doors against several battalions. To the right of the *Chaussée*, Quiot's 2 Brigade was engaged with Kempt's brigade and two Netherlands battalions. Donzelot's division had started to engage and Durutte's 1 Brigade was fast approaching Pack's position. Marcognet had swept all before him and was ascending the plateau. Napoleon was jubilant. He ordered Milhaud to send General Count Wathier with Travers' *cuirassier* brigade up the right side of the *Chaussée* in support of the attack and to combine with Dubois in the fol-low-up attack to exploit the breach.[37] Then, Milhaud was to hold Delort's cavalry division in readiness to exploit the developing situation. Keller-mann, too, was ordered to have his divisions ready. As d'Erlon's corps came to grips with Wellington's left and seemed to be prevailing, Napoleon grew increasingly confident that the motley Allied force would rout in panic, fulfilling the first part of his plan.

Fate, however, made a timely intervention in the shape of the Earl of Uxbridge. A few minutes earlier he had been above Hougoumont, arranging for Bull's howitzer troop to shell the French troops moving up through the wood, and offering Frazer the use of the guns attached to Grant and Dornberg's brigades. Returning to his vantage point just to the left of the *Chaussée*, he saw at once the gravity of the situation. Galva-nized, he ordered Somerset's Household Brigade '... to prepare to form line ...' then galloped over to Ponsonby's Union Brigade, some 200 yards behind Picton's division, and '... having told him to wheel into line when the other brigades did, instantly returned to the Household Brigade and set it in motion.'[38]

Uxbridge had also ordered Ponsonby to charge the moment he saw the 2nd Life Guards do so, as they were visible to him. Then, with perfect timing and trumpets sounding the charge, the heavy division of Uxbridge's cavalry moved off. Across the *Chaussée*, Dubois' brigade of *cuirassiers*, elated at having destroyed the Hanoverian Lüneburg battalion, advanced towards the crest of the ridge at the very centre of the Allied line. Then came the thunderbolt. Uxbridge and the Household Brigade erupted through the hedges lining the sunken road in the centre of the position. Leading the 2nd Life Guards, Uxbridge smashed into Dubois' leading squadron, driving them back across the *Chaussée*. In their flight many of the *cuirassiers* rode right over the edge of the drop above the Haye Sainte farmhouse, losing their horses and, many, their lives as well. Others sought to escape by galloping along the sunken Ohain road then cutting up the right side, only to discover that they had come out on the field in front of the Allied left and were ploughing into their own infantry. Uxbridge and the 2nd Life Guards, in hot pursuit, also emerged from the road on to the field, scattering the French line which was disputing the hedges in front of Kempt's and Bijlandt's brigades. They also caused the French columns still advancing to fall back in panic. Kincaid, who against the odds was still alive and sitting on his horse, related his amazement at this *deus ex machina*: '... for the next moment the cuirassiers were charged by our Household Brigade; and the infantry in our front giving way at the same time, under our terrific shower of musketry, the flying cuirassiers tumbled in among the routed infantry, followed by the Life Guards, who were cutting away in all directions. Hundreds of the infantry threw themselves down, and pretended to be dead, while the cavalry galloped over them, and then [they] got up and ran away.'[39]

Behind Pack's brigade, sheltering in a hollow from the French artillery fire, were the 2nd North British Dragoons, the Scots Greys. From where he sat on horseback their colonel, Inglis Hamilton, recognized that Pack's men were in danger. Ponsonby had ordered the Greys to remain in the second line as support, but the French cannonade had prompted them to move to the first line. There they saw the 92nd retire in disorder. This retirement was also observed from farther out on the Allied left above Smohain, where Lieutenant Ingilby of the Royal Artillery saw that '... our troops recoiled, and some Highlanders were in confusion...'[40] Colonel Hamilton immediately ordered the Greys to advance at a walk. General Ponsonby, with the Royals and Inniskilling Dragoons, moved forward simultaneously and in line with the Greys. The Greys walked up the reverse slope of the ridge – they did not trot, gallop, or charge – because of the impediments in their path: a muddy field, a steep rise, tall wet crops, and the 92nd. The Greys had to pass through the 92nd, who were giving way before the French and unable to open ranks to let the cavalry pass. This fact was appreciated by the Greys. One of their officers, Lieutenant Wyndham, remarked: '... The 92nd Highlanders appeared to be giving way when the Greys came to the top of the Hill where the hedge was situated...'[41] Sergeant-Major Crawford of the Greys wrote: '... The French columns which were causing our infantry to retire, upon which we advanced direct, and not as a supporting body. As we advanced we were met by a number of the 92nd Regiment, who turned and ran into the charge with us ...'[42] Some men of the 92nd were knocked to the ground by the Greys in their enthusiasm to close with the French.

In the front rank of Marcognet's division, sharing the elation of his men, Captain Duthilt observed the abrupt appearance of the Greys from the French point of view:

> '... Just as I was pushing one of our men back into the ranks I saw him fall at my feet from a sabre slash. I turned round instantly – to see English cavalry forcing their way into our midst and hacking us to pieces. Just as it is difficult, if not impossible, for the best cavalry to break into infantry who are formed into squares and who defend themselves with coolness and daring, so it is true that once the ranks have been penetrated, then resistance is useless and nothing remains for the cavalry to do but to slaughter at almost no risk to themselves. This is what happened, in vain our poor fellows stood up and stretched out their arms; they could not reach far enough to bayonet these

cavalrymen mounted on powerful horses, and the few
shots fired in chaotic mêlée were just as fatal to our own
men as to the English. And so we found ourselves defence-
less against a relentless enemy who, in the intoxication of
battle, sabred even our drummers and fifers without
mercy.'[43]

As Lieutenant Winchester of the 92nd commented: '... the Scots Greys
actually walked over this [French] column ...'[44]

To the right of the Greys and further towards Wellington's centre,
the Royal Dragoons also crossed the sunken Ohain road. Kempt's brigade
had pushed back the two leading columns of Quiot's brigade (four battalions), but Donzelot's massive divisional column was advancing on the
remaining core of Bijlandt's brigade, which had been pushed back. The
Inniskilling Dragoons charged headlong into Donzelot's column. Colonel
Muter, commanding the Inniskillings, described the action:

'... the cavalry, on reaching the crest, or a moment before
that, saw, from being a little raised on horseback, the solid
Columns, and increasing their speed, attacked with great
impetuousity ... The French Infantry made good use of
their muskets and fire, but had no time to throw themselves into square; any attempt to do so would, I think,
have been frustrated by the momentum which the cavalry
had gained by plunging over the hedges, and their
increased ardour by this time acquired.'[45]

The regiment of Royals to the right of the Inniskillings also moved
off, but slightly later as they had to pass through the intervals of Kempt and
Perponcher's brigades and negotiate the drop into the cutting. Their movement was described by Captain Clark Kennedy of the Royals:

'... The pause after wheeling into line did not exceed a few
seconds. The left of my squadron [the centre one] being
already in front of part of the enemy's column, I brought it
more so, and clear of our own Infantry, by inclining a little
to the left. How the others got on I cannot say. I came into
contact with the head of the column on the Brussels side
[north] of the hedges as it was going about, after having
given us a destructive fire at a distance of perhaps fifty
yards ... which brought down about twenty men, went
instantly about and endeavoured to regain the opposite
side of the hedges; but we were upon and amongst them
before this could be effected, the whole column getting
into one dense mass, the men between the advancing and

retiring parts getting so jammed together that the men could not bring down their arms, or use them effectively, and we had nothing to do but to continue to press them down the slope, the right squadron of the Royals naturally outflanking them, as the centre one (which I commanded) also did to a certain degree ... I can only speak of the 1st and 2nd squadrons ... I can give no account of the third.'[46]

The three squadrons of the Inniskillings ploughed into Donzelot's column, the left passing the French column's right flank and savaging it. The centre and right squadrons hit Bourgeois' brigade and sent it reeling. In the process Captain Clark Kennedy of the Royals captured the Eagle of the 105th Line Regiment in Bourgeois' force. The Royals' 3rd Squadron had to dress to its left to avoid Kempt's brigade and the steep drop in front of the road intersection.

This necessity delayed the squadron's entry into the action; and the delay was to produce remarkable results. The three squadrons of the Scots Greys had walked into and over Marcognet's column which was only 24 men deep. In the course of this, Sergeant Ewart, after a struggle, captured the Eagle of the 45th. Emerging at the back of Marcognet's ravaged column, the Greys noticed Durutte's 1 Brigade coming up the slope, acting as a link with its sister brigade attacking Saxe-Weimar.

The Greys had lost all semblance of order in moving through Marcognet's mass of men. On impulse, in the passion of battle, they spontaneously spurred their horses and charged down the slope toward their new quarry. Durutte's brigade column halted; the rear ranks closed three paces; and the four outer and rear ranks, including the file supernumeraries, turned outward. In less than a minute Durutte's men had formed square and levelled their muskets. Lieutenant Wyndham of the Greys related: '... in descending the hill, about three or four hundred yards from the hedge, the Greys came in contact with the 2nd French column or Square, regularly formed, the fire from which they received and which did great execution. The loss at this moment in men and horses was most severe ...'[47] Lieutenant Hamilton commented that the Greys were '... completely overpowered by a fresh column of Infantry firing upon us'.[48]

The Greys must have arrived before Durutte's brigade in a very ragged line, lacking any cohesion or momentum. The great volley they received at close range emptied scores of saddles. This was observed by Ensign Mountsteven of the 28th: '... I well remember the intense anxiety we felt when we saw some over-rash fellows, without stopping to form again, ride on headlong at what appeared to me an immensely strong Corps of support in perfect order ... On this column they, of course made no impression, but suffered some loss, although as far as I could see, a fire was only opened upon them from a portion of it.'[49] As a formation, the Scots Greys were spent; their effect on Durutte's brigade was like that of a wave on a rock. The shattered remnant of the Greys careered past Durutte toward the French lines.

The Royals' 3rd Squadron, which had been delayed in passing the hedges, emerged and, seeing Durutte's square, executed a left wheel as though on field parade. At the gallop the squadron hit Durutte's formation obliquely. The formation had very little depth (12 men). In moments the flank of the column had disintegrated. The Royals slashed and stabbed into Durutte's brigade with as much terrible effect as the Greys had on Marcognet's division. Men threw themselves to the ground to avoid being cut down. Panic ensued and the whole formation broke, the soldiers fleeing left and right. Lieutenant Shelton of the 28th observed this spectacular rout: '... I perfectly recollect a squadron of the Royals inclining considerably to its left to clear our left wing, which, after crossing the hedge, became separated from the right, and some way down the slope encountered a column of the enemy on its own left ... The column that was charged by the Royals was broken, and the greater part taken prisoner.'[50] Ensign Mountsteven also saw the charge of the Royals: '... The charge on the square which was broken took place some distance in our front, but a little to the left ...'[51]

Lord Uxbridge and the 2nd Life Guards who had followed him over the right-hand side of the road, driving some of Dubois' *cuirassiers* before them, ran straight into Travers' brigade advancing up the right side and along the road. Hitting Travers' men at speed, the Life Guards, closely followed by elements of the Union Brigade, sent the enemy infantry and cavalry falling back rapidly on its divisional supports. At the same time, across the *Chaussée* between Hougoumont and La Haye Sainte, the *cuirassiers* of Dubois and Charlet's brigade assaulting the farmhouse were struck by the remainder of the Household Brigade – the 1st Life Guards and the 1st Dragoon Guards, in perfect order, followed by the Royal Horse Guards acting initially as support, but coming into line to fill the frontage.

Thunderstruck and impotent, Napoleon and his staff watched the calamity unfold before them. Never had British cavalry been used in such a daring fashion and with such results. The 'sixty chances' which the Emperor had given his men against the enemy had been wiped out by Uxbridge's charge.

The two brigades of British heavy cavalry which had charged down the slope arrived in front of the French positions. The fighting strength of the Union Brigade had been considerably reduced, probably more through horses shot than men. Unhorsed cavalrymen, especially heavies, were rather ineffective on the field, encumbered as they were with heavy cuff-topped boots. In retiring back up the slope, the mounted remainder of these brigades suffered further casualties from the muskets of French infantry who had formed into rallying masses of various sizes -a tactic learned the hard way in Spain and Russia. Other troopers were occupied in herding prisoners back toward the Allied line.

Despite the toll taken of the British cavalry in their shock assault on d'Erlon's corps, the effect of it on the French infantry was both immediate and secondary. Immediate were the casualties caused by sabre and hoof, and secondary was the psychological effect on the remaining French infantry ranged on the slope and the crest of the ridge. The eruption of the Greys into Marcognet's division and the horror of the Royals' breaking of Durutte's brigade caused panic. The French foot, so near to breaking Wellington's left, were themselves broken and they knew it; they turned and ran. The men of Kempt's division and Bijlandt's brigade were enthusiastic in pursuit, and had to be restrained from going too far into the no man's land. One group of French were given an unexpected, and unintentional, chance to get clear. Bijlandt's brigade had rallied and charged past the 28th Foot[52] which had split into two wings. When these two wings went forward, they had fired on one of Bourgeois' columns from the front and flank. In the act of re-forming, one wing of the 28th mistook a rallied knot of French for some of Bijlandt's who had preceded them in the pursuit. As Ensign Mountsteven related: 'In advancing in pursuit of... [the French] the wings of the regiment separated, and I, carrying the King's Colour, went on with the right wing. When we had proceeded a little way we perceived through the smoke another body of troops in column immediately in our front, which we mistook for some Corps of the Allies, and many of the officers (I amongst them) cried out to the men, "Don't fire, they are Belgians!" Having just been passed by a Corps of Belgians during our advance. This caused a momentary check of our wing, when we quickly discovered our mistake by the enemy making off with all speed in the direction of the French Position.'[53]

Napoleon reacted to d'Erlon's heavy repulse with his usual speed and effectiveness, as he himself related:

> '... I saw that on his [Wellington's] left he was preparing for a big cavalry charge; I dashed there at the gallop. The charge had taken place; it had repulsed a Column of infantry [Marcognet's] which was advancing on the Plateau, had taken two eagles from it, and put seven guns out of action. I ordered a brigade of General Milhaud's cuirassiers, of the second line, to charge this cavalry. It went off with shouts of "Vive l'Empereur!"; the English cavalry was broken, most of the men were left behind on the Battlefield; the guns were retaken; the infantry protected ...'[54]

When Somerset's brigade arrived at the bottom of the valley, between the rear of Hougoumont and La Belle Alliance, they found themselves facing Milhaud's counter-charge and a heavy fire at close range from Bachelu's division. Ponsonby's brigade, elated at having overridden and routed d'Erlon's corps, arrived at the French lines thoroughly disorganized and having expended their momentum. Many of their horses were blown; they had no objective and were unable to rally; so they milled about in small bodies, some attacking guns, and some trying to find their way back to the Allied line. Suddenly they too were confronted by the mass of fresh, compactly ordered French cavalry which were Milhaud's *cuirassiers*.

However, the plight of the two dissipated British heavy brigades, set upon in the valley between the armies, had not gone unnoticed. General de Ghigny and The Netherlands 1 Light Cavalry Brigade, placed on the plateau behind Somerset's brigade, had watched d'Erlon's advance and repulse, and could see the predicament of Ponsonby's troopers and also that of Perponcher's men in Papelotte. De Ghigny decided on his own initiative to cross the *Chaussée* and assist. He reported: '... About half-past two in the afternoon I perceived a retrograde movement being made by some of our troops on our left [in the first line] immediately I ordered my Brigade to cross in squadrons to the left-hand side of the chaussee, whereupon I brought up the 8th Hussars to the front at a trot, followed by the 4th Light Dragoons in echelon ...'[55] In the meantime the brigades of Vandeleur and Vivian remained in their positions – constrained by Wellington's orders not to move except to exploit a local advantage – from which they could see their comrades being butchered below. Vandeleur and Vivian would later be accused of 'maintaining a masterly inactivity', but much as they wanted to intervene they would not risk the consequences of disobeying Wellington's order. General Müffling remonstrated with them to go to the assistance of the foundering heavies: 'Both agreed with me fully but shrugging their shoulders answered "Alas, we dare not! The Duke of Wellington is very strict in enforcing obedience to prescribed regulations on this point." I had afterwards an opportunity of asking the duke about these regulations ... The duke answered me: "The two generals were perfectly correct in their answer, for had they made such an onslaught without my permission, even though the greatest success had crowned their attempt, I must have brought them to a court-martial." '[56] To those brave, reckless British cavalrymen in the valley, who had alone broken a corps of French infantry and wrecked Napoleon's plan of attack, Wellington's principles would be cold comfort indeed.

While Napoleon himself threw Farine's brigade of *cuirassiers* at the British heavies, General Baron Jacquinot on the far right of the French battle line, supporting the attack on the Smohain complex, saw with disbelief the rout of d'Erlon's corps by a single division of enemy cavalry. Jacquinot, the archetypal light cavalryman, who had fought in every campaign since 1806, knew at once and instinctively what to do. Comprehending the action at a glance, he ordered Colonel Martigue to disengage his 3rd Lancers, leaving only Colonel Brô with the 4th Lancers to act as a screen to help Durutte's 2 Brigade disengage from the Smohain area. Then Jacquinot wheeled the 3rd Lancers into a line at right angles to the main French line.

Shouting 'Open order!', he unleashed his lancers on the flank of the milling British cavalry. The lancers, who moments before had seen their own men trampled and hacked by the men now at their mercy, in turn had no mercy. Instead of the usual 'Vive l'Empereur!' it was 'A mort!' as they swept forward, opening into an arc. 'Never did I realize before the great superiority of the lance over the sword,' said Durutte of the almost clinical slaughter he then witnessed.[57] None was spared; there was no surrender, no quarter. Anyone clothed in a British uniform, alive, wounded or already dead was speared without discrimination. Some of these hapless British cavalrymen were found to have received as many as eighteen lance wounds.

General Ponsonby, desperately trying to rally some of his command and carry out a fighting withdrawal, was identified by a French lancer officer named Urban. Having no defence against a man riding down on him with a lance, Ponsonby spurred his horse and galloped off. Unfortunately Ponsonby's horse, much heavier than Urban's mount, became bogged down trying to cross a muddy ploughed field, while Urban's did not. Overtaken, Ponsonby surrendered to Urban and might have survived the battle had not a party of Scots Greys seen his capture and determined to rescue their commanding officer. When Urban noticed the Greys riding towards him, he killed Ponsonby with a lance thrust and rode to meet them. The Greys parted to avoid the deadly reach of the lance, but three were nevertheless unhorsed and run down in less than a minute.[58] Many men in Kempt's division were horrified witnesses to this multiple execution.

Vivian's brigade, holding the extremity of Wellington's left flank, remained motionless; and, in light of Napoleon's dispositions and the disappearance of Marbot's regiment of Jacquinot's lancers into the surrounding woods earlier, this may have reflected sound judgement. Vandeleur, however, had stomached enough and, to his credit, ignored his orders. He led his brigade forward down the slope in support of his trapped compatriots. De Ghigny, unencumbered by the need to observe Wellington's prohibition, had also moved his men forward at speed to the aid of their allies. Leading his light brigade, de Ghigny rode down in a charge which drove a body of lancers before them until it brought him up against a regiment of Lobau's corps. Then, joined by Vandeleur's brigade, de Ghigny pursued the lancers. These men, however, were not Martigue's 3rd but Brô's 4th. De Ghigny described the action:

> '... We caused the whole of the cavalry which was in front
> of us, composed of lancers, to retire until it reached the
> flank of a very numerous battalion [part of Lobau's corps]
> formed in square on rising ground on the further side of
> the valley. Arriving at half distance from this battalion, I
> sounded the "Halt". My skirmishers were engaged with
> theirs, and immediately afterwards they detached a large
> number of skirmishers on foot from their front, assisted by

some companies which were behind them and supported by their cavalry on my left. As the enemy's fire became very vigorous, I ordered the "Retire" by echelon.'59

At the bottom of the valley below La Haye Sainte the Horse Guards, who had held themselves in good order, helped to extricate Somerset's brigade, while the King's Dragoon Guards and the 1st Life Guards rallied behind them. Covered in this way, the Household Brigade, hotly pursued by French cavalry, regained the crest of the ridge where they had begun their charge, and were joined by the remnant of the 2nd Life Guards who had crossed the *Chaussée* with the Earl of Uxbridge.

General Farine's brigade of *cuirassiers*, together with Jacquinot's lancers, swept the valley of Allied cavalry, then advanced up the slope towards Kempt and Bijlandt's men, who had lined the hedgerows and formed squares. However, the skilful withdrawal of Vandeleur and de Ghigny deterred the French cavalry from attempting to assault the Allied infantry formations. Uxbridge, returning to his position after his charge, had sought supports for a follow-up, but, for reasons of which he had no knowledge, these supports had already been committed and those that had returned were spent. In vain Uxbridge tried to rally them, but only a handful heeded his trumpet. He described the reaction that his charge had elicited from Wellington's tail of notables, and referred with becoming modesty to the great achievement his battle instinct had put in train: 'When I returned to our position I met the Duke of Wellington, surrounded by all the 'Corps diplomatique militaire', who had from the high ground witnessed the whole affair. The plain appeared swept clean, and I never saw so joyous a group as was this *"troupe dorée"* [gilded troop]. They thought the battle was over. It is certain that our squadrons went into and over several squares of infantry, and it is not possible to conceive greater confusion and panic [among d'Erlon's infantry] than was exhibited at this moment.'60

When d'Erlon's main force had marched up the slope towards the Allied main line, Durutte's 2 Brigade had advanced to engage the Allied troops occupying the Smohain complex. Château Frischermont was the nearest of the buildings to the French right flank. It was situated on the southern slope of the Smohain valley. The château was much smaller than that of Hougoumont but, like it, was abutted by a formal garden and had a wood interposed between it and the French positions. To the Allied right rear of Frischermont was the hamlet of Smohain, surrounded by broken ground and straddling the Smohain brook. Further right, and closer to the main battlefield, were the farmhouses of La Haye and Papelotte, situated on the northern slope of the Smohain valley. All these buildings were interconnected by a grid of narrow sunken dirt tracks bordered (in 1815) with hedges and trees.

Saxe-Weimar had disposed his brigade of 3,400 men throughout this area:

'The 2nd Battalion No. 28 formed in square; four companies of the 3rd battalion in column behind, both behind the village [of Smohain] and in reserve; the remainder of the troops were posted behind the hedges and other sheltered parts of the ground in the direction of Smouken [Smohain]; four companies of the 1st battalion regiment No. 28 occupied the Chateau of Frischermont, and a company of the 2nd battalion guarded the low-lying road of Smouken leading to the Chateau of M. Beaulieu [Frischermont].'[61]

Some of Jacquinot's troopers had been sent out to reconnoitre this area with a horse battery at about 10 in the morning, but had been driven off. Colonel van Nyevelt described the action as he saw it:

'The attack on the left wing proved only to be an act of reconnoitring, in order to find out whether our left wing joined the Prussian troops, and whether it would be possible to turn our left flank by way of Frischermont. In the first attack the enemy made use of no other troops than the cavalry and artillery, which were easily beaten off, after which these troops returned to regain their position in the army of the enemy.'[62]

However, General Durutte realized that Frischermont was of no tactical importance and could safely be ignored. He decided that his attack should fall principally on Papelotte, as it seemed to be the strong point of the Allied left wing (as La Haye Sainte was to the centre and Hougoumont to the right). Its possession, with La Haye, would allow a strong force to be sent by way of a north-running spur of the Smohain recess around to the rear of the Allied left flank. Also, the Papelotte farmhouse would serve the French well as a strongpoint which, when supported by cannon, would deter the Allied light cavalry from descending the ridge[63] (as indeed de Ghigny would have been deterred from taking the route he did). But to take Papelotte, Durutte knew he would first have to clear the dip around Smohain. For this task he had allocated only one brigade of 1,700 men, unaware that this gave the defenders the great advantage of 2-to-1 odds against their assailants.

At 1.30 p.m., therefore, Durutte, supported by his other brigade acting as a link with Marcognet's division, advanced along the edge of the Smohain dip, hoping to join up with the link brigade to the left of Papelotte, having cleared the dip of the enemy. Descending into the dip, his brigade was supported by Jacquinot's cavalry brigade and three horse batteries, one of Jacquinot's and two detached from Milhaud.[64] Horse batteries were felt to be needed for this attack because the ground was rough and the supporting artillery would have to be pulled up the other side of the dip as the advance proceeded.

Very soon eighteen French artillery pieces had commenced a dropping fire on the Allied positions in and around the hamlet of Smohain, which was the first obstacle in the path of Durutte's planned advance. Saxe-Weimar had placed three of his large, 400-man companies in the hamlet area, arrayed in skirmish order, and taking advantage of every bit of cover available: hedges, trees, buildings and outbuildings. The French skirmishers soon discovered that they were badly outnumbered, and Durutte was soon obliged to begin feeding battalions, in open order, into the several fire fights that had developed with the well-positioned enemy. He also sent four battalions in a flanking movement to the (French) left of the ground in an attempt to assault the Smohain position in flank. Durutte further called up a horse battery to close with the hamlet and begin firing canister into the enemy positions there. Durutte's other two battalions advanced and attacked Papelotte, which was held by Captain Rettenberg's light company of the 3/2nd Nassauers. The Nassauers had neglected to secure one of the gates of the farm and were driven out of it by one of the French battalions.[65]

Despite his numerical disadvantage, Durutte seemed to be succeeding in clearing the Smohain area when all but one regiment of Jacquinot's cavalry support disappeared towards the main battlefield. He rode up out of the dip to find out what was happening. It was then that he saw the destruction of his 1 Brigade, the routed remnant of the rest of d'Erlon's corps, and the wildly careering Allied cavalry. Clearly his position in the Smohain dip was no longer tenable, so he instructed a staff officer, Captain Parentin, to order a withdrawal under cover of his attached artillery and Brô's lancer regiment.

With this turn of the tide, Captain Rettenberg, reinforced by another three companies, the 10th, 11th and 12th of the 3/2nd Nassauers, executed a bayonet charge on the French battalion pulling back before him. The charge routed one battalion, sending it back on to the other accompanying it, and resulted in both bodies breaking and running back to their own lines.[66] The precipitate retreat of these French may have been prompted also by the sight of de Ghigny's light brigade of cavalry moving down the slope in their direction. The rest of Durutte's 2 Brigade withdrew in reasonable order and re-formed behind one of Lobau's battalions while Lobau's men repelled de Ghigny with the help of one of Durutte's foot batteries.

While d'Erlon's main attack had been in progress, Napoleon's attention had been drawn for a time to the diversionary assault on Hougoumont. Concerned at the growing cost in precious men of this diversion, he ordered several howitzer sections from Reille's corps artillery to combine as a battery above Hougoumont. Their place in Reille's artillery batteries was taken by Kellermann's other horse battery.[67] The howitzers began shelling the château with inflammable carcasse and it was soon ablaze, the soldiers within desperately trying to maintain their positions while avoiding being burned alive or buried under collapsing roof beams and debris. Wellington, observing the conflagration from his position behind an elm tree near the central crossroads, wrote to Colonel Francis Hepburn who, with his eight companies of the 2/2nd Coldstream Foot Guards, had taken command of Hougoumont: 'I see that the fire has communicated from the haystack to the roof of the Chateau. You must however still keep your men in those parts to which the fire does not reach. Take care that no men are lost by the falling-in of the roof or floors. After they have both fallen in, occupy the ruined walls inside of the Garden; particularly if it should be possible for the enemy to pass through the embers in the inside of the House.'[68] It must have been difficult to order men to remain in such imminent danger, but needs must, and Wellington gave sound advice to Hepburn on preserving his men from injury by fire.

On the Allied left, the unexpected rout of the French assault at this early stage in the battle had created a logistical problem: how to deal with about 3,000 prisoners? As senior surviving general on the left, following Picton's death, Kempt had responsibility for them, but could ill afford to detach enough men to take the prisoners to the rear. Wellington sent General Lambert's brigade forward from reserve to reinforce the left flank and ease Kempt's predicament.

The escorting to the rear of prisoners and wounded was a significant drain on the effective fighting strength of a unit. They had necessarily to be taken back by healthy effective soldiers who would be sorely missed in the line. Some wounded officers – rank having its privileges – were carried to the field hospital in blankets by as many as six fit men.[69] This practice was forbidden, but often honoured in the breach. This haemorrhage of effective manpower highlighted a deficiency in the organization of the Allied armies. Unlike the French army, they had no stretcher-bearers or ambulances, and the non-combatant auxiliaries such as bandsmen and camp-followers were inadequate to the task.

Attached to each unit was an assistant surgeon, equipped with dressings and tourniquets, who would administer a crude first aid to as many as he could, until his supplies ran out or until he himself became a casualty. This small measure did nothing to stem the flow of able-bodied men helping their wounded comrades to the rear.[70] The same *esprit de corps*, or fellow-feeling, which could often make the difference between victory and defeat, would also motivate the unscathed to concentrate on the well-being of their wounded comrades at the expense of the larger issues which preoccupied their commanders.

Kempt apparently discussed the problem of the prisoners with Perponcher. In the light of Wellington's positive order that no British officer or soldier should leave the ranks, even to help the wounded, it was decided that it would be best to make up prisoner escorts from among the Netherlands Militias. To take 3,000 prisoners back through the great forest of

Soignies to Brussels would have required at least 400 infantry, as van Nyevelt recounted: 'Many non-commissioned officers and soldiers having volunteered to escort the large number of prisoners we had made, it was found necessary to reorganize the different corps on the spot, which was immediately attended to.'[71] This depletion fell on Bijlandt's brigade and, on top of its more than 800 battle casualties incurred in bearing the brunt of d'Erlon's massive attack, reduced the unit to the size of two small battalions.[72] The prisoner foot escort might have had trouble controlling prisoners, especially if they were not dispirited by capture, who outnumbered them more than seven to one. As was customary a detachment of cavalry accompanied the party. Colonel Muter, who had assumed command of the remainder of the Union Brigade, delegated the duty to some Inniskilling Dragoons who had been only lightly mauled in action: '... A squadron of the Inniskillings was sent to the rear (Brussels, I believe) with the Prisoners ...'[73]

Upon its arrival at Brussels towards evening, this large body of prisoners, marching in formation and flanked by Netherlander Militiamen and Inniskilling Dragoons, was taken correctly to be a French column, but at first was thought to be under French command. The city alarm was sounded and a predictable panic ensued. Sergeant Costello of the 95th, who had been wounded on the 16th at Quatre Bras and had been evacuated to Brussels, to the designated holding area for non-commissioned British wounded, witnessed the confusion: '... It was about six o'clock in the evening of the 18th. I was entering a large square, and gazing on some hundreds of wounded men who were stretched out on some straw, when an alarm was given that the French were entering the city. In a moment all was in an uproar; the inhabitants running in all directions, closing their doors, and some Belgian troops in the square, in great confusion; loading my rifle, I joined a party of the 81st, who remained on duty here during the action. The alarm however, was occasioned by the appearance of about 1,700–1,800 French prisoners, under escort of some of our Dragoons.'[74]

In the reorganization of Wellington's left to make good for the loss a further 400 Netherlanders, on top of the 800 lost dead and wounded, Lambert's 'Peninsula' men attempted to fill the gap, but as Kincaid recalled: 'I was told it was very ridiculous, at the moment, to see the number of vacant spots that were left nearly along the whole line, where a great part of the dark dressed foreign troops had stood, intermixed with the British, when the action began.'[75] From above La Haye Sainte Sir Augustus Frazer had observed how what remained of Bijlandt's brigade had held post: '... The Belgian troops, though they yielded [gave ground tactically], yet returned to their posts'.[76] Bijlandt's brigade together with the 1/95th and the 92nd had received d'Erlon's hammer-blow, had not broken, but had paid a price. General Picton was dead, General Perponcher had two horses shot from under him and General Bijlandt, Colonel van Zuylen van Nyevelt, and three battalion commanders were wounded. Bijlandt had been wounded badly enough to have to pass command to Lieutenant-Colonel de

Jongh (he had already been wounded at Quatre Bras), who managed to control the rump of the brigade by having himself roped to his saddle. Almost every officer of the 92nd had been killed or taken to the rear wounded. Sergeant Robinson explained: '... When we resumed our old station, we found that we had lost a great many in the late affair ... We had no time as yet to ascertain the amount of loss, and was amissing, and that I was left in command of two companies, as we lost all the subaltern officers on the 16th ...'[77] Kempt's brigade had as yet suffered only light casualties because of his advantageous position. The remainder of Pack's division had seen little action, but all had suffered from the incessant cannonade, which had recommenced in full throat.

A pause in the action followed the clearing of the valley and the withdrawal from the assault of the Smohain complex. Napoleon needed some time to revise his plans, and his men needed more time to regroup, especially among d'Erlon's scrambled corps. Companies and regiments had become thoroughly intermingled in the rout. Brigade formations had ceased to exist. Specialist companies such as the flanking *voltigeurs* and grenadiers would be easier to re-form, but the milling masses of rank and file would take time to sort out. Many had also lost their weapons in their flight.

Regimental staff officers were staking out assembly areas and trying frantically to form their units on them. Lobau's small corps had moved to the extreme right flank of the French line to form a barrier against interference by any Prussian force. The only formed infantry immediately available on Napoleon's right flank was the Corps of the Imperial Guard, but Napoleon would not commit his only reserve to a second assault on Wellington's left. And on the right he had only 1½ uncommitted divisions: Bachelu's and one brigade of Foy's. However, Napoleon dared not show his weakness to Wellington by calling off the draining, purposeless attack on Hougoumont. For the moment, all he had with which to maintain pressure on Wellington was his artillery and his cavalry. He knew that his present situation, rebuffed with the loss of precious time and the prospect of heavy Allied reinforcement arriving at any time, required something exceptional.

Across the valley, the man who had bought Wellington the time he needed with the spectacular rout of an army corps by two brigades of cavalry, was trying to reorganize the remnant of his brigades. Losses of horses to musketry and grape shot were the greatest problem; without adequate remounts Uxbridge could form only a scant three squadrons, and they were a motley assortment from a variety of units. It is sad to reflect that Uxbridge, who had done so much to win the day at Waterloo, brooded for years afterwards over the terrible losses his men had suffered and was haunted by the regret that if he had not led that charge he might have been able to restrain the supports from joining in the mêlée, thus avoiding their losses from the French cavalry's counter-attack. What Uxbridge did not realize was that the sacrifice had not been in vain: the charge of his men had done incalculable harm to the carefully calculated and almost successful plan of one of the greatest captains of history.[78]

CHAPTER 13

18 June: 3.30 to 6.00 p.m.

'But if you argue that the fury with which the horses are driven to charge an enemy makes them consider a pike no more than a spur, I answer that even though a horse has begun to charge, he will slow down when he draws near the pikes and, when he begins to feel their points, will either stand stock-still or wheel off to the right or left. To convince yourself of this, see if you can ride a horse against a wall; I fancy you will find very few, if any – however spirited they may be – that can be made to do that.' – Niccolo Machiavelli, *The Art of War*, 1521.

Napoleon gazed across the strangely empty battlefield from La Belle Alliance. To his left he saw the debris of battle, human, animal and other, littered around Hougoumont which was burning fiercely and from which came a continuous rattle of musketry. Ahead, towards the Allied centre, the field was empty of movement, save for the wounded and dying men and horses that disfigured the ground. To his near right he saw d'Erlon's mob of men, some 10,000 to 12,000, with only one of Quiot's brigades in any semblance of order. D'Erlon would need at least an hour to get his troops sufficiently organized for them to be ready to fight again. And, somewhere beyond Lobau on the far right flank, in the hazy wooded heights above Smohain were the Prussians. At this point a messenger from Grouchy, Major le Fresnaye, stepped forward to hand the Emperor a dispatch which Grouchy had written at 11 a.m. from Walhain. Le Fresnaye had found Napoleon earlier, during Uxbridge's counter-attack, but had been kept waiting until now because the Emperor was too busy to receive messages. Grouchy's report informed Napoleon that:

'The I, II and III Prussian Corps, under Blücher, are marching towards Brussels. Two of these corps marched through Sart-à-Walhain, or passed just to the right of the place; they marched in three columns roughly keeping abreast of each other ... One Corps coming from Liège [Bülow's IV], effected its concentration with those that had fought at Fleurus (herewith a [Prussian] requisition in proof of this statement). Some Prussians in my front are directing their march towards the plain of the Chyse which is near the Louvain [to Namur] road, and some 2½ leagues [6 to 7 miles] from this town.

'It would seem as though they intend to concentrate there so as to give battle to their pursuers, or finally to join hands with Wellington; such was the reports spread by their officers, who, in their usual boasting spirit, pretend

313

that they only left the field of battle on June 16 in order to ensure their junction with the English army at Brussels. This evening I shall have massed my troops at Wavre, and thus shall find myself between the Prussian Army and Wellington, who, I presume, is retreating before Your Majesty. I need further instructions as to what Your Majesty desires me to do next. The country between Wavre and the plain of the Chyse is rough and broken and in some parts marshy.

'By the Vilvorde road I shall reach Brussels before the troops who have halted at La Chyse. Deign, Sire, to send me your orders so that I can receive them before commencing tomorrow's operations ...'[1]

Grouchy's news, and the enclosed Prussian requisition chit issued to a local peasant, confirmed what Napoleon already knew. Blücher was marching on him with all his men. Grouchy's missing Prussian corps (Bülow's), was already to his knowledge at Chapelle St-Lambert. Napoleon was certain, from his experience of battle with Blücher in two previous campaigns, that he would be moving every man he could towards Mont St-Jean. The rest of Grouchy's letter served only to inform Napoleon that Grouchy had little idea of Blücher's true intentions and was therefore irrelevant. Grouchy's indication that he fully expected Blücher, or part of the Prussian force, to turn on him reflected in part Grouchy's own respect for Blücher's known ability to let a pursuer come on hurriedly and in extended order, then turn him and defeat him in detail, as he had done to Macdonald at the Katzbach in 1813 and, by night, to Marmont at Laon in 1814. Hence Grouchy's expressed fear that the Prussians might concentrate 'so as to give battle to their pursuers'. This phrase might have told Napoleon all he needed to know about the pace at which Grouchy was likely to proceed. And in fairness, the previous day Napoleon, in his orders to his Marshal of the Right Wing, had emphasized the need to be wary of such a Prussian tactic, and to avoid risking his command by following too closely at Blücher's heels. He had stressed the need for vigilance, especially at night, when following a force three times his size: '... choose each evening a good military position, which has several avenues of retreat'. Grouchy, remembering the dressing-down Napoleon had given to Ney, one of the original Marshals, at Charleroi for not following the letter of his orders, would carry out his with punctiliousness.

Napoleon did not reply to Grouchy's dispatch, as he had already covered all of Grouchy's queries in the dispatch he had sent the Marshal an hour and a half earlier. This was the dispatch which had appended to it the important postscript: 'So do not lose a moment in drawing near to us, and effecting a junction with us, in order to crush Bülow whom you will catch in the very act of concentrating [with Wellington].'

At this moment Napoleon had other pressing concerns. Reille had 1½ divisions tied up around Hougoumont. These could not easily be disengaged because they had become dispersed in the woods and environs of the château. This left only Bachelu's division and one brigade of Foy's with which to hold his entire left between Hougoumont and the *Chaussée* at La Belle Alliance. On his right, between the inn and Lobau's position, he had only one brigade of Quiot's division in good order. Napoleon had begun the battle with 4,000 men and 90 pieces of artillery more than Wellington could field. With d'Erlon's reverse, he had lost double that difference in men, killed, wounded or taken prisoner. Further, to block an expected thrust by Blücher, he had placed Lobau to the far right with 10,000 men and 28 guns. If Wellington were to launch a general counter-attack now, Napoleon would only have 13,000 men in good order[2] and the 10,000 to 12,000 disorganized troops of d'Erlon's with which to meet it. And d'Erlon's routed men would break again if attacked before they had re-formed. But among his 13,000 effectives were the men of the Imperial Guard whom he dared not commit to battle except at a decisive point, they being his only remaining reserve and needed as a rearguard in case Wellington did attack, forcing Napoleon to fall back to consolidate his army. In the meantime he sought to mask his predicament with an artillery barrage, while he brought his military genius to bear on the problem of revising his plan in light of the new conditions. He was too weak to defend; he would have to attack. Accordingly he ordered Ney to launch an assault on the farmhouse of La Haye Sainte. Ney, in turn, ordered Charlet to carry out the order using Quiot's 2 Brigade.

Meanwhile, Wellington, believing it imperative to preserve his line of retreat, had no intention of calling for Prince Frederick to march to join him on his right. If Blücher did not arrive in time and in decisive strength, Wellington would need Prince Frederick where he was. So he did not exploit Napoleon's weakness. The Duke's plan of battle did not involve any movement from his defensive position. He intended to stand where he was until Blücher arrived to take Napoleon in flank. Wellington had no knowledge of Napoleon's distress and still feared lest it be the Emperor's intention to turn the Allied right flank, severing Wellington's line of retreat. He was not going to make any 'false movement' in front of Napoleon, whom he had never before met in battle. He would content himself with disbursing some of his ample right flank reserves forward to counter any turning movement by the French around Hougoumont, and continuing to feed reserves into the first line as necessary to maintain its integrity.

General Lambert's brigade of three battalions was placed in the second line of the Allied left, together with the two reduced Netherlands battalions. Kempt's and Pack's brigades now formed the first line of the left. Lambert sent the 1/95th forward again to assault the gravel pit and knoll, now held by the French, and General Perponcher rode over to Smohain to assume overall command of his 2 Brigade. Major Baring returned to La

Haye Sainte from the Allied main line where he had remained during d'Erlon's attack, without having requested of his brigade commander, Colonel Baron von Ompteda, any entrenching tools, pioneers or ammunition for his beleaguered men. Fortunately, however, Wellington had sent to reinforce the farmhouse garrison the three companies of the 1/2nd Nassauers of The Netherlands' 2nd Division who had been driven from the Hougoumont wood to the hollow way behind the château. They, and two companies of the KGL 1st Light Battalion, would support their German-speaking comrades holding the farmhouse and the barn without doors.

When Napoleon had sent Lobau to the far right he had also moved down his Imperial Guard infantry to La Belle Alliance, simply to appear to be part of the French line, as part of his efforts to conceal the weakness of his position. This move left only the 1st Grenadier Regiment and the 1/1st *Chasseur* Regiment, the oldest of the Old Guard infantry, still back between Rossomme and Le Caillou. In the interim Ney struggled manfully to make bricks out of straw. He detached one regiment of Bachelu's division to form an extended skirmish line between La Haye Sainte and Hougoumont, and sent three battalions of Donzelot's division forward on the right (eastern) side of the *Chaussée*. Ney prepared to lead Quiot's brigade in the attack on the farmhouse, and the whole advance was to be supported by Farine's *cuirassiers* riding behind to screen the nudity of the remaining French line.[3] On the extreme of the French right flank, Durutte held the angle of the main line facing Wellington and Lobau's line facing the expected line of approach of the Prussians. As part of the general French cannonade, he used three horse batteries to keep up a steady bombardment on the Allied troops in the Smohain dip.

The defences of La Haye Sainte farmhouse left much to be desired. Although some barricading had been accomplished, as a whole the buildings remained vulnerable. The barn, which led directly to the inner courtyard, had no outer door and nothing had been found with which to block the opening. One of the defenders, a Scotsman, Lieutenant George Graeme, of the 2nd Light Battalion, KGL, later wrote: 'We had no loopholes excepting three great apertures, which we made with difficulty when we were told in the morning that we were to defend the farm. Our Pioneers had been sent to Hougoumont the evening before. We had no scaffolding, nor any means of making any, having burnt the carts &c. Our loop holes, if they may be termed thus, were on a level with the road outside, and later in the day the enemy got possession of the one near the pond and fired in on us. This they also did during the first attack on the roadside.'[4] Graeme also related how the men had to use the small piggery roof as a firing platform and, unable to fire over the courtyard walls, were reduced to balancing on the barn roof to get a line of fire. The Nassauers, arrived from Hougoumont, emulated what they had seen done there and ripped the tiles off the slanting roofs and knocked out window frames to create a firing platform from the house overlooking the walls.[5]

The French cannonade may have been intended only to put up a bold front, but it also caused great damage. The thousands of rounds fired into Wellington's static array caused massive casualties and was terribly demoralizing. The sudden and capricious extinction and maiming of men by round shot was vividly described by young Ensign Leeke of the 51st Foot:

> 'The standing to be cannonaded, and having nothing else to do, is about the most unpleasant thing that can happen to soldiers in an engagement ... I do not exactly know the rapidity with which the cannon-balls fly, but I think that two seconds elapsed from the time I saw this shot leave the gun until it struck the front face of the square [he was in]. It did not strike the four men in the rear of whom I was standing, but the poor fellows on their right. It was fired with some elevation, and struck the front man about the knees, and coming to the ground under the feet of the rear man of the four, whom it severely wounded, it rose and, passing within an inch or two of the Colour pole ... The two men in the first and second rank fell outward, I fear they did not survive; the two others fell within the square. The rear man made a considerable outcry on being wounded.'[6]

And as one battalion of the 40th Foot in Lambert's brigade moved into position one veteran soldier recalled the march '... up to action in open column', when an exploding shell reduced two men to a bloody pulp and hurled the veteran '... at least two yards in the air', but left him only shaken. The effect on a recruit nearby had been paralyzing: he lay on the ground, rigid with fear, and would not budge regardless of words or blows. The veteran left him with a contemptuous remark: '... it's the smell of this little powder that has caused your illness.' Wellington, in an effort to reduce the rate of casualties among his exposed troops, ordered the infantry to retire 'one hundred paces', but this had almost no effect on the intensity of the barrage, while it had the disadvantage of leaving the Allied artillerymen, then almost beyond the range of the infantry's protective fire, feeling isolated.

As Ney's advance went forward, Bachelu's regiment, marching in column towards Hougoumont, intending to turn right facing Wellington's front and open up into skirmish order, was perceived by the Allies as yet another assault on Hougoumont. Any threat to Hougoumont caused Wellington grave concern because its loss would threaten his right and his route to the Scheldt. Thus, before the column of Quiot's brigade, moving behind the skirmishers to attack La Haye Sainte, could reach the wood to turn right into line to face Wellington's centre, a large volume of Allied artillery fire was brought down on it, causing very many casualties. The other French skirmish line, approaching the knoll and the gravel pit, fared no better. They came under concentrated rifle fire from the 1/95th and the flank companies of Kempt's and Pack's brigades. Quiot's already thinned and demoralized brigade also were subjected to heavy rifle fire. A terrible fusillade was poured into their ranks by riflemen occupying the farm. They were armed with sighted rifles that could be aimed and could bring the attackers under effective fire at a greater distance than could muskets. Quiot's men were dwindling so rapidly that before they had got halfway past the orchard they gave up the assault and retired.[7]

The Prussians, meanwhile, had been advancing since daybreak towards Mont St-Jean. Bülow had put 15 Brigade – his strongest – in the van, followed by 16 and 13, then his reserve artillery and cavalry, and 14 Brigade as rearguard. All the corps baggage had been sent to Louvain in keeping with Bülow's order: 'No carts will be allowed in the columns.'[8] Bülow advanced from Wavre by way of Point du Jour to St-Lambert, and was concentrated there by 3 p.m. Blücher and his staff left Wavre at 11 a.m., having ordered II Corps to follow IV Corps, and I Corps to advance by way of Point du Jour to Geneval, then by the Ohain valley to arrive on Wellington's left.

The roads between Wavre and Mont St-Jean were atrocious, even by the low standards of the day. Lieutenant-Colonel von Reiche, Chief of Staff of I Corps, later wrote: 'Our march to the battlefield was extremely difficult. Sunken lanes cut through deep ravines had to be negotiated; almost impenetrable forest grew on each side, so that there was no question of avoiding the road, and progress was very slow, all the more so because in many places men and horses could get through only one at a time. The column became very split up and wherever the ground allowed it, the heads of columns had to halt so as to give time for the detachments to collect themselves again.'[9]

Blücher had hoped that Thielemann's III Corps would also advance to Mont St-Jean, but before two of his brigades had crossed the bridges through Wavre, elements of Exelmans' cavalry were sighted. Thielemann halted, feeling vulnerable with his flank visible to the enemy. He sent a rider to Blücher and Gneisenau with a letter asking for orders in light of this new factor.

Blücher and Gneisenau, meanwhile, had sent two staff officers, Count Nostitz and Colonel von Pfuel, with a strong escort to scout the battlefield and its approaches. These officers reported that they had seen no enemy in the valley of the Lasne between the end of Paris Wood and the hamlet of Maransart. Blücher at once rode there with his staff. Count Nostitz related Blücher's reaction to his view of the battle in progress: 'The Prince, with the eye of a Hawk, surveyed the entire battlefield, saw clearly the way the fighting was going, and devoted his main attention to the dispositions of the English batteries.'[10] Gneisenau was convinced that Napoleon had fixed Wellington in position. He therefore advised Blücher to abandon the idea of giving heavy support to Wellington; and instead send into Wellington's left flank only the last corps to arrive, Zeithen's. Gneisenau argued in favour of taking advantage of the great opportunity of attacking Napoleon's right rear flank, cutting the Charleroi road, and entrapping and annihilating Napoleon's army. To the counter argument that at the approach of strong Prussian forces arriving on that quarter Napoleon would divert his main force against them as they came up piecemeal, Gneisenau replied '... that, on the contrary, I am convinced that Napoleon would then use his entire strength and effort in an attempt to breach the English line of battle and would bring to bear upon us only such forces as were needed to hold us up long enough to allow him to deliver his decisive blow against the English.'[11] Blücher concurred, but where Gneisenau was calculating, Blücher was passionate: he burned to accomplish a revenge, both personal and national, on Napoleon: revenge for Ligny, for the loss of Saxony, for Jena and for a thousand humiliations suffered from the French.

Gneisenau sent Thielemann specific orders that he was to hold Wavre with III Corps at all costs, but that in the event of his being forced to withdraw he should retire in the direction of Louvain, drawing Grouchy after him and away from the main Prussian army. Before receipt of these orders, Thielemann had pushed his 9 Brigade forward to warn him of the approach of Grouchy's main body. Blücher remarked to Gneisenau before the order was dispatched: '... it matters not if Thielemann and his men stand and die to the last man, as long as they keep the French away from Napoleon'.[12]

Napoleon was unaware of how close Blücher and his army were, but he had nevertheless decided on his course of action. His original plan ruined, he no longer had sufficient infantry to use decisively against Wellington. He could not use Lobau's corps because the Prussians could appear at any time. His artillery was, he thought, holding Wellington immobile, but he could not expect it to be too long before his enemy realized his weakness.

At this point Napoleon still had time to withdraw his army behind his mass of cavalry, then use Lobau's fresh troops as his rearguard and send word to Grouchy to withdraw and join him. This was the sensible strategic option in the circumstance; and it is what Napoleon probably would have done had conditions been as they had been in 1814 when he was still absolute ruler of the French. But now, in 1815, he had been back on the throne for less than three months, and with constitutional limitations to his power. He needed a quick, resounding victory, with its political repercussions, to maintain the aura of invincibility which had been rekindled on his march from Fréjus to Paris. To withdraw ignominiously back into France before Wellington and Blücher, inveterate enemies of his rule, and be obliged to fight a repetition of the demoralizing 1814 campaign on French soil, would encourage Austria and Russia to press on and join in at the kill.

There were also the Chambers to consider. In his need to harness the strength of republican sentiment rampant on his return, Napoleon had agreed to a constitutional monarchy. Now, in his absence from Paris, his enemies, such as Fouché[13] were using the new liberal freedom of the Chamber to foment opposition. A retreat, however orderly, would give further ammunition to political enemies in Paris. They would be able to adopt the Allied line of persuasion that it was only Napoleon personally who presented an obstacle to peace.[14] As Napoleon saw it, everything depended on Brussels: if he could defeat Wellington, causing Blücher to withdraw, and rush forward to capture Brussels, all would be well.

Surely, he reasoned, Grouchy would understand from his last dispatch the need to march his 33,000 men quickly to Napoleon's right flank. Once they came between him and Blücher the Prussians would have little choice but to retreat. Napoleon, the greatest general of the age, had made his decision; setting aside his incomparable experience as a soldier, he acted as Napoleon the Emperor, putting the political considerations before those of the military.

The time was now approximately 3.30 p.m. There was only one option available in the time to hand and Napoleon had already decided to use it. The last time he had been in this predicament had been on 8 February 1807 at Eylau in East Prussia, when he had been fighting the Russians in the middle of winter. There, too, he had lost one corps, routed by the enemy, and had nothing with which to plug the gap except his Guard, although he dared not use it. Instead, at Eylau Napoleon had sent in Murat with all his cavalry. Murat had smashed through the Russian centre, through two lines (echelons) of infantry, had broken six squares and captured sixteen standards. Napoleon had followed the first attack by sending in his Mounted Guard as support. They helped Murat break the third and final reserve, returning left and right and slaughtering the Russian infantry on the way.[15]

In accordance with the Emperor's new plan, Ney was ordered to prepare Milhaud's *cuirassiers* to attack the Allied line. Napoleon himself ordered the Grand Battery to intensify its fire on the English centre. General Count von Alten, commanding the British 3rd Division, said: 'Never had the most veteran soldiers heard such a cannonade.'[16]

Marshal Ney quickly sent his aides to gather all the cavalry to the right of the crossroads – Milhaud's corps and Lefebvre-Desnouëttes' Light Cavalry Division of the Guard – and to form them on the ground between and behind Hougoumont and La Haye Sainte. General Farine was about to move off with his two regiments in compliance with this order, but his divisional commander, General Delort, halted him. Ney rode over to see what was causing the delay, and Delort told Ney: 'We receive no orders, but from Count Milhaud.'[17] This was standard procedure, for Napoleon had specified in his orders of 16 June to Ney and to all corps commanders when he had given Ney and Grouchy command of each wing that: '*General officers*

Above: The remnants of the Household Cavalry and Union Brigade can be seen holding the gap between the corners of the squares. In the distance, General van Trip brings up his heavy cavalry through the smoke and pushes the French over the crest (detail from the panorama by Louis Moulin, Author's collection).

Below: The French cuirassiers attack a corner of a Nassau square and hack away at this vulnerable point. Several Nassau Grenadiers are cut down but always the gap is plugged from the rear. Behind can be seen the Prince of Orange leading up the Netherlands cavalry to assist (detail from the panorama by Louis Moulin, Author's collection).

Above: Desperate, the Militia battalion of von Kruse's contingent hold their formation surrounded on all sides. In the background through the smoke can be seen the farm of Mont St. Jean, used as a field hospital throughout the day (detail from the panorama by Louis Moulin, Author's collection).

Below: Napoleon, in desperation to break Wellington's centre, commits the Imperial Guard Cavalry to add to the attack. Napoleon on his white horse and with his escort can be seen in the distance (detail from the panorama by Louis Moulin, Author's collection).

Above: As the Guard Lancers attack, Reille's infantry can be seen attacking the vulnerable barn entrance behind the farm of La Haye Sainte (detail from the panorama by Louis Moulin, Author's collection).
Below: Near Hougoumont, Foy's infantry prepare to assault the Château (detail from the panorama by Louis Moulin, Author's collection).

Top left: As the cavalry clear the 'hollow way' its length can be discerned (detail from the panorama by Louis Moulin, Author's collection).

Above: Piró's horse battery unlimbers behind Hougoumont near the Allied line. (detail from the panorama by Louis Moulin, Author's collection).

Left: The French prepare an all-out assault on La Haye Sainte, the key to Wellington's position, at 1.30 p.m. (Author's collection).

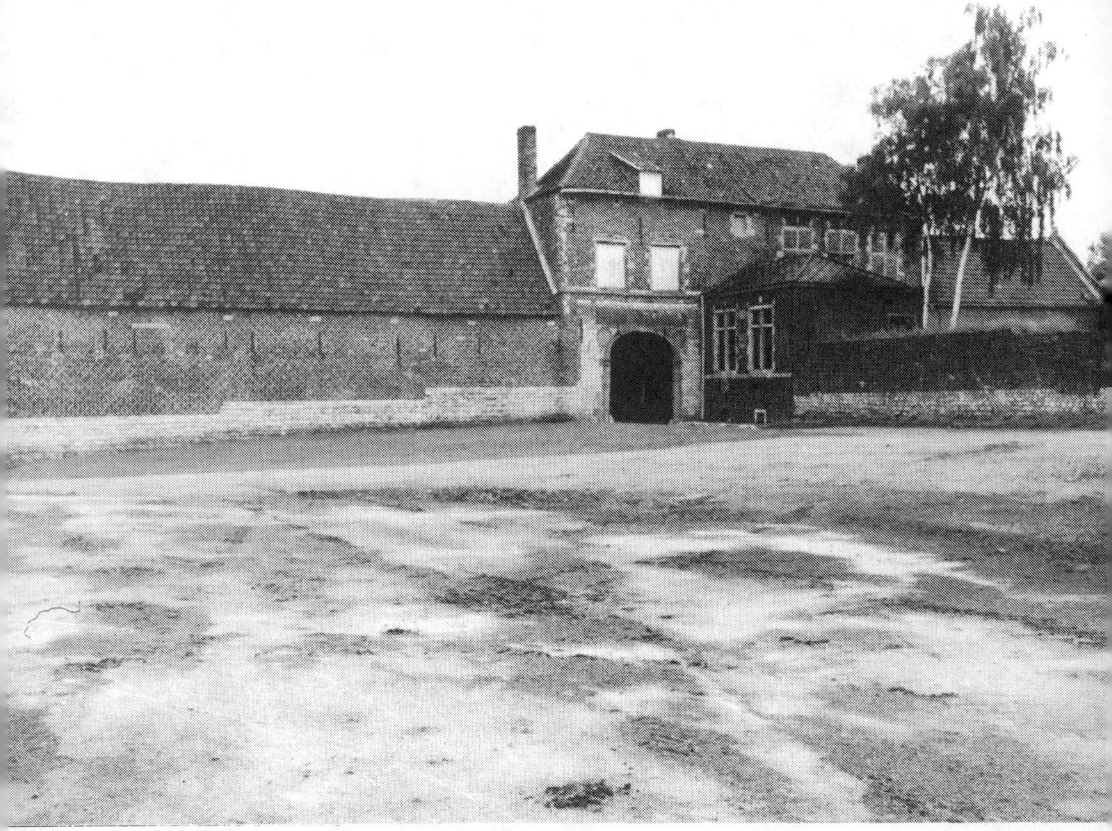

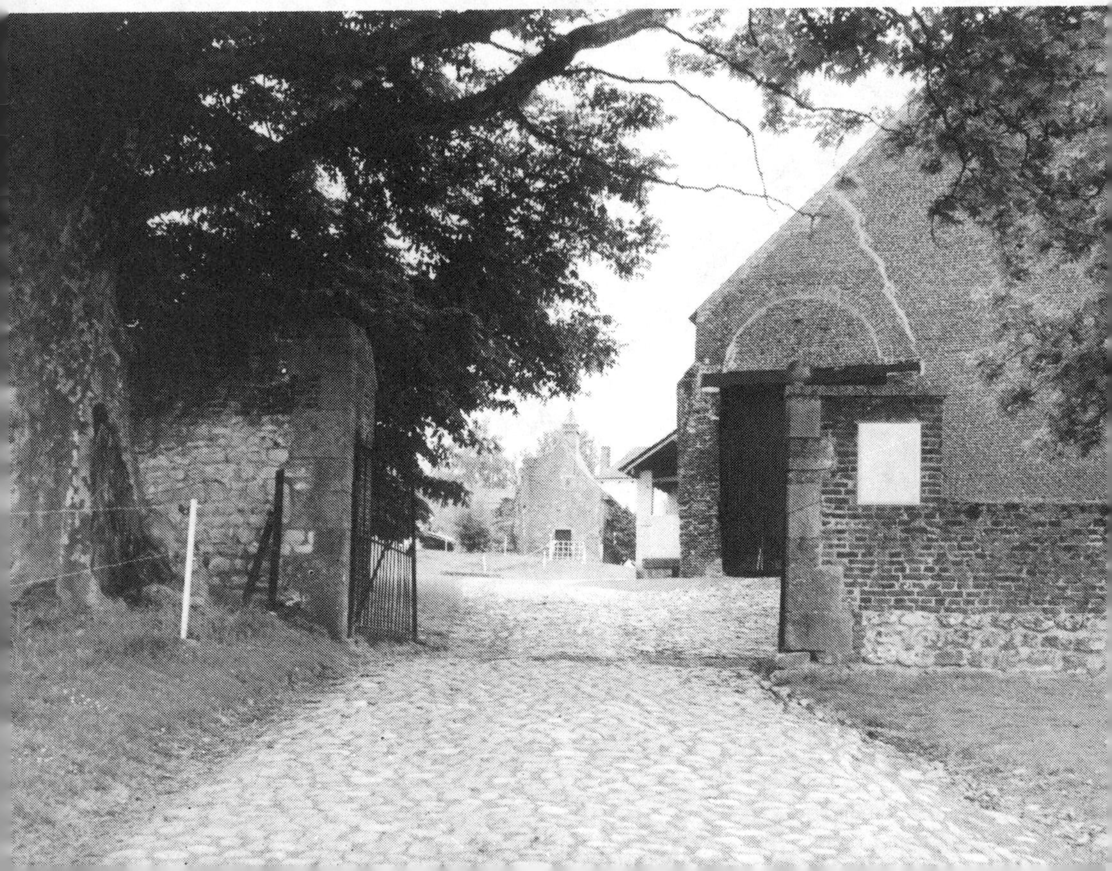

Left: The north gate of Hougoumont as it is today; the ruined chapel and the building above the south gate are visible (Richard Ellis collection).

Right: The south gate of Hougoumont. The extension with the plaque on it was not there in 1815. The Guards, Nassaus and, later, the Brunswickers fired down from the now blocked-up windows, from improvised firing platforms made by ripping holes in the roof and from the attic. (Richard Ellis collection).

Right: The south gate today from the site of the entrance of the burnt-down Château's right wing. To its right is the outbuilding used by the gardener for his implements etc., and to the right are the stables (Richard Ellis collection).

Left: The south gate of Hougoumont, scene of attempts all day to gain an entry. This is the view from where the woods would have begun in 1815 (Richard Ellis collection).

Right: The eastern side of Château Hougoumont as it is today, clearly showing the strength of the buttressed walls. The lower wall near the north gate was considerably higher in 1815. Note that this side of the Château afforded virtually no firing positions, so that here Jérôme and Foy's divisions could have formed up in relative safety to threaten Wellington's right. (Richard Ellis collection).

Above: La Belle Alliance today (Richard Ellis collection).
Below: La Haye Sainte farmhouse today. Note the wall is missing near the great barn; it had been battered and reduced in height by artillery fire in Ney's final assault and was demolished in the 1960s. (Richard Ellis collection).
Top right: Inside La Haye Sainte courtyard, showing the dovecote and outbuildings on the road-side of the wall, which were used as firing platforms (Richard Ellis collection).
Bottom right: La Haye Sainte courtyard, looking through the small gate adjacent to the great barn the doors of which had been burnt the night before. The French gained entry here during the garrison's withdrawal to the house (Richard Ellis collection).

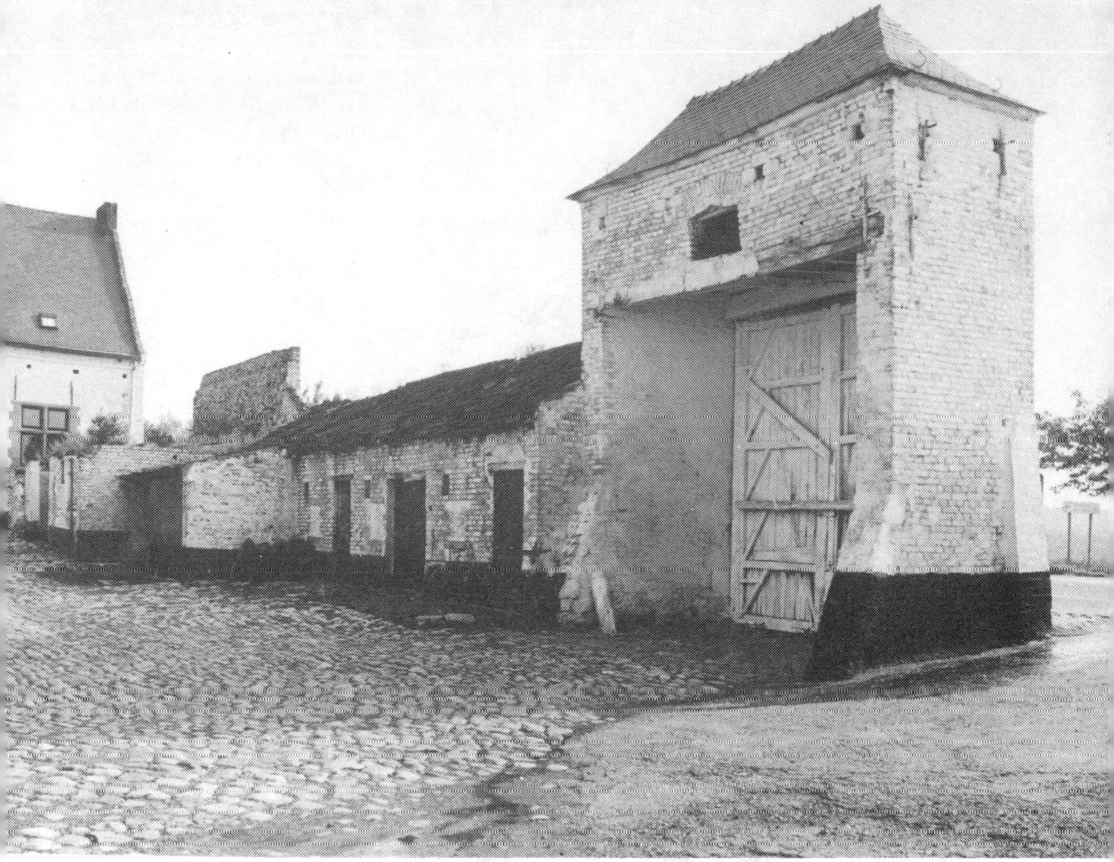

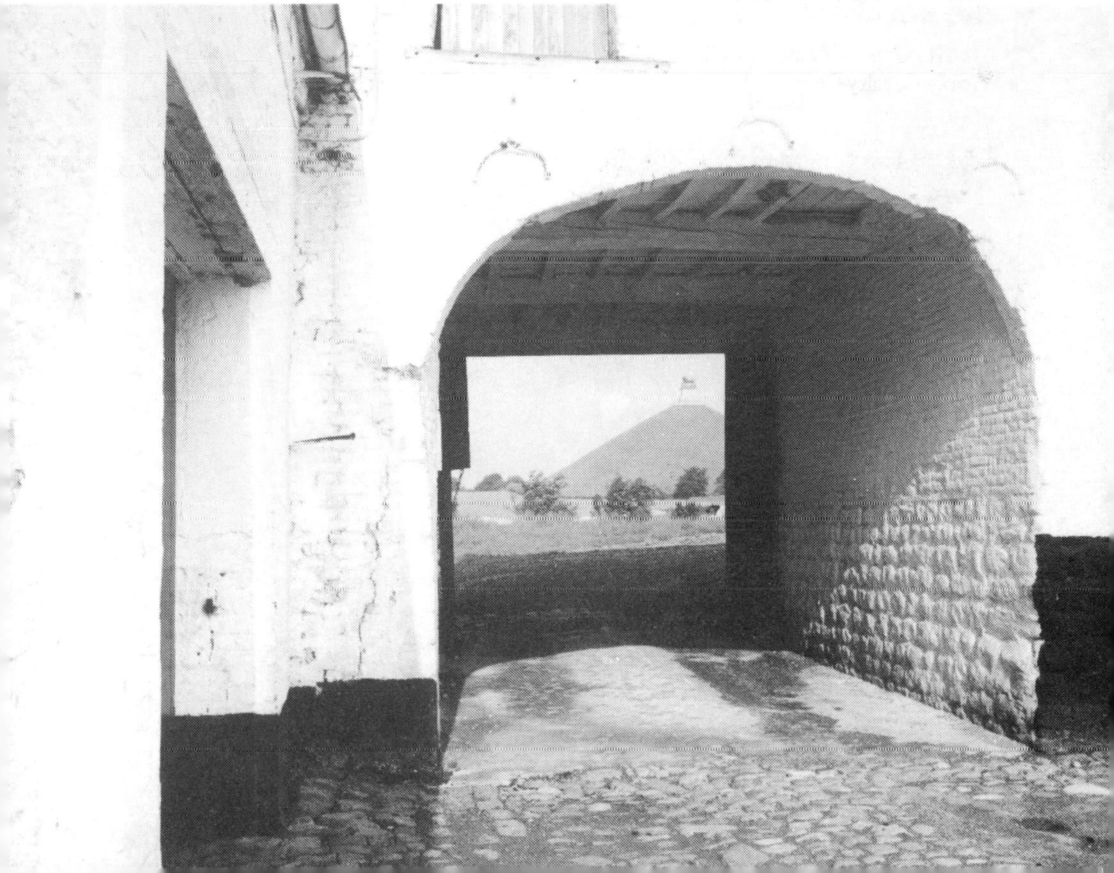

Right: The Old Guard goes forward at Waterloo; they are advancing in echelon of regimental squares from their right. A horse artillery section of two guns can be seen between this and the square to its right (Author's collection).

Above: General François Kellermann, commander of III Heavy Cavalry Corps.

Right: The entrance to the farm of Mont St. Jean today (Author's collection).

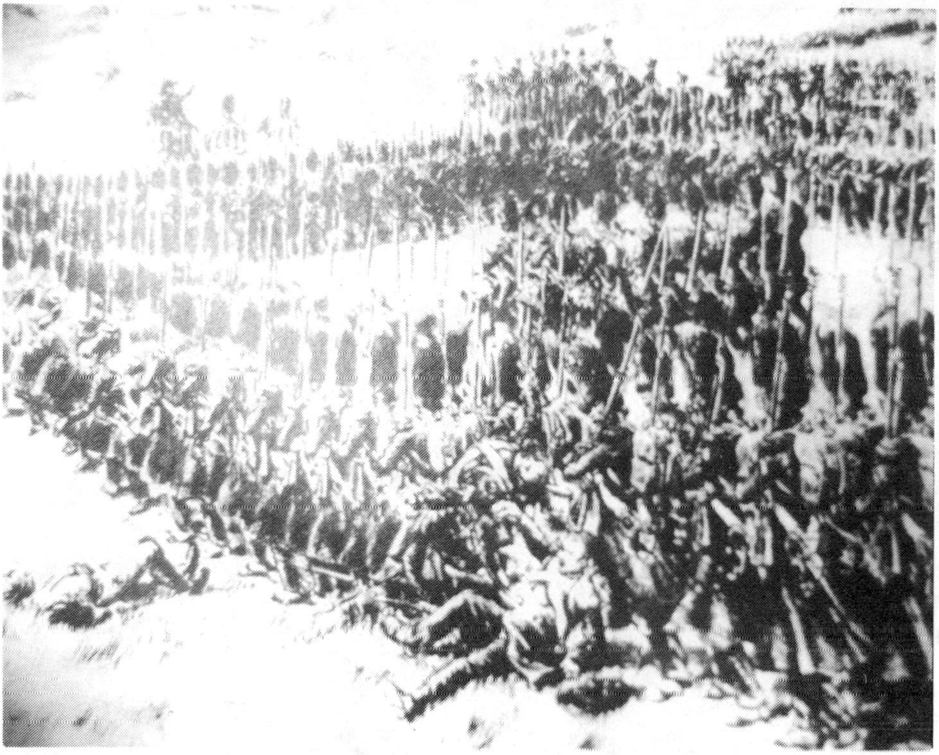

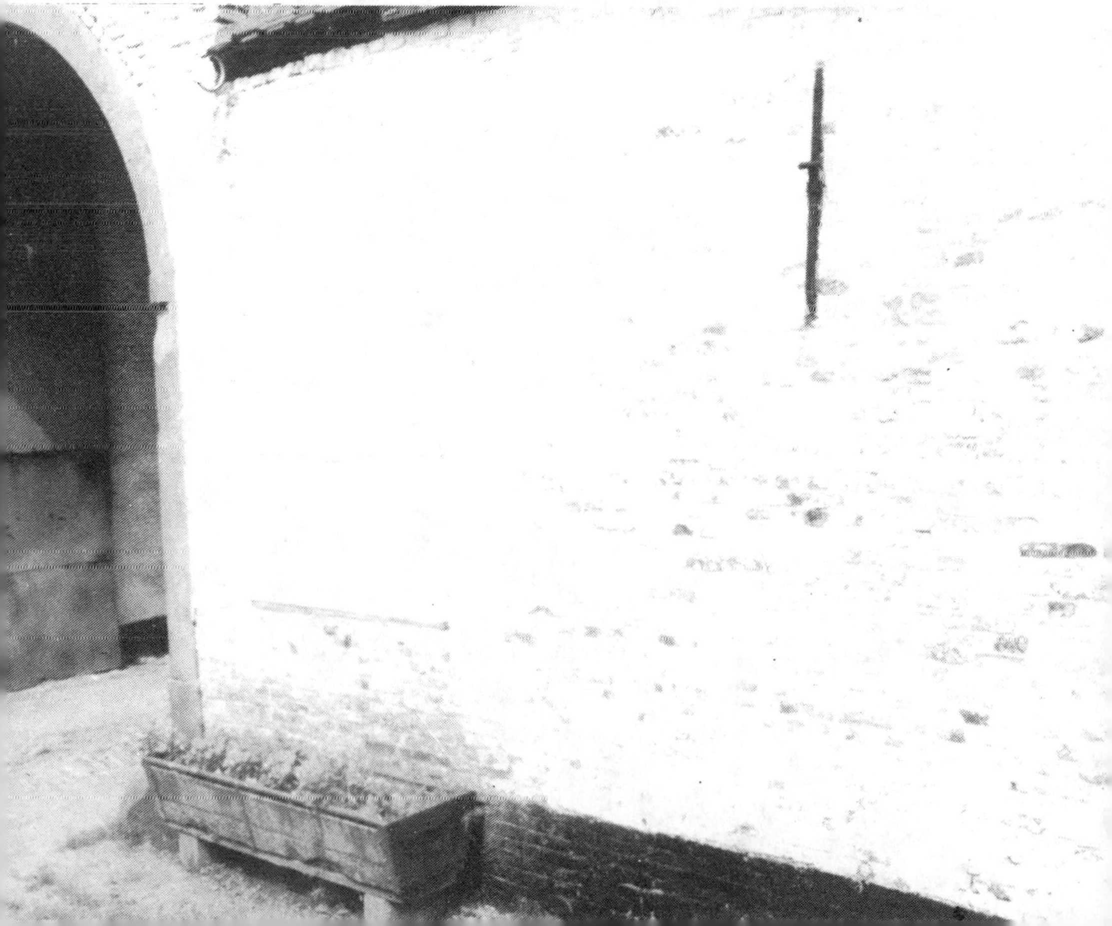

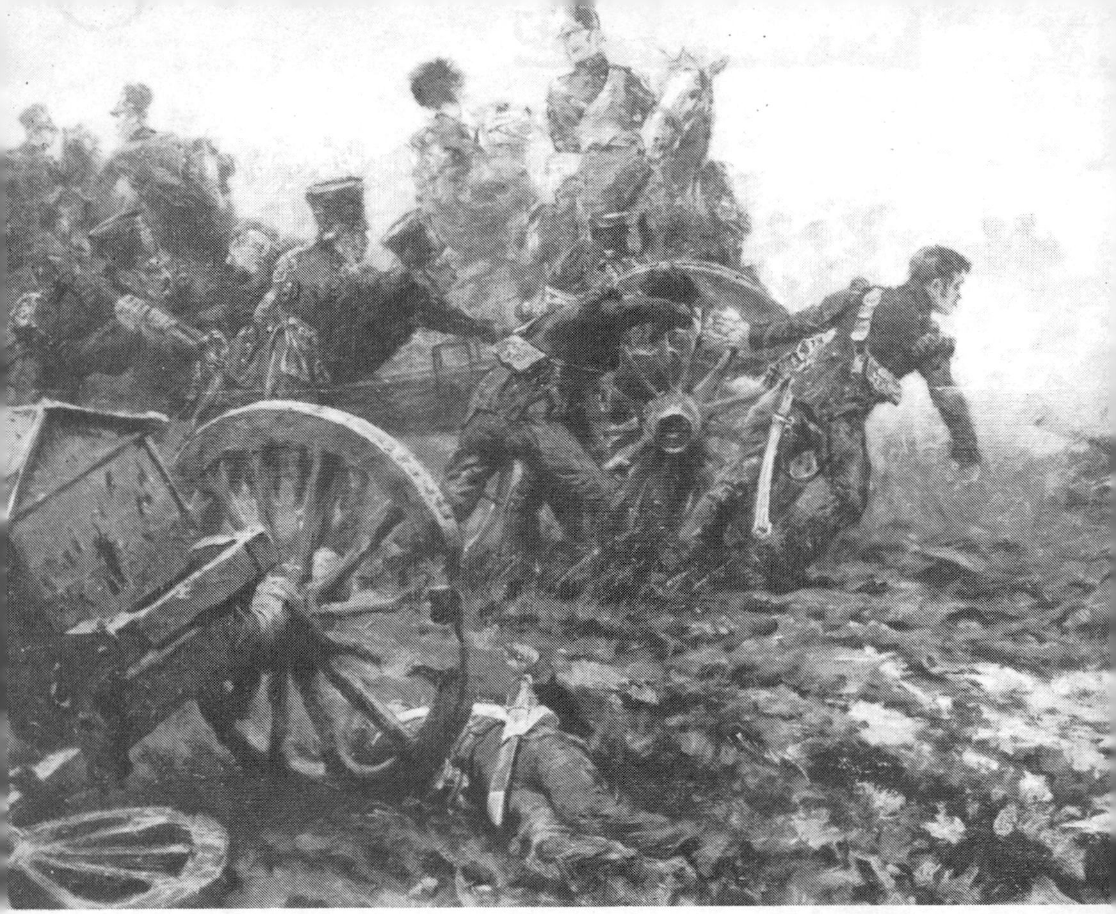

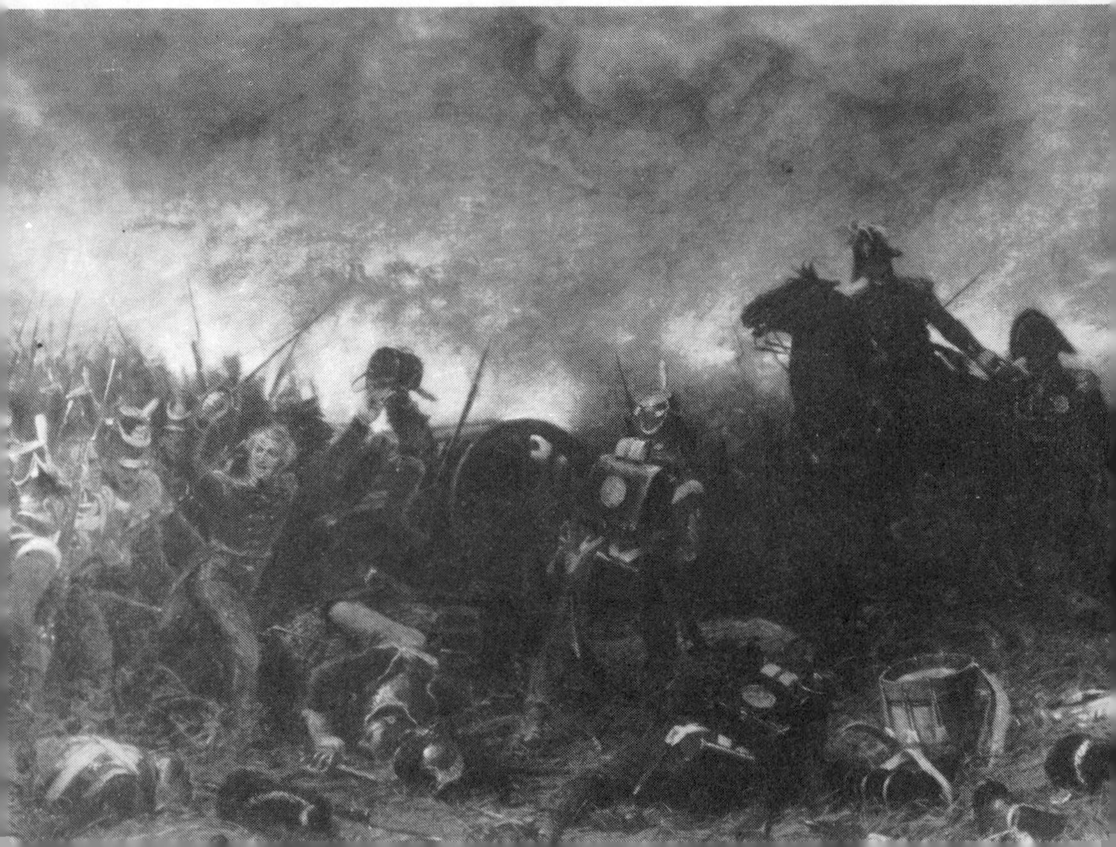

Top left: The Netherlands Horse Battery Krahmer de Binche, whose fire saved Captain Mercer's troop at the end of the day. Here it is seen preparing to fire canister into the advancing Imperial Guard in support of Halkett's brigade (painting by J. Hoynck van Papendrecht, courtesy of the Koninklijke Nederlands Leger en Wapen Museum, Delft).

Left: The capture of General Cambronne by General Halkett and the King's German Legion; in the centre can be seen the Old Guard holding the Genappe road, with La Belle Alliance and Napoleon in background (painting by Adolph North, courtesy of the Niedersächersisches Landesmuseum, Hannover).

Above: General Maximilian Foy, Commander of General Reille's 9th Division.

Twenty re-enactment soldiers ready to fire (above) and giving fire (below). The amount of smoke produced can be seen, and the reader can imagine the effect of fire given by nearly 180,000 men and 300 cannon by the end of the day. Gunpowder of the period hung about in low dense clouds that were slowly blown away, giving an effect similar to the London fogs of the 1950s – but of greater density (Author's collection).

commanding corps will take orders directly from me when I am present in person.'[18] Delort sent an aide to Soult, the Chief of Staff, who confirmed that Napoleon had ordered the cavalry to be placed under Ney's command.[19] Ney, conscious of the need to act quickly in light of the Prussian approach, exhorted Delort: 'Forward! The salvation of France is at stake.'[20] Delort moved off, followed by the other *cuirassier* division and the Imperial Guard light cavalry, formed up one behind the other, with the light cavalry to the rear to exploit the breach made by the heavies.

Wellington and his staff scrutinized these proceedings, which seemed to them rather strange. Kennedy, the staff officer attached to Alten's 3rd Division, wrote: 'To our surprise, we soon saw that it was a prelude to an attack of cavalry upon a grand scale. Such an attack we had fully anticipated would take place at some period of the day; but we had no idea that it would be made upon our line standing in its regular order of battle, and that line as yet unshaken by any previous attack by infantry.'[21] Kennedy and Wellington of course had no idea that Napoleon had no infantry to send in to shake his squares.

The order went along the Allied line to form 'Square!' and a chequer-board of twenty such formations, each of one or two regiments, soon covered the plateau. Wellington gave strict instructions to his artillery that they were to fire as many rounds as possible at the advancing enemy, then retire and take refuge in the nearest square until the enemy retreated, and when the French cavalry retired down the slope to run up and fire into their backs. The squares in the centre of Wellington's position contained some 18,000 infantry, and were fronted by 56 guns. Behind them were ranged the cavalry. Apart from the two reduced British heavy brigades and de Ghigny's brigade, most had as yet seen no fighting and were fresh to the fray. Wellington had at his disposal: Trip's Netherlands 3 Heavy Brigade, Merlen's 1 and de Ghigny's 2 Light Brigades, 7 Brigade of Colonel Arentschildt, Dornberg's 3 Brigade, Sir Colquhoun Grant's 5 Brigade, the Brunswick Contingent's Brigade of Lancers and Hussars; and the Cumberland Hussar Regiment of Colonel Estorff's Hanoverian Brigade. Including the 400-odd effectives left of the British heavy brigades, Wellington had a total of 5,054 cavalry.[22]

Marshal Ney now prepared to launch Milhaud's *cuirassiers* and Lefebvre-Desnouëttes' Light Cavalry Division numbering almost 5,094 men,[23] in a mighty onslaught to break Wellington's centre of 18,000 infantry, 5,054 cavalry and 56 guns. In the smoke-filled valley Ney gave the order and the French cavalry advanced in echelon of squadrons, the *cuirassiers* leading with the light horsemen and lancers in the rear echelons. Wave upon wave rode on to the plateau, a gap of several hundred yards being left clear behind the leading line, so that the following ranks would have space to avoid stricken horses and men. The Allied artillery, double-loaded with canister and roundshot, waited for them to close. At a slow canter the horses climbed the steep plateau over the soaked and muddy ground which had been churned up by earlier cavalry action. The batteries of Lloyd and Cleeves, almost at the centre of the point of the French attack, waited until the leading horsemen were about 100 yards away and then opened up with all their guns, mowing down almost the entire front rank of the French line, including Marshal Ney; the gunners then ran back to their supporting squares. All the guns along the Allied line followed suit and men and horses were brought crashing to the ground. The masses of horsemen rode through and around the first line of squares, whose fire wrought terrible execution.

Then began the deadly game of sabre against bayonet. The Allied soldiers in the squares stood four-deep, presenting a solid wall of gleaming bayonets. The front rank knelt, the butts of their muskets grounded, while the other ranks stood behind them, and all together they presented a bristling hedge of blades. Having already fired their muskets, the men were at first reluctant to put them down long enough to reload, and thus stood protecting themselves only with their bayonets. No horseman could bring his mount near such a hedge, but as they rounded the apex of a square or oblong, experienced French troopers were often able to cut down men in the corner files. This was due to an inherent weakness in the square formation: that the men who acted for both sides at the angle were most vulnerable and had constantly to keep their wits about them. Those who fell to the sabre were quickly replaced.[24]

Casualties were also inflicted on the squares by the French firing their large horse-pistols at point-blank range, and by the lancers who could overreach the steel hedge to skewer and blind unwary enemy foot.

The pressure from the French rear pushed the leading cavalry forward towards the rear of Wellington's position, where they received further volleys from the sides of squares that had not yet discharged their pieces. Finally, as they came through the smoke, the leading French troopers were hit by the full, formed squadrons of the mass of Wellington's cavalry, and were driven back.

Wellington, his staff and retinue, had taken shelter in the centre of a Brunswick square. The Duke was outraged when, at the commencement of the first charge, he saw Captain Sandham's British battery limber up and gallop hell for leather to the rear, leaving the unfortunate officer and his gunners to run after it.[25] As the overwhelming numbers of fresh Allied cavalry drove the French cavalry off the plateau to regroup in the valley below, the Allied artillery re-opened fire, causing many casualties. Wellington sent Sir Augustus Frazer to bring up a horse battery to fill the gap left by Sandham's battery. Captain Mercer recalled: 'It might have been, as nearly as I can recollect 3 p.m., when Sir Augustus Frazer galloped up, crying out, "Left! limber up, and as fast as you can!" The words were scarcely uttered when my gallant troop ... [moved] "At the gallop, march!"... he was leading us (about one-third of the distance between Hougoumont and the Charleroi road), and that in all probability we should immediately be charged on gaining our position. "The Duke's orders, however, are positive," he added, "that in the event of their persevering and charging home, you do not expose your men, but retire with them into an adjacent square of infantry."[26]

Ney remounted and prepared to lead another charge up the slope that was now littered with fallen men and horses. However, before the reformed French cavalry had started to trot, the massed French artillery fired round after round into the Allied squares, whose men were bunched tightly together for protection. Roundshot tore into the fronts of squares, reducing sometimes four or more men at a time to pulp, then ricocheting into another square and doing equal damage. Shellfire was even more distressing; balls landed in or near the squares, the burning fuzes making them spin like catherine wheels before exploding, killing as many as eight and wounding as many more in the packed formations. Up the slope again came the French horsemen, to be blown away again by the artillery whose men then ran again into the squares for safety. Captain Mercer, stationed in front of the two Brunswick squares, had no need to retire because his flanks were covered by the volleys of the front of each supporting square and his guns were protected by a raised embankment. After the first two volleys of canister from his six guns, the welter of dead Frenchmen and horses piled to his immediate front prevented any horsemen from reaching him. He and his men were therefore well protected and had no need to withdraw.[27]

Yet again Ney led the French cavalry charging up the slope in an attempt to break the Allied squares. This time his ranks were even thinner, having suffered severe losses of men and horses in the last charge. Ensign Gronow of the 1st Foot Guards described the onslaught:

'Not a man present who survived could have forgotten in after life the awful grandeur of that charge. You perceived at a distance what appeared to be an overwhelming, long moving line, which, ever advancing, glittered like a stormy wave of the sea when it catches the sunlight. On came the mounted host until they got near enough, whilst the very earth seemed to vibrate beneath their thundering tramp. One might suppose that nothing could have resisted the shock of this terrible moving mass. They were the famous cuirassiers, almost all old soldiers, who had distinguished themselves on most of the battlefields of Europe. In an almost incredibly short period they were within twenty yards of us, shouting 'Vive l'Empereur! The word of command, 'Prepare to receive cavalry!' had been given, every man in the front ranks knelt, and a wall bristling with steel, held together by steady hands, presented itself to the infuriated cuirassiers.

'I should observe that just before the charge the duke entered by one of the angles of the square, accompanied only by one aide-de-camp; all the rest of the staff being either killed or wounded. Our Commander-in-Chief, as far as I could judge, appeared perfectly composed; but looked very thoughtful and pale.'[28]

Once more the French death ride resumed its macabre dance around the squares, unable to cause any to break. Impotently the cavalry contented themselves with trying to kill any soldier caught with his guard down. Gronow pictures his square graphically: 'During the battle our squares presented a shocking sight. Inside we were nearly all suffocated by the smoke and smell of burnt cartridges. It was impossible to move a yard without treading upon a wounded comrade, or upon the bodies of the dead; and the loud groans of the wounded and dying was most appalling. At four o'clock our square was a perfect hospital, being full of dead, dying, and mutilated soldiers.'[29] Once again the Allied cavalry used its greater numbers to force the depleted French cavalry off the plateau, and again they received a hail of iron as they went back down the slope.

While these events had been unfolding on the central slopes of the Mont St-Jean battlefield, the infantry of Vandamme's corps in Grouchy's command began to appear in the distance in front of Wavre. Grouchy, obedient to his current orders and totally unaware of Napoleon's predicament, was marching on the town. At midday, when the cannonade from Napoleon's grand battery had reverberated across the few miles to Wavre for all there to hear, General Gérard, commander of IV Corps, had remonstrated with Grouchy, 'To march to the sound of the guns', but Grouchy refused. Gérard begged Grouchy to let him go with his corps of 15,500 men – 26 battalions of infantry, twelve squadrons of cavalry and 38 guns – to join the Emperor. Grouchy refused to allow such a large detachment on the valid grounds that to divide his force in front of the whole Prussian army would be disastrous. Instead, Grouchy force-marched northwards past the roads leading most directly to Plancenoit and St-Lambert, taking them farther from Napoleon.[30]

Colonel Ledebur's Prussian detachment, which had been observing the French since Mont St-Guibert, had filed through Wavre earlier that morning, leaving only General von Borcke's 9 Brigade of Thielemann's corps between the French and Wavre. As Vandamme's corps started to appear before Dion-le-Mont in strength, Borcke began to retire on Wavre, but found the bridge so heavily barricaded as to make a crossing impossible. He led his men downstream to Basse Wavre, half a mile away, where there was a bridge intact. He destroyed the bridge after his crossing, thus denying it to the French. He then marched his men towards Mont St-Jean, as he had been ordered to do earlier that morning, totally unaware that Gneisenau had changed these orders. However, Borcke, one of the new breed of Prussian officers, on his own initiative lined the hedges and trees on the bank of the Dyle with the sharpshooters of his 8th Regiment and those of the 1/30th Regiment under Major Dittfurth. These men covered the bank from Basse Wavre to Wavre, using every ounce of cover, loopholing every building and outbuilding that they found as well as using natural cover. Continuing to Wavre, he detached the 2/30th and two squadrons of cavalry to reinforce Colonel Zeppelin's force lining the town front. Borcke's men had also loopholed the buildings in and around Wavre and along the river bank facing the south. Borcke then marched off, unaware that Thielemann, his commander, and the rest of his corps were behind the town.

Thielemann, at the news of Vandamme's approach, had organized his corps thus: von Kamphen's 10 Brigade was directly behind Wavre and would feed in troops as required; Stulpnägel's 12 Brigade was behind the village of Bierges; von Luck's 11 Brigade was next to 10 Brigade on the other side of the Brussels road. The bridge at Bierges was barricaded and its mill (spanning the river) put in a state of defence with a horse artillery battery in front of the village.

Borcke would have been placed as a central reserve, but he had passed round his commander by way of La Bavette. Theilemann detached two more companies to reinforce Basse Wavre and three battalions and three squadrons of cavalry of Major Bornstaedt to guard the bridge at Limale.[31]

At about the same time as Marshal Ney was assembling the cavalry for his first attack, Vandamme, without waiting for Grouchy's instructions, ordered Habert's 10th Division to attack the village of Aisemont which lay spread along a road equidistant between Basse Wavre and Wavre. Habert quickly cleared the Prussian light troops from its environs. Supported by a cannonade from his two batteries of 12pdrs placed on each side of the road, he assaulted the Wavre bridge with heavy columns of companies. Almost immediately the entire far bank and its buildings erupted in musketry, supported by numerous cannon, all of which enfiladed the bridge. In a few minutes General Habert and 600 of his men had fallen. Two more attempts to storm the bridge were repulsed with terrible loss. The division fell back behind the walls and buildings along the river bank under constant fire and shelling from the Prussian howitzers. Slowly, company by company, 10th Division found shelter from the deadly fire, but in doing so became trapped. They could neither advance nor fall back without being exposed to the cannon fire and the masses of dispersed skirmishers holding a two-mile front. Yet if they remained where they were, they would gradually be picked off by the rifle-armed *Jäger* mixed in with the Prussian light infantry.

Grouchy, having now come up, decided to relieve the pressure on Vandamme by attacking both flanks of Wavre. He sent General Exelmans with his dragoons to Basse Wavre and ordered a battalion of infantry to try to cross the bridge at the mill of Bierges. At about 5 p.m., Napoleon's orders of 1 p.m. arrived, ordering the Marshal to lose no time in moving to join the Emperor's right and to take Bülow in flank at St-Lambert. Grouchy, unable to disengage Vandamme, sent orders for Pajol to force-march towards Limale, and ordered Gérard to advance on that village at once and engage the enemy. Grouchy's plan was for Gérard and Pajol, with more than half his command to attack St-Lambert, wading into what he thought would be Bülow's strung-out corps, while he used Vandamme and Exelmans to destroy what he thought to be a rearguard of one Prussian brigade, then advance on the rear of St-Lambert.[32]

The attempt by one French battalion to cross the bridge at Bierges was a disaster. They were completely outgunned, and the ground there was swampy, not (in 1815) having been drained. Hulot's division of Gérard's corps tried to storm the bridge, but was also beaten back with loss. The boggy ground slowed them and increased the length of time they were exposed to cannon fire. Grouchy, impatient to heed the Emperor's call, rode off to bring up the remainder of IV Corps and Pajol's force. Back at the river bank, several assaults at Bierges had failed, one of the casualties being General Gérard, who had fallen wounded to a Prussian sniper. Just before dark, however, Teste's division and Pajol's cavalry attacked the bridge at Limale. The Prussian commander there had failed to barricade or destroy the bridge, and thus had been unable to stop Pajol's hussar regiment from storming across four abreast and routing the Prussians, who fell back on their supports in the heights behind the village. Teste's division followed and took up position, followed in turn by Gérard's corps. Fighting continued during the night. Thielemann, convinced that the main fight was now around Limale, transferred his reserve brigades to cover that direction and sent a dispatch to Blücher to inform him that he was being attacked by the enemy corps. Grouchy, thinking that he had trapped Bülow, settled down to wait for morning before resuming operations.

At Mont St-Jean, Ney had returned to the front of the ridge of La Belle Alliance. His attempts to break Wellington's centre had been observed by Napoleon, who spoke of it to his Imperial aide, General Count Flahault, who recorded the conversation: "'There is Ney hazarding the battle which was almost won (the words are engraved in my memory), but he must be supported now, for that is our only chance." Turning then to me, he bade me order all the cavalry I could find to assist the troops Ney had thrown at the enemy's across the ravine.'[33] Flahault then, using the unquestionable authority of speaking 'in the name of the Emperor', ordered Kellermann's corps of heavy cavalry and the heavy division of the Imperial Guard cavalry to line up on the valley floor to join the attack. This added another 5,300 horsemen[34] to Ney's force, giving him with the losses already sustained nearly 9,000 horsemen: ten echelons of 900 men each, covering the 900-yard space between the road and the grounds of Hougoumont. While Ney prepared to lead yet another assault in the same ill-fated manner, the

French artillery poured more death and destruction into the Allied ranks; Brunswickers, Netherlanders, Hanoverians and Britons were falling all the time to the shot and shell pounding the squares on the plateau.

What Ney did not know, as he was about to lead this new wave forward, was that Lobau on the right flank was now under attack by Blücher and the Prussians. General Müffling, who had been posted on the heights over Papelotte, had sent one of his aides to Blücher to apprise him of the situation. Müffling states: 'On the receipt of my reports, it was resolved not to await the arrival of the whole of Bülow's corps on the plateau, but to advance out of the wood as soon as the two twelve-pounder batteries arrived. At four o'clock the Field Marshal [Blücher] began his advance against Planchenois [*sic*] ... From my station above Papelotte I could overlook the advance of the enemy's reserves from La Belle Alliance.'[35]

Initially Gneisenau and Blücher had had no intention of launching their attack until all the elements of IV Corps were closed up behind the woods. But in view of Napoleon's heavy attack on the Anglo-Allied centre and fearing that Wellington might break before his men could cut off the line of retreat of the French army, Blücher had decided to attack with his IV Corps cavalry and two brigades. At some time between 4 and 4.30 p.m. Nostitz brought Bülow the order to attack. Bülow had deployed his troops thus: two battalions and the Silesian Hussar Regiment were under cover of the thick wood. They were followed by 15 and 16 Brigades together with the reserve artillery and cavalry. All these troops were in camouflaged positions [within the woods] along a broad front and in close order on both sides of the track through the wood. The artillery was drawn up on the track itself, and everything was in readiness to break forth at the right moment towards the open heights of Frischermont opposite. The reserve cavalry were waiting behind the wood, ready to follow the infantry immediately.[36]

Bülow advanced his two brigades side by side,[37] Losthin's 15 Brigade on the right, to the west of the track to Plancenoit, and Hiller's 16 Brigade on the left side. Both these brigades sent out several of their light fusilier battalions on either side to give an appearance of greater strength. The leading brigade batteries, supported by the two reserve 12pdr batteries, immediately opened fire on the cavalry of Domon and Subervie on Lobau's left, who were watching the wood around Frischermont. As this surprise bombardment began, the two missing brigades came up one behind the other, Hacke's 13 Brigade behind and to the left of 16 Brigade, with the cavalry alongside.

Blücher had ordered the corps to advance obliquely in the direction of La Belle Alliance, but at the same time Gneisenau had indicated to Blücher that the key to the field was the village of Plancenoit which was as yet unoccupied by the French. If the Prussians took the village and could then sever the *Chaussée* and Napoleon's line of retreat, they could entrap all but the small part of the French army that could escape by the Nivelles road. Napoleon's army would have then ceased to exist.[38] Blücher amended his orders accordingly, and as the Prussian right engaged Lobau, its left advanced toward Plancenoit. Lobau, on the appearance of the Prussians, immediately engaged them. His men were all veterans who stood firmly rooted to their position as the 30,000 Prussians assaulted them at odds of three to one. At first Lobau used the cavalry to outflank and turn Bülow's right. For this purpose he sent Durutte once more against the Smohain area, to take the farmhouses as strongpoints to bolster the French line against a concerted attack from both Wellington and Blücher. The Smohain area now took on a new tactical importance as the juncture of the two right-angled French lines. Lobau perceived the Prussians' intention and quickly moved one of his reserve brigades into Plancenoit. These men had to run to beat the Prussians to it.[39] Lobau then decided to withdraw his small corps toward Plancenoit at an angle, reducing his frontage. The fight for Plancenoit thus began: a battle equal in intensity to Ligny in its violence. At this moment Thielemann's messenger reached Blücher and Gneisenau, reporting that his corps at Wavre was under attack by a vastly superior force and doubting that he could hold out for long. Gneisenau replied: 'Let Thielemann defend himself as best he can, it matters little if he be crushed at Wavre, provided we gain the victory here.'[40]

To Ney and the Allies at Wellington's centre, the Prussians and Lobau could have been warring on the moon for all they knew. With the massive cannonade from both sides, and the pounding of so many thousands of horses, combined with the massed musketry, little of what the Prussians were doing carried to them; but Napoleon knew, because Lobau and Marbot had sent him urgent messages saying that they were under attack, yet he had not halted Ney's charge. Napoleon realized that he was being assailed by only one corps at the moment, and Lobau was temporarily holding it in check. If Ney soon broke Wellington's centre and caused him to retreat, Blücher would still have to withdraw or be caught between the main French force and Grouchy.

Napoleon still believed that, as at Eylau, when he attacked on a small frontage his cavalry could ride over everything. But on that occasion he had had his brother-in-law, Joachim Murat, in charge of his cavalry. Murat may have had many failings, but not when it came to commanding cavalry. Marshal Ney, although 'the bravest of the Brave', who before the Revolution had been a sergeant-major in the Royalist Hussars, could lead cavalry, but that is not the same as to be in command of several huge cavalry corps, as Murat had been. For all his courage Ney had not Murat's expertise. Napoleon, piqued at Murat for his role in 1813 and for his campaign of 1815 in Italy,[41] had refused to employ or even see him. If Murat had been there now, he would have broken Wellington's squares in the first charge, as Napoleon had expected Ney to do. But Murat was not there. If he had been, he would have told his brother-in-law that Ney could not break Wellington's squares because the Emperor had denied him the means to do so. Napoleon had stripped Milhaud, Kellermann, Lefebvre-Desnouëttes and Guyot of their horse-artillery batteries to use elsewhere. Murat would have ensured that at the very least he had two of the eight horse-artillery batteries of six guns with him in his charge. Then on the plateau they would have opened up on the squares at close range with canister, blowing gaps in them which the milling cavalry would at once have exploited. The remainder of the broken squares would have disintegrated and his cavalry would have ridden over and slaughtered them. Further, as at Eylau, his mounted gunners would have used their headless nails to spike all the deserted Allied guns so that they would be unable to fire on the French cavalry if it had to withdraw.

But Murat was not here, and Ney reached the plateau with his men and no horse-artillery. They received further volleys of musketry and cannon fire which could not be silenced. And there was still the massed cavalry waiting behind the squares. Back and forth, Ney led the cavalry, having mounted horse after horse that afternoon. On and up the futile charges went. Captain Rudyard of the Royal Artillery in Lloyd's battery, placed before Alten's 3rd Division, recalled:

> "The Cuirassiers and Cavalry might have charged through the battery as often as six or seven times, driving us into the Squares, under our guns, waggons, some defending themselves. In general, as a Squadron or two came up the slope on our immediate front, and on their moving off at the appearance of our Cavalry charging, we took advantage to send destruction after them, and when advancing on our fire I have seen four or five men and horses piled upon each like cards, the men not having even been displaced from the saddle, the effect of cannister.'42

General Guyot's Mounted [*à cheval*] Grenadiers of the Imperial Guard, nicknamed 'The Immortals', tall men wearing huge black bearskins, mounted on large horses, the terror of many European battles, were mowed down, rank upon rank, for little purpose. The French cavalry gained some local victories: the Imperial Guard dragoons, returning to the bottom of the valley by way of the Nivelles road and the farm of Mont Plaisir, badly mauled the detachment of the 15th Hussars sent to watch Piré's lancers, and cut down many Brunswick and Guard skirmishers around the flank of Hougoumont, who were taken unawares, but these actions were peripheral and insignificant.

The men in the squares were continually making involuntary backward movements, but at least they were in British squares, held in place and given support by the sergeants in the rear ranks, who used their pikes sideways to restrain the rankers from bolting. These pikes were a relic of former times, retained as symbols of rank and to protect the Colours. Also, when punishment was to be meted out for one of a multitude of petty offences, they were used lashed together in threes to form a tripod, to which the ranker was tied for flogging. On this day, however, they were seeing more honourable, if bloodier, service.[43]

The struggle, long and bloody and futile, had now almost reached its conclusion. None of the untrained men in the squares – Brunswicker, Nassauer, Hanoverian or British – panicked, or gave ground, notwithstanding the absolute horror to which they were subjected by prolonged cannonade and repeated massed cavalry charges. Ensign Gronow observed:

> 'The artillery did great execution, but our musketry did not at first seem to kill many men; though it brought down a large number of horses, and created indescribable confusion. The horses of the first rank of cuirassiers, in spite of all the efforts of their riders, came to a stand-still, shaking and covered with foam, at about twenty yards distance from our squares, and generally resisted all attempts to force them to charge the line of serried steel.'[44]

Marshal Ney belatedly, but understandably given the press of events, sought to gain infantry support. As d'Erlon's corps had now reassembled in *ad hoc* battalions, Napoleon allowed Ney to use Bachelu's division and Foy's brigade, with Piré's horse battery in the assault. But this was to be too little and too late. Due to the restricted space with the cavalry coming and going in a disorderly procession, the three brigades of infantry advanced up the eastern flank of Hougoumont, whose woods were completely in French hands. The garrison of the château, trying to survive both French assaults and the flames that had engulfed the buildings, had no time to fire upon them. Indeed, it is doubtful whether they were even noticed. Foy's brigade led the advance up the slope from the wood, supported by Piré's battery which had unlimbered in the area of the hollow way. The Guards supporting the garrison had wisely formed squares. As Foy personally led his brigade forward, Du Plat's and Adam's brigades opened a withering fire, sweeping the general from his horse wounded and causing the French to retreat. Because of the cavalry charges the frontage on which he could advance was narrow and Bachelu decided that to attack with his own men on this width would be suicidal, so he called it off. Piré's battery was much more dangerous, causing a great deal of damage with several rapid rounds of canister. However, this was driven off the field with some loss by the Brunswick Hussars, led by their lancer squadron, which nearly overran Piré's gunners who lost two guns while escaping.[45]

It was now nearly 6 p.m. Ney called off any further attacks by the cavalry, which withdrew on blown horses, with vastly reduced numbers, and at least some of its wounded and exhausted men reduced to tears of frustration at having been deprived of victory, though suffering such loss. The field was strewn with the dead and wounded, men and horses. Napoleon, still optimistic, was convinced that Wellington's centre must have been tried now to the full extent of its endurance. He told Ney that the farmhouse of La Haye Sainte was the key to cracking Wellington. If Ney could but take the farmhouse they could penetrate the centre of Wellington's line. Ney, without his hat, his face blackened from gunpowder, his uniform torn by artillery fire and plastered in mud from the many times he had his horse shot from under him, prepared once more to launch another assault on Wellington's line for his Emperor.

CHAPTER 14

18 June: Evening

'This empire has been acquired by men who knew their duty and had the courage to do it, who in the hour of conflict had the fear of dishonour always present to them, and who, if ever they failed in an enterprise, would not allow their virtues to be lost to their country, but freely gave their lives to her as the fairest offering which they could present at her feast.' -Pericles, funeral oration for the Athenian dead, 431 BC, quoted in Thucydides' *History of the Peloponnesian Wars.*

While Marshal Ney prepared for his assault on the farmhouse of La Haye Sainte, Wellington re-arranged and consolidated his battered centre. Nothing that he had experienced in his long campaigns in the Peninsula had prepared him for the type of warfare that had been inflicted on him that day. Wellington had expected, as in the Peninsula, that the French would assail his position with swarms of skirmishers, which his own would push back. Then columns of French infantry would advance, to be repulsed by the linear tactics he had evolved in Spain. This would then be followed by cavalry charges to try to break his line. Wellington had not expected what did happen: a sustained artillery bombardment by more than 200 cannon for nearly seven hours, and assaults by nearly 12,000 cavalry launched repeatedly on his squares. Unable to fathom Napoleon's tactics, Wellington had sustained heavy casualties by his passive defensive strategy of maintaining his position without carrying out any counter-offensives. By so doing he had allowed Napoleon, with a much weaker force, to take the initiative; and consequently he had had to absorb all the punishment that Napoleon meted out.[1]

Napoleon, impelled by the need to drive Wellington from the field and capture Brussels, had overruled in his mind the strictly military considerations of the moment. Marshal Ney, the unforgiven reprobate of 1814, prepared to launch a third attempt to break Wellington's line. For this operation he ordered Quiot's entire division, much reduced as it was, to spearhead the assault, with Bachelu's division on its right, and with its divisional battery and the horse battery detached to it by Napoleon from Kellermann's corps. This attack was to be supported from behind by a brigade of Kellermann's cuirassiers. On the other side of the road Marcognet's reduced division, supported by Milhaud's cuirassiers, would keep abreast of the assault.

Quiot's division went forward once more against the farmhouse, supported by the other two and the cavalry, and this time enjoying the weighty assistance of artillery which tore large gaps in the wall surrounding the courtyard.[2] Quiot's division assaulted the building on all sides, and the German defenders shot down Frenchmen as fast as they could reload. The French soldiers, having overcome the Germans' fire by sheer weight of numbers, threw themselves against the walls and tried to pull the rifles out of the hands of the defenders. The makeshift loophole at ground level near the pond in the courtyard was taken by the expedient of French soldiers thrusting several muskets into the breach, firing into it and killing the defender. Then a French soldier fired through it, having numerous loaded muskets passed to him one after another by his comrades, making that part of the wall untenable to the defenders.[3] At the rear of the barn the French tried desperately to storm the breach, which was only denied to them by the rapid and continuous fire kept up by the defenders, cutting down the French almost as fast as they entered, and bayoneting those that had been missed, until a rampart of corpses walled the breach.

Major Baring's ammunition was becoming seriously depleted; the Hanoverian battalions had had only sixty rounds each when they had occupied the building. Baring now found that his men were down to half that amount. He sent a runner back to the main lines by the dangerous expedient of the man dropping down on to the main road from the garden while it was under assault, and running up along the undercut to the main Allied line.[4] But unknown to Baring no ammunition was available[5] and a second messenger was sent. Colonel Ompteda, apprised of Baring's desperate situation, sent the light company of the 5th Line Battalion under Captain von Wurmb, to reinforce him. The company managed to break through the French troops assaulting the garden, although Wurmb was killed in the process. Grateful as Baring was for this additional strength, it did not compensate the lack of ammunition. After another half-hour's desperate fighting, yet another messenger was sent. Whether he got through is not known, but no rifle ammunition was sent.

Enterprising French soldiers had thrown inflammable material into the barn and set fire to the roof. Smoke and flames billowed through the barn and at first Major Baring was at a loss as to what to do: '...our alarm was now extreme, for although there was water in the court, all means of drawing it, and carrrying it were wanting, every vessel having been broken up. Luckily the Nassau troops carried large field cooking kettles; I tore a kettle from the back of one of the men; several officers followed my example, and filling the kettles with water, they carried them, facing certain death, to the fire. The men did the same, and soon not one of the Nassauers was left with his kettle, and the fire was extinguished; but alas with the blood of many a brave man.'[6]

One Hanoverian light infantryman, Fredrick Lindau, was conspicuous by his gallantry in the defence of the great barn. Wounded twice in the head, he held the small door leading to the entrance to the barn. Repeatedly offered relief by Baring, he is reported to have answered: 'He would be a rogue indeed, that deserted now, as long as he still had a head on his shoulders.'[7]

The assault continued for more than an hour, the French on the high ground across the road firing into the farm. Quiot had also opened up at close range with his artillery on the walls that faced the road near the pond, tearing down masonry and blasting holes. Two riflemen of Baring's battalion who distinguished themselves during the cannonade were representative of the multitude of nameless heroes that day. Private Dahrendorf fought on after having received three bayonet wounds, until falling when his leg was shattered by canister. Private Lindhorst, defending one of the breaches made by the cannon, ran out of ammunition, but continued to hold the breached top of the wall with his sword-bayonet until it broke, then wielding a stick, and finally hurling chunks of masonry at the attackers.[8]

Baring's men were now down to four rounds apiece, and it was obvious to the attackers that the defenders' fire was diminishing. A concerted assault now took place, the French scaling the wall facing the orchard that had been reduced by artillery fire and coming through the barn. Masses of French troops, on gaining the walls, fired down on the defenders who had finally expended all their ammunition. Baring withdrew his men to the house, intending that they should hold it as long as possible, but without ammunition this was not feasible. The French soon got in and bayoneted everyone within, such was the bitterness engendered by the struggle. The farmhouse had fallen.[9]

Sir Charles Alten, seeing one of the French columns in pursuit of the retreating garrison and thereby approaching his position, ordered Colonel Ompteda to advance his 5th Battalion in line to attack it and give covering fire to the few of Baring's men who had managed to fall back. Ompteda protested, thinking it a useless sacrifice in men, and declared that he had seen French cavalry through the dense powder smoke that hung like fog over the battlefield, from the hundreds of thousands of artillery rounds fired that day. The Prince of Orange, Commander of I Corps, holding a Major-General's commission in the British army, overhearing this exchange, ordered the colonel to obey General Alten's commands without further argument.[10]

Colonel Ompteda mounted his horse and gave the order to advance in line. His battalion crossed the sunken road, and with a volley and a loud 'Hurrah!' rushed towards the French column which withdrew before contact was made. At that moment Ompteda's claim to have spotted enemy cavalry proved terribly correct. One of Kellermann's *cuirassier* regiments, which had been posted in a fold of the ground, came out and, catching the battalion in flank with muskets unloaded, rode over it, slaughtering its men, killing Colonel Ompteda and capturing its Colour. Only Lieutenant-Colonel von Linsingen and eighteen of his men escaped back to the main line. In their elation the *cuirassiers* came too close to the sunken road in which the remnant of riflemen of the 1st and 2nd Battalions had joined *ad hoc*. They opened fire. Sir Fredrick Arentschildt in person led forward the 3rd KGL Hussars to engage the *cuirassiers* in defence of his countrymen, but coming up in support of the *cuirassiers* were the Imperial

Guard lancers. The German hussars disengaged, both sides having lost about forty men. One German hussar who had been carried too far forwards returned wounded, only to be confronted by a wounded French *cuirassier* returning to his unit. In single combat reminiscent of the days of chivalry, carried out in the space between the opposing regiments, who refrained from interfering, the hussar suffered many wounds but managed to cut the *cuirassier* a back-handed blow across the face which killed him. The hussar then rode back unmolested to the cheers of his countrymen.[11]

As these events were unfolding Wellington correctly divined that Napoleon intended to break his centre and sent orders to General Chassé's 3rd Netherlands Division to march over from Braine l'Alleud to reinforce the centre of the Allied line. Major-General Müffling, using the authority given to him by Wellington, ordered Vivian and Vandeleur's brigades to the centre.[12] Wellington also ordered the Brunswick *Leib*-Battalion, 1st Light Battalion and *avant-garde* riflemen into the shell of the burnt-out Hougoumont to assist the exhausted garrison in keeping the French at bay.[13]

Meanwhile in the dip at Papelotte, Smohain and Frischermont, Durutte's entire division had launched a heavier, more urgent attack in the light of Lobau's request for its capture. Durutte, laying down a heavy barrage with one foot- and two horse-batteries, kept the mass of Saxe-Weimar's brigade pinned down in and behind Smohain. These he assaulted in an arc with his 2 Brigade, while the remnant of his 1 Brigade, reduced to 2½ battalions[14] and supported by one horse-battery, assaulted Papelotte farmhouse. This was taken using canister to sweep the defenders from the walls and to effect an opening through a gate. The brigade then fortified the position with its artillery placed in support.

While Ney had seized La Haye Sainte farmhouse and Durutte had taken Papelotte, Lobau's brigade barricaded in Plancenoit's buildings and holding the circular cemetery wall, which rose in the middle of the village and acted as strongpoint, resisted two attacks by Bülow's 16 and 14 Brigades. These had difficulty in using their advantage of numbers in the village. Near Frischermont Lobau's cavalry and infantry had used the ground to repel the attack of Bülow's 15 and 13 Brigades, and Blücher was becoming frustrated by the delay of his other army corps in coming up to join the fight. Further, fighting with Bülow's IV Corps on such a dispersed front was not the preferred method of the new Prussian army, in effect spreading itself almost in a linear formation.

As elements of Pirch's II's corps soon started to arrive, Blücher launched von Ryssel's brigade again into Plancenoit, and vicious hand-to-hand fighting flared up again. Two Prussian light cannon were brought up to fire canister on the cemetery which had become the bastion of the village. The Frenchmen behind its circular wall, which was lined with numerous trees, fired down on the Prussians, but were soon scythed down by canister fire of about fifteen minutes' duration. The devastating effect of this reduced the trees to stumps in line with the wall. Again the Prussians charged and put anyone they could reach to the bayonet, in a no-quarter struggle similar to that at Ligny.[15]

Lobau immediately called upon Napoleon for support to hold the village that was fast being lost to the Prussians. Fearing that his communications behind this village might be cut, Napoleon ordered General Duhesme, commanding the Young Guard division of the Imperial Guard, to retake and hold the village and its right flank as far as the woods near Lasne. Eight battalions, 4,200 men, went in at the charge and rolled up the exhausted men of Ryssel's brigade, stabilizing this flank and releasing Lobau's battered brigade for use in reserve.

Blücher and Gneisenau now became worried that their plan of entrapment might be thwarted. They decided to order General Zeithen and his I Corps, on its arrival, to turn left at Frischermont and join him attacking the French right flank at Plancenoit, instead of turning right there to support Wellington's left flank.[16]

It was now about 6.30 p.m. Marshal Ney, having captured the farmhouse, advanced up the main road and on both sides of it, taking up the road two pieces of the horse-battery and placing the other sections and another battery in front and to the left of the farmhouse. At under 100 yards, the cannon opened fire with canister which blew great gaps in the ranks of Lambert's brigade to the right of the crossroads. Then the French, in skirmish order, began a fire fight all along the line. The battery near the farmhouse sent shot and canister into the fronts of the brigades of Ompteda, Kielmansegge, Alten and Halkett. Of Wellington's staff, Colonels Gordon and De Lancey were mortally wounded. The Prince of Orange and Generals Alten, Kielmansegge and Halkett were carried wounded from the field. Ney had supported his attack with heavy cavalry which caused the Allies to form squares, and thus be more vulnerable to artillery. The packed squares were being reduced mercilessly by the French guns. Captain Shaw found himself, as a headquarters staff officer, the most senior officer available. Wellington's centre was starting to crumble and give.

Meanwhile, over near Hougoumont, Wellington had ordered some of his reserves there forward to consolidate his first line. The attempt to move some of these reserves, which were almost all over and above Hougoumont, met an equally warm reception. Captain Shaw relates:

> 'Du Plat's infantry brigade of the King's German Legion advanced across the Nivelles road and took up position to the NE angle of the Hougoumont enclosure, where it got into immediate contact with the enemy, and its leader fell. Halkett's Hanoverian brigade was also advanced across the Nivelles road, and formed in a second line in support of Du Plat's brigade. Adam's brigade, which, when the action commenced, stood near to Merbraine, was early in

action, moved forward to, and formed on, the right of the Nivelles road. It was moved across the Nivelles road at about the same time as Du Plat's brigade, and nearer the Guards; and was placed in the hollow which extended from near the right of the Guards to the Hougoumont enclosure. The brigade cleared from its front large numbers of enemy skirmishers, and was exposed in that position to a considerable cannonade and partial attacks by cavalry, which caused it to form sometimes in squares and sometimes in a four-deep formation. The 52nd was at one time in squares of wings, and afterwards, the companies having formed their left behind their right subdivisions, the battalion, by closing companies, formed a line four deep, and continued in that four-deep formation during the remainder of the action. The brigade, being too much exposed to the cannonade, was withdrawn from its advance position in the low ground, to the reverse slope.'[17]

The devastation wrought by Ney's attack was causing the Allied centre near the crossroads to give ground. The 1/95th Rifles behind the hedges on Kempt's right managed to pick off and disable the French gunners and horses of the section of two guns on the actual highway, but the pieces hidden by the ground and the farmhouse were still active, ripping holes in the line. General Lambert had placed the 27th Foot (Enniskillens) in a square formation above the crossroads cutting, on the Ohain side of the crossroads, so as to be able to fire down from two angles. This elevated target was only 300 yards from the farmhouse battery which poured canister into it, turning it into a shambles. Of the 698 men in the unit who had arrived on the battlefield that morning, 480 became casualties. Major von Weyhers, commanding the 1/1st Nassauers of Kruse's independent contingent, charged with his battalion across the road in an attempt to silence the battery, but one volley reduced them to shreds, and although Wellington ordered them to withdraw, the battalion's grenadier and *Jäger* companies remained in an open-order fire fight with the battery until they were slaughtered by the same French *cuirassiers* who had destroyed Colonel Ompteda's battalion.[18]

La Haye Sainte, the knoll and gravel pit were now firmly in French hands. Ompteda's brigade had been virtually annihilated, and Kielmansegge's brigade was so decimated that together they could barely hold their ground. The battle line holding the crossroads was retracting visibly. The Colours of the 73rd and 30th foot were wrapped around the bodies of sergeants and sent to the rear. Marshal Ney now sent his aide, Colonel Heymes, as fast as his horse could carry him to the Emperor, from whom he requested fresh troops to break through this rupture and turn Wellington's flanks left and right.

Napoleon, however, was preoccupied with Plancenoit and his line of retreat. Prussian cannon-balls were falling all around La Belle Alliance and the Genappe road. At about 7.00 p.m. General Gneisenau, taking personal command of 15 and 14 Brigades, had succeeded in pushing the Young Guard out of Plancenoit, as Colonel von Hiller related:

'In the second assault two battalions of the 14th Brigade also took part, while I kept the 1st Silesian Militia regiment in reserve. This attack was also repelled, but the troops did not lose their morale. Lieutenant-General Gneisenau was also here. With his influence and that of the officers of the 15th regiment it was possible to lead up the columns for a third time and with great success.'[19]

Napoleon immediately formed his Old and Middle Guard into eleven battalion squares deployed opposite Plancenoit along the road between La Belle Alliance and Rossomme.[20] The 1st *Chasseurs* remained as headquarters guard at Le Caillou, and Napoleon had ordered two battalions of the Old Guard, the 1/2nd Grenadiers under General Pelet, and 1/2nd *Chasseurs* under General Morand, to recapture Plancenoit. At this moment Colonel Heymes asked Napoleon for troops on Ney's behalf. Unsure of his position, he replied: 'Troops, where do you expect me to get them? Do you expect me to make them?' And with this answer Marshal Ney would have to be content. Meanwhile 1,100 men of Napoleon's Old Guard marched into Plancenoit with drums beating. He had ordered the village to be taken at the bayonet, and not one shot was fired by the Guard; at the sight of the fearsome 'Bearskins', the Prussians recoiled in terror, some 3,000 of them being killed in their precipitate retreat.

During 1813 and 1814 the Prussians had become accustomed to seeing the Guard appear on the battlefield only in force and only under Napoleon's direct command. They were therefore expecting to see some 7,000 more bearskins following the ones confronting them, and they expected them to be accompanied by the small man wearing the grey riding-coat and tricorn hat to appear with them. The psychological effect of the two battalions was electric. The Old Guard pushed back Bülow's two (divisional strength) brigades and nearly captured his corps artillery before the Prussians realized that this was not an all-out onslaught by the entire Imperial Guard. But by then the Young Guard had repossessed the village. Such was the impact of the Prussian withdrawal that Count Lobau, struggling with the brigades of Losthin and Hacke, had gained ground, stabilizing Napoleon's left flank.[21]

While the routed Prussians took time to regroup, Napoleon ordered the two Old Guard battalions to remain with the Young Guard to stiffen their defence of the key village. The Young Guard, having seen its two elder battalions, to whose ranks its men all aspired, rout fourteen

Prussian battalions, naturally enjoyed a high morale and were imbued with sentiments of heroic emulation. Napoleon now received a report from Lobau that the Allied troops attacking Durutte around Frischermont, Smohain and Papelotte were in turn being attacked in rear.[22] Napoleon was jubilant. Grouchy had obviously come between Bülow's corps and the rest of the Prussian army. This would account for the exceptional success of the two Guard battalions. Grouchy was obviously attacking the rear of Bülow. Now Napoleon would use his last reserve, his Old and Middle Guard, to complete Ney's attack and crush Wellington. Then on with his Guard to Brussels, his prime objective. He sent his aides up and down the line shouting the good news that Grouchy had arrived.

While these events were taking place Ney, having no fresh troops with which to effect a rupture, had to maintain his position and await Napoleon's Guard. Captain Shaw Kennedy, meanwhile, had ridden up to Wellington, who was overlooking Hougoumont at the time when his centre was beginning to crumble.[23] Shaw Kennedy explained the situation and Wellington reacted immediately by telling him and Sir Augustus Frazer: 'I shall order the Brunswick troops to the spot, and other troops besides; go you, and get all the German troops of the division to the spot that you can, and all the guns that you can find.'[24]

Marshal Ney, desperate for reinforcements, galloped back up the road to Napoleon near La Belle Alliance, to make a plea in person for troops. Napoleon, amid the Prussian shot and shell that rained down on the crossroads, told Ney that Grouchy had arrived and that he wanted Ney to lead forward the battalions of his Old Guard. Shaw Kennedy in the meantime had moved Vincke's brigade over from the left flank and brought forward the remaining Nassau battalions. Wellington himself put four Brunswick battalions into the front line and supervised them personally. Sir Augustus Frazer brought the remaining three reserve artillery batteries up to strengthen the line.

Napoleon ordered Drouot to bring down to the valley floor the nine remaining battalion squares of the Old and Middle Guard, in the same formation as they had adopted on the road between the inn and Rossomme.[25] Colonel Octave Levasseur recalls how General Dejean, the Emperor's aide, rode up to Ney and informed him that Grouchy was fast approaching:

"'Monsieur le Maréchal,' he said. "Vive l'Empereur! Voila Grouchy!" The Marshal at once ordered me to go right along the line and announce that Grouchy had arrived. I set off at the gallop and, with my hat raised on the point of my sabre, rode down the line, shouting: "Vive l'Empereur! Soldats, voila Grouchy!"; The sudden shout was taken up by a thousand voices. The exaltation of the troops reached fever pitch and they all shouted: "En avant! En avant! Vive l'Empereur!" I scarcely reached the far end of our line [near the dip], when I heard cannon fired behind us. Enthusiasm in me gave way to a profound silence, to amazement, to anxiety ... In utter consternation I rode up to the Marshal, who forbade me to go and find the cause of this panic. I turned to General [left blank], who said to me: "Voyez, Ce sont les Prussiens!" I turned back to Marshal Ney, but could not find him ... Up came Drouot and called out: "Formez le Carré!" [form Square]. I then saw the Emperor go past me, followed by his staff. When he came opposite his Guard he said: "Qu'on me Suivre?" [Who will follow me?] and he moved off in front along the road ... one hundred and fifty bandsmen now marched down at the head of the Guard, playing the triumphant marches of the Carrousel as they went. Soon the road was covered by the Guard marching by platoons in the wake of the Emperor.'[26]

The fourteen battalions of Napoleon's Old and Middle Guard were disposed thus: 1/1st *Chasseurs* at Le Caillou as headquarters guard; two battalions, 2/2nd Grenadiers and 1/2nd *Chasseurs*, in Plancenoit. Napoleon left the two most senior battalions, 1/1st and 2/1st Grenadiers, one each side of the road in front of Rossomme as a reserve, possibly for commitment to Plancenoit. As an immediate reserve and to conserve them as a possible second wave of attack on Wellington, there were placed in line betwen La Belle Alliance and Hougoumont the four battalions: 1/2nd Grenadiers (Christiani), 2/1st *Chasseurs* (Cambronne), 2/2nd *Chasseurs* (Monprez), and near Hougoumont, 2/3rd Grenadiers (Belcourt).[27]

The five battalions of the Guard, destined to spearhead the attack of the French army on Wellington, were formed up in echelons of squares to their right. They were: 1/3rd Grenadiers, 4th Grenadiers, 1/3rd *Chasseurs*, 2/3rd *Chasseurs* and 4th *Chasseurs*, drawn up in a line of squares. The Imperial Guard had eight companies per battalion as opposed to the six of the line regiments. They presented a frontage of two companies, as did the normal line battalions in attack, but with two companies in the rear and on each side in line of threes. Thus they formed a complete square of three ranks. In the centre of each square was placed the Eagle or fannon, and its Colour Guard and corps of drums. Each battalion was led by its colonel. In each gap between squares was a two-gun section of the horse-artillery of the Guard under Colonel Duchand. Ney was ordered to lead these forward, supported by an all-out attack by every man of Reille and D'Erlon's corps capable of standing, and behind them by the heavy cavalry. The Guard infantry would be supported by the Guard cavalry.[28]

The point of attack was to be between Adam's brigade at the north-east corner above Hougoumont and just before the crossroads. In that convex, from left to right, were the Allied batteries of Mercer, Rogers, Bolton, Sandham (which had returned) and Cleeves. Behind them were ranged the brigades of Adam, Maitland, Halkett, Brunswick and Kruse.

To the beat of their drums the Old Guard, supported on its flanks by Reille and d'Erlon's corps, and supported from behind by the cavalry, started its right-angled advance in echelon, down and then up the valley. The troops of Marcognet, Donzelot, and Quiot vigorously assaulted the Allies behind the hedges on the left flank. On the right the assailants of Hougoumont, fired up with the news that the Old Guard was going forward – a sign that always heralded victory – again drove murderously against the shell of the château. On the flanks of the Guard, Foy's brigade to its left, and Bachelu's division to its right, prepared the way. And, as the Guard moved off, the French artillery with jubilant *élan* fired into the Allied line.

As this advance was getting under way, back in the dip near Frischermont General Müffling had ridden down to stop Steinmetz's leading brigade from attacking The Netherlands troops of Perponcher. These Nassauers, the 28th Netherlands Line Regiment, were dressed in blue coats, grey trousers and white belting, and were therefore very similar in appearance to the French and had been attacked by mistake. General Müffling then ordered Steinmetz to march his brigade to Wellington's left flank. Lieutenant-Colonel von Reiche, Chief of Staff of Zeithen's I Corps, recorded these events:

'The first people I came upon were the Nassau troops forming the left wing of the English army, and it was not long before I met our General von Müffling, attached to Wellington's Headquarters. From him I learned that the duke was anxiously awaiting our arrival and had repeatedly declared that time was running very short, and that the duke had already strengthened his centre at the expense of his left wing, and that it was therefore urgent that Zeithen should link up with that wing; and I was to direct the corps accordingly ... On returning to the battlefield [from Müffling] I found that the situation had deteriorated. The Nassau ranks had given way and their guns were already moving back. I did my best to prevent anything worse happening, and assured them over and over again that the 1st Prussian Army Corps must arrive at any minute. I was hurrying back [from the Nassauers] towards the corps in order to report to Gerneral Zeithen, when Captain von Scharnhorst, now a Lieutenant-general and Inspector of Artillery but at that time on Prince Blücher's staff, dashed up to me, shouting that the 1st Corps must push on immediately to Blücher beyond Frischermont, because things were beginning to go badly there. I pointed out to him what had been arranged with Müffling, and emphasized that Wellington was relying implicitly on our arrival. But von Scharnhorst would not listen, and said that this was Blücher's order and he would hold me responsible for the consequences if it were not carried out...

'General Steinmetz, who commanded the advance-guard, came up to the halted troops at this moment, stormed at me in his usual violent manner, and insisted upon an advance. He was scarcely willing to listen to how things stood. My embarrassment increased not a little when General Steinmetz let the head of the column resume its march and himself went past the point where the road to Frischermont branches off [right to Papelotte, centre to Plancenoit and left to Plancenoit by way of the Chapelle St-Lambert road and Blücher] ... Fortunately General Zeithen came up at this critical moment. I hurried over to him and when I had given my report, he issued orders for the advance to be continued without fail towards the English army.'[29]

Steinmetz's brigade thus turned and took the central road up out of the dip towards Papelotte and the very hinge of Napoleon's two lines at right angles.

Marshal Ney, with Generals Friant, Rouguet and Michel, and all the other general officers of the Guard, rode at the head of the attacking columns; Ney's horse – the fifth this day – was shot from under him and he walked on next to Friant. At 600 yards from the Allied line the Guard passed Napoleon as if on review. The Emperor sat astride his horse in front of two batteries which were firing up the road in the general direction of Wellington's centre. The sun was beginning to sink and the appalling clouds of gunpowder smoke which hung all around the valley gave an eerie appearance to the Guard as the rays in the west threw their shadows up on to the smoke, giving the Allies the impression that the Guards were both taller and nearer than they actually were.

The Allied batteries opened fire on the advancing Guard with some 30 guns, double-shotted with canister. Captain Mercer's battery had barely fired a volley before the French battery near La Haye Sainte opened an enfilade fire along its flank. Mercer's battery, presenting such a large target, was reduced to a tangled mass of broken guns, limbers, wheels and men, and some 90 horses were killed.[30] The Netherlands horse-battery of Krahmer de Binche arrived providentially near to Mercer's position, unlimbered, and knocked out the threatening French battery, saving the rest of Mercer's command. In his poverty of spirit, Mercer could feel only chagrin and ingratitude at his deliverance.[31]

Bodies of men and horses lay so thick upon the ground on the slopes and the spur which projected into the middle of the Allied position, and the dense smoke was so obscuring, that the French echelons diverged from their diagonal advance, the 1/3rd and 4th Grenadiers keeping to their original line of advance, but the three others veering slightly to the left of the spur. The 1/3rd Grenadiers with Friant and Ney at their head overran the battery of Cleeves, started to push back one of the Brunswick battalions, and also pushed back the 30th and 73rd Foot. A few minutes later the 4th Grenadiers pushed into the other half of Halkett's brigade and pushed the 33rd and 69th backwards.[32]

At this moment Captain Krahmer de Binche's horse battery arrived and opened up with a volley of canister at less than 100 yards, disabling the 1/3rd Grenadiers. Ensign Macready of the 30th wrote in his diary: 'Some guns from the rear of our right poured in grape amongst them, and the slaughter was dreadful. Nowhere did I see carcasses so heaped upon each other ...(I believe) these guns to be Mr van der Smissen's. Whosesoever they were, they were served most gloriously, and their grand metallic bang, bang, bang, bang, with the rushing showers of grape that followed, were the most welcome sounds that ever struck my ears – until I married.'[33]

As the 1/3rd recoiled and the 4th Grenadiers pushed forward, General Baron Chassé launched the 3,000 men of Detmers' brigade of the 3rd Netherlands Division, to which Captain Krahmer's battery belonged. They poured past Macready and routed what was left of the 1,000 men of the two shattered Guard battalions that had endured the Allied artillery all the way up the slope, and Krahmer's canister at close range. This overwhelming avalanche by nearly four times their number was too much for the French and they retreated to avoid the bayonets. Macready, who had survived with 160 men of his regiment, wrote: 'A heavy column of Dutch infantry (the first we had seen) passed, drumming and shouting like mad, with their chakos on the top of their bayonets, near enough to our right for us to see and laugh with them.'[34]

Meanwhile the 1/3rd *Chasseurs*, who had almost been joined by the 2/3rd *Chasseurs* in their march left towards Maitland's brigade, were receiving the fire of Bolton, Rogers and Ramsay's (commanded by Lieutenent Sandilands) batteries. Just as they reached the Ohain road Maitland's Brigade of Guards, some 1,500 strong, stood up in the high-standing corn, four deep and at about 20 yards from the double column, and poured a withering fire into the 1/3rd *Chasseurs* which cut them to pieces. The Guards charged forward and sent the routed column pell-mell back down the hill, but the 4th *Chasseurs* behind rallied the 2/3rd and poured fire into the Guards who, elated, had advanced too soon, and sent them back to their lines post-haste. At this point Colonel Sir John Colborne on his own initiative wheeled his 1,000-strong élite 52nd Light Infantry into line so that its entire length, some 500 yards, was parallel with the flank of the French 4th *Chasseurs* and the remnant of the 2/3rd *Chasseurs*. The 52nd poured a volley into the column and it disintegrated. At the same time Colonel William Halkett's 3 Hanoverian Brigade, coming up from behind Hougoumont, fired into its rear, completing its destruction. Sir John then ordered an oblique advance in line with the bayonet.

While the Imperial Guard was being resisted, the French troops of Foy, Bachelu and d'Erlon's corps pressed the Allies to the last extremity, supported by the heavy cavalry behind that was keeping the Allies in a close formation.[35] All along the French line, which started at Hougoumont, extended to Papelotte where it turned right, and then curved backward to the road past Plancenoit, almost in the shape of a huge question mark, the Emperor's soldiers gave everything they had.

Suddenly, from the Smohain dip, rising to the crest of the miniature amphitheatre came Steinmetz's brigade, nearly 2,500 infantrymen in a Prussian brigade attack column which drove straight into the plain, its fusilier battalions fanning out right and left, rolling up d'Erlon's line and Lobau's left flank. They drove before them those few of Durutte's reduced command who had survived the onslaught by hiding in the dip. Behind them, moving rapidly up and out of the ground, came Lützow's cavalry brigade of 1,300 troopers, followed by von Treskow's brigade of another 2,000 men. These also turned their regiments left and right to hack, stab and overrun the French soldiers from the rear. General Zeithen placed his artillery near the crest of the dip, firing on both French flanks. The effect on French morale was shattering; Napoleon had announced to the army that Grouchy had arrived, and now here were the Prussians attacking them in the rear from behind the centre of both d'Erlon's and Lobau's positions, driving a wedge right towards La Belle Alliance some 1,000 yards behind them. Zeithen brought up his cannon to fire into the rear of both Lobau and d'Erlon.[36]

As d'Erlon and Lobau's lines suddenly contracted and withdrew away from the Prussians, thus widening the breach, Napoleon's army was cut into two halves. Panic rippled along the lines, giving rise to cries of 'Treason, save yourselves!' and 'The Prussians!'. Zeithen, the man who had prevented Napoleon from gaining his objectives on the 15th, and had fought so hard against him on the 16th at Ligny, had, by disobeying Blücher's orders, destroyed Napoleon's army utterly. Having used his corps to break Napoleon's line at its weakest point, Zeithen, coming up out of the Smohain hollow, had penetrated the French line with his mass where no reserves were available. It mattered not what the French did in front of Wellington or in front of Lobau and Plancenoit, for now whatever they did Zeithen and his infantry and cavalry were behind both their fronts.

In the French ranks panic spread like wildfire. The Guard first wave, having been defeated and stopped by the Allies under Wellington, were now driven back from the front and flank. Whatever Napoleon might have done with the second wave of Guard battalions would now be of little use; his line was broken, his centre ruptured and his flanks were being rolled up.

The remainder of d'Erlon's and Reille's men had but one wish: to gain the Genappe road before Zeithen closed it. A jubilant Gneisenau wrote to his King:

> 'General Zeithen arrived on the points of attack, near the village of Smouhen [sic] on the enemy's right flank, and instantly charged. This moment decided the defeat of the enemy. His right wing was broken in three places; he abandoned his positions. Our troops rushed forward at the pas de charge, and attacked him on all sides, while, at the same time the whole English line advanced. Circumstances were extremely favourable to the attack formed by the Prussian army; the ground rose in an amphitheatre, so that our artillery could freely open its fire from the summit of a great many heights which rose gradually above each other, and, in the intervals of which the troops descended into the plain, formed into brigades and in the greatest order; while fresh corps continually unfolded themselves, issuing from the forest on the height behind us.'[37]

Wellington, seeing this mayhem and the arrival of the Prussians from Maitland's position, stood up in his stirrups and waved his hat in the direction of the retreating French, ordering his first offensive move of the day. The whole Anglo-Allied line moved forward and followed General Chassé and Sir John Colborne's precipitated advance on the Imperial Guard. Some regiments such as the 30th Foot, however, who had had to stand all day and receive appalling punishment, were too exhausted to move. The spent men of that regiment, some 160 left standing, piled their arms and sat down or tried to find water.[38]

Napoleon's army had achieved marvels. It had been engaged by nearly double its numbers, and since 3.30 p.m. it had kept Wellington's superior army drawn up in a defensive posture, taking incredible punishment from artillery, cavalry and combined arms assaults. The French army had held the Prussians at Plancenoit with less than half the Prussians' numbers, while attacking Wellington's superior force with a lesser force and at one point (6-6.30 p.m.) nearly breaking his centre. In the end, however, Napoleon had been beaten by his own tactics. He had accepted a battle on two fronts, and had committed his last reserve only to have the attacker break through the weakest part of his line with a large fresh force – the 'mass of decision of Zeithen'.

Napoleon now had a routed army, but no reserves with which to form a rearguard behind which he could rally his forces and stop them becoming a panic-stricken mob. Giving one of his last orders, he sent General Piré to ride to the approaches to Genappe and try to stem the routing troops and restore some order.

In the hope of stemming this rout Napoleon had placed the four remaining Guard battalions in squares, with his four service squadrons of the Guard drawn up behind, hoping to prevent Wellington's forces from advancing along the *Chaussée* in pursuit, while the men of Reille, d'Erlon and the rest of the Guard rallied behind it. It was useless. On its right flank General Durutte, whose left hand had been nearly severed, was being closely pursued by the Prussians.[39] Napoleon, who had taken refuge in one of the squares, left the field with one squadron of Guard *chasseurs* to ride back to his two oldest battalions, where he would try to use his charisma, as at Arcis-sur-Aube in 1814, to stem the rout. On that occasion he had planted himself squarely on a bridge and demanded, 'Which of you will cross before his Emperor?' and his embarrassed troops had sorted themselves out.[40]

Between 8 and 9 p.m. these last four squares were assailed by the men of Adam and Halkett's brigades, Chassé's division and the cavalry brigades of Vivian and Vandeleur. This Allied advance, by the time it had covered the roughly 800 yards to the Guard squares, had become intermingled and more like a mob. Vivian's cavalry attempted to break the squares of the Old Guard and received a volley from them and a counter-attack by Napoleon's three élite *escadrons du service*, which soon drove them to seek easier prey, such as the backs of the routing infantry and cavalrymen.[41] Marshal Ney was unrecognizable, bare-headed and blackened face, uniform in tatters, his epaulettes shot off and holding the hilt of his shattered sword which, in frustration and fury, he had broken on a cannon after his fifth horse had been killed under him and he had failed to rally the men. Major Rulliere took the dazed Marshal into one of the squares. Rulliere was carrying the Eagle of the 95th and hoped to avoid its capture. Slowly, against incredible odds, the Old Guard squares moved off toward Genappe. They had no trouble repelling the Allied cavalry, but the infantry raked the squares and brought down men in ranks, which quickly closed. Soon artillery came up and opened fire with canister at point-blank range, quickly reducing the squares to triangles. The brigades of Adam and Halkett especially were determined to stop the Guard withdrawing. Step by step, over countless bodies, the Guard continued to move. Every fifty yards they halted to close up, and all the time their numbers dwindled under the fierce fire.

Some British officers called upon the stricken Guard to surrender, but the only reply was '*Merde!*'[42] The disorder on the field is hard to imagine; in the falling light, dismounted *cuirassiers* threw away their armour and ran, drivers cut free their horses and rode off, deserting their guns and wagons. Wounded men were trampled to death in the rush to leave the field. The four depleted Guard squares were the only organized French troops left on the plateau, and their slow, deliberate retreat blocked the road and paths to the enemy trying to race after their fleeing countrymen. Marshal Ney was assisted to horse and rode off toward Napoleon. By the time the first three squares had passed La Belle Alliance, Allied canister had reduced them virtually to nothing. Those of them who had not been killed took to their heels. Only the 2/3rd Grenadiers, commanded by Colonel Belcourt, fought on. Attacked by Vivian, the 2/3rd brought down nearly 200 horses, which then acted as a rampart. Another charge opened a corner, allowing fifteen riders to enter, but they were promptly bayoneted. The 2/3rd moved on again towards Rossomme, but by letting in French stragglers and wounded, it lost its cohesion and was advancing now in a triangular formation. Not long afterwards rounds of canister and cavalry charges finished it, and its men lay dead in a heap.

Near Rossomme, where Napoleon had halted his two élite battalions of the Grenadiers of the Old Guard, he placed a 12pdr battery of the Foot Guard artillery beside them. The battery had retired from the ridge in good order but without any ammunition. Napoleon hoped to rally his men here and form a rearguard, but on either side of the Old Guard and himself streamed French soldiers of all arms. The presence of these silent Guards did nothing to dissuade them, nor did any exhortations from their officers. Some Allied hussars rode forward towards the immobile squares which 'stood like granite blocks, two squares defying two armies', when a volley of canister from the 12pdrs brought them crashing to the ground. The artillerymen, although having no more ammunition, stood as if about to fire again, a bluff which worked for a few minutes until the cavalry charged again, sabring the gunners, but receiving a massive volley from the squares that reduced the hussars' yet further.

Meanwhile in Plancenoit the French found that the Prussian onslaught had not only increased but that they were being assailed from behind and from the north-east by Steinmetz's infantry. Plancenoit, whose burning buildings illuminated the darkening sky, still held ten battalions of the Guard, eight Young and two of the Old, as well as part of Lobau's corps. Plancenoit had become a cornerstone of the battle, and the defenders had fortified every dwelling as strongly as possible. The church, with its circular wall, was the central point and citadel, and was held by one battalion of the Young Guard. The main Prussian attack on the church was carried out by the 1st Pomeranian Regiment and the 5th Westphalian Militia – some 2,300 men. The village was attacked in detail from the south by the 25th Regiment of Pirch's II Corps.[43] House by house, and smallholding by smallholding, the village had to be taken, the defenders dying where they stood. In gardens and orchards, streets and houses, they shot and slaughtered one another. By the end of the evening very few French were left alive.

Blücher, leaving the slaughter of the encircled French in Plancenoit to Pirch, had with part of IV Corps gone around the village on to the Genappe road and had joined up with Wellington. They greeted each other cordially and Wellington explained that his army was exhausted: *'fatigué à en mourir'*[44] and could not continue the pursuit. Blücher, with his eternally vigorous hussar heart, and Gneisenau agreed to take over the role.

This says something about the ability of the Prussian army of 1815. Blücher had fought Napoleon throughout the 15th and 16th, suffering a technical defeat, and had retreated on Wavre during the 17th. From there, on the morning of the 18th, he had negotiated his army over ten appalling miles, fought the French for five hours, and now with one corps to his knowledge engaged with three French corps at Wavre more than ten miles away, he was prepared to carry out the pursuit of the rest of Napoleon's army. His men had had no rest since the 15th, and had suffered thousands of wounded. His train had been sent on to Louvain, so his army was was without supplies. Only the iron spirit of Blücher could have galvanized the exhausted Prussians 'to go the extra miles' to prevent Napoleon's army from rallying. Blücher, in a feeling of camaraderie, suggested that they name the battle after the inn of La Belle Alliance, in commemoration of their joint operation. Wellington did not reply to this suggestion, but later told his aide that he would continue his Peninsula practice, and name the battle after his headquarters – at Waterloo.

The two squares of the Old Guard were still unbroken. Presenting their bayonets, they had no intention of being swamped and overrun. On Napoleon's order they moved off in formation with him towards Le Caillou where he collected his papers, treasury, staff and the 1/1st *Chasseurs*, in whose square he marched off toward Genappe, followed by the other two battalions impregnable to all assaults upon them. At Genappe Napoleon left the Guard squares and found an absolute shambles. The three battalions of the Old Guard, wisely turning left by the village and crossing the Dyle at Ways la Hutte, proceeded towards Philippeville, France and immortality.

At Genappe Napoleon did everything he could to restore order. Hundreds of overturned vehicles – carts, guns, forage, baggage and ammunition wagons – clogged the winding path. Most of the horses had been cut free to be used by soldiers and drivers to flee. Thousands of panic-stricken troops crushed one another in their efforts to get across the stream. Most of them were unaware of the other two crossings. The bridge was only 2½ yards wide, and desperate men attempted to cut their way through, not realizing that the stream, impassible for vehicles, was only three yards wide and three feet deep. Napoleon, having reached his coach, found it impossible to move more than a few yards.

Soon the Prussians were upon the village. Napoleon took to his horse, and his escort beat a path through the throng. He barely escaped capture. The Prussians relentlessly attacked the human herd to their front. The *Uhlans* had butchered scores of French, before the French soldiers fought back. Nameless officers and NCOs took charge and improvised a barricade. The Prussians, however, soon brought up a battery of horse artillery and blew it apart. By now the French had discovered the shallowness of the stream, and were decamping as fast as they could. Roder's cavalry thundered down on through the village and slaughtered most of the French who had surrendered, wounded or not. They plundered the Emperor's coach which, besides his hat, sword and cane, contained diamonds worth a million francs. As an example of what the French could expect from the Prussians now that the tables had been turned, Napoleon's personal surgeon, Baron Larrey, wounded on the field by two sword cuts, was struck again by an *Uhlan*'s lance. The *Uhlan* then stripped and plundered him, and led the wounded doctor, almost naked with tied hands, to his general, who ordered Larrey to be taken out and shot. Just before a firing-squad could carry out the summary sentence, a Prussian surgeon, who had recognized Larrey from Berlin, intervened to save the eminent surgeon.[45]

Blücher halted his pursuit at the inn 'Roi d'Espagne' at Genappe, and wrote that night to his wife: 'I have been true to my word, on the 16th I was compelled to withdraw before superior forces; but on the 18th acting with my friend Wellington, I have annihilated the army of Napoleon.' Gneisenau, determined not to give Napoleon a chance, as in 1814, to rally his army, continued the pursuit until he reached Frasnes. All the way there, on his 'hunt by moonlight' he had a drummer-boy mounted on a horse at his side playing a march and trumpeters sounding the charge. At Frasnes Gneisenau halted exhausted and commandeered the use of the 'Sum Kaiser' inn, where he finished his report to the king:

> 'At Genappe, the enemy had entrenched himself with cannon and overturned carriages: at our approach we suddenly heard in the town a great noise and a motion of carriages: at the entrance we were exposed to a brisk fire of musketry; we replied by some cannon-shot, followed by a Hurrah, and, in an instant after, the town was ours... thus the affairs continued until daybreak. About forty thousand men, in the most complete disorder, the remains of the whole army, have saved themselves, retreating through Charleroi, partly without arms, and carrying with them only twenty-seven pieces of their numerous artillery.'[46]

Wellington, after his meeting with Blücher, rode back over the field, passing the four squares of dead French Guardsmen who had slowed the Allied advance. He went up the road and past the more than 400 dead of the 27th Foot's square, who looked as though they lay asleep, and back to the inn at Waterloo. But he did not seek his bed – this was occupied by his aide, Colonel Gordon, who was dying. Instead, he went to the table near the fireplace to write his official dispatch to London. One of his aides informed him that the Earl of Uxbridge, the man whose initiative had destroyed Napoleon's plan, had lost his leg and that the Duke's Military Secretary, Lord Fitzroy Somerset, had lost an arm. Wellington sat down and wrote his official report to the Earl of Bathurst, in which he stated:

> '... these attacks [of the French] were repeated till about seven in the evening, when the enemy made a desperate effort with cavalry and infantry, supported by the fire of artillery, to force our left centre, near the farm of La Haye Sainte, which, after a severe contest was defeated; and, having observed that these troops retired from this attack in great confusion, and that the march of General Bülow's corps, by Frischermont, upon Planchenois [sic] and La belle Alliance, had begun to take effect, and as I could perceive the fire of his cannon, and as Marshal Prince Blücher had joined in person with a corps of his army to our left line by Ohain, *I determined to attack the enemy, and immediately advanced the whole line of the infantry, supported by the cavalry and artillery.*'[47]

On the 19th, at 8.30 a.m., Wellington wrote his first letter, to Lady Frances Webster:

> 'I yesterday, after a most severe and bloody contest, gained a complete victory, and pursued the French till dark. They are in complete confusion; and I have I believe, 150 pieces of cannon; and Blücher, who continued the pursuit all night, my soldiers being tired to death, sent me word this morning that he had got 60 more ... The finger of providence was upon me, and I escaped unhurt.'[48]

Napoleon had reached Philippeville by morning. He was not stupified, nor dumbfounded; he still had a war to fight; and to lose a battle, as at Leipzig, was not to lose the war. Napoleon immediately wrote to his brother Joseph in Paris:

> 'All is by no means lost. I suppose I shall have 150,000 men available when my forces are once more united. The well-affected among the federated troops and the National Guards will give me another 100,000 men, and I shall obtain 50,000 more from the depot battalions. Thus I shall have 300,000 soldiers to oppose the enemy. I shall horse my artillery with carriage horses; I shall raise 100,000 conscripts; I shall arm the latter with muskets taken from the Royalists and from the disaffected of the National Guard [of Paris]; I shall call up the whole male populations of

Dauphiny, Lyonnais, Burgundy, Lorraine, Champagne; I shall crush the enemy; but it is essential that I am helped and assisted and not bewildered. I am now setting out for Laon; doubtless I shall find there some of my army. I have no news of Grouchy; if he is not taken, as I fear may be the case, then in three days I shall possess 50,000 men. With this force I shall confront and occupy the enemy's attention, and thus obtain time necessary for Paris and France to do its duty.

'The Austrians advance but slowly; the Prussians fear the country people and dare not push on rapidly, there is still time therefore to repair all. Write to me of the effect which this horrible muddle has produced in the Chamber. I believe that the deputies will recognize that their duty at this moment is to rally around me so as to save France. Therefore prepare to second my efforts suitably; above all let them show courage and resolution.'[49]

Napoleon might have lost this battle, but he had not yet lost the war. He still had nearly 400,000 men under arms in France, not counting Grouchy and the half of his army that was dispersed. He was certain that those so dispersed would rally. Since 15 June the Allies had sustained as many casualties as he had. Let them soak up some more on his northern fortresses, then he would see. He had lost more heavily after his campaign in Russia in 1812, then had raised more men and trounced the Russians and Prussians in 1813. After Leipzig in 1813, when he had lost many more men, the Allies had declared him defeated. Again, in 1814 he had raised another army and run rings round the Allies until Paris had been betrayed. Compared with such losses, those at Mont St-Jean were insignificant, strategically if not personally.

Aftermath: Wavre, Pursuit, Lost Opportunities

'The haft of the arrow had been feathered with one of the eagle's plumes.
We often give our enemies the means of our own destruction.' - Aesop,
The Eagle and the Arrow, 550 BC.

Throughout the night of 18/19 June, as the French fugitives made their way south, Marshal Grouchy, ignorant of the lost battle, continued his fighting around Limale, Bierges, Wavre and Basse Wavre. In the falling light, Grouchy deployed his battalions of Teste's division in front of Limale. Major Stengle's men maintained a brisk fire on these columns as they wound their way to their positions through the lanes and villages, with Pajol advancing his cavalry to the division's left flank.

Colonel Stulpnägel's 12 Brigade was now reduced to six battalions. As a reserve he left the fusilier battalion of the 5th Kurmark *Landwehr* and one battery in a small copse north of Bierges, and joined Stengel who, with the other five battalions, was now on his right. Stulpnägel's orders were to regain Limale and drive the French across the Dyle. He assaulted the French with an attack column composed of two battalions in the first line and three in support. His two squadrons of cavalry were sent to reinforce Stengel on his right. Darkness had descended so quickly that little cohesion was possible between units, and the attack fell to pieces more from confusion than opposition. Little was known in the dark of the formation of the ground; there were folds and a hollow lane into which the first line of the Prussian assault columns fell. French skirmishers on the other side fired into this mass of disorganized Prussians who tried to reply. The second line of Prussians coming up in support advanced too far to the left in the dark and became a front line itself, facing Pecheux's complete French division. Stengel, on the right, was charged by the French cavalry and compelled to retire. Stulpnägel, realizing that this fiasco if continued would only waste more Prussian lives, retired his men to the lee of the woods behind Point-du-Jour, leaving a strong picket line for the night.

The French, not prepared to make the same mistakes as the Prussians, declined to attack until daylight. At Wavre and the mill of Bierges, though, the fighting increased rather than abated. Vandamme's entire corps was engaged, assaulting the barricaded bridge time after time. Thirteen recorded attacks were repulsed by the Prussians, and on five occasions the defenders pursued the French back to the houses on the far side of the Dyle. On one occasion the French gained the far bank and occupied some of the buildings, only to be driven out by the Prussian reserves. Thielemann had but four battalions defending Wavre against the whole of Vandamme's corps, but while the attackers were exposed to canister and musketry in the open at each attempt, the defenders remained secure behind loopholed walls.

At Basse Wavre, lower down the Dyle, the French did not press home any attack. Exelmans' cavalry had been ordered to make a demonstration on this flank, supported by one battalion of infantry and a section of horse artillery. Since the bridge there had been blown by the Prussians, the stream was unfordable, and Exelmans was without sappers so his continued presence there was of little use. By 11 p.m., when all fighting had ceased, Grouchy had gained the northern bank at Limale, and he was sure that he had entrapped at least half of Blücher's army. It was too late to assist Napoleon at Mont St-Jean, but as the noise of battle had died out there he assumed that the Emperor had been victorious.

Grouchy took no steps to make contact as ordered with the left flank of Napoleon's army. Instead, he ordered Vandamme to move his corps across the Dyle at Limale and crush the Prussians in the morning. Thielemann by contrast had sent several messengers to Gneisenau by way of Ohain, and had ascertained by the early hours of the 19th that Napoleon's army had been utterly routed. It was therefore reasonable for Thielemann to have expected Grouchy to withdraw at first light. Naturally, in the circumstances, Major Stengel marched off to join his own troops (4 Brigade of I Corps) at first light, followed by Colonel Ledebur, to join his troops (19 Brigade of IV Corps), with his five squadrons and two guns, thus weakening Thielemann's force. Consequently, on the morning of the 19th, when Thielemann saw French troops still facing him, he assumed that these were Grouchy's rearguard. Thielemann ordered Colonel Marwitz, with the 8th *Uhlans* and two squadrons of the 6th Kurmark *Landwehr* cavalry, to attack Grouchy's left flank above Limale, while General Hobe with the 5th and 7th *Uhlans* was to support Marwitz's left. Colonel Stulpnägel's 12 Brigade was ordered to extend itself further to the right to cover the gap left by Major Stengel's departure. This weakened the brigade's strength and left a mere three battalions in reserve in the wood of Point-du-Jour.

On Stulpnägel's left, six battalions of Kamphen's 10 Brigade held a line between Bierges and the Dyle. In reserve were five battalions of *Landwehr* from von Luck's 11 Brigade, and two battalions from Stulpnägel were detailed to hold the bridge at Bierges. The remainder of Thielemann's force was extended along the Dyle in Wavre and Basse Wavre. Marwitz started his probing attack with fire from two batteries, one horse and one foot, on the French columns massed on the plateau above Limale. So great was the response from the French guns, however, that they soon silenced the Prussians, disabling five of their guns. As Vandamme had been been unable to disengage his corps and cross the Dyle at Limale, Grouchy prepared to attack the Prussians with just the four divisions of Gérard and Teste's corps, with Pajol's cavalry. He formed up Teste's, Vichery's and

Pecheux's divisions in columns in his first line. Teste was to attack Bierges and the mill; Vichery, the centre of the Prussian line; and Pecheux, Stulpnägel's right flank. Each of these columns was provided with a battery of artillery and was preceded by skirmishers. The remaining division of Hulot's was to act as a reserve in the rear, and Pajol's cavalry was to turn the Prussian right flank resting on Rixensart Wood. Unknown to Thielemann, 28 French battalions were preparing to attack ten Prussian battalions.

Thielemann, seeing the French build-up, reinforced his line with a further battalion which was all that he had to spare. The French columns soon forced back the Prussians who were trying to hold an extended line. Pajol and Pecheux took Rixensart Wood; and Stulpnägel fell back on his supports, the three battalions of the 11 Brigade, and took up a defensive posture behind the wood. Teste's attack on the mill foundered and the two Prussian battalions were reinforced with four battalions of 10 Brigade. Marwitz, on the Prussian right flank, used all twelve squadrons of his cavalry to secure Chambre and the Brussels road. At about 8 a.m. Thielemann received a definitive report about La Belle Alliance and the French rout, and the news spread along his line, increasing his troops' morale. They soon rushed forward and recaptured Rixensart Wood.

This unexpected attack at first prompted Grouchy to fear that the Prussians had greater strength than he had imagined or that they had been reinforced, but in fact Stulpnägel's effort was short-lived, and a French counter-attack again cleared the woods. At 9 a.m. Bierges at last fell to Teste. This was a severe blow to Thieleman, whose line was thus broken at its angle; his centre pierced, he could no longer defend the pressure of both wings and he withdrew. Vandamme meanwhile, although not assaulting the bridge, had maintained pressure on the troops there by a constant cannonade and sniping, with the threat of an imminent assault if Thielemann withdrew any of his men. Thielemann, well aware that Grouchy himself must soon retreat, decided not to waste any more men when the decisive battle had already been won; he therefore retreated as ordered towards Louvain, protected by a strong rearguard provided by Marwitz's cavalry. Wavre was evacuated and Vandamme immediately stormed into it in hot pursuit. In the rear of Wavre, in a hollow, two battalions of the 4th Kurmark *Landwehr* were waiting to cover the withdrawal of the corps, and these slowed the pursuit long enough for the defenders of the bridge to disengage. The Prussian cavalry held back the leading squadrons of Vandamme's cavalry and allowed Thielemann to withdraw toward Louvain by way of St-Achetenrode, where Thielemann took up a defensive position. He did not intend to retreat too far, being certain that later he would have to advance over the same ground in pursuit.

At 10.30 a.m. a staff officer brought Grouchy the news of Napoleon's defeat.[1] Grouchy was dumbounded and at a loss as to what to do. He could still march on Blücher's rear, but to do that now would place his inferior force betwen Thielemann and Blücher. Grouchy still did not know that Napoleon had been utterly routed. The Emperor, Grouchy believed, had simply been forced to quit the field as at Brienne in 1814. He knew that Napoleon had always managed to rally his men after a defeat. On the 19th he convened a General Officers' council of war. In light of his refusal to march to the sound of the guns, or permit General Gérard to do so, Grouchy felt he ought to justify his decision:

> 'My honour makes it a matter of duty to explain myself in regard to my dispositions of yesterday. The instructions which I received from the Emperor, left me free to manoeuvre in no other direction than Wavre. I was obliged, therefore, to refuse the advice which Count Gérard thought he had a right to offer me. I do ample justice to General Gérard's talents and brilliant vigour; but you are doubtless as surprised as I was, that a general officer, ignorant of the Emperor's orders, and the data which inspired the Marshal of France, under whose orders he was placed, should have presumed publicly to dictate to the latter, his line of conduct. The advanced hour of the day, the distance from the point where the cannonading was heard, the condition of the roads, made it impossible to arrive in time to share in the action which was taking place. At any rate, whatever the subsequent events may have been, the Emperor's orders, the substance of which I have just disclosed to you, did not permit of me acting otherwise than I have done.'[2]

At this meeting General Vandamme put forward a plan which he thought would disrupt the Allies and slow their advance toward France. He proposed that they should march on Brussels by way of Wavre, seize the capital city, release the thousands of French prisoners, gain the political prize and drive out the two Vienna kings. Then when the Allies, strung out in pursuit of the Emperor, fell back to succour the Belgian Netherlands capital, Grouchy's force should fall back to France by way of either Lille, or Enghien and Ath.[3] This innovative plan was rejected by Grouchy, who decided to retreat back to France by way of Namur, Dinant and Givet. At 11 a.m. he gave the orders for his army to commence its retreat.

From Genappe Napoleon had reached Quatre Bras on horseback with Marshal Soult, Count Bertrand and Drouot, accompanied by a dozen lancers of the Imperial Guard. He had hoped to use Girard's division, which had been left at Fleurus after Ligny, and which had been ordered there on the evening of the 18th, to be in position to stem the rout and form a rearguard. There were, however, no signs of the division – it had already retreated across the Sambre at Charleroi. Gneisenau's stratagem of pursuing quickly with light cavalry, mounted drummers and light infantry had kept the routed French in panic, like that of the Prussians after Jena in 1806. Napoleon was only as much use as the next man in this confusion, so he rode on to Philippeville, arriving there at 9 a.m. on the morning of the 19th. There he wrote two letters to his brother, King Joseph, one for public and one for private consumption. Joseph, as in 1814, however, disclosed both to the Council of Ministers, which included the Royalist agent Fouché. Armed with this crucial intelligence Fouché at once set about turning the Royalist wheels of subversion.[4]

Before the campaign had opened, Fouché had persuaded Napoleon not to execute the Bourbon Minster Baron de Vitrolles. Vitrolles had been captured trying to raise the royalists in the south and had intended handing Toulon over to the British Navy on Napoleon's return.[5] He had further alienated Napoleon by the treacherous part he had played in the *coup d'état* that overthrew Napoleon in 1814.[6] Fouché had asked Napoleon to keep Vitrolles alive to trade with the Bourbons for the crown jewels taken when they departed. In fact Vitrolles was a high-ranking officer of the secret Bourbon terrorist organization *Chevaliers de la Foi*, which had become a secret political party for d'Artois at the first Restoration,[7] and would be useful to Fouché in making an approach to the Royalist underground if Napoleon's bid to restore himself failed.

Already on 13 June Louis at Ghent had given unlimited powers to the Chevalier Hyde de Neuville, another high-ranking officer of the organization, to form an underground government and to carry out drumhead courts-martial of its enemies.[8] Hyde de Neuville's provisional 'government' was also instructed that:

> 'It shall cause the arrest of all who shall contravene this order, or shall attempt by violence or otherwise, to oppose the re-establishment of the rightful authority. It shall, by proclamation, declare that the King intends to put the Constitution again in force at the earliest possible moment.
> 'It shall cause the King's proclamation [ordinance] of the 6th of March last, against Buonaparte and his adherents and accomplices, to be published in Paris, as well as the Declaration of the Congress of Vienna, of the 13th of the same month.'[9]

In other words, Napoleon was to be executed if caught, as should any other person aiding the 'usurper'.

Already Fouché's plans for a *coup d'etat* were well under way, and involved playing on the republican spirit of disgruntled members such as the Marquis de Lafayette, who had betrayed his king in 1789, and had betrayed his country in 1792, when he went over to the Austrians. Now Lafayette was being set up to betray Napoleon who, as a victorious republican general, had obtained Lafayette's release from a sentence of death.[10]

Fouché easily persuaded the egotistical 'patriot' Lafayette that only he could save the country, and that the Allies had said that if Napoleon were removed France could determine its own government. He added that Napoleon again intended to declare himself absolute and dissolve the Chambers. Thus Fouché had given Cassius a dagger, a cause, a victim and the promise that he too might become Caesar.[11]

Fouché had not been idle in his role of Minister responsible for law and order. During Napoleon's absence from Paris on campaign, he had been busily replacing all the loyal Bonapartist members of the Paris Municipal National Guard with men loyal to him and the royalists, using the expedient of giving commissions to the rank and file in the provinces as a reward for their loyalty to the Emperor, and sending to the mobile battalions for garrison duties those reluctant to leave.[12]

Napoleon returned to Paris on 21 June after having instructed the border fortresses to hold out as long as possible so as to buy him time to field a new army from the 150,000 conscripts at the depots and exchange some of them for some of the 90,000 experienced men on the borders. He hoped that, with the probable 50,000 men who could be salvaged from the rout of the *Armée du Nord*, he could take the field with 200,000 men in a few weeks' time. Soult was given the task of bringing in the stragglers and making contact with Grouchy's force to bring it back towards the capital.

Napoleon, exhausted, arrived at the Tuileries in the early morning of 21 June. Fouché, having heard from his own sources that the Emperor had returned, arrived at the palace. Napoleon, dirty and exhausted by the exertion of the last six days, was advised by his brother Lucien and by Davout to prorogue the Chambers as was his right under the new constitution, declare a state of emergency and rule by decree. But Napoleon did not want to assume the mantle of dictator and give the Allies a propaganda weapon against him. Instead he said he would address the Chambers himself. Fouché agreed and declared that the nation was behind him.

Fouché had already arranged with the president of the lower house to bring forward the time that the Chambers sat due to 'a national emergency'. While Napoleon washed, changed and slept briefly, Fouché called on the great patriot Lafayette to speak. The once proud aristocrat, who had emulated George Washington, had had a bill passed through the Chambers which seemed on the surface as being for the national protection against royalists and traitors, and upholding the *tricolore*. The bill, drawn up in effect by Fouché, was really aimed at Napoleon. Its articles declared the Chamber immovable and inviolate, and called on the Municipal National Guard to defend the Chambers' building.[13] Without the consent of the Upper Chamber this course was illegal, but to Fouché that did not matter. If civil war or anarchy broke out, so much the better. That would show Europe that Napoleon had no authority save the army and that Paris was in rebellion against the usurper.

Napoleon, on hearing the news, refused to use force against the Chambers, sensing that the situation had been engineered and that it was hoped he would react arbitrarily.[14] Instead he trusted in the House of Peers to turn down the bill, thus making people see the proponents of the bill in the lower house as traitors. But Fouché had foreseen and prepared for this eventuality as well. When Carnot, Minister of the Interior, told the House (correctly) that he had been informed by Davout and Soult that the combined forces of Grouchy and the routed troops that had re-formed amounted to 60,000 men (in fact, 62,737), Marshal Ney rose and challenged the figure in his abrupt manner, calling it a lie. Ney said that there couldn't be more than 20,000 to 25,000 troops left under arms.[15] Marshal Ney had been provoked into this outburst by Fouché, who told him that he ought to defend himself against the accusation made in Napoleon's dispatch that he, Ney, had contributed to the disaster. Ney, exasperated by Napoleon's seeming ingratitude for all he had done for the Emperor since his return, now extracted a terrible revenge. He continued that no one knew better than he – or had as much to lose in a Bourbon restoration. Ney said that he had no reason not to tell the truth, and that he was convinced that the country would be overrun by the Allies within two weeks.[16]

The people, who were solidly behind Napoleon, had formed Militia battalions called *fédérés*, echoing the military units of the early Revolutionary period. These armed bands were outside the Chambers' building, howling against traitors. The Chambers, fearful of violent developments, recessed until a later date.

Napoleon had been left with little choice. He could seize power by force, using Davout's regulars against Fouché's National Guards positioned in the streets around the buildings (although Davout was not in favour of that course),[17] or use the *fédérés* and be seen as having the support only of a mob. Napoleon decided to try one last card: he offered to abdicate in favour of his son. The people of Paris were not in favour of this at all. The Chamber of Peers sat in fear of being lynched. Consequently, Fouché's supporters accepted Napoleon's abdication, but left open the succession, because of the tumult and the fact that Napoleon's son was being held hostage by the Austrians. Further, because of the dangerous situation in the streets and the need to restore order and consolidate the army for the national defence, it was proposed that a provisional government be set up following the acceptance of Napoleon's offer of abdication. The fact that it was conditional was ignored by Fouché and others.

Fouché, as he had intended, was nominated as president. Davout was made Minister of War, and Carnot, Lafayette and other *adaptibles* were given posts. The Chambers were 'temporarily' suspended because of the hostilities. Fouché created countless committees to occupy the other members of his government in discussions with the Allies concerning what form of government they would accept, even discussing a new constitution. While this was taking place Fouché, with Davout's assistance, connived to keep the army out of the Allies' path and to halt all resistance. Partisan groups were ordered to disband, and vital passes and bridges were abandoned. Only when the republican elements of the provisional government accused Davout of selling them out to the royalists, and under pressure from his own officers, did he engage Blücher in a limited skirmish.

Thus it was that, on 26 June, eight days after Waterloo, Napoleon was at Malmaison, and in Paris there were 117,000 troops of all arms, with 150,000 more equipped and in their depots. At Noyon, above Compiègne, Wellington was advancing with 52,000 men, after his casualties and detachments to besiege fortifications had been deducted. Blücher and Gneisenau were displeased with Wellington, despite their mutual victory: they felt that he was being too slow in his pursuit and they had asked Müffling to hurry the field marshal along. Müffling related:

> 'On the march to Paris, the Prussian army made longer marches than the English; and when in the morning [20th] I made my daily communications to the Duke, I took the liberty of respectfully calling his attention to this, and suggesting that it would be better if he kept the same pace as his ally. He was silent at first, but on my urging him again to move more rapidly, he said to me: "Do not press me on this point, for I tell you, it won't do. If you were better acquainted with the English army, its composition and habits, you would say the same. I cannot separate from my tents and my supplies. My troops must be well kept and well supplied in camp, if order and discipline are to be maintained. It is better that I should arrive two days later in Paris than discipline should be relaxed."'[18]

This seemingly pompous answer obviously angered the Prussian commanders, in light of the exertions already made and being made by them. But in making such a reply Wellington was being neither pompous nor truthful. He was merely carrying out his government's secret policy by dragging his feet until Louis XVIII could catch up. Among the Allied powers, it was only Britain that wanted the Bourbons back on the French throne. The Prussians were dismayed to realize that Wellington was carrying the Bourbon monarch back on his coat-tails, unilaterally and without prior discussions with his allies, despite the decision at Vienna that all the powers would decide this matter. Yet again Britain seemed to the Prussians as untrustworthy. The final straw was Wellington's refusal, in the event of his army capturing Napoleon, either to shoot him or agree to hand him over to the Prussians to be shot.[19] By 26 June, therefore, the Prussians were at Laon with 66,000 men, a day's march away from Wellington's 52,000 men, both in a position to be defeated in detail. Napoleon pleaded with Marshal Davout to let him use the 117,000 men Davout controlled to reverse his defeat at Mont St-Jean and then combine these with the 150,000 depot troops to use against the other Allies. He felt that everything lost could yet be regained. But Davout was now Minister of War and Commander-in-Chief of Fouché's provisional government, and had an eye to holding office under Louis. He refused Napoleon's plea. In fact, he went further and threatened that if Napoleon did not leave Paris he would have him arrested.[20]

Having lost the battle now called Waterloo, Napoleon had once again lost any chance of regaining his throne by military means. As in 1814, he had not lost the campaign or his throne through military defeat, but by the betrayal and treachery of men he had raised to prominence. That he had lost some 60,000 men killed, wounded and prisoners was not the cause of his defeat. Indeed, his resources after Waterloo in manpower, weapons and above all morale were much greater than after the appalling losses of men in the retreat from Russia in 1812 and after Leipzig in 1813. Napoleon still had more than 400,000 men available to him on 21 June and, but for the treachery of Fouché, Lafayette, Davout and the Royalists, he would have been able to continue fighting, as he had intended to do, with a reasonable prospect of success.

Deserted even by Davout, and with his enemy as head of government, Napoleon was isolated, without even his Imperial Guard to protect him. He had the choice of regaining control by civil war, thus allowing the enemy to defeat him and declare him a true usurper, or leaving with dignity and letting France and history judge the traitors. Napoleon left Paris for the Atlantic coast to board a ship provided by the provisional government before Fouché could hand him over to the Prussians as he intended to do.[21] It is likely that Napoleon would have made good his planned escape to America if the British Navy had not been alerted five days earlier by Fouché as to the place and mode of the Emperor's escape.

Fouché had released Vitrolles from prison on 23 June and had secretly set in motion the restoration of Louis XVIII. The part played by Fouché and the provisional government in preventing the French army from fighting the Allies and in handing over Paris and France without a fight was recognized in a secret letter from Wellington to Lord Castlereagh:

> 'The French people submitted to Buonaparte; but it would be ridiculous to suppose that the Allies would have been in possession of Paris in a fortnight after one battle fought, if the French people in general had not been favourably disposed to the cause which the Allies were supposed to favour [the right to determine their own government, barring the retention of Napoleon in power] ... The assistance which the King and his party in France gave to the cause was undoubtedly of a passive description [underground]; but the results of the operations of the Allies has [sic] been

very different from what it would have been if the disposition of the inhabitants of the country had led them to oppose the Allies.'[22]

Thus deprived of any military means to continue the fight, surrounded by enemies of all factions, condemned to death by Louis and the Prussians, and without the protection of his Imperial Guard, Napoleon made for the coast and the ship provided for him by Fouché's government: a ship which it had taken five days 'to make seaworthy'. Napoleon's last military campaign had thus ended, as had his liberty.

In the final analysis Napoleon was not brought down by the might of the Allied armies. His defeat had been caused by men that he himself had placed in positions of power and, although mistrusting them, had failed to remove, particularly Talleyrand in 1814 and Fouché in 1815. Napoleon had believed that his own ability, his genius, would suffice to keep these untrustworthy men under control. In this he had deceived himself. In 1814, before leaving Paris for the front, he could have imprisoned Talleyrand in Château Vincennes for the duration, as both a precaution and a lesson to others, instead of simply warning his brother Joseph to be wary of Talleyrand's treachery, and leaving Talleyrand with access to all in Paris, including the Empress, Ministers and the Allies. Likewise in 1815, although Napoleon was wary of the new Chambers, with his experience of Talleyrand's treachery in 1814, he should on leaving Paris have ordered Marshal Davout to imprison Fouché, which Davout would have done without a second thought. Without Fouché at liberty to lead them, the Chambers would have remained passive and Waterloo, although still a disaster, would not then have been a decisive battle in providing ammunition for Fouché to use against him.

Instead, Napoleon left Fouché in office, intending to use his talents to pacify the Vendean rebels, then remove him later. In so doing he had again sown the seeds of his own destruction. Napoleon was taken to the island of St. Helena, as a virus to be isolated from Europe. There he wrote what indeed could have become his own epitaph: 'If I had hanged just two men, Talleyrand and Fouché, I would still be on the throne today.'

AUTHOR'S NOTE. Because of considerations of space, I have treated the events after the Battle of Wavre on 19 June with great brevity. The events after Napoleon's removal from power and leading to his betrayal to the Royal Navy, the royalist lynch mobs, and judicial murders carried out during the second Restoration of Louis XVIII at the insistence of the British Government, together with Napoleon's unlawful detention at Torquay and subsequent murder on St. Helena through the British Government's connivance, are not relevant to this military account of Waterloo and will be dealt with in detail in *Napoleon: The Final Betrayal*, currently in preparation.

Notes

Introduction: Captain William Siborne
1. Sir Charles Oman, 'The Dutch-Belgians at Waterloo' in *Nineteenth Century Magazine*.
2. Ibid.
3. 'Captain William Siborne' in Dr. D.G. Chandler, *The Road to Waterloo* (National Army Museum, 1990), pp. 190-6. Under the subheading 'The Accuracy of the Model – Siborne the Historian under Investigation', Dr. Chandler stated: 'In a recent article [see note 4 below], D.C. Hamilton-Williams has pointed out that Siborne was highly selective in the evidence he chose to portray. It appears that many of the unpublished letters challenge points of detail on the model, and later expressed as historical facts in Siborne's two-volume History..., which has been much cited by military historians ever since. It would seem that many myths became incorporated in the book.'
4. D.C. Hamilton-Williams, 'Siborne the Unpublished Letters' in *The Bulletin*, The Military Historical Society, August 1987; D.C. Hamilton-Williams, 'Captain William Siborne' in *Journal of the Society for Army Historical Research*, vol. LXVI, No. 266, 1988.
5. Chandler, op. cit.
6. Ibid., p. 189. See also: Hamilton-Williams, 'Captain William Siborne', p. 73; and B.L. Add. MS. 34703.
7. Ibid.
8. *Wellington and his Friends* (London, 1968), Gerald, 7th Duke of Wellington, No. 24, endorsed by Lady Wilton, 23 April, 1840.
9. B.L. Add. MS. 34704, The Prince of Essling to Lieutenant William Siborne, 22 November 1832.
10. *United Services Institute Journal*, March – June 1845, for these historic arguments between Siborne and Macready.
11. F.O. Cont. 17 PRO, Clancarty to Castlereagh (No. 17), 15 April. See also: Wellington's *Despatches* [WD] vol. XII, pp. 416-7; and Wellington's *Supplementary Despatches* [WSD], vol. X, pp. 39, 80.
12. B.L. Add. MS. 34703.
13. General Sir J. Shaw Kennedy, *Notes on the Battle of Waterloo* (London, 1865), pp. 51-4.
14. Lieutenant-Colonel Charles Chesney, *Waterloo Lectures – A study of the Campaign of 1815* (London, 1868), p. 20.
15. WSD, vol. X, p. 513. Memorandum upon the plan of the Battle of Waterloo.
16. B.L. Add. MS. 34703, pp. 192-6, memorandum from W. Gordon to Lord Fitzroy Somerset 29/10/1831, with attached request from Siborne. This was a memorandum from Somerset to Gordon allowing the copy, on condition that Siborne use a professional draughts-

man, 1/11/1831. The de Craan Map from the Horse Guards – approved by Wellington – is in the King's Collection of Maps in the British Museum Map Library, reference King's Collection shelf mark 31885(1).
17. The present author recommends using the map in J. Keegan, *The Face of Battle* (London, 1984), pp. 124-5, for this experiment.

Chapter 1. The End and the Beginning
1. D.C. Hamilton-Williams, *The Fall of Napoleon: The Final Betrayal* (in preparation), Chapters 4-5.
2. Ibid., quoted with citations in Chapter 1. For further information on the difficulties of maintaining a blockade on Low Countries North Sea ports with sailing ships, and for Admiral Lord Keith's comments, see B. Lavary, *Nelson's Navy* (London, 1992), pp. 300-5.
3. Ibid. See also FO Russia. 60 Public Record Office [PRO] 19 January 1805.
4. Hamilton-Williams, op. cit., chapters 4-6, passim.
5. Ibid.
6. Ibid. Also, French National Archives [ANF], Folios F7-6500 to F7-6523. These contain the amalgamated government files on the Malet Plot, including army and police files, court examinations, and ministerial and imperial investigations.
7. Ibid., chapters 1 and 2, quoting the relevant documents.
8. Ibid.
9. Ibid.
10. Ibid.
11. Ibid. See also H. Nicholson, *The Vienna Congress* (London, 1948), Appendix IV Maritime Rights, pp. 285-7.
12. Hamilton-Williams, op. cit., chapters 4, 8, 9 and 11, passim.
13. Ibid., chapter 2.
14. Ibid., chapter 4.
15. Ibid., chapter 2.
16. Ibid.
17. Ibid. Contains all the relevant documents and citations.
18. Ibid., chapter 3, 10 February 1814, 'The Crisis of Troyes'.
19. Ibid.
20. Ibid., chapter 4.
21. Ibid., chapter 5. All relevant documents are quoted.
22. Ibid.
23. Ibid.
24. Ibid. Joseph's order to Marmont reads: 'If Marshal Mortier and Marshal Marmont can no longer hold their positions, they are authorized to enter into negotiations with

Prince Schwarzenberg and the Emperor of Russia facing them. They will withdraw to the Loire.' Montmartre, 12.15 noon. – Joseph, *Memoires et correspondance du Roi Joseph* Ed. Albert du Casse (Paris, 1854), 10 vols. vol X, pp. 23-4.

25. Ibid.

26. Ibid., chapter 2. Napoleon attacked the allied army of St. Priest in the city of Reims during the late winter's evening of 13 March 1814. The citizens illuminated the city by putting candles in their windows to enable Napoleon's troops to see the enemy better. They also constructed barricades to inhibit enemy troop movements and attacked isolated enemy units and men. By midnight the allied army was fighting on two fronts, one against Napoleon's army and the other against the people of Reims.

27. Ibid., chapters 5 and 6.

28. Ibid.

29. Ibid. See chapter 6 for a more detailed treatment and for Castlereagh's machinations.

30. Ibid.

31. Ibid., passim. The part played by d'Artois and his secret terrorist group/political party is documented throughout the book.

32. Ibid.

33. Ibid.

34. Ibid.

35. Ibid., chapters 6-8.

36. Ibid., chapter 8.

37. Ibid., chapter 6.

38. Ibid. Correspondences quoted in chapter 8.

39. Ibid.

40. Ibid.

41. Ibid. See the memorandum of Lord Liverpool from the Cabinet to Castle-reagh.

42. Ibid. See the Lord Chancellor's letter to Prince Lieven, Russian Ambassador, and Lieven's letter to the Tsar.

43. Ibid. See Castlereagh's letter describing his 'painful' interview with King Frederick William of Prussia.

44. Ibid., chapters 12 and 13.

45. Ibid., chapters 5 and 6.

46. Ibid.

47. Dr. D.G. Chandler, *Napoleon's Marshals* (London, 1987), p. 360.

48. A. Brett-James, *The Hundred Days* (London, 1964), p. 1.

49. Hamilton-Williams, op. cit., chapter 6, passim.

50. Ibid.

51. Ibid.

Chapter 2. The Return of the Eagles, which Fly from Steeple to Steeple

1. D.C. Hamilton-Williams, *The Fall of Napoleon: The Final Betrayal* (MS), chapters 3, 4, and 10, passim. These chapters contain a full discussion of the collusion between Castlereagh, Metternich, Talleyrand and Louis to invade Naples and remove Murat, having fabricated a plausible justification. But Wellington refuted their *causus belli*, and Parliament accused Castlereagh of a breach of faith. Although he denied this, state papers

prove him to have been 'economical with the truth'.

2. Ibid.

3. Ibid.

4. Ibid.

5. Ibid. See also Dr D.G. Chandler, *Napoleon's Marshals* (London, 1987), p. 470. This book is recommended to the reader for background information on the entire marshalate.

6. *Le Moniteur*, 7 March 1815 (ANF).

7. Hamilton-Williams, op. cit., quoted in chapter 6.

8. Ibid.

9. Ibid. Chapters 11 and 12 deal in depth with Fouché's actions, and give all citations. Fouché, it should be remembered, was the principal figure in the manoeuvring which led to the fall and execution of Robespierre. He was a formidable opponent.

10. *Le Moniteur*, 8 March 1815 (ANF).

11. Hamilton-Williams, op. cit., quoted in chapter 9.

12. Ibid., chapter 8. The full text can be found in Christopher Kelly, *A full and circumstantial account of the Memorable Battle of Waterloo: The second restoration of Louis XVIII; and the deportment of Napoleon Buonaparte to the island of St. Helena*, (London, 1817), pp 8-9.

13. Ibid. The discussion in chapters 12 and 13 includes the relevant letters and state papers.

14. Ibid., chapter 8.

15. Ibid. See also *Le Moniteur*, 8 March 1815.

16. Ibid., chapter 9. See also police reports, ANF, iv 1936, folio 12.

17. Ibid., chapter 8. Given verbatim.

18. Ibid.

19. Ibid.

20. Ibid.

21. Ibid.

22. C. Dickens, *A Tale of Two Cities*. Dickens carried out massive research for his novel. He was taken with a description given by a Vendean fighter of the mobile execution squads which transported guillotines among the villages and towns of the region and conducted mass executions. Many royalists have recounted in their memoirs the fear which these travelling guillotines engendered. See, for example, *Memoirs of the Marchioness De Larochejaquelin* (Edinburgh, 1816), pp. 520-30.

23. Hamilton-Williams, op. cit., chapters 12 and 13. Transportation of political dissidents was carried out by Britain over a period of nearly 200 years: Charles I sent his to the American Carolinas; Oliver Cromwell's went to the West Indies; James II's Monmouth rebels found themselves in the American colonies; while William and Mary, Anne and the Hanoverians also sent their Highland Jacobites and others to America. The revolutions in America and France, particularly the latter, gave rise to relatively mild manifestations of revolutionism in Britain. Perhaps the most dangerous occurred in 1797, when revolutionaries in the North Sea Squadron incited mutiny and for six weeks the squadron block-

aded London. Before the mutiny collapsed, there was even talk of taking the ships over to the French. The government's reaction to Jacobinism, real or imagined, in Britain included the Traitorous Correspondence Bill of 1793 and yearly suspensions for ten years of *Habeus Corpus*. Many convicted by these draconian measures were transported to the penal colony of New South Wales begun in 1788.
24. Ibid.
25. Ibid. Also: FO Cont. 14 Wellington to Castlereagh, Vienna, 12 March 1815 [PRO].
26. FO Cont. 14, Castlereagh to Wellington, London, 26 March 1815 [PRO].
27. Hamilton-Williams, op. cit., chapter 9. See the Tsar's letter to Constantine. Metternich, in his memoirs written years later, stated that the Tsar disregarded the copy of the treaty and that the Allies were in unison. This is highly unlikely. The Tsar was a man to whom honour and principles mattered; he knew Metternich had no such scruples and refused to have anything to do with him.
28. Ibid.
29. Ibid.
30. Ibid., chapter 10. See also: AF iv. 1936, Davout to Napoleon [ANF].
31. Ibid., chapter 3.
32. Ibid., chapter 10. See note 7.
33. *Correspondence*, Napoleon, no. 21755.

Chapter 3. The United Netherlands: The Allies Assemble
1. Duke of Wellington, *Wellington's Supplementary Despatches* [WSD], 2nd ed. (London, 1863), vol. X, pp. 5-6.
2. Sir John Fortescue, *The Campaign of Waterloo* (London, 1987), reprint of vol. X of *A History of the British Army* (1920), p. 19. See also WSD, vol. IX, p. 394.
3. WSD, vol. X, pp. 167, 218, 222.
4. Ibid., p. 8.
5. Ibid., p. 11.
6. Ibid., pp. 1-5. The reader wishing to understand the creaking antiquated quagmire of administration that controlled the British Army of the period should read S.P.G. Ward's definitive *Wellington's Headquarters*, OUP (London, 1957). See also P.J. Haythornthwaite, *Wellington's Military Machine* (Tunbridge Wells, 1989), pp. 64-6.
7. WSD, vol. X, pp. 20-25. Memorandum by Major-General Sir Henry Torrens to the Duke of Wellington, Dover, 4 April 1815.
8. Ibid.
9. Hansard, series 1, xxxv, pp. 334-60. For the Parliamentary debate and further relevant citations, see D.C. Hamilton-Williams, op. cit., chapter 9.
10. The Marquis of Angelsey, *One-Leg: The Life and Letters of Henry William Paget, First Marquis of Anglesey* (London, 1951), pp. 119-22. For the personal matters which alienated Wellington from Uxbridge – principally that Uxbridge ran off with Wellington's sister-in-law, see pp. 89-122.
11. *The Despatches of Field Marshal The Duke of Wellington* [WD], ed. Lieutenant-Colonel Gurwood (London, 1888), vol. XII, p. 358. Bruxelles, 8 May 1815. Wellington to Lord Stewart, the British plenipotentiary in Vienna. Wellington continues: '... in my opinion they are doing nothing in England. They have not called out the Militia either in England or Ireland; they are unable to send me anything; and they have not sent a message to Parliament about the money. The War spirit is evaporating as I am informed.'
12. Fortescue, op. cit., pp. 23-40. See also Torrens memorandum, op. cit.
13. WSD, vol. X, pp. 261-2.
14. Ibid., p. 217. On 1 April 1815 the 1st Battalion was ordered to Flanders. Its commanding officer, Colonel Upton, who was ADC to the Duke of York, obtained through his patronage the post of Military Attaché to the Bavarian army. If Upton's battalion went to Wellington, Upton would have to go with it and lose his lucrative appointment. For this reason Wellington was denied the seasoned 1st Battalion. See Hamilton, *Origin and Services of the Grenadier Guards*, chapter XXV, p. 9. Hamilton wrote from primary source documents.
15. Ibid., pp. 35-40.
16. Hansard, vol. xxxi, pp. 223, 265, 653. Status of George III, p. 55. Caps, pp. 76-7.
17. The reader should note that most of the denigratory allegations against the Dutch-Belgian army came from Siborne's collection of British officers' recollections, set down from 1838 onward. In 1831, after sixteen years of Dutch domination, the Belgians revolted and declared independence. The French sent an army to assist the Belgians, and this was seen at the time by the British as further proof of the Belgians' wish to be part of France. The revolt was a reaction to Dutch efforts to Hollandize Belgium: King William, for example, had tried to enforce Dutch as the official language of both countries; and in politics, the Belgians objected to 'Dutch arithmetic', the 'double Dutch' method of ballot counting whereby the votes of Dutch nationals were counted twice in the assembly. Britain, fearing to lose its 'military barrier' created an independent Belgium, tied to Britain by treaties which were still honoured in 1914. Anyone wishing to understand the reasons for the Belgian revolt should read Professor J.A. van Houtte, 'The Low Countries', in *The New Cambridge Modern History*, vol. IX, CUP, 1985, pp. 469-80. Captain William Siborne, it must be remembered, started collecting information from his contemporaries in 1838-44. Wellington's dispatches had by then been widely read, and memories of events that had taken place more than a quarter of a century earlier were inevitably coloured by Wellington's published views, later taken up by Fortescue and Oman. See *Introduction*.
18. WSD, vol. X, pp. 167-8. There are many similar examples, but the one cited towards the end of this section will serve.

19. Ibid., pp. 15-17. This memorandum from Clarke could hardly be ignored, but one can only speculate as to the convoluted or aberrant mental processes which led Clarke to his allegations. Clarke had risen in the French army bureaucracy from being an obscure topographical officer to the position of Minister of War. Having betrayed Napoleon in 1814 only to wittness the almost unanimous welcome he received on his return in 1815, Clarke seemed perversely to see treason in every ex-Napoleonic officer who had not betrayed Napoleon in 1814. Certainly, events were to prove Clarke's allegations to be totally unfounded: not one Netherlands officer or soldier deserted during the 1815 campaign; and before the campaign, only 358 Belgians had been recruited to the French forces.

20. WD, vol. XII, op. cit., pp. 324-6.

21. WSD, vol. X, pp. 167-8.

22. *Gedenksukken der Algemeene Geschiedenis van Nederland van 1795 tot 1840* (Documents on the General History of the Netherlands from 1795 to 1840), ed. H.T. Colenbrander (The Hague, 1905-22), vol. XVII, pp. 321-5. See also Dirk, Count van Hogendorp, *Memoires* (The Hague, 1887), pp. 430-41.

23. WD, vol XII, pp. 312-3.

24. Ibid., vol. X, p. 222.

25. Ibid., vol. XII, p 363.

26. Ibid., pp. 460-1.

27. WSD, pp. 160-2.

28. WSD, vol. X, pp. 313-5.

29. N.L. Beamish, *History of the King's German Legion* (London, 1837), 2 vols., vol. 2, p. 323. This classic work was first published in 1832, then again in 1837. It was the ONLY source on the KGL used by Siborne for his History and models. Beamish's book is a mine of information, but of course it only contains material from manuscript documents available at that time. To the author's knowledge, no use had been made by later English-speaking historians of the wealth of manuscripts, letters, journals, diaries and reports accumulated by the Hanoverian archives after 1831. In particular, I refer to those contained in the Niedersachersisches Hauptstaatsarchiv Hannover: Legionsgeschichte der King's German Legion enthalten die Akten Hann. 38D, Folios 18, 22, 188, 200, 230-43, 297; Hann. 41 XXI, Folios 92-99, 150-6; Hann. 48aI, Folios 99-137; and Hann. 92 XV-XIV-22c.

30. WSD, vol. X, p. 168.

31. WD, vol. XII, p. 336. Grant is considered to have been the first officially appointed head of military intelligence, and held that position in the manner of the present Royal Army Intelligence Corps. See C.J.D. Haswell, *The First Respectable Spy: The Life and Times of Colquhoun Grant, Wellington's Head of Intelligence* (London, 1969), p. 222. Also, for the role of an intelligence officer of the period, see J. Page, *Intelligence Officer in the Peninsula* (Tunbridge Wells, 1986), especially Appendix C.

32. Countess E. Longford, *Wellington: the Years of the Sword* (London, 1973), 4th imp., pp. 399-400. Lady Elisabeth has had greater access to the Wellesley/Wellington papers than any other author. The wealth of detail presented in this classic book is invaluable to an understanding of the character of the First Duke.

33. Fortescue, op. cit., pp. 31-2.

34. Again, due to the constraints of space, the author has refrained from giving background details on the majority of these important characters. For this information the reader is advised to consult the following excellent works: Dr D.G. Chandler, *Dictionary of the Napoleonic Wars* (London, 1979); *Napoleon's Marshals*, ed. Dr. D.G. Chandler (London, 1987); and P.J. Haythornthwaite, *The Napoleonic Source Book* (London, 1990).

35. Wellington has received much criticism over the years because of his introduction of the corps system to his army at this crucial time, rather than keeping to the standard British army practice of 1808-14 of having the division as the largest unit within the army. Some historians have written that much time was lost through the transmission of orders through titular corps commanders, rather than sending them directly to the divisional commanders, as was Wellington's practice. Wellington's use of the corps system for the 1815 campaign, although not his preference, proved to be a clever way to get the officers and men of five different nationalities to overcome chauvinism and co-operate with one another. Wellington's 1815 corps were not organic corps – that is, tactical units of all arms – but rather administrative entities. Had the British Cabinet declared war on France in time, Wellington could have had many more British troops and perhaps would not have needed to resort to such expedients.

36. *The Creevey Papers*, ed. J. Gore (London, 1963), p. 127.

37. Von Ollech, op. cit., pp. 19-23. Facsimiles of the original letters. Von Gneisenau's reply in German reads: '... *vielmehr, Herr Herzog, konnen Sie im Pall eines Angriffs auf den Beistand aller unserer verfugbaren Streitkrafte rechnen. Wir sindfest entschlossen, das Loos der Armee zu theilen, welche unter den Befehlen Ew. Excellenz steht.*'

38. WD (1852 ed.), vol. VIII, p. 72. This dispatch, written in French, has been overlooked by historians. Wellington to 'General officer commanding the Prussian troops at Charleroi', Brussels, 9 May 1815, 1.30 p.m.: 'It is my duty to inform you that all information I have from the frontier leads me to believe that the French troops arc collected between Valenciennes and Maubeuge, and rather about Maubeuge than Valenciennes ... I will cause you to be informed through the posts of the Low Countries of all news that I may obtain.' Correspondence concerning the transmission of reports was to take place with the Prince of Orange, and we read of the establishment of letter posts at certain places,

notably The Netherlands posts at Binche and Frasnes. Reports or alarms were to be transmitted by way of these posts, while matters of policy were to be conveyed directly between headquarters through the resident liaison officers. These arrangements were to have great significance at a later date.

39. WSD, vol. X, pp. 43-4.
40. Ibid., p. 52.
41. E.F. Henderson, *Blücher and the Uprising against Napoleon* (New York, 1911), p. 268.
42. G.H. Pertz, *Das Lebens des Feldmarschalls Grafen Neithardt v. Gneisenau* (Berlin, 1854-65), vol. IV, p. 321. This is a continuation of the work of Hans Delbruck.
43. G.L. von Blücher, *Memoirs of Field-Marshal Prince Blücher* (London, 1932), p. 37. G.L. Blücher was the great-great-grandson of the Field Marshal.
44. Hamilton-Williams, op. cit., chapter 2.
45. C. von Ollech, *Geschichte des Feldzuges von 1815 nas archivalischen Quellen* (Berlin, 1876), p. 14.
46. Hamilton-Williams, op. cit.
47. Von Gneisenau viewed Wellington with grave mistrust. Contrary to the assertions of some English historians, he was neither paranoid nor jealous. He knew that Wellington had been ambassador to the court of Louis before replacing Castlereagh in Vienna, and was intimate with all the political machinations regarding the formulation of the Franco-Austro-British policy of depriving Prussia of Saxony when Castlereagh had already agreed that Prussia could have it. The reversal of Castlereagh's initial position for Prussia was made to save him politically at home. For the political manoeuvrings revealed by the state papers, see Hamilton-Williams, op. cit., chapter 7. For von Gneisenau's opinion of Wellington, see *Leben Thaten und Charakter des Fursten Blücher von Wahlstadt, Ein Buch für Deutschlands Folk und Heer* (Leipzig, 1836), p. 236 *et seq.*; K. Griewank, *Gneisenau, Ein Leben in Briefen* (Leipzig, 1939), p. 300 et. seq.; and von Ollech, op. cit., pp. 124-8.
48. K. von Ollech, *Geschichte des Feldzuges von 1815 nas archivalischen Quellen* (Berlin, 1876), p. 14.
49. 'Bemerkungen uber die im englischen parlemente von dem Herzog von Wellington gethanen Ausserungen uber die disziplin in der preussischen und englischen armee', in *Militair-Wochenblatt* (Berlin, 1836), p. 92.

Chapter 4. A Pleasant Disposition
1. Chandler, *Napoleon's Marshals* , op. cit., pp. 323-4. Napoleon was referring to the Bourbon flag and cockade. The chapter on Mortier covers him adequately. Whether Mortier's attack of sciatica was 'diplomatic' is open to speculation as the condition is impossible to verify. A passage from Mortier's journal is produced as evidence of his loyalty to Napoleon, but the journal was written long after the events of 1815. As Mortier was soon

reinstated by the Bourbons while Ney, Brune and others were executed, it is fair to say that he was able to keep to the narrow ground of conduct which satisfied both camps.
2. See R. Horricks, *Marshal Ney – The Romance and the Real* (Tunbridge Wells, 1982). Also. A.H. Atteridge, *The Bravest of the Brave* (London, 1912).
3. See Hamilton-Williams, op. cit. This is covered in depth in chapter 9, with extensive evidence given in note 43. See F. Macirone, *Interesting facts relating to the fall and death of Joachim Murat King of Naples; the capitulation of Paris 1815 and the second restoration of the Bourbons &c* (London, 1817), pp. 143-4. Francis Macirone was a British subject who acted as liaison between Fouché and the Allied high command, including Wellington. Macirone had given Murat an Austrian passport. After Murat's death, Macirone was seized by d'Artois' secret police on a trumped-up charge and interrogated. As he had been an agent working with Fouché, he 'knew too much' and most probably would have been quietly murdered but for Wellington's intervention. Of his interrogation, Macirone relates, 'He [the interrogator] began with asking me whether I was acquainted with the circumstances of the death of Berthier, Prince of Neufchatel [*sic*]. I answered I had heard he had not met his death by accident, as had been reported, but that I was ignorant by whose order he had been put to death. On my appearing to be acquainted with the facts of Berthier's having been murdered, M. Menars expected that I should be able to furnish him with particulars of his death ... He added that the death of the personage [Murat] and the murder of Berthier were most particularly connected.'
4. P. Hayman, *Soult: Napoleon's Maligned Marshal* (London, 1990), p. 223. This author appears to have overlooked Soult's proclamation and ministerial orders, even though he quoted from the same sources as given above. This book covers the Hundred Days, but seems to exclude more than it reveals. For background on Soult, see Chandler, *Napoleon's Marshals*, op. cit., pp. 458-78.
5. Napoleon has often been criticized by historians for not giving Soult an active command. However, with what Napoleon knew of Soult's statements and activities during the period, he would not have dared to do so. The damaging effect of Marmont's defection, with an army corps, a year earlier would still have been vivid in Napoleon's mind. He was not prepared to risk a repetition of that fatal incident if Soult decided to betray troops under his command to the enemy. After Waterloo, Soult, in justifying his actions to the Bourbons, claimed that he had only accepted an appointment under Napoleon because, 'As a soldier it was my duty to defend France from the invader.' But in his *Mémoires Justificatives* (Paris, 1815), pp.9-10, written to counter a charge that he had incited army officers to adopt a treaso-

nous attitude towards their king, Soult was more revealing, 'I am accused of having provoked by various unjust and untimely measures, the discontent of the officers of the army. First: by neglecting them in favour of officers who are *chouans, Vendéens*, or *émigrés* . The Court well knows that the places and favours granted on both hands were granted by its own orders. None knows better than I how many French officers have not received the pensions and places they well deserved. I have constantly worked with the Comte de Bruges [d'Artois' aide], and have profited by his intelligence. He knew my work and my thoughts. My association with him and his reputation, should have been enough to preserve me from the reproach of 'treason'. In the confused aftermath of Waterloo, Soult was apprehended several times by murder squads of the royalist White Terror, but each time somehow managed to escape. When Marshal Brune, who had held a lesser position than Soult's under Napoleon's command, was caught by a mob organized and led by the White Terror, he was killed out of hand. While Marshal Ney, General La Bedoyère, aide-de-camp to Napoleon, and Postmaster-General Lavallette were tried for treason and executed, Soult was given parole by a royalist prefect and allowed to pass into exile unmolested, by order of d'Artois. We can only surmise that, as d'Artois was not known to be merciful or forgiving, Soult's gentle treatment by his order was because, as Soult put it, 'he knew my work'. Further evidence that Soult had been vouched for by d'Artois was that he sought and received asylum in Hardenburg in Prussia – not a state noted for its Bonapartist sympathies. Had Soult's exile in Prussia not been arranged by d'Artois, Soult would undoubtedly have been executed there or sent back to France in chains. However, Soult was permitted to live quietly there – the police reports on him are entirely favourable (Hayman, op. cit., p. 235) – until a decent interval had passed. He was allowed to return to France in 1819 and was even granted an audience with Louis.

6. General A. von Horsetzky, *Kriegs-geschichtliche Übersicht der wichtigsten Feldzuge seit 1792* (Historical review of the Chief Campaigns in Europe since 1792) (Vienna, 1909), p.7.

7. For the sake of brevity and narrative flow, when introducing a prominent figure, such as a general, I have refrained from giving the full recitation of his titles and peerage, unless he is referred to variously in quotation (e.g., General Savary, or Duc de Rovigo; Talleyrand, or Prince de Benevento). For details of this nature, see Dr D.G. Chandler, *A Dictionary of the Napoleonic Wars*, op. cit.; P.J. Haythornthwaite, *The Napoleonic Source Book*, op. cit.; and R. Horricks, *In Flight With the Eagle* (Tunbridge Wells, 1988).

8. Houssaye, op. cit., p. 21; ANF, iv, 1936, Davout to Napoleon, 11 June; ANF, iv, 1936, Carnot's report to the Chamber of Peers, 13

June; ANF, iv, 1936, Davout's report to the government commission, 23 June; *Correspondence*, op. cit., no. 21755, Napoleon to Davout, 23 March.

9. Marshal Brune, with the force he had, would have been well equipped to hold the narrow coastal strip between the Maritime Alps and the sea until Suchet could either have reinforced him or marched through Alpine passes to take in rear the enemy force engaged with Brune. Much has been said of the 'law of numbers': in this instance, that an Austrian army of 210,000 would steamroll over any force of 10,000-50,000. This law may well have applied in a later, more industrialized age, in which the tactics of attrition were practised – the American Civil War may be a good example. Commanders in the Napoleonic period, however, unlike General U.S. Grant, would not normally send line after line of men forward over the bodies of their fallen comrades. In any case, only a relatively small number of men at a time can advance in a restricted area. In such a situation, large numbers can become a logistic liability rather than an asset.

10. The defile of the valley between Basel and the Alps was in 1815 2½ miles across at the widest point (Ferraris & Capitaine map 1797, British Museum Map Library). If an Austrian army, even of 210,000 men, had been obliged to draw up in battle formation of three lines to fight their way out of this defile, allowing room to manoeuvre, they would not have been able to bring to bear more than 42,000, while the rest would be crowded behind. For a discussion on frontages for the period, see General Sir James Shaw Kennedy, *Notes on the Battle of Waterloo* (London, 1865), p. 88.

11. See Hamilton-Williams, op. cit., chapters 7 and 8, for the events leading up to the Battle of Tolentino. The author intends to discuss this campaign in another book, now in preparation: *Murat: The Last Battles, 1815*.

12. Ibid, chapters 2-5, passim.

13. At midnight on 15/16 March 1815, the Comte d'Artois went to the Faubourg St-Germain and entered the house of the Comte d'Escars. Monsieur met there with Joseph Fouché, Duc d'Otranto. Fouché, execrated by royalists as one of the three hundred who voted for the death of Louis XVI, had not been forgiven by d'Artois, or Louis XVIII, for the execution of their brother, but because he acted as a royalist agent in 1814, he was allowed to keep his life, his titles, and his wealth. At the eleventh hour of the first Bourbon restoration, he had been offered the post of Chief of Police for having betrayed the 'military *coup*' plans of d'Erlon and others. Now d'Artois, to solicit Fouché's further assistance in the present crisis, offered him the position of Chief Minister. But Fouché refused, explaining that it was all up for the Bourbons for the time being. He told d'Artois that he would take office under Napoleon and pretend to serve until the Allied armies

could bring about conditions like those of 1814. Then, at the critical moment, he would act openly to set Napoleon aside and restore the Bourbons. He said to d'Artois, 'Monsieur, save the King; I'll take care of saving the Monarchy.' Thus Fouché and d'Artois came to an arrangement. The next morning, to provide Napoleon with a proof of Fouché's 'loyalty', a charade was enacted. Fouché's coach was stopped in the street outside his house 'by order of the King'. There was a suitable amount of commotion, for the residents of the street to witness, about how the Prefect of Police had a warrant for Fouché's arrest. A National Guard unit arrived. Fouché declaimed for the ears of his neighbours that, 'One does not arrest a former Minister and senator of the Empire in this fashion.' Normally, for voicing such a Bonapartist sentiment, anyone would have been. Then Fouché and the police went inside his house while someone was sent to check the validity of the warrant. The National Guard had no authority to obstruct the police from executing a warrant; in fact, they were bound to assist in its execution. In the meanwhile, Fouché managed to slip through a secret door into his garden and, using a ladder fortuitously left there, over a wall adjoining the garden of Hortense de Beauharnais, step-daughter of Napoleon, and into a waiting coach. Pausing in his flight, he had informed the ex-Queen of Holland that his arrest was sought for having helped the abortive military *coup* in the north. That he had arranged for the coach some twelve hours before Monsieur called on him would indicate that their plan was already well advanced. This incident was reported to Napoleon in the favourable light Fouché had intended to be cast upon it, and Napoleon was apparently reassured that his trust in choosing him as chief of police was not misplaced. Thus d'Artois had secured a key agent deep within Napoleon's government. See J. Fouché, Duke of Otranto, *The Memoirs of Joseph Fouché Duke of Otranto* (London, 1825), vol. II, pp. 262-3. See also Macirone, op. cit., pp. 92-104. Also, for official confirmation, see FO Cont. 17 PRO, Castlereagh to Clanarty (Private and Secret), 15 April 1815, in which Castlereagh discusses royalists still active in Paris: '... some of them as Fouché are in situations of great trust ... the most essential services might be rendered by them to the general cause' See also chapters 9-12 of Hamilton- Williams, *The Fall of Napoleon: The Final Betrayal*, for an in-depth account.

14. Ibid.

15. Ibid. While serving Napoleon as Minister of State, Fouché passed on, through his agents, to Wellington, the complete order of battle of Napoleon's army. This will be cited below.

16. Napoleon sent many disguised officers into Belgium to gather intelligence. The British and Hanoverians were not familiar with the new uniforms just issued to the newly formed United Netherlands army, which were similar

in colour to the French. Also, only some of the British and Hanoverian officers spoke French. It was therefore difficult for them to distinguish between a French-speaking Belgian officer and a French officer in disguise. Captain Mercer, in his *Journal of the Waterloo Campaign* (London, 1870), gives several instances of suspected spies gathering intelligence in this fashion. See also Gourgaud, op. cit., pp. 29-30. Also Colonel Vachée, *Napoleon at Work* (London, 1914), pp. 33-76. These sources show such subterfuge to have been standard practice. For example, Napoleon wrote to Berthier on 19 July 1813, ordering him to send four wounded officers who could speak German to convalesce at Toplitz and Carlesbad. They were to be 'exceedingly clever men, to act as spies, and report everything that occurs'.

17. A.F. Becke, 'Waterloo: An Appreciation of the Situation, from the point of view of a French Staff Officer, on June 1st, 1815' in *United Services Magazine*, vol. XXXXVI, No. 541, 1908.

18. Vachée, op. cit., pp. 33-76. See also ANF, op. cit; and WSD, vol. X (London, 1863 ed.), pp. 439-81. These pages contain numerous references to French deserters coming forward and volunteering information, but it proved to be so misleading, as to the positions of the deserters' own units, and the locations of the Imperial Guard and Napoleon, that they could only have been deliberate lies. Yet, cleverly, they would contain some element of true, although militarily useless, information, sufficient to raise doubt, and thus at least partly succeed in their intent to confuse the Allies as to the true area of concentration of the French army.

19. Napoleon suspected that Blücher might avoid battle. In 1813-14, the Austrians and the Swedes devised a plan called the Trachenberg Policy, according to which any Allied army facing Napoleon himself would retreat without giving battle. The theory behind it was that Napoleon's army would exhaust itself in marching and counter-marching in an effort to bring the Allies to battle. This idea was apparently taken from the days of Marlborough, when army commanders made a fine art of manoeuvre. Although outmoded, it was adopted by these two nations because they felt they could not afford to have their armies suffer any major losses. However, this tactic was a two-edged sword, which took a toll of attrition on both pursuer and pursued alike, as both armies had to do the same amount of marching. Further, it was a boost to the morale of the French troops to see the enemy continually run before them, while of course for the Allied soldiers, having to retreat without fighting in the face of inferior numbers of French had a demoralizing effect such that the mere report of Napoleon being present among a French force would be enough to cause a near panic. See Hamilton- Williams, *The Fall of Napoleon: The Final Betrayal*, chapters 2–5.

20. Wellington's position was less flexible than is often appreciated. He was obliged to cover Antwerp, which was to remain the unspoken strategic key to British Continental policy until the age of steam. In his Memorandum on the Battle of Waterloo (WSD, vol. X, pp. 513-31), Wellington explained his difficult position, complicated by considerations of maintaining William's control of Brussels and Louis' court-in-exile at Ghent. Moreover, Wellington was not free to reveal his strategic and diplomatic constraints to his Prussian allies. Explaining his wide dispositions, extending to the coast, Wellington expressed his fear that if he concentrated sooner with the Prussians in anticipation of battle with Napoleon, 'The initiative for such a battle must still have been in the hands of Buonaparte. He might have avoided it merely by remaining with his main body within the French frontier; while with his Hussars and light troops he would have possessed Bruxelles and Ghent and the communications with England and Holland and Germany through Holland.' Wellington's fears of a secondary force outflanking him by a coastal sweep, seizing the major towns and ports and cutting his communications, is readily apparent.

21. The Prussians have been much criticized for their choice of cantonment areas, as though they were allowing Wellington to cover a wider section of front so that they could concentrate more rapidly. This was not the case. Von Gneisenau moved the Prussian army into Belgium in answer to Wellington's request that he do so. He would have preferred to remain on German soil, but he had already unequivocally pledged Wellington Prussian support in the event of an attack (Von Ollech, op. cit., pp. 19-20, original letters).

22. O. von Lettow-Vorbeck, *Napoleon's Untergang 1815* (Berlin, 1904), vol. I, p. 178.

23. G.L. von Blücher, *Memoirs of Blücher* (London, 1932), p. 37.

24. WSD, vol. X, p. 246.

25. Henderson, op. cit., pp. 278-9.

26. Ibid.

27. FO France, No. 116. Wellington also wrote to Sir Charles Stuart at Ghent to defend this decision on the grounds that both he and von Blücher had very raw troops and therefore could not advance into France and invest the border fortresses in safety (that is, their numbers would be too depleted by the detachment of investing units) until the Russians and Austrians had come up to the border and could co-operate in a general advance.

28. Ibid.

29. F.C. von Müffling, *Aus Meinen Leben* (Berlin, 1851), pp. 218-9, et. seq. Compare this with its English language version, F.C. Müffling, *Passages from my Life* (London, 1853), ed. Colonel P. Yorke, pp. 232-3.

30. Ollech, op. cit., p.14.

31. See Hamilton-Williams, *The Fall of Napoleon: The Final Betrayal*, chapter 5, et.

seq. Also compare the reports in Houssaye, op. cit., p. 21; ANF, iv, 1936, Davout to Napoleon, 11 June 1815; ANF, iv, 1936, Carnot's report to the Chamber of Peers, 13 June 1815; ANF, iv, 1936, Davout's report of 23 June to the government commission; and *Correspondence*, No. 21755, Napoleon to Davout, 23 March 1815, ANF, iv, 1936, with WD, vol. XII, 1888 ed., pp. 394-409. On 16 May Wellington wrote from Brussels to Lieutenant-Colonel Hardinge with a copy of a memorandum to Blücher, sent also to the kings of The Netherlands and Bavaria, and the Marshals Wrede, of Bavaria, and Schwarzenberg. The information contained in the memorandum on the troop strength and equipment of Napoleon's field army, about which Wellington stated, 'I have drawn from Intelligence I have recently received', is identical with the breakdowns given in the offical reports cited in the French sources above. For example, the memo notes that 'the Gendarmerie have supplied 4250 horse' (See Houssaye, op. cit.). Wellington's memorandum was written just 15 days after the meeting of the Council of Ministers in Paris at which the information was presented by Marshal Davout, and two days after Carnot's limited recital before the Peers. For information of this precise accuracy to have reached Wellington in Brussels in 15 days by way of England, it could only have come from someone who attended the meeting Davout addressed. In his memoirs, Fouché stated that he had been the source of the information (Fouché, op. cit., vol. II, pp. 290-1). Wellington stated that he was unaware of the source of the information, but see WSD, vol. X, pp. 60, 80, in which it is recorded that Fouché, supposedly at the behest of the Duc d'Orléans, sent an emissary to Wellington and the Allies, and especially to the Comte d'Artois. Further, on 22 May Wellington wrote to Lord Bathurst regarding intelligence, 'You have two good correspondents, one from whom Lord Castlereagh sent me the other day two original letters ...' (WD, vol. X, pp 416-7). Finally, there is the evidence of FO France, C C CXCVII, 16 May 1815, Castlereagh to Wellington, in which Castlereagh enclosed a report from '... a correspondent of the Comte d'Artois, who had access to the ministry of war papers'.

32. WSD, vol. X, p. 471.

33. Ibid.

34. WD, vol. XII, p. 462.

35. Henderson, op. cit., p. 278. Gneisenau adding in a further letter dated 12 June 1815, 'The danger of an attack has almost vanished.' p. 288.

Chapter 5. 'A Dependable Article': the Rival Commanders and their Tactics

1. The reader wishing to understand more of Napoleon's character and his method of warfare should read Dr D.G. Chandler's monumental *The Campaigns of Napoleon* (London and New York, 1966). Also Colonel

Vachée, *Napoleon at Work* (Paris, 1914), which gives an insight into the running of Napoleon's headquarters and method of fighting.

2. Chandler, *Campaigns*, op. cit., pp. 133-205.
3. *Correspondence*, quoted in Dr D.G. Chandler, *Waterloo the 100 Days* (London, 1980), p. 76.
4. Much has been written over the years about the inadequacy of Napoleonic weapons, especially their firepower. Some historians and 'weapons experts' have stated that statistically the muskets of the period did little long-range damage. Further, a plethora of accounts has been produced to show that the artillery of the period was ineffective, especially behind sloping ground. This may well have been true in the Peninsula when cannon were used in isolation and not massed. The first day of the Battle of the Somme, 1 July 1916, is often cited as the worst example of carnage on the battlefield of the 20th century when 60,000 British casualties alone fell to modern weaponry: high-powered, sighted rifles, machine-guns, high-explosive shells, and the co-ordination made possible by electronic communications. A terrible toll, and yet at the Battle of Borodino on 7 September 1812 the unsophisticated weapons of the day caused a massive 77,000 casualties out of a much smaller number of combatants than were at the Somme. See Chandler, *Dictionary*, op. cit., p. 67.
5. Chandler, *Campaigns*.
6. Vachée, op. cit., pp. 33-75. passim. Also, for headquarters set-up and map movements, etc., pp. 96-100.
7. *Correspondence de Napoleon*, XXVI No. 20398 of 32 vols. (Paris, 1858-70), pp. 78-9.
8. Vachée, op. cit., pp. 96-100.
9. Ibid., pp. 116-122.
10. Ibid., pp. 86-7. See also the letters of his general ADC, Comte de Flahaut in *The First Napoleon: Some Unpublished Documents from the Bowood Papers* (London, 1925), ed. The Earl of Kerry, pp. 66-132, but particularly p. 116, on which Flahaut is quoted as having said, 'I was directed to give them to Marshal Ney by word of mouth. I therefore gave them him as from the Emperor the order to move to Quatre- Bras.'
11. From the 15th to 19th centuries it was not at all unusual for Europeans to take service in the armies of other nations, even to fight against their own nation if required. Blücher, a Prussian, once served Sweden, then Prussia; Scharnhorst, a Hanoverian, served Prussia; Dornberg, a Hanoverian, fought under Napoleon instead of with the King's German Legion, and later served Hanover against France; Jomini, a Swiss, served first France then Russia; Moreau, a Frenchman, fought for Russia; Thielemann, a Saxon, was against France in 1805, with France until 1813, for Russia until 1814, then with Prussia in 1815. The Dutch and Belgians were at times with the French, at times with the Allies. The Swiss took service everywhere. In Britain,

where the Treason Law of Edward III had been in force since the 14th century, and remains so today, there was an understandable reluctance to take service abroad. Over the centuries, this prohibition produced an inbred feeling that to do so was traitorous. This sentiment combined with shock at the enthusiasm with which the French people rallied to Napoleon on his return and the remarks of General Clarke against The Netherlands troops, created in some senior British officers a serious mistrust of the fidelity of The Netherlands and Nassau forces because they had once served under Napoleon. They feared that at the sight of the Emperor these men would fall under his influence and flock to him.

12. G.L. von Blücher, *Blücher's Campaign* (reprinted Hamburg, 1866).
13. For Blücher's campaigns and his part in them, see Hamilton-Williams, *The Fall of Napoleon: The Final Betrayal*.
14. This designation of a divisional force as a brigade was a subterfuge initiated by the Prussians to circumvent the limitations on the size of their army permitted by the harsh terms of Napoleon's treaty with them in 1807. The anomaly was preserved as a new tradition.
15. P. Paret, *Yorck and the Era of Prussian Reform*, op. cit., pp. 111-249, also pp. 255-65 for Scharnhorst's essay on infantry tactics. See also von R. Diusburg und Essen, *Der Krieg der Franzofen gegen Russland, Preussen und Oestreich in ben Jahren 1812 bis 1815*, 4 vols., 1815, vol. iv, pp. 272-4. Also Professor P. Feddersen Stuhr, *Die Drei Letzten Feldzuge gegen Napoleon* (Lemgo, 1833), 2 vols., vol ii, pp. 538-60.
16. As an example of these theoretical brigade compositions, see Gneisenau's order constituting Steinmetz's 1 Brigade in May 1815 in *Das Preussische Heer der Befreiungskrieg*, vol 3, *Das Preussische Heer in den Jahren 1814 und 1815* (Berlin, 1914), p. 159. Historical section of the German Imperial General Staff. Source: Militargeschichtlisches Forschungsamt.
17. S.P.G. Ward, *Wellington's Headquarters* (Oxford, 1957), p. 25, from PRO document W.O. 3/592, p. 329.
18. Colonel J.D. Hittle, *The Military Staff, Its History and Developments* (Harrisburg, PA, 1952), pp. 62-5.
19. P.G. Tsouras, *Warriors' Words* (London, 1992), pp. 96-7.
20. Ward, op. cit., pp. 1-60. This book provides invaluable background and analysis on the British army.
21. Ibid., p. 13.
22. Tsouras, op. cit., pp. 51-2.
23. Longford, op. cit., p. 139, quoting Croker.
24. Paret, op. cit., p. 257.
25. This of course is an over-simplification for the sake of brevity. See Haythornthwaite, *Wellington's Military Machine*, op. cit. Also, for a fuller discussion on all of Wellington's units and their tactical uses, P.J. Haythornthwaite, *The Napoleonic Source Book* (Lon-

don, 1990).

26. E.J. Cross, 'The Misadventures of Wellington's Cavalry from the Peninsula to Waterloo' (Ohio State University), presented at the Waterloo Congress at Southampton University, July 1987, reproduced in *Journal – Waterloo Committee*, vol. X, No. 1, April 1988, pp. 18-28, passim.

27. Ibid., p. 23, quoted from WD, vol. IX, p. 240.

28. Much has been written about the firepower of British infantry in a line two deep. This subject was debated in the 1900s by Professor Sir Charles Oman and Commandant Jean Colin. Oman, in his monumental *History of the Peninsular War*, put forward evidence that a British battalion in line two deep (i.e., 500 men on a frontage of 250 yards) could bring all their muskets to bear on an advancing French column of double-column frontage (i.e., a frontage of 40 yards with only 50 muskets able to fire) and shoot them to pieces. But this was a statistical elaboration based on a false assumption. Oman had based his thinking on the routing of a French battalion by a British force at Maida in Italy in 1806. It was later learned that at Maida the British attacked in column and the French defended in line! Oman appears to have been influenced by the naval tactical dispute current at the time involving 'crossing the T', by which it was thought desirable to sail your line of battleships across the bows of an advancing enemy line to be able to deliver the maximum weight of broadside. But reports in the Siborne Manuscripts corroborate the excellent research contained in Dr. Paddy Griffith's *Forward into Battle* (Swindon, 1990), pp. 1-50, which shows conclusively that the British usually fired one or two volleys then attempted to rout the damaged enemy with a shout and a bayonet charge. The French point of view, put forward by Colin, was that the French of the day used columns for mobility, but intended to deploy before fighting. In fact, however, if the French columns could not punch a hole in the enemy line by either momentum or fear, they would disperse into skirmishing order and a firefight would develop, with the French feeding in more and more companies and battalions. If this failed, the French divisional or corps commander would attempt to find another, more vulnerable, point in the enemy line to break through. Napoleon himself had said: 'Columns do not break through lines, unless they are supported by a superior artillery fire.' Quoted in Dr. D. Gates, *The Spanish Ulcer: a History of the Peninsular War* (London, 1986), p. 21.

29. It should be noted, however, that squares, used by all armies of the day, could be quite vulnerable if threatened by cavalry supported by horse artillery. The horse artillery would draw up, unlimber at close range, and fire double canister, which would shatter the square, leaving it open to the cavalry. Seeing the first square destroyed in this devastating fashion, the supporting squares would generally panic and break, to be routed by the cavalry.

30. This is a grave historical error which originated in Siborne's period. The army that Wellington commanded between 1809 and 1814 bore no resemblance whatever to his army in 1815 in Flanders. Everything from his command structure down to its tactical units was different. The Flanders army under Wellington was certainly not 'the British Army' some have termed it. Wellington's control over three of its components was restricted by the sovereigns concerned, and Hanover refused to integrate its troops with their own countrymen in British service, except at an extortionate price. In the Peninsula at least, Wellington had the same authority over his allies' soldiers as he did over his own. In 1815 he did not have this authority from the King of The Netherlands or from the Dukes of Brunswick and Orange-Nassau.

Chapter 6. 12–14 June

1. WD, op. cit. (1888 ed.), vol. XII, p. 458.

2. Siborne Manuscripts, British Library Manuscript Dept., BL. ADD. Mss. 34708, general order, von Zeithen, Charleroi 2 May 15, certified by von Reiche, Chief of Staff, dated to Siborne 8 November 1845.

3. Mercer, op. cit., p. 76.

4. Ibid., pp. 108-9. Also correspondence manuscripts in the Braunschweigisches Landemuseum. Akten 178a. von Strombeck.

5. Regimental Archives of the Coldstream Guards, Regimental Order Book 12-20 June 1815, pp. 50-6.

6. *Letters and Journals of Field-Marshal Sir William M. Gomm* (London, 1881), p. 349.
7. WD, op. cit. (1888 ed.), vol. XII, pp. 470-2.

8. Ibid., pp. 466-9.

9. Ibid. (1838 ed.), vol. XII, pp. 469-70 (p. 140 of vol. VII of 1852 ed.).

10. WSD, op. cit., vol. X, pp. 464-5.

11. Ibid., pp. 440-8.

12. C. von Clausewitz, Hinterlassene Werke uber Krieg und Kriegfuhrung, vol. XVIII *Der Feldzug von 1815 in Frankreich* [The Campaign of 1815 in France] (Berlin, 1862), pp. 39-40.

13. Colonel F. de Bas and le Comte J. de T'Serclaes de Wommesom (Brussels, 1908), vol II, p. 240. Also Dr. N Vels Heijn, *Waterloo: Glorie zonder helden* (Amsterdam, 1990), pp. 53-7.

14. *Correspondence*, op. cit., No. 22,049.

15. *Correspondence*, op. cit., No. 22,053. This concise set of orders, which demonstrates Napoleon's precision in giving explicit instructions to his subordinates, is given *in extenso* in Appendix I.

16. Ibid.

17. Ibid.

18. Ibid.

19. Ibid.

20. Ibid.

21. Ibid.

22. Ibid.

23. For the orders of von Zeithen and the letters

of Steinmetz, Dornberg, and Pirch II (Clause-witz), see: von Ollech, op. cit., pp. 87-8. For the letters of Hardinge, Dornberg, etc., see: WSD, op. cit., vol. X, pp. 436-7, 454-5, 476.

24. Ibid.

25. WSD, op. cit., vol. X, p. 477. See also: Major-General Dornberg's own account of the transmission of Grant's information in Dornberg MSS Ak. Hann. 41 XXI. Nr. 150-6. Niedersachersisches Hauptstaatsarchiv Hannover.

26. Ibid.

27. WD, op. cit. (1888 ed.), vol. XII, pp. 416-7.

28. Ante. Chapter 3, note 38: WD, op. cit. (1852 ed.), vol. VIII, p. 72. The reader is again referred to this citation. Historians who have missed this directive have assumed that Zeithen was to dispatch a messenger post-haste to Brussels. This was not the case. His responsibility was to send as soon as possible to the agreed letter post, Mons. From there it was an Anglo-Allied responsibility to deliver the message to Brussels. Hence Wellington's later continual reference that he had to 'wait until he heard from Mons'.

29. Hamilton-Williams, *The Fall of Napoleon: The Final Betrayal*, op. cit., chapter 3. See also: H. Houssaye, *1814* (London, 1914), pp. 187-91.

30. Henderson, *Blücher*, pp.286-7. Many historians have criticized Gneisenau's wording of this movement order, but they should take into account the incidents forming the background to it and the prickly pride of the corps commanders. If Gneisenau had ordered Bülow, his senior in rank, to make all haste, it is probable that Bülow would have created havoc over it. The corps commanders senior to Gneisenau, including Bülow, resented his having been appointed over them. This view is verified by General von Müffling in his *Passages from my Life* , op. cit., pp. 225-7: 'But the more it became known that Gneisenau really commanded the army, and that Blücher merely acted as the bravest in battle ... the louder became the discontent of four Generals who had commanded armies in 1814, and were senoir to Gneisenau ... Bülow at Dennewitz, Kleist at Culm [sic] ... It is necessary also to mention here, that since the years 1811 and 1812, a mutual dislike had existed between these Generals and Gneisenau ... considering "it a point of honour not to be put under the command of a junior in commission". The same notion prevails in all armies where promotion by seniority is the rule ... The fourth Corps [*was*] intended as a reserve Corps in the Rhenish provinces, and [*was*] not expected to be brought into action under Bülow.'

31. WSD, op. cit., vol. X, p. 476. This letter, sent at 10 p.m. from Namur, had to travel 40 miles by mounted courier to Brussels. It would have reached Wellington's headquarters at about 2 or 3 a.m. It is doubtful whether Wellington would have been awakened upon its arrival.

32. Delbruck, *Das Leben des Feldmarschalls*

Grafen Neithardt von Gneisenau, Fortsetzung von G.H. Pertz (Berlin, 1880), vol. IV, p. 521.

33. British intelligence officers during this period often penetrated deep into enemy territory, relying on seclusion and the speed of their mounts to avoid capture. The penalty for being caught out of uniform was, of course, execution as a spy. When Major John Andre ignored this convention in 1780 in America during the War of Independence, he paid with his life. Napoleon also recognized this convention, sending his military spies whenever possible in uniform, often in the guise of deserters.

Chapter 7. 15 June

1. Arch. Serv. Hist., op. cit., Davout to Bertrand, 20 May 1815.

2. Ibid., Bourmont to Gerard, Florenne post-dated 11 June 1815. See also: Les Cent Jours en Belgique, Bibliotheque Universelle de Genève, July-August 1857.

3. Von Ollech, op. cit., p. 101. Ollech's recorded words were: 'Einerlei was das folk, für ein zeichen ansteckt! Hundesfott gleibt Hundesfott!'

4. Müffling, *Passages*, op. cit., pp. 232-3.

5. The reader wishing to see the terrain as it was in 1815 is advised to visit the Map Department of the British Library and look at the 1797 Ferraris & Capitaine maps of Belgium. These were used by Napoleon, Wellington, and indeed by all the nations involved in the campaign.

6. See Zeithen's account in von Reiche, *Der Krieg der Franzosen gegen Russland, Preussen und Oestreich in den Jahren 1812 bis 1815* (Duisberg and Essen), vol. IV, p. 212, *et seq.*

7. Houssaye, *1815*, op. cit., p. 65.

8. Von Reiche, op. cit.

9. Ibid.

10. Arch. Serv. Hist., op. cit. d'Erlon's report to Soult, Marchiennes, 15 June, 4.30 p.m.

11. Von Reiche, op. cit., p. 221.

12. Clausewitz, *1815*, op. cit., chapter XX. Clausewitz was chief of staff to Thielemann. He received the order for the Corps (25,000 men) to march from Gneisenau at 10 a.m. on the 15th. The Corps was in position at Ligny 24 hours later. Its dispersal area can be seen on the campaign map.

13. Ibid., pp. 219-25.

14. le Maréchal de Grouchy, *Observations sur la Relation de la Campagne de 1815, publiée par le Général, et Réfutation de quelques unes des Assertions d'autres écrits relatifs à la bataille de Waterloo* (Philadephia, 1818), p. 32. The order given to Ney to reach Quatre Bras has been hotly disputed for years. The 18 June 1815 edition of *Le Moniteur* published this bulletin on the morning of Waterloo: 'The Emperor gave command of the left-wing to the Prince of Moscow [Ney] who had that evening his headquarters at les Quatre-Chemins [Quatre Bras] on the road to Brussels.' See also: Houssaye, *1815*, p.339,

note 33. For the clash of personalities and Ney's distinct disadvantage at the start of the campaign, see: D.C. Hamilton-Williams, 'Marshal Ney and Quatre Bras' in *The Bulletin Journal of the Military Historical Society*, vol. XXXIX, 1987, pp. 63-75.

15. Ibid., p. 33, *et seq.*
16. The reader wishing to learn more of the Imperial Guard should see: Commandant H. Lachouque, *Anatomy of Glory*, tr. A.S.K. Browne (London, 1978). Also: P.J. Haythornthwaite, *Napoleonic Source Book* (London, 1990).
17. *Fragments Historiques relatifs à la Campagne de 1815* (Paris, 1829), pp. 12, 14. Appendix 4.
18. 'The Journal of Henri Niemann of the 6th Prussian Black Hussars', ed. F.N. Thorpe, in *The English Historical Review*, vol. III, July 1888. Also the original in P.F. Stuhr, *Die Drei Lekten Feldzuge gegen Napoleon* (Lemgo, 1833), pp. 546-7. See also: Colonel F. Maurice, 'Von Zeithen's Defence on the 15th June', in *The United Service Magazine*, No. 743, October 1890, pp. 73-9.
19. Ibid.
20. Dr N. Veils Heijn, *Waterloo: Glorie zonder helden* (Amsterdam, 1990), pp. 59 60. Also quoted in J.P. Jonxis, *Quatre-Bras* (Doesburg, 1875), pp. 178-9. The present author has included this Dutch eye-witness account written at the time, which corresponds exactly with the French commander's report (cited below), and invites its comparison with, for example, R. Horrocks, *Marshal Ney: The Romance and the Real* (Tunbridge Wells, 1982), pp. 215-6, so that the reader may distinguish an account based on primary source material from one based (in good faith) on the Siborne version of events.
21. Lieutenant-Colonel W.H. James, *The Campaign of 1815 Chiefly in Flanders* (London, 1908), pp. 74-5. Also: de Bas and de Wommeson, *Campagne de 1815*, op. cit., vol. III, pp. 253-4.
22. Colonel Heymes, in his *Relations*, published in *Documents Inédits de duc d'Elchingen* (Paris, 1833) [Doc. Ined.], puts Ney's arrival at nearly 10 p.m. Houssaye and others say that Ney arrived earlier, between 5.30 and 7 p.m., implying that had Ney pressed his overstretched and exhausted men, Quatre Bras could have been occupied that night. Thus, an enduring example of scapegoatism arose out of the efforts of some of Napoleon's more uncritical adherents to fix the blame for defeat at Waterloo on someone other than the great man. In fact, Ney could not have arrived before the 9.45 to 10 p.m. estimate of his aide, Colonel Heymes, or the report from Lefebvre-Desnouëttes of 9 p.m. from Frasnes would not have been written and sent in the manner it was. The unpalatable (for Napoleon's posthumous defenders) truth is that if Napoleon had confided in Ney on the 13th and given him command of the left wing from 3 a.m. on the 15th, with orders to reach and hold Quatre Bras, Ney would probably

have done so. To expect that Ney could assume command at 3.30 p.m. on the 15th, having been kept in the dark as to what Napoleon really wanted him to do, and then to accuse him of having been lax or suffering from shell shock, is unrealistic. No one censured Grouchy for failing to reach Sombreffe, which Napoleon had set as the right wing objective for the 15th, although Sombreffe's strategic value in Napoleon's plan of campaign equalled that of Quatre Bras. Grouchy's troops, like Ney's, had performed well, but had simply advanced beyond their support and supplies.

23. Vachée, *Napoleon at War*, op. cit.
24. De Bas and de Wommerson, op. cit., vol. III, pp. 252-3. Also: James, *1815*, op. cit., pp. 76-7, and Becke, *Napoleon and Waterloo*, vol. II, pp. 274-5.
25. Doc. Ined., vol. VI, p. 25.
26. *Napoleon à Waterloo: Souvenirs Militaires. Napoleon à Waterloo, ou Précis rectifié de le Campagne de 1815. Avec Documents Nouveaux et des Pièces Inédites* (Paris, 1866), p. 144. Appendix C, no. vii.: Dispatch from Marcognet's chief of staff (3rd Division), Marchiennes 3 a.m., 16 June to General Nogues, commanding his 1 Brigade, informing Nogues that 2 Brigade would remain at Marchiennes until the arrival of Allix's 1st Division. Thus by 3 a.m. on the 16th, unknown to Napoleon, 1½ divisions of Ney's command had not even crossed the Sambre. D'Erlon's corps was therefore not closed up by 11 a.m. on the morning of the 16th.
27. It is important to note that at this point Napoleon had no preconceived idea that Blücher, 'the Hussar General', would fight. Several times over the previous two years, as part of Allied policy, Blücher had refused battle with Napoleon's army while Napoleon was present, only to fall upon one of his marshals or corps commanders after Napoleon had taken the rest of his army off to engage another Allied army. See: Hamilton-Williams, *Napoleon: The Final Betrayal*, chapters 2 and 3.
28. Marshal Grouchy, *Observations*, op. cit., p. 32: 'I heard him [Napoleon] blame him [Ney] for having suspended the movements of his troops on the 15th at the sound of the cannonade between Gilly and Fleurus, for having halted Reille's Corps between Gosselies and Frasnes, and for having sent a division towards Fleurus, where the fighting was going on, in place of keeping himself to the execution pure and simple of his orders, which prescribed to him to march on Quatre-Bras.'
29. WD, op. cit., vol. XII, pp. 470-2.
30. E. Richardson, *Long-Forgotten Days* (London, 1928), pp. 373-4, containing extracts from Verner's diary.
31. Mercer, op. cit., p. 126.
32. Guards Archiv., op. cit., MS book, 15 June 1815.
33. WSD, op. cit., vol. X, p. 481.
34. Letter from Lieutenant R.C. Eyre to his mother, dated Brussels 28 June 1815, MS

copy in the possession of the Regimental Archives of The Rifle Brigade, supplied to the author by the Regimental Archivist.

35. In the Waterloo canon, much has been made one way or another of the 'missing dispatch' from Zeithen to Wellington, informing him of Napoleon's attack on the Prussians. Wellington, on 8 May (WD, vol. XII, p. 363), had informed the Prince of Orange that General Behr should not send his reports to Wellington directly but through the Prince: 'It appears to me that the General [Behr] had misunderstood the King's order; at least, he has not understood it as I do, that is to say, they [messages] ought to go first to your Royal Highness, and your Royal Highness would send me such as you would deem it necessary I should have a knowledge of.' Further, it was Wellington, writing to General Zeithen when he was in command of the Prussians prior to Blücher and Gneisenau's arrival, who had established that the route by which communications would be sent between the Anglo-Allied and Prussian armies would be by way of Mons. See: WD, 1852 ed., vol. VIII, p.72: '... I will cause you to be informed through the posts of the Low Countries of all news that I may obtain.' Baron Müffling, Quartermaster-General of the Prussian army, seconded to Wellington's headquarters as liaison officer, confirms these arrangements and in his *Passages from my Life*, p. 215, makes the point that the only communication between the two army commanders was to be conducted through either himself or Colonel Hardinge, Wellington's man at Prussian headquarters. Thus it was that Zeithen's message was obliged to travel 58 miles by way of Mons to cover what could have been a 38-mile journey. When Wellington stated that he had heard nothing of Napoleon's attack, save from a Prussian who had arrived at his headquarters at 3 p.m., it was perfectly true. The Prussian he referred to had been sent to inform Müffling of the attack, not Wellington. The 'missing dispatch' addressed to Wellington did not reach him until 5 p.m. In the twelve hours since Zeithen had sent it, the message had travelled an unnecessary twenty miles and had been read and retransmitted four times. For this delay Wellington had only himself to blame.

36. WSD, op. cit., vol. X, p. 480. Sir George Berkeley to Lord Fitzroy Somerset, Braine-le-Comte, 2 p.m., 15 June 1815.

37. Ibid., p. 481. Baron Behr to the Prince of Orange, Mons. le 15 Juin 1815.

38. Müffling, *Passages from my Life*, op. cit., pp. 228-9.

39. WD, 1838 ed, vol. XII, pp. 472-3. For many years historians have argued over the discrepancies between this record of the orders and the slightly different record contained in WD, 1852 ed., vol. VII, pp. 142-3. The author believes that the later edition quotes from a second set of orders sent out as duplicates to the first, but amended in certain respects by changed circumstances. Evidence of this in the second edition orders includes: emendations, marked with an asterisk, as in (1), where the wording '... collect this night at Ath ...' had been deleted and '... remain as they are at Enghien ...' substituted; the statement in (5) 'The same ...', indicating no change from the first set of orders; and the advice in (10) of a change in circumstances since the issue of the first orders, 'The Prince of Orange who is now at Alva's, otherwise no change ...' Major General C.W. Robinson dealt well with these two sets of orders in 'Waterloo and the De Lancey Memorandum' in *The Royal United Service Journal*, 1910, but he had considered the discrepancies as copying errors.

40. 'Recollections of Waterloo, by a Staff Officer' (Basil Jackson), in *Colburn's United Services Magazine*, 1847, Part III, Sept, Oct, and Nov. issues, p. 3. *Recollections*, written entirely by Basil Jackson in 1847, is very different in content from the posthumous edition published in 1903, *Notes and Reminiscences of a Staff Officer*, edited by R.C. Seaton. Seaton edited Jackson to conform to Siborne, and was so lightly acquainted with Jackson's original that he gave incorrect dates of publication for it of October and November of 1843 and March 1844. For an indicative example of Seaton's Orwellian tendencies, compare the following words put into Jackson's mouth on page 21 of Seaton, 'Some of our acquaintances belonging to the staff gave us, in the meantime, an account of the severe and bloody battle; all agreeing that our troops had never been more severely pressed in maintaining their position.', with Jackson's own words from page 7 of his original work, 'Some of our friends, belonging to the Staff, gave us in the mean time, an account of the battle; all agreeing that the Duke had never before been so severely pressed; or had so much difficulty to maintain his position.' Professor Chesney appears to have been right when he wrote in his Waterloo Lectures (op. cit., p.44), 'Time was when it was treasonable to doubt whether what Wellington arranged was the best thing possible on his part.'

41. Müffling, *Passages*, op. cit., pp. 228-9.

42. Ibid., p. 217.

43. Ibid., p. 230.

44. WD, op. cit., vol. XII, p. 474. Gneisenau has been much criticized by some British historians for not informing Bülow of the urgency of his orders, but no criticism was levelled from those quarters at Wellington, whose orders contain no indication of urgency, save possibly the word 'immediately', nor any indication that the units receiving the orders should expect to be going into action to oppose a French advance towards them rather than to participate in a general advance into France as they had expected.

45. Ibid., p. 473.

46. Starklof, *Herzog Bernard von Sachsen Weimar-Eisenbach* [N.D.], vol. 1, p. 181, *et seq*. The Prince, on deciding to hold Quatre Bras, informed his battalion commanders:

'Although I have no orders of any kind, I have never yet heard of beginning a campaign with a retreat, and therefore we will hold on to Quatre-Bras.'

47. In all his dealings with The Netherlands army, Wellington did not communicate directly with any Netherlands officer, but only through the Prince of Orange, as arranged. Although Wellington had been appointed a field marshal in The Netherlands army, his authority over that army was limited. Nor was their army subordinated to the British; and British military law did not apply to it. No British general would have dared to disobey Wellington's order, regardless of how dire he thought the consequences might be. General Constant Rebeque, however, decided to act in the best interests of The Netherlands. Some of the enigmas of the 1815 campaign stem from confusion over the distinct separation of The Netherlands and British armies.

48. Royal Archives, The Royal House, The Hague, The Netherlands. June 15, General Constant Rebeque to the Prince of Orange.

49. Müffling, *Passages*, op. cit., p. 239.

50. Sir H. Maxwell, *The Life of Wellington: The Restoration of the Martial Power of Great Britain* (London, 1899), vol. II, p. 13. Lady Hamilton Dalrymple remarked of Wellington's demeanour: 'Although the duke affected great gaiety and cheerfulness, it struck me that I had never seen him have such an expression of care and anxiety on his countenance. I sat next to him on a sopha [*sic*] a long time, but his mind seemed quite pre-occupied; and although he spoke to me in the kindest manner possible, yet frequently in the middle of a sentence he stopped abruptly and called some officer, giving him directions, in particular to the Duke of Brunswick and the Prince of Orange, who both left the ball before supper. Dispatches were constantly coming in to the Duke.'

51. Oldfield MS. The relevant copy was supplied to the author by The Royal Engineers' Museum Library, Chatham.

52. Delbruck and Pertz, *Das Leben des Feldmarschalls Grafen Neithardt von Gneisenau*, op. cit., vol. IV, p. 365.

53. Ibid.

54. J. von Pflugk-Hartung, *Vorgeschichte der Schlacht bei Belle-Alliance. Wellington* (Berlin, 1903), p. 292, quoting from the Dornberg MS. For the original, see: Ak. Hann. 41. XXI. Nr. 150-6. Neidersachsisches Hauptstaatsarchiv Hannover.

55. *A Week at Waterloo* (Lady De Lancey's narrative) (London, 1906), ed. Major B.R. Ward, pp. 44-5. She writes: 'About two, Sir William went again up to the Duke, and he was sleeping sound!' Because Lady Delancey was sent to Antwerp by her husband at 6 a.m. on the 16th, she apparently did not have the opportunity to learn whether he drew up the actual memorandum of dispositions for Wellington.

56. Jackson, op. cit., p. 4.

Chapter 8. 16 June: 2 a.m. to 2 p.m.

1. Napoleon, *Correspondence*, No. 22059. To Marshal Count Grouchy, Commanding the Right wing of the Armée du Nord. Charleroi, 16 June 1815.

2. Ibid.

3. Ibid.

4. Ibid. No. 22058. To Marshal Ney, Prince of the Moskowa, Commanding the Left wing of the Armée du Nord. Charleroi, 16 June 1815.

5. Ibid.

6. Ibid.

7. Wellington had given credence to the French deceptions which seemed to indicate a threat to his right flank and was reluctant to admit the seriousness of the threat indicated by Hardinge's reports from Prussian headquarters and his own outposts. This, in the absence of word from Grant, was why he sent out no movement orders on the 14th or 15th. Had General Constant Rebecque not disregarded Wellington's order to move Perponcher's troops to Nivelles, which no British general would have dared do, Napoleon would probably have achieved his objective – Brussels -on the 17th.

8. Müffling, *Passages*, op. cit., p. 221.

9. Mercer, *Journal*, op. cit., p. 127.

10. Ibid., p. 129.

11. Ibid.

12. For additional detail on the confusion in movements and the uncertainty of most British units as to their correct destination, see: the manuscript entries in the Brigade of Guards divisional, brigade and battalion order book, 15-19 June, Coldstream Guards Archives. See also: the following letters to Siborne in the British Library (Museum) Manuscript Department [Add. Mss.]: B.L. Add. MS 34703; Waymouth (2nd Life Guards), Clarke-Kennedy (1st Royal Dragoon Guards), Powell (1st Foot Guards), Walcott (Royal Horse Artillery): B.L. Add. MS 340705; Wallace (King's Dragoon Guards), Holmes (23rd Foot), Ingilby (Royal Horse Artillery): and B.L. Add. MS 340708; Banner (23rd Light Dragoons), Ellison (1st Foot Guards), and Muter (Inniskilling Dragoons).

13. Major N. Macready, 'On Part of Captain Siborne's History of the Waterloo Campaign', Parts I, II, and III (taken from his daily journal), in *Colburne's United Service Magazine*, 1845, pp. 389-90.

14. G.C. Smith, MA, *The Life of John Colburne, Field-Marshal Lord Seaton*, compiled from his letters, records, conversations and other sources (London, 1903), p. 215.

15. De Lancey had about six hussar orderlies at his disposal, with an additional eight junior Staff Corps officers and eight Deputy Assistant Quartermaster and Adjutant-General officers on his staff, and a further eight to ten of Wellington's extra aides, called gallopers. Thus, for this emergency Delancey had the use of about 30 riders. Each of the three sets of orders had to be delivered to ten different locations spread widely over hundreds of square miles of countryside, counting The

Netherlands divisions as one location – the Prince of Orange's headquarters being at Braine-le-Comte. Allowing for the distances to be covered, darkness and difficulty in finding some destinations, most of the riders would have been in the saddle for most of the night. The author is indebted to S.P.G. Ward, noted author of *Wellington's Headquarters*, for his advice on this matter.

16. *Letters of Colonel Sir Augustus Frazer, &c.* Major-General Sabine, ed. (London, 1859), p. 536.

17. WSD, op. cit., vol. X, p. 496. For a treatment in greater depth of the Memorandum, see: Major-General C.W. Robinson, 'Waterloo and the De Lancey Memorandum', in *The Royal United Services Journal*, 1910, pp. 582-98.

18. The Royal Archives, Royal House, The Hague [RAO]. The Prince of Orange to the King of The Netherlands. June 17 Nivelles, 2 o'clock in the Morning. See also: D.C. Boulger, *The Belgians at Waterloo* (London, 1901), pp. 20-1.

19. On 12 March 1944 a Royal Air Force bomber attempting to hit a V-2 rocket site in the Hague Wood overshot the target and destroyed the Dutch Military Archives, containing all The Netherlands' divisional reports for the year 1815. In 1908, Lieutenant-General François de Bas, Head of the Military History Section of the Netherlands Army, had completed a four-volume history, La Campagne de 1815 aux Pays-Bas, in co-operation with the Belgian Colonel of the General Staff, Count J. de T'Serclaes. During his research de Bas had copied all the original documents in the archives. In 1900 Demetrius Boulger wrote to de Bas for copies of the original reports, which appeared in the appendices of his book. Boulger, in his translations, made minor errors in some terminology. De Bas's original copies of the archive material still exist, and Professor Nico Vels Heijn of Ziest compared Boulger with de Bas and made corrections for the author. On 30 October 1986 Lieutenant-Colonel H.L. Zwitzer, Deputy-Head of the Military History Section of The Netherlands Army (Koninklijke Landmacht) certified these corrected copies [RNLA] to be faithful to de Bas's original manuscript copies from the destroyed archives.

20. *The Croker Papers 1808-1857*; correspondence and diaries of John Wilson Croker (London, 1884), Jennings, ed., vol. III, p. 173. Croker, who had successfully defended the Duke of York in the sale of commissions scandal, was given the lucrative post of 'Secretary of the Admiralty' which he held from 1809 to 1830. Wellington always maintained that from the Quatre Bras battlefield he could see Ligny and Sombreffe. Many historians and Napoleonic enthusiasts have attempted to duplicate this acheivement, even from the rooftops of the houses of Quatre Bras, but to no avail. In 1815, however, with a telescope it was possible to see Ligny and Sombreffe from

the heights behind Frasnes chapel.

21. General von Ollech, *Geschichte des Feldzuges von 1815* (Berlin, 1876). This letter, the existence of which had not been publicly known before it was photographically reproduced in von Ollech's book, had previously lain undisturbed in the Prussian Military Archives. Siborne and other historians writing of Waterloo before 1876 would have made their assumptions without knowledge of it. Von Ollech reproduced the letter as evidence that Wellington misled the Prussians into thinking that he would be coming to their assistance with at least one corps and his cavalry by 4 p.m. The superscript 'Upon the heights behind Frasnes' has been incorrectly interpreted as meaning at Quatre Bras. In fact it refers to the height behind the chapel of Frasnes, above the Bois Delhutte and a mile north of Frasnes village (the Ferraris & Capitaine map reproduced in this book clearly shows the two Frasnes).

22. In 1815, before the advent of chemical fertilizers, crops such as wheat, rye, corn, etc., grew to a much greater height than they do today, reaching six feet on average, and were therefore difficult to see through or over.

23. Gomm, *Letters and Journals*, op. cit., p. 352. Gomm was the Assistant Quartermaster-General attached to Picton's 5th Division. His diary entry for 15 June records: '... assemble[d] during the night and marched at 5 o'clock next morning on the Charleroi road, halting for two hours in the Bois de Soignies.' When, after about fifteen miles, the head of the marching column reached the road junction at Mont St-Jean, the division stopped as it had been ordered to do. In his entry for the 16th Gomm wrote: 'At one o'clock p.m. move on through Genappe to Quatre Bras, a post at which the roads from Brussels to Namur and Charleroi divide.' The other British infantry division in the army reserve, Lambert's 6th, would not reach Mont St-Jean for two days. The sovereign Duke of Brunswick, commanding his own corps, followed, with General von Kruse and his independent Nassau contingent (not in Dutch service) bringing up the rear. It is evident that more than 17,000 men in a marching column could not all have arrived at Mont St-Jean at the same time; they would have been stretched out along several miles of road. When Picton halted at the crossroads, most of his division would have been in the woods, as Gomm stated. Using the German *Manual for Commanders 1912* (Imperial War Museum), it is possible to compute the length and marching times of a column similarly equipped to that of Picton's. Assuming 23 infantry battalions of 600 men each, marching four abreast, five cavalry squadrons of 979 men, and three foot batteries with attendant train, these would occupy 6,875 metres, or 4.27 English miles. In this formation the column could move at three to four miles per hour. Thus the last units would leave 3–4 hours after the first, and not all units would

arrive simultaneously.

24. It seems apparent, when comparing the letter to Blücher with the chart in Appendix II, that the letter was written in consultation with the memorandum, notwithstanding General Robinson's explanations (op. cit.) as to De Lancey's document. General Müffling, an experienced Quartermaster-General responsible for army movements, recorded his embarrassment at having personal knowledge of the inaccuracy of the memorandum.

25. Müffling, *Passages*, op. cit., p. 234.

26. Ibid.

27. Von * R(eiche), *Der Krieg der Franzofen gegen Russland, Preussen und Ostereich in den Jahren 1812 bis 1815* (Duisberg and Essen, 1816), pp. 321-7. See also: Gneisenau's report of 19 June to the King of Prussia in Kelly, *Waterloo*, op. cit., p. 59. Kelly stated: 'Nevertheless, Field-Marshal Blücher resolved to give battle, Lord Wellington having already put in motion to support him a strong division [*Abteilung*] of his army, as well as his whole reserve stationed in the environs of Brussels, and the fourth corps of the Prussian army being also on the point of arriving.' Kelly probably interpreted the German word '*Abteilung*' as 'division' because that was the largest tactical unit in the British army, but a closer rendition of the original German would have been 'a strong part of his army', that is, all that could be brought to bear.

28. Müffling, *Passages*, op. cit., p. 236.

29. *The First Napoleon: Some Unpublished Documents from the Bowood Papers* (London, 1925), The Earl of Kerry, ed., p. 116. This book contains the actual letters of Comte de Flahaut and Admiral Viscount Keith. Napoleon, wishing to avoid a repetition of the disastrous consequences arising from the capture by the Prussians of his letter to the Empress in 1814, had issued a decree (*Correspondence*, No. 21898) that orders given verbally by an Imperial Aide de Camp were to be obeyed as though Napoleon himself had given them in person. Comte de Flahaut wrote: 'I was directed to give to Marshal Ney by word of mouth. I therefore gave him as from the Emperor ...'

30. Ibid., p. 117.

31. D'Erlon had failed to make use of all the pontoon bridges which Napoleon had made available to him to supplement the bridges at Thuin and Marchiennes, hence his extended position. Ney would not have committed such an oversight. See *Military Studies by Marshal Ney* (London, 1833), H.G. Gaunter, tr., Chapter 7 – River Crossings. Historians who have blamed Ney for not seizing Quatre Bras at first light on the 16th ignore the extended situation of the left wing. To have been able to have driven out the 2nd Netherlands Division, held the crossroads in strength, and been able to have supported Napoleon would have required at least seven divisions by Napoleon's own later estimate. Such uninformed second-guessing of a field commander of Ney's calibre brings to mind a quote from Napoleon's hero, Frederick the Great: '... the kind of person who could not lead a patrol of nine men is happy to arrange armies in his imagination, criticize the conduct of a general, and to say to his misguided self: "My God, I know I could do better if I was in his place!"'

32. It is apparent from this order that Ney had no idea Napoleon would meet any Prussian resistance at this point. Ney was expecting to march on Brussels, as Napoleon's orders had comtemplated. This division and cavalry would act as link between the two wings of the French army as they travelled up the two high roads to Brussels.

Chapter 9. 16 June: Quatre Bras and Ligny

1. *Archives du Service historique de l'état-major de l'armée château de Vincennes* [Mil. Arch.] Reille's account of the actions of 12-20 June 1815, C15/ series. See also: Houssaye, *1815*, op. cit., p. 112.

2. Ibid.

3. Ibid.

4. Starklof, *Herzog Bernard von Sachsen Weimar-Eisenach* [N.D.], vol. 1, p. 181 *et seq.* Letter from the Prince to his parents, dated 19 June 1815: 'I retired in good order through the wood in the vicinity of Hautain le Val.' RANL, Divisional report of Colonel Zuylen van Nyevelt: 'Keeping under observation the lines of communication to the right of the forest of Bossu and the avenues on the road of Hautain le Val.' If Ney were to block the passage of Wellington's forces from Nivelles towards the Ligny battlefield, it was essential to hold Hautain le Val as well. This village lay in the vale of the head of the river Thy. Forces approaching Quatre Bras from Nivelles could use the cover of the vale to outflank forces holding Quatre Bras. A covered flanking movement of this kind can have a devastating effect when the attacker suddenly assails the defender from an unexpected quarter. For the topography of the area, see the Ferraris & Capitaine map sheets: Belgique: 27-30, 35-38, 42-45, in the British Map Library, reference K.7 Tab. 42.

5. RANL, Divisional report of the 2nd Netherlands Division. Also de Bas. Transcripts of the originals are in the author's possession. See also the Boulger version, pp. 49-61, with the caveat that Boulger is slightly inaccurate.

6. Ibid.

7. Ibid.

8. Mercer, *Journal*, op. cit., pp. 130-7.

9. Ibid. It is plain that neither Bull nor Mercer knew where he was going, and neither had received any of the subsequent orders.

10. Ibid., p. 132.

11. Ibid.

12. Ibid., p. 133.

13. Ibid., p. 134.

14. For another such account, see: Lord Albermarle, *Fifty Years of My Life* (London, 1876), vol. II, p. 14. Albermarle was with the 14th Foot. His account of this episode reads:

'June 16th, – The following morning as I proceeded to fall in with my company as usual ... They had received the "route" to Enghien ... At Enghien we received a fresh route from Braine le Comte ... we were detained at Nivelles for two hours to allow some Belgian cavalry to pass through our ranks.' And for yet another view, see the Journal of Captain Powell of the 1st Foot Guards (B.L. Add. MS 3704): '... In the direction of Braine le Comte, where ... [the brigade] arrived about 9 a.m., having been joined by the second brigade on the march. We halted on the eastern side, having had great difficulty in getting through the town in consequence of the numberless wagons and baggage confusedly huddled together in the street.' Similar accounts can be found in the Siborne Letters (manuscript and published).

15. Letter from Captain A.G. van Bronkhorst to his mother, dated Péronne, 9 July 1815. Published by his descendants in *Ons Leger* (Our Army) (the Hague, 1983), pp. 32-8.

16. MS copy of the Journal of Captain Kincaid, Siborne Manuscripts, B.L. Add. MS 3408. Abridged versions were published in: 1830, as *Adventures in The Rifle Brigade*; 1835, as *Random Shots from a Rifleman*; and, further abridged and combined in 1909, as *Adventures in The Rifle Brigade and Random Shots from a Rifleman*. But the original manuscript copy is recommended over these digests.

17. This was a typical example of the problems arising from the mutual inability of many of the linguistic groups within Wellington's polyglot army to understand one another. Many of Wellington's British officers could not speak French, fewer spoke German, and almost none spoke Dutch, Flemish or Walloon. Also, at the time, there were four major, and markedly different, dialects of German. Further, within the British Army, in many of the Highland and Irish regiments, the men spoke mainly Gaelic and 'didn't have much of the English'. To the British, officers and men, most of whom had been in Flanders only about three months, all the other allies in their army were simply 'Belgic', because that is where they were. Before the 15th, Picton's division had been cantoned beyond Brussels. Like Mercer, they were unfamiliar with the terrain around Quatre Bras. The Dutch 27th *Jägers*, on the other hand, had been on this ground skirmishing intermittently with the French for nearly 24 hours. Having been forced back over the ground in question an hour before, they knew it well. Wellington, accompanied by Lord Somerset (later Lord Raglan of Crimean fame), had been on the scene less than half an hour before ordering the 95th to seize a village held by French troops five times their numbers, with artillery and 1,000 cavalry. The Dutch *Jägers*, unable to speak English, tried to indicate by gesture the situation they faced. But the view of the Dutch which the British formed is related by Kincaid: '... they were a raw body of men,

who had never before been under fire; and they could not be prevailed upon to join our skirmishers'. The *Jägers* were in fact probably the most experienced unit in The Netherlands army, having seen French service in the brutal campaigns of Spain and Russia, some even serving in Napoleon's Guard; and they had been holding the left flank of the Quatre Bras position unaided all morning. It was from such uninformed comments as Kincaid's that the British myth of the 'cowardly' Netherlanders grew. Had The Netherlands' troops really been cowardly or sympathetic to Napoleon, they would have run away the previous evening or betrayed their position, rather than do what they did: hold it alone against increasingly superior French forces, even against Wellington's orders, until the belated Anglo-Allied concentration on Quatre Bras could be effected. Siborne's attempts to impute cowardice on The Netherlands' troops was a red herring to distract history's attention from the inept preformance of Wellington's Headquarters staff officers.

18. RANL, Divisional report of the 2nd Netherlands Division. This famous episode was so widely known that even Siborne was obliged to report it accurately in his history.

19. *Ons Leger*, op. cit., p. 36. See also: Vels Heijn, *Waterloo: Glorie zonder Helder*, op. cit., p. 77; Lieutenant-General W.J. Knoop, Krijgskundige beschouwingen ('s Hertogenbosch, 1855), p. 121 *et seq.*; and, A.F. Becke, *Napoleon and Waterloo* (London, 1914), vol. I, pp. 190-1. So much for Professor Oman's statistics!

20. Olfermann, Prostler MS, extracts and letters. Courtesy translations were provided by Dr Christof Rohmer of the Braunschweigisches Landesmuseum.

21. A. James, *Retrospect of a military life during the most eventful periods of the last war: Journal of Sergeant James Anton 42nd Highlanders* (Edinburgh, 1841), pp. 190-5. See copy of manuscript (unpublished, because Anton was not an officer!) sent to Siborne: B.L. Add. MS 34705 19 April 1839.

22. After Waterloo, it was discovered on examination of Picton's body that he had received a canister wound from this engagement to which he had made no reference.

23. Herzog Bernard von Sachsen Weimar-Eisenbach, op. cit., vol. I, p. 184.

24. Ibid.

25. When the fresh young officers of the Guard passed these Nassau troops at Hautain le Val, some three miles by main road from Gemioncourt (but only 1,200 yards through the Bois de Bossu), they misapprehended what they saw. Years later, between 1840 and 1844, they would write to Siborne that 'Hundreds of cowardly Belgics were seen unwounded several miles from the battle.' Siborne took up these remarks with enthusiasm, unable or unwilling to understand that the Nassau 'Belgics' were at their designated ammunition resupply park.

26. Macready, op. cit., pp. 389-90.

378

27. Von Ollech, op. cit. Wussow's letter is reproduced on pages 139-40.
28. General Girard died in Paris on 25 June 1815, from wounds received at Ligny. Napoleon had created him Duc de Ligny on the 21st, but the restored Bourbons denied the title to his heirs.
29. *Journal du capitaine François: 1793-1830, publié d'après le manuscrit original par Charles Groleau* (Paris, 1903-4), vol. II, pp. 879-81.
30. Captain Batty, *Historical Sketch of the Campaign of 1815* (London, 1820), Appendix XII B, p. 154. Batty was with the 1st Foot Guards.
31. Ibid., Appendix XIII, p. 154.
32. 'Souvenirs de Général de Salle' in *Nouvelle Review*, Paris, 15 January 1895.
33. De Salle's testimony is confirmed by the Chief of Staff's register (Major-General), Nat. Arch./ Mil. Arch., op. cit. 17 June, Fleurus, Soult to Ney: 'Had Count d'Erlon executed the movement ordered by the Emperor on Saint-Amand, the Prussians would have been totally destroyed.' 17 June, Soult to Davout: 'Count d'Erlon has received wrong directions, for if he had executed the movement enjoined by the Emperor, the Prussian Army was irremediably lost.' 26 June (published 29 June 1815 in *Journal de l'Empire*), Marshal Ney to Duc d'Otranto [Fouché]: 'I was going to send forward the 1st Corps, when I heard that the Emperor had disposed of it.' And finally, General Durutte published 8 March 1838 in *Sentinelle de l'Armée*: 'The Emperor sent Count d'Erlon the order to attack the left (the right) of the Prussians, and to try and take possession of Brye. The 1st Corps passed near Villers-Perouin to execute this movement.'
34. Ibid.
35. Ibid. Durutte relates that when I Corps was near Villers Perouin several orderly officers arrived from Ney with his order for I Corps to turn round and march to Quatre Bras. The officers reported to d'Erlon that '... Marshal Ney was engaged with superior numbers who had beaten off his attack at the cross-roads'. Durutte's was the lead division of I Corps and at the time was approaching Wagnelee.
36. Notizen MS, General Commando MS and Kielmansegge MS in Legionsgeschichte der King's German Legion Akten Hann. 38D – Nr. 18, 22, 188, 200, 230-43, 297. Niedersachersisches Hauptsaatsarchiv Hannover.
37. The Prince of Orange has been much criticized by English-language historians for his actions both here and at Waterloo. Siborne was the first, followed by many, including more recently, the American historian, Jac Weller, whose *Wellington at Waterloo* (New York, 1967) was marred by an over-reliance on Siborne and avoidance of non-English language sources. Among other things, the Prince was blamed for being too young, at 23, for his rank, Major-General, and to hold a corps command. However, there was ample precedent for this, as nearly 300 French generals, including Napoleon, had held this rank at the same age, as indeed had the Duke of York in his day. Further, it was the British establishment that had bestowed this appointment on the Prince, in 1813, and it was Wellington who appointed him to a corps command in 1815. Even if it is assumed that the appointment was made solely to enable Wellington to have effective command of the 30,000 Netherlands troops, the Prince cannot be criticized for accepting it. Rather might the government of Britain, the wealthiest nation in Europe at the time, be blamed for sending its field marshal to war without providing him with an army, or even declaring war. The truth behind the calumnies put about against the Prince of Orange is more simple and more venial. Siborne, the initiator of these slanders, was subsidized financially in writing his history by some of the British officers who had participated in the campaign of 1815. Siborne expressed his gratitude to these benefactors by portraying the British role much larger than life and with partisan sympathy. Not content with this inflation, Siborne also denigrated the efforts and maligned the motives of the British allies, so to magnify by comparison the British achievement in the campaign. Siborne's patrons would not have liked to think, and did not see in his account, that the Duke could have been caught unawares at the Duchess of Richmond's Ball. Instead, Siborne asserted that Wellington knew before attending that Ball that Napoleon had crossed the Sambre, and that the Duke's appearance at the Ball was to pacify the Belgian people who were ready to revolt in favour of Napoleon. The first assertion is merely untrue, but the second is patently absurd. The Belgian people had no more in common with the Duchess of Richmond and her guests than that they breathed the same air. Had they been in the mood to revolt, the sight of foreign officers, with their wives, mistresses and myrmidons, swanning around in a rarified social atmosphere from which mere mortals were excluded should, if anything, have precipitated rather than prevented insurrection. The historical record is replete with instances, such as this one, whereby a lie has been accepted as truth through iteration.
38. War Arch. Kellermann's report to Soult, Frasnes, 10 p.m., 16 June 1815.
39. B.L. Add. MS 3706. Captain B. Piggot to Captain William Siborne, 7 July 1844. According to Piggot, 'Major Lindsay regretted the order until the day he died.' Siborne ignored Piggot's eye-witness testimony, preferring to cast the blame for this rout of British troops on the Prince of Orange's order to form a line. Although the British troops may not have seen the French horsemen coming through the tall rye, they certainly heard and felt the thundering hooves of 1,000 heavy horses bearing down on them at the charge, and would have been in squares in time.
40. This is another fantastic example of the per-

petuation of historical error through the uncritical repetition of secondary source material. The error seems to have originated with Thiers, who in the course of preparing his massive 21-volume *Histoire du Consulate et L'Empire* (Paris, 1845-74) consulted Comte de Flahaut, Napoleon's ADC, who had remained all day on the 16th at the Quatre Bras battle. Flahaut tried to put Thiers right on the ridiculous version of Kellermann's escape which by then (1861) had already gained currency, and which persists to the present day. Flahaut recorded his view of the legend: '... "Kellermann, whose horse was killed, remains for some time at the enemy's mercy. He escapes on foot by clinging to the bits of two of the troop horses." Can you imagine a more ingenious way of effecting one's escape? for what is it he clung to – the manes, the boots or the horses' tails? Not at all! He hung on to their bits, which would inevitably have prevented them from moving and caused them to fall. It really is burlesque; nevertheless it is sad to see the *Revue des Deux Mondes* admitting such articles ... I trust in heaven that, in spite of party spirit, the public will have the good sense to treat such foolishness as it deserves.' – Bowood, op. cit., pp. 121-2.

41. Jackson, in *Colburne's United Service Magazine*, September 1847, pp. 5-7. This is the original account by Jackson, not to be confused with the 1903 distortion 'edited' by Seaton. Jackson reported no cowardly foreigners fleeing along the Brussels road, only those foreigners who were aiding Allied wounded or were themselves wounded.

42. Ibid., p. 7. Seaton, in his recreation of Jackson's record, *Reminiscences of a Staff Officer*, op. cit., p. 19, altered Jackson's '... all agreeing that the Duke had never been so severely pressed, or had so much difficulty in maintaining his position' to '... all agreeing that our troops had never been more severely pressed in maintaining their position'.

43. It would have been virtually impossible, even with field glasses, to distinguish at a distance of a mile or more whether the approaching troops were Netherlanders of the 1st or 2nd Divisions, or French from the left wing. Both wore black shakos, navy blue tunics, grey trousers, and white leather equipment.

44. From Gneisenau's report in Von Ollech, op. cit., p. 48.

45. 'The Journal of Lieutenant von Reuter' in *The United Service Magazine*, October 1891, pp. 43-50. Translated by Captain E.S. May. Copy courtesy of Lieutenant von Reuter's grandson.

46. Batty, op. cit., p. 154.

47. Docs. Inédits., op. cit., p. 64. Count d'Erlon to Duc d'Elchingen (Ney). See also: Le Maréchal Drouet, Comte d'Erlon, *Vie Militaire, etc.* (Paris, 1844), pp. 93-6.

48. According to Durutte's verbatim account in K. von Damitz, *Geschichte des Feldzugs von 1815 in den Niederlanden und Frankreich als Beitrag zur Kriegsgeschichte der neuren Kriege* (Berlin, 1837-8), vol. I, pp. 141-2. Such a column as d'Erlon's, numbering 21,000 men, would, according to the method of computation prescribed by the German *Manual for Commanders 1912* (see Note 23 to Chapter 8), have been about five miles in length.

49. Damitz, op. cit.

50. Ibid.

51. D'Erlon, op. cit., p. 96.

52. Von Reuter, op. cit., p. 47.

53. Kelly, *Waterloo* (London, 1817). For Gneisenau's report of 19 June 1815, see p. 60.

54. *Memoiren des koniglich preussischen Generals der Infanterie Ludwig von Reiche, herausgegeben von seinem Neffen Louis von Weltzien* (Leipzig, 1857), vol. II, pp. 201-3.

55. Von Ollech, op. cit., p. 162 *et seq.* Gneisenau's report to the King of Prussia, 2 a.m., 17 June 1815. See also: Damitz, op. cit., vol. I, p. 143.

56. The already considerable mistrust with which Gneisenau viewed Wellington over the treaty of 3 January 1815 was greatly intensified by Gneisenau's reading of the appearance and disappearance of what seemed to be a large Anglo-Allied force on the French left flank. After all, the conference at Brye had concluded with Wellington, through Müffling, giving Gneisenau to understand that he would send help to Ligny that day, the 16th. Other Prussian officers received the same message as Gneisenau had. Von Reiche, who was present at the conference, wrote that 'Having promised powerful support and co-operation, Wellington left soon after half-past one ...' (Von Reiche, op. cit.). This view also concerts with Müffling's *Journal*. Wellington's proviso about not being attacked himself must have seemed rather captious to the Prussians, especially as they and Wellington all knew that Napoleon with his main force faced the Prussian army and that Wellington had indicated he would have his entire army at Quatre Bras by 4 p.m. A French force not exceeding two corps could hardly be expected to prevent Wellington, with 80,000-90,000 men from pushing through to the Ligny battlefield. At about 5 p.m., Gneisenau's staff officer, Major von Wussow, had been informed that Wellington intended to use 20,000 men '... to launch a powerful attack which would benefit the Prussian army'. Naturally when the unidentified force which was d'Erlon's appeared from the expected direction shortly thereafter, causing panic among the French left, the Prussians could be excused for thinking it was an Anglo-Allied force fulfilling Wellington's promise. Bitterness toward the perfidious Wellington must have run in full flood on the evening of the 16th among the Prussian generals, as they reflected on how Wellington, by committing the force which he had seemed to have brought to the edge of the field at the critical point in the battle, could have prevented the Prussian defeat and perhaps ensured a victory. After all, it was hardly credible that a

French force would have marched away, effectively saving them from destruction.

57. Capitaine H. de Mauduit, *Les Derniers Jours de la Grande Armée* (Paris, 1847), pp. 187-9. Mauduit belonged to the 2/1st Grenadiers of the Old Guard.

58. Pertz and Delbruck, *Gneisenau*, op. cit., vol. IV, p. 522.

59. Ibid., pp. 298-9. See also: Henderson, *Blücher*, p. 240.

60. A. Brett-James. *Hundred Days*, op. cit., quoted on pp. 82-3.

61. Von Ollech, op. cit., pp. 139-40.

62. Von * (R)eiche, Krieg Der Franzofen, op. cit., p. 274. See also: von Stuhr, *Feldzuge gegen Napoleon*, op. cit., pp. 559-61.

Chapter 10. 17 June: Strategic Withdrawal

1. Netherlands, Archives of the Royal House. 'Headquarters at Nivelles the 17th June 1815, 2 o'clock in the morning.' Translated for the author by Dr. N. Vels Heijn. At the time the Prince was ordered to Nivelles, Wellington still had very little cavalry at Quatre Bras and could not offer him a mounted escort. The 27th *Jägers*, who had seen more action than most other Allied units, needed to return to Nivelles for their baggage, equipment and ammunition. It was natural that they would escort their Prince through an area where enemy cavalry patrols could be active. These brave men were viewed with ignorant denigration by some British officers such as Captain Mercer, who passed them on the Nivelles road and recorded his misguided impression: 'The road was covered with soldiers, many of them wounded, but also many apparently untouched. The numbers thus leaving the field appeared extraordinary. Many of the wounded had six, eight, ten, and even more, attendants ... My countrymen will rejoice to learn that amongst this dastardly crew not one Briton appeared. Whether they were of Nassau or Belgians, I know not; they were one or the other – I think the latter.' Mercer, op. cit., pp. 137-8. One can only speculate as to the thoughts of the battle-weary *Jägers*.

2. Jackson, op. cit., p. 7. Jackson, who was familiar with cavalry, has left an accurate account of the Earl of Uxbridge's dexterity as a cavalry commander. Uxbridge, having seen the congestion on the road from Nivelles to Quatre Bras, had the presence of mind to divert much of the cavalry that had not already passed on to the Vieux Genappe road, which took them to Genappe and down the main Brussels road to Quatre Bras. It was Uxbridge's use of this bypass that gave Wellington most of his cavalry on the morning of the 17th.

3. Müffling, *Passages*, op. cit., pp. 240-1. Müffling, as he himself asserts, had not previously been informed of the Prussian movement. Of course he knew of Gneisenau's profound mistrust of Wellington, and more than anyone knew what had been said and what had been understood in the conference at Brye on the 16th. In his role as mediator he sought to use

the incident of Winterfeldt's wounding to smooth over an embarrassment. He knew that Winterfeldt had carried no such message. Much of the misunderstanding which prevailed between the two Allied army commands over June 14-17 must be laid to Müffling's well-intentioned obfuscation.

4. Kelly, *Waterloo*, op. cit., p. 153. According to Hansard, on 23 June 1815 Lord Bathurst, the Colonial Secretary, addressed these remarks to the House of Lords: 'The position of Waterloo was one well known to Lord Wellington: in the summer of last year his Grace went there on his way to Paris, and on that occasion he took a military view of it. He declared, that if ever it was his fortune to defend Brussels, Waterloo would be the best position he could occupy.'

5. Dr. K. Griewank, *Gneisenau Ein Leben in Briefen* (Leipzig, 1939), p. 319. Letter No. 180, Wavre, Nr. Brussels June 17th, 1815.

6. WD (1852 ed.), vol. VIII, p. 144. De Lacy Evans' footnote reads: 'Copied from the Duke's writing. Saw the Duke write them while seated on the ground. They are my own original copies, taken at the moment.'

7. These Netherlands troops were sent to Mont St-Jean at Wellington's order (through the misunderstood mechanism of the political/military command structure of the 1815 Anglo-Allied army) to form an advance guard behind which the army, arriving piecemeal, could form. The British soldiers at Nivelles, who had not been taken into their field marshal's confidence, believed these Netherlands cavalry to be deserting in the face of the enemy. According to Private Wheeler of the 51st Foot of Colville's 4th Division: 'The next morning [of the 17th] we continued our march until we came to Nivelles, a smart sized town. This place was crowded with heavy cavalry beonging to Belgium, they were in a great hurry to get through the town and our Colonel thought they were changing their positions, we halted to let them pass, but afterwards found they were running away, helter skelter, The Devil take the hindmost. They looked like and as much resembled our Blues [Household Cavalry], but this is all that can be said of them except they were the rankest cowards that ever formed a part of an army.' – The Letters of Private Wheeler (London, 1951), Capt B.H. Liddell Hart, ed., p. 169. Of Private Wheeler and his like-minded comrades, it may be said that the natural fear of the hazards of war may have caused them to impute to the apparent retreat of the Netherlanders motives which any sane man would have entertained though he did not act upon them. Of historians and others who have subsequently, in the light of Wellington's orders and relevant Netherlands papers, allowed or encouraged such a calumny to stand, little can be said by way of mitigation.

8. Müffling, *Passages*, op. cit., p. 241. See also: von Ollech, *Feldzuges von 1815*, op. cit., p. 180; Siborne Add. MS 34705; WSD, op. cit., vol. X, pp. 526-7; Houssaye, *1815*, op. cit., p.

145.

9. Kerry, Bowood Papers, p. 119.

10. Archives of Duc d'Elchingen, 'To his Excellency the Duke of Dalmatia [Soult], Frasnes, 16 June 1815, 10 p.m. See also: General A. Pollio, *Waterloo* (Paris, 1908), photographic facsimile of the original given on pp. 248-9; and Becke, *Napoleon and Waterloo*, op. cit., vol. II, p. 287.

11. Bowood, op. cit.

12. Mil. Arch., Major-Generals' register. To the Marshal Prince of the Moskowa, Fleurus, Between 7-8 a.m., 17 June 1815. See also: Becke, *Napoleon and Waterloo*, op. cit., vol. II, pp. 288-9; Siborne, *Waterloo*, op. cit., pp. 357-8; Houssaye, *1815*, op. cit., pp. 126-7. Houssaye's account omits 'If Count d'Erlon had carried out the movement on S. Amand, prescribed by the Emperor ...' and 'Yesterday the Emperor remarked with regret that you had not massed your divisions', although they appear clearly in the register from which he quoted. Another example of the lamentable practice of Houssaye, Siborne and their ilk, of tailoring historical evidence to fit a preconception: that the particular hero was incapable of error. Neither Napoleon nor Wellington would have condoned such hagiographic treatment.

13. Mil. Arch., 'Exelmans to Grouchy, in front of Gembloux, before noon, June 17, 1815. See also: Houssaye, *1815*, op. cit., p. 378, note 45.

14. Grouchy, *Observations*, op. cit., p. 11. With regard to wasting time, Napoleon (as General Bonaparte) when speaking to Piedmontese emissaries in 1796 made a remark that continued to characterize his actions throughout his career: 'It may happen to me to lose battles, but no one shall ever see me lose minutes, either by over-confidence, or by sloth.'

15. Mil. Arch., 'Exelmans to Grouchy, in front of Gembloux, 17th June 1815.' See also: Houssaye, *1815*, op. cit., p. 129.

16. Somerset de Chair, *Napoleon's Memoirs*, op. cit., pp. 550-1. Napoleon observed: 'He [Wellington] ought to have crossed the Forest of Soignies in the night of the 17th to 18th, by the Charleroi road; the Prussian Army ought similarly to have crossed it by the Wavre road; the two armies ought to have effected their junction on Brussels at first light and have left a rearguard to defend the forest ... and have let me manoeuvre as I liked. Would I, with an army of 100,000 men, have crossed the Forest of Soignies, in order to attack, on issuing from it, the two armies joined together, more than 200,000 strong and in position? That would certainly have been the most advantageous thing that could have happened to the Allies. Would I have been content to take up a [defensive] position myself? My inaction could not have lasted long, for 300,000 Russians, Austrians, and Bavarians etc., would have arrived on the Rhine. They would be on the Marne within a few weeks, which would force me to hasten to the rescue of my capital.' These remarks, made on St. Helena and long dismissed as sour grapes on the part of the loser, provide a key to understanding Napoleon's actions in the campaign, the importance he attached to control of the main roads to Brussels from the Charleroi area, and especially his fears on the 17th as to what Wellington and Blücher's intentions might be.

17. Houssaye, in *1815*, pp. 373-4, cites ten different accounts of Napoleon's verbal order, recorded by members of his entourage. The author has given the substance common to the ten.

18. Comte de Flahault was in attendance on Napoleon when Grouchy received his verbal order and later wrote: 'We got to our horses to look around the battle-field. After this we made our way to the high road leading from Namur to Quatre Bras, and it was here that the Emperor gave his final instructions to Grouchy. As to what M. Quinet [a writer] says about there being no possibility of communication by any lateral road, I can on my honour affirm that the Emperor said to Grouchy, "*Allons Grouchy, poursuivez les Prussiens, l'epée dans les reins; mais communiquez toujours avec moi par votre Gauche* [Go Grouchy, pursue the Prussians, sword in the back; but always communicate with me by your Left.]" Surely this was as good as telling him that the maintenance of communication was an essential point in his orders.' – Kerry, *Bowood Papers*, op. cit., pp. 119-20.

19. Capitaine H. de Maduit, *Les Derniers Jours de la Grande Armée* (Paris, 1847), vol. II, pp. 209-10. This order, dictated by Bertrand, was quoted extensively by French and other European historians before 1850. It disappeared sometime between 1854 and 1867, during the editing of the 32-volume *Correspondence de Napoleon Ier*. Comte de Flahault had been appointed by Napoleon III as one of the commissioners for the publication of the work. Manuscript letters of his contained in the Bowood Papers in England show that the papers were edited in a Houssayean spirit, with a desire to present only an unblemished heroic view of the first Napoleon. For example: Flahault to Laborde, 1862 [no month or day given], 'I now come to the danger which might be incurred by the printing of documents such as the one (Nr. 10060) you sent me, and have no hesitation in saying that its publication would do grievous harm to whom it was the Emperor's [Napoleon III's] intention to set up.' When volume XII appeared, the document published as Numero 10060 was an innocuous note concerning the operation of the Marseilles criminal court. In a letter to Flahault written on 3 December 1863 Napoleon III made plain his expectations with regard to the *Correspondence*: 'I stopped the publication of the Emperor's letters because I perceived that letters had been published which would have been better suppressed.' Of the roughly 60,000 letters examined by the commission, only about 22,000 were actually published; while the rest are

presumed destroyed. Such 'editing' constitutes a far more heinous crime against history than Sibornic 'editing' because irreplaceable source material was deliberately destroyed and an attempt was made to pretend it had never existed. Siborne at least did not burn the memoirs sent to him. See: Kerry, *Bowood Papers*, op. cit., pp. 271-88.

20. Archives of the Duc d'Elchingen, 'To the Marshal Prince of the Moskowa', In front of Ligny, Noon, 17 June 1815. See also: Mil. Arch., Major-Generals' register, 17 June 1815; and Becke, *Napoleon*, op. cit., vol. II, p. 289.

21. General Baron de Jomini, *The Political and Military History of the Campaign of Waterloo* (New York, 1862), p. 150. Tr. by Captain S.V. Benet, US Army, from the 1839 Paris edition. There is little doubt that Jomini transcribed this document from its original manuscript copy, which was probably destroyed between 1854 and 1865 during Napoleon III's purge of his uncle's papers. Certainly it is most unlikely that Napoleon (the 1st) would have neglected to order a reconnaissance of this area.

22. Archives privées des Archives Nationales. The papers of General Gourgaud 314 AP. 'To His Excellency the Duke of Dalmatia [Soult], Frasnes, 6.30 a.m., 17 June 1815.' See also: Houssaye, *1815*, op. cit., p. 372, note 15. This letter explains Ney's actions on the morning of the 17th. It is another probable victim of Napoleon III's purge. Napoleon the 1st had attempted to blame his reversal at Waterloo on Ney in an effort to retain popular support in Paris after Waterloo and later on St. Helena in playing to the audience of posterity. Its appearance in the *Correspondence* would indeed have embarrassed Napoleon III.

23. Soult, as Napoleon's Chief of Staff, was not required to formulate complex orders, but rather to take down what Napoleon dictated and generate orders from it. Although there is no documentary proof extant, it is difficult to believe that a general officer of Soult's experiece could inadvertently have so mishandled his straightforward task. It is interesting in this light to note that, after Waterloo when loyal Marshals such as Ney were being executed or shot out of hand like Brune, Soult received very different treatment. He was captured by one of the Comte d'Artois' ultra-royalist murder bands, but curiously was not beaten, imprisoned nor even brought to trial. He was allowed parole on d'Artois's orders, and was further permitted to publish a justification for his apparent return to Napoleon in 1815 in which he stated that d'Artois 'knew my mind'. Soult opportunely managed to 'escape' custody in France, being granted exile in Prussia where Bonapartist sympathy was non-existent, until he was permitted to be reconciled with Louis XVIII. See: D.C. Hamilton-Williams, *The Fall of Napoleon: The Final Betrayal*, in preparation.

24. Jackson, op. cit., p. 11. See also: The Mar-

quess of Anglesey, *One-Leg* (London, 1961), pp. 129-30.

25. Houssaye, *1815*, op. cit., p. 146. Citations given in full by Houssaye.

26. Mercer, op. cit., p. 145.

27. Angelsey, *One-Leg*, op. cit., p. 128.

28. Ibid., p. 129.

29. Ibid., pp. 147-8.

30. D'Erlon, *Vie Militaire*, op. cit., p. 96.

31. General Gourgaud, *The Campaign of 1815* (London, 1818), p. 80.

32. J. Dumaine, *Napoleon è Waterloo: Souvenirs Militaires, ou précis rectifié de la Campagne de 1815. Avec des Documents nouveaux et des pièces inédites. Par un ancien officier de la Garde Impériale, qui est resté près de Napoléon pendant toute la Campagne.* (Paris, 1866), pp. 185-6.

33. Sir W. Gomm, op. cit., p. 357. Gomm stated that: 'His [Napoleon's] guns are silenced by the superior fire of a battery at La Haye St.' In fact Napoleon had used a ploy to unmask Wellington's position.

34. Mauduit, op. cit., vol. II, pp. 230-2.

35. Mil. Arch., Major-Generals' register, Soult to Grouchy, Le Caillou, 10 a.m. 18 June 1815, cited in von Ollech, op. cit., p. 170. A minor skirmish occurred between three platoons of French *cuirassiers* sent to reconnoitre this movement and the Prussian cavalry skirmishers covering the column of Colonel von Sohr's brigade.

36. *Wider Napoleon! Ein deutsches Reiterleben 1806-1815. Herausgegeben von Friedrich M. Kircheisen* (Stuttgart, 1911), reprint of 1861 ed., vol II, pp. 320-1.

37. *Der Feldzug von 1815 in Frankreich. Hinterlassenes werk des Generals Karl von Clausewitz* (Berlin, 1862), p. 95.

38. B.L. Add. MS 34705. Copy sent to Captain William Siborne by Colonel von Reiche of the Prussian General Staff. Dated Wavre 6 p.m., 17 June 1815. Cited in Siborne, *Waterloo*, op. cit., vol. I, pp. 278-9. In his book, however, Siborne did not give the place or hour.

39. Von Ollech, op. cit., p. 187. Blücher to Müffling, Wavre, 11 p.m., 17 June 1815.

40. WD (1888 ed.), vol. XII, p. 476.

41. Ibid., pp. 476-7.

42. Ibid.

43. Ibid., p. 478.

44. WSD, vol. X, p. 501. This letter, alerting Lady Frances and the Mountnorris's, who in turn of course alerted others in the British community, gave rise to an air of panic, coming as it did from the 'horse's mouth'. This would have made it quite a bit more difficult for Sir Charles Stuart to carry out Wellington's abjuration to 'keep the English quiet', although in the event Stuart spread the warning as well.

45. Napoleon, *Mémoires pour servir à l'histoire de France en 1815* (Paris, 1820), pp. 120-1.

Chapter 11. 18 June: Morning

1. Mil. Arch., 'Grouchy to Napoleon', Gembloux, 10 p.m., 17 June 1815.

2. Hamilton-Williams, op. cit., chapter 12.

3. ANF, Foreign Affairs, iv 1933, copy of letter to

the Emperor, Berlier to Bassano, 16 June 1815. See also: Houssaye, *1815*, op. cit., p. 156 and citations.

4. The political value of Brussels to Napoleon cannot be over-emphasized; its capture would probably have won him the war, hence Wellington's strategy. Wellington stressed this to Clausewitz: 'He [Clausewitz] is sensible of the advantage derived by the enemy from such impressions. He is aware of the object of Buonaparte to create throughout Europe, and even in England, a moral impression against the war, and to shake the power of the then existing administration in England. He is sensible of and can contemplate the effect of the moral impression upon the other armies of Europe, and upon governments in whose service they were, resulting from the defeat or even want of success of the Allied armies under the command of the Duke of Wellington and Prince Blücher. But he is not sensible of, the moral impression resulting from the loss of Bruxelles and Ghent, the flight of the King of The Netherlands, and of the King Louis XVIII., the creatures of the treaties of peace, and of the acts of the Congress of Vienna; and this with the loss of [the British] communications of the army under the Duke of Wellington with England, Holland, and Germany. – Wellington.' The opinion of the Field Marshal, diplomat and later Prime Minister is, I think, conclusive. WSD, op. cit., vol. X, pp. 520-1.

5. D'Erlon, *Vie Militaire*, op. cit., pp. 196-7.
6. Mil. Arch., Reille's account.
7. *Documents Inédits*, op. cit., p. 52.
8. Napoleon, *Mémoires*, op. cit., p. 124.
9. Ibid., pp. 124-5.
10. Lieut.-Colonel de Baudas, *Etudes sur Napoléon* (Paris, 1841), p. 224.
11. *Correspondence*, op. cit., No. 15,933.
12. Houssaye, *1815*, op. cit., p. 178. Quoted from Thiers who was given it by Reille.
13. M. de l'Ain Girod, *Vie Militaire du Général Foy* (Paris, 1900), pp. 278-9.
14. Mil. Arch., 'Soult to Grouchy, Before the Farm of Le Caillou, 10 a.m., 18 June 1815.'
15. Houssaye, *1815*, op. cit., pp. 181, 407 (note 41 for Houssaye's citations from the memoirs of Grouchy, Gérard and Marbot).
16. *Napoléon à Waterloo*, op. cit., pp. 344 *et seq*.
17. In describing the battlefield, I, like M. Houssaye, have consulted the De Craan map, which is reproduced in colour in the present book.
18. The author visited the battlefield in June 1992 in the company of Colonel Cyril Desmet, formerly Senior Lecturer at the Belgian Ecole Militaire. While we were standing near the inn of La Belle Alliance, the current Commandant of the school rode up on horseback accompanied by some twenty military attachés whom the commandant was conducting on a tour of the field. They then rode off, taking the present track west of the inn towards Hougoumont. Several times as they rode through depressions not discernible to

us from the apparently flat ground, they seemed to disappear and reappear.

19. Anglesey, *One-Leg*, op. cit., quoted on p. 133.
20. In his official dispatch to Lord Bathurst early in the morning of 19 June Wellington wrote: '... the enemy with the exception of the 3rd corps, which he sent to observe Marshal Blucher, in the range [ridge] to our front ...' – WD, vol. XIII, 1888, p. 481. Being in possession of Napoleon's complete order of battle, Wellington knew that the French detachment observing Blücher, one infantry and two cavalry corps, were the only units of Napoleon's army unaccounted for. In answer to Clausewitz's criticism of his having left Prince Frederick's force out of the battle all day, Wellington, referring to himself in the third person, replied: 'The Duke of Wellington [was] right in thinking that, from the evening of the 16th, Buonaparte would have taken a wiser course if he had moved to his left, have reached the high road leading to Mons to Bruxelles, and to have turned the right of the position of the Allies by Hal. It is obvious that the Duke was prepared to resist such a movement.' – WSD, vol. X, pp. 530-1. What was not obvious was the reality of such a threat. General Estorff, the Allied cavalry commander at Hal, had reported no enemy sighted within the range of his patrols, and General Behr at Mons had reported to Prince Frederick no enemy within five miles of Mons. The only plausible explanation can be that Wellington kept Prince Frederick, with 20 per cent of Wellington's army, where he did to maintain a line of retreat to the Scheldt.
21. Unpalatable though the fact may be, it is obvious that Wellington, *in extremis*, planned to withdraw his forces behind his strong right and fall back behind the force at Hal. As cited, he had already informed Blücher on the 16th that if Blücher could not support him at Mont St-Jean 'he would fall back behind the Scheldt'. Further, and more conclusively, he had stated to Lady Frances Webster at 3 a.m. that very morning: 'The course of the operations may oblige me to uncover Bruxelles for a moment, and may expose that town to the enemy.' (Loc. cit.) Wellington could hardly uncover Bruxelles by retreating towards it through the forest. Neither was he placed (as we shall see) to retreat east towards Blücher if the latter were coming by that route. It concludes that Wellington had provided, quite rightly as being responsible for his army, an avenue of retreat if needed. It would hardly have been prudent to have explained this point to the British public and to Clausewitz many years after the battle when the event had not been necessary and – as the 'hero' of the battle – this planned retreat might have been rather embarrassing.
22. Much confusion concerning the command structure of the Anglo-Allied army at Waterloo stems from the fact that Wellington had overall command of forces of five nationalities: British (including KGL), Hanoverian, Netherlands, Brunswick, and Nassau.

Because his correspondence contains almost no reference to reports from the non-British forces, and because of the smothering effect of the gospel according to Siborne, it was easy for Victorians to believe, as they fervently wished to do, that it was the British army that defeated Napoleon. In his rebuttal of Clausewitz's critcisms Wellington wrote of his army's complex command structure: 'It is forgotten by General von Clausewitz, that the army the Duke of Wellington commanded was not, like the army under Prince Blücher, composed of troops of all arms, and establishments of and belonging to one nation, but they belonged to several, the infantry, cavalry, and artillery in some cases belonging each to different nations; that the several corps [bodies] of troops composing the Allied army in question were not of uniform strength of numbers, whether considered by nations, by battalions, by brigades, or by divisions ... It was necessary to organize these troops in brigades, divisions, and corps d'armées with those better disciplined and more accustomed to war, in order to derive from their numbers as much advantage as possible. But these arrangements in allied armies, formed as this one was, are not matters of course. The same national feeling respecting its armies, even in the least powerful nation ... is not without its influence in the formation of such arrangements of organization. No troops can be employed in an allied army excepting each corps and detachment is under the immediate command of its own national officer ... and under the command of what officer, become therefore, and became in this case, a matter which required great attention and labour, and of great difficulty.' WSD, vol. X, pp. 517-8.

23. Bijlandt's 1 Brigade of Perponcher's 2nd Netherlands Division was placed on outpost duty covering the army's left flank during the night of the 17th. Wellington used this opportunity to break up Perponcher's division, placing one of his brigades in the middle of Picton's division. Bijlandt's brigade had been holding Quatre Bras when Picton arrived to reinforce them. Wellington had seen this and may have felt that those two units had formed a mutual respect, as both had fought well, and therefore would fight well together again. In battle, Bijlandt's brigade would normally have been positioned behind Saxe-Weimar's 2 Brigade as a reserve, but at Mont St-Jean Wellington had placed two Hanoverian brigades there instead. However Picton did not command Bijlandt's brigade; Perponcher retained command of the whole of his division. No British officer below Wellington and Lord Hill had authority over any Netherlands unit; and Wellington and Hill held their authority from King William. Throughout most of the 18th, Perponcher remained with Bijlandt's brigade. The report to King William from the 2nd Netherlands Division's Chief of Staff, Colonel van Zuylen van Nyevelt, referring to d'Erlon's attack of 1.30 p.m. stated

that: 'In this engagement the Lieutenant of the Staff (Van Harem) was killed, General Perponcher had two horses shot dead under him.' See also the report of the Prince of Orange to King William, 3 July 1815. [RAO]

24. Wellington's army is treated in greater detail in this exposition of dispositions in an attempt to shed more light on the locations of the various national forces within Wellington's polyglot army, especially as some dispute attends the subject.

25. General Sir James Shaw Kennedy, *Notes on the Battle of Waterloo* (London, 1865), pp. 100-1. See also: Unpublished letter to William Siborne dated 11 August 1839, B.L. Add. MS 34705. There is little difference of substance between Shaw Kennedy's letter to Siborne and his published account. The present author has excluded reference to the 3rd Division in isolation because, as Shaw Kennedy stated in his unpublished letter: 'The Duke of Wellington ordered all the army to adopt this defensive posture.' This assertion is borne out by most of the first-hand accounts, some of which will be cited below.

26. *History of the Royal Corps of Engineers*, op. cit., pp. 378-9. Quoted from the diary and journals of Lieutenant Sperling and Captain Oldfield. Oldfield wrote on the morning of the 18th: 'Soon after Col. Smyth had left, Captain [blank] came in and told me that he was in arrest by the Colonel, who it seems met him at the entrance of the village [Waterloo], whither he had come in place of Braine-le-Leud [*sic*] and hearing from the Major that British troops had left it the previous day [the 16th], he moved his people forward to Waterloo.' As a consequence Colonel Smyth refused to recommend any of the officers or men connected with this incident for the Waterloo honours or pecuniary advantages. Because of these 350 men having been in the wrong position, La Haye Sainte was not placed in a state of defence, with loopholes, firing platforms or earthworks.

27. Longford, *Wellington*, op. cit., pp. 447-9.

28. Müffling, *Aus Leben*, op. cit., pp. 209-10. This letter is not included in the English editions.

29. Captain A. von Nostitz, *Tagebuch des Generals der Kavellerie Grafen von Nostitz* (Berlin, 1884-5), pp. 36-7.

30. Hamilton-Williams, *The Fall of Napoleon*, op. cit., chapter 7.

31. O. von Lettow-Vorbeck, *Napoleons Untergang* (Berlin, 1904), vol. I, p. 527.

32. Von Ollech, op. cit., pp. 181, 190.

33. *Correspondence*, op. cit., No. 22,060.

34. *Docs. Inédits*, op. cit., p. 53.

35. Captain and Lieutenant-Colonel Batty, 1st Guards, *Historical sketch of the Campaign of 1815* (London, 1820), p. 88.

36. Wellington had specifically ordered his artillery not to expend ammunition in counter-battery fire, so as to save it for use against advancing infantry and cavalry. French gunners were not placed under any such prohibition; when possible they would

concentrate fire to disable an enemy battery to spare French troops the casualties their fire could have inflicted. This disparity in artillery standing orders may stem from the fact that Napoleon had begun his career as an artillery officer and had always promoted the co-ordinated use of all arms in mutually supporting roles; while in the British army, artillery was organizationally separate.

37. RANL, Report of the 2nd [Netherlands] Division, op. cit.: 'At nine o'clock His Royal Highness [the Prince of Orange] ordered 800 men of the division to be despatched to strengthen the right wing, for which the 1st Battalion of the 2nd Regiment Light Infantry Nassau was told off. This battalion, under command of Captain Buschen [Major Sattler, its appointed commander having fallen at Quatre Bras], took possession of the farmhouse of Hougoumont, situated between the roads of Nivelles and Genappe leading to Waterloo, and by this proceeding covered the front of the right wing of the army. This farmhouse was a large building, standing in the midst of a large-sized garden, enclosed by a wall, in which loopholes were made, as also in the windows and doors. Just in front of the farmhouse was a small copse, terminating on the road of Nivelles; three companies were placed in this copse, the three others entrenching themselves in the garden and in the house as well as the short time left at their disposal before the expected assault would allow.' See also Captain Buschen's account: Buschen MS, Nr 26-27 Kriegsdepartement Staatsarchiv Wiesbaden (VIII Nassau). Also: Boulger, op. cit., p. 60. The view that only the British Guards held Château Hougoumont stems from the seven or so British officers' accounts used by Siborne from 1838 to 1844 in his creation of what came to be the accepted British version of the battle. In the Siborne manuscript letters there is a certified copy dated 23 April 1840 of the 2nd Netherlands' 1815 Divisional report (B.L. Add. MS 34705), on the back of which Siborne had written in pencil: 'Written by an unknown K.G.L. officer.' See also the introduction to this book.

38. Mil. Arch., Reille's account, op. cit. He stated that Prince Jérôme was ordered '... to keep in the hollow behind the wood [in front of the buildings] meanwhile maintaining a strong skirmish line (tirailleurs).'

39. Frazer, Letters, op. cit., pp. 555-6. Dated 20 June 1815, 9 a.m. As a rule, whenever possible, the present author will use the edition of a first-hand account which was set down as soon as possible after the event recounted.

40. Sir Julian Paget and Derek Saunders, Hougoumont (London, 1992), pp. 45-7. They include the account by Lieutenant Diederich von Wilder of the 1/2nd Nassauers, but refer to him as a Hanoverian, perhaps confusing Wilder with Lieutenant Henry Wilding of the 1st KGL line battalion. However, in the absence of citations, it is impossible to be certain.

41. Mil. Arch., Marshal Grouchy to Napoleon, Gembloux, 6 a.m., 18 June 1815.

42. ANF, Major-Generals' Register. Soult to Grouchy, From the Battlefield of Mont St. Jean, 1 p.m., 18 June 1815. See also: the photographic facsimile in the 59th edition (1907) of Houssaye, 1815, op. cit.

43. Napoleon, Mémoires, op. cit., p. 139. Soult to Grouchy in de Baudas, Etudes, op. cit., vol. I, p. 226.

44. Soult to Grouchy in de Baudas, op. cit., vol. I, p. 226, postscript to quote above.

Chapter 12. 18 June: 1.30 p.m. to 3.30 p.m.

1. Napoleon, Mémoires, op. cit. p. 142.

2. Ibid., p.141-2. See also: Gourgaud, Papers, op. cit., p. 90; and Von Ollech, op. cit., p. 192. Many historians of the battle find it difficult to explain why at this stage Napoleon detached these 10,000 men, both infantry and cavalry, to his right flank. The best defence against Bülow's corps would have been to post initially a cavalry screen, proceed to defeat Wellington with a true Napoleonic stroke, then turn a large force on the Prussian advance guard. The two infantry and two cavalry divisions, together with the Young Guard division (which were needed as a reserve after Lobau's corps had been committed), another 4,780 men, should have been used to assail Wellington's position. The truth of course was that Napoleon had already calculated that Blücher was coming with his entire army, and that these numbers needed to hold them until Grouchy arrived while Napoleon concentrated on destroying Wellington. The Prussians had already diverted the equivalent of one corps (15,000 men) away from Wellington even before the initial attack had begun.

3. Lübeck MS, Braunschweigisches Landesmuseum [Hanover].

4. WSD, op. cit., vol. X, pp. 535-7: The official report of Major-General Sir James Kempt, 19 June 1815.

5. RANL, Official report of Colonel van Zuylen van Nyevelt, 25 October 1815, op. cit. This translation is certified as a correct and true copy of the actual manuscript documents copied by Colonel F. de Bas from the originals. The translation was done for the present author by Dr N. Vels Heijn, and was certified as being correct by the Military History Section of The Netherlands Army on 10 October 1986. See also: de Bas and de Wommerson, La Campagne de 1815 (Brussells, 1908), Tome III, pp. 570-2. This account was given and signed by three senior officers of the Nassau Regiment. See also: Boulger, op. cit., pp. 45-56.

6. Ibid. Sir Herbert Maxwell, Life of Wellington (London, 1899), vol. II, p. 19. The myth that Bijlandt's brigade of some 2,900 men stood on the exposed slope some 150–200 yards in front of Picton's division until the advancing French arrived, and then ran away was propounded by Siborne and taken up by others. Bijlandt's brigade two-deep would have occu-

pied 1,200 yards of frontage. The French 12pdr cannon placed 250 yards in front of La Belle Alliance would have been 500 yards from this brigade. The effective canister range for a French 12pdr was 600 yards (see Chandler, *Dictionary*, pp. 22-3) and would have reduced such a large target as a brigade formation to a human rubble in less than 20 minutes – let alone 1½ hours of intensive bombardment. Even had this not been the case and Bijlandt's men had been subjected only to round shot and shell from 84 guns for the same period, they would still have ceased to exist as a coherent unit. The author wishes to acknowledge the kindness of the late Major-General B.P. Hughes, of the Royal Artillery Institution, for his expert opinion on this matter.

7. RANL, op. cit.

8. Kincaid, *Adventures in The Rifle Brigade and Random Shots from a Rifleman* (London, 1909), p. 164.

9. D. Robertson, *Journal of Sergeant D. Robertson Late 92nd Foot* (Perth, 1842), p. 154.

10. Unpublished letters of Colonel Wyndham to Captain Siborne – and the unpublished manuscript letters of Lieutenant A.J. Hamilton, 19 June – courtesy The Trustees of the Scottish National Museum and The Scottish United Services Museum.

11. Kincaid, op. cit., p. 164.

12. H.E. Siborne, *The Waterloo Letters* (London, 1891), Nos: 7, 150, 151, 157. Where the extracts in this book do not differ from the originals and are reliable, that is where the writer had no financial interest in Siborne's models, or where extracts were quoted from previous journals or diaries of the sender, for the reader's convenience the author has quoted the more accessible book. However, in all other cases where foul play is suspected, i.e., suppression, filleting, or changing the context, quotes are from the original manuscript letters in the Manuscript Department of the British (Museum) Library.

13. Archives du Historique de l'Etat-major de l'armée. Château de Vincennes [Mil. Arch.], nos. C 15/22 and C15/23.

14. It has been stated by several historians that his formation was caused, not by the discussion of the French Generals, but by faulty staff work which transposed the words *'bataillons'* and *'divisions'*. This is both ridiculous and absurd. No doubt not understanding the formations of the period these writers have tried to fit a theory to explain what they did not understand. First, we may make a mistake with the idiom and grammar of a foreign tongue, but not experienced staff officers in their own language. Secondly, historians have stated that this unwieldy mass did not have the slightest chance either to deploy or to defend itself against cavalry; both these assumptions are wrong. On the first count, it was not intended that these columns should deploy (these were not columns of companies, needing extra firepower) against an expected two-deep line, but columns in line ready to fire. There were three such columns plus the brigade of Quiot's division. If we allow 50 yards between each formation for manoeuvring to avoid congestion (and each of these three columns is nearly 200 yards in width), we have a figure of 750 yards. If we add to this the frontage of Quoit's brigade of two regimental columns with intervals, another 150 yards frontage, giving a total of 900 yards, which covered almost the complete fighting area, which would rule out any thought of deploying into line at all. On the second count, these columns, some 180 men wide and 24 files deep, could quite easily deploy in a defensive formation by closing the distances between the three ranks of each battalion, and ordering the four outer files to face outwards. This complete procedure would only take about 30 seconds to execute. The Russian, Prussian and especially Austrian battalions of the period used a set formation to accomplish this (the 'Battalion Mass' and Prussian attack columns). This was well known by commanders of the period. It would have been inconceivable for formations since 1813 not to have used it, so closely related are they to the French manoeuvre 'colonne serre'. Siborne had his own reasons for describing the attack as coming forward in regimental columns.
For more in-depth information and the relevant regulations for executing this manoeuvre and the other formations mentioned, see: *Exerzir Reglement für die Infantrie die Koeniglich Preussischen Armee* (Berlin, 1812) for Prussia; *Règlements 1719* (Paris, 1811) for France; and R. Smirke, *Review of a Battalion of Infantry* (London, 1810) – for Britain.

15. Siborne, *Waterloo Letters*, op. cit., Nos. 148, 152, 157.

16. Ibid., no. 102.

17. Baring MS, Hann. 41 XXI Nr.99-137, Niedersachersisches Haupstaatsarchiv Hannover [Baring]. See also: Major-General Baron von Baring, 'Relations of the Part taken by the Second Light Battalion of the King's German Legion in the Battle of Waterloo' in *The Hanoverian Military Journal*, Part II, Hanover, 1831.

18. Ibid.

19. Ibid.

20. H.E. Siborne, *Waterloo Letters*, op. cit., No. 16.

21. RANL, van Zuylen van Nyevelt, op. cit.

22. H.E. Siborne, *Waterloo Letters*, op. cit., No. 102.

23. *Souvenirs d'un Grognard Belge (1804-1848), Les Mémoires du Colonel Scheltens* (Brussels 1880), p. 23 *et seq.*

24. Kincaid, op. cit., p. 166.

25. H.E. Siborne, *Waterloo Letters*, op. cit., No. 163. See also: *Manoeuvre VII*, R. Simkins, op. cit., and Kennedy, op. cit., pp. 99-102.

26. Scheltens, op. cit.

27. H.E. Siborne, *Waterloo Letters* , op. cit., Nos. 163, 167. See also The Historical

Records of the 44th, Chelmsford Museum, Essex; and Kennedy, op. cit., pp. 61-2.

28. H.E.Siborne, *Waterloo Letters*, op. cit., No. 153.
29. Ibid., No. 154.
30. Ibid., Nos. 150, 151.
31. Scheltens, op. cit.
32. H.E.Siborne, *Waterloo Letters*, op. cit., Nos. 162, 163, 164, 168.
33. Ibid., No. 168.
34. Dunhilt, quoted in *Waterloo illustré*, No. 5 (2/11) 41-42 (publication historique, Brussels), from: Duthilt: *Les Mémoires du Captaine Dunhilt* publiées par Camille Levi (La Société duquerquoise pour l'Encouragement des Lettrers, des Sciences et des Arts, Lille, 1909).
35. H.E. Siborne, *Waterloo Letters*, op. cit., No. 9.
36. Ibid., No. 162.
37. Mil. Arch., Milhaud's account.
38. *Waterloo Letters*, op. cit., No. 5.
39. Kincaid, op. cit., p. 167.
40. Unpublished letters of Colonel Wyndham to Captain Siborne, courtesy William A.G.F. Boag and the Trustees of the United Services Museum, Edinburgh. Consult the same source for the unpublished manuscript letters of Lieutenant A. J. Hamilton, 19 June 1815. Also see: *Waterloo Letters*, op. cit., No. 81.
41. B. L. Add. MS 34706.
42. B.L Add. MS 34704.
43. Duthilt,. loc. cit., p.42.
44. B. L. Add. MS 34706.
45. *Waterloo Letters*, op. cit., No. 44.
46. Ibid., No. 36.
47. Ibid., No. 41.
48. Ibid., Lt. A. J. Hamilton.
49. Ibid., No. 151.
50. Ibid., No. 150.
51. Ibid., No. 151.
52. RANL, Van Zuylen van Nyevelt, op. cit.
53. *Waterloo Letters*, op. cit., No. 151. Note in the original: Captain Mountstevens of the 28th's letter has a complete paragraph omitted in the published letter cited. The original in the Manuscript Department of the British Library: B. L. Add. MS 34703, 19 August 1839 contains the phrase: 'Having just been passed by a Corps of Belgians during our advance', which was excluded from the 1891 Siborne published extracts on page 351 indicated by ... ;See Introduction.
54. Napoleon's *Mémoires* (London, 1946), eds. de Chair, Somerset.
55. RANL, Van Zuylen van Nyevelt, op. cit., Report of General Ghigny.
56. Müffling, *Passages*, op. cit., p. 245, see text and footnote.
57. Houssaye, *1815*, op. cit., p. 199.
58. Ibid. Most British accounts of the Napoleonic Wars tend to deride the lance as a weapon, but it was soon adopted with gusto by Britain, and all European powers in emulation of Napoleon's lancers; by the time of the First World War every regiment including the heavy cavalry had adopted it.
59. RANL, Van Zuylen van Nyevelt, op cit.,

60. The Marquess of Anglesey, *One-Leg* (London, 1961), p.141.
61. RANL, Van Zuylen van Nyevelt, op. cit., Report of the 2nd Division.
62. Ibid.
63. ANF, *Sentinelle de l'Armée*, Paris 8 March 1836 gives Durutte's acccount verbatim [Durutte].
64. Mil. Arch., Milhaud, op. cit.
65. Nassau, op. cit., VII, Nr. 532.
66. Durutte, op. cit.
67. Reille, op. cit.
68. From the original in the Wellington Musuem, Apsley House, London.
69. *Waterloo Letters*, op. cit., No. 40.
70. Lieutenant-General Sir N. Cantile, *A History of the Army Medical Department* (London, 1974), p. 388. It is interesting to note the double standard operating in this regard, as in many others, in the British army of the period. Other ranks were forbidden to assist their wounded comrades to medical help, but a wounded officer could commandeer as many men as he liked to help him. Cantile, quoting Surgeon Gibney, tells us on p. 389: 'An assistant surgeon of the 7th Hussars, after collecting as many of his own wounded as possible from the field had them carried to Mont St. Jean [field hospital]. He found himself in a gathering of assistant surgeons with 500 wounded on their hands. His regimental surgeon had been calledto the front to attend his colonel and was no more seen that day or for several days after, for he went with him to Brussels.' Rank had its privileges in Wellington's British contingent.
71. RANL, Van Zuylen van Nyevelt, loc. cit., p. 62.
72. This was later to add to the myth that they 'ran away'.
73. *Waterloo Letters*, op. cit., No. 43. See also 45.
74. E. Costello, *Adventures of a Soldier – Memoirs of Edward Costello, etc.* (London, 1852), pp. 195-6. The similarity of the French and Netherlanders' uniform, i.e., blue tunics, grey trousers, black shako, and the common language (French), accounts for the reports from many hysterical British civilians of seeing large, regular formed bodies of Dutch-Belgian troops arriving in Brussels while the battle was still being waged: '... deserting as a body with their muskets still in their hands ...' The Netherlanders wore a uniform almost identical with that of the French, and would have had armed files on the outside of such a column which could be misinterpreted by hysterical British onlookers, who at that time were ready to decamp at a moment's notice if Napoleon were to arrive. It is easy to understand how the myth of 'the runaway' Netherlanders began to find supporting evidence.
75. Kincaid, op. cit., p. 167.
76. *Letters of Sir Augustus Frazer* (London, 1859), ed., Major-General E. Sabine, p. 560.
77. D. Robertson, *Journal of Sergeant D. Robertson Late 92nd Foot* (Perth, 1842), p. 157.

78. Anglesey, *One-Leg*, op. cit., p. 141-2. What Uxbridge did not know and could not have known were the reasons that impelled The Greys to disobey his orders. Without that disobedience, Napoleon's plan would probably have succeeded. The heavy brigades had been reduced, but at such a cost to Napoleon as to be incalculable. Had he not always quoted his own maxim: 'I can give you anything but time'? Uxbridge had bought that time for Wellington.

Chapter 13. 18 June: 3.30 p.m. to 6.00 p.m.
1. Mil. Arch., Grouchy to Napoleon, Sart-les-Walhain, 11 a.m., 18 June 1815.
2. Napoleon had immediately to hand the Imperial Guard Infantry of approximately 10,000 men (less Ligny's casualties), Foy's 2 Brigade (Jamin) of 1,900 (less heavy losses on the 16th at Quatre Bras) and Durutte's 2 Brigade (Brue) of 1,100 men; altogether some 13,000 infantry.
3. Gourgaud, op. cit., pp. 93, 96. See Kennedy, op. cit., p. 114; WSD, vol. X, p. 534 (Kempt's report of the 19th June); *Waterloo Letters*, op. cit.; and Baring, op. cit.
4. H.E. Siborne, *Waterloo Letters*, op. cit., p. 407. Major G. D. Graeme to Captain William Siborne, 6 December 1842. Compare with the original: B.L. Add. MS 34707. On p.407, Graeme ends: 'This they also did during the first attack on the roadside', followed by ***. The missing paragraph reads: 'We suffered from several blind areas afforded by being unable to see over the wall, which the enemy used to move men round to the outer entrance of the barn and set fire to it.' *Letters* p.407 then continues verbatim.
5. Nassau, VIII, op. cit., Nr. 129.
6. W. Leeke, *History of Lord Seaton's Regiment at the Battle of Waterloo* (London, 1866), vol. I, pp. 30-1.
7. WSD, vol. X, p. 534; Baring, op. cit.; *Waterloo Letters*, op. cit., pp. 52, 354, 391, 404, 406.
8. Nostitz, op. cit., p. 40.
9. Von Reiche, op. cit., vol. II, p. 209.
10. Nostitz, op. cit.
11. Ibid. See also: von Ollech, p. 227.
12. Von R*, op. cit., vol. IV, p. 261.
13. The part played by Fouché in Napoleon's downfall in 1815 is treated in depth in the present author's book in preparation, *The Fall of Napoleon: the Final Betrayal*. But as this matter loomed large in the formation of Napoleon's decision to fight Wellington when prudence dictated otherwise, it is necessary to understand that Napoleon knew that there was trouble in the Chambers, but he had no time to deal with it because of his military commitments. Marshal Davout, his military governor of Paris, had already warned him that morning that only a victory would calm the situation and silence Napoleon's secret republican and royalist enemies in the Chambers. As to Fouché being the main conspirator, the evidence for that is given by the Royalist Minister plenipotentiary, Baron Hyde de Neuville, who was given sweeping powers to

form a Royalist government in France on 13 June 1815. De Neuville states: 'It was said that Fouché had had two interviews with the King and the Count d'Artois on March 20th. The gravity of the situation, and the terror that prevailed [amongst the royalists], could alone justify such a step. The clever and supple mind of the Duc d'Otranto, his willingness to undertake and accept anything, regardless of dignity or honour, hid his disdain of men and things, had secured to him a certain influence with the Emperor of Russia and Prince Metternich. 'He was one of those men who serve a government, not so much in order to help it to maintain its position, as to render themselves necessary in the day of its fall. Having become a Minister of Napoleon, on the 21st March, he was aware, and indeed made no secret of it to his friends, that the Emperor's fall was inevitable; hence his overtures to men of influence, and his imprudent criticism of a government of which he was an agent. Napoleon suspected but durst not punish these intrigues; and events hurried on, leaving him no time to unmask the treason of Fouché. '*Memoirs of Baron Hyde de Neuville* (London, 1914), tr. F. Jackson, vol II, pp. 33-34.
14. Hamilton-Williams, *Napoleon*, op. cit., for the situation in the Chambers.
15. For the similarities between Napoleon's situation at Waterloo at 3.30 p.m., after d'Erlon's attack, and at 10.30 a.m. at Eylau on 8 February 1807, when Marshal Augereau's corps ceased to exist, see: Chandler, *The Campaigns of Napoleon* (London and New York, 1966), pp. 535-51. On page 543 Chandler writes: 'Apart from his jealously conserved Guard, the only men still available were the 10,700 troopers of Murat's cavalry reserve. These were now ordered ... to take position in the shattered French centre and charge ...' See also: A.H. Atteridge, *Marshal Murat: King of Naples* (London, 1911), pp. 161-5.
16. Lieutenant-General Count von Alten to His Royal Highness the Duke of Cambridge (Governor-General of Hanover), 20 June 1815, Brussels, Royal Archives, Windsor: 'Whole files of men were torn away by roundshot, each shell killed several men and wounded many others. Your Royal Highness cannot picture the devastation caused by the enemy's artillery, truly it caused more losses than can be imagined. Many ammunition carts and gun-carriages were destroyed by this bombardment.'
17. ANF, Gourgaud's papers, op. cit., Account of General Delort.
18. *Correspondence*, op. cit., No. 22058.
19. After Waterloo, Ney was made a scapegoat for many of the ills of the campaign. Napoleon, in several accounts, states that Ney led the cavalry forward either one hour or 45 minutes (depending on the source) too soon. General Gourgaud, while indicating that Napoleon had ordered Ney to charge, gives the reason for the one-hour delay that Napoleon wanted to see what the Prussians

were doing. This came after the event and after Napoleon tried to blame the failure of the campaign, for political reasons on Ney. However, it is obvious that Napoleon did give Ney the order. First, General Delort relates that he refused to obey without confirmation from Soult his corps order quoted to Ney in *Correspondence* No. 22058. Secondly, the Imperial Guard cavalry would not have moved without orders directly from Napoleon. Thirdly, Prince Jérôme , the Emperor's brother, writing on 23 June to his wife, states: 'The Emperor ordered Marshal Ney to bear on the enemy's centre with the bulk of his cavalry.' *Mémoires et correspondence du Roi Jérôme et de la Reine Catherine* (Paris, 1861-66, vol. VII, p. 23. Fourthly, we have Napoleon's own boast to Jérôme and General Foy (already cited) after breakfast that morning at Le Caillou: 'I will bring my artillery to play, order my cavalry to charge, and march with my Old Guard.'

The evidence that Ney charged too soon (there appears to be no reason why one hour would have made any difference) comes directly from Napoleon's account in his Bulletin to the Army of 21 June, published in Paris, in *Le Moniteur* on the 23rd (ANF), in which Napoleon stated: 'The Reserve Cavalry crowned the heights of Mt. St. Jean, and charged the English infantry, having noticed a retrograde movement made by the English to shelter themselves from our batteries whose fire had already caused them to suffer serious loss. This manoeuvre, made at the correct time and supported by the Reserves, must have decided the fate of the day, but made in an isolated fashion and before affairs on the right were satisfactorily settled, it was fatal.' This communication was issued by Napoleon only to save face, and would in itself have great repercussions for him later. But it simply does not state the truth, and was written with hindsight. Napoleon, at the time of the cavalry attack, had no visible enemy on his right to settle with first, having already detailed Lobau for that role. Neither did he have any reserves with which to support the attack, except the Imperial Guard, which as we will see he would not use to support this attack, or a later more important attack. Count d'Erlon himself stated that his corps was not operational, save two brigades, before 5.30 p.m. Further, d'Erlon, in giving his account to the French House of Peers (reported in *Le Moniteur*, 24 June [ANF]) stated that: 'Marshal Ney was ordered by the Emperor to charge the centre of the English line with the Heavy Cavalry, Marshal Ney told me that he was certain of its success.' Also generally overlooked by historians has been the length of time required to assemble three divisions (in the first attack) of cavalry into attack lines within the area in queston. It would have taken at least half an hour or more for the commanders to bring to the required positions and form into line some 5,000 horsemen on a front of only 900 yards.

Consequently, Napoleon could have halted this charge if he had thought it premature to his scheme of attack. He did not think so, and let it go forward. I wish to thank the notable cavalry authority, Major The Most Hon. The Marquess of Anglesey, for his advice and guidance in this matter, especially as to the time required to assemble the French cavalry.

20. ANF, Delort's account.
21. Kennedy, op. cit., p. 114.
22. S. Bowden, *Armies at Waterloo* (Arlington, Texas, 1983), pp. 260 (Brunswick), 269. I have used Bowden as the most reliable source readily available for reference. See Appendix II of the present book for notes on unit strengths.
23. Ibid., p. 84; Imperial Guard Light Cavalry division, p. 131, Milhaud's corps. 24. Mil. Arch., Milhaud's account,
25. WSD, vol. XIV., (1858 ed), pp. 618-20, Paris 21 December 1815 (six months after the battle). Wellington to the Earl of Mulgrave, Master of the Ordnance: 'The army was formed in squares immediately on the slope of the rising ground, on the summit of which the artillery was placed, with orders not to engage with artillery, but to fire only when bodies of troops came under fire. It was very difficult to get them to obey this order. The French Cavalry charged, and were formed on the same ground with our artillery, in general within a few yards of our guns. We could not expect the artillery men to remain at their guns in such a case. But I had a right to expect that the officers and men of the artillery would do as I did, and as all the staff did, that is to take shelter in the Squares of the infantry till the French cavalry should be driven off the ground, either by our cavalry or infantry. But they did no such thing; they ran off the field entirely, taking with them limbers, ammunition, and everything; and when in a few minutes, we had driven off the French cavalry, and could have made use of our artillery, we had no artillerymen to fire them; and, in point of fact, I should have had NO artillery during the whole of the latter part of he action, if I had not kept a reserve in the commencement. Mind my dear Lord, I do not mean to complain; but what I have mentioned is a fact known to many; and it would not do to reward a corps under such circumstances. The artillery, like others, behaved most gallantly; but when a misfortune of this kind has occurred, a corps must not be rewarded. It is on account of these little stories, which must come out, that I object to all the propositions to write what is called a history of the battle of Waterloo.

If it is to be a history, it must be the truth, and the whole truth, or it will do more harm than good, and will give as many false notions of what a battle is, as other romances of the same description have. But if a true history is written, what will become of the reputation of half of those who have acquired reputations, and who deserve it for their gallantry, but who, if their mistakes and casual misconduct were made public, would NOT be so well off? I am certain that if I were to enter into a critical discussion of everything that occurred from the 14th to the 19th June, I could show ample reason for not entering deeply into these subjects.' Captain William Siborne wrote many times to Captain Sandham on this matter, and the only reply that he received was: 'I have marked, as nearly I could, the position of my battery, and I believe I have nothing more to add about the time alluded [to] in your circular letter that it was charged by Cuirassiers.' Colonel Adye, who commanded the artillery of the 1st division, was with my battery the whole day, and from whom it received its orders has probably been able to give you fuller information.' *Letters*, op. cit., No. 95.The asterisks in the printed extract relate to Siborne's specific question: 'I understand from other officers that your battery was driven off the field by French Cuirassiers. Is this true? or can you deny it?' B.L. Add. MS 34704, Siborne to Captain C. F. Sandham 22 April 1835. Colonel Adye in reply to Siborne's identical questions answered: 'The guns continued in nearly the same position the whole day, a short time previous to the advance, they were suddenly and furiously charged by a body of Cuirassiers, and some of the guns in the confusion fell back on the road in their rear, leading from Brussels to Nivelles. They afterwards resumed their original position NEARLY.' *Waterloo Letters*, op. cit., No. 94. They could not resume their old position because Captain Mercer's horse battery on Wellington's orders had been called up and had occupied that ground. The reader checking these sources will also find no reference to this incident in Siborne's History, or any later British versions of the battle. The late Major-General B.P. Hughes of the Royal Artillery Institution did not accept this incident as ever having occurred, and informed the author that: 'Wellington always vented his spleen on the artillery. After having subsequently been sent by the author copies of all the Siborne correspondence, Major-General Hughes conceded that if Colonel Adye had admitted it then he accepted that it had occured, but wondered why the author '... as an Englishman, wished to raise an issue best forgotten that had little relevance except to foreigners'. Major-General Hughes' candid remark is expressive of a prevalent view, and reflects not in the slightest on his undoubted personal integrity. The incident involving the cavalry-shy batteries was not unique. Just after Sandham's battery retired precipitately, Captain James Sinclair's battery retired because, as Sinclair said, he had run out of ammunition, temporarily losing one gun in the process. However, there is reason to presume that Sinclair was afraid of the prospect of losing his guns and of the effect this might have on his blemished career. Sinclair had been Artillery Adjutant at

the Battle of Maya (25 July 1813), and his four were the only guns lost that day to the French. Although these pieces were Portuguese, under British supervision, Sinclair's career took a sideways turn because of the loss, until Waterloo. These two incidents, taken together, provoked Wellington's refusal, six months later, to endorse the recommendation that the Royal Artillery Corps receive a special distinction from the Master of the Ordnance, as they had done after the Battle of Vitoria, i.e., a large monetary award. (My thanks to Philip Haythornthwaite for providing me with a copy of Sinclair's statement of service.)

26. Mercer, op. cit., p. 169.
27. Captain Mercer, like the French Colonel Marbot, was of course a very brave man, but both did tend to blow their own trumpets rather strenuously. Mercer, in his account to Siborne nineteen years after Waterloo, being by then a 'Waterloo Man' and 'a hero', states that the Brunswick troops to his rear: 'Commenced a feeble and desultory fire; for they were in such a state that I momentarily expected to see them disband.' *Letters*, op. cit., No. 69 (p. 218). Nowhere in this document or the manuscript original (B.L. Add. MS 34704, 26 November 1834, entitled 'A true and complete copy of the entries from my journal, kept during the glorious campaign') is there any mention of being concerned that the Brunswickers might panic, neither is there anything at all about running to squares. In Mercer's *Journal* (op. cit.) published by his son in 1870, long after Mercer had retired with the rank of general and had begun editing it for publication, his account suddenly became entirely different from that sent to Siborne 30 years before, or 49 years after the event. Mercer stated on page 170 of the 1870 edition that he and his men did not take refuge in the Brunswick squares because: 'To have sought refuge amongst men in such a state were madness – the very moment our men ran from their guns I was convinced, would be the signal for their disbanding.' This unfounded presumption on the part of Mercer has received a prominence far out of proportion to the facts. First, the Brunswick soldiers were no less inexperienced than the majority of the new British recruits who were in the second battalions and present on the field that day, and who outnumbered those with combat experience. Secondly, these same Brunswick soldiers had already experienced cavalry combat at Quatre Bras and had held in square against Kellermann's and Piré's cavalry charges and knew what to expect. Thirdly, if they had had any inclination to run away it is probable that they would have done so when Sandham's battery of the Royal Artillery had run off the field in front of their very eyes. Fourthly, Mercer's battery of six guns and ammunition limbers, manned by 160 men, including gunners, a surgeon, farriers, etc., presented to the milling cavalry a large, visible target of nearly 100

yards length, and although his front was unassailable, his flanks were not. If the musketry of the Brunswickers had not been totally effective, this battery and men, 100 yards to the Brunswickers' front, would have been cut to pieces by the veteran French cavalry that soon became frustrated looking for somewhere to strike. Finally, the last nail in the coffin of this disreputable slur comes from no less a person than Lord Hill who, in his report to Wellington from Nivelles on 20 June 1815 (WSD, op. cit., vol. X, pp. 544-5), stated: 'I particularly remarked the firm manner with which two battalions of Brunswick infantry, commanded by Major Proestler and Major Holstein (formed in squares in support of the artillery) received the repeated attacks of the enemy's cavalry.' As to Mercer's original statement to Siborne of 1834, taken from his actual journal: Captain Mercer, a gunner, may not have realized that rather than discharge all their muskets at once the Brunswickers were firing by platoons. This slow, rolling fire was effective in keeping his battery safe. It if had not been they would have been cut down. Mercer, as his own journal reveals, constantly disobeyed orders. This statement appears to have been a convenient excuse to justify his flagrant disobedience of Wellington's order given by his commanding officer Frazer. This lie grew over the years in the telling. The author has dealt with this matter exhaustively to dispel this slur on the Brunswick troops, and because of his amazement that historians such as A. F. Becke, *Napoleon and Waterloo* (London, 1914), vol. II, p. 89, can state: 'Too much praise can hardly be given to Captain Mercer for the responsibility he accepted so fearlessly in this matter. He certainly saved this portion of our line from being pierced; and no one can say what serious result might not have followed the penetration of our right centre. At any rate, in all probability all the unreliable units would have broken up and streamed away; and then the whole battle line might have gone to pieces. From this risk the Anglo-Dutch army was saved by Captain Mercer's prompt and soldierly action.' This is a patently ridiculous statement which, if we are to believe it, and all the anti-Allies statements that British historians repeat from these sources, it poses two questions: first, why did Wellington refuse to stand without the assistance of two corps of Prussians if his British contingent was so invincible?; and, secondly, why did Wellington not fight without the handicap of being encumbered by all these unreliable allies, and simply face Napoleon with the 24,000 invincible Britons who were propping up the 43,661 useless allies?

28. *The Reminiscences and recollections of Captain Gronow, being Anecdotes of the Camp, the Court, and the Clubs, and Society to the Close of the last war with France* (London, 1900) (reprint of 1862 ed), vol. I, pp. 69-72.

29. Ibid., vol. I, pp. 190-2.

30. Grouchy, *Mémoires*, op. cit., p. 19-25. In this earliest account of his operations Grouchy states that, on the night of 15/16 June, when he had been present at the meeting between Ney and the Emperor (already cited), Napoleon had heavily censured Ney for deviating from his advance on Quatre Bras to pursue the Prussian rearguard and also because Ney had sent General Girard towards Fleurus and the 'sound of the guns'. Grouchy, bearing Ney's dressing-down in mind, would not commit the same error. Later, when Napoleon started to give new versions of his defeat at Waterloo in which he heaped odium and infamy for the disaster on the dead Ney and Grouchy himself, Grouchy began to fabricate justifications against the weight of such a formidable attack. The evidence seems to support Grouchy's 1818 account, written before Napoleon's St. Helena version started to circulate, as the most honest version from his viewpoint.

31. B. von Treuenfeld, *Die Tage von Ligny und Belle-Alliance* (Hanover, 1880), p. 221 *et seq*.

32. Grouchy, *Observations*, op. cit., p. 44-5. Also: Mil. Arch., Exelmans' account.

33. Bowood, Kerry, op. cit., p. 33. Here again is positive evidence that Napoleon personally ordered the cavalry charges to break Wellington's centre. If, as Flahault states, Napoleon blames Ney for 'Hazarding a battle almost won', it must be seen as Napoleon already trying to apportion blame, in case the manoeuvre failed, there being no other explanation. If Napoleon had had any intention of supporting Ney's attack with infantry, now would have been the time to order them to follow Ney, and if it can be argued that he did not want to do this because the deployment area was insufficient, he could have ordered Ney to halt the attacks until any infantry that he could conjure up was ready to assist. But in fact Napoleon compounded this supposed 'error' by sending in another 5,300 heavy cavalry which could have been used later to facilitate the army's retreat. No greater evidence is available to prove that Napoleon deliberately ordered all his cavalry to attack by design and not prematurely by Ney without support, than the fact that Napoleon had ordered in this second attack of 5,300 men, his last cavalry reserves. One does not compound one mistake with another. Napoleon, not having any infantry to spare, hoped that by emulating his actions at Eylau, sending in the rest of the cavalry, Ney would overwhelm the battered squares.

34. Bowden, op. cit., p. 84, 131.

35. Müffling, *Passages*, op. cit., p. 247. Müffling added this footnote on p. 248: 'Captain Siborne appears not to have been the least aware that in the position I held with the Duke of Wellington, I was stationed on his left wing, nor to have heard what charge [responsibility] I had. I never heard anything of an independent movement on the part of

general Vivian, nor did I ever hear that the Duke had verbal negotiations, through his aides-de-camp, with other Prussian generals besides me. This would be contrary to the agreements, with which Captain Siborne was unacquainted.'

36. Lettow-Vorbeck, op. cit., p. 249.
37. Von Ollech, op. cit., p. 242. Von Ollech recited a verbal order, but this substance is confirmed in Treuenfeld, op. cit., p. 476.
38. Von R*, op. cit., p. 274.
39. Lettow-Vorbeck, op. cit, p. 430.
40. von Ollech, op. cit., p. 195. This message was almost identical with the one sent an hour earlier by Blücher, which would have reached Thielemann at that time.
41. For the in-depth reasons for Napoleon's rejection of his brother-in-law, the reader is referred to the relevant chapters of *The Fall of Napoleon: The Final Betrayal* by the author now in preparation. As to the reasons why Murat was defeated in Italy, the author will deal with this campaign in depth in *Murat 1815: The Last Battles*, to be published from the author's manuscript.
42. *Letters*, op. cit., No. 99.
43. *United Service Journal*, London 1834, pp. 555-6, 'Use of the Pike by Serjeants' (*sic*) quoting from a sergeant of the 3/1st Foot Guards at Waterloo: 'The fight, at one time was so desperate with our battalion, that files upon files were carried out the rear from the carnage and the line was held up by the serjeants' pikes placed against the rear – not for want of courage on the men's parts (for they were desperate), only for a moment our losses had so unsteadied the line.'
44. Gronow, op. cit., pp. 190-2.
45. Brunswick, op. cit.

Chapter 14. 18 June: Evening

1. This is meant to be a true appraisal of the situation and should not be construed as 'Wellington bashing'. To quote Lieutenant-Colonel Charles Chesney, Professor of Military Art and History at the Imperial Staff College, from his book, *Waterloo Lectures* (London, 1868), p. 44: 'Time was when it was treasonable to doubt whether what Wellington arranged was the best thing possible on his part.' The present author trusts that these observations will not now be deemed treasonable.
2. Hannover, op. cit., manuscript account of Captain Christian Wynecken.
3. Ibid.
4. Hannover, op. cit., manuscript account of Captain Christoph Heise.
5. Ibid. Heise states that this lack of rifle ammunition was due to the ammunition cart having been overturned on the Brussels road during some confusion when the Cumberland Hussars, under their Colonel Hake, refused to charge the French cavalry and had galloped off towards Brussels, where they reported the battle lost, and that the Hussars plundered the baggage wagons en route. This is not true. The ammunition parks were nowhere near

the road. The KGL light battalions were armed with the British Baker rifle supplied by the British Government, and as the 1/95th in Picton's division, and the other KGL light infantry behind them were using the same ammunition, this reason grows rather thin. Rather, the author would offer the answer given by General Sir James Shaw Kennedy, acting Quartermaster-General of the 3rd Division, which seems the more logical: 'Much has been said of Baring's having sent repeatedly for ammunition, and that none was sent to him. This matter had certainly been grossly mismanaged. The arrangement for the brigades getting their spare ammunition was, that each brigade should communicate with the guard over the ammunition, and order forward what was wanted. How the brigade failed to do this has not been explained, as so many of its superior officers fell in action. Baring could not account for it, which I know from our having slept together on the ground close to the Wellington tree on the night of the action... The unexplained want of ammunition by Baring's battalion is placed in an extraordinary view when it is considered that the Battle of Waterloo lasted eight hours and a half, and that all three brigades of the division got the ammunition they required, with the exception of this one battalion. The simple fact of Baring's application for spare ammunition having been made by him so late in the day, when, because of the enemy's position, there could be no certainty of its being got in place [into the farmhouse] proves an extraordinary oversight. The spare ammunition should have been sent for early in the morning. What were 60 rounds per man for the defence of such a post?' Shaw Kennedy, op. cit., pp. 123-4. In effect it was probably impossible to get the ammunition to the farmhouse as the bearers would have been killed. Further, Baring had been twice negligent in not bringing down a supply, at the commencement and when he returned from the main line after his repulse at 1.30 p.m. A glance at the de Craan map will also show the positions of the ammunition parks, which were nowhere near the Brussels road or the baggage on the road. This is but another old Waterloo chestnut.

6. Hannover, op. cit., Baring MS.
7. Ibid. The text in Beamish (op. cit.) gives the same substance but differs in translation. The author is grateful to Captain Reinhart Ott of the German Embassy in London for his expert translations of the originals (Hann 38D, Nrs. 230-43).
8. Hannover, op. cit. (Guelphic MSS) Hann. 92 XV-XIV 22c.
9. This gallant defence was doomed to fall to an attack in force. Much has been written about the ammunition supply, but given that the great barn doors had been burnt, the defenders lacked the means to make adequate loopholes, and the use of artillery by a major assault force to breach an ordinary brick wall, it is doubtful whether any amount of ammu-

nition could have staved off the inevitable.

10. Hannover, op. cit., Report of the 5th Battalion, MS Hann. 48A, Nrs. 100-30. Also: Wynecken MS, op. cit. These eye-witness reports have never been cited in any of the British accounts which, in the Sibornic tradition, try to blame the Prince of Orange, hoping to make him appear incompetent, thus artificially augmenting Wellington's role in the campaign. The Hanoverian 5th Battalion was ordered forward for a sound reason: to destroy an oncoming French column. Ompteda was ordered by his Hanoverian divisional General, Alten, not the Prince, to make the movement. The Prince of Orange, as Corps Commander, merely ordered Ompteda to obey his superior's orders. Ompteda could have refused to carry out the order and have been removed from command, and his refusal would later have been vindicated by events. However, the brave officer went with his men, and the Prince of Orange was blamed for the consequences of the order which he had not given. The evidence to this cited above is given by Hanoverian eye witnesses and not by supposition.

11. Hannover, Baring narrative.

12. Müffling, *Passages*, op. cit., p. 247-8. Müffling stated: 'This march of the brigades of Vandeleur and Vivain from the left wing to the centre of the English line of battle, is very correctly described, as far as time, and occasion, and execution in the report of the battle by the English Captain Siborne. But the author has been misinformed as to WHO gave directions for this movement ... Captain Siborne appears not to have been the least aware that in the position I held with the Duke of Wellington I was stationed on his left wing, nor to have heard what charge [authority] I had.' Generals Vivian and Vandeleur had been ordered by Wellington to move off to the centre when advised to do so by General Müffling, when he, Müffling, deemed that the Prussians had arrived in sufficient force to ensure the safety of the left flank.

13. Brunswick, op. cit. There is in the Braunschweigisches Landesmuseum a fine painting by Leberecht of these troops in action in the ruined château. Siborne of course puts this much later, at 8 p.m. What use that would have been can be known only to him and the British officers who funded his project.

14. Mil. Arch., Durutte's account.

15. von Ollech, op. cit., p. 294 *et seq.*

16. Lettow-Vorbeck, op. cit., p. 433. Also: von Ollech, p. 234; von Reiche, op. cit., vol. II, p. 209-13.

17. Shaw Kennedy, *Notes*, op. cit., pp. 124-5.

18. Nassau, op. cit.

19. von Ollech, op. cit., p. 248, Report of Colonel von Hiller.

20. Mauduit, op. cit., vol ii, pp. 394-5. See also: Vicomte A. d'Avout, *L'Infanterie de la Garde à Waterloo* (Paris, 1905), pp. 23-6., Facsimile of the letter of General Petit, commander of the 1st Grenadiers, dated Bourges, 18 May 1835. This book contains facsimiles of all the relevant letters of the Officers of the Guard. My thanks to M. Jacques Logie for supplying me with this and other material.

21. D'Avout, op. cit., Petit's account; Mauduit, op. cit., vol. II, pp. 400-4. Also: von Ollech, p. 248 (Hiller's account).

22. ANF, Durutte's account, op. cit.; Charras, op. cit., pp. 299-300.

23. Kennedy, op. cit., account of, pp. 126-9. This also dispels the Victorian myth that Wellington was always in the right place at the right time.

24. Ibid.

25. There has been much controversy over the formation in which the Guard advanced. General Petit, who was there, states that they went forward in square. We know that they had been formed in square on the Genappe road, and marched down in that formation. Most British authorities, obsessed with the Peninsular War and continually making comparisons, base their arguments on the eye-witness reports that the Guard presented a double-company front. This, of course, is true. Whichever formation used a double-company front would have been seen from any of the four sides. These students of the Peninsular War have neglected to study the use of the square by the French in other theatres of operations. For example, at La Fère-Champenoise on 25 March 1814, six divisional squares of the National Guard under General Pacthod marched more than four miles while being attacked by more than 20,000 cavalry of the Russian, Austrian and Prussian armies. The squares were only halted when the Russian Guard infantry, supported by three batteries of guns and cavalry, forced them to halt and reduced them with canister. See: Houssaye, *1814* (London, 1914), pp. 296-317. Further, the French had used these formations on numerous occasions, notably in Egypt. Perhaps the difficulty arises because the British army, with its antiquated linear formation, was able to stand like a rock in square, but had not been trained to attack or move over distances in this formation. Therefore the ability of the French to do so is discounted. Finally, and most pertinently, Napoleon always jealously protected his Guard, which was in fact a separate entity from the line troops, and having seen the devastation wreaked on d'Erlon's corps, he was not prepared to allow his Guard to suffer similarly. Besides, the formation did not decrease the units' firepower; rather, it gave weight to the front double-companies in assault and they could deploy easily if required. The serious student should consult: the letters of the surviving officers in d'Avout, op. cit.; J. Logie, *Waterloo, L'évitable défaite* (Paris, 1989), pp. 132-9; Houssaye, op. cit., pp. 223-9. *The Life of John Colborne Field-Marshal Lord Seaton, compiled from his letters, etc.* (London, 1903), ed. G.C. Moore, Appendix F, pp. 421-8. Lord Seaton (then Sir John Colborne) agreed with General Petit and stated (on

p.424): 'The Great Column was formed in [composition] ... squares of battalions.'

26. O. Levasseur, ed., *Souvenirs Militaires d'Octave Levasseur, officier d'Artillerie, aide-de-camp du Marshal Ney, 1802-1815* (Paris, 1914), pp. 303-4.

27. D'Avout, op. cit. Also: Logie, *Waterloo*, op. cit., pp. 138-45. Monsieur Logie, one of the most respected Napoleonic historians and experts, recommended to the author by HIH the Prince Napoleon and by Professor Humbert of Les Invalides, has covered the positions of the Imperial Guard squares from all the primary source materials, which were not available at the time to either M. Houssaye or Captain Siborne. M. Logie's judgement is considered definitive by the author.

28. Logie, pp. 138-9.

29. Von Reiche, op. cit., vol. II, pp. 209-13. Also: Müffling, *Passages*, op. cit., pp. 248-9.

30. Mercer, op. cit., pp. 177-8: 'The rapidity and precision of this fire were quite appalling. Every shot almost took effect, and I certainly expected we should be annihilated. Our horses and limbers, being somewhat under cover from the direct [fire] in front; but this plunged right amongst them, knocking them down by pairs, and creating horrible confusion. The drivers could hardly extricate themselves from one dead horse ere another fell, or perhaps themselves. The saddle-bags in many instances, were torn from the horses' backs, and their contents scattered over the field. One shell I saw explode under the two finest wheel horses in the troop – down they dropped. In some instances the horses or gun or ammunition wagon remained, and all the drivers killed. The whole livelong day had cost us nothing like this. Our gunners too – the few left fit for duty of them – were so exhausted that they were unable to run the guns up after firing ... and as we pointed the two left guns towards the people that annoyed us so terribly, they soon came together in a confused heap, the trails crossing each other, and the whole dangerously near the limbers and ammunition wagons ... I sighed for my poor troop – it was already a wreck.' See also: Frazer, *Letters*, op. cit., p. 317: 'I find my late troop (G) has lost ninety horses.'

31. Ibid. p. 180. This is typical of the xenophobic attitude of the late General Mercer; when producing his journal for publication he included his sour grapes comments. What words of gratitude did he have for the gallant Netherlands horse battery that had saved him and his men from destruction, and gained for its commander, Captain Krahmer, singled out by Wellington for his part in repulsing a column of the French Guard, the Knights' Order of Wilhelm, equivalent to the Order of the Bath? 'These Belgians were all beastly drunk, and, when the first came up, not at all particular as to which way they fired; and it was only by keeping an eye on them that they were prevented from treating us, and even one another. The wretches had probably

already done mischief elsewhere – who knows? My recollections of the latter part of the day are rather confused; I was fatigued, and almost deaf.' Perhaps Mercer intended to imply that the Netherlanders were of such a higher calibre than their British counterparts that they should be held to a higher standard.

32. For the French account see: d'Avout, op. cit., Letters of all the Guard commanders, notably Petit; *Waterloo Letters*, op. cit., Nos. 75, 139, 140, Note on p. 319, Nos. 61, 124, 146; WSD, op. cit., vol. X, pp. 534-5. General Alten's divisional report to Wellington, Brussels, 19 June 1815: 'The squares had by this time been so reduced in number by the continued fire of cannon, musketry, and ultimately grape shot of the enemy, that they had hardly men enough left to remain in squares, and therefore were withdrawn from the position by Count Kielmansegge; and the remains of the Legion and Hanoverian brigades, and part of the British brigade [Halkett's], reformed on the high road in the rear of the village of Mont St. Jean.' Also, General Alten's subsequent report to Wellington on 22 June, WSD, pp. 559-60. 'Towards the close of the action, and immediately previous to my being wounded, I found one of the squares of Count Kielmansegge's brigade, on which the fire of grape was so tremendous that the four faces of the square are marked by the bodies on the field of battle, give way a little. As I found myself at that time with another square, which was equally critically situated, I remained with it, and directed the Count [Kielmansegge] to stop the square which was giving way, and bring it up again ... I was immediately after wounded and obliged to quit the field; and it was from the circumstances which was mentioned to me that the remainder of the division had been collected at the rear of the village of Mont St. Jean.' See also: *United Service Journal*, March-May 1845, Major Macready and the officers of the 30th foot on Captain Siborne's history.

33. Macready, op. cit., p. 398. Macready, as did Wellington in his official report to the King of the Netherlands, 19 June 1815, Royal House, op. cit., referred to the gallantry of 'Van der Smissen'; the officer so named was Krahmer's Lieutenant. It is though that either the name of the Netherlands artillery commander of the 3rd Division was also Smissen or that Major van der Smissen's name was given in error. When Wellington's aide asked Lieutenant van der Smissen the battery commander's name [Krahmer], he gave his own through lack of understanding. Krahmer however was awarded the Knight's Cross and was the subject of the famous painting illustrated in this book.

34. Ibid, p. 401. WSD, vol. X, 1863 ed., pp. 544-5. Lieutenant-General Lord Hill to Field Marshal the Duke of Wellington, Nivelles, 20 June 1815. 'I Have also to mention the steady conduct of the 3rd Division of the troops of the Netherlands, under the command of Major-General Chassé, which was moved up

in support of Major-General Adam's brigade, to repulse the attack of the Imperial Guard. The Brigade of Belgian artillery also deserves my best thanks for their steady conduct and well directed fire during the last mentioned attack.' Also: RANL, op. cit., Report of The Netherlands 3rd Division: 'General Chassé perceived that the English artillery placed in front of us on the height without completely ceasing its fire, perceptibly slackened it, and hastened to the spot to ascertain the cause. Learning that ammunition was wanting, and seeing at the same time that the French guard was making a movement to attack the English artillery, [he] ordered a battery commanded by Major van der Smissen, to advance up to the crest and to commence a very sustained fire ... His Excellency [Chassé] then re-united all the battalions of the first brigade and advanced against the enemy in close column at the head of the brigade ordering the charge. With shouts of "Long live the House of Orange!" and "Long live the King!", the brigade rushed forward, despite a very heavy musketry fire, and although threatened on the flank by an attack of cavalry, when suddenly the French Guard, against whom our attack was directed, left its position and disappeared before us.'

35. The myth that the 4,000-odd men of the Old Guard on their own attempted to break Wellington's line is rather ridiculous. The author has been unable to determine the origin of this assumption. He can only conclude that in the years after the battle, and prior to Siborne's history of 1844, each British regiment in the vicinity was so preoccupied in claiming the distinction of having destroyed the most formidable military force of some 15 years' standing, that they did not bother to recount what else occurred on the field. The farmhouse having been taken by Ney, the rear and road was used by Quiot and Bachelu to assail the men of von Kruse and Lambert; Marcognet and Donzelot pushed Pack, Kempt and Best hard also. Unfortunately, because so many officers were wounded here, for example, Sergeant Robertson of the 92nd was left to command two companies, Siborne did not bother to inquire of them what occurred after D'Erlon's repulse. See the following examples: *Letters*, op. cit., No. 153, that from Major Calvert of the 32nd Foot in Kempt's brigade stated: 'Attacks similar to the above [d'Erlon's] were renewed several times during the evening, and always with similar results.' No. 155, op. cit., B.L. Add. MS 34704, Lieutenant Leslie, 79th Highlanders to Siborne, Wilton, Cork, 12 April 1843: 'This attack was late in the day, and we had not long regained our position when, at the period to which you allude [7-8 p.m.] the enemy in front of us seemed moving forward a fresh column for a simultaneous attack to that on the right of our line. This was checked by the appearance of the Prussians breaking from the wood on the left of our position [Frischermont]. This eruption caused

all the French to our front and as far as the eye could see to recoil and depart as fast as they could.' Letter No. 160, Brevet-Major Leach of the 1/95th: 'From the time that La Haye Sainte fell into the hands of the French until the moment of the general advance of our army, the mode of attack and defence was remarkable for its sameness. But I speak merely of what took place immediately about our part of the position. It consisted of one uninterrupted fire of musketry (the distance between the hostile lines was probably rather more than 100 yards) between Kempt's and some of Lambert's regiments posted along the thorn hedge, and the French infantry lining the knoll and the crest of the hill. Several times the French officers made desperate attempts to induce their men to charge Kempt's line, and I saw more than once parties of the French spring up from their kneeling position and advance some yards towards the thorn hedge, headed by their officers with vehement gestures ... During this musketry contest, which I firmly believe was the closest and most protracted almost ever witnessed, some apprehension was entertained that the French would endeavour to force their way along the Chaussee, and attack the rear of the troops lining the thorn hedge.' There are many more such accounts which could also be cited. For French accounts of the concerted attacks in conjunction with the Guard, see: d'Avout, op. cit.; ANF, op. cit., d'Erlon's speech to the Chamber of Peers reported in *Le Moniteur* 24 June 1815; Foy, op. cit., daily account.

36. Von Ollech, op. cit., p. 252; Lettow-Vorbeck, op. cit, p. 436; Gneisenau's report to the King of Prussia, 22 June 1815 (destroyed by the Russians at Potsdam in 1945), copy in WSD, vol. X, 1836 ed., pp. 502-6. See p. 505. Also: Kelly, op. cit., pp. 58-62, which gives an accurate translation. My thanks to Captain Mai of the Embassy of the Federal Republic of Germany for examining both texts for me.

37. Ibid. Gneisenau's report.

38. Macready, op. cit., p. 403. Here Macready takes issue with Siborne's numbers. Macready, who had fought in the battle, tells Siborne, who had not: 'In the returns of Captain Siborne's history, the numbers of the 30th are given as 615 men. Whereas 460 bayonets was the outside of what the 30th marched into the field of Quatre Bras ... had it been otherwise, the 30th, 615 strong, having lost fifty-one before the 18th (and several missing, who returned), ought to have stood 560 strong at Waterloo, when its loss of 230 would have left it at the close 330 men, whereas 160 rank and file was our stength when we piled arms.' A British battalion had ten companies ranging at full strength as in the Guards and elite regiments (52) of 100 men, but averaged 40-50 in ordinary line regiments at Waterloo. The 30th had less than three companies strength left at the close of day with an average of 16 men per company.

39. ANF, op. cit., Durutte's account.

40. Houssaye, *1814* (London, 1914), p. 250. There, on 21 March 1814, Napoleon had faced an Allied army of 100,000 men with 30,000 and withdrew in good order, having been undefeated.

41. I have given little credence to the accounts of General Vivian for the following reasons: (1) his accounts of what happened changed drastically three times, twice after he had lent Siborne large sums of money for his models (B.L. Add. MS Nos: 34703, 34705, 34707), the last time just before the publication of Siborne's *History*, a staggering sum of £1,000, which Siborne was unable to repay and was never asked for; (2) Siborne was Vivian's military secretary and further obligated to him, thus this objectivity must have been compromised; (3) as historical evidence should, like juridicial evidence, be founded on creditable witnesses. I cannot accept this evidence; and (4) officers of his brigade such as Captain Taylor of the 10th Hussars contradict his account entirely. In fact, part of Taylor's replies in *Letters*, op. cit., No. 75, make clear that Vivian is allowed by Siborne to make comment on their answers. However, the author tends to agree with Captain Taylor's remark to Siborne in answer for verifications of Vivian's claims that they 'were a hoot!' I have therefore consigned Vivian's account to the same category as those of Marbot and Mercer – a good read but economical with the truth.

42. General Cambronne was credited with this *mot*, which translates as 'shit!'. However, General Cambronne was wounded at the time and later told his son that he never uttered the word nor the other phrase attributed to him, 'The Guard may die but never surrenders', which although true, was not uttered by him, but by some fanciful romantic. It seems the most logical explanation that it was shouted by one of the old 'grumblers' who, although highly trained, were allowed the unusual privilege of airing their views aloud when they felt like it, such as at Austerlitz and at Wagram.

43. Von Ollech, op. cit., pp. 248-9.

44. Chesney, *Lectures*, op. cit., p. 209.

45. Baron Larrey, *Mémoires de Chirurgie Militaire et Campagnes du Baron D. J. Larrey* (Paris, 1817), pp. 10-13.

46. Gneisenau's report to King William, op. cit.

47. WD, op. cit., vol. XII, 1888 ed., p. 482: 'Wellington's official despatch written the night of the battle'.

48. WSD, vol. X, p. 531.

49. *Lettres Inédites de Napoléon*, op. cit., Napoleon to King Joseph, Philippeville, 19 June 1815, No. 1225.

Chapter 15. Aftermath: Wavre, Pursuit, Lost Opportunities

General note: Most of the controversial material in this chapter is dealt with in depth in Chapter 12 of the author's book: *The Fall of Napoleon: The Final Betrayal*, currently in preparation. As space is not available here to cover in depth and with citations the matters raised, the author has cited the new material to show the reader that his statements are not unfounded supposition and that evidence exists to support his statements.

1. Mil. Arch., General Hulot's report, 20 June 1815.
2. Ibid.
3. Mil. Arch., Vandamme to Simon Lorière, Ghent, 10 February 1830.
4. D.C. Hamilton-Williams, *The Fall of Napoleon: The Final Betrayal*, in preparation, Chapter 12.
5. Ibid.
6. Ibid.
7. Ibid.
8. Ibid.
9. *Memoirs of Baron Hyde de Neuville* (London, 1914), tr. F. Jackson, vol. II, pp. 39-40.
10. Hamilton-Williams, op. cit., Chapter 12.
11. Ibid.
12. Ibid.
13. Ibid.
14. Ibid.
15. Ibid.
16. Ibid.
17. Ibid.
18. Müffling, *Passages*, op. cit., p. 231.
19. Hamilton-Williams, op. cit., Chapter 12.
20. Ibid.
21. Ibid.
22. Public Record Office, Castlereagh's Correspondence vol. XII, Wellington to Castlereagh, Most Secret, Paris, 11 August 1815.

Appendix I. Orders of March for the *Armée du Nord*

1. *Correspondences*. No. 22053. A further dispatch was later sent at 3.15 p.m. on June 15 commanding General Gérard to support the right and move across the Sambre at Châtelet 4 miles below Charleroi.
2. *Ibid*. No. 22053

Orders of March
for the *Armée du Nord*

Beaumont 14 June 1815

'Tomorrow, the 15th, at 2.30 a.m., General Vandamme's Light Cavalry Division will advance along the Charleroi road. Patrols will be sent out in every direction to reconnoitre the country, and to capture the enemy's advance posts; each patrol will consist of not less than fifty men. Before marching off General Vandamme will make sure that the cavalry are provided with small-arms ammunition.

At the same time Lieut.-General Pajol will parade the 1st Cavalry Corps, and will follow the advance of General Domon's Division; the latter is placed under General Pajol's orders. The divisions of the 1st Cavalry Corps will furnish no detachments, the 3rd Division will furnish such as are necessary. General Domon's Horse battery will follow, marching immediately behind the leading battalion of III Corps, and consequently will come under General Vandamme's orders.

Lieut.-General Vandamme will have *Réveil* sounded at 2.30 a.m., and at 3 a.m. his corps will move off in the direction of Charleroi. All his baggage and impedimenta will be parked in rear, and will not take the road until the whole of VI Corps and the Imperial Guard have defiled. The baggage, etc., will come under the orders of the Director-General of Transport, together with that of VI Corps, of the Imperial Guard, and the Headquarter Staff, and the afore-mentioned officer will issue their march orders to the baggage of these units.

Each division of III Corps will march complete namely, accompanied by its battery and ambulance wagons; but every other vehicle seeking to accompany the column will be burnt.

Count Lobau will cause *Réveil* to be sounded at 3.30 a.m., he will follow at 4 a.m. and act as a support to the latter. His order of march will be identical with that already laid down for III Corps, and the same orders hold good for his troops, artillery, hospital equipment and baggage. The baggage of VI Corps will be collected with that of III Corps, under orders of the Director-General of Transport, as already detailed.

The Young Guard will have *Réveil* sounded at 4.30 a.m., and it will march off at 5 a.m., along the Charleroi road, in rear of VI Corps.

The Chasseurs of the Guard will sound their *Réveil* at 4 a.m., and will follow in the rear of the Young Guard at 5.30 a.m. The Grenadiers of the Guard will sound their *Réveil* at 5.30 a.m., and will follow in the rear of the Chasseurs at 6 a.m.

The Imperial Guard will observe the same march orders with reference to artillery, ambulances and baggage, that have already been laid down for III Infantry Corps.

The baggage of the Guard will join that of III and VI Corps, and come under the orders of the Director-General of Transport, who will arrange to issue its march orders to it.

Marshal Grouchy will cause the Cavalry Corps, which is bivouacked nearest to the main road, to be ready at 5.50 a.m., and he will order it to follow the advance on Charleroi; his other two corps will follow in succession at one hour's interval between each. Marshal Grouchy will be careful to arrange that his corps use lateral roads for their advance, marching on each side of the main road used by the infantry, in order to avoid crowding; and also that his cavalry may preserve a better formation.

He will order the whole of his baggage to remain behind in bivouac, parked and collected, until orders arrive for its disposal from the Director-General of Transport.

Count Reille will have *Réveil* sounded at 2.30 a.m., and will march off II Corps at 3 a.m. He will march to the bridge at Marchiennes, and will arrange to reach that place before 9 a.m. He will cause all the bridges over the Sambre to be guarded, and will allow no one to cross them, the picquets which he leaves in charge will be relieved in due course by I Corps; but Count Reille will do his utmost to forestall the enemy at the bridges, in order to prevent their demolition, and especially to seize that of Marchiennes, which will enable him to cross to the other bank, and which he will arrange to have repaired immediately, if he finds that it has been damaged.

At Thuin, and at Marchiennes, as well as at the villages en route, Count Reille will interrogate the inhabitants, so as to get the latest news of the enemy's situation. He will cause the letters in the post-offices to be seized, and will open them, forwarding any information thus gained to the Emperor.

Count d'Erlon will march off I Corps at 3.30 a.m., and will advance on Charleroi, following the march of II Corps, the left of which he will gain as soon as possible, so as to be able to support it in case of need. He will keep one Cavalry Brigade in rear to screen himself and to keep up connection, by small posts, with Maubeuge. He will also push patrols beyond this town in the direction of Mons and Binche; they are to advance right up to the frontier so as to get news of the enemy, and they are to report immediately anything ascertained; these patrols will be careful not to compromise themselves, and they are not to cross the frontier.

Count d'Erlon will arrange to occupy Thuin with a division, and if the enemy has destroyed the bridge there, it is to be repaired at once, and a bridge-head will be traced and constructed on the left bank with another bridgehead at this place.

II Corps will conform to the same march orders as those already detailed for III Corps, with reference to their artillery, ambulance, and baggage. I Corps will do likewise. The impedimenta of these two corps will be collected on the left of I Corps, and will come under the orders of the Senior Transport Officer.

IV Corps (Army of the Moselle) has received orders today to take up a position in front of Philippeville. If this movement is completed, and the divisions of this corps are concentrated, Lieut.-General Gérard will march them off tomorrow at 3 a.m., and will advance on Charleroi.[1] He will be careful to keep in line with III Corps, with which corps he will arrange to keep in touch, so as to arrive in front of Charleroi at the same time that General Vandamme's Corps reaches that point; but General Gérard will reconnoitre to his right, and observe especially all roads leading to Namur. He will march closed up and in order of battle, and will leave all his baggage and impedimenta at Philippeville, so that his corps may be able to manoeuvre better, as it will be free of encumbrances.

General Gérard will order the 14th Cavalry Division (due to reach Philippeville today) to follow IV Corps to Charleroi; on arrival at the latter place this Cavalry Division will join IV Cavalry Corps.

Lieut.-Generals Reille, Vandamme, and Gérard will arrange that all the Engineers belonging to their corps march in rear of the leading Light Infantry Regiment, and the Engineers will be accompanied by all the necessary material for the repair of bridges; the Lieut.-Generals will order their Engineer officers to repair all bad places, to open up lateral communications, and to bridge those streams that would wet the infantry when fording them.

The Marines, the Sappers of the Guard, and Sappers of the reserve, will follow the leading regiment of III Corps. Lieut.-Generals Rogniant and Haxo will march at their head, they will be accompanied by only 2 or 3 vehicles, and the remainder of the Engineer Park will march on the left of III Corps. If the enemy is encounterd these troops will not be engaged, but Generals Rogniant and Haxo will use them for bridging rivers, constructing bridgeheads, opening up communications, etc.

The Cavalry of the Guard will follow the advance on Charleroi, marching off at 8 a.m.

The Emperor will accompany the advanced Guard on the Charleroi road. The Lieut.-Generals will take care to keep His Majesty informed of their various movements, and transmit all information which they happen to collect.

They are warned that His Majesty intends to have passed the Sambre before noon, and to cross the whole army over to the left bank of that river.

The bridging train will be divided into three parts, each consisting of 5 pontoons and 5 Advanced Guard Boats, so as to throw 3 bridges over the Sambre. There will be a company of pontoon personnel accompanying each of these subdivisions. The first section will follow in the rear of the Engineer Park, and after III Corps. The second will remain with the

Artillery Reserve Park, in the baggage column, it will have with it the fourth company of the bridging train [personnel].

The Emperor's baggage, and that of the headquarters staff, will be collected and marched off at 10 a.m.: as soon as they have defiled, the Director-General of Transport will put in motion that of the Imperial Guard, followed in succession by that of III and IV Corps; at the same time he will send orders to the baggage columns of the Cavalry Reserve to proceed in the direction already taken by the cavalry.

The ambulances of the army will follow the headquarters, and will march ahead of the baggage; but in no case will the baggage, or Artillery Reserve Park, or the second section of the bridging train equipment, approach within three leagues [8 miles] of the army, without express orders from the Major-General [Chief of Staff], and they will only cross the Sambre when specially ordered to do so.

The Commissariat-General will have collected in this column all the administrative baggage and transport vehicles, and precise places in the column will be assigned.

Carriages which are delayed will go to the left, and will only be able to leave their allotted place under orders from the Director-General of Transport.

The Emperor commands that all transport vehicles found in the Infantry, Cavalry, or Artillery columns are to be burned, as well as the vehicles in the baggage columns which leave their allotted place and thus change the order of march, unless they have previously obtained permission to do so from the Director-General of Transport.

For this purpose a detachment of 50 Military Police will be placed under the orders of the Director-General of Transport; and the latter officer is held personally responsible, as well as the officers of the Military Police and also the Military Police themselves, for the due execution of these arrangements on which the success of the campaign may depend.[2]

By Order of the Emperor
Marshal of the Empire and Major-General
Duke of Dalmatia [Soult]'

APPENDIX II
Orders of Battle on the Eve of the Campaign

The following Army lists are derived from many sources and must be accepted as being a guide only. After ten years of constant research, I have found that after this passage of time (178 years) it is virtually impossible to reconcile the different archival returns with those conflicting returns sent in immediately after the battle. Siborne's numeration of the troops involved based on the returns given in Wellington's Despatches are – as with his history, atlas and models, flawed by error. Siborne used only the columns marked 'rank and file', thus excluding all officers, NCOs and musicians. This figure also included 'sick absent', those on detached duties and in hospital, missing and prisoners.

Because this total represented all these men 'on paper', as actually being in the ranks, whether there or not, and did not take into account those actually wounded on the 16th, or away on detached duties: provost, escort, batmen and field-post office; it showed some units at Waterloo as being stronger than they actually were. Over the years the constant repetition of Siborne's numbers, because most historians have automatically accepted them as being correct, has lent them authority as being definitive, which they are not.

The next area of problem was: what was actually meant in the Napoleonic wars by 'missing'? In the conflicts of later periods 'missing' meant exactly that, not 'missing presumed dead' or, as Victorian historians who applied a different standard to our Allies interpreted it, 'missing – ran away'. In 1815 'missing' meant: 'missing, unaccounted for at time of role call'. In Wellington's Despatches, vol. XII (1888 ed.) p.485, Major-General Edward Barnes, the Adjutant-General, states: 'The greater number of the men returned missing had gone to the rear with wounded officers and soldiers, and joined afterwards. The officers are supposed killed.'

If this were the case with the British soldiers it is reasonable to assume that it was the same with the other nationals. The Brunswick, Nassau, Hanoverian and Netherland returns in Siborne and the Wellington Despatches do not correspond with those in the respective national archives. For example, Siborne's totals for the British contingent differ from the official ones in Despatches, which in turn differ from those in each regimental archive; which again in turn disagree with those submitted in the returns for the Waterloo medal. As a further example, Siborne and most British sources list the Brunswick Contingent as having at Waterloo: 154 killed, 456 wounded and 50 'missing' (all ranks). However, the Brunswick Landesmuseum archives show: 260 killed, 918 wounded and 378 missing. Not only is this figure more accurate, having been taken from the

Brunswick manuscript rolls, but it shows again how Siborne attempted to play down the role of the Allies and extol those of his fellow countrymen, implying greater bravery to the British contingent by giving lighter losses to the Allies and thus insinuating less involvement by comparison with greater British losses, making the latter appear in a more heroic light.

Thus I have attempted to cull my figures from the most reliable – in my estimation – archival sources available. They are by no means accurate and are given as a rough guide. To relate all my findings in this area alone would require a book in its own right, but I doubt that it would be at all accurate. Indeed, Scott Bowden spent many years compiling a massive work on the order of battle of the three contending forces: *Armies at Waterloo* (Empire Press, Texas 1983), but even that book is not definitive, much use of IMPs (Inherent Military Probabilities – or guesses) being made. Again, even in this work dedicated only to the three armies involved, the sources are incorrect. To give but one example, on page 166 Bowden states that the Prussian 6pdr artillery battery commanded by Captain von Reuter was 'still in mobilization process and joined the army after the action of June 15–18'. This was not so. Captain E.S. May, in an article published in *The United Services Magazine*, London, October 1891, entitled 'A Prussian Gunner's Adventures in 1815', gives a translation of Captain von Reuter's journal given to him by von Reuter's grandson. In this Captain von Reuter gives a graphic description of his battery's part both at Ligny and Waterloo. Arriving late, his unit had been attached to a different Corps.

I leave the last word on this subject to Major Macready of the 30th Foot, in refutation of Siborne's *History* when first published in late 1844: 'In the returns of Captain Siborne's history the numbers of the 30th are given as 615 men, whereas 460 bayonets was the outside of what the 30th marched into the field at Quatre Bras. It is not for me to say what portion of the residue went to guards, hospital, commissariat, provost, stores or what not, but I know that near 50 effective soldiers were away from the battle as servants and batmen. Had it been otherwise ... [then at the end of the Battle of Waterloo] its loss of 230 men would have left it at the close 330 men, whereas 160 rank and file was our strength when we piled arms.' – *The United Services Magazine*, March 1845, p.403.

L'ARMÉE DU NORD
(14 June 1815)

NAPOLEON
ARMY GQG
(Soult, Chief of Staff, 600)

LEFT WING – NEY
I Corps (D'Erlon, 20,950)
1st Division (Quiot)
1st Cavalry Division
  (Jacquinot)
2nd Division (Donzelot)

Artillery (Desales, 46guns)
3rd Division (Marcognet)
4th Division (Durutte)
II Corps (Reille, 25,100)
5th Division (Bachelu)
2nd Cavalry Division (Pire)
6th Division (Jerome)
Artillery (Pelletier, 46 guns)
7th Division (Girard)
9th Division (Foy)

RIGHT WING – GROUCHY
III Corps (Vandamme,17,150)

8th Division (Lefol)
3rd Cavalry Division
  (Domon)
10th Division (Habert)
Artillery (Doguereau, 38
  guns)
11th Division (Berthezene)
IV Corps (Gerard, 15,700)
12th Division (Pecheux)
7th Cavalry Division
  (Maurin)
13th Division (Vichery)
Artillery (Baltus, 38 guns)

14th Division ((Bourmont)
Hulot)

RESERVE
VI Corps (Lobau, 10,300)
Division (Simmer)
Division (Jeannin)
Artillery (32 guns)
Division (Teste)

GUARD CORPS
(MORTIER, DROUOT, 20,278)
Old Division (Friant)
Cavalry Division (Guyot)
Cavalry Division (Lefebvre-
Desnouëttes)
Middle Division (Morand)
Artillery (St Maurice, 96
guns)
Young Division (Duhesme)

RESERVE CAVALRY –
GROUCHY
I Cavalry Corps
(Pajol, 3,100)
4th Division (P.Soult)
Artillery (12 guns)
5th Division (Subervie)
II Cavalry Corps
(Exelmans, 3,290)
9th Division (Strolz)
Artillery (12 guns)
10th Division (Chastel)
III Cavalry Corps
(Kellermann, 3,700)
11th Division (L'Heritier)
Artillery (12 guns)
12th Division (D'Urbal)
IV Cavalry Corps
(Milhaud, 3,000)
13th Division (Wathier)
Artillery (12 guns)
14th Division (Delort)

Total: 123,000 men, 366
guns

THE ALLIED ARMY
(Anglo-Allied) (14 June)

WELLINGTON
ARMY GHQ (De Lancey,
QMG acting as C. of S.,
1,240)

I Corps (Orange, 31,500)
Guards division (Cooke)
Cavalry Division (Collaert)

1 Dutch/Belgian Brigade
(Trip)
2 Dutch/Belgian Brigade
(Ghigny)
3 Dutch/Belgian Brigade
(Merlen)
3rd Division (Alten)
2nd Dutch/Belgian Division
(Perponcher-Slednitsky)
Artillery (64 guns)
3rd Dutch/Belgian Division
(Chasse)

II Corps (Hill, 27,250)
2nd Division (Clinton)
Cavalry Brigade (Estorff,
Hanoverian)
4th Division (Colville)
Artillery (40 guns)
*Under nominal command
of Prince Frederick:*
1st Dutch/Belgian Division
(Stedman)
Indonesian Brigade
(Anthing)

Cavalry Corps (Uxbridge,
11,800)
HEAVY CAVALRY
1st Cavalry Brigade
(Somerset)
2nd Cavalry Brigade
(Ponsonby)
Cavalry Artillery (30 guns)
LIGHT CAVALRY
4th Cavalry Brigade
(Vandeleur)
5th Cavalry Brigade (Grant)
3rd Cavalry Brigade
(Dornberg)
6th Cavalry Brigade
(Vivian)
7th Cavalry Brigade
(Arentschildt)

General Reserve
(Wellington, 23,000)
5th Division (Picton)
6th Division (Lambert
(Cole))
Nassau Brigade (Kruse)
Artillery (56 guns)
Brunswick Division (Duke
of Brunswick)

Garrisons (13,000, 36 guns)
Ghent, Nieupoort, Ostend,
Antwerp, Ypres

Total: 107,000 men, 216
guns

THE PRUSSIAN ARMY
(14 June) (Exclusive of
Kleist von Nollendorf's
detached corps in Luxem-
burg, 25,000 men)

BLUCHER
ARMY GHQ (QMG and C.of
S. Gneisenau, C.of General
S. Grolmann)

I Corps (Ziethen, 32,500)
1 Brigade (Steinmetz)
Cavalry Brigade (Roder)
2 Brigade (Pirch II)
3 Brigade (Jajow)
4 Brigade (Donnersmarck)
Artillery (Lehmann, 96 guns)

II CORPS (Pirch I, 33,000)
5 Brigade (Tippelskirch)
Cavalry Brigade (Wahlen-
Jurgass)
6 Brigade (Krafft)
7 Brigade (Brause)
Artillery (Rohl, 85 guns)
8 Brigade (Langen (BOSE))

III Corps (Thielmann,
25,000)
9th Brigade (Borche)
Cavalry Brigade (Hobe)
10 Brigade (Kamphen)
11 Brigade (Luck)
Artillery (Mohnnhaupt, 48
guns)
12 Brigade (Stulpnägel)

IV Corps (Bülow, 32,000)
13 Brigade (Hacke)
Cavalry Brigade (Prince
William of Prussia)
14 Brigade (Ryssel)
15 Brigade (Losthin)
Artillery (Bardelben, 88
guns)
16 Brigade (Hiller von Gar-
tringen)

Garrisons (6,000)

Total: 128,000 men (excluding Kleist), 312 guns

Wellington's Movement Orders, 15/16 June

The table overleaf presents:

(1) The orders issued between 5 p.m. to 9 p.m., usually referred to by historians as the 6 or 7 p.m. orders. I believe these were two sets, the second slightly amending the first in the light of new information (see Chapter 7 footnote 38).

(2) The 'after orders' of 10 p.m.

(3) The subsequent orders issued by de Lancey between 3 and 6 a.m. on 16 June, referred to as 'subsequent orders'.

(4) The actual position of the troops in the forenoon of 16 June. (5) the Duke of Wellington's dispositions contained in his letter to Marshal Blücher of that morning which, when compared with (7) the Memorandum issued to him at 7 a.m. by either de Lancey or a member of his staff, can be seen as the basis for the Duke's letter.

The table shows clearly that the 'estimated' positions furnished to the Duke of Wellington were erroneous and did not take into account the belated departure of some units as a consequence of their movement orders being changed several times and no urgency being stressed in them, and no consideration having been taken of the immense bottleneck that would occur by the Army having to move to its left in the subsequent orders through Braine-le-Comte and Nivelles to Quatre Bras.

Finally it will be seen that Wellington had every reason to believe from this information supplied by his staff that his units could have attained the positions that he stipulated in his letter to Blücher, and that Gneisenau on the basis of this letter had every reason to believe that Wellington, even if attacked by the French, would be able to assist him with at least a third of his army with the rest arriving during the conflict.

In conclusion it can be seen that in the light of the letter from Wellington, Gneisenau had every reason to feel somewhat let down by the Duke's inability to assist him. Wellington cannot be held responsible for this delay because the 'routes' of movement were de Lancey's responsibility, while Wellington himself was sorely pressed to hold his position at Quatre Bras because of this poor staff work.

UNITS	FIRST OR 'COLLECTION' ORDERS OF 15 JUNE	STATION WHEN ORDER ISSUED	AFTER-ORDERS, 10 p.m. 15 JUNE	SUBSEQUENT ORDERS
Dörnberg's Cavalry Brigade & Cumberland Hussars	To march to Vilvorde this night	About Malines	Move on Mont St Jean [3]	—[4]
English Cavalry	Collect at Ninhove this night[2]	Grammont, Ninhove, and along Dender	Move on Enghien	Continue move on to Braine-le-Comte
1st Infantry Division	Enghien and neighbourhood[2]	Enghien	Move on Braine-le-comte	Continue to Braine-le-Comte immediately
2nd Infantry Division	Ath[2]	Ath with 1 Brigade King's German Legion, and 2 British Brigade; 3 Hanoverian Brigade at Lens	Move on Enghien	Move to Braine-le-Comte on 16th, subsequently ordered to march on Quatre B
3rd Infantry Division	Braine-le-Comte[2]	Soignies, Braine-le-Comte, and towards Enghien	Move on Nivelles	—[4]
4th Infantry Division	Grammont, except troops beyond Scheldt there at Oudenarde	Oudenarde, 6 Hanoverian Brigade at Nieuport	Move on Enghien	—[4]
5th Infantry Division and 4 Hanoverian Brigade of 6th Division[1]	—[2]	Brussels and neighbourhood	Move on Mont St Jean[3]	—[4]
10 Brigade[1]	To march to Brussels	Ghent	—	—[4]
Brunswick Corps	Road between Brussels and Vilvorde - ready to march in the morning[2]	Brussels and neighbourhood	Move on Mont St Jean[3]	—[4]
Nassau Troops	Louvain Road - ready to march in the morning[2]	On Louvain road, near Brussels	Move on Mont St Jean[3]	—[4]
2nd and 3rd Dutch-Belgian Divisions	Nivelles. If this attacked call up 3rd British Division, but not till certain attack on Prussian right and English left	2nd, Nivelles; 3rd, Roeulx, and towards Binche	—[4]	—[4]
1st Dutch-Belgian Division and Dutch-Indian Brigade	Sotteghem – ready to march at daylight	Sotteghem, the Dutch-Indian Brigade at Alost	—	—[4]
Reserve Artillery	Ready to move at daylight	Brussels	—	Ordered to Quatre Bras on 16th

1   This division was formed of 10 British and 4 Hanoverian Brigades. 10 Brigade was at Ghent. It was ordered to Brussels, reached Assche on the afternoon of the 16th, moved to Brussels on the 17th, halted till the 18th, when it marched to Waterloo. This brigade had only recently been completed. The 81st Regiment remained in Brussels guarding treasure.
2   Ready to move at a moment's notice.
3   To the junction of the road from Nivelles with that from Namur - i.e., Mont St Jjean.
4   No information, but there can be no doubt from the position recorded in the next column that the whole army was ordered to its left.
5   4 Hanoverian Brigade probably on road from Brussels towards Waterloo behind 5th Division.
6   A portion seems to have arrived at Quatre Bras during the night of the 16th.

TUAL POSITION, 1. 16 JUNE	DUKE'S LETTER TO BLUCHER	'DISPOSITION' 7 a.m. 16 JUNE	TROOPS AT QUATRE BRAS, MORNING, 17TH
bably between Brussels and Waterloo	Beyond Waterloo, marching to Genappe and Quatre Bras	Beyond Waterloo, marching to Genappe and Quatre Bras	Quatre Bras
rching on Quatre Bras. me reached that night	Nivelles at noon	Braine-le-Comte, marching to Nivelles and Quatre Bras	Quatre Bras
ached Braine-le-Comte 9 a.m. t till twelve, and then on to Quatre Bras	Nivelles	Do.	Quatre Bras
ly received orders 10 a.m. this day. Reached Enghien 2 p.m. ine-le-Comte midnight	Braine-le-Comte	Do	—
ived Nivelles noon; atre Bras between five and six	Nivelles	Nivelles, marching to Quatre Bras	Quatre Bras
bably about 20 to 30 miles from ghien	—	Oudenarde, marching on Braine-le-Comte	—
terloo 10 a.m.; atre Bras about 3 p.m.[5]	Marching on Genappe, where it will arrive at noon	Beyond Waterloo, marching to Genappe	Quatre Bras
che afternoon of 16th	—	—	—
id to Quatre Bras – arrived there ut 4 p.m.	Marching on Genappe, where it will arrive at noon	Beyond Waterloo, marching to Genappe	Quatre Bras
lowing 5th Division and noverian Brigade of 6th Division	Do.	Do.	Quatre Bras
, at Quatre Bras; 3rd at Nivelles	Nivelles and Quatre Bras	Nivelles and Quatre Bras	Quatre Bras
	—	Sotteghem, marching to Enghien	—
ssels[6]	—	—	Mostly at Brussels, or marching down to Waterloo

Index